NOT IN FRONT OF THE CHILDREN

ALSO BY MARJORIE HEINS

Sex, Sin, and Blasphemy: A Guide to America's Censorship Wars

Cutting the Mustard: Affirmative Action and the Nature of Excellence

Strictly Ghetto Property: The Story of Los Siete de la Raza

NOT IN FRONT OF THE CHILDREN

"Indecency," Censorship, and the Innocence of Youth

MARJORIE HEINS

HILL AND WANG

A division of Farrar, Straus and Giroux

New York

Hill and Wang
A division of Farrar, Straus and Giroux
19 Union Square West, New York 10003

Distributed in Canada by Douglas & McIntyre, Ltd.
Printed in the United States of America
First edition, 2001

Library of Congress Cataloging-in-Publication Data

Heins, Majorie.
Not in front of the children : "indecency," censorship, and the innocence of youth / Marjorie Heins.
p. cm.
Includes bibliographical references and index.
ISBN 0-374-17545-4 (alk. paper)
1. Censorship—United States—History—20th century. 2. National characteristics, American—History—20th century. 3. Obscenity (Law)—United States. 4. United States—Moral conditions—History—20th century. 5. Youth—United States—Social conditions—20th century. I. Title.

Z658.U5 H42 2001
303.3′76′0973—dc21

00-47274

The research and writing for this publication were supported by a grant from the Individual Project Fellowship Program of the Open Society Institute.

For Ben Kaplan,

extraordinary mentor

"Satan lays the snare, and children are his victims. His traps, like all others, are baited to allure the human soul."

—ANTHONY COMSTOCK, *Traps for the Young*

"There is no more enduring struggle in the culture wars than the one for our children's hearts, minds, and libidos."

—JEFF STRYKER AND MARIA EKSTRAND, *San Francisco Examiner*, March 17, 1997

"You start out talking about condoms in this country, and you end up fighting about the future of the American family. Teens just end up frozen like a deer in the headlights."

—SARAH BROWN, director of the National Campaign to Prevent Teen Pregnancy, *Time*, June 15, 1998

CONTENTS

ACKNOWLEDGMENTS

I owe an immense debt of gratitude to the Open Society Institute (OSI), which supported my vision for this book both financially and intellectually. Copious thanks to its entire staff, and especially to Gara LaMarche, director of OSI's U.S. Programs, and Gail Goodman, program officer for OSI's Individual Project Fellowships.

My colleagues in free-expression work have been a steady source of friendship, intellectual stimulation, and moral support. Particular thanks to Joan Bertin, Leonore Tiefer, and Judith Levine of the National Coalition Against Censorship; David Greene at the First Amendment Project; Chris Finan at the American Booksellers Foundation for Free Expression; Michael Roberts and Diana Ayton-Shenker at PEN American Center; Paul McMasters at the Freedom Forum; and Ann Beeson, Chris Hansen, and Steve Shapiro at the ACLU. Their insights and hard work guided this project for years before the book took shape.

I am also grateful to First Amendment lawyers Robert Corn-Revere, Robert Balin, Burt Joseph, Eric Lieberman, and John Crigler for their dedicated labors and willingness to share their thoughts; to Dean Catharine Stimpson, whose confidence in this project enabled me to be a Visiting Scholar at New York University in 1998; and to Michael Carrera, Richard Green, Jonathan Freedman, Daniel Linz, Susan Rose, Henry Jenkins, Debra Haffner, and Victor Strasburger for their many insights about social science, censorship, and youth. Thanks also to colleagues who reviewed and critiqued portions of the manuscript: Hendrik Hartog; Leonore Tiefer; David Garrow; Robert Horwitz; Philippa Strum; my agent, Anne Depue; and my wise and patient editor, Lauren Osborne.

The Cambridge University Law Faculty and Wolfson College, Cambridge, were my generous hosts for the six months that I spent in England. Special thanks to Jack Beatson, Tony Smith, Tom Viles, Sir David Williams, and the Cambridge Law Faculty and library staff. The librarians at the International Planned Parenthood Federation (IPPF) in London were incredibly helpful, as were Monica Pini and Vicky Claeys of IPPF in Brussels, and Stefaan Verhulst at the Oxford University Programme in Comparative Media Law and Policy. Richard Swetenham and David Hughes of the European Commission were generous with their time and educated me about the intricate workings of that fascinating bureaucracy.

International free-expression advocates Yaman Akdeniz, Malcolm Hutty, Avedon Carol, Alex Hamilton, John Wadham, and Meryem Marzouki provided invaluable assistance as I attempted to understand and navigate the complicated censorship politics of Europe. In Britain, thanks also to Nigel Williams, Colin Shaw, Bill Thompson, David Kerr, Mark Stephens, and James Ferman for sharing their time and thoughts.

A specially affectionate thanks to Siobhan Dowd and Sally Sampson, my beloved London friends, frequent hosts, and sources of much wisdom, erudition, humor, and common sense.

For insights on Japan, I am grateful to Milton Diamond and Ayako Uchiyama. Thanks also to Satoshi Mishima for good counsel (and an unforgettable meal at Myoshin-ji Temple).

The New York Public Library is an amazing resource in whose microfilm and reading rooms I spent many rewarding hours unearthing obscure treasures. I don't know the staff members individually, but I would like to thank them collectively for their assistance. Thanks also to Amy Levine, the capable librarian at the Sexuality Information and Education Council of the United States (SIECUS); and to the staffs at the Library of Congress manuscript division (home of Justice Brennan's papers) and at the Kinsey Institute.

Finally, thanks to my daughter, Catherine Heins, for the inspired title, and to her brother Matthew for aiding in its creation.

NOT IN FRONT OF THE CHILDREN

INTRODUCTION

From Plato to Computers

> A young person cannot judge what is allegorical and what is literal; anything that he receives into his mind at that age is likely to become indelible and unalterable; and therefore it is most important that the tales which the young first hear should be models of virtuous thoughts.[1]

In 1998, citing this famous passage from Plato's *Republic*, judges on the U.S. Court of Appeals rejected the legal claims of a high school drama teacher who had been punished for choosing a controversial play called *Independence* for her advanced acting class. (The play addressed themes of divorce, homosexuality, and unwed pregnancy.) The judges ruled that school officials in North Carolina did not violate Margaret Boring's right to academic freedom when they revoked her advanced acting assignment and exiled her to a middle school in response to complaints about the play.

This reliance, by judges sworn to uphold the First Amendment, on the pedagogical advice of Plato was remarkable. For whatever the Greek philosopher's literary or intellectual virtues, his doctrine of rigid censorship was about as hostile to our modern ideas of free expression as one can imagine. In the *Republic*, his prescription for an ideal state, Plato explained that writers must be censored because they give "an erroneous representation" of gods and heroes; indeed, even if their tales of divine and heroic misdeeds were true, they "ought certainly not to be lightly told to young and thoughtless persons." Plato likewise urged the suppression of "indecency" in sculpture and "the other creative arts" and of all music that did not promote temperance and military courage.[2]

Judicial adoption of Plato's indoctrination theory was in a sense the logical culmination of a decade in which all branches and levels of American government were busy censoring youth. The same year as *Boring*, courts in other states also upheld punishments imposed by local school boards—in Missouri, of a creative writing teacher who failed to purge her students' stories of profane language; in Colorado, of a history teacher who showed his class a celebrated film by Bernardo Bertolucci, *1900*, which contained moments of nudity, violence, and implicit sex.[3] Indeed, censorship of public school curriculum materials and library books had become so common in the United States by the 1990s that hardly any work was immune from challenge. Among the more frequent targets were Maya Angelou's *I Know Why the Caged Bird Sings* and Toni Morrison's *Beloved*; John Steinbeck's *Of Mice and Men* and Mark Twain's *Huckleberry Finn*.

In Congress, meanwhile, the zeal to protect youth was manifested in a series of laws restricting "indecency" on television and the Internet and censoring sex education. As part of its massive 1996 welfare reform, Congress appropriated $250 million for local sex ed programs—but only if they preached abstinence until marriage and taught that any "sexual activity outside of the context of marriage is likely to have harmful psychological and physical effects."[4] Under this "abstinence till marriage" curriculum, potentially lifesaving information on safer sex and contraception was suppressed, on the theory that even learning about such subjects would lead youngsters to believe that sexual activity was encouraged.

Censorship in the name of child protection was not always solemn or health-threatening, however; sometimes it was simply comic. In 1996, the Bad Frog Brewery applied to the New York State Liquor Authority for permission to market its designer beer, with a label that featured "a frog with the second of its four unwebbed 'fingers' extended in a manner evocative of a well known human gesture of insult."[5] The Liquor Authority rejected Bad Frog's application, largely because it felt the label could have "adverse effects" on "children of tender age." A federal trial judge agreed that the Authority had a legitimate interest in "protecting children" from "profane" advertising.[6]

This exercise in government-enforced etiquette was eventually reversed, but not because the appellate judges questioned the underlying assumption that minors would be harmed by seeing the frog's crude gesture on a grocery label. To the contrary, the judges recited what had by then become a truism in U.S. constitutional law—that states have "a compelling interest in protecting the physical and psychological well-being of minors," an interest that includes shielding them from "the influence of literature that is not obscene by adult standards."[7] The only reason for a First Amendment violation in the *Bad Frog* case, according to the appellate court, was that given "the wide currency of vulgar displays throughout contemporary society, including comic books targeted directly at children," the Liquor Authority's ban amounted to removing only a few insignificant "grains of offensive sand from a beach of vulgarity."[8] In essence, it appeared, New York's problem was that it had not taken more *extensive* steps to censor advertising and other expression in the interest of protecting youth.

The *Bad Frog* judges never indicated why they thought exposure to the beer label would be psychologically harmful. But clearly they were acting on widely shared beliefs about harm to minors from art, literature, advertising, and other forms of communication. The assumption was that even if coarse entertainment or provocative materials are tolerable for adults, children and adolescents either are too fragile to handle vulgarity, sex, and controversy or lack the intellectual freedom rights that the First Amendment grants adults—or both.

Of course, the assumption that minors are harmed by reading, watching movies, or surfing the Internet is usually framed in terms of gratuitous violence or pornography, not controversial works of theater, silly beer labels, or novels by John Steinbeck and Toni Morrison. But terms like "pornography" and "gratuitous violence" are elastic, and if the underlying philosophy is one of protection through censorship, then it is only a matter of opinion whether gratuitous violence means *Schindler's List* or *Terminator 2*, whether safer-sex films that illustrate the unrolling of a condom are salutary or immoral, or whether Judy Blume novels that discuss masturbation or premarital sex are pornographic. Even if adults could agree, moreover, on what is truly inadvisable for young people, the rarely asked question remains, In what sense is it harmful? And does it justify censorship?

I became intrigued by these questions during my tenure as director of the American Civil Liberties Union's Arts Censorship Project (1991–98). Not only were children and teenagers the most frequent targets of censorship in these years, but they became the justification for restrictions that affected adults as well. Thus, we saw Internet rating and filtering installed on public library computers; stores refusing to carry popular music that contained warning labels; and laws prohibiting "indecency" on cable television.

The 1996 Communications Decency Act, or CDA, was undoubtedly the most sweeping of these "child protection" initiatives that infringed on the free-speech rights of adults.

The CDA made it a crime to send a minor any "indecent" Internet communication or to "display in a manner available to minors" any online expression that "in context, depicts or describes, in terms patently offensive as measured by contemporary community standards, sexual or excretory activities or organs."[9] Because nearly everything on the Internet was available to any minor who had the equipment and knowledge to access it, the "display" provision of the CDA in essence criminalized "patently offensive" or "indecent" speech online. (The two terms—developed in previous decades to describe speech deemed harmful to youth—were usually considered synonymous.)

To address this dramatic problem of "overbreadth," the CDA provided a defense if online speakers took steps to identify and screen out minors from their e-mail listserves, discussion groups, chat rooms, or World Wide Web sites. But such screening was a near-impossible task: the vast majority of speakers and publishers in cyberspace did not have the technological or economic means to determine the ages of those who accessed their ideas. The CDA thus essentially purged from the Internet any sexually oriented expression that a federal prosecutor somewhere in the United States thought might be "indecent" or "patently offensive."

I was one of the lawyers in *Reno v. ACLU*, the constitutional challenge to the CDA. Our plaintiffs—among them Planned Parenthood, Human Rights Watch, and the Queer Resources Directory—wanted to persuade the courts that their communications, even if "indecent" or "patently offensive," had value for minors as well as adults. So, for example, the plaintiff Critical Path AIDS Project targeted urban teenagers for its online information on condoms and other safer-sex techniques. Another plaintiff, Stop Prisoner Rape, communicated graphic descriptions of violent sexual experiences to youngsters at risk of incarceration. The ACLU itself had a teen chat Web page that included a discussion of masturbation, inspired by President Clinton's firing of Surgeon General Joycelyn Elders in 1994 because of her suggestion that sexuality education might straightforwardly address this common, safe, but still often shame-inducing activity.

Much of this evidence found its way into the judicial opinions in *Reno* striking down the CDA. Judge Dolores Sloviter, in the trial court, noted the possible application of the law to erotic sculptures on Hindu temples, the film *Leaving Las Vegas*, and Tony Kushner's Pulitzer Prize–winning play,

Angels in America.[10] Justice John Paul Stevens, writing for the Supreme Court the following year, mentioned "serious discussion about birth control practices," homosexuality, prison rape, safer sex, artistic nudes, and "arguably the card catalogue of the Carnegie Library."[11] The Supreme Court in *Reno* thus recognized for the first time that explicit, even "patently offensive," information and ideas about sex might be educational rather than harmful for minors.

But the recognition caused hardly a ripple in the political world. Within a month after the Supreme Court decision, the White House convened an "Online Summit" to explore alternative means of protecting kids in cyberspace, and a larger conference later that year featured colorful displays of the myriad software packages now available for blocking minors' access to "inappropriate" online content. Vice President Al Gore in a keynote speech equated the presumptive psychological harm of disapproved speech to poisons in the family medicine chest.

Inevitably, this touting of voluntary "parental empowerment" filtering software gave way to more coercive initiatives. Senator John McCain proposed legislation making Internet filters mandatory in schools and libraries that receive federal aid. In 1998, Congress passed "son of CDA," a "Child Online Protection Act" that again criminalized material deemed "harmful to minors" (a narrower legal standard than "indecency"). Campaigns against media violence also intensified: the 1996 CDA mandated television v-chips; Nassau County, New York, had already criminalized the sale to minors of trading cards depicting perpetrators of "heinous crimes"; and in 1999, the massacre at Colorado's Columbine High School by two disturbed teenagers sparked an orgy of media blaming.

The events that followed *Reno v. ACLU*, and the continued popularity of censorship designed to protect, shield, indoctrinate, or socialize young people, dramatized the durability and emotional power of the belief that minors are harmed by sexual expression—or, depending upon one's values, by speech about violence, drugs, alcohol, suicide, religion, racism, or other troublesome themes. Unexamined assumptions continue to dominate this debate, with questionable consequences not only for the First Amendment freedoms of all of us but for the moral and intellectual development of youngsters themselves. In *Not in Front of the Children,* I explore the origin of these assumptions, trace the history of "harm to minors" censorship, and attempt to get beyond the emotionally charged but sometimes dubious rhetoric that surrounds it.

Youth and Censorship: A Road Map

Not in Front of the Children begins at the beginning, with the pedagogical theories of Plato and Aristotle. Given a sweep this ambitious, my narrative of necessity moves swiftly through the evolution of beliefs in Western civilization about childhood, sexuality, socialization, and the effects of art and literature on youth.

Historians are hardly of one mind on these fundamental questions. Philippe Ariès, probably the most famous of the scholars plowing these waters, posited that modern concepts of childhood as a peculiarly vulnerable state arose only in the 17th century. Ariès has had his share of critics, but few experts dispute his basic conclusion that the concept of youth as a time of sexual innocence is a relatively recent historical phenomenon.[12]

Contemporary concerns about shielding children and adolescents from corrupting sexual ideas are traceable directly to Victorian-era fears that libidinous thoughts would lead to the "secret vice" of masturbation. Proscriptions against arousing literature, relatively rare before 1800, thus became pervasive in the century that followed. Evangelical religion, social reactions to the stresses of urbanization and industrialization, and "moral purity" movements in Europe and the United States during the 19th century drove the development of obscenity and "harm to minors" law. Censors like Anthony Comstock in the United States seized and destroyed tons of literature, art, advertisements, and contraceptive devices, and free-love advocates went to prison, all in the interest of protecting youth.[13]

Michel Foucault identified the perceived need to control the "masturbating child" as one of the four "strategic unities" that the 19th century contributed to the story of human sexuality. Foucault argued that while controlling sexual behavior has always been an issue for political and religious authorities, it was only in the last few centuries that sex became an obsessive subject of discourse, professional intervention, and institutional control.[14] Sigmund Freud, a product of this 19th-century fascination with sex, discussed the subject with a liberating new level of explicitness, and as a consequence changed both human culture and censorship law in the century that followed. Although Freud believed the sexual impulse had to be sublimated in the interest of civilization, others have argued that, on the contrary, societies have had to "invent an importance for sexuality"—to make it dangerous, hidden, or "essentially violative," in order to maximize reproductive behavior.[15] But it is clear that our current political and legal concepts of obscenity evolved from the 19th-century belief that youngsters must be shielded from libidinous thoughts.

When, in the mid–20th century, courts began to realize that censorship of the reading matter of adults should not turn on what might be thought appropriate for a child, new doctrines ("variable obscenity," "indecency") were created to maintain society's special interest in restricting the information, ideas, and entertainment available to youth. The Supreme Court's pronouncements in this period zigzagged dizzily—on the one hand recognizing minors' free-expression rights and on the other moralizing about government's interest in protecting them from a too vigorous exercise of those rights, particularly when the subject was sex. The high—or low—point in this judicial history came in the 1978 case of *Federal Communications Commission v. Pacifica* when, relying on the purported need to shield the ears of youth, the Court upheld the FCC's ban on radio or television broadcast of "indecent" or vulgar words. Justice William Brennan, who had been the architect of the "obscenity exception" to the First Amendment earlier in the century, and thus hardly a consistent opponent of sexual censorship, was sufficiently incensed by this decision in *Pacifica* that he accused his fellow justices of forcing their personal standards of taste, morality, and child rearing on the diverse American public.

Following *Pacifica*, there was a series of challenges to the FCC's indecency regime in the interests of, among others, Allen Ginsberg, whose poem "Howl" was an early casualty of the decision. The CDA litigation (*Reno v. ACLU*, or *Reno I*), eighteen years after *Pacifica*, was a milestone because of the plaintiffs' effort to persuade the courts to examine their assumptions about harm to minors. The aftermath of *Reno I*—the intoxication among policymakers with Internet classification and blocking schemes—relied on the same harm-to-minors assumptions that drove more direct forms of censorship like the CDA.

The history of harm-to-minors censorship is, by and large, a legal history, and therefore it will come as no surprise that much of *Not in Front of the Children* traces, chronologically, judicial struggles over "indecency," "variable obscenity," and public school censorship. Although this legal history is colorful in its own right, I have also attempted throughout to set the cultural and political scene rather than to present the legal story in a vacuum. And because not all history fits neatly into a chronological format, there are separate chapters on sexuality education; on cultural differences between the United States and other countries regarding what is considered harmful to youth; and on the all-important subject of "media effects"—a shorthand term for the whole complex of studies, theories, and debates about the effects of art, literature, and electronic communications on human attitudes and behavior, particularly those of youth.

For the chapter on cultural differences, I spent six months in Europe in 1999 in an attempt to learn how at least one section of the world outside the United States approaches the issue of presumed harm to youth. Much, I found, is similar to the U.S. approach, in terms of the tension between protectionism and rights; and much is different because each European culture is different. While most societies in Europe are anxious about *something* in the world of modern culture and how it might impair the young, their substantive understandings of harm to minors vary considerably. These cultural differences suggest that we really know very little about how sexual, violent, or other media content will affect any individual young person; but that censorship initiatives whose articulated justification is protecting minors nevertheless serve symbolic purposes and rarely encounter much political resistance.

What, then, is the actual basis for the harm-to-minors assumption? When people are asked what harm they think flows from violent, sexual, or other controversial art or entertainment, their answers range from the broadly moral (kids should not be "robbed of their innocence") to the developmental and psychological (fear, nightmares, anxiety, oversexualized behavior), to the specifically imitative (they will mimic violence or sexual activity that they see on TV). "Social learning" psychologists, whose perspective was popular in the 1970s, claim that youngsters will imitate attitudes and behaviors they see in the media—indeed, many insist that experiments have irrefutably proved the point—but they tend to differ in identifying both the objectionable media content and the adverse effects. A more nuanced approach—acknowledging that art and entertainment can produce catharsis as well as imitation—is scorned as obsolete; indeed, one leading expert warned me to "get rid of catharsis" (at least as a possible chapter title), lest I appear "naive."[16] Yet catharsis was a phenomenon noted by Aristotle more than two thousand years ago, and whether or not experiments can quantify it, there has been too much real aesthetic experience over centuries to dismiss the notion that violent, disturbing, or sexually charged content in art and entertainment can sometimes reduce rather than heighten human anxieties or aggression.

As MIT professor Henry Jenkins tried to explain to Congress in 1999 after the gruesome murders at Columbine, belief in widespread adverse media effects is "an inadequate and simplistic representation of media consumption and popular culture." It "often empties media images of their meanings, strips them of their contexts, and denies their consumers any agency over their use."[17] Positing a consistent, predictable causative relationship between "violent" media content and bad behavior thus blinds us to the fantastically complex way in which ideas, images, and stories affect individuals, and to the much more significant factors, from genetic predisposition to family and community environment, that influence child and adolescent development.

But although social science has not proved any identifiable subject or medium to cause significant, predictable changes in children's attitudes or behavior, provocative ideas in art or entertainment do affect the human psyche in myriad ways. It is just that these effects cannot be quantified. They undoubtedly include, in some instances, persuasion, reflection, revulsion, catharsis, excitement, and mindless enjoyment. And, of course, imitation. An often cited example is the Bible: full of sex and violence, it has, not surprisingly, inspired psychotic acts as well as charitable ones.

Media effects studies in the 1970s and 1980s were at bottom simply a quantitative variation on a cultural concern that goes back to Plato—that without censorship, minors will pick up bad ideas about sex or other controversial subjects. Attempting to shield them from disturbing information or ideas may not make them chaster, safer, nicer, or more honorable, but it has symbolic value, both for those who agree with writer/activist Andrea Dworkin and law professor Catharine MacKinnon that pornography degrades women and eroticizes male domination and for those who adhere to traditional conservative sexual morality. Many others genuinely seeking to ameliorate problems such as youth violence or teen pregnancy, as well as politicians who simply want to appear to be doing something to fix social ills, have seized on this symbolic value as well. Childhood "is an age that we disguise by embellishing, by using it to embody our ideals," as historian Paul Veyne says.[18] Or, in Henry Jenkins's words, censorship to preserve the myth of childhood innocence fulfills the "symbolic demands" of adults; it shifts attention "away from material problems affecting children and onto the symbolic terrain."[19]

The argument here is not that commercial pornography, mindless media violence, or other dubious forms of entertainment are good for youngsters or should be foisted upon them. Rather, it is that, given the overwhelming difficulty in even defining what it is we want to censor, and the significant costs of censorship to society and to youngsters themselves, we ought to be sure that real, not just symbolic, harm results from youthful pursuit of disapproved pleasures and messages before mandating indecency laws, Internet filters, and other restrictive regimes. Perhaps there are better ways to socialize children—among them, training in media literacy and critical thinking skills, comprehensive sexuality education, literature classes that *deal with* difficult topics rather than pretending they do not exist, and inclusion of young people in journalism and policymaking on this very issue of culture and values. In all of these areas, youngsters who are economically and educationally deprived are likely to benefit most from additional sources of information and ideas.

Which leads to a final theme of *Not in Front of the Children*: the intellectual freedom interests of young people themselves. This is a concept too often impatiently dismissed by child protectionists. Minors are thought insufficiently mature or socialized to understand and resist the ideas that a majority of adults think are not good for them—or, as one federal court put it, youngsters' access to speech must be restricted lest they "get lost in the marketplace of ideas."[20] But is this really the best way to prepare youngsters for adult life in a democratic society? The simultaneous titillation, anxiety, and confusion spawned by forbidden speech zones may do more harm than good. Certainly healthy upbringing, education, and community values are likelier than taboos to immunize them against violent, degrading, or simple-minded ideas. Censorship may also frustrate young people's developing sense of autonomy and self-respect, and increase their feelings of alienation. Some older children and adolescents are able to process information and make coherent decisions at the same level as many adults.[21] They *need* access to information and ideas precisely because they are in the process becoming functioning members of society and cannot really do so if they are kept in ideological blinders until they are 18.

These are not simple questions, for they touch not only on our commitment to intellectual freedom but on our society's whole attitude toward educating youth. Feelings that children are raised too permissively, without adequate boundaries on sexual or other behavior, and that adolescents are both directionless and out of control, drive much of the energy that is poured into protectionist censorship campaigns. Authors like Rochelle Gurstein and Neil Postman unabashedly argue for a return to a culture of sexual prudery and shame in which adults keep sexual secrets from children.[22] As the history of childhood shows, none of these adult fears and attitudes is new. But what *are* the best ways to socialize and educate youth—about drugs, violence, racism, and responsible, pleasure-affirming sexuality? Until these questions are confronted, the quick fix of censorship to "protect" the young will continue to have political appeal.

Clarifications and Caveats

Frequently when I begin to talk about censorship and harm to minors, listeners mistakenly assume that the subject of my book is child pornography.

But child pornography involves actual physical abuse, not exposure to words, images, or ideas. Indeed, the tendency to conflate the two separate issues is worrisome precisely because it threatens the foundation of the First Amendment: the distinction between free speech and thought on the one hand and punishable acts on the other. Allowing youngsters access to information and ideas about sex is decidedly not the same as engaging them in exploitative sexual conduct. The censorship issues raised by ever harsher and broader child pornography laws are worthy of concern, but they are not the concern of this book.

Another caveat relates to semantics. *Not in Front of the Children* uses different terms more or less interchangeably to refer to sexually explicit information and ideas. "Erotica," "pornography," "literature with sexual content," "sexuality education"—all have different connotations that vary not only with cultures but with individuals' own preconceptions. I use "sexually oriented" or "sexually explicit" here without judgmental implications, simply to describe speech with sexual content. I use "erotica" and "pornography" interchangeably to refer to literature, films, and other forms of expression that are primarily designed for sexual arousal. Reams have been written attempting to distinguish the two on stylistic or ideological grounds, but the distinctions are highly subjective, ultimately resting on differing, and hotly disputed, viewpoints about the nature of sexuality.

The term "censorship" is equally value- and emotion-laden. In Europe its connotation is less negative than in the United States; and even in the United States, with our constitutional commitment to free expression, not all censorship is illegal or necessarily wrong. But there is a distinction between censorship—suppressing speech because of disapproval of its content—and editorial, academic, or artistic judgment about what to publish, teach, or show in a museum. Unlike editorial or artistic decision making, censorship of information and ideas, whether in the presumed interests of youth, civil society, or morality in general, *is* fundamentally contrary to a defining principle of our democracy: that state power should not be used to suppress speech considered subversive or immoral, thus leaving "the government in control of all the institutions of culture, the great censor and director of which thoughts are good for us."[23] It is precisely because this is so basic a principle that "harm to minors" has become the primary justification for censorship and classification schemes in the United States.

Confusion also sometimes arises over the terms "free expression" and "free speech." For purposes of the First Amendment, and the values of intellectual freedom that it embodies, freedom of speech necessarily includes the right to read, view, hear, and think about the expression of others. This right of access and intellectual discovery, in fact, is what is usually involved when we talk about censorship based on harm to minors.

One final point of clarification: objectivity. I have long been a civil liberties advocate, but this book is not an ACLU tract or, indeed, an argument against censorship in any form. If speech is proven to cause direct harm—to personal privacy, to a fair trial, to physical safety, to the right to work, study, or vote—there is a good argument for suppressing or punishing it. The question is whether any similar, directly identifiable harm can be traced to minors' access to sexual or other controversial information or ideas, or whether the issue is really a more generalized ideological one—censorship in the interest of moral values and symbolism. In exploring that issue, I have taken pains to be scrupulously accurate both in recounting the history of harm-to-minors and indecency law and in presenting the psychological questions. I think that neither indecency laws nor censorship of school libraries, neither v-chips nor Internet filters, are great ways to socialize youth and prepare them for an uncertain world; but my primary goal is to raise the questions.

One

"TO DEPRAVE AND CORRUPT"

Minors, Censorship, Sex, and History

The judges who quoted Plato's *Republic* in their 1998 ruling against the drama teacher Margaret Boring reflected a familiar and obviously ancient child-rearing philosophy. As one scholar observed not long ago, "the greatest part of contemporary criticism of television depends on a moral disapproval which is identical to Plato's attack on epic and tragic poetry in the fourth century B.C."[1]

The notion that young people need special protection from improper ideas was not a moral tenet of the ancient world, and in this sense Plato was a rebel. The ancient Greeks associated children with grossness and lewdness, not innocence.[2] Youngsters had to be tamed and educated, but not kept ignorant of sexual realities. On the contrary, the most highly prized sexual relationship in ancient Athens was between an adult man and an adolescent boy; it was viewed as critical to male socialization.[3] Ethicists may have pondered the intricacies and agonized over the pleasures of "Greek love," but Plato's preference for nonsexual affections was largely a protest against things as they were.[4] The same is true of his desire to ban literary descriptions of the gods' erotic activities because they would "engender laxity of morals among the young."[5]

The puritanical Plato, fundamentally suspicious of creative art, rejected the humanism and democracy of Athens and "embraced the barbarism of Sparta," Athens's militaristic rival.[6] That the Spartan program resulted in "a narrow and brittle personality is appalling," according to one historian, but "certainly these virtuous prehistoric people had nothing to learn from us about the possibilities of molding the child."[7]

Plato's pupil Aristotle took a more nuanced view of the imitative effects of art and entertainment. Spectators at tragic dramas, Aristotle said in his *Poetics*, do not imitate the dreadful acts depicted onstage but instead, through the phenomenon of *katharsis*, are purged of violent and unruly emotions.[8] Artists, critics, and philosophers have debated, expanded upon, and modified Aristotle's catharsis theory ever since.[9] But although Aristotle's aesthetics were a break from Plato's more simplistically didactic approach, the younger philosopher was also not exactly a libertarian when it came to minors. In his *Politics*, Aristotle urged that "all unseemly talk" be "kept away from youth," for "the unseemly remark lightly dropped results in conduct of a like kind." Thus, "younger persons" should not be permitted "at comedies or recitals of iambics" (a poetic meter "often used for scurrilous purposes").[10]

As in Greece, boys in ancient Rome were often sexual partners for "gentlemen of quality." Wives, it is said, were greatly relieved when the youths reached puberty and were expected to abandon their "passive" sexual roles for more "manly" forms of erotic activity.[11] A boy's first ejaculation "was celebrated by his family at the feast of the Liberalia." On the other hand, virginity was "sacrosanct" for girls, at least those of the upper classes.[12] But because young females were married by 12 or 14, they also were not ignorant of sexual realities for very long. Youngsters in Roman households were exposed to "foul songs" and other ribaldry. The uninhibited eroticism of frescoes that adorned living spaces in ancient Herculaneum and Pompeii suggests that little effort was made to hide sexually explicit images from young viewers.[13]

Plato and even Aristotle may have disagreed with such exposure of minors to erotic art or ideas, but it was Christianity that radically changed attitudes about sexual knowledge. With the ascendancy of the peculiarly Christian notion that sexual desire is sinful,[14] children's virginity now assumed interior, spiritual value. Simultaneously and paradoxically, Christianity viewed children as untamed vessels of depravity and Original Sin.[15] Up to this point, as historian John Sommerville says, "even the few authors who reflected on the child's needs had considered children to be only potentially human"—infanticide, abandonment, and sales into brothels being among their frequent fates. The precepts of Jesus "exactly reversed the expectations of his hearers" by elevating the helplessness of children, and their ignorance of social convention, to a state of grace.[16]

At the same time, the Christian societies of late antiquity and the early Middle Ages married young people "as close to puberty as possible," not only to maximize the possibilities for childbearing, but to "mitigate through lawful wedlock the disruptive tensions of sexual attraction."[17] In a world where average life expectancy was about 30 years, and infant mortality about 45 percent,[18] an early start at childbearing was probably well advised. So eager were parents to marry off their children that even the minimum legal ages (generally, 12 for girls and 14 for boys) were sometimes overlooked. One court in 11th-century Byzantium invalidated a marriage because the girl was not yet 12.[19]

Christian sexual proscriptions clashed with economic and practical realities. In medieval and early modern Europe, adults and children often slept together around a common fire. A child "learned about intercourse by being in the same bed with parents when they did it."[20] This youthful familiarity with the "primal scene," later thought by Freud to be a source of neurosis, persisted into the 17th century.[21]

At the same time, virginity for girls remained tightly guarded. It was a commodity to be bartered in exchange for an advantageous marriage; it ensured the legitimacy of offspring as well as the husband's ownership of his wife.[22] Children in the Middle Ages and early modern Europe were thus bargaining chips in the business of economic alliance building through marriage, not the coddled innocents of later Western imagination. Infant and child mortality was still high—too high, according to some historians, for parents to invest much emotion in their young.[23] Tight swaddling—essentially immobilizing the young child for upward of a year after birth—was convenient for parents but not likely to advance autonomy or muscular development. The common practice of sending infants away from home to wet nurses did not enhance either mother-child bonding or the likelihood of physical survival. Early apprenticing-out of both middle- and working-class youngsters completed the picture of a social system in which children were viewed more as financial assets than as vulnerable beings.[24]

Records from the Middle Ages, the Renaissance, and early modern times nevertheless reflect some familiar conflicts over youth and sexuality. Children educated in monasteries were strictly controlled in order to prevent sexual contact. Their instructors' fears "were evidently well-founded," for youngsters' hormonal drives and sexual curiosity were manifest even in strict monastic settings.[25] But those sent to nonmonastic schools in the late Middle Ages, at ages as young as 14, often lived a free and bohemian life.[26] Images of juvenile sexuality pervaded Christian iconography, with depictions of the Christ child in sexual situations, and pairings of adult men and adolescent boys. Renaissance artists "revived the use of adolescent figures which the ancients had used to represent Eros."[27]

Censorship of sexual expression was primarily a function of the Church. Savonarola's campaign against indecency in late-15th-century Florence culminated in a "Bonfire of the Vanities" that consumed lewd pictures, books, cards, and trinkets. The Church's first official *Index Librorum Prohibitorum* half a century later banned books "treating of lascivious or obscene subjects," but made an exception for "works of antiquity, written by the heathen," because of "the elegance and propriety of the language."[28] The primary targets were impiety and heresy. The Church censored Boccaccio's bawdy *Decameron*, for example, only to the extent of expurgating "the uncomplimentary references to the clergy." The "amorous incidents" were left untouched, but priests and nuns were replaced with "a citizen, a nobleman, or a bourgeoise."[29]

If minors were not singled out for protection from sexual knowledge or literature, they *were* subject to their parents' commands, and nowhere more so than in the realm of courtship and marriage. Historian Lawrence Stone argues that for Elizabethans watching Shakespeare's *Romeo and Juliet*, the teenagers' rebellion against parental demands was not heroic or admirable, but a violation of duty; their tragedy was "the way they brought destruction upon themselves" by violating social norms.[30] Whether or not we agree with Stone's interpretation, the problem for Romeo and Juliet was clearly not sexual precocity or adolescent lust; these Shakespeare takes for granted. Juliet's wedding-day speech, "Spread thy close curtain, love-performing night," makes the point:

> *Come, civil night,*
> *Thou sober-suited matron, all in black,*
> *And learn me how to lose a winning match,*
> *Played for a pair of stainless maidenheads:*
> *Hood my unmanned blood bating in my cheeks*
> *With thy black mantle . . .*
> *O, I have bought the mansion of a love,*
> *But not possessed it, and, though I am sold,*
> *Not yet enjoyed.*[31]

The Invention of Childhood?

Philippe Ariès argued in his 1960 book, *Centuries of Childhood,* that the modern concept of childhood as a period of prelapsarian innocence was an invention of the 17th century. In the 1500s, "[e]verything was permitted in their presence: coarse language, scabrous actions and situations." "The idea did not yet exist that references to sexual matters . . . could soil childish innocence," because "nobody thought that this innocence really existed." It was only toward the end of the 16th century that "certain pedagogues . . . refused to allow children to be given indecent books any longer." Until then, "nobody had hesitated to give children Terence [the bawdy Roman playwright] to read, for he was a classic. The Jesuits removed him from their curriculum."[32]

Ariès concluded that the idea of a separate and uniquely innocent childhood produced anxieties and neuroses that are still with us. Children had to be taught to conceal their bodies from each other. The new moral climate produced "a whole pedagogic literature for children." As a result, the modern world "is obsessed by the physical, moral, and sexual problems of childhood" in a way that did not occur to ancient or medieval minds. An "increasingly severe disciplinary system" in boarding schools deprived youngsters of the freedom they had previously enjoyed among adults.[33]

Centuries of Childhood has had tremendous influence, and many critics. Historian Natalie Zemon Davis, describing adolescent rituals and escapades in the Renaissance and Middle Ages, concludes that a separate preadult period of maturation was recognized before the 17th century.[34] Lawrence Stone is even more dismissive of theories that adolescence, "and the nuisance it causes to society," were not recognized as problems at least by the Renaissance.[35] John Sommerville points out that not all Christian pedagogues advocated censorship: Martin Luther, for example, "objected that children could not be protected from ribaldry but must conquer it instead."[36] Psychohistorian Lloyd de Mause faults Ariès for minimizing the brutality of beatings, rapes, and other forms of child abuse that existed from earliest times.[37]

Much of the criticism of Ariès is well taken, but does not really undermine his basic insight. All historical periods embody tensions between conflicting social trends. In 19th-century England, Victorian sexual repression coexisted with—even stimulated—a brisk trade in erotica, while simultaneously in the United States rigidly antisexual "Comstockery" thrived, while contending against a vocal movement promoting free love. Thus, Linda Pollock's evidence (to take a nonsexual example) that many 16th-to-18th-century parents doted on their offspring does not negate the fact that other children and adolescents in the same period were starved, beaten, and psychologically abused.[38] Stone's account of English apprentices' precocious social life from the 16th century on suggests that youthful sexuality flourished even while, as Ariès documents, pedagogues were inventing new rationales to control it.[39] As historian David Archard argues, Ariès's claim was not so much that the separate nature of childhood was not recognized in the Middle Ages but that our modern sense of what that nature *is*—uncorrupted, asexual, and psychologically vulnerable—evolved later.[40] And with the modern perception came heavier, more institutionalized censorship and control.

Michel Foucault took Ariès a step further. It has only been in recent centuries, Foucault said, that childhood sexuality began to be isolated, examined, and viewed as sinful precisely so that authority could be exerted to control it. One has only to "glance over the architectural layout," the "rules of discipline," and the "whole internal organization" of secondary schools in 18th-century Europe to see that "the question of sex was a constant preoccupation." "The space for classes, the shape of the tables, the planning of the recreation lessons, the distribution of the dormitories (with or without partitions, with or without curtains), the rules for monitoring bedtime and sleep periods—all this referred, in the most prolix manner, to the sexuality of children." Eventually, "a whole literature of precepts, opinions, observations, medical advice, clinical cases, outlines for reform, and plans for ideal institutions" developed to control the sexuality of the young.[41]

Certainly, the 17th and 18th centuries brought the West closer to contemporary ideas about childhood and sexual expression. Historians note a stronger sense of parental involvement in 17th-century England and America, "new methods of child-rearing, based on the small, nuclear family," a reduction in the number of children being sent from home to become apprentices, and a proliferation of medical interventions and parental-advice manuals.[42] Seventeenth-century Puritanism viewed children as carriers of Original Sin, who must be controlled and indoctrinated into right behavior, but it also led to John Locke's 1693 *Thoughts Concerning Education,* which dramatically influenced pedagogy and child rearing for the next several centuries.

Locke argued for a reasoned, humane, and noncoercive style of teaching and socializing youth. His theory of learning was based on "sensationalist epistemology"—the idea that the human mind is a tabula rasa and that parents and educators are therefore responsible for children's development. Implicitly denying Original Sin, Locke set the stage for increasing state interference in children's upbringing to correct any failings by the formerly autonomous patriarchal father.[43] Some of the effects were salutary—swaddling and wet-nursing declined; revulsion against flogging and other brutalities increased.[44] But new, institutionalized concern for youngsters had its ominous side. If the authoritarian child rearing of Puritan days was justified in the interest of saving youth from sin and damnation, so the more nurturing philosophies that succeeded it rationalized repressive practices as necessary to protect youth from frailty, disease, or corruption. Censorship became a concern because "sensationalist epistemology" assumed that amoral literature could create "impressions as real to the mind as those made by other experience."[45] The most repressive and brutalizing manifestation of the new protectionism was the collection of myths and practices directed toward suppressing youthful masturbation.

The publication in 1710 of a lurid English tract entitled *Onania, or the Heinous Sin of Self-Pollution, And all its frightful Consequences, in both Sexes, Considered,* marked the beginning. The "frightful consequences" ranged from pimples and lapses of memory to hysteria, impotence, bodily pains and itching, tumors, and insanity.[46] *Onania* reportedly passed through at least eighty editions; it was translated, studied, and duly incorporated into medical tomes.[47] By far the most influential of these was the Swiss physician Samuel-Auguste Tissot's 1758 work, *L'Onanisme, Dissertation sur les Maladies produites par la Masturbation,* which drew on *Onania* even while acknowledging that the earlier work was "a perfect chaos," full of "moral trivialisms." Claiming the authority of science that his predecessor lacked but also relying on moral and religious exhortations, Tissot reported many dreadful consequences of youthful self-gratification, including consumption, incontinence, jaundice, loose teeth, sallow complexion, and a variety of psychological ills that—to the extent Tissot's secondhand reports were accurate—were probably caused by the overwhelming shame and guilt foisted on youngsters who indulged in the natural, common practice.[48]

Literary historian Walter Kendrick explains *L'Onanisme* as based "on the ancient theory of the humors," bodily fluids thought to govern "everything from excretion to thinking." To masturbate meant, "according to a clear if barbaric logic," to waste precious semen. "Performed in childhood, masturbation rechanneled the life force that should have gone toward healthy physical and moral development. Its result was weak, sickly, and impotent adults."[49] As for girls, the "economic metaphor" of wasted sperm "worked less well," yet Tissot thought the damage wrought by female masturbation was even more severe, and included "a horrifying list of specifically female complaints," from "attacks of hysteria or frightful vapors" to cramps, discharges, "falling and ulceration of the womb," "lengthening and scabbing of the clitoris," and, finally, "uterine fury, which deprives them at once of modesty and reason and puts them on the level of the lewdest brutes."[50]

It is not easy to understand why adults began in the 18th century so severely to punish their children for responding to a natural impulse. One is even tempted to consider Lloyd de Mause's theory (not credited by most historians) that parents, doctors, educators, and government officials had reached a "psychohistorical" stage at which children became the unfortunate scrims on which adults projected their own sexual anxieties.[51] But whatever the cause of the obsession, for the next 150 years, as Peter Gay recounts, preventive measures ranged from the relatively mild "avoidance of tight lacing, licentious novels, featherbeds, and similar luxuries" to horrifying practices like "cauterization of the sexual organs, infibulation, castration, and clitoridectomy," and elaborate mechanical restraints: "modern chastity belts for girls and ingenious penile rings for boys or straitjackets for both, all designed to keep growing or adolescent sinners from getting at themselves."[52] Havelock Ellis summarized: Tissot and his followers were responsible for much of "the suffering, dread, and remorse experienced in silence by many thousands" of young people over several centuries.[53]

A few years after Tissot published his influential work, European intellectuals were devising sunnier, less punitive, but not necessarily more balanced views of youth and sexuality. *Émile, or On Education,* Jean-Jacques Rousseau's fictionalized 1762 treatise on child rearing, insisted on the natural innocence of youth, urged withdrawal of adolescents from the libertine and "scandalous morals" of 18th-century French life, and imposed detailed prescriptions for an ideal education. Although Rousseau acknowledged that sexual potency comes with puberty, he wanted to postpone initiation and even instruction until the age of 20. In the meantime, he urged, adults must avoid arousing youngsters' erotic curiosity. "Put their nascent imaginations off the track with objects which, far from inflaming, repress the activity of their senses."[54] Although Rousseau has been credited with at least "calling attention to the needs of children,"[55] his pedagogical theories had an authoritarian edge; and despite his sentimentalizing of childhood, he left his own five illegitimate children at foundling homes.[56]

If Rousseau's recommendations for ignoring adolescent sexuality and Tissot's obsessive focus on controlling it represented two extremes of 18th-century thought, the artists of the era presented a more balanced view. One of the century's most memorable teenagers, Cherubino in the Mozart/Da Ponte opera *Le Nozze di Figaro,* expresses the sexual turbulence and curiosity of adolescence in the famous aria "Non so più": "I don't know anymore what I am or what I'm doing / Now I'm burning, now I'm made of ice . . . /

Every woman makes me change color, / Every woman makes me throb."[57] These spontaneous expressions of sexual emotion suggest that adolescents in the 18th century were understood to be not so much innocent as merely inexperienced, hormone-driven, and confused.

By the middle of the 19th century, the contradictory ideas of youthful sexuality embodied in the randy Cherubino, the naive Émile, and Tissot's lurid masturbating child merged to produce the beginnings of modern obscenity law. The view of children as "both inherently wicked" and "totally innocent, angels, not yet corrupted by the wickedness of the temporal scene,"[58] became simultaneous, mutually reinforcing justifications for a new form of censorship directed specifically at preventing juvenile corruption. Kendrick put the matter in literary terms: a "hypothetical institution called 'the Young Person,'" invented by the character Mr. Podsnap in Charles Dickens's novel *Our Mutual Friend,* had, at all costs, to be protected from anything that would cause her to blush. The Young Person was innocent and fragile but simultaneously "a frightening dynamo, anarchic and profligate in her actions." Not just pornography but romantic novels were likely dangers: physicians advised parents to channel their daughters' minds away from such "vicious" reading habits.[59] Even opera was thought too dangerously arousing for youthful viewers,[60] while Shakespeare had been purified as early as 1807, when Thomas Bowdler and his sister Harriet published their first expurgated edition of the Bard. Hoping that they had "removed 'everything that can raise a blush on the cheek of modesty,'" the Bowdlers excised large sections of *Hamlet* and eliminated *Romeo and Juliet* altogether. (It did reappear in Bowdler's second edition, "with the Nurse playing an exceedingly diminished role.")[61]

"Protecting the Young and Immature"

Heresy and sedition were the primary targets of censorship before the 19th century. Censors simply "did not think it worth their while to concern themselves with chap-books and similar light literature, some of which was very coarse."[62] Although there were a few prosecutions in the 18th century, resulting in a new "common law" crime of obscene libel, enforcement was sporadic, and such Enlightenment classics as John Cleland's *Memoirs of a Woman of Pleasure (Fanny Hill)* and Benjamin Franklin's *Advice to a Young Man on the Choice of a Mistress* circulated freely. The "few shots fired" were "mostly blanks."[63]

The English case traditionally cited as the precedent for obscenity law had nothing to do with art, literature, bawdy chapbooks, or erotica. In 1663, the poet and reveler Sir Charles Sedley threw bottles of urine over the balcony of the Cock Tavern in London while he "with eloquence preached blasphemy to the people."[64] Samuel Pepys's contemporary account has Sedley naked on the balcony, "acting all the postures of lust and buggery that could be imagined," preaching "a Mountebanke sermon," and saying that "he hath to sell such a pouder as should make all the cunts in town run after him."[65] Sedley was convicted of a misdemeanor, and the government cited the case forty-five years later when it first tried to prosecute a work of pornography (entitled *Fifteen Plagues of a Maidenhead*). The prosecution was dismissed on the ground that while a crime "that shakes religion, as profaneness on the stage, etc., is indictable," simply "writing an obscene book" is not.[66]

The first real obscenity-law precedent (as opposed to the dubious precedent of *Sedley*) came in 1728, when political pressures mounted to silence "the grubbiest publisher in Grub Street," Edmund Curl. The work in question this time was *Venus in the Cloister, or the Nun in Her Smock*, which combined anti-Catholicism with "several lewd passages."[67] Relying again on *Rex v. Sedley*, but this time with more success, the Attorney General argued that if an action or publication was "destructive of morality in general," then it constituted "an offence of a publick nature." He cited a case in which a publisher had been indicted "for printing some obscene poems" by the notorious Lord Rochester, which tended "to the corruption of youth; upon which he went abroad, and was outlawed; which he would not have done if his counsel had thought it no libel." This argument by inference persuaded the Court of King's Bench, which now overruled the earlier ruling in favor of *Fifteen Plagues of a Maidenhead* and created a new common-law crime of obscenity.[68] It was subsequently invoked against the antiroyalist gadfly John Wilkes, but for essentially political reasons: Wilkes's polemics infuriated King George III. The obscenity charge against Wilkes followed a tumultuous reading in the House of Lords of his *Essay on Woman*, a parody of Alexander Pope's celebrated *Essay on Man*. Wilkes's version began: "Let us (since life can little more supply / Than just a few good fucks, and then we die) / Expatiate free o'er that lov'd scene of Man; / A mighty Maze! For mighty Pricks to scan."[69]

The United States, like England, had only a smattering of obscenity prosecutions in the 18th century.[70] Massachusetts did pass a law in 1711 that banned "any filthy, obscene, or profane song, pamphlet, libel, or mock sermon," but the essence of the offense was in the "mimicking of preaching, or any other part of divine worship."[71] It was not until 1835 that the law was modified to criminalize "obscene or indecent" speech divorced from religious impiety—if it "manifestly" tended "to the corruption of the morals of youth."[72] In the interim, Massachusetts used the "common law" of obscenity, borrowed from England: in 1821, it charged a publisher with contriving "to debauch and corrupt" the morals of youth as well as "other good citizens," and to "create in their minds inordinate and lustful desires," by "wickedly, maliciously and scandalously" publishing a "lewd, wicked, scandalous, infamous and obscene" book. The object of the prosecutors' ire was *Fanny Hill*.[73]

Pennsylvania was also a trendsetter. As early as 1815, it prosecuted the exhibition of a painting from the Naples Museum that was said to depict "a man in an obscene, impudent and indecent posture with a woman, to the manifest corruption and subversion of youth, and other citizens of this commonwealth." The defendant, relying on the British distinction between ecclesiastical and secular courts, argued that the alleged offense was not a punishable crime; but the presiding judge insisted that "actions of *public indecency* were always indictable [in England], as tending to corrupt the public morals."[74]

These early state cases suggested that "obscene" expression could be censored to protect the morals of youth and other impressionable folk, but prosecutions were rare.[75] It was not until 1842 that Congress enacted the first federal ban, authorizing the U.S. Customs Service to confiscate "obscene or immoral" pictures or prints and bring judicial proceedings for their destruction.[76] Legal historians James Paul and Murray Schwartz comment on the swiftness and lack of debate that marked this radical legal change: "In hindsight it was a novel measure, a type of censorship statute and the first of its kind in this country. Yet it slipped into the law unnoticed." Its significance "as a technique to control reading and press freedom was not appreciated."[77]

This first federal sex-censorship law reflected a confluence of new social pressures. Industrialization and urbanization in Europe and the United States were breaking down traditional demographic patterns and making urban poverty, crowding, prostitution, drinking, gambling, and other "vices" increasingly visible. The 18th century's relatively relaxed sexual standards, partly a reaction against Puritanism, gave way to new evangelical strands of Christianity, which in turn spawned moral-purity crusades, YMCAs, and "sex hygiene" campaigns that encouraged celibacy by detailing the ravages of venereal disease. Immigration to the United States heightened nativist fears that foreigners with "low morals" would not only gain political power but "outbreed" Americans whose ancestors had arrived a few generations (or, in some cases, centuries) before. The spread of literacy and consequent availability of sex education tracts and cheap novels to workers and adolescents (including females) only heightened middle- and upper-class anxieties. "Licentious" books and prints were visible and symbolically important targets.[78]

Children and adolescents were not the only objects of the purity crusaders, but they were increasingly important ones. The culture's growing attention to children's separate status culminated in Romantic- and Victorian-era celebrations of youthful sexual innocence. The loosening of patriarchy meanwhile led to increased reliance on law to police youthful morality. The social-purity movement, with support from government and professional groups, now justified censorship by denying the existence of, or else maintaining the need to repress, the sexual interests of youth. Institutionalization and medicalization of public health, welfare, and education created new opportunities for control. By the close of the century, the new "science" of psychology was turning adolescence into a conceptually separate and vulnerable stage of life, worthy of scholarly study as well as institutional concern. Responding to pressures for purity and campaigns against prostitution, particularly among working-class girls with limited economic alternatives, legislators increased statutory ages of sexual consent—from medians of 10 or 12 to 14, 16, 18, or (in the case of U.S. federal territories) 21.[79] Historian Alison Parker summarizes: by the late 19th century, "focus on the morality of youth was central to the public's support of all censorship campaigns."[80]

A paradoxical aspect of the new repression, as Michel Foucault notes, was the increasing *centrality* of sex—especially of youthful interest in sex—as a public concern. Even "the refusal to talk about it," as one Foucaultian explains, "marks it as the secret and puts it at the heart of discourse."[81] It was thus Victorian prudery that fed pornography, which "flourished as never before" alongside the new obscenity bans.[82] At the economic level, there was a brutal irony in the simultaneous myth of childhood innocence and the exploitation of actual children in the Industrial Revolution's mines and factories.[83] By the late 19th century, adolescents in Massachusetts were on average providing one-third of their family's income; in the United States overall, only about 7 percent were in high school, with most of the remainder presumably at work;[84] but social purists were busy trying to shield them from corrupting literature.

In 1865, Congress expanded the federal obscenity ban from controls on importation to restrictions on domestic use of the mails. Salacious literature was being sent to Union soldiers, and the Postmaster General had been confiscating these packages without statutory authority. The 1865 law was largely intended to legitimize the seizures. Some congressmen did raise questions about both the invasions of privacy and the unrestrained censorship likely to result from a legislative grant to administrative officials of broad, discretionary authority to seize art and literature of which they disapproved.[85] But this first obscenity mail ban passed without significant controversy. It provided that no "obscene, lewd, or lascivious book, pamphlet, picture, print, or other publication of vulgar and indecent character shall be admitted into the mails,"[86] on pain of criminal penalties, and became the basis for a broad-ranging bureaucratic censorship of the mails that went unchallenged for most of the next century.

Like the United States, Britain passed its first obscenity statute in the mid–19th century. (The earlier prosecutions had been under the common law of obscene libel.) The Obscene Publications Act of 1857 was the handiwork of Lord Chief Justice John Campbell, who had started the legislative ball rolling by asking his fellow aristocrats in the House of Lords whether something should not be done about the free circulation of "a poison more deadly than prussic acid, strychnine or arsenic—the sale of obscene publications and indecent books," which were now so modestly priced that they were "sold to any person who asked for them."[87] Campbell's brethren were not swept away by his charged rhetoric; indeed, they put up a much greater struggle than Congress did in 1865, or would do in 1873 when it expanded the U.S. government's censorship powers. Lord Brougham, for example, with more than a hint of irony, said "he was sure that no one was more competent to judge of the extent of the evil" of pornography than "the noble and learned" Lord Campbell, but asked "how did he propose to define what was an 'obscene publication'? " Brougham reminded his "noble and learned Friend, that, in the works of some of their most eminent poets there were some objectionable passages."[88] Lord Lyndhurst chimed in with two examples from visual art: Correggio's "Jupiter and Antiope," showing "a woman stark naked, lying down, and a satyr standing by her with an expression on his face which shows most distinctly what his feelings are"; and "Danaë," showing "a naked woman lifting her eyes to heaven, but standing in a very strange attitude, the shower of gold descending upon her, a little Cupid peeping over her shoulder pointing with his dart, and other circumstances which I will not describe." Lyndhurst mentioned also the bawdy plays of the English Restoration: there was "not a page in any one of them," he said, "which might not be seized under this Bill." One of Congreve's characters is

"Lady Wishfor't," he said, and Dryden "is as bad as any of them," having translated Ovid's *The Art of Love*.[89]

Campbell replied that his proposed law was "intended to apply exclusively to works written with the single purpose of corrupting the morals of youth, and of a nature calculated to shock the common feelings of decency in any well-regulated mind."[90] With support from the clergy and the Society for the Suppression of Vice, he continued to insist that the young must be shielded from the licentious and "abominable" works available at any railway station.[91] Lord Campbell's Act passed despite the protest, giving police (with a warrant) the power to seize books or pictures they believed to be obscene and to destroy them unless the owner appeared before two justices and disproved the government's accusation. Eleven years later, in the landmark case of *Regina v. Hicklin*, the new law received an expansive, youth-oriented judicial interpretation that would dominate English and American law for most of the next century.

The literature at issue in *Hicklin* was an anticlerical pamphlet, *The Confessional Unmasked*, distributed by the Protestant Electoral Union and designed to oppose the election of Catholics to Parliament by "shewing the depravity of the Romish priesthood, the iniquity of the Confessional, and the questions put to females in confession."[92] One Henry Scott, from whom a collection of the pamphlets had been seized, claimed the work was not obscene because it was written and distributed for legitimate political purposes. A lower court agreed, and quashed the order of seizure (Benjamin Hicklin was one of the judges). But Chief Justice Alexander Cockburn, writing for the Court of Queen's Bench on appeal, held that legitimate intentions were no excuse for publishing or disseminating obscenity. The standard for judging the work, said Cockburn, was "whether the tendency of the matter charged as obscenity is to deprave and corrupt those whose minds are open to such immoral influences and into whose hands a publication of this sort may fall."[93]

How was one to identify those whose minds might be "depraved and corrupted" by "immoral influences"? As Cockburn explained, a medical treatise "with illustrations necessary for the information of those for whose education or information the work is intended, may, in a certain sense, be obscene, and yet not the subject for indictment; but it can never be that these prints may be exhibited for any one, boys and girls, to see as they pass." *The Confessional Unmasked*, like this hypothetical medical text, was obscene because it "would suggest to the minds of the young of either sex, and even to persons of more advanced years, thoughts of a most impure and libidinous character."[94] The purpose of obscenity law was thus to prevent immoral literature from falling into the wrong hands, whether they be those of servants, the mentally deficient, women, or minors. That women and mental defectives were included among the classes to be "protected" was consistent with the ideology of an era when, as Peter Gay recounts, women were also classed with "criminals, idiots, and minors" for purposes of property and inheritance law.[95] By the early 20th century, as egalitarian sentiments began to replace sexual and class hierarchies, shielding the young became ever more pivotal as the justification for obscenity laws.

Contrary to Lord Campbell's assurances, the Obscene Publications Act was soon used to suppress not merely pornography or even racy anticlerical pamphlets but also works of high literary art. The prosecution and imprisonment of the publisher Henry Vizetelly in 1888 for making the works of Zola, Flaubert, Daudet, and Maupassant available to the British public was one dramatic early consequence of the *Hicklin* test. Vizetelly, elderly and ailing, was jailed for three months in 1889 and died five years later "a ruined man."[96] The first volume in Havelock Ellis's massive *Studies in the Psychology of Sex* was suppressed in 1898; the author, incensed, refused to publish the other volumes in England until the 1930s.[97] The condemnation of Ellis's *Studies*, says sociologist Bill Thompson, "put British sexology into hibernation for over 60 years."[98] England exported its Victorian culture, including its obscenity standard, and censorship tests almost identical to *Hicklin* soon appeared in India, Australia, and of course the United States.

Free Love, the Comstock Law, and "Secret Entertainment"

Thanks to the ingenuity of George Bernard Shaw, who gave the noun "Comstockery" to the English language, the historical image of Anthony Comstock is more comic than threatening. Cartoonist Robert Minor in 1915 depicted him in the radical *Masses* magazine as a sexually obsessed Puritan dragging a poor woman into court on the criminal charge of giving birth to a "naked child" (see illustrations).[99] But Comstock was a smart and energetic man who, whatever the neuroses that drove him, arrived on the political scene at an opportune moment, knew how to make use of it, and wielded power over journalism, arts, and letters in the United States for forty years.

Born in 1844 "to devout Connecticut farm parents," as Paul Boyer writes, "this child of destiny arrived in New York City in 1867, a Civil War veteran with five dollars in his pocket." He tried clerking in a dry-goods store, but in 1872 "realized his true calling when he noticed the shocking books and pictures his fellow-employees were surreptitiously passing about."[100] Comstock had one malefactor arrested, discovered his talent for publicity, and soon attracted financial support from prominent businessmen, with whom he founded the New York Society for the Suppression of Vice.

Comstock's biographers suggest that, like many young men of religious background, he was tortured by guilt over masturbation.[101] Certainly, his writings betray an obsessive fascination with the subject. In his 1880 book, *Frauds Exposed,* Comstock warned that evil reading "breeds lust," which "defiles the body, debauches the imagination, corrupts the mind, deadens the will, destroys the memory, sears the conscience, hardens the heart, and damns the soul." Like a "panorama," he went on, "the imagination seems to keep this hated thing before the mind, until it wears its way deeper and deeper, plunging the victim into practices he loathes."[102] Three years later, Comstock's *Traps for the Young* enlisted the same lurid prose: there is "no more active agent employed by Satan in civilized communities to ruin the human family than EVIL READING." The "moral vulture" of obscenity "steals upon our youth in the home, school, and college, silently striking its terrible talons into their vitals, and forcibly bearing them away on hideous wings to shame and death."[103]

Comstock did not have a monopoly on overheated rhetoric. Boy Scout manuals also warned that "semen had to be hoarded"; that " 'secret bad habits' led to hysteria and lunacy"; and that "degeneracy" was transforming "a large proportion of our robust, manly, self-reliant boyhood into a lot of flat-chested cigarette-smokers, with shaky nerves and doubtful vitality."[104] The annual reports of the New York society and its Boston counterpart, the Watch and Ward Society, warned that even "the briefest of stimulating passages" in literature "could plunge the helpless reader into that 'state of excitement in which principle is overcome by passion and nothing but opportunity is wanted for unbridled indulgence.' " To avoid corruption, "only stern measures would suffice: 'The mind must not be permitted to dwell for a moment upon improper subjects. All reading and conversation must be of the most pure and elevating character.' "[105]

These references to "unbridled indulgence" and "secret vice" were hardly subtle. A century after Dr. Tissot's warnings of the fearful effects of youthful masturbation, it was ever more urgently the issue; and as with other disapproved sexual conduct, suppression became a matter of social, medical, and government concern. Comstock tapped into "both the fears and the longings of mainstream America . . . the specter of sexuality unleashed from traditional controls."[106] His Society for the Suppression of Vice cannot be credited with all of the censorship that took place, but it was the most prominent among the organizations in the moral-purity campaign. Enrolling corporate and civic leaders, progressives and feminists, the purity movement had little notion that literary censorship might violate the First Amendment (neither did most judges at the time). Censorship probably did not seem different in principle from providing young people with wholesome alternative nonsexual pastimes at the local YMCA or fighting prostitution and venereal disease. Indeed, the American Library Association, later to become a stalwart defender of minors' First Amendment rights, began by carefully screening youngsters' reading for immoral themes.[107]

As the director and moving spirit of New York's newly formed Society for the Suppression of Vice, Anthony Comstock "needed a big case" in 1872 to make his reputation.[108] He found it in the pages of *Woodhull and Claflin's Weekly*, a paper published by the radical feminist sisters Victoria Woodhull and Tennessee Claflin. The *Weekly* had published allegations of an adulterous affair between the famed preacher Henry Ward Beecher and Elizabeth Tilton, a local admirer. The language was decorous: the most Comstock had to seize upon were the words "token" and "virginity" (the latter from another article in the *Weekly*); but the sisters' free-love preachings, outspoken support for the 1871 Paris Commune, and unconventional lifestyles had aroused sufficient indignation in legal circles to push the prosecution forward. Comstock swore out a warrant under the 1865 obscenity law (which had been recodified in 1872); Woodhull and Claflin were arrested at their Wall Street brokerage firm (these sisters were nothing if not versatile); and federal marshals seized and destroyed 3,000 copies of the *Weekly* in addition to press and office equipment. Ultimately, the prosecution was dismissed because the 1872 law did not cover newspapers, but by then Comstock had successfully lobbied for a new one.[109]

He arrived in Washington in January 1873 carrying "a great cloth bag" filled with "lowbrow publications and their advertisements, gadgets purportedly designed to stimulate sexual potency, . . . bogus sexual literature, contraceptive and abortifacient matter, and other 'abominations' which were sold via the ads."[110] Denouncing his opponents "as lechers and defilers of youth and American womanhood,"[111] Comstock steamrolled a new obscenity law through Congress in just two months. It clarified the government's powers of confiscation and destruction, and expanded the 1865 law by adding to the laundry list of banned items "any article or thing designed or intended for the prevention of conception or procuring of abortion," or, indeed, "any article or thing intended or adapted for any indecent or immoral use or nature."[112] President Grant signed the Comstock Act on March 3, 1873, and two days later, the Post Office appointed Comstock its special agent to seize publications and devices he considered immoral and to prosecute their senders.[113]

The Comstock law was an unexceptional product of its time—after all, if libidinous literature might lead to the "secret vice" and its consequent dangers, it was the least the state could do to outlaw it. But late-19th-century moral attitudes were not monolithic, as the brief success of such radical publications as *Woodhull and Claflin's Weekly* demonstrated. At the same time that anti-vice societies were attacking abortifacients and lustful literature, anarchists and libertarians were challenging repression and preaching the virtues of free love. England had its outspoken sex radicals—Havelock Ellis, Edward Carpenter, Oscar Wilde and his circle. In the United States, the charismatic Emma Goldman, the notorious Victoria Woodhull, and the lesser-known Ezra Heywood and Moses Harmon were among the leaders of a noisy, passionate assault on Victorian morality and reticence. The same year the Comstock Act was passed, free-love advocates held a convention with the announced goals of women's suffrage, access to birth control, and an end to the sexual double standard. Not surprisingly, Harmon and Heywood were among Comstock's earliest targets for obscenity prosecution.[114]

One problem, of course, was that the terms "obscene, lewd, or lascivious," "indecent," and "immoral" were not defined in the 1873 Comstock law. "I know it when I see it" may have been the initial assumption then, as it became for Supreme Court Justice Potter Stewart a century later,[115] but it was the 1868 English decision in *Regina v. Hicklin*, with its "deprave and corrupt"/vulnerable-minors standard, that provided U.S. courts with a definition for punishable obscenity. Two years after Lord Cockburn penned the memorable prose of *Hicklin*, a Pennsylvania judge approved a jury's consideration of whether a medical text with explicit illustrations could appropriately be sent to families, "handed to their sons and daughters, and placed in boarding-schools for the beneficial information of the young and others."[116] Nine years later, in *United States v. Bennett*, the U.S. Court of Appeals for the Second Circuit squarely adopted the *Hicklin* standard.

Bennett was the culmination of Anthony Comstock's campaign against the free-love activist Ezra Heywood. Heywood's colleague De Robigne M. Bennett had decided to challenge the constitutionality of the Comstock law by sending Heywood's twenty-three-page pamphlet, *Cupid's Yokes, or The Binding Forces of Conjugal Life*, through the mail in response to one of Comstock's favored tactics, a decoy letter requesting material.[117] *Cupid's*

Yokes was a rhapsodic argument for sexual freedom, against the restrictions of marriage, and not coincidentally against Comstock himself and his "National Gag Law," as Heywood termed the 1873 act. Censors like Comstock, Heywood wrote, suppress both adults' and children's ability to get honest sexual information; Comstock was an inquisitor and "a religious monomaniac" whom "the mistaken will of Congress and the lascivious fanaticism of the Young Men's Christian Association have empowered to use the Federal Courts to suppress Free Inquiry."[118]

Neither Heywood nor Bennett was a stranger to obscenity law when the *Bennett* case began. Massachusetts had convicted Heywood of obscenity in 1878 for distributing *Cupid's Yokes*; following the era's cultural script, the prosecutor's summation had emphasized "the terrible effect such a pernicious doctrine as free love would be likely to have upon boys and girls in school, and upon others who had not reached the age of mature judgment." Heywood was sentenced to two years in the Dedham jail, but pardoned six months later by President Hayes after a vigorous campaign by free-speech advocates.[119] As for Bennett, Comstock had already prosecuted him for a scientific pamphlet of veterinary bent entitled *How Do Marsupials Propagate?*[120] and in August 1878, just two months after Heywood was jailed in Massachusetts, state authorities arrested Bennett and two colleagues for selling *Cupid's Yokes* at a meeting of the New York Freethinkers Association. This state case never went to trial, but the federal charge against *Cupid's Yokes* resulted in conviction, and this time no pardon from President Hayes was in sight.

On appeal, the Second Circuit rejected all of Bennett's legal arguments in a long meandering opinion. There was no issue of freedom of religion or of the press, the court said; Bennett and Heywood may hold any views they wish, but they may not, under the law, "publish them in connection with obscene matter." The appellate judges thus approved an instruction that the trial judge had given the jury based on the *Hicklin* "deprave and corrupt" test—that is, the work was obscene "if it would suggest impure and libidinous thoughts in the young and inexperienced." As in *Hicklin*, even one indecent passage in a work was sufficient for conviction.[121] The judges noted that two years earlier the Supreme Court had approvingly cited the Comstock Act in *Ex parte Jackson*, a decision upholding a Post Office ban on lottery circulars. The Supreme Court had assumed in *Jackson* that an obscenity ban, like a restriction on mailing lottery material, was a proper exercise of government power to protect "public morals."[122]

Obscenity laws in both England and the United States were now explicitly premised on the presumed need to prevent youthful libidinous thoughts.

It seems hardly necessary to note that although many suffered as a result, the effort was not destined to succeed. A German doctor, as Peter Gay recounts, reported in 1912 that "71 percent of all German secondary-school students are onanists, while Russian, German, and Hungarian researchers had discovered even higher, downright appalling percentages of self-abuse." One professor "declared the number of adolescent masturbators in Germany to be 100 percent," while another "reached the same total for America's youth, male and female alike."[123]

As for Ezra Heywood, Comstock continued to pursue him as relentlessly as Victor Hugo's Inspector Javert pursued Jean Valjean. Heywood's health was eventually ruined by his repeated stays in prison. But his wife, Angela, carried on the family tradition: in 1893, she wrote in the couple's newspaper, *The Word:* "What mother can look in the face of her welcome child and not religiously respect the rigid, erect, ready-for-service, persistent male organ that sired it?"[124]

Some Judges Start Asking Questions

American courts quickly lined up behind the prestigious Second Circuit's embrace of *Regina v. Hicklin*. In 1881, for example, a Missouri federal court held an illustrated medical pamphlet, intended for general circulation, to be obscene because even though "much of the offensive matter is taken from books upon medicine and surgery, which would be proper enough for the general use of members and students of the profession," the same publication, when "sent through the mail to persons of all classes, including boys and girls, would be highly indecent and obscene."[125] An 1891 prosecution against Moses Harmon, publisher of the free-love magazine *Lucifer*, also resulted in conviction. A Wisconsin judge the same year ruled that the pamphlet *A Monitor for Men*, answering questions about sexual disorders, was obscene because "liable to fall into the hands of the immature," for whom it "might well be deemed corrupting."[126]

It evidently did not occur to these judges that the Comstock law's criminal ban would also deprive educated adults of edifying information or entertainment. That insight began to find its way into occasional judicial opinions, but the Supreme Court would not embrace it until 1957. The standard having been set, moreover, most cases never got to court. As the historians of U.S. Post Office censorship put it, "informal administrative procedures" were used to suppress countless literary works based on "broad criteria which used possible impact on the minds of children." From its inception in the 1870s until the 1930s, this administrative decision making "was virtually unpoliced by the courts."[127]

At least one judge in the 1890s did express doubts about the breadth of the *Hicklin* test. The case involved "rare and costly editions" of various classics that were held in receivership, including *The Arabian Nights*, Ovid's *Art of Love*, Boccaccio's *Decameron*, Fielding's *Tom Jones*, and Rousseau's *Confessions*. The receiver sued Comstock in New York State court, seeking judicial instructions regarding final disposition of the works. Comstock, who had state as well as federal authority, maintained that the books were "unfit for general circulation" and accordingly must be excluded from the receiver's sale. But the trial judge found that suppressing these bawdy classics would be "quite as unjustifiable" as condemning the works of Shakespeare, Chaucer, or Laurence Sterne. Even here, however, it was important that the books be confined to the upper crust: the judge noted that these were expensive editions that "would not be bought nor appreciated by the class of people from whom unclean publications ought to be withheld. They are not corrupting in their influence upon the young, for they are not likely to reach them."[128]

So matters stood in 1896 when the U.S. Supreme Court for the first time took up the obscenity issue. Lew Rosen had been convicted for mailing—in response to a Comstock decoy letter—a paper called *Broadway* that contained "pictures of females . . . partially covered with lamp black that could be easily erased with a piece of bread." Justice John Harlan (who that same year was to dissent from the Court's *Plessy v. Ferguson* decision upholding racial segregation) wrote an opinion affirming the conviction. Rejecting Rosen's claim that he was not on reasonable notice that his paper was obscene, Harlan said that everyone who uses the mails "must take notice of what, in this enlightened age, is meant by decency, purity, chastity in social life, and what must be deemed obscene, lewd, and lascivious." His only explanation of what obscenity did mean was his approval of the trial judge's charge to the jury based on the "deprave and corrupt" standard of *Hicklin* and focusing on whether the publication would "suggest or convey lewd thoughts and lascivious thoughts to the young and inexperienced."[129] Two justices dissented on the ground that the indictment failed to state what exactly in the newspaper was supposed to be obscene. None said a word about the First Amendment implications of the Comstock law, or the fact that the *Hicklin* protection-of-minors test had the effect of reducing the adult population to a level of purity deemed necessary for a child.

The New York decision protecting Boccaccio and other bawdy classics, meanwhile, did not put an end to literary censorship. Although another New York court, in 1909, did hold Voltaire's *Philosophical Dictionary* and

Maid of Orleans not obscene,[130] judges elsewhere were less liberal. The scholar and free-speech activist Theodore Schroeder reported in 1907 that in England "a publisher, to escape criminal punishment, has consented to destroy his stock of Rabelais and Boccaccio." In Indiana, a bookseller "was induced to plead guilty" to mailing "an obscene book, to wit, *Decameron* of Boccaccio."[131] The Customs Bureau lifted its ban on importing Rabelais's two classics, *Gargantua* and *Pantagruel*, only in 1930, and even then only for some editions.[132]

The first truly thoughtful judicial opinion on obscenity came in 1913 from the scholarly Learned Hand, then a federal trial judge in New York. The defendant was Mitchell Kennerley, publisher of *Hagar Revelly*, "a novel of manners presenting the life of a young woman" who is "impulsive, sensuous, fond of pleasure, and restive under the monotony and squalor of her surroundings." According to the court's summary, "some of the scenes are depicted with a frankness and detail which have given rise to this prosecution."[133]

Judge Hand reluctantly rejected a motion to dismiss the charges against Kennerley, explaining that the *Hicklin* test was now widely accepted in the federal courts, so that "it would be no longer proper for me to disregard it," and that under *Hicklin* a few passages in the novel "certainly might tend to corrupt" those "whose minds were open to such immoral influences." But Hand protested: "however consonant it [the rule in *Hicklin*] may be with mid-Victorian morals," it "does not seem to me to answer to the understanding and morality of the present time."[134] Hand questioned the wisdom of keying censorship to a standard of "all which might corrupt the most corruptible." In a passage that became famously influential, he said: "it seems hardly likely that we are even to-day so lukewarm in our interest in letters or serious discussion as to be content to reduce our treatment of sex to the standard of a child's library in the supposed interest of a salacious few."[135]

The language was felicitous, the judge prestigious, and the sentiments unquestionably reasonable, but it was to be another forty-four years before the Supreme Court embraced the simple proposition that, if there was to be literary censorship, "a child's library" was not the appropriate standard. In the interim, it was not only attitudes about candor and sexuality that had to change but, as historian Nicola Beisel writes, the deeper social anxieties that account for the periodic successes of Comstockery. In the late 19th century, these anxieties included fear of immigrants, perceived threats to the power of social elites, and changes in the role of women. Similar social upheavals, Beisel suggests, may account for the revival of rhetoric about moral dangers to youth in our own time.[136]

Two

MORE EMETIC THAN APHRODISIAC

Freud, the First Amendment, and a First Round with Ulysses

The same year Judge Learned Hand wrote in *United States v. Kennerley* that "the understanding and morality of the present time" rejected Victorian-era sexual repression, Dr. Sigmund Freud published an article describing the influence of his psychoanalytic theories of dream interpretation, childhood sexuality, and neurosis on virtually every facet of modern culture. Eight years earlier, Freud's soon to be famous *Three Essays on the Theory of Sexuality* had detailed "the universality and normality of infantile and childhood sexuality." Another essay, "The Sexual Enlightenment of Children," had labeled society's usual reasons for keeping youngsters sexually ignorant "absurd."[1] Freud's "unblinking candor about sex"[2] distinguished him from earlier critics of Victorianism, and his historic 1909 lectures at Clark University in Massachusetts brought the issue squarely into American cultural life.

No intellectual revolution arrives without antecedents, of course; and despite its well-earned reputation for prudery, the late 19th century was obsessed with the question of sex. Its elaborate mechanisms of repression and campaigns for social purity were ways of talking and writing incessantly about the subject. Michel Foucault explains: "From the bad habits of children to the phthises of adults, the apoplexies of old people, nervous maladies, and the degenerations of the race, the medicine of that era wove an entire network of sexual causality to explain them."[3] The plentiful anti-vice tracts and guides to "sex hygiene," as other historians have observed, had "all the trappings of soft-core pornography and undoubtedly titillated quite a number of readers."[4]

Havelock Ellis was as sexually explicit as Freud, but more empirically grounded and tolerant of sexual variety. Ellis's six-volume *Studies in the Psychology of Sex*, published in the early decades of the 20th century, challenged the orthodoxy of such Victorian pundits as Lord William Acton, who denied the existence of female sexual response (except among immoral women) and urged stern repression of youthful masturbation. Ellis surveyed the universality of "auto-eroticism" among youth, and although not entirely discounting the possibility of "harmful consequences," noted its "primarily sedative effect."[5] Although Ellis was initially condemned as a pornographer, his fact-based approach eventually came to dominate 20th-century thinking about sex.[6]

Freud and Ellis created a new openness in public discourse that the "party of reticence" noted with ambivalence, if not trepidation. In 1914, the vice president of the U.S. Social Hygiene Association wrote ominously to *The Nation*: "The silence is now broken and whatever may be the wisdom or folly of this change of attitude, it is a fact, and it constitutes a social emergency."[7] Adding to the ferment were anthropologists like Bronislaw Malinowski, who reported on societies where childhood and adolescent sexuality were encouraged and adults shared sexual talk with the young.[8]

Neither Freud's nor Ellis's approach to sexuality could have taken hold, of course, without acolytes to spread the word. Among those in America who heralded the new dispensation were Mabel Dodge, the hostess of a bohemian Greenwich Village salon where Dr. A. A. Brill, Freud's chief U.S. promoter and translator, spoke in the winter of 1913; G. Stanley Hall, the president of Clark University, who had invited Freud to give his 1909 lectures; and Theodore Schroeder, head of the Free Speech League and leading opponent of obscenity laws.[9] By the 1920s, Freud's descriptions of unconscious life and his emphasis on sexuality as key to human personality and health had influenced not only these avatars of cultural fashion but virtually everyone concerned with literature, the arts, science, and philosophy, including legal intellectuals like Learned Hand.[10] From surrealism in visual art to stream of consciousness in literature, Freudianism and its many offshoots made the rigid and "formulaic mumbo-jumbo"[11] of *Regina v. Hicklin* appear fully as anachronistic as Judge Hand had suggested in *Kennerley*.

Freudianism was, inevitably, oversimplified and misinterpreted as it penetrated first highbrow, then popular culture. In 1913, Mabel Dodge's salon converted the editors of the socialist *Masses* magazine to Freudian psychoanalysis, but in the process imbued the theory with an optimism that "echoed American progressivism" far more than "orthodox Freudian theory." That is, while Freud "never intended psychoanalysis to serve as a tool of the more extreme forms of sexual liberation and certainly was no advocate of free love," his radical American followers "generated a variety of misinterpretations that provided them with theoretical rationalizations of their sexual explorations."[12] Indeed, Freud, unlike his radical followers, was Victorian in his insistence on heterosexual intercourse as the only mature, well-adjusted form of sexual behavior and on the "latency period" of childhood as free of sexual interests or concerns. Likewise, his theory that sublimation is essential to civilization and the creative arts was arguably just "one more addition to the long list of rationalizations about the need to restrict premarital sex."[13]

G. Stanley Hall added his theories of adolescence to the Freudian brew. The teenage years, Hall wrote in his two-volume 1904 tome on adolescence, are a time of high excitement and vulnerability during which emotional and hormonal changes trigger both sexual awakening and religious conversion. Hall mixed masturbation myths and unreflective sexism with exclamations on the importance of attending to teenagers' temptations and dilemmas lest they fall victim to the "perversion," "hoodlumism," and "secret vice" that he saw developing "in earlier years in every civilized land."[14] Adolescence is "a new birth," Hall rhapsodized; "the higher and more completely human traits are now born." But the dangers are grave, especially given the "temptations, prematurities, sedentary occupations, and passive stimuli" of urban life. He criticized feminists who wanted education for girls: they failed, he said, to appreciate that "sex and its wider irradiations overshadow all else during her ripening period," so that at the very least she must withdraw from activity when menstruating. "[P]uberty for a girl is like floating down a broadening river into an open sea."[15]

As for males, for Hall the primary victims of onanism, his book was only slightly less operatic than Dr. Tissot's jeremiad against masturbation 146 years earlier. Hall deplored the astounding prevalence of this "easiest and most spontaneous of all vices," particularly among 12-to-14-year-old boys; and listed among its causes "compulsive heredity, . . . idleness and laziness, weakness of will, . . . warm climates, improper clothes, rich food, indigestion, mental overwork, . . . sitting cross-legged," and "springtime." He parted company with such earlier writers on adolescence as Anthony Comstock, however, when it came to literature. Erotic reading and theater, Hall opined, were not the causes of youthful corruption. In fact, he encouraged youngsters to read Captain Kidd, Dick Turpin, and "other gory tales," on the theory that "Aristotelian catharsis" would arouse "the higher faculties" and help "deplete the bad centers and suppress or inhibit their activity."[16]

Hall inspired what historian Joseph Kett calls a "massive reclassification of young people as adolescents and the creation of institutions to segregate them from casual contacts with adults." The newly created public high school, for example, with its busy extracurricular schedule, was a means of channeling teenagers into approved activities and away from "sleazy dance halls in the neighborhood." Compared with college administrators of the 1890s, "who did not object to occasional skylarking by the undergraduates, high school officials in the early 1900s were virtually obsessed with instilling conformity and obedience in students."[17] Pundits like Hall thus generated not so much youthful liberation from Victorian repression as newer, more institutionalized styles of control. Historian Constance Nathanson adds that by creating an ideology of adolescent irresponsibility, psychologists paved the way for reform schools and homes for unwed mothers, repressive institutions whose purposes were to shame and control young women if their behavior departed from "age- and gender-based norms of sexual propriety."[18]

One of Freud's U.S. enthusiasts, Theodore Schroeder, was also the era's leading proponent of free speech on sexual subjects. Decades before the founding of the American Civil Liberties Union, Schroeder's Free Speech League was supporting the libertarians Moses Harmon and Ezra Heywood and arguing that the First Amendment protected speech about sex. Courts ignored Schroeder—even the fledgling ACLU in the 1920s refused to oppose theater censorship when the claimed justification was "morality"—but his uncompromising stance set a standard for other advocates as they began to challenge the *Hicklin* concept of harm to minors.[19] One of the first such skirmishes involved a long, complicated book, widely excoriated as filthy and obscene, but destined to become the most celebrated novel in English in the 20th century.

James Joyce had been working on *Ulysses* since 1914. A modern, "pacifist version" of the *Odyssey*,[20] *Ulysses* recounts the literary, philosophical, sexual, and scatological thoughts and actions of its three main characters in Dublin on June 16, 1904. Although literati on both sides of the Atlantic had heard rumors of the work in progress, with its intricate symbolism, stylistic dexterity, and radical stream-of-consciousness technique, it was not until 1918, when Margaret Anderson and Jane Heap began to publish early chapters of the still-evolving novel in *The Little Review* that Americans were able to read bits of the scandalous work. The U.S. Post Office confiscated and burned four separate issues of the *Review*, and in January 1920 told Heap and Anderson that it would put them out of business if they continued to publish *Ulysses*.[21]

Anderson and Heap tried to placate the censors by expunging explicit sections of the work in progress, but a legal confrontation was inevitable. John Sumner, Comstock's successor at the New York Society for the Suppression of Vice, bought a copy of *The Little Review* in Greenwich Village in September 1920 and charged the editors with violating New York's obscenity law. The issue in question contained portions of the "Nausicaa" episode, in which Joyce's hero, Leopold Bloom, quietly masturbates while watching the young Gerty McDowell display her thigh and undergarment.[22]

Anderson and Heap's defense at trial in February 1921 included the testimony of literary critic John Cowper Powys that *Ulysses* was "a beautiful piece of work in no way capable of corrupting the minds of young girls," and of another expert who praised Joyce's achievement in "unveiling . . . the subconscious mind, in the Freudian manner." But despite Freud's influence in artistic circles, his name was still "as new to the judges, and therefore as suspect, as that of Joyce" himself.[23] Anderson recalled that one judge refused to allow passages to be read aloud because there were females present (the defendants). She and Heap were convicted and fined.[24] Commenting on the trial, *The New York Times* dismissed the literary pretensions of this "writer by the name of Joyce," but nevertheless thought that making "pseudo-martyrs" of Anderson and Heap was unwise.[25]

By this point, a few Supreme Court justices had begun to think about whether the First Amendment might impose some limits on government censorship. But the context was political dissent, not art or literature, and certainly not art or literature about sex.[26] The Court remained oblivious to the constitutional problems with the Comstock law and with an obscenity standard that turned on the capacity of speech to "deprave and corrupt" the young. In 1926, it did reverse a Comstock Act conviction for mailing an advertisement for "The Queen Anne Private Home for unmarried women during pregnancy and confinement," but it approvingly repeated the *Hicklin* test. The Solicitor General, defending the case, had acknowledged that the ad was unlikely to "undermine morals or induce delinquency," and the justices agreed—"notwithstanding the inexcusable action of petitioner in sending these advertisements to refined women."[27]

Hicklin also continued to reign supreme in most states. In 1927, Boston banned Sinclair Lewis's *Elmer Gantry*, Upton Sinclair's *Oil*, and Theodore Dreiser's *An American Tragedy*, despite a defense team in the Dreiser case that included Clarence Darrow and an ACLU stalwart, Arthur Garfield Hays. The trial judge allowed the prosecutor to rely on selected passages of

Dreiser's novel and precluded the defense from introducing the rest into evidence. Anticensorship forces staged a free-speech rally, complete with satiric skits, while the trial was in progress. Birth control crusader Margaret Sanger, who had only recently been forbidden to speak in Boston, sat on the stage with a large piece of tape across her mouth.[28]

The Massachusetts Supreme Judicial Court affirmed the *American Tragedy* conviction in 1930, rejecting the publisher's argument that Dreiser's story of unprincipled ambition and unmarried sex was on the whole both nonprurient and moral. The justices' rationale turned explicitly on protecting minors:

> The seller of a book which contains passages offensive to the statute has no right to assume that children to whom the book might come would not read the obnoxious passages or that, if they should read them, they would continue to read on until the evil effects of the obscene passages were weakened or dissipated with the tragic denouement.[29]

Minors and Obscenity in the '30s and '40s

By the 1930s, the effects of Freudianism, feminism, artistic innovation, and post–World War I cultural upheavals could be perceived in the courts. The first jurisprudential dent in the *Hicklin* harm-to-minors standard came with a modest sex education pamphlet by Mary Ware Dennett, a birth control and women's suffrage leader. Dennett had written *The Sex Side of Life* in 1915 because her 11- and 14-year-old sons were asking questions. She found the available sex education literature "very misleading and harmful"; many points were avoided, "partly from embarrassment, but more, apparently, because those who have undertaken to instruct the children are not really clear in their own minds as to the proper status" of sex education.[30] *The Sex Side of Life* was hardly a raunchy thriller, as evidenced by its popularity among YMCAs and other social service organizations. But in 1929 John Sumner arranged a mail-order decoy; Dennett responded; and after fourteen years of relatively unmolested existence, *The Sex Side of Life* became a target of the Comstock Act.

In addition to its relative explicitness, *The Sex Side of Life* may have offended Post Office authorities because of what today would be called its sex-positive approach. Dennett waxed lyrical about "the climax of sex emotion" as "an unsurpassed joy, something which rightly belongs to every normal human being."[31] She also tried to allay fears about masturbation: there is "no occasion for worry unless the habit is carried to excess." (Here, she repeated the still-common myth that "the sex secretions are specially needed within your body, and if you use them wastefully before you are grown, you are depriving your body of what it needs.")[32] Her advice may not have been as accepting of self-pleasure as William Butler Yeats's contemporaneous poetic reference to "boys and girls, pale from the imagined love of solitary beds,"[33] but it was certainly an advance from Victorian hysteria. Given that *The Sex Side of Life* was written for minors, the prosecution of Dennett directly posed the question whether they are harmed by straightforward, guilt-free sexual information.

Dennett argued that her benevolent educational motive in writing *The Sex Side of Life* demonstrated its lack of capacity to deprave and corrupt. The trial judge was not convinced; he instructed the jury to apply the *Hicklin* test (that is, to decide whether the pamphlet would harm the most vulnerable readers). Dennett was duly convicted; but in 1930 the Second Circuit Court of Appeals reversed in an opinion by Augustus Hand, Learned's cousin (Learned by this time was also on the federal appeals court). The appellate ruling did not disagree that, under the Comstock law, it was the content of a work and not its author's motive that counted; but A. Hand rejected the notion that every publication that "*might* stimulate sex impulses" was therefore obscene. If that were true, he said, then "much chaste poetry and fiction, as well as many useful medical works" would be unlawful. As for minors, Hand said he "assumed that any article dealing with the sex side of life and explaining the functions of the sex organs is capable in some circumstances of arousing lust. The sex impulses are present in every one . . . and without doubt cause much of the weal and woe of human kind." But

> it can hardly be said that, because of the risk of arousing sex impulses, there should be no instruction of the young in sex matters, and that the risk of imparting instruction outweighs the disadvantages of leaving them to grope about in mystery and morbid curiosity and of requiring them to secure such information, as they may be able to obtain, from ill-informed and often foul-mouthed companions, rather than from intelligent and high-minded sources.[34]

Hand's *Dennett* decision thus did not reject *Hicklin*, but narrowed it. His reasoning rested on a stylistic distinction: explicit speech even to minors is acceptable, as long as it is not conveyed in "clearly indecent" terms.[35] This was an advance from the rigors of *Hicklin*, in that it recognized a legitimate social interest in satisfying the sexual curiosity of youth, but it left open the large question of when language becomes "clearly indecent," and who is to decide.

The influential Second Circuit Court of Appeals relied on *Dennett* later in 1930 to rule that a condom manufacturer who sold only to licensed druggists or jobbers did not violate the Comstock law's contraceptive ban. As in *Dennett*, the judges read the law to require an "indecent or immoral" intent.[36] Of course, there was nothing in the Comstock Act suggesting an exemption for medical use: Comstock himself certainly believed all contraception immoral. What had changed were the times. Decades of work by activists like Mary Ware Dennett and Margaret Sanger had moved opinion leaders, including judges, to the point where sex for purposes other than reproduction might not be considered sinful.

Although judges in the Second Circuit were thus narrowing *Hicklin*, its assumptions remained politically powerful. In Congress in 1930, Senator Reed Smoot fulminated against the recently published (but quickly banned) *Lady Chatterley's Lover*, the *Kama Sutra*, and works by Casanova and Rabelais in the course of exhorting his colleagues to resist a proposed liberalization of obscenity provisions in the tariff law that would, he said, "strike at the morals of every young boy and girl in the United States."[37] The reformers were reacting to Customs Bureau seizures of Balzac's *Droll Stories*, Boccaccio's *Decameron*, and Flaubert's *Temptation of St. Anthony*, among other works. Ultimately, a compromise law was passed, which required that Customs assess books in their entirety and gave the Treasury Department discretion to admit "so-called classics."[38]

The fate of *Hicklin* in the U.S. courts now converged with the literary fortunes of the century's most scandalous novel. Parts of *Ulysses* had already been adjudicated obscene under New York law in the 1920 *Little Review* case. Although the complete novel was published by Shakespeare & Company in France in 1922, and seven book-length studies of its literary intricacies had also appeared by the early 1930s, it was still not available in the United States or England except clandestinely.[39] Four hundred copies had been burned by U.S. Customs in 1922; the British government destroyed five hundred the following year, while its Director of Public Prosecutions, Sir Archibald Bodkin, tried to prevent F. R. Leavis, then a young Cambridge don, from teaching the novel to "boy and girl undergraduates."[40] (Bodkin also distinguished himself by calling Freud's work " 'filth' and threatening its publishers with prosecution unless they restricted its circulation to those doctors and professors who were prepared to give their names and addresses."[41])

In 1933, Bennett Cerf of Random House, having secured a contract with Joyce for a U.S. edition of *Ulysses*, attempted to bring a copy into the country. The Customs Bureau seized the book and filed a forfeiture application in federal court. Judge John Woolsey, who had previously relied on the *Dennett* precedent to rule an English sex education book—Dr. Marie Stopes's *Married Love*—not obscene or "immoral,"[42] was assigned the *Ulysses* case.

Woolsey studied the massive novel over many weeks. In his decision, he noted with obvious understatement that *Ulysses* "is not an easy book to read or to understand." In writing it, Joyce "sought to make a serious experiment in a new, if not wholly novel, literary genre"—that is, not only to recount what his characters did in Dublin on June 16, 1904, but to record "what many of them thought about the while." Joyce's use of what are "generally considered dirty words" was psychologically necessary to the artistic purpose. Because Woolsey found nowhere in *Ulysses* "the leer of the sensualist," he concluded that the book did not tend to "stir the sex impulses or to lead to sexually impure and lustful thoughts," and was thus not obscene within the meaning of recent decisions like *Dennett*. The standard should be the average person—"what the French would call *l'homme moyen sensuel*"—not the most vulnerable reader. Woolsey wound up by opining that while the effect of *Ulysses* was "undoubtedly . . . somewhat emetic, nowhere does it tend to be aphrodisiac."[43]

Judge Woolsey's rightly famous *Ulysses* opinion was more literary review than legal analysis, but the Second Circuit remedied the oversight in its 1934 decision affirming that the bulky tome was not obscene. A. Hand's opinion for himself and cousin Learned now repudiated the *Hicklin* harm-to-minors test and in its place enunciated an obscenity standard that considered the "dominant effect" of a work, "taken as a whole," on the average person, rather than the possibly libidinous impact of selected passages on the most vulnerable child. Though Hand found *Ulysses* overall a depressing read, inspiring "pity and sorrow for the confusion, misery, and degradation of humanity," he recognized that if the erotic passages were to "make the book subject to confiscation," then

> by the same test Venus and Adonis, Hamlet, Romeo and Juliet, and the story told in the Eighth book of the Odyssey by the bard Demodocus of how Ares and Aphrodite were entrapped in a net spread by

the outraged Hephaestus amid the laughter of the immortal gods, as well as many other classics, would have to be suppressed.[44]

Like Woolsey, Hand did not mention youthful readers; the obscenity standard was now keyed to the libidinous inclinations of average adults. And that standard, in turn, was applied in a way that sanitized *Ulysses*, denuding the novel of its sexual import in the interest of avoiding the underlying conflict between literary freedom and legally enforced disapproval of lascivious thoughts. Judge Martin Manton, in dissent, at least did not purify Joyce's at once heroic and scabrous work; he would have censored *Ulysses* on the basis of the presumed governmental power to protect those most vulnerable to lewd ideas.[45]

The new *Ulysses* obscenity test, turning not on "the young and immature" but on the average adult, was adopted by many but far from all U.S. judges. Massachusetts, most notably, clung to *Hicklin* through the 1940s and '50s, condemning Erskine Caldwell's *God's Little Acre* (the high court rejected evidence of literary merit as irrelevant) and Lillian Smith's *Strange Fruit*, a nonexplicit novel about an interracial love affair (ruled obscene because likely to corrupt "the morals of youth").[46] Federal courts in Ohio also stuck with *Hicklin*: in one case, although the judge did order police to stop a campaign of threats against booksellers, he noted the importance of preventing "the distribution of all forms of lewd and indecent literature, with its demoralizing effect upon the young."[47] Even using the *Ulysses* "taken as a whole" standard, a New York judge in 1946 found the memoir *Call House Madam* obscene because, "in the hands of the adolescent and easily suggestible of both sexes," it "may do considerable harm."[48] The Post Office retained on its unmailable list works by Margaret Mead, Simone de Beauvoir, and that fabulist who caused so much difficulty in the first place, Sigmund Freud.[49]

Even in the Second Circuit, as Learned Hand said in a 1936 case, there might be circumstances where obscenity should be judged by the capacity to deprave adolescents. The case involved two pseudo-anthropological works, *Secret Museum of Anthropology* and *Crossways of Sex*, and a novel, *Black Lust*; the buyer of one of the books may have been a youth. In future cases, Hand said, the court might consider "the possible injury to such a youthful reader."[50] Hand did not specify the nature of the "possible injury," but presumably it was the same inspiration to bad behavior or libidinous thoughts that had worried courts and legislators since Anthony Comstock's day.

It was probably inevitable that as the new academic fields of psychology and sociology gained respectability, scholars would try to quantify these presumably bad effects. Thus, in the 1930s, the Motion Picture Research Council, with a grant from the Payne Foundation, sponsored a series of studies of cinema's impact on impressionable youth. Although the "most conclusive" of the Payne studies "showed that the movies did not have any significant effect in producing delinquency," it also found that "boys and young men, when suitably predisposed, sometimes have used gangster films to stimulate susceptible ones toward crime," or "have idealized themselves imaginatively" to engage in the same "romantic activities as gangster screen heroes."[51] Another study in the Payne series argued that although only 11 percent of inmates interviewed at a juvenile correction facility felt movies had "some definite influence on their criminal careers," there was a wide range of indirect harms, including demonstration of crime methods, glamorization of "the fast life," and "emotional possession of a sexual character."[52] The technology may have changed—cinema rather than 19th-century dime novels or bodice rippers—but the perceived danger to youth was much the same.

At the Supreme Court, the Post Office's freewheeling censorship finally did produce a reprimand. In 1946, the Court ruled that the denial of second-class mailing privileges to *Esquire* magazine on the ground that the journal's risqué features rendered it "morally improper" exceeded the Postmaster's statutory authority.[53] The *Esquire* decision was important mainly for its recognition that even in the provision of a "privilege" such as second-class mailing, government officials cannot discriminate on the basis of their assessment of a book or magazine's moral propriety. This was a significant advance from the 1877 logic of *Ex parte Jackson,* when the justices assumed that federal power over "the entire postal system" entitled the government to refuse to deliver material that it "deemed injurious to the public morals."[54] Now, William O. Douglas's opinion in *Esquire* said "grave constitutional questions" would be raised if use of the mails could be granted or withheld based on subjective notions of "good literature" or "refined public information." Requiring literature to "conform to some norm prescribed by an official smacks of an ideology foreign to our system."[55]

This was encouraging language for those eager to bring some coherence to the law of obscenity and harm to minors, but *Esquire* involved only an interpretation of the Post Office law, not of the Constitution. The underlying issues remained: did the First Amendment allow government to police the morality of sexual ideas or impose censorship in order to preserve minors' sexual ignorance? The justices had an opportunity to address these issues the very next year.

The case involved none other than Edmund Wilson, the country's preeminent literary critic. In 1947, New York's high court had followed the *Hicklin* test in affirming an obscenity finding against Wilson's book of stories, *Memoirs of Hecate County*, despite its undisputed literary value and seriousness of purpose.[56] (The one dissenting judge at trial described *Hecate County* as an honest work, concerned with "the complex influences of sex and of class consciousness on man's relentless search for happiness."[57]) The Supreme Court, evidently not eager in 1947 to make a major statement about obscenity law's continuing clash with literary freedom, affirmed the New York decision, without writing an opinion, on a 4–4 vote. (Justice Frankfurter, as a friend of Wilson's, abstained.) As William Lockhart and Robert McClure later observed in an influential article documenting the judicial chaos, this was a "strange litigation in which Doubleday [the publisher] was convicted, and the conviction affirmed by three courts, without a single opinion except the lone unpublished dissent of one of the trial judges."[58]

By the late 1940s, the suppression of a work by as celebrated a literary figure as Wilson caused embarrassment among the middlebrow as well as the intellectual elite. It fell to a judge on the Second Circuit to articulate that concern the following year. A progressive veteran of government service during the New Deal, Jerome Frank had written an influential book, *Law and the Modern Mind*, which drew on psychology to challenge traditional theories of impartiality in judicial decision making. The case involved Samuel Roth, who had already been sued for publishing pirated sections of *Ulysses* back in 1927. Now, in *Roth v. Goldman*, he was challenging the Post Office's seizure of several of his publications without any prior determination that they were obscene.[59]

The Second Circuit upheld the confiscations, primarily on grounds of misleading advertising. But the judges did tackle the obscenity question for one book, *Waggish Tales from the Czechs*, which they said was "obscene or offensive enough by any refined standards." Then they muddied the issue by opining that in any event the judgment of the Post Office should not be second-guessed.[60] Judge Frank was horrified by this judicial deference to bureaucrats untrained in the niceties of First Amendment rights. His unusual concurring opinion began by explaining, with scarcely concealed irony, that "[b]ecause of my judicial inexperience in this field, I yield in this case to the more experienced judgment of my colleagues," but "I do so with much puzzlement, and with the hope that the Supreme Court will review our decision, thus dissipating the fogs which surround this subject. For . . . those fogs are indeed thick, and I find no clear light penetrating them either in my colleagues' opinion in this suit or elsewhere."[61]

Frank reviewed the literary censorship problem. "In the light of the First Amendment," he said, "it is not, I think, frivolous to ask a question about the constitutional power of Congress to authorize an official to bar from the mails, and probably thus largely to suppress, any book or writing he finds obscene." He questioned obscenity law's traditional justification, the suppression of sexual excitement:

> I think that no sane man thinks socially dangerous the arousing of normal sexual desires. Consequently, if reading obscene books has merely that consequence, Congress, it would seem, can constitutionally no more suppress such books than it can prevent the mailing of many other objects, such as perfumes, for example, which notoriously produce that result.

No proof existed that reading arousing books actually "conduces to socially harmful sexual conduct," Frank added; indeed, the recently published report by Alfred Kinsey and his colleagues, *Sexual Behavior in the American Male*, suggested the opposite.[62]

The Supreme Court declined to review Roth's case, but an impassioned appeal from a prestigious jurist like Jerome Frank made legal news. An even more remarkable outpouring came at about the same time from a county judge in Philadelphia, Curtis Bok. At issue this time were a variety of literary works, including James T. Farrell's *Studs Lonigan* trilogy and William Faulkner's *Sanctuary* and *Wild Palms*. Dismissing the obscenity charges, Judge Bok produced a detailed, scholarly history of censorship from ancient times. His critique of *Hicklin* was unrestrained: "strictly applied," he said, the test "renders any book unsafe, since a moron could pervert to some sexual fantasy to which his mind is open the listings in a seed catalogue." Bok argued that the First Amendment test of "clear and present" danger ought to apply here just as in other contexts where speech is censored. As for minors, including his own "young daughter," he opined that "by the time she is old enough to wish to read" these books, "she will have learned the biologic facts of life and the words that go with them"; there is "something seriously wrong at home if those facts have not been met and faced and sorted by then."[63]

Judge Bok's proposal that government should have to show a clear and present danger in order to justify literary censorship never attracted significant support from scholars or other judges, but he had at least raised the issue of precisely what harm sexually explicit speech causes to anyone, including the young. A New Jersey court added to the chorus of questioners four years later, in a decision enjoining a state prosecutor from suppressing "objectionable" publications by circulating a list compiled by a local "citizens' committee," then sending police to visit stores and newsstands to check compliance. After reviewing the history of harm-to-minors censorship, the state judge asked "just what the effect of a book on a young person may be," and responded by citing surveys of youngsters who rarely mentioned "dirty books" among their sources of sex information. He concluded: "The influences which operate on a child in the swift movement of our society are as infinite as they are varied. One may not single out the printed page as the one source of moral infection."[64]

Juvenile Delinquency, Social Science, Comic Books, and Professor Kinsey

The time was approaching when the Supreme Court could no longer avoid the urgent questions raised by obscenity law. Jerome Frank and Curtis Bok had challenged the Court to bring some coherence, and constitutional protection, to sexual speech. Their protests had inspired debate among practitioners and scholars.[65] What, if any, definition of obscenity should apply? Should the standard be different for minors and adults? More fundamentally, how did obscenity law square with the constitutional guarantee of free speech and access to ideas?

Early 1950s America was not the most hospitable environment for asking such questions. Arguments against censorship of any sort had rough sledding in a political atmosphere dominated by investigations of seditious speech, loyalty tests for employment, and blacklists of suspected Communists or their sympathizers.[66] Sexual unorthodoxy was associated with left-wing politics; homosexuals particularly were attacked as a "corrosive influence" on fellow employees and corrupters of "young and impressionable people."[67] At Senate hearings in 1950, Undersecretary of State John Peurifoy testified that most of the ninety-one employees recently fired by the department for "moral turpitude" were homosexuals; and Republicans eager to brand the Truman administration as subversive "pounced upon Peurifoy's remarks," warning that "sexual perverts," who were "perhaps as dangerous as actual communists," had "infiltrated our government."[68]

Artists who painted nudes or—worse—abstractions that might be filled with "mysterious but surely dirty symbols" were also suspect.[69] The radical psychoanalyst Wilhelm Reich, theorist of the origins of authoritarianism in sexual repression, was pursued by the Food and Drug Administration throughout the 1950s; in 1957, six tons of his writings including *The Mass Psychology of Fascism* were burned by court order, and he died in prison while serving a sentence for contempt of court.[70] Congressional hearings in 1955 and again in 1959 built an ideological connection between left-wing politics and exposure of minors to "obscene materials." One legislative report concluded that the "loose portrayal of sex" in literature "serves to weaken the moral fiber of the future leaders of our country."[71]

It was in this unpromising atmosphere that Professor Alfred Kinsey's Institute for Sex Research at Indiana University published *Sexual Behavior in the American Male* (1948), followed by *Sexual Behavior in the American Female* (1953). These hefty tomes applied the painstaking classification techniques of Kinsey's academic specialty, zoological taxonomy, to human sexual behavior. Based on sexual history interviews with about 12,000 volunteers, Kinsey's research revealed, among other things, that oral sex and other perceived deviations from conventional missionary-position heterosexuality were widespread in the United States; that masturbation was among the most frequent and, in orgasmic terms, efficient of sexual activities; that the experience of premarital, including adolescent, sexual activity was common, and, particularly among females, correlated with more satisfying sex during marriage; and perhaps most disturbing given the prevailing homophobia, that 37 percent of American males had had at least one homosexual experience leading to orgasm.[72] Even accepting the probable overrepresentation of homosexuals and men in prison (Kinsey interviewed where he could, and random sampling was not possible), these figures were striking. Thanks in part to Kinsey's public relations skills, his messianic sense of purpose, and his support from the Rockefeller Foundation–funded National Research Council, his graph- and statistic-laden reports were extensively publicized, popularized, and debated. *Sexual Behavior in the American Male* sold over 200,000 copies in the first two months of 1948.[73]

Of course, many reviews and comments resorted to euphemisms, and others simply refused to publicize Kinsey's findings lest they contribute to the destruction of sexual morality or insult "American womanhood."[74] But Kinsey's arguments against the soul- and body-distorting harms of sexual repression, and in favor of sexual diversity and the needs of youth, carried legitimacy because of his scientific approach and the imprimatur of the National Research Council. Historian Paul Robinson, hardly an uncritical fan, calls Kinsey's advocacy of the sexual rights of youngsters a major contribution to less guilt-ridden views about sex.[75]

The backlash to Kinsey was intense. In a widely circulated article in *Christianity and Crisis,* Union Theological Seminary's Reinhold Niebuhr criticized the Indiana professor's "absurd hedonism" and "moral anarchism." Critic Lionel Trilling faulted Kinsey for his sometimes extreme subjectivity and failure to make "any connection between the sexual life and the psychic structure." Indianapolis's Catholic bishop, Paul Schulte, complained of the "great harm" caused by making information in the reports available to "the young, the unlearned, the mentally deficient." One letter writer accused Kinsey of "aiding the Communist's aim to weaken and destroy the youth of your country," views echoed by J. Edgar Hoover, who wrote in a 1948 *Reader's Digest* symposium that Kinsey's work was a threat to "our civilization" and "our way of life," and ordered the FBI to compile a dossier on the Institute for Sex Research and its founder.[76] (The controversy over Kinsey's accuracy, and his own sexual proclivities, continues to this day.[77])

Politicians who saw opportunities to link sex and Communism joined the fray. Shortly after *Sexual Behavior in the American Female* appeared, a congressional committee chaired by B. Carroll Reece of Tennessee began to investigate the funding of "Communists and socialists" by tax-exempt foundations.[78] Although the Reece Committee's report blasting Kinsey's research and by inference the Rockefeller Foundation did not have a major impact, the investigation had its effect in helping persuade the foundation's new president, Dean Rusk, to cancel further funding.[79] But the revolution wrought by Kinsey in opening up discourse about sex turned out to be more lasting than either the antisubversion purges of the 1950s or the equation of Communism and sexual unorthodoxy.

While Kinsey's application of empirical methods to the study of sex enhanced the legitimacy of his arguments and findings, the apparent certitude of science was also becoming a rhetorical tool for those favoring more controls on expression. The studies of film sponsored by the Payne Fund in the 1930s had relied on early social science techniques—statistical compilations of youngsters' answers to questionnaires. Now in the 1950s, New York psychiatrist Fredric Wertham invoked science to bolster his campaign against comic books. Wertham's methods—asking young offenders about their reading habits without testing his hypothesis through comparison with a control group—were flatly unreliable; had he bothered to ask, he would have found that many nondelinquents also read comics. But as one student of the era writes, Wertham achieved credibility because he was a professional and "couched his findings in scientific terms."[80] His luridly illustrated 1953 book, *Seduction of the Innocent*, was widely praised despite its overwrought style and its attribution of juvenile ills, from nightmares to murder, to the influence of crime and adventure comics.[81]

Wertham claimed in *Seduction* that his research showed "a significant correlation between crime-comics reading and the more serious forms of juvenile delinquency." In one case of arson, a judge found that the young perpetrators "favored a particular comic book which has on its cover a burning human being." Western, sci-fi, jungle, and superhero adventures were all corrupting—*Batman* especially so because of the "subtle atmosphere of homoeroticism which pervades the adventures of the mature 'Batman' and his young friend 'Robin.' "[82] Wertham had no patience with defenders of comics who called them "the modern version of fairy tales," riposting that there are no "heroin addicts in Grimm, marihuana smokers in Andersen, or dope peddlers in Mother Goose." He attacked those who posited multiple causes for criminal behavior—"unconscious factors, infantile experiences," and so forth—these were "pseudoerudite and utterly false."[83]

Wertham's scientific bona fides did not escape criticism. Education professor Frederic Thrasher said Wertham's studies lacked "the most essential element of scientific validity, a control group," and illustrated "a dangerous habit of projecting our social frustrations upon some specific trait of our culture, which becomes a sort of 'whipping boy' . . . or scapegoat for parental and community failures to educate and socialize children."[84] A *New Republic* reviewer likened Wertham to other psychiatrists who "have deluded themselves" with fallacies about the impact of fiction; while the author of a child-rearing advice book argued that violent media were "not the *cause* of aggression in our youngsters. The aggression, as we know by now, is already there," and the child "gets a vicarious thrill" from watching fantasy characters act it out.[85]

This author reflected the more permissive attitudes heralded by a popularized Freudianism and articulated most prominently in the 1950s by Dr. Benjamin Spock. The supposedly repressed 1950s also saw new interest in anthropologist Margaret Mead's descriptions of cultures where "casual nudity, social masturbation, and sex play (both heterosexual and homosexual)" were common.[86] But neither the popularity of Mead and Spock nor measured critiques of Wertham had significant impact on the politics of child protection. By 1955, two states had legislated against comic books, while Los Angeles County passed an ordinance criminalizing the sale to anyone under 18 of comics depicting the commission of a crime. (The state high court struck it down.)[87] Congress meanwhile held hearings on the media's effects on juvenile behavior three times between 1950 and 1954; in the last of these, Senator Estes Kefauver displayed a cover from EC Comics' *Crime SuspenStories* depicting a man holding a bloody ax and a severed head (see illustrations) while other popular titles such as *Tales from the Crypt* and *Vault of Horror* were excoriated, and Wertham testified against *Superman* because it created in children "phantasies of sadistic joy in seeing other people punished . . . while you yourself remain immune."[88]

Given the luridness of the hearings, the Senate Judiciary Committee's 1955 report, *Comic Books and Juvenile Delinquency*, was comparatively measured. By this point, though, the industry had responded to the brouhaha by creating two good-conduct codes, one in 1948 (which the Senate committee said was ineffective) and a second in 1954—an extensive list of dos and don'ts complete with a Comics Code Authority that would review stories, art, and advertising to assure compliance with such values as "honorable behavior" and "respect for parents." Participating publishers displayed a Code seal of approval, and distributors refused to handle comic books without the seal. In short order, twenty-four of the twenty-nine publishers of crime and violence comics had gone out of business.[89] The Senate report applauded this industry self-censorship, even while expressing skepticism about Wertham's more extreme statements. As the report noted, some experts believed that reading about zombies, vampires, and other staples of comic book literature had a cathartic effect.[90]

The comic book industry had modeled its self-censorship on the by then entrenched Hollywood Production Code, or Hays Code, established in the early days of talkies in an unsuccessful attempt to forestall governmental licensing for movies. Until the 1960s, a multitude of city and state licensing boards practiced film censorship alongside the industry-imposed strictures of the Hays Code. These boards granted or denied permission for film exhibition based on varying local standards—pictures with racial themes, for example, often being denied permits in southern states—but the suppression of sexual subjects was almost universal. In New York, licensing was handled by the education department, which, as one critic commented, tended to fix its standards "at the intellectual level of school children."[91]

It was shortly before the comic book campaign, in 1948, that the Supreme Court first addressed the harm-to-minors issue. New York courts had found the magazine *Headquarters Detective—True Cases from the Po-*

lice Blotter to violate a state law banning publications "principally made up of" criminal news or police reports or "pictures or stories of deeds of bloodshed, lust or crime." (The ban had originally been aimed at minors, but was "later broadened to include all the population.") In *Winters v. New York*, the Supreme Court invalidated the law because terms like "bloodshed" and "lust" were too vague to put publishers on notice of what was illegal; but it acknowledged "the importance of the exercise of a state's police power to minimize all incentives to crime, particularly in the field of sanguinary or salacious publications with their stimulation of juvenile delinquency."[92] The justices thus seemed to assume that youngsters would imitate the "sanguinary and salacious" deeds about which they read—an assumption on which Justice Felix Frankfurter focused in his *Winters* dissent. Frankfurter did not claim there was any proof that certain kinds of literature incited youthful crime, but he argued that psychological judgments should be left to legislatures and not second-guessed by courts. New York's lawmakers had a right to believe that crime publications "cater to morbid and immature minds," with the consequence that "deeply embedded, unconscious impulses may be discharged into destructive and often fatal action," especially given "the destructive and adventurous potentialities of boys and adolescents."[93]

The *Winters* case is best known for rejecting the argument that a publication's trashy style robs it of First Amendment protection. As Justice Stanley Reed wrote in the majority opinion: "We do not accede to appellee's suggestion that the constitutional protection for a free press applies only to the exposition of ideas. The line between the informing and the entertaining is too elusive for the protection of that basic right."[94]

Intellectual Rumblings

Despite *Winters*'s invalidation of New York's ban on "bloodshed, lust, or crime" stories, by the mid-1950s the Supreme Court still had not addressed the constitutional implications of obscenity law. A 1942 decision had suggested in passing that the "lewd and obscene," along with "the profane" and "the libelous," are "no essential part of any exposition of ideas, and are of such slight social value as a step to truth that any benefit that may be derived from them is clearly outweighed by the social interest in order and morality."[95] This "step to truth" limitation on the First Amendment had originated not with the Supreme Court but with a Harvard professor, Zechariah Chafee, Jr., who wrote in a 1941 book that "profanity and indecent talk and pictures, which do not form an essential part of any exposition of ideas, have a very slight social value as a step toward truth, which is clearly outweighed by the social interests in order, morality, the training of the young, and the peace of mind of those who hear and see."[96] Some twenty years before, Chafee's writings had persuaded Justice Oliver Wendell Holmes, Jr., that proof of clear and present danger should be required before government can ban political protest,[97] but Chafee's solicitude for speech did not extend to "indecent talk and pictures." The Supreme Court borrowed from Chafee, and the "exposition of ideas" limitation became an established tenet of constitutional law.

The notion that First Amendment protection was limited to "the exposition of ideas" should not, one would think, have survived the Supreme Court's recognition six years later in the *Winters* case that "the line between the informing and the entertaining is too elusive" to supply a coherent standard for literary censorship. But when it came to sexual speech, intellectual coherence would not be the Court's strong suit. The distinction between great and "slight" social value was to dominate the justices' thinking when they finally confronted the obscenity issue in 1957.

The years preceding that momentous decision were filled with intellectual rumblings. In their influential article (published in 1954), Professors Lockhart and McClure invoked the *Memoirs of Hecate County* case to dramatize the oddity of a legal state of affairs in which a state could suppress a work by one of the nation's brightest literary lights without even a word about the First Amendment from the Supreme Court.[98] They wrote their article, they said, "in the belief that it is essential for this issue to be raised and carried to the Supreme Court in a strong case in order to establish that literature dealing with sex is entitled to the same freedom of expression as literature dealing with any other significant social problem." Such a ruling, they said, "would go far toward bringing about a quick restoration of sanity when periodic orgies of censorship break out."[99]

Having sounded the call to arms, however, Lockhart and McClure did not argue for an end to obscenity laws, or even propose a "clear and present danger" test as Pennsylvania's Judge Bok had done in 1949. Instead, after reviewing the development of obscenity law from *Hicklin* through *Dennett* and *Ulysses*, and the possible effects of salacious books on readers' thoughts, on conduct (including what they called "the sexual perversion of autoeroticism"), and on community standards, the two proposed a multifaceted "balancing of interests" of the same type that the Supreme Court had used three years before in affirming convictions of Communist Party leaders for advocating the overthrow of the government. This test was so convoluted that readers might have been forgiven for wondering why Lockhart and McClure had bothered to argue against prevailing standards of obscenity in the first place. For a court, under their proposal, would have to balance "the seriousness of the evil or evils" and "the probability that the book or article in question will be a substantial factor in bringing about the evils or evils,"

> against the value of the particular book or article, the value generally of literary treatment of sex matters, and the effect the application of the statute to this particular book or article may have upon the freedom of others to write and to read literature touching upon sex and related social problems.[100]

The bottom line under this multipart balancing test was that an argument for complete freedom "would be hard to maintain in the face of published material that seems designed to stimulate sexual appetites, contributes nothing to the expression of ideas, and is without literary merit."[101] Lockhart and McClure undoubtedly understood that their proposed balancing test contained a number of highly subjective, indeed ineffable, factors. But at the time, they either could not imagine or could not countenance the prospect of eliminating government censorship of sexual expression.

They also recognized that the issue of harm to minors was even trickier. Although urging the Supreme Court to reject *Hicklin* because it relegated the adult population to the level of a vulnerable child, they nevertheless suggested that if a book is "aimed at a youth audience, a court in passing upon the constitutional question can properly consider its probable effect on the sex conduct of that audience."[102]

The year after Lockhart and McClure's article, another legal journal devoted a symposium to the unsolved conundrum of obscenity. Legal, psychological, historical, and anthropological views were represented, the last of these reminding readers of the relative character of almost all sexual censorship. We must "guard against any facile assumption that our parochial patterns, however deeply engrained both emotionally and legally, necessarily constitute human absolutes," Professor Weston La Barre wrote. Ancient Peruvian civilizations, for example, decorated their pottery with scenes of "coitus and other sexual acts." These jars were now kept in a "reserved section" of a university museum, and shown only to "qualified persons." The "point to be made" was that

> the existence of this segregated "reserved section" is an ethnographic commentary on our own society, not that of the ancient Peruvians.

> The same principle holds for the Christian tourist viewing the "obscene" carvings on the famous Hindu temple at Benares; he may have met all these things before in Krafft-Ebing, but he finds them unexpected or out of context in a religious edifice.[103]

The symposium editor was more modest in his ambitions than La Barre. He noted the contentiousness of morality-based censorship, as well as the importance of new theories of causation in the debate, and hoped simply that the articles might "in a small way" contribute to "a rational resolution of a compelling social problem."[104]

Judge Jerome Frank proposed such a "rational resolution" the following year. The occasion was *United States v. Roth*, another case involving the indefatigable Samuel Roth, who had now been prosecuted under the Comstock Act for mailing a variety of publications, including *American Aphrodite*, an erotically oriented quarterly with literary pretensions. The issue included the artist Aubrey Beardsley's prose rendition of the myth of Venus and Tannhäuser, complete with a titillating description of the love goddess's performance of oral sex on her pet unicorn.

The Second Circuit affirmed Roth's *American Aphrodite* conviction in an opinion that focused on the "continuing social problem" of commercial pornography.[105] Judge Charles Clark wrote that despite the absence of scientific certainty, "we are hardly justified in rejecting out of hand the strongly held views of those with competence in the premises as to the very direct connection of this traffic with the development of juvenile delinquency."[106] Frank concurred in the judgment, as he had in *Roth v. Goldman* seven years before, but again his opinion read more like a dissent. First, he attacked Clark's reliance on "strongly held views" about juvenile delinquency, pointing out that it had been Second Circuit law at least since *Ulysses* that "the correct test" of obscenity "is the effect on the sexual thoughts and desires, not of the 'young' or 'immature,' but of average, normal, adult persons." More fundamentally, said Frank, "no one can now show that" obscenity has "any effect on the behavior of normal, average adults," and even as to minors, it is "most doubtful" that "anyone can now demonstrate that children's reading or looking at obscene matter has a probable causal relation to the children's anti-social conduct." Indeed, existing studies indicated that young criminals did not read much of anything.[107]

Frank also questioned the historical basis for obscenity law. The literature available in the library of "a colonial planter in Virginia or a colonial intellectual in New England" was likely to have included "Tom Jones,

Tristram Shandy, Ovid's Art of Love, and Rabelais." In view of the liberality of those times, "it seems doubtful that the constitutional guaranty of free speech and free press could have been intended to allow Congress validly to enact the 'obscenity' act." Indeed, the social attitude "towards writings dealing with sex" that gave rise to obscenity legislation "arose decades later, in the mid-19th century." Courts should adhere to the Framers' 18th-century expectations, not "the later 'Victorian' Code."[108]

Finally, Frank detailed an unusual correspondence with Dr. Marie Jahoda, whose report on psychological assumptions in the censorship debate had been cited by Clark in his majority opinion. Frank had asked Jahoda for a summary of the report in order to "avoid any possible bias in my interpretation." She responded that in the "vast research literature on the causes of juvenile delinquency,"

> there is no evidence to justify the assumption that reading about sexual matters or about violence leads to delinquent acts. Experts on juvenile delinquency agree that it has no single cause. Most of them regard early childhood events, which precede the reading age, as a necessary condition for later delinquency.

Jahoda did not discount the possibility of imitation from literature, at least where "childhood experiences and subsequent events" have predisposed youngsters to delinquency; but, she said, it was equally likely that reading "could provide for a substitute outlet of aggression in fantasy, dispensing with the need for criminal action. There is no empirical evidence in either direction."[109]

Frank ended his concurrence in *United States v. Roth* on a less scholarly note. "Youngsters get a vast deal of education in sexual smut from companions of their own age," he opined. "A verbatim report of conversations among young teen-age boys (from average respectable homes) will disclose their amazing proficiency in obscene language."[110] Frank's view would not prevail when *Roth* made its way to the Supreme Court the next year, but the questions he raised about youthful innocence and psychological harm would continue to simmer just beneath the surface of obscenity, harm-to-minors, and "indecency" law.

Three

THE GREAT AND MYSTERIOUS MOTIVE FORCE IN HUMAN LIFE

The Supreme Court Speaks—Finally

Samuel Roth's case was now headed for the Supreme Court, but two months before it was argued, the Court briefly and elegantly interred the century-old "deprave and corrupt" obscenity test of *Regina v. Hicklin.* It was a bit of an anticlimax.

The case of *Butler v. Michigan* involved a typical state obscenity law that criminalized any publication with a tendency "to incite minors to violent or depraved or immoral acts, manifestly tending to the corruption of the morals of youth."[1] Alfred Butler was convicted in state court for selling "an admittedly serious" novel,[2] *The Devil Rides Outside,* to a police officer, despite his argument that a censorship standard for adults could not, under the First Amendment, turn on what might corrupt minors.

Felix Frankfurter's opinion for the Supreme Court (on appeal of Butler's conviction) avoided one obvious basis for reversal: the vagueness of Michigan's legal standard. Certainly, "manifestly tending to the corruption of the morals of youth" was as nebulous as New York's "bloodshed, lust, or crime" ban, held unconstitutionally vague in the *Winters* case nine years before. But the implications that such a vagueness ruling would have for the Court's imminent announcement on obscenity were plain. The alternative, which the Court adopted, was to disavow the *Hicklin* test.

"It is clear on the record," Frankfurter wrote, that Butler was convicted because Michigan "made it an offense for him to make available for the general reading public" a book that had "a potentially deleterious influence upon youth." The State's defense was that, "by thus quarantining the general reading public against books not too rugged for grown men and women in order to shield juvenile innocence, it is exercising its power to promote the general welfare." But surely, said Frankfurter, "this is to burn the house to roast the pig." The Michigan law was "not reasonably restricted to the evil with which it is said to deal." The result was "to reduce the adult population of Michigan to reading only what is fit for children."[3] Frankfurter's views had evidently evolved since his 1948 dissent in *Winters*, where he had said a law designed to prevent juvenile delinquency was justified despite its encroachments on the free-speech rights of adults.

With harm to minors now dead as a general censorship test, the Supreme Court heard oral argument in April 1957 in Samuel Roth's appeal from his conviction for mailing the high-toned if titillating *American Aphrodite* and other works. *Roth* and its companion case, *Alberts v. California*, presented a straightforward First Amendment challenge to both the federal Comstock Act and a typical state obscenity law. Friend-of-the-court briefs had been submitted by the ACLU, the Authors League, the American Book Publishers Council, and a new journalistic entity, *Playboy* magazine. All stressed the absence of scientific evidence that sexually explicit art or entertainment caused antisocial conduct.

The Justice Department's strategy in response was to submit to the Court a box of pornography that had no connection to Roth or Alberts, that was not part of the record in the case, and that the lawyers for the other side had not even seen. This secret box was designed to persuade the justices, as Assistant Solicitor General Roger Fisher said at oral argument, that obscenity caused several types of "clear and present danger," including "immediate" imitation of "photographs of sexual perversion," "breaking down of morals," and "psychological harm of the housewife who opens the morning mail and finds one of Mr. Roth's circulars." Similarly, the lawyer for California, condemning Albert's sale of an illustrated edition of the Kinsey reports, among other items, raised the specter of "terrified children" and the presumed harm of sending gynecological pictures to high school boys.[4]

A few weeks after oral argument, the American Law Institute, a prestigious organization of legal scholars and practitioners, suggested a definition for punishable obscenity. This portion of the ALI's proposed *Model Penal Code* was a political compromise: it noted the importance of free expression, but relied on psychological arguments to justify sex censorship. As the *Tentative Draft* of the *Code* explained, "[p]sychiatrists and anthropologists see the ordinary person in our society as caught between normal sex drives and curiosity, on the one hand, and powerful social and legal prohibitions against overt sexual behavior." The purpose of banning obscenity is to prevent the "commercial exploitation" of "this psychosexual tension." "A thing is obscene," therefore, said the ALI, "if, considered as a whole, its predominant appeal is to prurient interest, i.e., a shameful or morbid interest in nudity, sex, or excretion, and if it goes substantially beyond customary limits of candor in description or representation of such matters."[5]

This notion of "prurient interest," the *Tentative Draft* said, should be judged by reference to "ordinary adults." After *Butler*, it was clear that a general censorship test could no longer turn on presumed harm to the young. But the ALI had not forgotten about the special problem of youth, and so proposed that a different standard should govern if the material in question is "designed for or directed to children or other specially susceptible audience." On the other hand, if otherwise obscene material is disseminated to "institutions or individuals having scientific or other special justification" for possessing it, the obscene should be no longer obscene.[6] Here in essence was the concept of "variable obscenity."

The ALI's focus on a work's "predominant appeal" to the "prurient interest" of adults had two significant implications—it accepted, first, that government had the authority to shield grown men and women from sexual arousal, at least when it was of a "shameful or morbid" nature; and second, that police, prosecutors, juries, and judges would decide when sexual expression crossed the line from sober description or even healthy erotica to "prurient" interest in "nudity, sex, or excretion." But at least, under the ALI proposal, the work would be judged as a whole, not on the basis of isolated passages. This was, in essence, the definition that newly appointed Justice William Brennan would adopt for the Supreme Court majority in *Roth*.

Just a week before *Roth* and *Alberts* were decided, the Court released four decisions that reflected a considerably more relaxed attitude toward controversial speech than it had displayed through most of the 1950s. The decisions placed constitutional limits on some of the more egregiously repressive political initiatives of the day—investigations of radical professors; criminal prosecutions of suspected subversives; firings of federal employees for alleged disloyalty.[7] The combined impact of the four cases was bracing: as the journalist I. F. Stone enthused, "June 17, 1957, will go down in the history books as the day on which the Supreme Court irreparably crippled the witch hunt."[8] According to law professor Morton Horwitz, the decisions were the most dramatic step in the Warren Court's "gradual dismantling of McCarthyism in American life and law."[9] The prospects for a First Amendment–friendly ruling in *Roth* seemed promising.

Like the American Law Institute, however, the Supreme Court crafted a political compromise. Disappointing the scholars, advocates, and lower court judges who had been arguing that the First Amendment did not permit censorship based on the perceived immorality or prurience of expression, Justice Brennan's opinion for the *Roth* majority started with the proposition (citing colonial-era libel laws) that the First Amendment's purpose was never "to protect every utterance," but only, or at least fundamentally, "to assure unfettered interchange of ideas for the bringing about of political and social changes desired by the people." Thus, "all ideas having even the slightest redeeming social importance—unorthodox ideas, controversial ideas, even ideas hateful to the prevailing climate of opinion"—have First Amendment protection. But "implicit in the history of the First Amendment is the rejection of obscenity as utterly without redeeming social importance." Here, Brennan quoted the Court's 1942 decision opining that some categories of speech—including the "lewd and obscene"—are "no essential part of any exposition of ideas" and of such "slight social value as a step to truth that any benefit that may be derived from them is clearly outweighed by the social interest in order and morality."[10] Brennan ignored the Court's rejection nine years earlier of precisely this "slight social value" theory of First Amendment protection in the *Winters* "bloodshed, lust, or crime" case. And as Harry Kalven, Jr., later commented, Brennan's use of historical sources in *Roth* was "so casual as to be alarming."[11]

The announcement that obscenity was outside the First Amendment umbrella was crucial to the Supreme Court's holding in *Roth*. For it meant that government did not have to satisfy the "clear and present danger" test that applied when political speech was suppressed, or, indeed, any other standard of justification, before criminalizing expression deemed to be obscene.[12] The Court thus avoided the psychological morass into which many lower courts, the American Law Institute, the friend-of-the-court briefs in *Roth*, and even the government, with its box of dirty pictures, had fallen: trying to assess the actual behavioral effects of sexual speech. Simply announcing that "obscenity" is unprotected by the First Amendment begs the question by skipping it entirely, as Justice John Harlan noted in his partial dissent.[13] These question-begging legal gymnastics would be equally crucial when, eleven years later, Justice Brennan constitutionalized the concept of variable obscenity to deal with the issue of harm to minors.

What, then, was this obscenity that "is not within the area of constitutionally protected speech or press"? Here, Brennan arrived at the part of his *Roth* opinion that civil libertarians love to quote. "[S]ex and obscenity are not synonymous," he said.

> The portrayal of sex, *e.g.*, in art, literature and scientific works, is not itself sufficient reason to deny material the constitutional protection of freedom of speech and press. Sex, a great and mysterious motive force in human life, has indisputably been a subject of absorbing interest to mankind through the ages; it is one of the vital problems of human interest and public concern.[14]

This celebrated language was not in fact entirely Brennan's: it had been borrowed from Justice Wintringham Stable's instructions to a jury three years before in an English obscenity case. Sex, Stable had opined, is a "great mystery," one that he viewed "with profound interest and at the same time a very deep sense of reverence"; "one of the great motive forces in human life."[15] Stable actually went further than Brennan would in *Roth*, for he noted that authors "create imaginary worlds for our edification, amusement, and sometimes, too, for our escape." That is, expression is valuable not only when (as Brennan was to say) it involves the "exposition of ideas." Stable added that sexual literature is particularly important when a "boy or girl reaches . . . that perilous stage which we call 'adolescence,' " for "it is the natural change from childhood to maturity that puts ideas into young heads." Adults, so far as possible, must "see that those ideas are wisely and naturally directed to the ultimate fulfillment of a balanced individual life."[16]

Inspired by Stable, Justice Brennan in *Roth* concluded his own peroration on the mysteries of sex by noting the value of literature "which does not treat sex in a manner appealing to prurient interest," and therefore rejecting *Hicklin*'s reliance on "the effect of an isolated excerpt" of a work "upon particularly susceptible persons." Drawing from the ALI's fortuitously released *Model Penal Code*, Brennan announced that the true test is "whether to the average person, applying contemporary community standards, the dominant theme of the material taken as a whole appeals to prurient interest." In a footnote, he defined "prurient" by reference first to Webster's Dictionary ("having itching, morbid, or lascivious longings"), then to the ALI's proposed *Code* ("shameful or morbid").[17]

Brennan now asserted that he was merely following a consensus among lower courts that had already rejected *Hicklin* and adopted the dominant theme/prurient interest formula. But the cases Brennan cited did not support his claim, for they ranged from Massachusetts's restrictive *Hicklin*-inspired ruling that the novel *Strange Fruit* was obscene despite its literary merit to Judge Curtis Bok's argument for proof of clear and present danger before sexually explicit expression could be banned.[18] As for Roth's and Alberts's arguments (relying on the 1948 *Winters* case) that the obscenity standard was too vague, Brennan simply asserted that "lack of precision" in the Comstock Act and the California obscenity law was "not itself offensive" to the Constitution—a view he would disavow sixteen years later when he ruefully acknowledged that "none of the available formulas" for defining obscenity "can reduce the vagueness to a tolerable level."[19]

Chief Justice Warren wrote a concurrence in *Roth* that was to have repercussions eleven years later when the Court addressed the issue of harm to minors. For Warren, aware that the "line dividing the salacious or pornographic from literature or science is not straight and unwavering" and that any test of obscenity is therefore likely to risk censorship of valuable speech, the important question was not so much the content of the literature in question as the motivation and conduct of its publisher. It was the commercial exploitation of people's "morbid and shameful craving for materials with prurient effect" that most disturbed the chief.[20] Criminality should therefore be judged by a variable concept of obscenity in which literature might or might not be unlawful depending on how it was marketed and to whom. Warren's concern here with the youthful audience was consistent with an incident reported by *Newsweek* in 1964: "Shaking a sample of a dirty work in his fist, Warren blurted angrily to a colleague, 'If anyone showed that book to my daughters, I'd have strangled him with my own hands.' "[21]

Justices Douglas and Black were the two predictable dissenters in *Roth*. They saw no reason for political compromise, for under the First Amendment the "legality of a publication should never be allowed to turn either on the purity of thought which it instills in the mind of the reader or on the degree to which it offends the community conscience." Because there was no scientific basis to believe that "impurity of sexual thoughts impelled to action, whether by juveniles or adults," obscenity laws were constitutionally unjustified.[22] Horwitz acknowledges that Black and Douglas "were right all along," particularly in light of the "sexual revolution that was about to burst on the scene and thoroughly transform the most intimate aspects of American life"; but given the puritanism of the 1950s, he defends Brennan's more moderate, compromise position in *Roth*.[23]

Yet from the time of Havelock Ellis and Freud, sexuality *had* been explicitly discussed in America. By the 1950s, Molly Bloom's lascivious monologue had been read by a generation of college students; and the Kinsey Reports, with their discussions of masturbation, oral sex, and other common events of sexual life, had been best-sellers. Even in the button-down atmosphere of the '50s, the success of *Playboy* magazine and the popularity of novels such as Grace Metalious's *Peyton Place* suggested that American society could probably have tolerated the trauma, had the justices in *Roth* decided to do away with obscenity laws entirely.

Roth was nonetheless liberating. Allen Ginsberg's "Howl," William Burroughs's *Naked Lunch*, Vladimir Nabokov's *Lolita*, D. H. Lawrence's *Lady Chatterley's Lover*—and Edmund Wilson's *Memoirs of Hecate County*—all were legally published in the United States after the decision.[24] And although many adults might have thought such works should be kept from minors, it was a familiar enough rite in American high schools to pass around dog-eared copies of these classics in the ensuing years.

Protecting Young Psyches After Butler *and* Roth

The Supreme Court's announcement in *Roth* that sex is a "great and mysterious motive force in human life" might have been composed with the next major censorship battle in mind. *Lady Chatterley's Lover* had been available only underground, or in expurgated form, in England and the United States since its 1928 publication. Now in the wake of *Roth*, Barney Rosset of Grove Press announced that he would publish an unexpurgated *Lady Chatterley* in the United States despite fears among opponents of censorship that this "act of wild extremism" was "suicidal."[25]

Rosset's gamble worked: a federal court in New York declared *Lady Chatterley* not obscene in 1959, based on its obvious literary value and exposition of ideas.[26] Although not all sectors of American society concurred in the new tolerance, the not notoriously avant-garde *Field & Stream* magazine had a relaxed response. Its mock review of *Lady Chatterley* late in 1959 noted the work's "considerable interest to outdoor-minded readers" because of its "many passages on pheasant raising, the apprehending of poachers, ways to control vermin, and other chores and duties of the professional gamekeeper"; the review warned, however, that "[u]nfortunately one is obliged to wade through many pages of extraneous material in order to discover and savor these sidelights on the management of a Midlands shooting estate."[27]

England also finally freed *Lady Chatterley*, after a considerably longer and more hotly contested battle in which "harm to minors" played a major role. In 1959, England had finally updated its obscenity law to recognize a defense of "public good," similar to the "redeeming social value" that the U.S. Supreme Court had used two years earlier in *Roth* as a means of distinguishing obscenity from constitutionally protected speech. The 1959 Obscene Publications Act created a two-part procedure under which judges or juries first decided whether a work tended to "deprave and corrupt"—England could not free itself of *Regina v. Hicklin*—and only then, if the "deprave and corrupt" standard were met, considered whether the work nevertheless had sufficient value to serve "the public good."[28] The paradoxical result was that expression could be found corrupting and beneficial at the same time. *Lady Chatterley*, the first case to test this paradox, followed within the year. A U.S. court had just cleared the novel of obscenity charges under the Comstock Act, and it was a matter of some moment in literary Britain whether the work of one of its leading modern authors would continue to be banned in his homeland. Penguin Books decided to publish an unexpurgated *Lady Chatterley* shortly after the U.S. decision; the public prosecutor took the bait; and *Regina v. Penguin Books* was under way.

The new Obscene Publications Act dealt with shielding minors not by creating a separate "variable obscenity" test, as the U.S. Supreme Court was soon to do, but by using the same all-purpose law and applying it differently depending on the likely audience. At least eight of the defense experts in *Penguin Books* focused on this critical element in the obscenity equation by testifying that *Lady Chatterley* had wholesome value for young readers. Among them were the Bishop of Woolwich (Church of England), a classics mistress at a girls' school, an educational psychologist, a chaplain who chaired the Battersea Youth Commission, and a grammar school headmaster.[29]

In one of the more counterproductive legal strategies in the history of obscenity law, *Penguin Books* prosecutor Mervyn Griffith-Jones emphasized in his opening argument the danger that "the minds of those hitherto pure" might be exposed to "contamination and pollution" by reading *Lady Chatterley*, which, at a price of just over three shillings, "the merest infant" could afford to buy. Griffith-Jones asked the jurors

> to consider whether you would approve of your young sons, young daughters—because girls can read as well as boys—reading this book. Is it a book that you would have lying around in your own house? Is it a book that you would even wish your wife or your servants to read?

C. H. Rolph, who edited the *Lady Chatterley* transcript for publication, commented that "this last question had a visible—and risible—effect on the jury, and may well have been the first nail in the prosecution's coffin."[30] Defense counsel Gerald Gardiner countered Griffith-Jones by arguing that "many of the people I am calling" as witnesses "have adolescent children of their own, and it is something on which views may differ." (Gardiner also feigned concern about "upset[ing] the Prosecution by suggesting that there are a certain number of people nowadays who as a matter of fact don't *have* servants.") Griffith-Jones was not discouraged, however; and in his closing argument he sardonically questioned the sex-affirming pieties in the Bishop of Woolwich's testimony for the defense. Would "young boys" who left school at age 15, he rhetorically asked, really read *Lady Chatterley* "as a treatment of sex on a holy basis"? Would "girls working in the factory . . . read this book—as something sacred?"[31]

The jury acquitted *Lady Chatterley*, but the issues of obscenity and harm to minors were hardly settled in Britain. A year after *Penguin Books*, the courts ruled that the *Ladies' Directory*, a guide to local prostitutes, was obscene under the 1959 Act.[32] In 1964, British police seized the otherwise legally available *Fanny Hill* from a bookshop because the shop was frequented by children.[33] In 1965, the Court of Queen's Bench found two racy film brochures "indecent or obscene" under the 1953 Post Office Act, whose standard of criminality was even looser and more subjective than the obscenity law's "deprave and corrupt" test. The brochures had been sent to a 14-year-old boy, in response to his request.[34] By contrast, a distributor was acquitted of obscenity in 1962 because the only proven purchaser of the work in question was a policeman who testified that he was unaffected by it. The victory was Pyrrhic, though: the defendant was convicted of the more serious charge of conspiring to corrupt public morals.[35]

In the United States, legislators, judges, and prosecutors now faced a dilemma. The Supreme Court's *Butler* and *Roth* decisions had rejected the *Hicklin* test of juvenile vulnerability as a measure of literary censorship for adults, but the problem of minors remained. Justice Frankfurter in *Butler* had noted that Michigan's total ban on writings that might "incite" youngsters to depraved acts was not necessary because the state had a separate law directed specifically at "furnishing to any minor child" obscene material "tending to the corruption of the morals of youth."[36] This suggested that a law targeted at distribution of "corrupting" material to minors would resolve the problem. But how should such corrupting literature be identified? And because by definition it would encompass expression that was constitutionally protected for adults, would the state have to make some showing of actual harm to justify censorship?

Professors Lockhart and McClure proposed a series of answers. Their second major obscenity article, published in 1960, examined the problems remaining after *Roth*, including the obscurities of a legal test that turned on "contemporary community standards" and "prurient interest," and the variations in motivation and circumstance (particularly commercial exploitation) that Chief Justice Warren had said in his *Roth* concurrence ought to be relevant to an obscenity finding.[37] The scholars noted a federal court decision shortly after *Roth* that upheld the right of researchers at the Kinsey Institute to import clearly pornographic material for scientific purposes; this, they said, was an excellent application of the concept of variable obscenity. It would allow genuine researchers access to explicit literature that, in less disinterested hands, might simply be used for "sexually immature" erotic imaginings. (No mature person, the authors insisted, would have the slightest desire for pornography.)[38]

The Supreme Court decided a number of obscenity cases after 1957, but without confronting the harm-to-minors problem or, indeed, advancing much in specificity beyond *Roth*'s prurient interest test. In *Bantam Books v. Sullivan* (1963), it condemned the methods of the Rhode Island Commission to Encourage Morality in Youth, which threatened distributors with prosecution if they did not remove from circulation works that the commission thought "objectionable" (or, in the words of the state's obscenity law, "manifestly tending to the corruption of youth"). Writing for the Court, Justice Brennan commented that because the commission's domain was "the whole of youthful morals," it was impossible to know whether any book or magazine on its list was deemed harmful to young readers or obscene for adults. Indeed, Brennan said, the commissioners "did not make this distinction in their own minds."[39] *Bantam Books* thus reiterated *Butler*'s disapproval of censorship that "reduced the adult population to reading only what is fit for children," but did nothing to resolve the question left open by *Butler*: how minors could be separately censored.

The jurisprudential confusion was epitomized in Justice Potter Stewart's famous quip in a 1964 case that he could not define obscenity, but "I know it when I see it."[40] (The decision reversed an obscenity judgment against French director Louis Malle's only modestly torrid film *Les Amants*.) Two years later, a majority of the Court agreed that a fiction considerably more titillating than anything essayed by Louis Malle was not obscene. The work was *Memoirs of a Woman of Pleasure (Fanny Hill)*, and Justice Brennan's opinion for himself, Earl Warren, and Abe Fortas explained that because the work was not "utterly without redeeming social importance," it could not be legally obscene despite its classically pornographic structure (a sentimental narrative punctuated by erotic adventures).[41]

The case against *Fanny Hill—Memoirs v. Massachusetts*—established three definitional components for obscenity: "predominant appeal to prurient interest," utter lack of social value, and "patent offensiveness" as judged by "contemporary community standards relating to the description of sexual matters."[42] Brennan borrowed this third element from a 1952 case in which the Court had described some magazines as not sufficiently offensive to "affront current community standards of decency—a quality that we shall hereafter refer to as 'patent offensiveness' or 'indecency.' "[43] But adding "patent offensiveness" to the definition hardly made the line between obscenity and constitutionally protected expression any easier to discern. And Brennan's three-part definition did not command a majority of the Court: there were seven separate opinions in *Memoirs*. Byron White dissented on the ground that dominant appeal to the prurient interest made a work obscene regardless of its merit; William O. Douglas repeated his insistence that there was no constitutional basis for obscenity law; Tom Clark, in dissent, cited a variety of reputed experts on the presumed link between pornography and antisocial conduct—among them J. Edgar Hoover, Fredric Wertham, and New York's Francis Cardinal Spellman.[44]

The *Memoirs* case thus produced a new obscenity definition, a welter of conflicting opinions, and continuing judicial chaos. Brennan planted one seed for the variable-obscenity doctrine, though. *Memoirs* was a civil proceeding against a book, he said; the value of *Fanny Hill* had therefore to be judged in the abstract. In a different case, evidence that a book was "commercially exploited for the sake of prurient appeal to the exclusion of all other values, might justify the conclusion that the book was utterly without redeeming social importance."[45] The value of a work, it seemed, could vary depending on the elegance or lack thereof with which it was promoted.

Brennan played out the implications of this dictum in the second of the Supreme Court's 1966 obscenity decisions. *Ginzberg v. United States* was an appeal from Comstock Act convictions against the indefatigable litterateur Ralph Ginzberg, for sending through the mails his hardcover magazine *Eros*, a newsletter called *Liaison*, and a small book, *The Housewife's Handbook on Selective Promiscuity*. These were slick productions that had some artistic merit and considerably less explicit sex than the just liberated *Fanny Hill*. A Supreme Court majority nevertheless affirmed Ginzberg's convictions because of the pandering manner in which the justices thought the works had been marketed. Writing for the Court, Brennan "assume[d] without deciding" that Ginzberg could not have been convicted otherwise. Ginzberg was faulted for having had the comic presumption to seek mailing privileges in the towns of Intercourse and Blue Ball, Pennsylvania; when that failed, he mailed his publications from Middlesex, New Jersey.[46]

Ginzberg v. United States was vociferously criticized even by those otherwise sympathetic to the goals of obscenity law. First Amendment expert Edward de Grazia reports that Brennan later told him it was "the worst mistake" he ever made.[47] Black, Douglas, Harlan, and Stewart each wrote dissents: Stewart complained that Ralph Ginzberg was going to jail for a crime with which he was not charged—pandering; and Black angrily pointed out that the publisher had now been "condemned to serve five years in prison for distributing printed matter about sex which neither Ginzberg nor anyone else could possibly have known to be criminal."[48] An ad hoc "Committee to Protest Absurd Censorship" placed a full-page ad in *The New York Times* asking what Ralph Ginzberg had done to merit imprisonment; among the signatories were Arthur Miller, Rex Stout, and Hugh Hefner.[49]

But whether misguided or not, Lockhart and McClure's "variable obscenity," with its emphasis on both audience vulnerability and distributors' motives, had become constitutional law. Works protected by the First Amendment could become obscene and unprotected if their publisher or distributor misbehaved. "Variable obscenity" was now poised to address the harm-to-minors problem. The case involved another defendant named Ginsberg—different spelling and different profession, but similar fate.

In the aftermath of the *Butler* decision invalidating a law that reduced the adult population to reading only what was considered fit for children, a number of states had revised their obscenity schemes to focus separately on the distribution of "harmful" material to minors. Other states already had harm-to-minors laws in place—a Chicago film ordinance, for example, empowered the police commissioner to bar anyone under 21 from films that he thought might create "a harmful impression on the minds of children." A federal court declared this ordinance unconstitutional after a movie version of Eugene O'Neill's *Desire Under the Elms* was classified for adults only.[50]

New York had long had a separate harm-to-minors law banning the distribution to youngsters of magazines that would appeal to their "lust" or arouse their "curiosity as to sex or to the anatomical differences between the sexes."[51] It was replaced in 1967 with a law that tracked the recently announced three-part *Memoirs v. Massachusetts* obscenity test. Thus, New York prohibited the sale to anyone under 17 of material that "(i) predominantly appeals to the prurient, shameful or morbid interest of minors, . . . (ii) is patently offensive to prevailing standards in the adult community as a whole with respect to what is suitable material for minors, and (iii) is utterly without redeeming social importance for minors."[52]

In 1965, Sam Ginsberg, who with his wife operated a luncheonette in

Bellmore, Long Island, sold "girlie" magazines to a 16-year-old boy whose mother had sent him into the store for the specific purpose of initiating a prosecution. The magazines, in the words of the New York trial judge, contained "female nudities" as well as "verbal descriptions and narrative accounts of sexual excitement and sexual conduct."[53] They were plainly not obscene under the *Roth/Memoirs* test, as Justice Brennan's opinion for the Supreme Court in *Ginsberg* would acknowledge.[54] Nor was there any proof that the nude pictures would cause psychological or social harm, as Brennan also agreed. New York's legislature had justified the law in frankly ideological terms—as an attempt to stop sexual materials from "impairing the ethical and moral development of our youth."[55] In the words of the trial judge, the legislation was

> to protect minors of high school and junior high school age . . . an age of awakening of sex desires, but also an age where the minors have insufficient maturity to deal with and to properly evaluate the plethora of material dealing with illicit sex, lust, passion, depravity, nudity and immorality.[56]

Invocations of morality, however, did not ordinarily satisfy the "clear and present danger" standard that the Court had embraced in the 1940s and '50s to test censorship laws against the First Amendment. Absent proof of such danger, Justice Brennan needed some means of relieving the government of its obligation to show that girlie magazines were objectively harmful to youth. He found it by labeling the material targeted by the law as constitutionally *un*protected, like the publications in *Roth*, so that no showing of justification by the state was necessary.[57] But how could this be so, when the magazines were admittedly *not* obscene? The answer was variable obscenity.

The intellectual sleight of hand accomplished here was considerable. In *Roth*, Brennan had said that there was a line between obscenity and constitutionally protected speech about sex. The line was difficult to draw, the definitions were hazy, and the Court continued to modify them. But at least theoretically, there was a line. Now in *Ginsberg*, Brennan said the line was variable—not only because different judges' or juries' standards of "patent offensiveness," "redeeming social importance," or "prurient interest" vary, but also because when it comes to minors, the obscenity test itself varies. In this world of jurisprudential sliding doors, works fully protected by the First Amendment nonetheless *lose* that protection if distributed to minors.

Thus, according to Brennan's opinion in *Ginsberg*, no constitutional rights were at stake, and only a "rational basis" was needed to justify the law. He found two such rationales—the right of parents "to direct the rearing of their children," for which they are "entitled to the support of laws"; and the state's "independent interest in the well-being of its youth." Whether girlie magazines in fact impaired "the well-being" of youth was immaterial, so long as the legislature's belief that they did so was "not irrational."[58]

Here, Brennan appended a long footnote citing authorities. The most intriguing of these was an article by psychiatrist Willard Gaylin. Gaylin acknowledged the absence of empirical harm from pornography but argued that nevertheless it is in "the period of growth," when

> patterns of behavior are laid down, when environmental stimuli of all sorts must be integrated into a workable sense of self, when sensuality is being defined and fears elaborated, when pleasure confronts security and impulse encounters control—it is in this period, undramatically and with time, that legalized pornography may conceivably be damaging.

Thus, said Gaylin, many psychiatrists made a distinction

> between the reading of pornography, as unlikely to be per se harmful, and the permitting of the reading of pornography, which was conceived as potentially destructive. The child is protected in his reading of pornography by the knowledge that it is pornographic, i.e., disapproved. It is outside of parental standards and not a part of his identification processes. To openly permit implies parental approval and even suggests seductive encouragement. If this is so of parental approval, it is equally so of societal approval—another potent influence on the developing ego.[59]

In other words, Gaylin seemed to say, youngsters must learn that sexual fantasies—and their likely outcome, masturbation—are not condoned by adults, even though "the reading of pornography" is "unlikely to be per se harmful." But it was unclear why the feelings of conflict and guilt that this regime is likely to produce should be considered psychologically healthy. Perhaps Gaylin was implying (as historians of sexuality have sometimes opined) that taboo and transgression are necessary elements of sexuality in the modern world, and erotica their equally necessary if forbidden vehicle.

The citation of experts like Gaylin added a patina of scientific respectability to arguments that censorship was necessary to the proper socialization of youth even if, at bottom, these arguments were no different from the more frankly ideological ones that had turned on Victorian attitudes. Justice Douglas made this point in his and Justice Black's not very temperate *Ginsberg* dissent. Brennan's opinion, Douglas said, was revived Comstockery; and to illustrate, he quoted Comstock's 1883 book, *Traps for the Young*, along with psychoanalytic studies of censorship arguing that the real dangers to sexual health were in repression. Contrary to the view that "obscene" books have "a deleterious effect upon the young," Douglas doubted "the wisdom of trying by law to put the fresh, evanescent, natural blossoming of sex in the category of 'sin.' " He quipped that if rationality is all that is required, "I see no reason to limit the legislatures to protecting children alone. The 'juvenile delinquents' I have known are mostly over 50 years of age."[60]

Justice Fortas also questioned the wisdom of giving the state "a role in the rearing of children which is contrary to our traditions and to our conception of family responsibility." Many parents might in fact "wish their children to have uninhibited access" to publications or artworks that might fall within the definition of variable obscenity as interpreted in fifty different states.[61] But child psychologists did not agree with Fortas—or at least not those cited in a *New York Times* article published two months after the *Ginsberg* decision, who opined that "the reading of salacious literature encourages a morbid preoccupation with sex" and that masturbatory fantasies may interfere with schoolwork.[62]

As in *Roth* a decade earlier, the Supreme Court in *Ginsberg* rejected arguments that the obscenity standard was unduly vague. But the Court did use the vagueness doctrine the same day to invalidate a Dallas, Texas, film censorship scheme that prohibited anyone under 16 from viewing any movie labeled "not suitable for young persons." Dallas defined "not suitable" as film content that portrays either "brutality, criminal violence or depravity" in a manner "likely to incite or encourage crime or delinquency on the part of young persons," or "nudity beyond the customary limits of candor in the community, or sexual promiscuity or extra-marital relations or abnormal sexual relations."[63] Under this law, the city had classified *Viva Maria!* (starring Brigitte Bardot and Jeanne Moreau) as "not suitable for young persons."

The recently appointed Thurgood Marshall's majority opinion in the Dallas case dismissed the city's argument that its "salutary purpose of protecting children" justified the film ordinance. Laws "aimed at protecting children from allegedly harmful expression," Marshall said, "—no less than legislation enacted with respect to adults"—must be "clearly drawn," with standards "reasonably precise so that those who are governed by the law and those that administer it will understand its meaning and application." Following *Winters v. New York*, Marshall ruled that Dallas's classification standards were too vague: what might encourage delinquency or promiscuity was left totally to "the censor's discretion."[64]

Applying Marshall's reasoning in *Dallas* to the prurience, offensiveness, and "redeeming social importance" test upheld the same day in *Ginsberg* yields the unavoidable conclusion that the vagueness doctrine was simply not being applied to the censorship of sexual expression. For in addition to the inherent vagueness of such terms as "patently offensive," the variable-obscenity test spanned a capacious age range and an even larger set of possible "community standards." But if an odor of inconsistency permeated the simultaneous decisions in *Ginsberg* and *Dallas*, it derived from the sexual politics that had driven obscenity law since *Hicklin* a century before.

Ginsberg v. New York, with its embrace of variable obscenity or harm to minors as a new legal category, left a host of unanswered questions. The New York law, for example, applied to those under 17, but for many legal purposes 18 or even 21 is the age of majority. When is a minor a minor for purposes of the legislature's interest in directing her "ethical and moral development" through censorship? Similarly, state ages of consent under statutory rape laws vary considerably; should youngsters mature enough to consent to sex nonetheless be denied communications about it if deemed unsuitable for them by a jury of adults in their community? Most important, how is "redeeming value" to be determined for minors who vary widely in age, cognitive ability, literary inclination, and level of maturity? If *Fanny Hill*, constitutionally protected for adults, is thought to lack value for 15-year-old high school juniors, what about 17-year-old college freshmen? If the more difficult but equally explicit *Ulysses* is not harmful to teenagers, what about the high-minded but verbally uncouth *Lady Chatterley*?

Beneath these unanswered questions lay a more fundamental one: Do minors have First Amendment rights? If they do, then the government should no more be able to shield them from ideas it disfavors than it can shield adults, at least not without demonstrating a clear and present danger, or in more contemporary constitutional parlance, a "compelling state interest." And this is true regardless of whether the ideas the government thinks immoral concern sex or (in the words of a 1959 Supreme Court decision invalidating New York's ban on a film version of *Lady Chatterley*) "adultery, socialism, or the single tax."[65] Brennan essayed a sort of response in *Gins-*

berg when, explaining why no constitutional issue was involved, he said that minors have "more restricted" First Amendment rights than adults; and Potter Stewart, concurring in *Ginsberg*, agreed: because minors are not "possessed of that full capacity for individual choice which is the presupposition of First Amendment guarantees," he said, they are analogous to a "captive audience" that the state can protect from unwelcome speech.[66]

But neither Brennan nor Stewart claimed that free-expression ideals have no application to those under 17, 18, or some other chosen age. Indeed, in areas outside the sexual, constitutional law was moving in the opposite direction.

Buttons, Armbands, The Little Red School Book, *and Rupert Bear*

Nineteen sixty-eight was an odd year for the Supreme Court to announce, as it did in *Ginsberg*, that minors have more restricted First Amendment rights than adults. By the late 1960s, the political and sexual rebellion of youth was a fact of life that could scarcely be ignored in the United States or Europe, and teenagers were loudly expressing their opinions—on sex and many other matters—in underground newspapers, buttons, clothing, armbands, and other protest symbols. Increasingly, "protection" resembled repression, for it seemed anomalous at best to be shielding minors from ideas of their own creation.

As if to compensate for the paternalism of *Ginsberg*, the Supreme Court's next decision involving youngsters reached a discernibly more speech-friendly result. The case was *Tinker v. Des Moines Independent School District*, and the political, nonsexual nature of the speech at issue accounted for much of the difference in the Court's approach. Thirteen-year-old Mary Beth Tinker, her 15-year-old brother John, and Christopher Eckhardt, age 16, had been suspended from school for wearing black armbands to protest the Vietnam War. They challenged the suspensions in federal court, and although the trial judge thought the school authorities within their discretion in banning symbols that they feared might lead to classroom disruption, the Supreme Court disagreed, announcing that neither students nor teachers "shed their constitutional rights to freedom of speech or expression at the schoolhouse gate." That public schools are " 'educating the young for citizenship,' " Justice Fortas explained for the majority in *Tinker*, "is 'reason for scrupulous protection of Constitutional freedoms of the individual, if we are not to strangle the free mind at its source and teach youth to discount important principles of our government as mere platitudes.' " Young people "may not be regarded as closed circuit recipients of only that which the State chooses to communicate." Only if there was a real basis to believe that disruption would ensue could school authorities ban peaceful student expression.[67]

Tinker was a barometer of the Supreme Court's general disaffection with school censorship in the 1960s. Nine years earlier, the Court had ruled that schoolteachers could not be forced to disclose their political associations as a test of loyalty, explaining that the "vigilant protection of constitutional freedoms is nowhere more vital than in the community of American schools."[68] It repeated the idea in 1968, just a few months before *Tinker*, in a case striking down an Arkansas law that forbade public schools from teaching evolution.[69] In 1967, it put an end to McCarthy-era loyalty tests for teachers, noting that the First Amendment "does not tolerate laws that cast a pall of orthodoxy over the classroom."[70]

Neither school administrators nor judges were uniformly thrilled with the Court's proclamation of youthful free-speech rights in *Tinker*. In the 1970s, judges wrestled with First Amendment challenges by students to schools' restrictions on political leafleting, distribution of underground newspapers, agitation for a "high school bill of rights," or dissemination of information about marijuana.[71] Where the expression involved sex or vulgar words, they were particularly likely to find support in *Ginsberg*'s protectionism rather than *Tinker*'s recognition that youngsters are not "closed-circuit recipients of only that which the State chooses to communicate."

A court in Dutchess County, New York, for example, granted a district attorney's request to bar the distribution at a local high school of an alternative newspaper, *Common Sense*, which contained articles on ecology, poverty, homosexuality, and women's liberation. Among the paper's offerings were a photograph of "two nude males in a homosexual embrace" and a cartoon "depicting a young child doing gymnastics on a man's erect penis drawn to exaggerated scale."[72] The DA claimed that *Common Sense* was obscene as to minors, in violation of the same state law that had recently been upheld in *Ginsberg*. The judge agreed, relying in particular on a psychologist's testimony that the photograph of the two men "not only depicted an act of homosexuality but that the verbal matter associated therewith did endorse such practice." The bottom line for this judge was that despite the law's "unending, profound concern that unconstitutional restraints not be imposed upon the young lest their education and quest for knowledge be stifled or stultified," there also "abides the solicitude of parents and the State that the young not be corrupted."[73]

The Supreme Court of New Hampshire went further in a case two years later when it upheld the conviction of a "head shop" owner for contributing to the delinquency of a minor after he sold a button bearing the message "Copulation Not Masturbation" to a 14-year-old girl. The court rejected arguments that the crime was incomplete without some showing that the minor had actually become delinquent. The "Copulation Not Masturbation" button was obscene as to minors under the *Ginsberg* test because its mere possession might convince the girl that sex at her age "was an acceptable act."[74] An Ohio court likewise stretched *Ginsberg* the following year by ruling that Claude Brown's *Manchild in the Promised Land* and Ken Kesey's *One Flew Over the Cuckoo's Nest,* both chosen as readings for high school courses, were obscene as to minors. The judge acknowledged the books' literary merit for adults, but said they had no value for teenagers, notwithstanding the contrary assessments of their teachers.[75]

While these state judges were stretching *Ginsberg*'s harm-to-minors rationale, the Supreme Court was taking an important step away from the notion that the First Amendment protected only polite and rational discourse. In 1971, it upset the criminal conviction of a Vietnam War protester for disturbing the peace after he had worn a jacket emblazoned with the slogan "Fuck the Draft" in the hallway of a California courthouse. The state court had noted in support of the conviction that "women and children" had been exposed to Paul Cohen's sartorial display; but Justice Harlan, explaining the Supreme Court's reversal, said the words served a crucial expressive function: "We cannot indulge the facile assumption that one can forbid particular words without also running a substantial risk of suppressing ideas in the process." While "the particular four-letter word being litigated here is perhaps more distasteful than most others of its genre," Harlan said,

> it is nevertheless often true that one man's vulgarity is another's lyric. Indeed, we think it is largely because governmental officials cannot make principled distinctions in this area that the Constitution leaves matters of taste and style so largely to the individual.[76]

Language "serves a dual communicative function," Harlan went on: "it conveys not only ideas capable of relatively precise, detached explication, but otherwise inexpressible emotions as well." In fact, "words are often chosen as much for their emotive as their cognitive force."[77]

But if children's exposure to a "Fuck the Draft" message was not enough to justify censoring Cohen's jacket, their actual rights to ideas and information were still precarious. A year after *Cohen*, the interests of Amish teenagers in receiving education were barely noticed by the Court in a decision upholding their parents' claim of exemption from their state's compulsory education law. The parents insisted it was essential to their strict religious community that youngsters after age 14 be sheltered from secular knowledge and temptation. The Supreme Court majority bought the argument and gave the parents an exemption. Only Justice Douglas noted, in dissent, that the youngsters might have an interest in receiving sufficient education to enable them to make informed decisions about their future. Douglas cited Jean Piaget, Lawrence Kohlberg, and other psychologists for the proposition that 14-year-olds often have cognitive and decision-making abilities equal to adults'.[78] This was not to suggest that adolescents' interest in expanding their intellectual horizons must necessarily trump their parents' wishes; simply that the youngsters' views might have been considered.

By the early 1970s, speech-sensitive decisions like *Cohen*, and the *Roth/Memoirs* "utterly without redeeming social value" test, encouraged publishers, entertainers, and their legal champions to predict the end of obscenity as an exception to the First Amendment.[79] In 1970, the National Commission on Obscenity and Pornography, appointed by Congress in 1967 and headed by Professor (by then Dean) William Lockhart, released a comprehensive report finding no discernible social or behavioral harm from sexually explicit entertainment. Twelve of the seventeen commissioners urged the repeal of all federal, state, or local legislation that interfered with the right of adults "to read, obtain, or view explicit sexual materials."[80]

The commissioners found that it was not speech about sex but "disorganized family relationships and unfavorable peer influences" that generally accounted for "harmful sexual behavior or adverse character development." A few studies suggested in fact that sexual offenders "have seen markedly *less*" of sexual materials "while maturing." Moreover, "explicit sexual materials are sought as a source of entertainment and information by substantial numbers of American adults" and may "facilitate constructive communication about sexual matters within marriage." The Supreme Court's "vague and highly subjective aesthetic, psychological and moral tests" of prurience, patent offensiveness, community standards, and redeeming social value "do not provide meaningful guidance for law enforcement officials, juries, or courts." Finally, national standards of morality "are currently in a process of complex change" caused by "a number of powerful influences, among which are the ready availability of effective methods of contraception, changes in the role of women in our society, and the increased education and mobility of our citizens." Pornography could not be blamed for perceived changes in sexual morality.[81]

The Lockhart Commission did not extend its bracing reasoning to minors. It acknowledged that empirical research failed to disclose any causal relationship between delinquency or emotional disturbance and youthful exposure to erotica. But the evidence was less thorough because of ethical constraints against studies that exposed youngsters to sexual expression. There were also political considerations—the support of "a large majority of Americans" for restricting minors' access to erotica. Even though exposure to sexually explicit material sometimes actually facilitated "much needed communication between parent and child," censoring youth was still a political imperative.[82]

The Lockhart report reflected the more relaxed sexual values of a nation that had just experienced a decade of social turmoil; but '60s rebellion triggered '70s reaction. President Nixon and a majority of the Senate vociferously rejected the recommendations. Commissioner Charles Keating (a founder of the fundamentalist Citizens for Decency Through Law, and later a federal convict for his role in the savings and loan scandals of the 1980s) filed a passionate dissent from the report, with citations to the New Testament epistles of St. Paul, attacks on the ACLU, charges of "tyranny" by "the Commission Chairman and the runaway staff," and complaints about the "pure pornography" and "filth" of a recent production of the Kenneth Tynan play *Oh! Calcutta!* in "a sleazy, disreputable" district of New York.[83]

While the cultural changes of the 1960s and early 1970s generated hot rhetoric like Keating's, across the Atlantic two spectacular harm-to-minors cases were unfolding. British censorship law, with its focus on protecting youth, had a more ample armory of legal theories than was available in the United States, where the First Amendment imposed some brakes on eager prosecutors. The British government, for example, could choose to ignore the *Hicklin* "deprave and corrupt" test in favor of an even looser "indecent or obscene" standard, which applied to the mails, customs, various local ordinances, common-law offenses like "outraging public decency," and, until 1977, cinema censorship.[84] "Indecent or obscene" for the purpose of these laws had been expansively defined as "offending against the recognized standards of propriety, indecent being at the lower end of the scale and obscene at the upper end."[85]

Britain's most striking instance of definitional elasticity in the interests of protecting youth had been its 1967 chewing gum card case. The Court of Queen's Bench had reinstated an obscenity prosecution (after acquittal at trial) because the defendant company's chewing gum cards depicting battle scenes were sold to schoolchildren. The trial court, following the general rule for obscenity cases, had not allowed expert psychiatric testimony on the capacity of the cards to deprave and corrupt the youthful clientele; but the appellate judges created an exception to the rule when it came to youth.[86] As this case illustrated, the English concept of harm to minors was not limited to matters of sex—a proposition that had been established two years earlier when the Queen's Bench ruled that the novel *Cain's Book* was obscene because it encouraged drug-taking. Although in the past obscenity law had "always been treated as having regard to sexual desires and sexual behaviour"—indeed, this was the explicit premise of *Hicklin*'s focus on "libidinous thoughts"—the court in the *Cain's Book* case said these precedents did not "conclude the matter." The novel posed a "real danger" that impressionable readers might be tempted "to experiment with drugs and get the favourable sensations highlighted by the book."[87]

British law was thus poised, as the 1970s began, to challenge the emergent counterculture. In 1971, the government prosecuted both the publisher of an antiauthoritarian sex education pamphlet, *The Little Red School Book*, and the scruffy editors of an alternative journal, *Oz*, who had invited teenagers to be guest editors of a special "School Kids" issue. *The Little Red School Book*, originally published in Denmark, advocated radical changes in education and had been selling briskly elsewhere in Europe. It encapsulated the "general spirit of sexual liberalisation during the 1960s and 1970s";[88] but it did not appeal to Margaret Thatcher, then Education Secretary in the Tory government, or to Mary Whitehouse, Britain's closest counterpart to Jerry Falwell and the Moral Majority in the United States. Whitehouse's evangelical campaign for cleaner television had already made her an English household name.

The *School Book*'s alleged criminality consisted of an introduction headed "All grown-ups are paper tigers," and sections addressing masturbation, orgasm, intercourse, petting, contraceptives, wet dreams, pornography, impotence, homosexuality, venereal disease, and abortion. The young publisher, Richard Handyside, was charged with obscenity and convicted in magistrate's court in July 1971. Some 1,000 confiscated *School Books* were destroyed, though most of the press run of 25,000 escaped the authorities.[89]

While Handyside's appeal was pending that summer, Britain was treated to six weeks of a much noisier prosecution. The charges against the editors of *Oz* included not only obscenity under the 1959 law but mailing "indecent or obscene" matter under the Post Office Act, and conspiracy to corrupt the morals of young people, which carried a maximum penalty of life in prison. *Oz*'s School Kids issue had been created by its 14-to-18-year-old guest editors; as defendant Richard Neville explained, "one of the reasons we invited adolescents to edit this special issue of *Oz* was to combat this tendency for everyone to try and shut them up."[90]

A mélange of graphic styles and garish colors, the School Kids issue featured an elegant cover illustration of two nude women, and inside, photos and biographies of the guest editors, followed by reportage of events at various schools, a "headmaster of the year" award, and a drawing of a schoolmaster masturbating. Articles discussed drugs, sex, rock music, "the revolution," and authoritarianism in education. Ads in the personals section were largely sexual; one, seeking young male models, particularly distressed the government, while another mentioned "the joys from the female aspect" of oral sex. Probably the most provocative of the young editors' choices were a drawing of three schoolmasters lined up—the first is flogging the second, while the third seems to have an object in his anus; and a comic strip in which one of the teenage editors had superimposed the "familiar and lovable" image of the children's book hero Rupert Bear onto a cartoon by the underground artist Robert Crumb depicting a fellow with a giant erection charging Gipsy Granny, with accompanying poetic doggerel (" 'Oh good, that door is open wide,' / Pants Rupert, as he runs inside").[91] "Forty-eight blurred pages of schoolboy ebullience" was how defense counsel/author John Mortimer described the School Kids issue.[92]

The trial was at least as much a reaction to the counterculture and the insouciance of the School Kids issue as to its sexual content, for at the time much more explicit and less edifying sexual fare was available in British bookshops, magazine stalls, and cinemas. As the Oxford University newspaper protested, the "apostles of radical change and not the pedlars of sexual fantasies are being indicted as the depravers and corrupters of British youth." The *Oz* prosecutor, Brian Leary, confirmed this view when he argued that the School Kids issue was "the very epitome" of the "permissive society"; it was "nothing more or less than propaganda," and "not a proper vehicle for the assessment of ideas."[93] Leary's claim notwithstanding, issues like permissiveness do involve "the assessment of ideas"; and as one expert witness opined apropos of Rupert Bear, the cartoon was merely satirizing the adult belief that "this kind of rubbishy sentimentality," "this horrible sentimental little bear," is appropriate for minors instead of "the more realistic activities of a male human being."[94]

Despite a formidable defense team (including Mortimer and his young assistant Geoffrey Robertson) and an array of experts at least as voluble as those in the *Lady Chatterley* trial, among them a professor of social psychology who praised the drawing of the three schoolmasters as healthy and cathartic, the jury convicted Neville and his two co-editors of violating both the Obscene Publications Act and the Post Office Act; they were acquitted of conspiracy to corrupt minors' morals. On appeal, the Post Office convictions were affirmed but those under the Obscene Publications Act reversed—on the ground, in part, that the judge had confused the two separate legal standards while instructing the jury.[95] The appellate court noted ruefully that the School Kids issue had been intended to provide youngsters a vehicle for expressing their views, contained many serious articles, and had some "charming and humorous" illustrations that "would not cause the slightest flutter in any well conducted Victorian household."[96] The judges seemed to recognize the irony in a prosecution whose stated purpose was to protect teenagers from the corrupting influence of their own ideas.

Richard Handyside, meanwhile, had appealed his *Little Red School Book* conviction; a new trial was held in the London Court of Quarter Sessions in October 1971. Both defense and prosecution presented psychological and educational experts on the question whether minors would suffer harm from reading the *School Book*'s authority-defying and occasionally explicit text. The judges found the conflicting testimony more puzzling than useful, noting that educational philosophies, like modes of upbringing, vary greatly; the "almost infinite variation in the religious background of the children who would be in one way or another affected by the book" made it "difficult to speak of 'true facts' in this case." In the absence of certain knowledge, they said, "a high degree of responsibility ought to be exercised by the courts"—that is, they should err on the side of suppression—particularly where the work "was intended for children passing through a highly critical stage of their development."[97] Despite its many virtues, moreover (among them excellent discussions of homosexuality and contraception), the court thought the *School Book* could be harmful because it did not present alternative moral views. It largely ignored marriage, and it described pornography not only as "a harmless pleasure if it isn't taken seriously and believed to be real life," but as a possible source of "some good ideas" about things "that you haven't tried before." In sum, the *School Book* "would tend to undermine, for a very considerable proportion of children, many of the influences, such as those of parents, the churches, and youth organizations" that might encourage sexual "restraint."[98]

Handyside reprinted the *School Book* in expurgated form. He softened the section on pornography, added the fact that sexual intercourse with a girl under 16 was illegal, and eliminated a suggestion for contraceptive vending machines at every school. The toned-down *School Book* was now permitted in Britain, but Handyside decided to pursue his argument against the original censorship; and the only place left to do so was the European Court of Human Rights. This international tribunal, located in Strasbourg, France, was the arbiter of the European Convention on Human Rights, part of the 1950 Treaty of Rome that a battered Europe had constructed after World War II.[99] British lawyers had drafted the Convention, but now, twenty-one years later, Britain was the only nation in Western Europe that had not incorporated Convention rights into its domestic law—a situation that did not change until 1998.[100]

Handyside brought his primary claim under Article 10 of the European Convention. Article 10 has two paragraphs: the first announcing the right to expression in broad terms—"freedom to hold opinions and to receive and impart information and ideas without interference by public authority and regardless of frontiers"—and the second listing an impressive array of exceptions. These include "such formalities, conditions, restrictions or penalties as are prescribed by law and are necessary in a democratic society . . . for the protection of health or morals."[101] It was, of course, this "protection of morals" exception on which Handyside's case would turn.

In its 1976 decision in *Handyside*, the European Court said that Britain's seizure of the *School Book* and criminal conviction of its publisher obviously violated the first paragraph of Article 10; the question was whether the violation was, in the nebulous words of paragraph 2, "necessary in a democratic society." Struggling to give meaning to this sweepingly subjective phrase, the judges resorted to an international law concept, the "margin of appreciation," under which different nations have wide discretion in deciding issues of social morality. Thus, although the margin of appreciation is not unlimited and although, as the Court proclaimed, free expression is "one of the essential foundations of a democratic society" and includes ideas that "offend, shock or disturb the State," in the end it deferred to Britain's judgment that *The Little Red School Book* could "have pernicious effects on the morals of many of the children and adolescents who would read it" and might encourage them "to indulge in precocious activities harmful for them or even to commit certain criminal offenses." To the defense argument that more explicit and less educational material was not prosecuted in Britain, and that the case was therefore not about harm to minors but about suppressing anti-authoritarian views, the Court responded that the more pornographic publications were not aimed at adolescents and children.[102]

Justice Brennan Changes His Mind

While *Handyside* made its way through European courts, those in the United States who predicted an end to obscenity law were preparing for the Supreme Court's first major confrontation with the issue since its 1968 *Ginsberg* and *Dallas* decisions. The Court accepted five obscenity cases for its 1972–73 term, but its ideological makeup had changed since the late 1960s. Abe Fortas, a reliable vote against censorship laws, had been forced to resign in 1969 as a result of political and financial scandals. Fortas had been a candidate to succeed Chief Justice Warren, who retired in 1968. President Nixon appointed appeals court judge Warren Burger as chief instead; he then (after abortive attempts to appoint Clement Haynsworth and G. Harrold Carswell) designated Burger's "Minnesota Twin," Harry Blackmun, to succeed Fortas. Compounding Nixon's good fortune, Justices Hugo Black and John Harlan, both aged and ailing, retired in September 1971. Nixon filled these slots with Lewis Powell and William Rehnquist.

There followed what Edward de Grazia describes as a three-year struggle by Chief Justice Burger to "wrest leadership on obscenity decisions" from William Brennan, the author of *Roth, Memoirs,* and of course the variable-obscenity doctrine of *Ginsberg*. By 1973, de Grazia writes, "the maneuvering among the brethren" was "close and complicated." When the five cases were first conferenced, "Brennan nearly collected a majority behind a draft opinion in which he proposed to abandon *Roth*" in favor of "an approach that would have invalidated all obscenity laws except those narrowly geared to the protection of children and the prevention of unconsented-to transactions between adults." Indeed, materials in the Brennan Papers at the Library of Congress show that his original drafts were only later turned into dissents.[103]

Chief Justice Burger thus wrote the majority opinion in *Miller v. California,* the lead obscenity decision among five handed down on June 21, 1973. The Court's four new "Nixonburger" justices (joined by Justice Byron White) not only rejected arguments to eliminate obscenity laws but broadened them in two important ways. First, *Miller* abandoned the *Roth/Memoirs* "utterly without redeeming social importance" test and substituted a looser concept, "serious literary, artistic, political, or scientific value." If a work was found to lack such "serious value," and if it met the other two parts of the obscenity test—patent offensiveness and prurience—it could be ruled obscene. Second, these other two definitional prongs were now to be judged by local, not national, "community standards." This was a radical shift for the Court, which Burger justified by saying that "our nation is simply too big and too diverse" to require "fixed, uniform national standards of precisely what appeals to the 'prurient interest' or is 'patently offensive.'" National standards, he said, are "hypothetical and unascertainable."[104]

This was true enough, but it was unclear why the necessary conclusion was that individuals living in localities with censorious majorities must suffer criminal penalties for buying or selling literature that is constitutionally protected elsewhere in the country. Burger's famous line—the "people of Maine or Mississippi" should not have to "accept public depiction of conduct found tolerable in Las Vegas, or New York City"[105]—essentially read local nonconformists out of the First Amendment. Instead, he said (in a companion case to *Miller*), it was sufficient for state or local legislatures

> to conclude that a sensitive, key relationship of human existence . . . can be debased and distorted by crass commercial exploitation of sex. Nothing in the Constitution prohibits a State from reaching such a conclusion and acting on it legislatively simply because there is no conclusive evidence or empirical data.[106]

Justice Brennan, for sixteen years the main architect of obscenity law, now led the dissenters. He had finally concluded that obscenity laws were unworkable: no definition supplied by legislatures or judges could cure the vagueness and subjectivity of such concepts as prurient interest, patent offensiveness, and serious value, which necessarily vary "with the experience, outlook, and even idiosyncrasies of the person defining them. Although we have assumed that obscenity does exist, and that we 'know it when [we] see it,'" Brennan wrote, "we are manifestly unable to describe it in advance except by reference to concepts so elusive that they fail to distinguish clearly between protected and unprotected speech."[107] He later told a reporter: "I put sixteen years into that damn obscenity thing. . . . I tried and tried, and I waffled back and forth, and I finally gave up. If you can't define it, you can't prosecute people for it."[108]

Brennan's conclusion that any legal definition of obscenity would be hopelessly vague of course extended to harm-to-minors laws. He acknowledged as much in his judicial mea culpa by expressing "grave doubts" that the variable-obscenity test he had created in *Ginsberg v. New York* "could be sustained today." But Brennan, like the Lockhart Commission, continued to believe that "the state's interests in protecting children" stood on a "different footing" from the generalized moral concerns asserted in support of adult obscenity laws. He knew that "[d]ifficult questions," including the problem of vagueness, "must still be faced" if laws were to be upheld restricting minors' access to sexual speech.[109]

Vague as they might be after *Miller v. California*, U.S. obscenity and variable-obscenity laws still did have their limits. Indeed, the emphasis in *Miller* and its companion cases on "commercial exploitation" of sex suggested that obscenity might now encompass only commercial pornography. This was not a congenial prospect for some local governments, and one response was the enforcement of anti-nudity laws, designed to shield youths and offended grown-ups from glances of flesh on drive-in movie screens. In 1975, the anti-nudity ordinance of Jacksonville, Florida, reached the Supreme Court.

Erznoznik v. City of Jacksonville epitomized the tension between *Ginsberg* (girlie magazines) and *Tinker* (black armbands) over minors' constitutional rights. Justice Powell described the problem: "It is well settled that a State or municipality can adopt more stringent controls on communicative materials available to youths than on those available to adults. See, e.g., *Ginsberg v. New York*." On the other hand, "minors are entitled to a significant measure of First Amendment protection, see *Tinker v. Des Moines School Dist.*" Thus, said Powell, "only in relatively narrow and well-defined circumstances may government bar public dissemination of protected materials" to youngsters. "Speech that is neither obscene as to youths nor subject to some other legitimate proscription cannot be suppressed solely to protect the young from ideas or images that a legislative body thinks unsuitable for them," and the Jacksonville ordinance was accordingly unconstitutional.[110]

But *Erznoznik* did not make clear what "other legitimate proscription" might mean or why, if minors have First Amendment rights, including rights to receive information about sex, they can also be censored. Nor did it indicate where their First Amendment rights end and censorship legitimately begins.[111] This tension persisted not only in First Amendment law but in the social values that it reflected: by the 1990s, with the arrival of the Internet, teenagers and even preadolescents were communicating online and creating Web sites on the very subjects that censorially inclined adults thought should be kept from them.

In the 1970s, the tension between protectionism and minors' free-expression rights was increasingly being played out in America's public schools. An early case rejected a First Amendment lawsuit challenging a Brooklyn school board's order to remove Piri Thomas's memoir *Down These Mean Streets* from district libraries. The federal court of appeals explained that some parents believed the book "would have an adverse moral and psychological effect on 11-to-15-year-old children, principally because of the obscenities and explicit sexual interludes." The plaintiffs had countered with affidavits from psychologists asserting that the book was valuable and would have no adverse effect. Justice Douglas, dissenting from the Supreme Court's refusal to review the case, protested that the "right to know" is "nowhere more vital than in our schools and universities."[112]

Other courts were more sympathetic to students' claims. In 1978, a federal judge invalidated the Chelsea, Massachusetts, school board's removal of an anthology of adolescent poetry from a high school library. One poem, by a 15-year-old girl, referred to "one million horney lip-smacking men / Screaming for my body." The judge quoted *Cohen v. California* on the importance of strong, shocking, and emotive speech, and described libraries as "mighty resource[s] in the marketplace of ideas" where "a student can literally explore the unknown."[113] A Nashua, New Hampshire, judge similarly ordered the return of *Ms.* magazine to the high school library after the school board had removed it because of "advertisements for 'vibrators,' contraceptives, materials dealing with lesbianism and witchcraft," and ads for recordings by "known communist folk singers."[114]

These cases represented a high point in judicial recognition of minors' First Amendment rights: by the 1980s, the Supreme Court had begun to retrench. Although a 1982 decision, *Board of Education v. Pico,* held by a narrow majority that school authorities could not remove books from libraries for "partisan" or ideological reasons, the justices limited the ruling by suggesting that sexual content or vulgarity *could* be censored. The books in question—by Richard Wright, Langston Hughes, Kurt Vonnegut, and Eldridge Cleaver, among others—had been purged because the school board considered them "anti-American, anti-Christian, anti-Semitic, and just plainly filthy."[115] (Indeed, they had some raunchy passages.) Justice Brennan's opinion in *Pico* quoted the Chelsea, Massachusetts, poetry case on libraries as "mighty resources in the marketplace of ideas," but only two other justices joined him, and his apparent exemption of sex left youngsters without any right of access, at least on school grounds, to information about that "great and mysterious motive force in human life" that he had celebrated in *Roth* twenty-five years before.

By the 1980s, then, the conflict between minors' First Amendment rights and the censorial impulses of many who held positions of power was no closer to resolution. Sex and crude language remained the major flash points for regulations whose claimed justification was the protection of youth.

Four

POLICING THE AIRWAVES

Oral Sex, and "the Public Convenience, Interest, or Necessity"

On February 21, 1973, the host of the popular *Femme Forum* talk show on radio station WGLD-FM in Illinois began a conversation with a caller:

Q: OK, Jennifer. How do you keep your sex life alive?
A: Well actually, I think it's pretty important to keep yourself mentally stimulated . . . you think about how much fun you're going to be having. . . . [I]f that doesn't work there are different little things you can do.
Q: Like?
A: Well—like oral sex when you're driving is a lot of fun—it takes the monotony out of things.
Q: I can imagine.
A: The only thing is you have to watch out for truck drivers.
Q: Uh-hum, OK, that sounds like good advice.[1]

A social historian might have appreciated this tongue-in-cheek exchange as a manifestation of sexual openness as pioneered by Sigmund Freud, Havelock Ellis, Alfred Kinsey, and their successors, William Masters and Virginia Johnson, in the 1960s,[2] but the Federal Communications Commission was not amused. Assigned by Congress to regulate broadcasting, which included enforcing a law that banned "any obscene, indecent, or profane language" on the airwaves, the FCC decided that the oral sex segments of

Femme Forum were not just "indecent" but "obscene"—that is, so "patently offensive," prurient, and without "redeeming social value" under the Supreme Court's then-reigning *Roth/Memoirs* obscenity test as to lack any First Amendment protection.[3] The agency relied largely on the concept of variable obscenity that had recently been elaborated by Justice Brennan; as in *Ginzberg v. United States*, the 1966 "pandering" case, it said, the producers of *Femme Forum* sought "to garner large audiences through titillating sexual discussions." And because broadcasting is uniquely "pervasive and intrusive"—it both saturates public space and invades the privacy of the home—a more expansive standard of obscenity should apply.

Finally, the Commission said, impressionable youngsters might tune in to *Femme Forum*, for radio "is almost the constant companion of the teenager." It was clear that Sonderling Broadcasting, the owner of station WGLD, knew minors were in its audience, for a program earlier in February had segued from a discussion of orgasm directly to one about turning 16 and getting your driver's license. Under the concept of variable obscenity, this presence of vulnerable youth lowered the threshold for an obscenity finding still further.[4]

A liberal commissioner, Nicholas Johnson, protested in a pointed dissent that both the "variable obscenity" and (as yet undefined) "indecency" prohibitions in the FCC law were hopelessly vague, and questioned how *Femme Forum* could be "patently offensive" according to prevailing community standards when it was the area's top-rated radio show.[5] Indeed, the genre of sexually uninhibited, or "topless," radio was thriving in many communities by the early 1970s.

Sonderling Broadcasting did not appeal the $2,000 fine that the commission imposed to punish *Femme Forum* for its jocular sex recipes. Instead, the company acquiesced by banning all sexual discussion. By the time of the FCC's *Sonderling* decision, other broadcasters had also eliminated topless radio. A coalition of radio listeners did go to court, and the resulting judicial decision in 1974, affirming the FCC's power to stop "titillating and pandering" radio productions in the interest of protecting children, set the stage for the next three decades of broadcast censorship.[6]

Ever since the 1927 Radio Act, the federal government had licensed and regulated broadcasters in a way that would have raised immediate First Amendment hackles had the targets been newspapers or books. The justification was "scarcity"—the availability, at least initially, of only a limited number of broadcast frequencies. The scarce resource of the airwaves, it was said, should be used to further the public interest rather than the editorial predilections of the few who secured broadcast licenses.[7] One problem with this apparently commendable approach, however, is deciding what constitutes "the public convenience, interest, or necessity"—the open-ended standard announced by the Radio Act and its successor, the Communications Act of 1934.[8] As in England, where for centuries the print medium was subject to licensing, political abuses are inevitable when government has the power to decide in advance who may speak. In the FCC's case, the licensing power was used not only to squelch political opponents, but through the subjective, vague indecency ban, to impose governmental standards of sexual and linguistic propriety.[9]

At the outset, the Radio Act's ban on uttering "any obscene, indecent, or profane language" did not look very different from obscenity proscriptions in the Comstock and tariff laws that referred to "obscene, lewd, lascivious," or "indecent" material. That is, these laundry lists of proscribed speech all presumably denoted the same thing—the kind of "lewd or obscene" expression that did not merit constitutional protection, as explained by the Supreme Court back in 1942.[10] And certainly, early court rulings did not suggest any constitutional problem with the indecency ban. In 1931, for example, the Ninth Circuit upheld a punishment by the Federal Radio Commission (predecessor to the FCC) of a radio announcer who had used such terms as "damned" and "by God" while fulminating against local political corruption. If the federal government could control the content of mail, the court reasoned, it could also control the airwaves by punishing a broadcaster who had threatened to "put on the mantle of the Lord and call down the curse of God" on public officials.[11]

The DC Circuit followed suit the next year by upholding the Commission's refusal to renew the Trinity Methodist Church's radio license because it had broadcast attacks on judges and other public servants. Surely, the court said, the agency could refuse renewal to a station whose programs it thought false and defamatory, just as it could punish broadcasters that "offend youth and innocence by the free use of words suggestive of sexual immorality."[12] And in 1937, the now renamed Federal Communications Commission upbraided NBC radio for broadcasting a satirical Adam and Eve skit in which an assertive Eve (played by the redoubtable Mae West), bored with life in Eden, had spiced up the text with her "usual plummy tones and suggestive innuendo."[13]

The Supreme Court reinforced the FCC's power over radio six years later when it upheld the agency's "Chain Broadcasting Rules." The rules barred local stations from agreeing with one national network not to broadcast the programs of another. Because radio was "inherently . . . not available to all," Justice Frankfurter explained, government regulation was essential.[14] His approval of the vague "public convenience, interest, or necessity" standard left intriguing possibilities for FCC censorship in the area of morality.

This power lay largely dormant in the 1950s. Despite occasional departures from conventionality, radio was relatively quiescent; and the new medium of television, seeking a broad national viewership, also tended to avoid controversy.[15] In 1952, the National Association of Broadcasters even promulgated a private industry censorship code, forbidding "offensive language, vulgarity, illicit sexual relations, sex crimes, and abnormalities during any time period when children comprised a substantial segment of the viewing audience." The code would be periodically revised in response to congressional pressures (usually involving TV violence); it was not discontinued until the 1980s.[16]

One broadcaster that did run afoul of the FCC's undefined indecency ban in the 1950s was Mile High Radio in Denver, whose announcer joked during a 1958 program about "flushing pajamas down the toilet (with sound effects of a toilet flushing)," "inflating 'cheaters' with helium," and "the guy who goosed the ghost and got a handful of sheet." For these transgressions, the FCC began a license revocation proceeding. The station owner pleaded that the remarks had been unauthorized and the announcer fired, whereupon the agency satisfied itself with a cease-and-desist order.[17]

By this point in constitutional history, the Supreme Court had begun to dismantle the "right-privilege distinction" on which its early mail censorship cases had been based—the notion that if the government grants a benefit such as use of the mails, it may rely on any criteria it chooses in deciding who receives the service. The Court had pointed out the dangers of such freewheeling discretion in 1946 when it invalidated the Postmaster General's decision to bar *Esquire* magazine from second-class mail on grounds of immorality. But the judiciary's solicitude for publications did not extend to broadcasting; and as the 1950s gave way to the more culturally rambunctious '60s, FCC vigilance over radio grew more aggressive.

The Commission launched its first full-dress assault on radio indecency in 1962. "Uncle Charlie," host of South Carolina's *Charlie Walker Show*, had a fondness for ribald wordplay on the names of nearby towns ("Ann's Drawers" for Andrews; "Bloomersville" for Bloomville) and favored such daring phrases as "let it all hang out." The Commission ruled that he had abused the airwaves by subjecting housewives, teenagers, and young children to these offensive remarks, and refused to renew the station's license. Affirming the decision, the DC Circuit avoided ruling on the station's claim of a First Amendment right to be raunchy, although Judge J. Skelly Wright, in a concurrence, noted that recent Supreme Court decisions required considerably more specificity in the regulation of speech than could be located anywhere in the FCC's indecency regime.[18]

As a community-based medium, radio was well situated to reflect the political and cultural rebellion of the '60s, so it was not surprising that the four stations affiliated with the left-leaning Pacifica Foundation attracted FCC scrutiny. In 1964, the Commission investigated Pacifica for broadcasting readings by Edward Albee, Lawrence Ferlinghetti, and Robert Creeley, and a discussion among eight homosexuals entitled *Live and Let Live*. Ultimately, it vindicated Pacifica, noting the "very great discretion" that the Communications Act "wisely vests in the licensee," and opining that if Pacifica were sanctioned for these shows, then "only the wholly inoffensive, the bland could gain access to the radio microphone or TV camera." But despite these comforting words, the investigation cast a pall over Pacifica; Commissioner Robert E. Lee wrote a separate concurrence specifically to express his disapproval of the show on homosexuality. A discussion of "sexual aberrations" was not necessarily "a violation of good taste," Lee said, but a panel of "eight homosexuals discussing their experiences and past history does not approach the treatment of a delicate subject one could expect by a responsible broadcaster."[19]

A year later, the Commission was less gentle with Pacifica. By a 4–3 vote, it gave the foundation's West Coast stations only a one-year renewal, during which time they were to be on notice that they had better behave. The stations' managements had already apologized for "isolated errors" in programming. There was still no definition of what the FCC thought was indecent.[20]

Jerry Garcia and a Definition for Indecency

The FCC inched closer to defining indecency in 1970. The Jack Straw Memorial Foundation (Jack Straw led the 14th-century English Peasants' Revolt) operated KRAB radio in Seattle, which had aired autobiographical readings by Paul Sawyer, a local Unitarian minister, that included a few vulgar words. The Commission chastised the station management for its lax supervision and gave only a short-term, provisional license renewal, during which time, it said, "it is expected that appropriate steps will be taken" to assure tighter control of program content.[21] The *Jack Straw* decision never specified what words were considered indecent, but it did put broadcasters on notice "that at least some four-letter words would put them at risk."[22]

The liberal Nicholas Johnson was now joined by another commissioner, Kenneth Cox, in protesting FCC censorship. KRAB should be praised, not sanctioned, Johnson wrote: it was not "some marginal operation which pumps out aural drivel," and in contrast to broadcasters whose licenses were regularly renewed despite their airing of "33 minutes of commercials an hour," KRAB devoted almost all of its resources to "the performing arts, public affairs, news, and general educational programming." Cox's dissent focused on the vagueness of "indecency"; indeed, he said, it was "a nonexistent standard." Licensees "do not know even now what the dangerous words are because the majority have not listed them."[23]

Jack Straw's license was fully renewed in 1971, despite some additional FCC warnings—about vulgarity during a bluegrass music show, a speech by civil rights leader James Bevel, and a tape entitled *Murder at Kent State,* in which were heard "about a half dozen obscenities including an epithet directed at the Vice President of the United States."[24]

The need for a definition of broadcast indecency had now become pressing. And it was fitting that the guilty party in the case that supplied the definition was Jerry Garcia, lead guitarist of the Grateful Dead. Interviewed in January 1970 by WUHY Radio–Philadelphia, Garcia held forth on music, ecology, philosophy, and politics in his characteristic uninhibited style. Four-letter words abounded, "mostly as either adjectives or as substitutes for 'et cetera,' and occasionally as an introductory expletive," as in: "I must answer the phone 900 fuckin' times a day, man," and "Political change is so fucking slow." The FCC ruled the language indecent, which it now defined as "patently offensive by contemporary community standards and wholly without redeeming social value."[25] The definition was obviously borrowed from the Supreme Court's then current *Roth/Memoirs* obscenity test, with the FCC's version lacking only the requirement that the "dominant theme" of the material appeal to the "prurient interest."

The Garcia interview was clearly not obscene, as the FCC acknowledged. Its "dominant theme" was not prurient and, indeed, did not even focus on sex. But in regulating broadcasting, the FCC said, it was not limited to banning only constitutionally unprotected obscenity. Garcia's language was not illegal, but that did not mean there was a right to use it in "public arenas." Broadcasting can be regulated because "it comes directly into the home and frequently without any advance warning of its content." In addition, there were "very large numbers of children" in the broadcast audience. "No one would ever know, in home or car listening, when he or his children would encounter what he would regard as the most vile expressions."[26] As in previous (and subsequent) cases, the Commission did not explain the nature of the harm to minors that it assumed would flow from hearing "most vile expressions," but protecting the young continued to be the hook by which it justified its indecency patrols.

As in *Jack Straw*, so in *WUHY*, Commissioners Johnson and Cox dissented. "What this Commission condemns today is not words but a culture," Johnson lamented, "a lifestyle it fears because it does not understand." Cox added that "people who do not like the ideas or the language" of the counterculture "do not need to listen to programs of this kind." Garcia "was not trying to shock or titillate the audience. Apparently this is the way he talks, and I guess a lot of others in his generation do so too." Cox reminded his fellow commissioners that they had found WUHY guilty of a crime, though "I suspect that the United States Attorney in Philadelphia has more important matters to occupy his time" than to bring criminal charges against a radio station whose guest complains that political change is too "fucking slow."[27]

The FCC fined WUHY $100—too small an amount to justify a constitutional challenge to the new indecency standard. As it happened, judicial review might have been salutary, even if the courts had approved the FCC's definition. For that definition was to alter dramatically five years later when Pacifica radio was again in trouble, this time for its New York affiliate's broadcast of a gross, vulgar, and uproarious monologue by comedian George Carlin. The FCC, in this most famous of its indecency cases, would simply drop the "wholly without redeeming social value" requirement—or indeed, any deference to the merits that a challenged program might possess.

But before the *Pacifica* case began its slow trek through the agency and courts, the FCC had one more clash with the counterculture. The subject was rock 'n' roll, and the opening fusillade was fired by Vice President Spiro Agnew in a September 1970 speech complaining about the "blatant drug culture propaganda" of some popular songs. Six months later, the Commission took up Agnew's theme by issuing a "Public Notice" that unsubtly reminded broadcasters of their duty to be aware of the content of the songs they aired, specifically including lyrics that might "promote . . . illegal drug usage." Failure to review song lyrics, the agency said, would raise "serious questions as to whether continued operation of the station is in the public interest."[28] Shortly afterward, it released a list of twenty-two songs, previously identified by the

U.S. Army as containing "so-called drug-oriented lyrics." They included the Beatles' "Lucy in the Sky with Diamonds" and "With a Little Help from My Friends," Bob Dylan's "Mr. Tambourine Man," the Jefferson Airplane's "White Rabbit," Steppenwolf's "The Pusher" (despite its plainly antidrug message), and the children's favorite "Puff the Magic Dragon."[29]

Commissioner Johnson's dissent from the "Public Notice" again charged his colleagues with "harass[ing] the youth culture," and with joining the Nixon administration's attempt "to divert the American people's attention" from pressing political problems, among them the Vietnam War, racial prejudice, hunger, poverty, and urban blight.[30] But the radio industry generally acquiesced: some stations dropped all music referring to drugs; one told its employees that no lyrics dealing with politics or sex would be allowed; and another banned all Bob Dylan songs "because management could not interpret the lyrics."[31]

Five weeks later, the FCC issued a "Memorandum Opinion and Order" protesting that it had been misunderstood. No songs had been banned, it said: the list of disapproved songs had been furnished by "a Commission employee" in response to a station's request, and did not represent "any official or even unofficial pronouncement by the Commission."[32] But the agency reiterated that a broadcaster "could jeopardize his license" by failing to exercise "responsibility in this area." "It was a neat trick," as legal historian Lucas Powe says. "Drug lyrics were not banned, but should a station play such songs, it could lose its license. That, of course, has been the charm of licensing from its inception."[33]

Yale Broadcasting filed suit to challenge the drug music ultimatum, likening it to the thinly veiled threats against book distributors that the Supreme Court had condemned in its 1963 *Bantam Books* case. But the FCC contended that there was nothing unusual, unconstitutional, or censorious about simply reminding radio stations of their obligation to be aware of what they are airing. A receptive panel of the DC Circuit agreed, over the angry dissent of Chief Judge David Bazelon. "Talk of 'responsibility' of a broadcaster in this connection is simply a euphemism for self-censorship," Bazelon protested. The only evidence in the case regarding the presumed causal relation between songs and drug use was "the statement of the Director of the Bureau of Narcotics and Dangerous Drugs expressing strong doubt that there is any connection between 'drug-oriented song lyrics' and the use of drugs." Bazelon posed a question that the Supreme Court was to face five years later in the context of George Carlin's scabrous satire—whether the government can ban constitutionally protected expression from the airwaves in the announced interest of shielding youth.[34] Justice Douglas, dissenting from the Supreme Court's refusal to review the rock 'n' roll case, was blunter:

> I doubt that anyone would seriously entertain the notion that consistent with the First Amendment the Government could force a newspaper out of business if its news stories betrayed too much sympathy with those arrested on marihuana charges, or because it published articles by drug advocates such as Timothy Leary. . . . Songs play no less a role in public debate, whether they eulogize the John Brown of the abolitionist movement, or the Joe Hill of the union movement, provide a rallying cry such as "We Shall Overcome," or express in music the values of the youthful "counterculture." The Government cannot, consistent with the First Amendment, require a broadcaster to censor its music any more than it can require a newspaper to censor the stories of its reporters.[35]

Shielding Young Ears from the Seven Dirty Words

On the afternoon of October 30, 1973, Pacifica radio's New York affiliate, WBAI, broadcast George Carlin's twelve-minute "Filthy Words" monologue as part of a program that addressed "contemporary society's attitude toward language."[36] Six weeks later, John Douglas, a member of the national planning board of the procensorship watchdog group Morality in Media, complained to the FCC that "he had heard the broadcast while driving with his young son."[37] "Filthy Words" was a commentary on taboos surrounding "seven dirty words" that, according to Carlin, one "couldn't say on the public airwaves." To quote from the monologue itself: "I heard a lady say bitch one night on television and it was cool . . . And, uh, bastard you can say, and hell and damn, so I have to figure out which ones you couldn't ever and it came down to seven . . . shit, piss, fuck, cunt, cocksucker, motherfucker, and tits." Carlin goes on to dissect each taboo term: shit, for example, "the middle class has never really accepted," although "a lady now in a middle-class home, you'll hear most of the time she says it as an expletive . . . She says, 'Oh shit, oh shit,' if she drops something or burns the broccoli." Other uses: "I don't want to see that shit anymore"; "He don't know shit from Shinola"; "Built like a brick shit-house"; "Up shit's creek"; "Holy shit, tough shit, eat shit, shit-eating grin," and so on.[38]

The FCC received John Douglas's complaint at a political moment when it was under severe pressure to "do something" about both vulgarity on radio and violence on television. Concerns about media violence going back to the 1950s—the days of Fredric Wertham and Congress's juvenile delinquency hearings—had inspired psychologists and scholars in the burgeoning field of communications to fashion studies attempting to prove that children would imitate violence that they saw on-screen; a 1963 *Look* magazine article by a leading psychologist of the "social learning" school, Albert Bandura, had popularized this imitation theory.[39] Political agitation in the late 1960s had led to a federal study of TV violence, released in 1972 by the Surgeon General and the National Institute of Mental Health. Although this report, accompanied by five appendices describing dozens of government-funded experiments, was cautious and qualified,[40] politicians and advocates cited it in support of demands to remove violence, sexual subject matter, and even mild vulgarities from television. Congress threatened to cut off FCC funding "should the Commission fail to act" against electronic violence, vulgarity, and sex.[41]

FCC chairman Richard Wiley was reluctant, but as two historians of the era recount, the Commission did not realize "that the fusion of obscenity and violence had lengthened the congressional attention span."[42] In June 1974, Congress directed the agency to submit a report by year's end "outlining the specific, positive actions taken or planned by the Commission to protect children from excessive violence and obscenity."[43] In response to the congressional heat, Wiley began a campaign of "jawboning" with the goal of persuading the National Association of Broadcasters to amend its 1952 Television Code to create a "family viewing hour." Under this scheme, the first hour of TV prime time and the preceding hour "would not consist of programming unsuitable for viewing by the entire family."[44] The family viewing hour was in place by April 1975, to the distress of the Writers, Directors, and Screen Actors guilds, which sued both the FCC and the networks, claiming that the "hour" was a product of joint government-private censorship, and threatened such popular shows as *All in the Family*, *The Mary Tyler Moore Show*, and *M*A*S*H*. Initially, they won their case, but on appeal, the DC Circuit decided not to decide: it ruled that under the legal doctrine of "primary jurisdiction," the FCC itself should have the first crack at determining whether it had engaged in undue coercion.[45] The agency, to nobody's surprise, eventually decided that its jawboning of TV executives to create the family viewing hour had been proper.[46]

The FCC, meanwhile, was awaiting word from the courts in the topless radio case, to learn how far it could constitutionally go in censoring naughty ideas or vulgar words. The agency had been sitting on John Douglas's complaint about the "Filthy Words" monologue since late 1973. When, the next year, the DC Circuit affirmed the FCC's punishment of topless radio based on a variable-obscenity test which stressed the presumed need to protect children from raunchy banter,[47] the Commission had the judicial backing it needed for a politically desirable resolution of the Pacifica matter. Censoring sex and vulgarity while avoiding a constitutional battle with the TV industry over violence was the chosen solution. In February 1975, it ruled on Douglas's *Pacifica* complaint, announcing a new, broader indecency standard. A week later, its report to Congress on "The Broadcast of Violent, Indecent, and Obscene Material" relied on that new, broader standard to allay congressional pressures.[48]

The FCC's *Pacifica* ruling thus did not rely on the variable-obscenity test that the DC Circuit had just approved in the topless radio case. Instead, it focused on indecency—a bigger category, so it claimed, even though the Supreme Court in previous cases had interpreted "obscene," "indecent," "lewd," and so forth to be synonymous. Moreover, the Commission announced, it was "reformulat[ing] the concept of 'indecent' " by dropping the part about "redeeming social value" that it had included in its indecency definition in the Jerry Garcia case three years before. The definition of broadcast indecency was now to be simply "the exposure of children to language that describes, in terms patently offensive as measured by contemporary community standards for the broadcast medium, sexual or excretory activities and organs." There was no need to show that the language appealed to the "prurient interest," nor could it be "redeemed by a claim that it has literary, artistic, political or scientific value." The reason for the switch: "Obnoxious, gutter language . . . has the effect of debasing and brutalizing human beings by reducing them to their mere bodily functions, and we believe that such words are indecent within the meaning of the statute and have no place on radio when children are in the audience."[49]

Carlin's monologue, with its inspired repetition of "gutter language," was assumed to be "patently offensive" and therefore indecent under this new, expanded definition. Because it aired the piece when children might be listening, WBAI radio had violated the just-created indecency standard. This meant that indecent speech was banned for nearly the entire broadcast day, for the FCC assumed that children are in the listening audience during all but late-evening hours (many are present then as well). Pacifica's characterization of Carlin as a "significant social satirist of American language and manners in the tradition of Mark Twain and Mort Sahl" was irrelevant: serious value no longer saved indecent language.[50]

The FCC's justification for vastly expanding its indecency definition was not, as in the early broadcast cases, the scarcity of the electromagnetic spectrum, but the "invasiveness" of radio, and its ready availability to children. In an analogy that later impressed Supreme Court Justice John Paul Stevens, the Commission likened its regulatory power to the law of "public nuisance," which channels rather than flatly prohibits inappropriate behavior: "The law of nuisance does not say, for example, that no one shall maintain a pigsty; it simply says that no one shall maintain a pigsty in an inappropriate place, such as a residential neighborhood."[51] One difference, of course, was that pigsties had more places to locate than indecent language had times when, under the FCC's regime, it could be heard on television or radio. If all broadcasting was to be a "pigsty"-free zone, then the century's most powerful communications medium would be sanitized by government in a manner that would be immediately recognized as unconstitutional for newspapers or books.

A change in personnel contributed, if not to the result, at least to the absence of any dissents in the FCC's *Pacifica* ruling. Nicholas Johnson and Kenneth Cox were gone. Concurrences by Commissioners James Quello and Charlotte Reid were even more vociferous than the majority opinion in their condemnation of Pacifica. Only a concurrence by Commissioners Glen Robinson and Benjamin Hooks raised any constitutional or policy questions about the breadth of the power the FCC was asserting. "I acknowledge that the logic of this 'nuisance' test of obscenity or indecency could carry us much further into the realm of censorship than would be proper," Robinson wrote. "But I also think that the attempt to accommodate the powerful sensibilities that attach to free speech on the one hand, and modesty on the other, is worth the effort." Most adults do think vulgar language inappropriate for children, Robinson said; "the only possible way to take a mediate position on issues like obscenity or indecency is to avoid dogmatism and its meretricious handmaiden, the Ringing Phrase, and to split the difference, as sensibly as can be, between the contending ideas."[52]

Robinson's concurrence reflected a pragmatic, weary acceptance of bureaucratic realities, which had much to do with politics and little to do with objective assessments of harm to kids. It did not advance understanding or even curiosity, though, about *why* political pressures are so strong when it comes to censoring the language, information, intellectual stimulation, or entertainment available to youngsters, or what harms might befall them from censorship itself. Robinson himself came to agree: twenty years later he confessed embarrassment at his "complicity" in the FCC's *Pacifica* decision.[53]

The Radio-Television News Directors Association filed a petition for "clarification or reconsideration" of the FCC ruling, protesting that it would have "a deleterious impact on accurate and insightful" news reporting. The agency responded with a supplementary order in March 1976, assuring broadcasters that *Pacifica* "was issued in a specific factual context" and should not "inhibit broadcast journalism." "We intimated," the commissioners said, that vulgar language "could be broadcast in a news or public affairs program or otherwise when the number of children in the audience was reduced to a minimum, if sufficient warning were given to unconsenting adults and if in the context used the language had 'serious literary, artistic, political or scientific value.' "[54] If this "clarification" offered little real editorial guidance, *Pacifica* did at least have one comforting limitation. The "number of words which fall within the definition of indecent is clearly limited,"[55] the Commission had said in its initial decision, although it did not enumerate them. Perhaps George Carlin had been right and there were only seven.

The Commission imposed no sanction against Pacifica, beyond placing its decision in "the station's license file" for easy reference in case WBAI sinned again. The decision, as the FCC frankly proclaimed, was designed to "to clarify the applicable standards" for the industry.[56] Pacifica nonetheless appealed, and in contrast to its previously complaisant responses to FCC censorship, the DC Circuit ruled in 1977 that this time the agency had gone too far.

Judge Edward Tamm's decision explained that by banning words and dispensing with any judgments about a program's overall value, the FCC had practiced censorship in violation of its own governing statute and in the process had reduced virtually all of broadcasting to the level of a child. The result, Tamm said, invoking the memorable phrase that Justice Frankfurter had coined in *Butler v. Michigan* twenty years before, was "a classic case of burning the house to roast the pig." Under the FCC's indecency standard, passages from Shakespeare and the Bible could not be broadcast, in addition to "works of Auden, Beckett, Lord Byron, Chaucer, Fielding, Greene, Hemingway, Joyce, Knowles, Lawrence, Orwell, Scott, Swift and the Nixon tapes."[57]

Chief Judge Bazelon agreed with Tamm but faulted him for relying solely on the anticensorship provision of the communications law and thus avoiding a more obvious and pressing deficiency in the FCC's indecency scheme: its offense to the First Amendment. "Indecent" but nonobscene speech is constitutionally protected, as Bazelon pointed out, and may include work with "overriding literary, artistic, political or scientific value." None of the FCC's arguments justified the banning of constitutionally protected speech from the airwaves for virtually all of the broadcast day. The child-protection rationale in particular—"the argument most strenuously advanced by the Commission"—not only contradicted the *Butler* principle that adults cannot be reduced to hearing only what is fit for children, but relied on "several undocumented" and possibly erroneous assumptions: for example, "that most parents consider any mention of dirty words to be unsuitable for their children" and that parents are unable to control their children's radio listening. Bazelon also reminded his readers that minors have "a 'significant measure of First Amendment protection,' " which bars government from censoring their access to literature and entertainment unless it meets the *Ginsberg v. New York* variable-obscenity test.[58]

The third member of the DC Circuit panel, Harold Leventhal, could hardly have disagreed more; and his dissent in *Pacifica* reinforced just how little consensus there was among judges, or intellectuals generally, about indecency and harm to minors. Leventhal reiterated the FCC's argument that it was simply engaged in time-channeling or nuisance-zoning, not outright censorship. He admitted there were problems with the FCC's order—it was not clear why "tits," for example, was banned, "because it is neither a sexual nor excretory organ." But these trivial details had not been part of Pacifica's appeal, and Leventhal saw no reason to overturn the order on its face. The Commission's decision had been narrowly limited to particular language broadcast at a particular time. Parents need all the help they can get "in their protection of young children during the uniquely prolonged period of development needed to permit the emergence of a competent and consenting person." Society must let children know what is disapproved, Leventhal said, citing Justice Brennan's use ten years before in *Ginsberg* of Dr. Willard Gaylin's argument about the importance of inculcating sexual taboos. That is, although children will certainly "hear these words somehow, somewhere, and even at a relatively early age, . . . it makes a difference whether they hear them in certain places, such as the locker room or gutter, or at certain times, that do not identify general acceptability."[59]

Leventhal's dissent was clearly a brief for Supreme Court review, as the FCC's lawyers understood, and they followed it scrupulously in preparing their petition for certiorari. The DC Circuit majority, they argued, had been unduly imaginative in pointing to literary works that would now presumably be banned from radio. Instead of sticking out their judicial necks by striking down the new indecency rule on its face, the judges should have given the agency leeway to refine it one case at a time. The whole dispute was really just about one offensive broadcast that everyone agreed was indecent, they said—disingenuously, for the agency's *Pacifica* ruling had been explicitly framed as a general warning to the industry.[60]

Pacifica in the Supreme Court

With much at stake for broadcasting, it was to be expected that amicus curiae briefs would be filed in the Supreme Court by the networks as well as by free-expression groups, among them the ACLU, the Association of American Publishers (AAP), and PEN American Center. What *was* surprising was that the Solicitor General's office, the government's official representative before the Supreme Court, also filed an amicus brief, rather than representing the FCC, and that the brief took the part of Pacifica. Whatever the legitimate limits of indecency enforcement, Solicitor General Wade McCree argued, the FCC had gone too far. (Indeed, the Solicitor General's office would admit to the Supreme Court at oral argument that its support of the FCC in the Court of Appeals was "an embarrassment.")[61]

The amicus briefs in *Pacifica* illustrated just how contentious the harm-to-minors presumption had become. The ACLU and AAP argued that the FCC had no basis for its conclusion that "indecent words standing alone, and regardless of context, are patently offensive or harmful in any way to minors." They pointed out that many parents might disagree with the agency's attitude toward vulgar words; indeed, "there are children's books which use some of these words and yet have won awards."[62] At the Supreme Court argument on April 18, 1975, however, the justices evidenced a different view of the harm that might flow from George Carlin's vulgarities. Suppose that a station "just decided that for an hour it would put on a record consisting of one four-letter word, repeated over and over again," one of the justices asked Harry Plotkin, Pacifica's attorney. "Under your definition would the FCC be powerless because of the censorship statute to affect that?" Plotkin's answer—"I think it would be powerless to tell them to stop doing it"—was constitutionally sound but not very politically prudent.[63]

The changes wrought by Richard Nixon in Supreme Court personnel determined the outcome in *Pacifica*, as they had in *Miller v. California* five years before. All five justices joining the majority ruling (Stevens, Burger, Powell, Blackmun, Rehnquist) had been appointed by Presidents Ford or Nixon; the four dissenters (Brennan, Stewart, White, and Marshall) had been chosen earlier. When *Pacifica* came down on July 3, 1978, the five-justice majority adopted Judge Leventhal's and the FCC's argument that the case was really a narrow one, involving only an indecency ruling against one obnoxious monologue as broadcast at 2 p.m. But the Court's decision necessarily also approved the Commission's freewheeling definition of indecency.

There was no majority opinion. John Paul Stevens, who had already indicated his leanings by writing in a 1976 "adult zoning" case that "few of us would march our sons and daughters off to war to preserve the citizen's right to see 'Specified Sexual Activities' exhibited in the theaters of our choice,"[64] wrote a plurality opinion that Rehnquist and Burger joined. Stevens started off by approving the FCC's interpretation of "indecency" as far broader than "obscenity." The indecency definition ("patently offensive as measured by contemporary community standards") was acceptable, said Stevens, even though it covered constitutionally protected speech, because broadcasting is peculiarly invasive, and "uniquely accessible to children, even those too young to read."[65] Besides, the agency was not really banning indecent speech—only channeling it to times when children are unlikely to be listening. (In practice, this meant after 10 p.m.) Adopting the FCC's analogy to the law of nuisance, Stevens said vulgar words on radio were like "a pig in the parlor instead of the barnyard"—they are "in the wrong place." Brushing aside the *Butler v. Michigan* rule that adults cannot constitutionally be reduced to the level of children, Stevens suggested that those who want indecency can find it at their local nightclub or record store.[66]

Stevens emphasized the "narrowness" of his ruling. The FCC had issued its order in a "specific factual context," and had reserved questions "concerning possible action in other contexts" for the future. The indecency rule, after all, was not being applied to "a two-way radio conversation between a cab driver and a dispatcher, or a telecast of an Elizabethan comedy." Even if crude, these communications might not offend the FCC because the indecency concept "requires consideration of a host of variables," including the likely "composition of the audience." Thus, even a "prime-time recitation" of Chaucer's bawdy "Miller's Tale" "would not be likely to command the attention of many children who are both old enough to understand and young enough to be adversely affected by passages such as: 'And prively he caughte hire by the queynte.' "[67] Stevens's faith here in the FCC's discretion ignored the obvious chilling effect that the agency intended its indecency standard to have on broadcasters, but at least it enabled First Amendment lawyers in later cases to argue that *Pacifica* was so narrow as to be "limited to its facts."

The most controversial part of Stevens's plurality opinion was probably its assertion that "patently offensive references to excretory and sexual organs and activities surely lie at the periphery of First Amendment concern." A "requirement that indecent language be avoided," he said, "will have its primary effect on the form, rather than the content, of serious communication. There are few, if any, thoughts that cannot be expressed by the use of less offensive language."[68] This seemed to clash head-on with Justice Harlan's recognition of the emotive power of vulgar words in *Cohen v. California* (the "Fuck the Draft" case). Certainly, D. H. Lawrence, James Joyce, Joyce's judicial expositor Judge John Woolsey, and many others would have disagreed with Stevens's literary opinion; but it became a frequent source of support for those defending censorship in the years after *Pacifica*. As late as *ACLU v. Reno* in 1997 (the "Communications Decency Act" case), the government argued that a total ban on indecency was constitutional because it affected only the "form," not the substance, of expression.

As for the Carlin monologue, which obviously could not substitute polite for charged words without losing its point entirely, Stevens acknowledged that it "does present a point of view" about dirty words—"that our attitudes toward them are 'essentially silly' "—but he responded with a non sequitur: that the FCC did not censor the broadcast because of its political viewpoint.[69] This was like saying that California did not censor Paul Cohen's "Fuck the Draft" jacket because of its political viewpoint but only because of its taboo word—that is, it was irrelevant to the censorship issue.

Stevens gave no explanation why minors needed protection from vulgar words, nor did he respond to the ACLU's and AAP's argument that there was no factual basis to assume psychological damage. He said only that while the written message of contempt for military conscription on Cohen's jacket "might have been incomprehensible to a first grader," the Carlin monologue "could have enlarged a child's vocabulary in an instant." Justice Powell, who wrote a separate concurrence, was slightly more expansive on this point: because children are "not 'possessed of that full capacity for individual choice which is the presupposition of First Amendment guarantees,' " he said, they "may not be able to protect themselves from speech which, although shocking to most adults, generally may be avoided by the unwilling through the exercise of choice. At the same time, such speech may have a deeper and more lasting negative effect on a child than on an adult." Powell did not elaborate on the nature of this "more lasting negative effect," noting only that Carlin's monologue was a "verbal shock treatment," and "the language involved in this case is as potentially degrading and harmful to children as representations of many erotic acts."[70]

Powell wrote his concurrence (in which Harry Blackmun joined) primarily to distance himself from Stevens on the constitutional status of dirty words:

> I do not subscribe to the theory that the Justices of this Court are free generally to decide on the basis of its content which speech protected by the First Amendment is most "valuable" and hence deserving of the most protection, and which is less "valuable" and hence deserving of less protection.[71]

For Powell, the reason for allowing the FCC to ban Carlin's "verbal shock treatment" along with other constitutionally protected but indecent speech turned not on the assertedly low value of taboo words but on the unique properties of broadcasting—its "invasion" of the home and its accessibility to children. But here Powell ignored the fact that, as Judge Harry Edwards later wrote in a law review article, "Joe Couch Potato" might well "wonder whether the Justices ever noticed the 'off' button on their remote controls as an efficient mechanism with which to fend off intrusive and pervasive television."[72]

The Stevens and Powell opinions in *Pacifica* were not models of lucid constitutional analysis, but they responded to a political reality. Broadcasting is not a tangible thing that can be distributed only to those who look grown-up. Radio and TV do not exactly invade the home, but they *are* ubiquitous; and parents who care about the point probably cannot prevent their children from hearing vulgar speech if producers choose to air it. The tenuous balance of obscenity law—protecting adults' free-speech rights (*Butler*) while imposing stricter restrictions on kids (*Ginsberg*)—was not really workable for broadcasting. The choice was either to restrict the rights of adults and broadcasters—along with the cutting-edge capacity of the medium—or to risk the presumed shock, "negative effect," and "degrading" impact on minors. For the five justices in the *Pacifica* majority, the correct political answer was obvious.

For the four dissenters, though, it was not obvious at all; and their disagreement simply dramatized the extent to which this was a debate about personal moral values, rather than psychological harm to minors—or constitutional law. As Justice Brennan wrote, "surprising as it may be to some individual Members of this Court, some parents may actually find Mr. Carlin's unabashed attitude towards the seven 'dirty words' healthy, and deem it desirable to expose their children to the manner in which Mr. Carlin defuses the taboo surrounding the words." Such parents

> may constitute a minority of the American public, but the absence of great numbers willing to exercise the right to raise their children in this fashion does not alter that right's nature or its existence. Only the Court's regrettable decision does that.

The majority's approval of the FCC indecency regime flatly contradicted *Butler*, Brennan said, but "equally disturbing" was Powell's and Stevens's

> depressing inability to appreciate that in our land of cultural pluralism, there are many who think, act, and talk differently from the Members of this Court, and who do not share their fragile sensibilities. It is only an acute ethnocentric myopia that enables the Court to approve the censorship of communications solely because of the words they contain.[73]

Justice Stevens never explicitly disowned his opinion in *Pacifica*, though he did produce an apologia of sorts fifteen years later, in a speech at Yale Law School, when he blamed the dubious result on poor litigation strategy by Pacifica. "[I]t seems to me that the attempt to craft black-letter or bright-line rules of First Amendment law often produces unworkable and unsatisfactory results," Stevens warned, "especially when an exclusive focus on rules of general application obfuscates the specific facts at issue and interests at stake in a given case." *Pacifica*, he said, "illustrates the point."

> Ever since the case was argued, I have thought the result might have been different if the broadcaster had simply contended that the particular order was erroneous because the evidence of actual or probable offense to the listening audience was so meager. Instead, however, the station took the position that the Commission was entirely without power to regulate indecent broadcasting . . . no matter how inappropriate for children. . . . Instead of attempting to sell the Court such a rigid and unattractive proposition of law, adopting a less

> ambitious strategy might have better served the interests of both litigants and the law.[74]

Deconstructed, Stevens's muted apologia seemed to acknowledge that *Pacifica* did not well serve "the interests of . . . the law." Perhaps it was a response to the forensic ammunition that the decision gave censorship advocates in the decades that followed. Despite *Pacifica*'s "narrow holding," they began regularly to argue for an indecency standard, rather than the more rigorous (if almost equally vague) variable obscenity or harm-to-minors. Although indecency/patent offensiveness bans after *Pacifica* were often invalidated on First Amendment grounds, it was not until *Reno v. ACLU* in 1997 that the Supreme Court cast any doubt on the viability or even intelligibility of the standard itself.

Pacifica was a watershed case. Intellectually and constitutionally indefensible, the decision nevertheless responded to political and cultural imperatives, at least in the view of five justices. The rationale was deeply regressive, backward from cases like *Butler* and *Roth*, backward even from the variable obscenity of *Ginsberg*. An agency of the U.S. government was now empowered to ban constitutionally protected, socially valuable speech, on a theory that subordinated the rights of adults to the 19th-century logic of *Regina v. Hicklin*.

Five

THE REIGN OF DECENCY

The FCC, the Meese Commission, and Art About AIDS

The FCC had insisted that the *Pacifica* case was narrow, involving only George Carlin's provocatively repetitious riffs on the seven naughty words. And the agency was as good as its word, initially. In the first eight years after the Supreme Court's decision, it focused its indecency rule on the taboo terms and little else.

Barely two months after *Pacifica*, the Commission dismissed complaints against Boston's public television station for airing segments from *Monty Python's Flying Circus* that allegedly included "scatology, immodesty, vulgarity, nudity, profanity and sacrilege." A ruling five years later exonerated a Pacifica announcer who had used several of the forbidden words because they were not equivalent to George Carlin's "verbal shock treatment." The agency rejected complaints about the radio shock jock Howard Stern's incessant sexual banter.[1] Broadcasters thus felt reasonably secure if they simply avoided the taboo words that Carlin had so presciently identified, with a few fairly obvious additions.

In fact, between 1978 and 1987 the FCC did not find a single violation of the indecency standard. The hands-off approach coincided with Reagan-era deregulation. As Mark Fowler, the Reagan-appointed FCC chair, suggested apropos of indecency, "if you don't like it, just don't let your kids watch it."[2]

But deregulation of broadcasting was one thing for the economic market and quite another for the marketplace of ideas, particularly in a decade when moral-values conservatism had increasing influence in national politics. Attorney General Edwin Meese's initiation in 1985 of a new commission to investigate pornography signaled the primacy for the Reagan administration of the "culture war" issue of sexual speech.

Well before Meese assembled his commission, antipornography activists Catharine MacKinnon and Andrea Dworkin had inspired a modification of traditional censorship arguments to conform to their view that sexual entertainment is most harmful where it conditions males to respond to images or ideas of domination.[3] An ordinance drafted by MacKinnon and Dworkin had been proposed in several localities, finally passed in Indianapolis, and struck down by the federal courts in a lawsuit led by the American Booksellers Association. A friend-of-the-court brief from anticensorship scholars active in women's rights outlined the harm *to women* caused by speech restrictions ostensibly enacted to protect them.[4] Judge Frank Easterbrook, writing for the federal appeals court, pointed out that the Indianapolis law could affect everything from "hard-core films to W. B. Yeats's poem 'Leda and the Swan' (from the myth of Zeus in the form of a swan impregnating an apparently subordinate Leda), to the collected works of James Joyce, D. H. Lawrence, and John Cleland." Easterbrook acknowledged that bad ideas may "influence the culture and shape our socialization," but "all is protected as speech": "Any other answer leaves the government in control of all the institutions of culture, the great censor and director of which thoughts are good for us."[5]

This legal setback left MacKinnon/Dworkin supporters frustrated, and seeking other outlets and alliances. Despite ideological differences, they joined forces with the Meese Commission as it got under way in 1985.[6] The result was a year of often circus-like hearings in which code words like "subordination of women" came to replace more traditional moral-values arguments. Women who had been abused by husbands or partners gave emotional testimony attributing their sufferings to pornography, while free-speech advocates like the ACLU's Barry Lynn critiqued the Commission's preconceptions. "I'm afraid there is a train marked 'censorship' which has just left the station," Lynn quipped in May 1985. And indeed, most of those chosen as commissioners had settled antipornography views.[7]

When the Commission arrived for hearings in New York, the National Coalition Against Censorship organized a press event at which Kurt Vonnegut, Colleen Dewhurst, and Betty Friedan, among others, denounced its ideology and methods. The director of the Sex Information and Education Council of the United States (SIECUS) spoke about the victims, not of pornography, but of censorship: the "children who are growing up not understanding their bodies and feeling guilty and confused about sexuality," and the "millions of adolescents who are pregnant, becoming parents, getting abortions, [and] dropping out of school" because they "have not been helped to understand and handle their sexuality."[8]

Although the Meese Commission's *Final Report* in 1986 concluded (over two dissents) that social science studies showed violent pornography to have adverse behavioral effects, scholars protested that their data had been misinterpreted. The experiments to which the Commission referred generally involved male college students who were shown violent sexual materials in an artificial laboratory setting, then deliberately angered, and finally tested on their willingness to perform some act (for example, administering electric shocks) that was considered a proxy for real-world aggression. Such willingness is "a long way from real aggression," as Edward Donnerstein, one of the leading researchers, explained.[9] More important, the Meese Commission's conclusions were essentially moral, not empirical, as it acknowledged:

> To a number of us, the most important harms must be seen in moral terms. . . . Issues of human dignity and human decency, no less real for their lack of scientific measurability, are for many of us central to thinking about the question of harm.[10]

This moral concern, as the Commission's *Final Report* said, was particularly critical for youngsters. Like the liberal Lockhart Commission before it (which had urged the scrapping of most obscenity laws), the conservative Meese Commission had no empirical evidence of harm to minors; yet both recommended maintaining restrictions on youthful access to sexual material. The Meese Commission's reasons were frankly pedagogical: "For children to be taught by these materials that sex is public, that sex is commercial, and that sex can be divorced from any degree of affection, love, commitment, or marriage is for us the wrong message at the wrong time."[11]

Needless to say, pornography's function as fantasy material, not pedagogy, was lost in the Commission's analysis. And its assertion that harm to minors is fundamentally a question of suppressing immoral or disapproved ideas about sex only highlighted the constitutional dilemma, for as Judge Easterbrook had just explained in the Indianapolis case, the First Amendment is premised on the idea that government may not become "the great censor and director of which thoughts are good for us."

While the Meese Commission was traversing the country, Surgeon General C. Everett Koop had assembled a group of experts in a less heated atmosphere for a two-day workshop on the effects of pornography. Koop had assured Henry Hudson, chair of the Meese Commission, that even though the Commission was not doing any scientific research, the Public Health Service would "study the issue and 'feed material to you.' "[12] But as one workshop participant recalls, "for a host of trivial reasons," the papers assigned by Koop reached the Commission only after its *Final Report* had been issued.[13] A report of the Surgeon General's workshop was eventually published, but it was little publicized and, although an official government publication, became very difficult to find.

In contrast to the Meese Commission, the Surgeon General's workshop approached the issue of harm skeptically. Attitudes and behavior, it said, are "[n]ot necessarily linked in a straight causal pathway." Long-term effects of pornography on human conduct are essentially unknown. As to minors, although some experts believe that later-life "sexual and emotional patterns" could be affected by early viewing of erotica, others think young children are unaffected because they lack "the cognitive or emotional capacities needed to comprehend the messages of much pornographic material." Youngsters' responses and susceptibilities vary widely, and in the end, it is "rather difficult to say much definitive about the possible effects of exposure to pornography on children."[14]

While these sober and undramatic conclusions were little noticed in 1986, and the Meese Commission's were simultaneously touted and reviled, the FCC and its chairman, Mark Fowler, found themselves in a new political swamp. Morality in Media and the National Decency Forum, incensed at the agency's lax enforcement of its indecency standard, initiated a letter-writing campaign to Congress, correspondence with Fowler himself, and picket lines opposing his renomination as FCC chief. Fowler responded by inviting Brad Curl of the National Decency Forum to meet with him and FCC general counsel Jack Smith, Jr., to discuss the indecency standard. After that meeting in early July 1986, Curl wrote to Fowler agreeing to call off the pickets and assuring him: "[i]f we are satisfied that there is significant response to our deep concerns about the material reaching our children we will abandon our growing campaign to secure new F.C.C. leadership."[15]

Fowler and Smith met with Curl again on July 21; Paul McGeady of Morality in Media also attended. As *The Wall Street Journal* later recounted, Smith "advised Mr. Curl to make tapes or transcripts of offensive broadcasts. Morality in Media conveyed that advice" to supporters, several of whom then taped the off-color radio ramblings of Howard Stern in Philadelphia and mailed the tape to the FCC. Complaints were also filed against Pacifica's KPFK affiliate about a broadcast, after 10 p.m., of excerpts from the sexually graphic play *Jerker*, which dealt with the devastation of AIDS and had recently opened in Los Angeles.[16] Jack Smith meanwhile corresponded with the Mississippi fundamentalist leader Donald Wildmon, who had objected to a television broadcast of *The Rose*, advising Wildmon that the film did not present "the kind of air-tight case that you want to push at this time," and assuring him that the agency was "inquiring into a couple of other cases which we think may be more clear violations."[17]

Thus, by the latter months of 1986, "as anti-pornography conservatives attacked his appointment for a second term and picketed the FCC," Chairman Fowler "sharply changed direction" and announced his intention "to drive lewd programming off the air."[18] Fowler had not been studying child psychology, however, or otherwise ruminating over the harm that might have befallen youngsters in the previous eight years of decency nonenforcement. Indeed, the welfare of minors was about the furthest thing from the FCC's mind as it responded to the right's political pressures in 1986 and '87.

ACT I, *the Irrepressible Mr. Stern, and Perhaps Molly Bloom*

The FCC's new indecency regime was unveiled in April 1987, in four decisions that replaced the simple, specific "dirty words" test with a "generic" approach that took full advantage of the broad, vague contours of *Pacifica*—prohibiting anything that was "patently offensive." Under the new rule, sexual innuendo and double entendre could now be banned along with taboo words, if "the context of the references in question rendered them explicit."[19] At an open meeting on April 16, two weeks before formal announcement of the new standard, the commissioners acknowledged that judging indecency now would not be "an easy task"; Commissioner Patricia Diaz Dennis observed that scenes in *Macbeth* and *The Taming of the Shrew* "refer to excrement and to sex in fairly graphic terms," yet she did not think anyone would want to bar them from prime time.[20]

The Commission also announced that it was eliminating its 10 p.m. "safe harbor" for indecent speech. This had been a critical element of the Supreme Court's argument in *Pacifica* that the indecency ban was really just a form of time-channeling. But as the Commission explained, "recent evidence for the markets involved" indicated that "there is still a reasonable risk that children may be in the listening audience" after 10 p.m.[21] Protesters pointed out that abandoning the safe harbor defied the *Butler v. Michigan* principle that adults' free-expression rights cannot be sacrificed on the altar of the vulnerable child. But the FCC demurred: not only was eliminating the safe harbor consistent with the First Amendment, it said, but there was no constitutional reason why indecency regulation could not extend to all media, including books and magazines.[22] This was a startlingly aggressive interpretation of *Pacifica*, but one necessitated by the fact that two of the four programs the FCC chose to illustrate its new approach were aired after 10 p.m.: KPFK's literary offering of *Jerker* and a song, "Makin' Bacon," by an English punk rock band, broadcast by the student radio station at the University of California, Santa Barbara.

The FCC decisions detailed offending excerpts from *Jerker*, Howard Stern's broadcasts, and "Makin' Bacon." *Jerker* was indecent because it included such lines as "I'll give you the gentlest fuck west of the Mississippi" and a description of anal sex. Stern's subjects were conscientiously listed as "masturbation, ejaculation, breast size, penis size, sexual intercourse, nudity, urination, oral-genital contact, erections, sodomy, bestiality, menstruation and testicles." "Makin' Bacon" consisted of a long, hyperbolically macho sexual rap (example: "Come here baby, make it quick / Kneel down there and suck on my dick . . . Get down baby on your hands and knees / Take my danish and give it a squeeze").[23] The FCC had not paid much attention to the song until the complainant wrote to Tipper Gore's Parents' Music Resource Center, whereupon "Kaboom!" he later said, "they took my letter to the White House and sent Patrick Buchanan [the administration's communications director] to the FCC, where he read them the riot act" in August 1986.[24]

The FCC acknowledged that its April 1987 decisions signaled a radical change. Accordingly, it issued only declarations and "warnings," but it put the broadcast industry on notice that subsequent sanctions for "patently offensive" speech could include hefty fines as well as license revocations.[25] Commissioner James Quello protested that KPFK deserved a "substantial forfeiture" for *Jerker*, and applauded the agency's decision to forward the file to the U.S. Attorney for criminal prosecution.[26] But the Justice Department thought better of going forward: as the director of its new National Obscenity Enforcement Unit wrote to the FCC, "it would be difficult to prove, 'beyond a reasonable doubt,' that Pacifica *intended*" to violate the criminal law, "where prior Commission policies indicated that: (a) broadcasts after

10:00 p.m. were immune from prosecution; and (b) where the Commission had previously restricted the meaning of 'indecent' to the repetitive use of the same 'Filthy Words' held to be indecent in the *Pacifica* case."[27]

As for Mark Fowler, the turnabout did not save his job. His term as FCC chair expired just a day before the April 1987 decisions were announced.[28]

Industry and public interest groups led by Action for Children's Television (ACT) now filed a "Petition for Reconsideration" of the indecency rulings, arguing that the FCC should not have changed to a new, generic standard without at least an opportunity for input by the public; and that the elimination of any safe harbor reduced adult audiences to hearing only "what is fit for children."[29] Pacifica chose a more literary mode of attack; barely a week after the April rulings, it asked the FCC whether WBAI Radio in New York could safely broadcast a long-planned reading of a novel, scheduled for June 16 at about 11 p.m. The work, which Pacifica did not identify, included such choice phrases as "kissing my bottom," "put it in me from behind," "lovely young cock," "fucked yes and damn well fucked too," and "stick his tongue seven miles up my hole." Pacifica's coyness evaporated over the next few weeks as June 16 approached and the FCC failed to respond; it explained in supplementary papers that the work was *Ulysses*, that June 16 was "Bloomsday" (the day when the events in the novel take place), that the reading was an annual Bloomsday event, and that the raunchy quotations came from the "Penelope" episode, Molly Bloom's stream-of-consciousness recollections of her erotic life.[30]

Despite the totemic literary status of *Ulysses*, Pacifica's concerns were hardly frivolous, for Mrs. Bloom's ruminations were no different in spirit or explicitness from the sexual descriptions that had just been condemned in "Makin' Bacon" and *Jerker*. Indeed, Commissioner Quello publicly opined that *Ulysses* was indecent: this is "stuff you deck someone over," had been Quello's evaluation; "I'm amazed it made it as a classic."[31]

The Commission refused to render the requested declaration—for fear, as it explained, of imposing a "prior restraint on expression." After noting the great fame of *Ulysses* and quoting Judge Woolsey's 1933 decision proclaiming its value, the Commission's Mass Media Bureau concluded that Pacifica would simply have to make its own "informed decision" whether broadcasting "the subject program is the desirable course in light of the first amendment and other concerns addressed herein."[32] Pacifica now filed an Application for Review to the full Commission (there were only six days left until Bloomsday), in which it urged both a decision on Molly Bloom and a reconsideration of the April rulings, in particular the FCC's condemnation of *Jerker* without consideration of its context and relevance to the national trauma of AIDS. It appended in support of this argument an editorial cartoon showing "FCC Radio Police" arresting Surgeon General Koop "for broadcasting AIDS warnings that contained sexual innuendo"[33] (see illustrations).

The Commission still would not rule on Bloomsday. Approving the broadcast, on the one hand, would seem to violate the generic rule it had just announced, and could be viewed as discrimination in favor of New York intellectuals and against rock music in Santa Barbara or gay theater in LA; but disapproving it would invite charges of yahooism, and give Pacifica a case to appeal to the courts that was considerably more sympathetic than *Jerker*. WBAI did go forward with Bloomsday, and although an indecency complaint was filed, the agency eventually dismissed it because the offending passages had been aired after midnight.[34] But an immediate result of the uncertainty, and of Pacifica's already hefty legal costs, was its decision later not to broadcast Allen Ginsberg's "Howl" in celebration of the poem's thirtieth anniversary. Thus began an era of literary vetting at Pacifica during which the stations' attorney, John Crigler, spent one holiday editing Steinbeck's *Grapes of Wrath* for a Thanksgiving broadcast.[35] As for Allen Ginsberg, he was incensed, and began a crusade against the FCC censors that would last till the end of his life.[36]

The FCC in due course rejected the requests of ACT and its colleagues for reconsideration of the April rulings, but it did make some modifications. In November 1987, it issued a new opinion reaffirming the "patent offensiveness" test and clarifying that in deciding whether speech was indecent, it would consider "merit" not as a defense but only as "one of many variables." "Contemporary community standards" would be national, not local—based on the "views of the average person" patronizing "the broadcast medium." Finally, realizing that its elimination of the 10 p.m. safe harbor was constitutionally dubious, the agency indicated that its "current thinking" was to recognize a new midnight–to–6 a.m. period "when it is reasonable to expect that it is late enough to ensure that the risk of children in the audience is minimized and to rely on parents to exercise increased supervision over whatever children remain."[37]

A long battle now began, known in legal annals as the *ACT* cases. Challenges to the April 1987 rulings went directly to the DC Circuit. Timothy Dyk, the Washington lawyer leading the legal team in this and three subsequent ACT suits, told the press that the FCC's generic indecency test was "incomprehensible," while Pacifica's director, David Salniker, was less lawyerly: "It is our belief that they never were interested in protecting children," he said. "All they wanted . . . was to appease the right wing."[38]

At oral argument in June 1988 in the case that became known as *ACT I*, Judge Ruth Bader Ginsburg betrayed impatience with the FCC. Why was the agency setting itself up as a "superparent," she wanted to know, without even seeking public input on the desirability of its pre-midnight indecency ban? It seemed that the commission was "acting in a rather high-handed manner. It doesn't want to hear from the group it is supposedly defending—parents. . . . I don't think it has an expertise in child development."[39]

Judge Ginsburg's questions surfaced in the decision she wrote for the DC Circuit two months later. She upheld the generic indecency standard, as she felt she must in light of *Pacifica*. ("If we have misunderstood Higher Authority," she quipped, she would "welcome correction.") But on the safe harbor issue, she took the FCC sharply to task. It had sloppily extrapolated from gross listener ratings in Los Angeles and Santa Barbara in order to conclude that significant numbers of young people had heard the post–10 p.m. broadcasts of *Jerker* and "Makin' Bacon." Even more troubling was the FCC's reliance on statistics for radio listening among 12-to-17-year-olds. At the time of *Pacifica*, the Commission had focused on children under 12. If it was now "widening its sights," Ginsburg wrote, "that apparent change in policy warrants explanation." Indecency is, after all, constitutionally protected, and the FCC's only asserted purpose in restricting it was to aid parents "in protecting unsupervised children," not "to act *in loco parentis* to deny children's access *contrary to* parents' wishes." Accordingly, the agency "must endeavor to determine" through coherent fact-finding and rule-making procedures "what channeling rule will most effectively promote parental—as distinguished from government—control."[40]

From the harm-to-minors viewpoint, Judge Ginsburg's distinction between government imposition of its own moral standards and government action "to *assist parents*" comprised the most interesting part of the *ACT I* decision. "Assistance," obviously, was not something that all parents necessarily welcomed; nor were parental views uniform regarding what language was inappropriate for youngsters. As Ginsburg phrased it, the issue was one of "language and descriptions" that were simply "offensive" to some parents—not objectively or uniformly understood as harmful.[41]

The FCC did not have a chance to follow Judge Ginsburg's instructions. Three days before *ACT I* was decided, Senator Jesse Helms had introduced legislation replacing the agency's post-midnight safe harbor with a twenty-four-hour-a-day indecency ban. Fulminating about "garbage" on the airwaves and alluding specifically to "Makin' Bacon," Howard Stern, and *Jerker* (which he termed "a sick, sick discussion between two homosexuals on how they perform their perversion"), Helms drew for his colleagues an image of corrupted youth in Comstockian terms:

> [W]hat happens when a child unintentionally tunes in and hears or sees material describing, by innuendo, how to have sex? Or when an 8-year-old girl turns on her radio to hear the deejay describe sex acts by the use of metaphors? . . . How much damage will be done? I hope that we will not have to find out.[42]

Helms appended to his senatorial presentation a legal memorandum from Citizens for Decency Through Law asserting that a total ban on broadcast indecency would not violate the First Amendment, and a more circumspect letter from Bruce Fein of the Heritage Foundation urging that even if the First Amendment did not permit a wholesale ban, Congress should pass the law and leave it to the courts to decide its constitutionality.[43] Congress obliged by passing the Helms law several months later.[44]

The FCC now decided it would be prudent to assemble some empirical data supporting Helms's total ban on indecency. It accordingly issued a Notice of Inquiry (NOI) requesting public input. John Crigler and William Byrnes, on behalf of Pacifica, PEN, Allen Ginsberg, and community radio stations, were among those who submitted briefs in response. The proceedings were "not about children, but politics," they wrote. "The primary purpose of the NOI is not to protect children from inappropriate materials, but to protect the FCC from congressional criticism."[45] Certainly, it was true that the results were a foregone conclusion: the FCC was hardly in a position to issue fact-findings that did not support Helms's twenty-four-hour-a-day indecency ban.[46] The DC Circuit in due course invalidated the law when the case returned to court as *ACT II*.

This time, the decision was written by Judge Abner Mikva (with circuit judge Clarence Thomas on the panel), and it followed the analysis of *ACT I*: indecency is constitutionally protected and cannot be banned from broadcasting altogether; some safe harbor is necessary lest adults be reduced to the expressive level deemed appropriate for children.[47] The Supreme Court denied review and Congress promptly responded with a 6 a.m.–to–midnight ban.[48] The challenge to this law became known—of course—as *ACT III*.

Outside the still-contested safe harbor, meanwhile, the FCC was energetically enforcing its generic indecency rule. In 1988, even before *ACT I* had been resolved, the agency concluded that the R-rated film *Private Lessons*, broadcast on Kansas City television, was indecent because the "story line of the seduction of a 15-year-old boy by an older woman, together with the inclusion of explicit nudity, would have commanded the attention of children."[49] Two years later, the Commission subjected KQED-TV in San Francisco to an investigation lasting more than a year into the highly praised BBC series *The Singing Detective*. "Dismissing the complaint should have been a simple matter," wrote Robert Corn-Revere, an FCC attorney at the time of the investigation.

> To the extent the FCC seriously considered merit as an important factor in making indecency determinations, *The Singing Detective* did not present a close case. . . . But the FCC did not consider the program as a whole. Indeed, the Commission did not even know what the show was about. Its review was riveted on images of nudity and a short scene in which a child witnesses a non-graphic sexual encounter.

The agency "was paralyzed," Corn-Revere recalled. "The matter languished for months and finally was forgotten. No order was ever issued." To him, it was "the most egregious" of the FCC's censorship episodes after the 1987 policy change.[50]

Chicago's *Steve and Garry* talk show was another target. The FCC fined it for airing discussions of a widely publicized photo spread in *Penthouse* magazine featuring the former Miss America Vanessa Williams. Other offenses included a call-in listener's rendition of the nonexplicit if tasteless satiric song "Kiddie Porn" and a mildly homophobic joke about an exchange at a gay bar ("May I push your stool in for you?"). The Commission was unimpressed by the argument of *Steve and Garry*'s lawyers that "spontaneous, free-wheeling discussions of controversial issues in a creative, informal, and humorous manner are the essence of good AM broadcasting."[51]

The FCC likewise punished a Miami station for the songs "Candy Wrapper" (a long double entendre using candy brand names for sexual parts or acts), "Walk with an Erection," and "Penis Envy"—this last a feminist satire by the Seattle rock group Uncle Bonsai ("I'd take it to parties / I'd stretch it and stroke it and shove it at smarties / I'd take it to pet shows and teach it to stay / I'd stuff it in turkeys on Thanksgiving day"). The agency fined a Michigan station $2,000 for a silly but tame exchange about possible titles for a story about a man whose "left testicle was sucked into a hot tub drain" (among the suggestions: "Man's honeymoon goes down the tubes," "Man ties knot, loses nut," and so forth). It punished a St. Louis station for a conversation about the alleged rape of Jessica Hahn by the entrepreneur/evangelist Jim Bakker, and in the course of the decision reiterated its position that the merit or news value of a work is not a defense to an indecency charge but "simply one of many variables" to be considered.[52]

Finally, the FCC continued to pursue an unrepentant Howard Stern for his unending jokes about penis size, bathroom functions, and myriad related matters, including TV entertainer Pee-wee Herman's 1991 arrest for masturbating in a movie theater.[53] Among the more instructive of the Commission's citations against Stern was the following exchange with his partner Robin Quivers:

> RQ: You'd better be a good boy.
> HS: No, I can't be good because it's the weekend.
> RQ: You're going to lose all of us our jobs.
> HS: You think I'd say penis?
> RQ: Oh no.
> HS: I don't care what the FCC says. Where is the FCC?
> RQ: Somebody stop him.
> HS: Hey, FCC, penis.
> RQ: Put your hand over his mouth.
> HS: I don't care, it's the weekend, baby.
> RQ: It's a stampede in there, you can't say that [stampede sound effect].
> HS: Yeah, I don't care. I do draw the line at vagina. Whoa, whoa, I can't believe I just said that word.
> RQ: That's it. Here they come.
> HS: Oh, ooh, here comes the thought police. I don't believe it, baby. Oh my goodness. Oh, look at those horses. They're going to trample over you, Robin.[54]

By February 1994, the FCC had levied well over $1 million in cumulative fines against Infinity Broadcasting for such irreverence on Stern's show, and Commissioner Quello was calling ever more vociferously for harsher sanctions, including denial of Infinity's pending applications to acquire new stations.[55]

There was no court review of any of these indecency rulings. For a combination of political and economic reasons—primarily the desire not to antagonize the agency and endanger broadcast licenses, and the delays running to several years before indecency proceedings were completed—broadcasters always ended up settling. Evergreen Media, proprietors of the *Steve and Garry* show, was the first actually to refuse to pay a forfeiture and assert in court its constitutional right to joke about Vanessa Williams and *Penthouse*, but it settled the case—thereby dropping its constitutional challenge to the indecency regime—before the judge could rule. In exchange for an empty promise by the FCC to clarify its definition of "patently offensive" (years later, the agency still had not done so), Evergreen paid $10,000. Infinity for its part complained of the massive fines levied against it and signaled an intent to sue, but with additional licenses and profits in the balance, it too began to censor Stern, and eventually opted for a settlement that included a $1.7 million "donation" to the U.S. Treasury in exchange for expungement of the indecency findings.[56]

Infinity nonetheless won a victory of sorts, for Howard Stern continued to be outrageous, popular, and somehow less of an issue as the 1990s progressed. Even Commissioner Quello admitted: "I'm almost ashamed to say it, but I find him tremendously funny. He's a very entertaining smart-ass."[57] During the 1998 media frenzy over Monica Lewinsky, the online magazine *Slate* pertly announced that shock jock Stern, long the bane of the FCC, had become obsolete. "Time has passed him by," *Slate* eulogized; what Independent Counsel Kenneth Starr can say in his impeachment report to Congress, "Stern can't. On a recent episode of his show, the censors bleeped over Stern saying the word 'anal,' as in 'Do you have (bleep) sex?' . . . In the Starr report, one footnote matter-of-factly refers to 'oral-anal contact' between the president and Monica Lewinsky."[58]

Sealed Wrappers, Blinder Racks, and Dial-a-Porn

The FCC's indecency standard was subjective and sweeping, but as a matter of law it was peculiar to broadcasting—or at least that was the presumption behind the *Pacifica* decision: radio and TV were uniquely "invasive" and uniquely accessible to children. Other government attempts to shield the eyes and ears of youth still had to use the more speech-friendly standard of *Ginsberg v. New York*—the harm-to-minors or variable-obscenity test. When city or state laws went beyond variable obscenity, courts would usually slap their hands, and sometimes even make reference to the First Amendment rights of youth.

So, for example, a California court in 1976 invalidated a Los Angeles ordinance regulating news racks because it departed from *Ginsberg* and prohibited sales of any material "displaying nudity"—including, as the judges pointed out, "a line drawing of the Venus de Milo."[59] A New York court struck down Buffalo's "Anti-Obscenity and Display to Minors" ordinance because its ban on nude or partially nude figures if "posed or presented in a manner to provoke or arouse lust or passion" was unconstitutionally vague.[60] On the other hand, a harm-to-minors law that conformed to *Ginsberg* was upheld by the Florida Supreme Court when applied to punish the admission of a 15-year-old to two X-rated films—over the dissent of one judge who protested the "political opportunism and demagoguery" that led to the "puritanical spasms" of censorship law.[61]

In these cases, courts modified the variable-obscenity test created by the Supreme Court's 1968 decision in *Ginsberg* by conforming it to the newer, three-part definition of obscenity five years later in *Miller v. California*. Thus, states or localities could ban youthful access to literature only if—adjusting the words of *Miller*—it lacked serious value for minors, appealed to the "prurient" interest of minors, and was patently offensive for minors according to "contemporary community standards." Laws barring sale or "display" to youngsters were generally upheld if they tracked the language of this "*Miller* Lite" test. And so, requirements of segregated bookstore sections, blinder racks, or sealed wrappers for literature deemed harmful to minors came into vogue.

Of course, any law restricting book and magazine displays inevitably affects adults. Adults-only back rooms, shrink-wrapping, and blinder racks all make people nervous, and thus psychologically as well as physically inhibit browsing. In the 1980s, booksellers began to challenge display laws on just these grounds. Although their suits were not wholly successful, they sometimes did result in narrowing the reach of the laws. In Virginia, for example, the courts rejected bookstores' arguments that the state's law prevented them from displaying *The New Our Bodies, Ourselves*, Judy Blume's *Forever*, Joyce's *Ulysses*, and *The Penguin Book of Love Poetry*. The judges accepted the Virginia Attorney General's contention that if a work had serious value for "a legitimate minority" of "older, normal (not deviant) adolescents," then it did not meet the definition of variable obscenity.[62] The result was to narrow the variable-obscenity or harm-to-minors definition so that it differed by only a hair from the *Miller v. California* adult obscenity test.[63]

This narrowing of variable obscenity nearly to the vanishing point hardly sat well with those desiring more, not fewer, restraints on curious or disobedient youngsters' access to what was often briskly categorized as "smut." For one thing, if the variable-obscenity test did not cover material having serious value for a "legitimate minority" of 17-year-olds, then what was left as a censorship standard for young children? Replacing variable obscenity with the more commodious indecency test, as pioneered by the FCC and approved by the Supreme Court in *Pacifica*, became a favorite cause of Senator Helms, among others, and in the highly fraught family-values politics of the 1980s, the arrival of cable television and commercial phone services only intensified efforts to expand indecency law beyond the limited realm of broadcasting.

In the sphere of cable TV, Utah was the dogged pioneer. Its anti-indecency laws were repeatedly invalidated, but it kept trying. In 1981 (while the FCC was still in low-enforcement mode), Utah passed the first of two laws prohibiting any distribution "by wire or cable" of "any pornographic or indecent material."[64] Home Box Office successfully challenged the law, persuading a federal court that the First Amendment does not permit bans on constitutionally protected "indecent" speech outside the context of broadcasting. Notably, the court (citing *Erznoznik*, the Supreme Court's 1975 drive-in movie case) observed that "minors are entitled to a significant measure of First Amendment protection," and "only in relatively narrow and well-defined circumstances may government bar public dissemination of protected materials to them." If applied to motion pictures on cable, the court said, Utah's law "would encompass a number of Academy Award-winning films," including *The Godfather*, *Annie Hall*, and *Coal Miner's Daughter*.[65]

Less than a year after the HBO case, Roy City, Utah, was in court defending a local ordinance that required cable operators to ban "pornographic or indecent material." Again, the federal court invalidated the law, suggesting that it might embrace Walt Whitman's *Leaves of Grass*, and rejecting Roy City's asserted "power to improve morals" and "concern for children who may hear and see things they should not."[66]

Undeterred, Utah enacted another cable indecency law four months after the *Roy City* decision. Courts invalidated this one on grounds of both free speech and federal preemption,[67] for by this time Congress had weighed in with a massive Cable Communications Policy Act, superseding state legislation in the area. This 1984 federal law acknowledged the constitutional problem with flat indecency bans and therefore opted for a requirement that cable operators supply customers with lockboxes enabling them to screen out raunchy programming if they chose.

Congress since the early '80s had also been trying to regulate commercial phone services (or "dial-a-porn"), ostensibly to keep their masturbatory messages from the ears of youth. After three rounds of litigation over laws requiring various forms of blocking, scrambling, and credit card checking, Congress in 1988 voted to ban "obscene or indecent" phone services completely. "Indecent" was not defined, but the legislative history made clear that the lawmakers had the *Pacifica* test of "patent offensiveness" in mind.

The inevitable lawsuit followed. A California federal judge enjoined the "indecency" part of the ban, and in April 1989 the case of *Sable Communications v. FCC* was argued before the Supreme Court. The stakes were high—the implications far broader than the future of phone sex. For in expanding *Pacifica* from broadcasting to telephone and eliminating even the pretense of time-channeling or safe harbors, the lobbyists, politicians, and think tanks pushing indecency laws were not only replacing *Ginsberg*'s variable-obscenity or harm-to-minors standard, which protected speech having serious value, with the FCC's wide-ranging, virtually limitless concept of "patent offensiveness," but they were cutting off adult access to sexual speech and vulgar words as well.

The problem, of course, was that in the electronic media, shielding youthful eyes, ears, and minds naturally meant restricting adults' listening and viewing options also. In essence, the old "deprave and corrupt" rationale of *Regina v. Hicklin*, resurrected in *Pacifica* for broadcasting, was now hovering in the wings for telephone, cable, and even print. As Tim Dyk wrote in an amicus brief for ACT, the ACLU, and others in the *Sable* case, the FCC had used its indecency standard to investigate a remarkably broad range of interesting, useful, constitutionally protected speech: "social satire, political advertising, informational programs, classic works of literature, modern drama addressing social issues, and motion pictures."[68] Harvard law professor Laurence Tribe's brief for Sable likewise reminded the Court that even in the context of phone services, the indecency ban threatened not just lusty talk but "dial-a-joke services that replay suggestive or scatological comedy routines" and " 'rap' music messages, in which expletives and vulgar street language are de rigueur."[69]

The Supreme Court's 1989 decision in *Sable*, per Justice Byron White, was a victory, or so it seemed, for those on the free-speech side of the indecency wars. The Court reiterated that "[s]exual expression which is indecent but not obscene is protected by the First Amendment," and distinguished *Pacifica* as "an emphatically narrow holding" that involved neither a total ban on indecency nor the regulation of anything other than broadcasting. It is true, Justice White said, that government can regulate constitutionally protected speech, but only when it "chooses the least restrictive means to promote a compelling interest"—that is, when there is no alternative method, less oppressive to First Amendment rights, available to accomplish the state's "compelling" goal.[70] Because the government had not demonstrated that methods short of a total ban would fail to block minors' access to phone sex, the dial-a-porn law was unconstitutional.

It was here, though, that *Sable* signaled a seismic shift in the Court's thinking about harm to minors. Government obviously has a compelling interest, said White, in "protecting the physical and psychological well-being of minors," and this interest extends to shielding them "from the influence of literature that is not obscene by adult standards."[71] What fell in this "not obscene by adult standards" category? White noted only that the dial-a-porn ban was "not a narrowly tailored effort to serve the compelling interest of preventing minors from being exposed to indecent telephone messages."[72]

Thus casually slipped into the ostensible First Amendment victory in *Sable* was a dramatic new concept: government has a compelling interest in protecting minors from indecent speech, and it evidently need not produce any evidence to prove the point. *Pacifica,* with its narrow "invading the home" focus and "nuisance" rationale, had not enunciated such a sweeping proposition. Indeed, Justice Brennan had crafted *Ginsberg* twenty-one years before on the explicit—if intellectually slippery—premise that variable obscenity was *not* protected by the First Amendment, and therefore no showing of a compelling state interest, or indeed, any evidence of harm, was needed to suppress it.[73] Indecency, by contrast, *was* constitutionally protected—it was not necessarily prurient and might have significant literary, artistic, or other value. Sliding noiselessly from "variable obscenity" to "indecency," the Supreme Court in *Sable* now seemed to be saying that government need not submit any proof of need for laws censoring constitutionally protected art, literature, entertainment, or ideas.

Justice White cited only two cases as precedents to support this sweeping expansion of government censorship power: *Ginsberg* itself and *New York v. Ferber*, a 1982 decision holding that child pornography is not protected by the First Amendment.[74] But child pornography laws are premised on the need to protect minors from actual sexual exploitation, not from disfavored ideas. And *Ginsberg,* of course, hewed to a variable obscenity standard, not the broader indecency test in which the literary or educational value of everything from political satire to raw drama, feminist music, and bawdy humor was just one factor that the censor might choose to consider.

Sable did make one crucial concession to the free-expression values that inevitably suffer when harm to those deemed most vulnerable becomes the censorship standard. However "compelling" the justices thought the need to protect youth from the "influence of literature" might be, it was apparently not so great that the shield must be impenetrable. That is, as Justice White said, less restrictive approaches to dial-a-porn, such as credit cards and scrambling, might be "extremely effective," with "only a few of the most enterprising and disobedient young people" managing to penetrate the barriers.[75] Obviously, the *most* effective means of censoring youth in any given situation will be a total ban; as the FCC's struggle with safe harbors showed, anything less creates a risk that *some* "enterprising and disobedient young people" will access indecency. But the First Amendment, per *Butler v. Michigan*, does not allow the sacrifice of adult speech rights in the interest of total efficiency.

Congress responded to *Sable* with new, narrowed restrictions on dial-a-porn, banning "indecent" commercial phone communications to "any person under 18 years of age." The FCC's implementing regulations prescribed credit cards, scrambling, or access codes as permissible means of blocking minors' access. Two federal appeals courts, rejecting constitutional challenges to this new dial-a-porn law, now relied on Justice White's language in *Sable* about the compelling interest in shielding minors from indecency. They referred only briefly, and unquestioningly, to the presumed harm to minors who might hear libidinous telephone talk.[76]

The analytically careless judicial attitude toward harm to minors reflected in *Sable* and other dial-a-porn cases was a far cry from Ruth Bader Ginsburg's more probing analysis of the issue back in 1988 in the *ACT I* case. There, Ginsburg had explained harm to minors as a question of offense, civility, and parental prerogative rather than psychological damage. The new context—telephonic sex fantasies rather than all of broadcasting—probably explained some of the difference in approach; but additional years of Helmsian rhetoric in Congress, and an increasingly conservative judiciary, also accounted by the late 1980s for the courts' uncritical acceptance of the idea that "indecency" causes harm.

A Few Judges Think About Indecency and Harm

In 1992, Congress went after cable television, or at least after those parts of the industry least able to fend off mandatory censorship schemes. Although most of the erotica on cable was found on premium channels such as Spice and Playboy, or pay-per-view offerings from cable operators themselves, Congress in the 1992 Cable Consumer Protection and Competition Act targeted indecency only on so-called public and leased access channels. This was programming that the cable operators—generally media giants like Viacom or Time Warner—did not want to carry, but that either Congress in its original 1984 cable law or the municipalities that granted cable franchises required the big companies to accommodate in order to prevent their total monopolization of local TV content.

Public access (actually, "public, educational, or governmental" access, or "PEG") was generally a condition of local franchises and included programs produced by community groups, schools and colleges, government agencies, and assorted enterprising individuals who, whether by choice or circumstance, had not penetrated the slicker world of commercial television. Although sometimes mildly subversive or even addressed to sexual subjects, PEG programming was rarely pornographic. Leased access, by contrast, was commercial programming that the 1984 federal law required cable operators to permit by setting aside a few channels for independent producers to rent at "reasonable" rates. In practice, rates were rarely reasonable enough for many independent producers other than purveyors of erotica, supported by ads for phone sex and escort services, to afford. Leased access cable, consequently, became associated with sex—most prominently, with a tasteless New York City offering called *Midnight Blue*, which Jesse Helms attacked in the Senate as proof of the need for leased access indecency restrictions.[77]

The 1992 cable law rejected parentally controlled lockboxes as sufficient protection for youth and, oddly, substituted the big cable companies as the medium's moral guardians. The law required the companies either to block leased access programming that they deemed indecent until a subscriber, in writing, requested unblocking or to ban completely any leased access show that they "reasonably" believed "describes or depicts sexual or excretory activities or organs in a patently offensive manner as measured by contemporary community standards." Similarly, for public or PEG access, the law delegated to cable operators the power to censor shows that contained "obscene material, sexually explicit conduct, or material soliciting or promoting unlawful conduct."[78]

Like much legislation governing television, the 1992 Cable Act's leased and PEG access provisions required the FCC to create a regulatory scheme. This leisurely process was accompanied by voluminous filings on the part of industry and public interest groups. The agency in due course disgorged its regulations, in two separate orders, the first concerning leased access and the second, PEG access. The Alliance for Community Media, a coalition of public access programmers, led the list of plaintiffs in the lawsuit that followed, and a three-judge panel of the DC Circuit invalidated the law on First Amendment grounds.[79] But the government sought rehearing before the full bench of eleven judges, and in a bizarre 1995 decision, seven of them ruled that the sections of the law that delegated judgments about indecency to cable operators presented no constitutional issue because the actual censorship decisions would be made by private companies, and the First Amendment only limits the actions of government. This ruling that no "state action" was involved in the 1992 law was almost surreal, because the entire scheme was after all mandated by the legislature. As for the section requiring companies to block any indecent shows that they did not "voluntarily" ban, the DC Circuit recognized that this, at least, *was* government action, but thought it acceptable because it was the "least restrictive means" available to serve the "compelling interest in protecting the physical and psychological well-being of minors."[80]

Judge Patricia Wald filed a dissent, objecting to the sophistries of the "no state action" ruling and noting that under the "broad definition of 'indecency' used in this regulation, affected speech could include programs on the AIDS epidemic, abortion, childbirth, or practically any aspect of human sexuality." She offered by example the shows aired on leased access by the Denver Area Educational Telecommunications Consortium, which provided "information and opinion on a broad range of subjects in a self-described 'unvarnished' cinema-verité style." These included "segments on how to do a self-help gynecological exam, a documentary on the controversial Robert Mapplethorpe art exhibit, and a traditional fertility festival in Japan featuring a procession of marchers carrying images of human genitalia."[81] Eventually, the Supreme Court reversed the DC Circuit's tortured ruling on the state-action issue, but in the process it would further muddy the doctrinal waters and for the first time extend *Pacifica* from broadcasting to cable.

The question whether minors of any particular age are really injured by "indecency" did finally receive serious attention as the inevitable *ACT III* litigation began—the third round in the broadcast industry's fight with the FCC over its shifting safe-harbor rules. *ACT III* challenged Congress's relegation of indecency to a midnight–to–6 a.m. safe harbor (with a post–10 p.m. exception for public broadcasters who signed off before midnight). The plaintiffs, including this time the Pacifica Foundation, PEN, and Allen

Ginsberg in addition to the previous congeries of industry and public interest groups, claimed that the new law was vague, discriminatory in its preferential treatment of public broadcasters, and insufficiently justified by data regarding minors' viewing or listening patterns or, indeed, by any evidence of harm to youth. On this last point, the ACT plaintiffs relied on an analysis that ACT had submitted to the Commission, written by the social science researchers Edward Donnerstein, Barbara Wilson, and Daniel Linz. In this document, the three professors opined that there is "serious reason to doubt" that exposure of children under 12 to indecent material "has an effect, in view of the general sexual illiteracy of this age group" and their "lack of ability to understand—and likely lack of interest in" sexual topics. As for adolescents, the professors said, they "may understand 'indecent' material," but

> they are likely to have developed moral standards which, like adults, enable them to deal with radio and television more critically. Moreover, adolescents are subject to other influences that may mediate any effects that might flow from exposure to such material. In general, studies of adult behavior fail to find any antisocial or harmful effects for materials such as those found by the FCC to be indecent.[82]

ACT III arrived at the same DC Circuit as the cable indecency case, and met the same fate. A three-judge panel struck down the post-midnight safe harbor on the ground that it did not adequately respect the free-expression rights of adults; the full bench vacated that decision and upheld the law.[83] The Justice Department was now asserting a "compelling" government interest not only in assisting parents but in shielding youngsters from indecency whether their parents liked it or not. The full bench of the DC Circuit readily accepted this philosophy of surrogate parenting and rejected ACT's argument that the FCC had failed to prove any harm to minors from indecency. "[C]linically measurable injury" and "scientific demonstration of psychological harm," it said, are unnecessary when it comes to shielding youngsters from "sexually explicit, indecent, or lewd speech."[84]

Judge Harry Edwards, one of four dissenters in *ACT III*, found this new surrogate-parent argument to be both appalling and intellectually incoherent. "I do not comprehend how the two interests can stand *together*," he said. Then, quoting from his earlier dissent in the cable case, he continued:

> "Congress may properly pass a law to facilitate *parental supervision of their children, i.e.*, a law that simply segregates and blocks indecent

> programming. . . . However, a law that effectively *bans* all indecent programming . . . does not facilitate parental supervision. . . . [M]y right as a parent has been preempted, not facilitated, if I am told that certain programming will be banned."

Presumably, Congress could "take away my right to decide what my children watch" if it had evidence that they were "in fact at risk of harm from exposure to indecent programming"; but, Edwards said, no such risk had been shown. Although the *ACT III* majority "strains mightily to rest its finding of harm on intuitive notions of morality and decency (notions with which I have great sympathy), the simple truth is that '[t]here is not one iota of evidence in the record . . . to support the claim that exposure to indecency is harmful—indeed, the nature of the alleged "harm" is never explained.' "[85]

Patricia Wald also made a point of shredding her brethen's unsupported assumptions about harm to minors. Her dissent flatly said that Congress when it passed this latest FCC law had no real evidence "regarding the magnitude of psychological or moral harm, if any, to children and teenagers who see and hear indecency."[86] And although her views did not prevail, some other judges were beginning to echo them. In Massachusetts, for example, federal judge Rya Zobel chastised the local transportation authority for censoring clever but mildly risqué safer-sex announcements that had been slated for posting in subway trains. Citing Wald's original panel decision in *ACT III*, Zobel opined that minors do have a legitimate interest in receiving sexual information—an interest that, at some point, trumps the censorial urges of government officials.[87]

Four appellate judges had now expressed serious skepticism about the harm-to-minors rationale for indecency laws. (Judges Judith Rogers and David Tatel had joined Wald's *ACT III* dissent.) But in the political and judicial climate of 1995, the DC Circuit's generalized notions of morality carried the day. The majority did agree with the plaintiffs that the 10 p.m. safe harbor for public broadcasting was discriminatory, and ordered the FCC to establish a 10 p.m. rule for everybody.[88] The Supreme Court denied review, leaving the FCC and the broadcast industry, after nearly a decade of *ACT* litigation, with the same 10 p.m. safe harbor as in the years just after *Pacifica*.

The DC Circuit proved more scrupulous in scrutinizing harm-to-minors claims when the subject was not sex or dirty words. Around the same time as the *ACT III* litigation, the FCC had permitted an Atlanta TV station to time-channel political campaign advertisements featuring images of bloody fetuses because, even though not "indecent," they were thought potentially harmful for children. The Court of Appeals, reviewing this decision, referred sardonically to the highly subjective business of determining what is "too shocking for tender minds," and ruled that it would violate the equality provisions of FCC law to exile some ads to "broadcasting Siberia" late at night.[89]

There was one *ACT* case still to come. Infinity Broadcasting was reeling from the more than $1 million in indecency fines that the FCC had imposed on account of Howard Stern and from threats by now–Acting Chairman Quello of even more punishing sanctions. The agency had fined other broadcasters, too, particularly those favoring the talk show/call-in format. None of these indecency rulings had been reviewed by a court, but the Commission relied on them to make licensing decisions and decide on the severity of future penalties. In practice, then, the highly discretionary indecency regime functioned in a bureaucratic cocoon, impervious to the constitutional standards applied by courts.

ACT IV was an unsuccessful challenge to this scheme. What was unusual, however, about the DC Circuit decision by Judge Douglas Ginsburg (no relation to Ruth) was its acknowledgment of exactly the problem the plaintiffs described. "In an extreme case," Ginsburg conceded, "a broadcaster could wait as long as six or seven years" for judicial review of an indecency ruling, during which it "runs the risk of incurring an increased forfeiture for any subsequent indecency violation." Meanwhile, "individual Commissioners have taken an active public role in criticizing broadcasters for airing indecent material and have let it be known that sanctions for such activity are likely to increase." Yet Ginsburg dismissed the *ACT IV* case, citing a variety of procedural and jurisdictional defects.[90]

Harry Edwards wrote a concurrence that exuded a sense of exhaustion. The DC Circuit had, in one year, rejected three challenges to indecency laws; and in all of them, Edwards said, the court's First Amendment analysis seemed "to border on the whimsical." He joined the *ACT IV* majority, though, because "I believe that it is essentially correct in stating and applying extant law. This is not to say that the extant law makes any sense."[91]

School Censorship, Heinous Crimes, and Violent Videos

While decency reigned in Congress and at the FCC, public schools were also finding many dangers to youth in art and literature. A 1981 case signaled the new dispensation by upholding a school superintendent's decision to cancel a student production of the musical *Pippin* because a parent complained that the show mocked religion.[92] Other courts were also moving away from the Supreme Court's hymn to minors' First Amendment rights in *Tinker*, its 1969 black armband case. Five years after the contretemps over *Pippin*, the Supreme Court decided that school authorities were within their rights in punishing a budding politician named Matthew Fraser for delivering a dopey speech laden with sexual puns at a student government assembly.

Chief Justice Burger, writing for the Court, expressed a kind of paternalism that outdid anything to be found in *Pacifica*. "By glorifying male sexuality, and in its verbal content," Burger said, young Fraser's speech was "acutely insulting to teenage girl students." Indeed, it "could well be seriously damaging to its less mature audience, many of whom were only 14 years old and on the threshold of awareness of human sexuality."[93] Burger cited no empirical basis for his twin assumptions that 14-year-olds are seriously damaged by sexual jokes or that teenage girls are offended by (and would themselves never engage in) sexual innuendo. As Justice Stevens noted in dissent, Matthew Fraser "was probably in a better position to determine whether an audience composed of 600 of his contemporaries would be offended by the use of a four-letter word—or a sexual metaphor—than is a group of judges who are at least two generations and 3,000 miles away from the scene of the crime."[94]

Two years later, the Court again weighed in on the side of official pedagogy by approving a high school principal's censorship of two student newspaper articles, addressing divorce and teenage pregnancy. The paper was a curricular activity, the Court said in *Hazelwood School District v. Kuhlmeier*, and the principal's "legitimate pedagogical concerns" about the propriety of the articles were sufficient reason for their expurgation.[95] A year afterward, an appeals court reluctantly applied *Hazelwood* to school authorities' removal of Aristophanes' *Lysistrata* and Chaucer's "Miller's Tale" from an advanced literature course. The judges did "seriously question" how "young persons just below the age of majority can be harmed by these masterpieces of Western literature," but said that under *Hazelwood* censorship of the bawdy classics did not violate the students' First Amendment rights.[96]

There were nevertheless occasional student free-speech victories in these years. The California courts in one 1989 case invalidated the removal of Gabriel García Márquez's *One Hundred Years of Solitude* and John Gardner's *Grendel* from literature classes; in another, they condemned an administrator's ban on four books by the hippie scribe Richard Brautigan. The judges acknowledged that some readers might find the "loose sexual mores and occasional profanity of the flower children depicted by Brautigan" to be "indecent," but opined that "no reasonable trier of fact could find the books, judged as a whole, are 'harmful matter' as to minors" within the meaning of California's variable-obscenity law. Moreover, "book-banning is the archetype symbol of repression of free speech," a problem "all the more serious" when it takes place "in front of the children."[97] In the 1990s, Kansas students and parents, after a long and expensive struggle, similarly won a case challenging the removal of the lesbian-themed novel *Annie on My Mind* from local school libraries. The school board members had frankly acknowledged that their motive was to suppress any positive information about homosexuality. Had the board members been less candid and claimed they were concerned with sexual content, vulgarity, or "mature" themes, the students' chances of success would have been considerably more tenuous.[98]

T-shirt aficionados in western Massachusetts also had a free-speech victory in the mid-1990s, though the judges in this convoluted case ultimately avoided addressing the students' First Amendment claim. Jeffrey Pyle and his brother Jonathan challenged their high school's ban on clothing with messages that were "vulgar" or "profane." Jeffrey had been forbidden to wear a "Coed Naked Band. Do It to the Rhythm" T-shirt that his mother had given him as a Christmas gift. In subsequent attempts to discern the parameters of the dress code, the brothers wore shirts declaring "Coed Naked Civil Liberties. Do It to the Amendments" and "Coed Naked Gerbils. Some People Will Censor Anything." A federal judge upheld the vulgarity ban in reliance on Matthew Fraser's case involving sexual innuendo at the school assembly.[99] On appeal, the Pyles argued that standards like "vulgarity" are not only vague but "laced with upper-class contempt for lower-class modes of expression," and especially pernicious when "intended to protect the so-called 'weaker sex,' " for they have "the effect (and often the purpose) of confining women to domestic roles and in linguistic ghettos that have historically deprived them of economic and intellectual opportunities." " 'Good taste,' " said the Pyles, "has little to do with taste, but much to do with enforcing stereotypic sex roles, including preventing females from being sexually forward, or from considering human sexuality humorous."[100] Eventually, the Massachusetts Supreme Judicial Court ruled that the T-shirt censorship violated a state law that barred school administrators from restricting student speech unless it was likely to cause actual disruption.[101]

State judges and state laws thus partially compensated for the rollback in youngsters' expressive rights wrought by the *Fraser* and *Hazelwood* cases. But these pockets of recognition for youthful intellect, protest, or humor were rare. By the 1990s, judges and school officials generally embraced the philosophy that students, even of high school age, must be shielded from the presumed shock or moral corruption of sexual subjects, or at least socialized to regard them as taboo. Thus (to take only a tiny sampling from a vast range of literature attacked and often removed from public schools in the 1990s): a Wisconsin court in 1995 upheld a school district policy prohibiting the showing of R-rated movies (the work at issue was *Schindler's List*); a New Hampshire school board removed Shakespeare's *Twelfth Night* because it "has the effect of encouraging or supporting homosexuality as a positive lifestyle alternative"; and a Texas town banned *Moby Dick* and *The Scarlet Letter* from an English advanced placement reading list because they "conflict with the values of the community."[102]

As these school censorship controversies suggested, protecting youthful psyches now had to do with more than simply fear of sex. Blaming fantasy violence for real or imagined social malaise enjoyed a new vogue in the 1980s and '90s, with arguments differing only in rhetorical flavor, not in substance, from Anthony Comstock's earlier exhortations against "blood and thunder" stories or Dr. Wertham's against superhero comics. And the violence issue only gained in intensity with the arrival of the VCR in the 1980s.

The U.S. response to horror videos—"video nasties," to use the English term—included harm-to-minors legislation in some states that added violence to sex in the statutory definition of variable obscenity. Thus, Missouri banned the sale or rental to minors of videos that the average adult would find "cater or appeal to morbid interest in violence for persons under the age of seventeen"; depict violence in a "patently offensive" way, according to "contemporary adult community standards with respect to what is suitable for persons under the age of seventeen"; and, taken as a whole, lack "serious literary, artistic, political, or scientific value for persons under the age of seventeen."[103] In a challenge by the Video Software Dealers Association, a federal appeals court found the law unduly vague in delineating which among the multitude of violent images and ideas that populate cinema would actually appeal to the "morbid interest" of those under 17. The law was in any event unconstitutional because "not narrowly tailored to promote a compelling state interest." Like Judges Edwards and Wald in *ACT III*, these judges were skeptical of the state's highly generalized claim of concern for the well-being of youth.[104] The Tennessee Supreme Court came to similar conclusions regarding a similar law the following year.[105]

Movies and TV were the main targets of those believing that images of violence caused the real thing, but media-blaming also extended to the old-fashioned medium of trading cards. In response to the production of some tasteless "serial killer" cards in the early 1990s, several states considered legislation banning the sale of the cards to minors, although only Nassau County, New York, actually passed such a law. It barred the dissemination to anyone under 17 of "any trading card which depicts a heinous crime, an element of a heinous crime, or a heinous criminal and which is harmful to minors." Like Missouri in the video case, Nassau County took the variable-obscenity legal formula and simply substituted violence for sex as the targeted subject.[106] Eclipse Enterprises, producer of many trading card sets in addition to "Serial Killers," including "Crime and Punishment," "Drug Wars," and "Friendly Dictators" (describing U.S. support of authoritarian regimes), brought a First Amendment challenge to the law. To demonstrate how far beyond serial killers the law could reach, Eclipse introduced hundreds of these cards into evidence (see illustrations).

Observing that the subject of crime is "an inescapable part of our cultural landscape" and has always enjoyed First Amendment protection, Eclipse argued for a quick ruling in its favor. But the judge wanted an evidentiary hearing to determine whether, as Nassau insisted, the ordinance was "narrowly tailored" to serve "the County's compelling interest in providing for the well-being of minors."[107] For probably the first time, then, a federal court would hear evidence from social scientists on the relation between violence in the media and children's behavior. The apparent assumption was that if evidence of a causal link were sufficiently strong, an exception to the First Amendment could be created.

The 1994 evidentiary hearing in *Eclipse*, however, was not the titanic battle of experts that might have been anticipated. Nassau's lawyers did not call as witnesses any of the scholars who had studied media violence. Instead, they presented a child psychiatrist, Sandra Kaplan, along with a priest, a rabbi, a victims' rights advocate, and a social worker. Dr. Kaplan testified that children would "be inclined to imitate the crimes depicted on the cards"; opined that a "Jolly Roger" card from Eclipse's "Pirate" series was "not very good for teenagers" because it described a grisly beheading; and after some equivocation decided that a card depicting Indonesia's General Suharto, from the "Friendly Dictators" series, could be harmful because "his face looks heroic" and the text contained a graphic description of Suharto's slaughter of suspected Communists.[108] Like the county's other witnesses, Kaplan admitted that she knew of "no studies connecting crime trading cards or any other reading material to violent behavior in children" and "no particular incidents of violent behavior in children that could be attributed to crime trading cards."[109] The trial court, and eventually the Court of Appeals, invalidated the law primarily on this basis. They pointed to the testimony of Eclipse's experts, psychologists Joyce Sprafkin and Jonathan Freedman, that, contrary to popular belief, research studies on TV violence have yielded, at best, inconsistent results, with evidence of actual effects on children's behavior being either weak or nonexistent. But the appellate judges also suggested that television would have presented a stronger case for censorship than trading cards, because TV is a "far more powerful medium."[110]

Like the case involving the Bad Frog Brewery's crude beer label (decided a month later in the same Second Circuit Court of Appeals), the *Eclipse* decision thus seemed not so much to discourage legislation censoring minors as to invite government to do a better job identifying its targets and to find better expert witnesses. Indeed, Judge Thomas Griesa wrote a concurrence in *Eclipse* that lauded Nassau's efforts "to ensure the welfare of juveniles" and faulted the ordinance only for its vagueness.[111] Griesa seemed oblivious not only to the evidence that had been assembled refuting any claim of psychological harm but also to the larger questions that jurists like Patricia Wald and Ruth Bader Ginsburg had been asking. As the California judge in the Richard Brautigan case had suggested, censorship ought particularly to be questioned when it happens "in front of the children."

Six

THE IDEOLOGICAL MINEFIELD: SEXUALITY EDUCATION

Modesty, Virtue, and Early Battles over Sex Ed

In 1999, a recent college graduate named Wendy Shalit published *A Return to Modesty*, a book lamenting her generation's sexual freedom. Shalit argued that too many youngsters "know far too much too soon" about sex, and "as a result they end up, in some fundamental way, *not* knowing."[1] Her variation on harm-to-minors ideology—the notion that sexual knowledge in itself is damaging—had received a more scholarly exposition in Rochelle Gurstein's *The Repeal of Reticence* several years before. These authors contended that it somehow destroyed the mystery of sex for young people to learn explicit facts about contraception, reproduction, or sexual response. Their views were one foundation for the continued opposition to comprehensive sexuality education in the United States at the end of the 20th century.

In its early manifestation as "social hygiene," sex ed in the United States preached celibacy outside marriage through a combination of moral injunctions and scare tactics. Courses "often culminated with a slide show of suffering from tertiary syphilis: skin covered in carbuncles, noses eaten away by ulcers."[2] Biological facts were conveyed without reference to the pleasures or varieties of sex; even detailed descriptions of anatomy were avoided.[3] Instruction confused morality with biology, as evidenced by continued arguments that male masturbation and premarital sex were dangerous because semen "should not be wastefully expended."[4] The antimasturbation tracts of cereal king John Harvey Kellogg and others were fully as lurid as Dr. Tissot's had been: "shriveled countenance," "ulcerous, toothless gums," and "suppurating blisters and running sores" were among the predicted results of the dreadful practice.[5]

Margaret Sanger articulated a less superstition-bound approach to anatomy, masturbation, and other aspects of sexuality in her columns in the newspaper *The Call* (later published as a short book, *What Every Girl Should Know*); but she had to contend with the efforts of Anthony Comstock and the Post Office to suppress them.[6] Freud's early essay "The Sexual Enlightenment of Children" was also a challenge to the Wendy Shalits of his day,[7] but it was not until birth control advocates like Dr. Mary Calderone turned their attention to the shredding of taboos that a more comprehensive approach to sexuality education took shape.

Calderone was "far more than a female doctor championing a cause," as one obituary noted in 1998. "Her theatrical training, coupled with her carriage, poise, and authoritative voice, helped her to get her message across that children are born sexual beings and remain so until they die and that people of all ages need and deserve a proper sexual education."[8] With Lester Kirkendall and others, she co-founded SIECUS (Sexuality Information and Education Council of the United States) in 1964 after the National Education Association and the American Medical Association jointly endorsed "family life" and sex education starting in kindergarten. By the mid-1960s, most public school boards had introduced sexuality curricula, although their content and comprehensiveness was, to say the least, uneven. Calderone, for example, "was an unstinting advocate for the acceptance of masturbation as a wholesome, normal and almost universal practice for people of all ages,"[9] but it was hardly a subject featured in most classes.

The campaign for sexuality education was "tempestuous," with SIECUS the "target of virulent attacks" from groups like MOMS (Mothers Organized for Moral Stability) and PAUSE (People Against Unconstitutional Sex Education).[10] Some of these opponents were inspired by the Reverend Billy James Hargis's Christian Crusade or by the John Birch Society, which called sex ed "smut," "destructive of religious belief," and a "filthy communist plot."[11] In response to the pressures, communities in thirteen states restricted their sexuality curricula in the late 1960s, while twenty legislatures considered bills to investigate or restrict them.[12] Although much of Europe by this point had accepted sex ed, in the United States, where curriculum decisions are more decentralized, no affirmative national policy developed. State and local programs varied enormously; local groups pressured many school boards to eliminate or water down instruction.

Opponents also tried to stop sex ed by going to court. In 1969, a group of

Maryland taxpayers sued school administrators in an unsuccessful attempt to stop a program that had been created in response to a perceived teen pregnancy problem. A few years later, judges in New Hampshire and California rejected parents' rights arguments against sexuality education, noting that children have a right to receive information and ideas beyond those approved at home—or, in the California court's words, parents do not have "a monopoly over the thoughts of their own children or anyone else's." In Wisconsin, a judge ordered a district attorney to stop threatening obscenity charges against officials of the Unitarian Church for offering a sex ed course, and cited *Roth v. United States* on the importance of sex in "art, literature, and scientific works."[13]

But not all judges were equally solicitous of youngsters' educational needs. In 1974, a Michigan court rejected a challenge by a physician and teachers to a state law that banned discussion of birth control in public schools.[14] Three years later, students at New York's Stuyvesant High School lost a legal challenge to an administrative edict forbidding them from distributing a questionnaire to classmates on sexual experiences and attitudes. The Stuyvesant case became a near-comic battle of experts, as the administrators filed affidavits from psychologists asserting that the mere reading of the questionnaire could "create anxiety and feelings of self-doubt" among fragile adolescents, some of whom might be pushed into "a panic state or even a psychosis." The students countered with expert affidavits averring that most teens were familiar with sexual subjects; that even anxious ones were unlikely to be traumatized; and that any student "sufficiently fragile to suffer serious anxiety or depression upon reading questions which (s)he may ignore with impunity or respond to anonymously, is a youngster too fragile to have survived the trip from home to school."[15]

The trial judge, Constance Baker Motley, upheld the ban on the questionnaire for ninth and tenth graders, but ordered the administrators to let it be distributed to older students. Even this compromise, however, was reversed by the Second Circuit Court of Appeals, which thought the officials had met their burden under *Tinker* (the Supreme Court's black armband case) of proving they had a "substantial basis" to believe that the questionnaire "would result in significant emotional harm to a number of students." One judge dissented, protesting that the majority's unquestioning trust in the school officials' vague assertions of harm would allow nearly any censorship, "under the guise of 'protecting' . . . students against emotional strain."[16] And other courts at the time did invalidate school censorship of youthful efforts at sex education, noting, for example, that "responsible presentation of information about birth control to high school students is not to be dreaded."[17]

In 1977, the Supreme Court also had to grapple with this politically fraught issue of minors' access to contraceptive information. A New York law outlawed not only the dissemination of contraceptives to anyone under 16 but any advertising or display of contraceptives, and prohibited anyone other than a licensed pharmacist from distributing them. In *Carey v. Population Services International*, a majority of the justices said all three parts of the law were unconstitutional, but could not agree on why.

The state's lawyers argued that allowing advertising and display of contraceptives "would legitimize sexual activity of young people."[18] The ban, in other words, was symbolic, as Justice Stevens explained in a concurrence: "[i]n essence, the statute is defended as a form of propaganda," of "communicating disapproval of sexual activity by minors." But symbolism has its limits, especially when its effect is to increase the risk of real harm—in this case, unplanned pregnancy and venereal disease.[19] Justice Brennan added that "with or without access to contraceptives, the incidence of sexual activity among minors is high, and the consequences of such activity are frequently devastating." Forcing girls either to go through an unwanted pregnancy or face "the physical and psychological dangers of an abortion" was an unduly punitive, and counterproductive, way to dissuade them from sex.[20]

But even Brennan, who recognized a right of privacy for minors to buy contraceptives, did not say this included a right to have consensual sex.[21] Other justices (Byron White and John Paul Stevens) described as "frivolous" the argument that "a minor has the constitutional right to put contraceptives to their intended use, notwithstanding the combined objection of both parents and the State." Justice (not yet Chief Justice) Rehnquist dissented from the entire ruling because he thought it unduly tied the hands of the state legislature in dealing with "the problem of promiscuous sex and intercourse among unmarried teenagers."[22]

Five years after *Carey*, the Court revisited the issue. A drug company challenged a section of the Comstock law banning the unsolicited mailing of contraceptive ads. Thurgood Marshall, writing for the majority, agreed with the Justice Department's argument in defense of the ban that the interest in helping parents "control the manner in which their children become informed about sensitive and important subjects" like birth control was "substantial." But the law did little to advance this goal, since parents can easily dispose of unwanted mail, and in any event "must already cope with the multitude of external stimuli that color their children's perception of sensitive subjects." Marshall rejected analogies to *Pacifica*, quipped that the "level of discourse reaching a mailbox simply cannot be limited to that which would be suitable for a sandbox," and noted that minors are "entitled to 'a significant measure of First Amendment protection.' " Indeed, he said, given that over one-third of teenage girls are sexually active, adolescents "have a pressing need for information about contraception."[23]

Teen Pregnancy and Sex Respect

Contraceptive education had become a major issue because of statistics indicating that, by the mid-1970s, almost half of the 15-to-19-year-old girls in the United States had had sexual intercourse, with fewer than a third of them consistently using birth control. By the end of the '70s, there were more than a million teen pregnancies annually, and more than 600,000 live births. U.S. adolescent pregnancy rates were fifteen times higher than in Japan, twice as high as in sexually emancipated Scandinavia, and significantly higher than in the Netherlands, Poland, Portugal, Italy, and Great Britain.[24]

Melvin Zelnik and John Kantner, two leading researchers, offered no simple explanation for the failure of so many U.S. teenagers to use birth control, but posited a variety of reasons, including widespread ignorance of basic reproductive facts; cultural myths regarding "the cherished spontaneity" of sex and romance; guilt and conflict—also culturally bred—over acknowledging sexual activity or planning for it; adolescent mental processing, which in some cases involves "planning horizons" that "barely stretch beyond the next weekend"; and sexuality education that comes too little or too late.[25] Some of these possibilities had empirical support, but the ones that turned on disparaging generalizations about adolescents' ability to plan or think rationally had one logical drawback: they did not explain why the great majority of youngsters in European countries with similar rates of teen sexual activity did manage to prevent pregnancy.

The Alan Guttmacher Institute cited the Zelnik and Kantner statistics in two publications that helped create a national perception of a teen pregnancy "epidemic."[26] In reality, the highest rate of U.S. teenage births had occurred in 1957, when girls had much less access to contraception.[27] But more teenage mothers were married in the 1950s and '60s, and their sexual behavior was less visible. The cultural upheavals of the '60s and '70s, the increasing visibility of teen sexuality, the low level of contraceptive use, and the relative dearth of sex education drove the new sense of crisis.[28]

None of this went unnoticed by an increasingly active and powerful religious right. As federal grants for contraceptive outreach and education multiplied, the right countered with alternative curricula that promoted chastity. Phyllis Schlafly of the Eagle Forum protested that "nearly all existing sex education curricula . . . taught teenagers (and sometimes children) how to enjoy fornication without having a baby and without feeling guilty." Questionnaires "are pornographic in their explicitness," she declared; New York City's program "forces explicit discussions of sexuality and genitalia on little children."[29]

Sex Respect, the most successful of the right's alternative curricula, was created in the mid-1980s under the auspices of the Schlafly-inspired Committee on the Status of Women. Designed for grades seven to nine, *Sex Respect* was followed by a counterpart high school curriculum, *Facing Reality*, and a number of other texts, parent/teacher guides, and audiovisual aids. The materials pushed abstinence until marriage based on exaggerated fears of emotional devastation, sexually transmitted diseases (STDs), and death from premarital sex, and eschewed any information about contraceptives, except to emphasize their failures.[30] They incorporated religious doctrines, sometimes overtly—as in *Sex Respect*'s advice to "[a]ttend worship services regularly"—and sometimes in a manner only thinly veiled—as in the remark that "nature seems to be making a statement about the wisdom of keeping sex within marriage through the current epidemic of STDs and teen pregnancy."[31] *Sex Respect* asserted that "there's no way to have premarital sex without hurting someone," that the human immunodeficiency virus (HIV) can pass through latex condoms and be contracted by kissing, and that a "male can experience complete sexual release with a woman he doesn't even like, whereas a woman usually can't do so unless she loves her partner."[32] *Facing Reality*'s parent/teacher guide characterized as "mythology" the idea that condoms can prevent pregnancy or STDs, and catalogued forty-five separate perils of premarital sex, including "inability to concentrate on school, syphilis, embarrassment, abortion, shotgun wedding, . . . heartbreak, infertility, loneliness, cervical cancer, poverty, loss of self-esteem, loss of reputation, being used, substance abuse, melancholy, loss of faith, possessiveness, diminished ability to communicate," and death.[33] In one video designed for use with *Sex Respect*, a student asks an instructor, "What if I want to have sex before I get married?" "Well, I guess you'll just have to be prepared to die," the instructor replies.[34]

During the Reagan years, champions of *Sex Respect* were able to advance their version of sexuality education with hundreds of thousands of government grant dollars for promotion, curriculum development, and pilot projects. As a contributor to *Conservative Digest* gratefully wrote, the 1981 Adolescent Family Life Act "was written expressly for the purpose of diverting money that would otherwise go to Planned Parenthood into groups with traditional values"; if not for "the seed money provided by the federal government, *Sex Respect* might still be just an idea sitting in a graduate student's thesis."[35] Critics meanwhile complained of *Sex Respect*'s bias in favor of the traditional two-parent family and "its disparaging comments about divorced and single-parent families as well as gays and lesbians." The lives of the mostly inner-city, low-income, and minority students who populated the targeted schools "did not mirror these middle class clichés."[36]

By the 1990s, according to one estimate, a quarter of the nation's schools were using an abstinence-only curriculum and one in eight was using *Sex Respect*, even though public health experts called it "dangerously inaccurate, biased and moralistic."[37] Some communities engaged in ferocious political battles as newly elected school board majorities substituted *Sex Respect* for more comprehensive, less ideologically loaded texts. In one case that went to litigation, a Louisiana court ruled that using *Sex Respect* and *Facing Reality* in public school violated state law proscriptions against the teaching of religious beliefs or medically inaccurate information.[38]

SIECUS and its allies countered in 1991 with *Guidelines for Comprehensive Sexuality Education*. A coalition of more than one hundred organizations, from the American Academy of Child and Adolescent Psychiatry to Catholics for a Free Choice, participated in developing *Guidelines*.[39] The major premise was that sexuality education should be a lifelong process beginning in childhood, which encompasses not just biology but "sociocultural, psychological, and spiritual dimensions of sexuality." It should promote "a positive view of sexuality," help students "acquire skills to make decisions now and in the future," and enable them to "develop the capacity for caring, supportive, non-coercive, and mutually pleasurable intimate and sexual relationships." *Guidelines* stressed abstinence as "the most effective method of preventing pregnancy and STD/HIV" but avoided fearmongering and encouraged students to think about their choices. The very use of the term "sexuality" rather than "sex" was an attempt to emphasize the social and human context.[40]

Guidelines divided sexuality education into six subject areas and four developmental levels starting at age 5. So, for example, elementary school classes would discuss reproduction, masturbation, and puberty (in advance of its arrival). Contraception, gender roles, varieties of sexual behavior, and discussion of homosexuality would be covered in level three. Level four would explain, among many other more detailed facts, that most women "need clitoral stimulation to reach orgasm" and (probably a relief to many adults) most couples "do not experience simultaneous orgasm during vaginal intercourse." Nonjudgmental information regarding different religions' sexual attitudes was scattered throughout. Finally, *Guidelines* encouraged media literacy—noting, for example, that soap operas and talk shows "may give inaccurate and unrealistic" portrayals of sexuality.[41]

Guidelines was indeed comprehensive, and rarely implemented in its entirety. Given the extreme decentralization of education in the United States and its peculiar susceptibility to local political pressures, it was not surprising that even before the passage in 1996 of a federal abstinence-unless-married law, only 5 to 10 percent of schoolchildren were receiving comprehensive sexuality education.[42] Most courses lasted just a few weeks; many were taught by ill-prepared, anxious teachers, or tucked into physical education programs. Even those that were simply "abstinence-based" rather than "abstinence-only"—that is, that urged celibacy without suppressing health information—gave only limited instruction on contraception and avoided the more controversial issues of "sexual pleasure, masturbation, homosexuality, and abortion."[43] By the late 1990s, moreover, eight states required or recommended teaching that "homosexuality is not an acceptable lifestyle and/or that homosexual conduct is a criminal offense under state law," while only one (Rhode Island) instructed schools to "teach respect for others regardless of sexual orientation."[44] Queried after completing one typical six-hour program in a midwestern city, students said they would have liked more information about pregnancy options, homosexuality, masturbation, sexual response, and sexual and reproductive health services. One student commented that a recent TV sitcom had offered better and more thoughtful coverage of unplanned pregnancy options than the "bogus" message in a film that was included in the course.[45] As SIECUS executive director Debra Haffner summed up, sexuality education in the United States continued to consist primarily of "disaster prevention and organ recitals."[46]

Given the fearful approach to contraception in U.S. sex ed classes in the 1980s and '90s, it was not surprising that the incidence of teen pregnancy remained far higher than in any other major industrialized nation, despite similar rates of adolescent sexual activity. By the late '80s, the U.S. teen pregnancy rate was about one in ten, and more than half of those pregnancies, or 51.3 per 1,000, resulted in live births. The corresponding teen birthrate for Japan was 4 per 1,000; for Denmark, 16; for Italy, 23; for France, 25; for Canada, 28.[47] U.S. youngsters scored lowest of thirteen nations in the

1980s on a test of basic sexual and reproductive knowledge.[48] Meanwhile, not only were *Sex Respect* and its counterparts discouraging birth control, but the U.S. mass media still generally refused to air contraceptive information. Sociologist Ira Reiss describes one sad episode in 1988 when Surgeon General C. Everett Koop attempted to persuade the networks to lift their ban:

> The U.S. Centers for Disease Control prepared the announcement but decided to avoid even using the word *condom*. They also failed to get the announcement shown during prime time. The final video portrayed a barefoot man sitting on a chair saying: "If I told you that I could save my life just by putting on my socks, you wouldn't take me seriously because life is never that simple." Then he starts to put a sock on his bare foot and says: "But watch . . . OK, you're right, that wouldn't really save my life. But there's something just as simple that could." Then you are to guess what that "something" is![49]

Adolescent pregnancy and birth rates in the United States did decrease by the late 1990s, but they remained by far the highest among industrialized nations. For girls 15–19, the U.S. pregnancy rate was 101 per 1,000 in 1995, down from a peak of 117 in 1990.[50] In a 1998 tally of childbirth rates for young women through age 19, Bangladesh and Côte d'Ivoire ranked the highest, with India, Kenya, Ghana, and Zimbabwe not far behind. Mexico, Bolivia, Colombia, Brazil, Indonesia, and Egypt followed. Then came the United States, with a teen childbirth rate higher than any European country, and many non-Western ones as well.[51]

Abstinence Unless Married

Despite the sobering statistics, minors' access to basic sex information in the United States continued to be an ideological minefield. In a typical year (1994), the textbook *Human Sexuality* was banned from use in Fulton County, Georgia, because it placed too little emphasis on abstinence and was "too graphic" (a drawing of the female anatomy was cited as "the most egregious example"). In Helena, Montana, some parents objected to sex ed films because they discussed homosexuality and masturbation, and one showed a boy getting an erection while looking at bikini-clad women at a swimming pool—an attempt, according to a local expert, to assure boys "that it's natural for them to become aroused at what may be inappropriate times." Holt, Rinehart & Winston announced that it would not sell a high school health textbook in Texas because doing so would require hundreds of revisions: the state's education officials had demanded abridgment of passages on homosexuality and deletion of illustrations of a self-examination for testicular cancer.[52]

In Massachusetts, on the other hand, the Hot, Sexy and Safer Productions Company, which had been hired by Chelmsford High School in 1993 to give a sex ed workshop, was cleared of sexual harassment and invasion of privacy charges brought by a group of parents and students who objected to the explicitness and humor of the presentation. The federal appeals court noted that the right to privacy does not include the power "to dictate the curriculum at a public school," and that Hot, Sexy and Safer's "graphic sexual discussions . . . could not reasonably be considered physically threatening or humiliating so as to create a hostile environment."[53]

These local skirmishes were overshadowed in 1996 by the federal abstinence-unless-married law. A late addition to that year's massive welfare legislation, the law provided $50 million a year for five years, to be matched by the states in a 4:3 ratio, for local sex ed programs that have as their "*exclusive* purpose teaching the social, psychological, and health gains to be realized by abstaining from sexual activity."[54] With matching funds and increased chastity education financing under another federal program, the Adolescent Family Life Demonstration Project, the package amounted to almost $88 million per year to be deflected from comprehensive sexuality education or family planning and devoted to abstinence-only programs.[55]

Congress specified eight attributes for a funded program. These included teaching that "abstinence from sexual activity is the only certain way to avoid out-of-wedlock pregnancy, sexually transmitted diseases, and other associated health problems"; that "a mutually faithful monogamous relationship in the context of marriage is the expected standard of human sexual activity"; and that "sexual activity outside of the context of marriage is likely to have harmful psychological and physical effects."[56] Under this regime, contraceptive and safer-sex techniques could not be discussed, except to emphasize their failures, and thus discourage their use. The law's ideological requirements denigrated gay men and lesbians, single parents, and unmarried couples, not to mention the vast majority of Americans who were not virgins when they married (and who were therefore presumed to have suffered "harmful psychological and physical effects").[57]

Educators and public health officials bridled at the strictures of the new program. "No sex until marriage is a religious concept," said one New Jersey family planning leader. "These kids need to talk about sexual issues and not be preached at."[58] A Maine official explained that the "limits on what you can say are so restrictive that we decided we could not use the money for classroom programs or anywhere else where there was face-to-face contact. Youths might raise issues you couldn't address under the law."[59] Wyoming and Connecticut said they would not accept the federal money (they later changed their minds), while Maryland decided to continue teaching about birth control in regular sex ed classes and use the federal funds for after-school activities.[60] Charleston County, South Carolina, voted against accepting the federal money; the school board chairman explained, "Let's not live in a fantasy land" or "play Russian Roulette with the lives of our students."[61]

SIECUS, Advocates for Youth, Planned Parenthood, and other groups tried to counter claims that fear-based abstinence curricula would reduce adolescent sexual activity. They cited studies by the World Health Organization, the National Campaign to Prevent Teen Pregnancy, and other researchers that showed no decrease, and often an increase, in the age of "sexual debut" after programs that included contraceptive and safer sex information.[62] They emphasized that comprehensive sexuality education does advocate abstinence—at least until maturity, if not marriage—but not to the exclusion of essential, often lifesaving information.

By late 1998, though, every state had applied for and received the abstinence-unless-married funds. (California and New Hampshire ultimately declined to use them.) Some used the money for media campaigns rather than school curricula; but six incorporated the federal mandate into their official sex ed programs. The Pennsylvania Senate proclaimed "Chastity Awareness Week" and urged "Chastity Day" presentations at public schools. Franklin County, North Carolina, cut three chapters out of its ninth-grade textbook because they dealt with contraception and STDs, and the school board had not held a hearing, required by state law, before state-mandated abstinence-till-marriage could be replaced with a comprehensive curriculum. Virginia also pursued an abstinence-unless-married agenda, but the city of Richmond withdrew from participation, its Director of Health declaring that the program was "ill-conceived" and "did not help children who were already sexually active or gays and lesbians."[63]

SIECUS's Debra Haffner put a positive spin on the abstinence-till-marriage law. It had at least made sex ed less controversial, she said, now that it had the imprimatur of federal funding: "We've won the battle . . .

we're fighting skirmishes."[64] Given the pedagogical constraints of the law, it took real imagination to be so optimistic. At the end of 1999, three years into the abstinence-unless-married regime, fewer than half of U.S. public schools were offering information on where to get birth control, and more than one in three districts used a curriculum that permitted discussion of contraception only in its failures. "I think parents should be concerned," said a vice president of the Guttmacher Institute. "What is the impact of hundreds of thousands of kids across the country being taught that contraception doesn't work well?" In 2000, the White House Office of National AIDS Policy agreed, writing in a report that "it is a matter of grave concern that there is such a large incentive to adopt unproven abstinence-only approaches." And a national survey of American parents the same year found that the overwhelming majority wanted public schools to offer much more than preachings about abstinence; they wanted discussion of contraception, abortion, safer sex, homosexuality, and negotiation and coping skills.[65]

But Haffner was right about one thing: the availability of contraceptive and safer-sex information for teens, along with advice about sexual technique, had outstripped government attempts to control it. From the groundbreaking feminist health book *Our Bodies, Ourselves* in 1971 to popular magazines and the Internet in the 1990s, explicit sex information was available, if not always wholly accurate or accessible to the economically disadvantaged. Although a study in 1996–97 showed astonishing ignorance among U.S. teenagers of basic sexual and reproductive facts,[66] Web sites and other media outreach were to some extent filling the gap. A newsletter and Web site called *SEX, ETC.*, for example, written for and largely by teens, was distributing 1.8 million copies nationwide by 2000–1. Its guiding spirit, Susan Wilson of the Network for Family Life Education at Rutgers University, described student leaders' "electrifying" response when the idea of the journal was first broached: "They spoke of the weaknesses of their [school] programs and how they came too late in their lives to help them make decisions," and "complained that many teachers withheld information from them because of parental or administrative pressures."

Another Web site, gURL.com, put out a "brash, nonjudgmental guide entitled *Deal with It! A Whole New Approach to Your Body, Brain, and Life as a Gurl.* It discussed fellatio, among other topics, in frank terms, "as girls give each other hints on how to do it well, and how to gracefully handle the aftermath."[67]

Models of Sexuality Education

While "abstinence unless married" reigned as official U.S. policy, in Western Europe teen sexuality had long since become a "public health, not a political or religious, issue." In many countries, free or low-cost contraceptive services and information were readily available, and youngsters received "open, honest, consistent information about sexuality from parents, grandparents, media, schools and health care providers." Governments funded "massive, consistent, long-term public education campaigns using television, radio, discos, billboards, pharmacies and clinics to deliver clear, explicit portrayals of responsible sexual behavior."[68]

One measure of the difference in attitude was the European Parliament's explicit recognition of sexuality education in its 1992 Charter of Rights of the Child. In addition to incorporating minors' rights from other international documents, the Charter specifies a right to information about birth control and "the prevention of sexually-transmitted diseases."[69] That the politicized and diverse European Parliament could have agreed on birth control and safer-sex education for minors as matters of not only propriety but legal entitlement was telling—for it would have been nearly unthinkable for the U.S. Congress to have passed a similar resolution at the time.

According to Vicky Claeys, Director of Public Information for the European Network of the International Planned Parenthood Federation (IPPF), no country in Europe has faced right-wing opposition to sex and contraceptive education nearly as severe as in the United States.[70] Indeed, it was one of the ironies of European life in the 1990s that Italy, overwhelmingly Catholic and home to the Vatican, had the lowest birthrate on the Continent. Italy's Family Planning Association (FPA), the Unione Italiana Centri Educazione Matrimoniale e Prematrimoniale, offered sexuality education for youth in Turin, Milan, Genoa, Rome, and Palermo, and since 1989 also presented programs in public schools. Its materials covered contraception, STDs, frigidity, orgasm, masturbation, homosexuality, and other issues from the viewpoint and in the language of adolescents.[71]

Denmark and Sweden have been the leaders in sexuality education, with syllabi starting as early as third grade. The Danish experience is informative, as sociologist Susan Rose observes, "because the rates of teen pregnancy and attitudes toward sexuality were not so different there than in the U.S. 50 years ago."[72] The basis for Danish sex education was laid in the 1930s, when family planning leaders went to prison to establish women's rights to contraception and abortion, and sex ed became an integral part of the reproductive rights movement.[73] In 1945, Copenhagen began sex education in state schools. A national curriculum was developed in the 1960s after a government commission reported on steps that might be taken to reduce unplanned pregnancies. In 1970, the Danish Parliament made sexuality education compulsory in primary schools.[74]

Six years later, the European Court of Human Rights described the Danish system in a landmark case. Sex instruction is integrated into "the natural context of other subjects" starting in the early years. By the middle grades, the curriculum covers "the sexual organs, puberty, hormones, heredity, sexual activities (masturbation, intercourse, orgasm), fertilisation, methods of contraception, venereal diseases, sexual deviations (in particular homosexuality) and pornography." The course is value-neutral, exposing youngsters to "different views on sexual life before marriage; sexual and marital problems in the light of different religious and political viewpoints; the role of the sexes, love, sex and faithfulness in marriage; divorce, etc." Teachers are instructed "not to use vulgar terminology or erotic photographs; not to enter into discussions of sexual matters with a single pupil outside the group and not to impart to pupils information about the technique of sexual intercourse." Because sexual information is woven into the curriculum over many years, the Court said, it would be impossible to honor parental demands for exemption.[75]

Three Danish couples challenged their country's system as a violation of the "right to education" provision in the European Convention on Human Rights. The provision announces that "no person shall be denied the right to education," but then interposes a qualification: "the State shall respect the right of parents to ensure such education and teaching in conformity with their own religious and philosophical convictions." Interpreting this Janus-like text, the European Court in its 1976 *Kjeldsen* decision refused to elevate the parental proviso above the child's "fundamental right to education"; the curriculum was permissible because it was not designed to indoctrinate but to instill sexual knowledge "more correctly, precisely, objectively and scientifically" than youngsters were likely to imbibe from other sources. If parents could "object to the integration of such teaching or education in the school curriculum, all institutionalised teaching would run the risk of proving impracticable."[76]

The European Court did not try to reconcile its recognition of minors' right to sexual education with its decision the same day in Richard Handyside's case, which allowed Britain to suppress *The Little Red School Book* on grounds of sexual immorality. What the two cases had in common was the

Court's deference to national governments' policies regarding sexual information and youth. That the policies of Britain and Denmark were so vastly different only highlighted the cultural and political variations across the globe in views about what is harmful to minors.

Neil Rasmussen, director of the Danish Family Planning Association, wrote in 1996 that the key to the success of Danish sexuality education is a "widespread consensus that youth should share the same fundamental rights and enjoy the same welfare as adults."[77] In the 1980s and '90s, young Danes did not generally have their sexual debuts earlier than their American or British counterparts—the average age in the 1990s was almost 17—but 80 percent of them used contraceptives at first intercourse. The rate of adolescent pregnancy declined from 47.3 per 1,000 in 1964 to 8.7 in 1994.[78]

Sweden's story is similar: contraceptives were banned until 1938; reproductive rights pioneers took serious risks in distributing diaphragms and teaching about sex. But by 1955, sexuality education was compulsory in the nation's schools.[79] As a result of the "most comprehensive and sophisticated approach to the subject in any country,"[80] Swedish youngsters became far more knowledgeable than their U.S. or British counterparts about basic sexual and reproductive facts and had far lower teen pregnancy and venereal disease rates.[81] The Swedish Association for Sex Education (RFSU), although praising these accomplishments, said in 1990 that there were still "serious shortcomings" in the system, partly owing to inadequate numbers of trained teachers and partly to a health-prevention mentality that tended to view sex as "a kind of dangerous substance" rather than an integral part of a healthy life.[82]

Like Denmark, Sweden did not achieve comprehensive sexuality education without a struggle. But centralized educational policy, combined with decentralized decision making about details, prevented political stalemate. Public leaders went to "enormous lengths" to address areas of controversy and "elaborately justify the formulas adopted."[83] By the 1990s, RFSU was helping the new nation of Estonia develop sex ed publications, kits, and videos, and collaborating with the Family Planning Association of Tanzania to create local programs geared toward African culture and covering condoms, spermicides, STDs, psychosexual development, gender differences, masturbation, menstrual pain, wet dreams, fears of impotence, female orgasm, and penis size.[84]

Britain, by contrast with Scandinavia, has been closer in moral culture to its former American colony. In the 1980s, Prime Minister Margaret Thatcher and Tories in Parliament "had a field day attacking value-neutral sex education."[85] A 1987 Education Department circular advised against any teaching "which advocates homosexual behaviour" or "presents it as the 'norm' " and announced that despite a 1985 ruling by the House of Lords permitting teenagers to obtain contraceptives, in some circumstances, without their parents' knowledge, it might be a crime for teachers and counselors to assist with contraceptive information.[86]

The 1985 House of Lords case had been a striking declaration of minors' rights. Victoria Gillick, the mother of five daughters, had challenged a local government circular suggesting that doctors at family planning clinics could in "exceptional circumstances" prescribe contraceptives to girls under 16 (Britain's age of sexual consent) without informing their parents. In rejecting Gillick's claim, Law Lord Walter Ian Reid Fraser wrote that "growing up is a gradual process" and it is "contrary to the ordinary experience of mankind, at least in Western Europe in the present century, to say that a child or a young person remains in fact under the complete control of his parents until he attains the definite age of majority." Lord Leslie Scarman observed in a separate opinion that if the law should "impose on the process of 'growing up' fixed limits where nature knows only a continuous process, the price would be artificiality and a lack of realism in an area where the law must be sensitive to human development and social change."[87]

But reaction to *Gillick* soon set in. In 1993, Parliament incorporated basic sex ed in England's compulsory National Curriculum, but pointedly excluded "aspects of human behaviour," as well as STD prevention. These more controversial areas could be taught, but were not mandatory, and schools had to honor parents' requests for exclusion.[88] The parental veto made no provision for youngsters' own opinions to be heard—an oversight that was noted and critiqued by the United Nations Committee on the Rights of the Child.[89] Britain's political struggles over sex ed were reflected in its teen pregnancy rate, the highest in Europe in the 1990s, seven times higher than that of the Netherlands, where "similar numbers" were having sex but were "more likely to use contraception."[90]

Yet Britain remained free of the abstinence-unless-married extremism that beset the United States. In 1999, the Health Education Authority sponsored a "Lovelife" Web site for teens "who are or are about to become sexually active" in order to give them explicit, nonjudgmental information about safer sex and condoms.[91] Such a government-funded initiative would have been nearly unthinkable in the United States at the time. Britain also managed to accept contraceptive information on TV; one program, "placed in the early evening to draw an audience of young people, demonstrated the fitting of a condom, a piece of unprecedented frankness." A 1987 public service ad showed a "working-class couple making out on a sofa."

> Delighted when his girlfriend quickly agrees to his overtures, the young man is shocked and crestfallen when she assumes he has his "rubber-johnnies" with him. He pleads. She's unmoved, citing concern about contracting AIDS. "Nobody knows these days," she says, "so if you want humpy-pumpy, it's pop-it-in-a-bag time."[92]

Societies opposing sexuality education—most notably Muslim countries in Asia and the Middle East—do so based on strong religious and cultural taboos.[93] The United States, however, was the only country in the industrialized world to have, at the turn of the 21st century, legislated "abstinence unless married" as official policy. (It was also the only industrialized country still embroiled in debates over evolution vs. creationism.[94]) Albania, with a large Muslim population, was working with the local FPA (Family Planning Association) in the 1990s to develop contraceptive and sex education. Heavily Catholic Poland struggled with the issue but by 1986 was requiring at least two hours per month of family life and sex education in schools. The curriculum included "erotic life," "psychosexual development," "sex drive," "love and emotions and their social-historical conditioning," contraception, abortion, and fidelity.[95]

After the collapse of the Iron Curtain in 1989, International Planned Parenthood's European Network expanded to cover formerly Eastern Bloc countries. By 1998, it was working in thirty-three nations, stretching as far east as Kazakhstan. Advancing sex education and contraceptive services in this vast new territory was daunting: some Central Asian governments wanted neither public school sex ed nor nongovernmental organizations disseminating contraceptive and safer-sex messages.[96] Ideological conflict meanwhile stalled the sexuality education and birth control goals set by the 1994 Conference on Population and Development in Cairo. Five years after the conference, "a comparatively small group of conservative Roman Catholic and Muslim developing countries, with strong support from the Vatican," objected to confidential contraceptive advice for teens and to a Mexican proposal for sexuality education that would "protect adolescents from 'pregnancy, unsafe abortion and sexually transmitted diseases.' "[97]

Most experts share the Scandinavian view that sexuality education must begin early, because children already have many questions about their sexual feelings and the behavior of their elders. They are able to grasp fundamental facts about reproduction and sexuality and should be prepared for puberty well before it arrives.[98] If they are not given basic facts, they will construct their own, "often of the mythological variety."[99] Sexuality education starting only at or after puberty is "poorly timed" because by then major components of children's "sexual scripts have already been formed and reinforced by experience"; adolescents are already "beyond the point when [new] information could be easily integrated into their ongoing sexual lifestyles."[100]

"Family values" conservatives of course disagree. They insist that at least until age 12 ignorance is better than knowledge and that prepubescent development is distorted by sexual information.[101] To this the British author David Archard replies that considering childhood a period of asexual innocence can be dangerous because it is often the very ideal of "purity, virginity, freshness and immaculateness which excites by the possibilities of possession and defilement."[102] Pediatrician Victor Strasburger, who objects to much of the sexual content on television, nevertheless supports early sex ed; the notion that teaching kids about sex makes them more likely to "do it," he says, is "the worst myth of all."[103]

Educators also believe that programs are more successful when they are "holistic"—addressing not just mechanics but educational and social issues. "Giving out contraceptives is easy," says Dutch family planner Doortge Braeken, "the problem is how to help young people cope with their sexual problems."[104] Dr. Michael Carrera's Adolescent Sexuality & Pregnancy Prevention Program in New York City is one model. "In addition to sexuality and family life education, teenagers in this program receive medical services, tutoring, career planning, employment, and sports opportunities."[105]

Finally, educators have discovered the importance of peer participation. Both the 1994 Cairo Conference and the Fourth World Conference in Beijing the following year recognized "the need for young people's active involvement in the design, development, and evaluation of activities which affect their lives," including sexuality and reproductive education.[106] FPAs in Europe involve youngsters through special clinics and services, youth groups, volunteer opportunities, participation in organizational governance, training of peer leaders, telephone hotlines, school talks, youth magazines, leaflets, and videos.[107] In the United States, the Advocates for Youth Web site says peer education is effective because it creates "positive peer pressure"; teenagers "tend to do what they believe their friends" are doing.[108]

A group of St. Louis eighth graders demonstrated the point in 1999 "after witnessing a cheerleader pick up her baby after a football game." They developed and were allowed to teach a sex ed curriculum for forty of their fellow students. In a Michigan town, students pressed for sexuality education beyond the existing program, which one boy described as "just a unit in a book" that most of his peers "don't take seriously." The school board agreed to consider changes, but refused the students' request for condom machines in rest rooms because it would have violated state law.[109] The National Campaign to Prevent Teen Pregnancy reported in 1997 on a variety of local initiatives in which youngsters became peer leaders. In one program that included a poster campaign, the director was summoned to a local high school "by angry teens who wanted to express how insulted they were. . . . They were adamant that teens must be involved in creating media messages in order for them to be acceptable and effective."[110]

Sex ed materials around the world are varied, imaginative, and sometimes charmingly frank. In the Dominican Republic, the FPA Profamilia has a *Manual de Educación Sexual* that covers sex role stereotypes in the media, describes the "dehumanized" images of sexuality in "*los 'porno-shows,'*" discusses male and female orgasm, and contains explicit and amusing illustrations—among them a cartoon of a young fellow who has just masturbated and looks worried about his future virility (see illustrations). The *Manual* deflates such myths about "*la masturbación,*" including the notion that it produces "*la idiotez,*" "*la locura,*" and "*la impotencia.*" On the contrary, it confides, the common harmless activity "is normal in boys, men and women of all ages."[111] Profamilia, with a national program of outreach to teens (including mass media), has used its curriculum, with reliance on peer instructors, in neighborhood clubs and some Santo Domingo schools.[112]

Profamilia's willingness to discuss "*los 'porno-shows'*" was important. Pornography, among the touchiest of subjects in sex ed, is often evaded. After all, how can youngsters be taught about something that they are not supposed to see? Those who distinguish between sexuality education (explicit but good) and pornography (explicit and bad) fear either that youngsters will get the wrong ideas or that those opposing balanced and comprehensive sexuality education will seize on the "pornography unit" as rhetorical ammunition to attack the entire program. But human sexuality cannot be understood without attending to one of its hardiest and longest-lived cultural manifestations. If commercial pornography is indeed wrongheaded and degrading (a by no means universal opinion), at the very least teaching about it in sex ed is likely to have an "immunizing" effect.[113]

Another subject about which Americans have been notoriously squeamish is masturbation. Despite the theme's frank and humorous treatment in some popular films of the late 1990s—Todd Solondz's *Happiness* and Sam Mendes's *American Beauty* come to mind—discussion of the "sin of Onan" was still largely avoided in U.S. classes.[114] By 1999, even the Vatican was doing better. According to a revision of its *catechism* that year, the Church was relaxing its condemnation of masturbation. Psychological factors such as "anxiety and maturity," the revision advised, could now reduce the moral culpability of the offender "to a minimum." A British theologian explained: "The act itself is still regarded as unsatisfactory. But the culpability of the agent is considerably diminished. We are not saying, fine, go ahead and enjoy yourselves. It is still objectively wrong, but subjectively, it might not always be sinful."[115]

Seven

INDECENCY LAW ON TRIAL: *RENO V. ACLU*

Panic over Cyberspace

The same year that Congress made "abstinence unless married" official government policy, it also passed its biggest, most sweeping anti-indecency law. Among the many ironies of this 1996 Communications Decency Act, or CDA, was that the youngsters it was ostensibly passed to protect generally knew more about the Internet and how to explore its wonders than the politicians, mostly middle-aged or beyond, who had enacted it.

The CDA applied the broad indecency standard that the Supreme Court had upheld for broadcasting in *Pacifica* to the new realm of cyberspace, with its vast archives of literature, information, video, music, and art; its private e-mails and communal chat rooms. Unlike the FCC's indecency regime, moreover, this was not some regulatory form of time-channeling. The CDA flatly banned "indecent" or "patently offensive" speech, with criminal penalties of up to two years in prison and $250,000 in fines.

The Internet was undergoing dramatic change in the mid-1990s as Congress wrestled with various drafts of what would become the CDA. The brilliant point-and-click technology of the World Wide Web had rapidly transformed cyberspace from the participatory, communitarian network of its early days into a huge online shopping mall. Yet the amount of noncommercial information available—from libraries, nonprofit organizations, and university Web sites, among other sources—was formidable. It was these nonprofit education and advocacy groups that would form the core of the plaintiff roster in the lawsuit that became known as *Reno v. ACLU*, or later simply *Reno I*.

The CDA, part of the massive Telecommunications Act of 1996, was a masterwork of internal confusion. It had sections on cable television and the v-chip as well as Internet indecency. (Only the Internet provisions were challenged in *Reno I*.) One section criminalized any use of a "telecommunications device" to make, create, or solicit, and "initiate . . . the transmission of," any "obscene *or indecent*" communication, "knowing that the recipient . . . is under 18 years of age," or to permit "any telecommunications facility" to be used for this purpose. A separate but overlapping section forbade the use of an "interactive computer service" to "send to a specific person or persons under 18 years of age" or "*display in a manner available to*" a person under 18 any communication that, "in context, depicts or describes, in terms patently offensive as measured by contemporary community standards, sexual or excretory activities or organs."[1] This "patent offensiveness" language, of course, was borrowed nearly verbatim from the FCC's definition of indecency, as approved by the Supreme Court in *Pacifica*. But Congress in the CDA did not bother to say whether it meant "indecent" as used in one part of the law to be the same as "patently offensive" as used in the other, nor did it explain how the reference to a "telecommunications device" might differentiate the "indecency" portion of the CDA from the "interactive computer service" that was subject to the "patent offensiveness" ban.

It was clear, though, that in crafting the Internet provisions of the CDA, the House-Senate Conference Committee had rejected a proposed compromise substituting for "indecency" the less sweeping variable-obscenity or harm-to-minors standard. The Christian Coalition and other influential groups had even opposed a clarification recommended by House Speaker Newt Gingrich that would have protected "serious works of literature, art, science, and politics." The same groups stopped a proposed exemption from the law for nonprofit libraries and schools.[2]

The announced purpose of the CDA, of course, was to ban indecent or patently offensive communications to minors. But virtual reality is more complicated than real-world cinemas and bookshops. Most online speakers and publishers cannot know the ages of those who may read their words or view their images. The "send" and "transmit" provisions of the law were dubious enough—applying, so it seemed, not only to one-on-one e-mail but to group messages or online discussions among hundreds of people, if even one minor is present. But the provision criminalizing "display in a manner available" to minors was the truly loose cannon in the CDA. It applied to all of cyberspace—Web sites, archives and libraries, discussion groups, and "mail exploders" or "listserves" (e-mails sent to multiple recipients). And it did not require an identifiable young reader, merely the possibility of one. As the evidence in *Reno I* was to demonstrate, most of the speech in cyberspace is displayed in a manner "available" to anyone of any age who possesses the knowledge and equipment needed to find it.

In an attempt to avoid the obvious problem of reducing the adult population of cyberspace to reading or viewing only what was "fit for children," Congress had written defenses into the CDA for those indecent or patently offensive communicators who try to identify and screen out minors through credit card verification, adult identification codes, or other "good faith, reasonable, effective, and appropriate actions."[3] Such screening methods were both expensive and technologically limited, however, so that most individuals and nonprofit organizations lacked the financial or technical ability to use them. More important, of course, the groups that joined as plaintiffs in *Reno I wanted* to communicate about sexual subjects to young people. Among them were the ACLU, which hosted a discussion of masturbation after Joycelyn Elders was fired as Surgeon General for mentioning the subject; Human Rights Watch, which offered sometimes graphic descriptions of sexual torture and rape; Planned Parenthood, the Safer Sex Web Page (see illustrations), and the Critical Path AIDS Project, all of which provided explicit descriptions of contraception and safer sex; and Wildcat Press, which published an online magazine for gay and lesbian teens.[4]

If the CDA's censoring of adults' as well as minors' access to the vast resources of the Internet was its most obvious constitutional defect, its use of vague language was equally disquieting. (The courts eventually assumed that Congress intended "indecent" and "patently offensive" to mean the same thing.) The *Pacifica* indecency test did not require that the speech in question be lascivious or appeal to "prurient interests" in order to be regulated; it needed only to be "patently offensive" according to "contemporary community standards." More important, indecent or patently offensive speech could have "serious literary, artistic, political, or scientific value," as the House-Senate Conference Committee understood and as the FCC had demonstrated in its indecency rulings over the previous decade. This meant that all manner of political, literary, or otherwise educational material was potentially criminal if displayed in cyberspace and thought patently offensive by a local prosecutor, jury, or judge. One of the many ironies of *Reno I* was that anyone who posted online the text of George Carlin's "Filthy Words" monologue would be committing a federal crime, for this was the one expressive work that had actually been ruled indecent by a court. The

Supreme Court had published the monologue as an appendix to *Pacifica*, and it was accordingly available at online law libraries, and at the Web sites of the ACLU, the Electronic Privacy Information Center (EPIC), and the Electronic Frontier Foundation (EFF), all plaintiffs in *Reno I*.

What had inspired this ambitious censorship law? The politics of sexual morality primarily, turning as it frequently does on the specter of pornography corrupting youth. A well-publicized but misleading 1995 study by a Carnegie-Mellon graduate student, Marty Rimm, had exaggerated the proportion of explicit sex online and fueled demands for control. Highlights from the Rimm article were sensationalized in a July 1995 *Time* cover story.[5] As Henry Jenkins recalled:

> The figure of the endangered child surfaced powerfully in campaigns for the Communications Decency Act, appearing as a hypnotized young face awash in the eerie glow of the computer terminal on the cover of *Time*, rendering arguments about the First Amendment beside the point. As one letter to *Time* explained, "If we lose our kids to cyberporn, free speech won't matter."[6]

But regardless of *Time*'s (and Rimm's) sensationalism, there was no question that plenty of sexual subject matter *could* be found in cyberspace—in participatory newsgroups, chat rooms, and bulletin boards as well as nonprofit and for-profit Web sites. Senator James Exon, the originator of the CDA, proclaimed that "the worst, most vile, [and] most perverse pornography" was "only a few click-click-clicks away from any child," while his colleague Dan Coats noted that the danger was particularly severe because children were "the computer experts in our Nation's families."[7]

How could Congress control all this online sex, available to anyone with a modem, software, and a youngster willing to show them how to use it? "Obscenity," of course, was already illegal, but the *Miller v. California* three-part test for proving it included a requirement that the expression lack any serious value, which would frustrate prosecutions in many Internet cases. Few juries in the 1990s were likely, for example, to rule the *Playboy* Web site obscene; yet surely, at least so the legislative thinking went, it was not appropriate for minors, nor were the many other sexually oriented pictures, writings, and conversations that were available online but were not hard-core enough to be prosecuted under *Miller*. Variable obscenity, a watered-down variant on the *Miller* test, also had its problems as a censorship standard for cyberspace (as the Conference Committee evidently understood). It would not ban materials, no matter how lascivious, that had serious value for youngsters; and if judicial decisions in some of the variable-obscenity display cases were followed, the serious-value test would be pegged to the interests and abilities of older adolescents, and thus differ very little from adult obscenity.

The 1978 *Pacifica* decision, approving the indecency/patent offensiveness standard for broadcasting, was a tempting alternative, especially given the Supreme Court's reference in its *Sable Communications* "dial-a-porn" case to the government's "compelling interest" in shielding minors "from the influence of literature that is not obscene by adult standards," including indecency. The reliance by two federal courts in subsequent phone sex cases on this casual reference in *Sable* were the primary precedents to which champions of the CDA could point for an FCC-style indecency test. Neither industry nor free-expression advocates could persuade Congress that indecency or patent offensiveness, questionable enough as a censorship standard for broadcasting, was far too sweeping and subjective to govern cyberspace.

The ACLU had a young lawyer on its national legal staff, Ann Beeson, who was already an experienced Internet traveler. This was the first ACLU case in which the clients and attorneys did most of their communicating online, and Beeson was the primary networker. The lead attorney in the case, Christopher Hansen, was a talented trial lawyer who had worked in the areas of children's rights and institutional reform for much of his ACLU career. Beeson and Hansen filed suit in Philadelphia on February 8, 1996, just as President Clinton was signing the CDA into law.[8]

Philadelphia is part of the Third Circuit, whose Court of Appeals six years earlier had invalidated a Pennsylvania law requiring adults to apply for access codes in order to receive "sexually explicit" telephone messages. As in the Supreme Court's *Sable* decision on dial-a-porn in 1989, the Third Circuit judges found that less burdensome methods of screening out minors were available to serve the legislature's purpose. The desire to prevent "a few of the most enterprising and disobedient young people" from accessing sexual messages was not adequate justification for a law whose effect was to reduce "the content of adult telephone conversations to that which is suitable for children."[9] Even more significant, for purposes of *Reno I*, the judges rejected arguments turning on the state's desire to censor youngsters whose parents had chosen not to do so:

> In this respect, the decision a parent must make is comparable to whether to keep sexually explicit books on the shelf or subscribe to adult magazines. No constitutional principle is implicated. The re-

> sponsibility for making such choices is where our society has traditionally placed it—on the shoulders of the parents.[10]

The author of this prose was Judge Dolores Sloviter. By 1996, she was chief judge of the circuit.

Perhaps recognizing the constitutional questionability of the CDA, Congress had provided for legal challenges to be brought before a tribunal of three judges, rather than the single judge who ordinarily hears federal cases. An appeal from the three-judge ruling would go directly to the Supreme Court. The *Reno* case would be on a particularly fast track not only because of this provision for expedited review but because the ACLU sought a preliminary injunction to stop the law's enforcement while the case was being litigated. There is always a possibility that evidence presented and rulings made at the preliminary injunction stage will end up deciding a case, as indeed happened in *Reno*, but this meant that the entire litigation (which ordinarily would take years) was compressed into a few frenetic months.

Each of the twenty plaintiffs submitted an affidavit describing both the information posted on its Internet site and the difficulty of complying with the law's "good faith" or adult ID defenses, even assuming that they wanted to block minors from their sites. Thus, the president of the Journalism Education Association explained how its teacher members helped high school journalists with Internet research. Some of the topics—"media treatment of women," for example—included explicit sexual material. The director of Stop Prisoner Rape described his group's efforts to slow the epidemic of prison sexual assaults through the posting of graphic testimonials from rape survivors. Sister Mary Elizabeth, the systems operator, or "sysop," for the AIDS Educational Global Information System (AEGIS), described the sex-related databases to which AEGIS was linked, and opined that for minors "who may not feel comfortable" discussing sex with family or friends, or who "live in areas where they may not feel safe discussing sex with anyone," resources like AEGIS "provide an important venue."[11]

Judge Sloviter assigned a district court judge, Ronald Buckwalter, to hear the plaintiffs' request for a temporary restraining order, or TRO, an attempt to prevent the law from taking effect even before hearings on the preliminary injunction motion. She appointed herself, Buckwalter, and Stewart Dalzell to comprise the three-judge court that would handle the rest of the case. Buckwalter granted the TRO, but only in part: he thought that "indecent," standing alone in the "transmission" section of the CDA, was too vague to be constitutional; but "patently offensive," in the "send" and "display" clauses, was acceptable.[12] The result was that federal prosecutors were temporarily restrained from enforcing the "indecency" ban against the plaintiffs, but not the broader, more problematic prohibition on "display" of "patently offensive" speech. The government was ultimately persuaded to refrain from enforcing any section of the CDA until the preliminary injunction proceedings were over.

By this time, a second lawsuit had been filed in Philadelphia and consolidated with *ACLU v. Reno*. It had twenty-seven plaintiffs, including the American Library Association; industry giants America Online, Microsoft, and CompuServe; the popular online magazine *HotWired*; and a coalition of nonprofit entities and individuals called the Citizens Internet Empowerment Coalition.[13] They were represented by the Washington law firm Jonner & Block, with a legal team headed by First Amendment specialist Bruce Ennis. In a former life, Ennis had been legal director of the ACLU.[14]

The litigation schedule in the combined cases of *ACLU v. Reno* and *American Library Association v. Reno* tested the lawyers' endurance. Compressed into a few months was a pretrial process that included sixteen depositions (questioning of potential witnesses), legal briefing on a host of subsidiary issues, preparation of dozens of witness declarations, lengthy, detailed stipulations (agreements on facts that were not in dispute), and selection of thousands of documents to introduce as exhibits. All this culminated in five days of testimony in April and May 1996. For the first time, the U.S. Courthouse ceremonial courtroom in Philadelphia was wired for computer access.

The lawyers had to educate themselves and the three judges on the intricacies of cyberspace. Convoluted testimony from Internet pioneers, including the Web's inventor, Tim Berners-Lee, had to be translated into comprehensible English—an endeavor that was not always successful. The operation of "proxy servers" had to be explained in order to persuade Judges Sloviter, Buckwalter, and Dalzell that adult ID systems and credit card validations were not feasible methods to identify and screen out minors.

Among the stipulations of fact that the contending lawyers hammered out were details about software programs like Cyber Patrol and SurfWatch that rated and blocked different categories of online content and that, the plaintiffs claimed, were less burdensome means of accomplishing the state's interest in protecting minors than the broad criminal ban of the CDA. This "less burdensome alternative" strategy was a typical one in First Amendment cases, but it had its share of legal and political traps. The first of these was the unquestioned assumption on which the various rating and blocking schemes were based—that certain expression (such as pornography) is harmful to minors. The second was that filtering programs were vastly overinclusive: that is, they did not distinguish pornography—however that elastic word is defined—from other information, discussion, literature, or art concerning sex, or even the human nude. Keyword-based blocking, of necessity used by most filtering programs, led to frequently ludicrous results: eliminating access to sites, for example, that mentioned the word "breast" (as in "breast cancer") or "sex" (as in "Middlesex County" or "Anne Sexton"). Employing squads of individual human screeners to use their own judgment in deciding how to rate at least some of the millions of Internet sites was almost equally problematic: they had to make hasty, discretionary decisions about whether and how to label countless words, ideas, and images based on slippery, intangible categories of disapproved subject matter. Some of these disapproved categories, moreover, bore no conceivable relation to protecting minors—for example, speech critical of filtering software.[15]

The perils of filtering became apparent just before the *Reno* hearings began. In the near-empty Philadelphia courtroom, Bruce Ennis was preparing Ann Duvall, the president of SurfWatch, for her testimony. She was to show the judges the wonders of Internet surfing, then demonstrate how SurfWatch blocked "inappropriate" online content. As Duvall explained that SurfWatch would block any site containing the word "sex," including sex discrimination, sexual harassment, and secondary sex characteristics, it became clear that this particular "less burdensome alternative" entailed massive censorship risks of its own.

In filtering's defense, of course, enthusiasts argued that, whatever the crudeness of the software, at least the choice to use it is voluntary, and therefore it is less oppressive than a coercive criminal law like the CDA. But as the preliminary injunction hearing in *Reno* approached, the major corporations that increasingly controlled Internet access were already beginning to introduce rating and blocking systems directly onto computer browsers. The primary method for doing so, still in development as the hearings began, was PICS, the Platform for Internet Content Selection. PICS could read content labels assigned by any company or group that chose to undertake the massive task of rating Internet sites. This embedding of rating and blocking technology directly into computer browsers threatened to make filtering the rule rather than the exception for the hitherto freewheeling world of Internet speech. As one of the stipulations put it, until a majority of sites had been rated by a PICS rating service (an unlikely prospect), PICS would function as a " 'positive' ratings system in which only those sites that have been rated will be displayed." The "default configuration for a PICS-compatible Internet application will be to block access to all sites which have not been rated by a PICS rating service."[16]

In other words, the default setting on the computer would screen out the vast majority of Internet communications. This might not have been *government* censorship—the traditional prerequisite to a First Amendment violation—but it had the potential to be an extremely effective substitute. And PICS-compatible ratings—like stand-alone blocking software—did not even, ironically, have the advantages of government censorship. For under the relevant Supreme Court decisions, government restrictions on speech must contain standards that are clearly defined, publicly known, and subject to court review. Private rating companies, by contrast, treat their technologies as proprietary business information, and have only discretionary procedures for resolving complaints that sites have been wrongfully blocked. The circle is completed when government agencies begin to rely upon or even mandate the use of private, unregulated rating and blocking systems, all in the interest of protecting youth.

The strategy of arguing that filtering software is an alternative means of protecting minors, less burdensome than the harsh and sweeping CDA, clashed with yet another part of the ACLU's case: the decision to introduce evidence of the valuable, nonharmful character of much online communication about sex, nudity, and even vulgar words. The plaintiffs' declarations described material on their sites that could well be considered patently offensive or indecent, and attached copious documents to illustrate the point. Thus, the judges were supplied with downloaded pages full of sexual and reproductive information; erotically charged literature and art; and political discussions on homosexuality, feminism, and human rights abuse. But if all these examples of potentially indecent speech were not in fact harmful to minors, and in many instances might be educational or enlightening, then it became difficult to argue that the crude "parental empowerment" software was any kind of reasonable alternative to the CDA.

Of course, lawyers frequently argue "in the alternative"; it was hardly unheard-of for the ACLU and the American Library Association to contend that the government had not proved its case that minors are harmed by indecency, but that, even if it had, voluntary blocking software was a less burdensome means of shielding the young than a criminal ban. Nor was it necessarily inconsistent to say that regardless of the validity of the harm-to-minors presumption, blocking mechanisms were available for parents who, for whatever reason, wanted to use them. But there was an undoubted *air* of inconsistency about the approach, and the reliance on blocking software came back to haunt the plaintiffs after *ACLU v. Reno* was won.

The Wired Courtroom

The strategy of questioning the whole idea that "indecency" is harmful to youth did not arouse much enthusiasm from the ACLU's colleagues in the companion case of *American Library Association v. Reno*. Not only was it politically risky; not only had court decisions from *Pacifica* to *Sable* assumed that indecent speech was harmful; but it was arguably unnecessary since the unfeasibility of the "good faith" defenses meant that the CDA amounted to a total ban on indecency online—a result that unconstitutionally reduced adults to reading or communicating only what was "fit for children." Bruce Ennis and his team, accordingly, concentrated on proving the unworkability of the "good faith" defenses and arguing that filtering software was a less burdensome, more effective way of protecting youth. The ACLU lawyers, by contrast, thought the CDA such a grossly excessive application of the already problematic indecency standard that it seemed imperative to focus the courts on actually analyzing (perhaps even reconsidering) past statements about the importance of protecting kids from patently offensive speech. If the only thing wrong with online indecency bans was the lack of cheap and efficient technology to screen out youngsters, then harm-to-minors legislation would continue to be passed and the interests of both online speakers and minors themselves in art and information about sex (or literature whose language strayed from Victorian propriety) would continue to be hostage to largely unexamined moral and psychological assumptions.

The ACLU group of plaintiffs accordingly submitted testimony that focused on value, not harm, to minors from sexually explicit speech. Kiyoshi Kuromiya, who operated the Critical Path AIDS Project, described his Web site's multiple links to other sexual-health and gay-positive Internet locations and its use of frank language to respond to requests from its youthful audience. Although Kuromiya did not know what "indecent" or "patently offensive" meant, he was confident that Critical Path's candid style of discussing sexuality and illness would offend some readers. Nor was the organization willing to screen out minors: its mission was to reach them.[17]

Patricia Nell Warren, an author of gay-themed novels, likewise described her online work with the YouthArts Project, a program for economically disadvantaged and "computer-poor" gay teenagers. YouthArts "e-zines" (electronic magazines) were an important forum for these youngsters, and were often sexually explicit. "Gay and lesbian youth are not damaged from exposure to materials like those found in YouthArts," she said, but instead find a "creative outlet" for their "frustrations, fears, and anxieties." Two gay teenagers submitted statements describing how YouthArts helped them and other economically disadvantaged youngsters take advantage of the Internet.[18] Other declarations detailed Human Rights Watch's sometimes graphic news bulletins; the need for confidentiality among gay youngsters trolling the Queer Resources Directory; and the ACLU Web site's feature on George Carlin's famous monologue that "allows users to guess" the "seven dirty words."[19]

Among the witnesses in the companion case of *American Library Association v. Reno*, Robert Croneberger, director of Pittsburgh's Carnegie Library, testified that the library's online catalogue included such titles as *So Fucking What?* and *The Ice Opinion: Who Gives a Fuck?* by the rap musician Ice-T. Popular magazines like *Cosmopolitan*, *Playboy*, and *Vanity Fair* were available on computer in full text, as was the notorious, and explicit, Marty Rimm study of online pornography. Croneberger said he had neither the staff nor the financial resources to screen all of this material for "indecency" or "patent offensiveness," even if he could determine what the terms meant. The cost of creating an adults-only site with monitoring and preregistration requirements "would be astounding." At least fifteen new staff members would be needed, "at an annual cost of $195,000 simply to enable us to complete this task of pre-registration of just existing cardholders," and another $30,000 for software to "review our online material and attempt to select out 'keywords' that might signal that the information could potentially be deemed 'indecent' or 'patently offensive' by some community standards." Nor would keywords be enough: "any segregation of our online materials into acceptable and potentially inappropriate for minors categories would have to be done by hand, using human judgment (presumably, with the assistance of legal counsel)." With more than two millions items in the catalogue, many accompanied by abstracts, he estimated that the Carnegie Library would have to hire 180 additional employees to review and rate it all, "at a cost of approximately three million dollars."[20]

In the face of this evidence, the Clinton Justice Department chose to defend the CDA primarily by deluging the three judges with raunchy examples of online pornographic texts and images, meticulously downloaded, where possible printed in vivid color, and submitted in a large loose-leaf binder that the judges took to calling "Mr. Coppolino's book." (Anthony

Coppolino was the Justice Department's lead trial lawyer.) One of the more creative items in Mr. Coppolino's book was a long printout from an interactive site named "Bianca's Smut Shack" and reminiscent of the board game Clue. Visitors to the virtual "shack" could contribute their sexual fantasies as they traveled through its many chambers.

The government's point here was in part simply to predispose the judges in favor of the CDA by showing them the shocking things available online; but it was also to persuade them that although the law's language was loose, the target was only, or at least *mostly*, "pornography," so that publishers of safer-sex pages or gay rights bulletin boards did not really have to worry. (Moreover, they said, prosecutors would be sensible in applying the law.) But the very selection of "Bianca's Smut Shack" as an indecent site demonstrated how fuzzy the government's proposed distinction was, for the site was not a typical commercial purveyor of glossy nudes. It was interactive, it had humor, and it invited participants to create their own stories. As Judge Sloviter was to explain later, relying on government promises of prosecutorial reasonableness "would require a broad trust indeed from a generation of judges not far removed from the attacks on James Joyce's *Ulysses*."[21]

The administration also argued to the three judges, as it later would to the Supreme Court, that cyberspace should be more strictly regulated than nonvirtual communications because it invades the home, is pervasive, and is particularly accessible to children. These descriptors were, of course, borrowed from *Pacifica*, which had justified the FCC's regulation of broadcasting based on the same set of supposedly unique characteristics. But many forms of communication are pervasive and accessible to children. The Philadelphia judges rejected the government's argument for diminished First Amendment protection in cyberspace. As Dalzell was to write, as "the most participatory form of mass speech yet developed," the Internet "deserves the highest protection from government intrusion."[22]

The five days of preliminary injunction hearings in *Reno* combined mind-boggling Internet technicalities with moments of sly humor. Sloviter and Dalzell actively voiced concerns about valuable expression that was at risk under the CDA. Dalzell asked one of the government's two expert witnesses, Howard Schmidt (a federal agent specializing in computer pornography), about the community standards of an archetypically conservative municipality—Brainard, Minnesota, for example. If the CDA were upheld, Dalzell said, and a group of parents or content providers asked Schmidt's advice on whether an HIV prevention Web site that showed "erect penises" and "how to put on a condom" violated the law, what would he say?

Schmidt, evidently prepared for this type of hypothetical, responded that the material must be viewed "in context"; because the safer-sex information "appears to be an educational type context, not something done purely for pleasure purposes," he would not "go to a prosecutor with that type of information."

Dalzell persisted, however, and Schmidt's "educational context" gave him little help on the next example—an online version of the famous *Vanity Fair* cover showing a naked and pregnant Demi Moore. "What do I do," Dalzell asked Schmidt, "to prevent you from coming after me under the Communications Decency Act of 1996?"

"[I]n that context," Schmidt answered, "it's a visual image for fun, basically. Not an educational—it could be educational, but for fun more than anything else. And I would tell them . . . , depending upon the community in which that image could be viewed, that standard would probably apply towards the—pursuant of the—rules of this law."

JUDGE DALZELL: So, it would be different in Brainard, Minnesota, perhaps, than New York City.

THE WITNESS: That's quite possible, yes, your Honor.

. . .

JUDGE DALZELL: Okay, so what should they do on the Internet then, with their Web site?

. . .

THE WITNESS: My recommendation is to, once again, in order to try to come up with some sort of a standard . . . that's the reasonable person in that area. If it's in Brainard, Minnesota, put those standard disclaimers, adult content, it may allow someone in the community that feels that's offensive to not have—allow their children to have access to it, but . . . for those that don't find it that way, they can still have unlimited access through some sort of a user ID or a pass code.[23]

If there was one moment during the hearings that prefigured the likely outcome of *ACLU v. Reno*, this was it. The government's expert had just testified that posting the photograph of a naked pregnant celebrity that had appeared on the cover of a mass circulation magazine might be a felony under the CDA.

The government's other expert found himself in a similar dilemma a few days later. Dan Olsen, a professor at Brigham Young University, had devised a plan for self-rating and blocking of questionable Internet sites, which the government claimed would satisfy the "good faith" defenses of the CDA. Under Olsen's proposal, Internet speakers would "tag" their online communications "–L18" if they were potentially indecent or patently offensive (under whose community standard, he did not say). The tags could then be read and blocked by PICS. Dalzell gave Olsen a hypothetical about an online chat group discussing the CDA, with participants "varying in age from 13 to 18. And in the course of the chat an 18-year-old, exasperated by his or her view of the law, types in 'Fuck the CDA.' Is it your proposal that before he types in 'Fuck the CDA' he should tag that minus L18?"

THE WITNESS: Yes.
JUDGE DALZELL: I beg your pardon?
THE WITNESS: Yes. . . . If they want to identify their speech that is one way they can do it, yes.
JUDGE DALZELL: And protect themselves because, after all, that is one of the seven dirty words.
THE WITNESS: Okay.[24]

The judges had still other examples. Sloviter wondered out loud whether *National Geographic* photos of Hindu statues of copulating couples, news reports of female genital mutilation, J. D. Salinger's *Catcher in the Rye*, or Henry Miller's once-banned *Tropic of Cancer* would now be illegal. (She mentioned that she had read it before she was 18.)[25]

The most politically fraught moment in the hearings came during the testimony of the *ACLU* plaintiffs' witness William Stayton, a Baptist clergyman, psychologist, adjunct professor at the University of Pennsylvania, and sex therapist. Stayton's written declaration had asserted that children need accurate sexual information in order to "develop criteria and skills for making sexual decisions." Young people who "act out on their sexuality in promiscuous, dangerous, and irresponsible ways" generally do so because they are "desirous of information and experiment out of ignorance." The explicit online material provided by plaintiffs like Critical Path, Planned Parenthood, and the Safer Sex Web Page would be "extremely valuable" for minors. Although some of the sexual information in cyberspace is offensive or inaccurate, the best remedy is parental discussion with children. Because "not every parent shares the same values and not every child is the same, these decisions need to be made by individual parents who best know their children."

On cross-examination by Patricia Russotto, one of the Justice Department attorneys, Stayton explained: pornographic images in magazines like *Playboy*, *Penthouse*, and *Hustler* are not in themselves psychologically harmful to minors. Russotto showed him sexy pictures of (mostly) women in semi-undress, gleaned from Mr. Coppolino's book. Stayton said that even this unedifying erotica, although it reflects "a socialization process" that uses "women as sex objects" (Russotto's phrasing), was not by itself harmful because "it's only one part of all the input" that children receive. Russotto read an excerpt from Stayton's deposition, in which he had said that some pornographic pictures did not promote "a healthy view" of women or men "as sexual beings."

Q. What is it about those pictures that you think may not promote a healthy view of women and men as healthy sexual beings?
A. Well, it's so typical of the way people are socialized that women are like sex objects. You know, this just doesn't depict real life.
Q. And yet you don't believe that exposing minors to these types of sexually explicit images is harmful to them, do you?
A. Not in and of itself, no.
Q. And you don't think that minors would be socialized to view women as sex objects by exposure to these kinds of images?
A. No. They're going to get that from other parts of their input, from family, society, peer group.

. . .

Q. And you wouldn't have a problem if a six-year-old was exposed to those kinds of sexually explicit images, would you?
A. No. I would want to be the one to give my value system as I worked with . . . a six-year-old. But there's nothing inherently harmful that would hurt a six-year-old. Hundreds of thousands of people have seen pictures like this and never been harmed.[26]

There were gasps from the courtroom's spectator section during this exchange. Indeed, the alleged compelling government interest in protecting minors from explicit sexual imagery had for so long been a self-evident proposition in legal and policy circles that the Justice Department lawyers seemed surprised the ACLU was even questioning it. Yet the examination of Stayton was illuminating, for it highlighted the nature of the government's compelling interest as the Justice Department saw it: a desire to socialize youngsters into proper views about women and men as "sexual beings" by suppressing their exposure to contrary ideas. This was, of course, the same rationale used to defend the Catharine MacKinnon/Andrea Dworkin antipornography ordinance that had been ruled unconstitutional a decade before.[27]

On redirect examination, Hansen elicited from Stayton that his views were in "the mainstream" among sex educators and therapists. Judge Buckwalter interjected: "You believe that it ought to be in the hands of parents?"

> THE WITNESS: Yes.
> JUDGE BUCKWALTER: But it probably is not, though, is it?
> THE WITNESS: Unfortunately what happens is the parents abdicate their role. I would like to see us do more training of parents to be sex educators. In fact we do that. I'm doing it with a Methodist church this weekend.[28]

Dr. Stayton's testimony was not mentioned again, nor did it figure in the three judges' preliminary injunction decision. Frankly, there were less controversial ways to strike down the massively overbroad CDA without stepping into the political minefield of whether minors are really harmed by viewing pornography.

A Never-Ending Worldwide Conversation

Fittingly, the three judges' June 11, 1996, decision striking down the CDA arrived at the ACLU via computer, and the legal team crowded into Chris Hansen's office as the pages appeared on the screen. Sloviter, Buckwalter, and Dalzell each wrote separately, after joining in lengthy "findings of fact." These findings pointed out that online communications are available worldwide regardless of different community standards, so that, for example, when the University of California Museum of Photography posts "nudes by Edward Weston and Robert Mapplethorpe,"

> those images are available not only in Los Angeles, Baltimore and New York City, but also in Cincinnati, Mobile, or Beijing—wherever Internet users live. Similarly, the safer sex instructions that Critical Path posts on its Web site, written in street language so that the teenage receiver can understand them, are available not just in Philadelphia, but also in Provo and Prague.[29]

Judge Sloviter's separate opinion returned to her favorite example of the CDA's overbreadth—pictures of "the sculptures in India of couples copulating in numerous positions." She added that the widely acclaimed *Angels in America*, a play that "concerns homosexuality and AIDS," might be criminal under the CDA because its graphic language and themes were "far less acceptable in smaller, less cosmopolitan communities of the United States" than in New York City. The government had made no showing "that it has a compelling interest" in preventing older teenagers from accessing these works. Nor could the Justice Department rely on the existence of hard-core pornography, already subject to prosecution under obscenity law, to justify a statute of such massively broader sweep as the CDA. And the government had not established that Professor Olsen's tagging proposal was feasible or would satisfy the law's "good faith" defense. There was "no agreed-upon 'tag' in existence," and no Web browsers or user-based screening systems were currently "configured to block tagged material." In any event, Sloviter said, "even if the technology catches up, as the government confidently predicts, there will still be a not insignificant burden attached to effecting a tagging defense." For "the many not-for-profit entities which currently post thousands of Web pages," this burden of reviewing all their online material for "patent offensiveness" "would be impossible to sustain."[30]

Sloviter wound up by agreeing with Judge Buckwalter that the CDA was also intolerably vague. Buckwalter had decided by this time that both "patently offensive" and "indecent" were indecipherable as legal standards for criminalizing speech. Nor did the Justice Department improve matters by arguing that speech would be criminal under the CDA only if patently offensive "in context," Buckwalter said. In fact, this defense of the law only highlighted its vagueness:

> [O]ne government expert opined that any of the so-called "seven dirty words" used in the Carlin monologue would be subject to the CDA and therefore should be "tagged," as should paintings of nudes displayed on a museum's Web site. The Government has suggested in its brief, however, that the Act should not be so applied. . . . Even Government counsel was unable to define "indecency" with specificity. The Justice Department attorney could not respond to numerous questions from the court regarding whether, for example, artistic photographs of a nude man with an erect penis, depictions of Indian statues portraying different methods of copulation, or the transcript of a scene from a contemporary play about AIDS could be considered "indecent" under the Act.[31]

Dalzell's opinion was to become the most frequently quoted. The Internet was "the most participatory form of mass speech yet developed," he said;

"a never-ending worldwide conversation." "Just as the strength of the Internet is chaos, so the strength of our liberty depends upon the chaos and cacophony of the unfettered speech the First Amendment protects." Dalzell reviewed the FCC's string of broadcast indecency rulings, which nicely illustrated their breadth, unpredictability, and lack of concern with news or literary value. As for the government's interest in protecting minors, Dalzell was ambivalent: the interest was "as dangerous as it is compelling," because it had "no limiting principle. . . . Regulations that 'drive certain ideas or viewpoints from the marketplace' for children's benefit . . . risk destroying the very 'political system and cultural life' . . . that they will inherit when they come of age."

Dalzell's most memorable flight of rhetoric employed a simple conceit. He had no doubt that a "Newspaper Decency Act, passed because Congress discovered that young girls had read a front page article in the New York Times on female genital mutilation in Africa, would be unconstitutional." So would a "Novel Decency Act, adopted after legislators had seen too many pot-boilers in convenience store book racks," or a "Village Green Decency Act, the fruit of a Senator's overhearing of a ribald conversation between two adolescent boys on a park bench," not to mention a "Postal Decency Act, passed because of constituent complaints about unsolicited lingerie catalogues."[32]

With *Reno I* now on its expedited way to the Supreme Court, a new complication emerged. Just weeks after the Philadelphia judges' decision, the Supreme Court decided *Denver Area Educational Telecommunications Consortium v. FCC*, the constitutional challenge to Congress's 1992 law giving cable companies the power to censor indecency on leased and public access channels. The Court in *Denver* rejected the DC Circuit's bizarre holding that the law's appointment of cable operators as censors presented no First Amendment problem because it did not amount to "state action"; and it struck down two of the anti-indecency provisions. But it upheld a third, allowing the companies to ban anything they "reasonably" thought indecent on leased access cable shows. Justice Stephen Breyer's plurality opinion gave no principled rationale for the distinction between public and leased access; he simply asserted that leased access presented more of a threat to minors. As for the indecency standard, Breyer said cable was close enough to broadcasting—invasive, pervasive, and uniquely accessible to kids—for *Pacifica* to apply. Anthony Kennedy and Ruth Bader Ginsburg, in dissent, criticized Breyer's failure to apply First Amendment "strict scrutiny" and pointed out that indecency "may have strong communicative content, protesting conventional norms or giving an edge to a work by conveying 'otherwise inexpressible emotions.' " But Ginsburg and Kennedy, like the other justices, agreed without analyzing the question that Congress has "a compelling interest in protecting children from indecent speech." Neither Breyer nor his brethren mentioned the Philadelphia judges' recent findings in *Reno* that much patently offensive or indecent expression not only does not harm minors but is likely to enlighten them.[33]

It was difficult to predict what effect the murky and fragmented *Denver* decision would have on the Supreme Court's upcoming review of *Reno v. ACLU*. (The names in the case were now reversed because the government was appealing.) The Internet was substantially different from cable television; the facts presented in *Reno* were vastly more illustrative of the range of valuable expression chilled by an indecency standard; and the Court in *Denver* had, after all, invalidated two of the three challenged provisions of the cable law. Breyer's opinion, moreover, had reiterated the Court's statement in the *Sable* dial-a-porn case that the possibility of a few determined youngsters accessing pornography was not an acceptable justification for reducing the adult population to hearing, reading, or viewing "only what is fit for children."[34]

Once the Supreme Court accepted review in *Reno I*, publicity predictably focused on the familiar—the government's need to protect youth from "smut." Thus, *The New York Times* quoted a comment by Cathy Cleaver of the Family Research Council that the Court "now had the chance to 'reverse the radical ruling which gave Bob Guccione the right to give his Penthouse magazine to our children on the Internet.' "[35] There was no reference in this lengthy *Times* article to Planned Parenthood, Human Rights Watch, or the mounds of other valuable and arguably nonsmutty speech that would be chilled by the CDA.

Yet the factual record in *Reno* on the issue of harm (or help) to minors was ample, whether or not one considered the psychological testimony of William Stayton. Apparently recognizing the centrality of this issue to the case, and the Justice Department's disinclination to address it in any detail, the Enough is Enough antipornography campaign organized a friend-of-the-court brief on the government's side, joined by twenty-six other groups or individuals ranging from the Salvation Army to Omaha for Decency, and focusing on the alleged damage caused by pornography to the hearts and minds of youth. With its citation to psychological sources, the Enough is Enough brief plainly aspired to scientific status. It contended that youths viewing pornography would suffer "the centerfold syndrome," masturbating to "airbrushed sexual images of women" instead of establishing "relationships with an actual person"; and cited a pamphlet by psychologist Victor Cline, published by Morality in Media, which asserted that "pre-teen or adolescent males" are "particularly vulnerable" to the "negative and addictive effects" of pornography.[36]

But Cline's science was hazy, his claims of harm based on anecdotes or clinical cases, not samples of the general population. As sex educator Michael Carrera commented, scientific researchers "would have a field day" with conclusions like Cline's, drawn from a handful of case studies.[37] At bottom, the Enough is Enough brief, like the Meese Commission's *Final Report* in 1986, did not differentiate between moral or pedagogical arguments and psychological ones. "Sexually explicit speech" harms minors, it said, because it distorts "the natural development of personality," and "encourages neither tenderness nor caring" in sexual relations.[38]

In contrast to Enough is Enough, the government's Supreme Court brief in *Reno I* said remarkably little about harm to minors. Emphasizing Howard Schmidt's testimony that online searches using such apparently innocuous terms as "Little Women" or "Sleeping Beauty" could lead to pornographic Web sites, the brief simply assumed that a child stumbling on such material would suffer damage to her "psychological well-being." The closest the government came to defining the harm was in a footnote that adverted to the symbolic or socializing function that Justice Brennan had relied on thirty years before in *Ginsberg v. New York*. The "harm to children is exacerbated," it said, "where access to indecent material by children is readily permitted, because of the implied societal approval of the material that accompanies such a regime."[39]

The Supreme Court received several other amicus briefs—on the government's side from Morality in Media (arguing that safer-sex information was indecent); the American Center for Law and Justice (contending that "indecency" was neither vague nor overbroad); and twenty-five members of Congress; and on the plaintiffs' side from Feminists for Free Expression; Playboy Enterprises; a coalition that ranged from the American Society of Journalists to SIECUS; and a group of artists, writers, filmmakers, and arts organizations. This artists' brief had an appendix with fifteen color reproductions of potentially indecent works, including an African phallic sculpture, Rodin's "The Kiss," and Egon Schiele's "Autoportrait Se Masturbant"; and text excerpts from *Lysistrata*, *Angels in America*, Alice Walker's *The Color Purple*, and Cole Porter's "Love for Sale."[40]

At oral argument, Seth Waxman of the Solicitor General's office chose a dubious analogy to defend the CDA. A group of adults discussing sex, he said, would surely change the subject if a minor entered the room, so it was not problematic for Congress to expect adults to do the same in their online discourse. This was a remarkable proposition, as most of the justices quickly recognized: adults may or may not censor their sexual conversations in the presence of youngsters, but it is quite a leap to suggest that those who do not should go to jail.

Justice David Souter asked Waxman whether a parent would risk criminal prosecution by sending his 17-year-old college student son or daughter information about sex or birth control. Waxman admitted that there was no exemption from the CDA for parents. Justice Breyer gave another example: two teenagers communicating via e-mail regarding their sexual adventures or imagined adventures. This is known to happen in high school, said Breyer, smiling; Waxman conceded they could be prosecuted.

The Supreme Court argument in *Reno* was heavily publicized, with Enough is Enough's telegenic leader, Donna Rice Hughes, much in the spotlight. And if the argument itself had focused on the CDA's implications for contraceptive information and the like, Hughes brought it back to "airbrushed centerfolds," "women engaging in sex with animals," and online newsgroups with names like "alt.sex.snuff.cannibalism."[41]

The Supreme Court's decision three months later was a near-unanimous endorsement of free speech online. John Paul Stevens's majority opinion rejected the Justice Department's argument that cyberspace should enjoy less First Amendment protection than books, magazines, or movies. On the contrary, said Stevens, "this new marketplace of ideas," whose growth "continues to be phenomenal," essentially *includes* all these other categories of communication—"not only traditional print and news services, but also audio, video, and still images, as well as interactive, real-time dialogue."

> Through the use of chat rooms, any person with a phone line can become a town crier with a voice that resonates farther than it could from any soapbox. Through the use of Web pages, mail exploders, and newsgroups, the same individual can become a pamphleteer. As the District Court found, "the content on the Internet is as diverse as human thought."[42]

Strict First Amendment scrutiny was therefore needed; and under this standard the CDA was plainly overbroad. The terms "indecent" and "patently offensive" were so expansive as to threaten with criminal prosecution "large amounts of nonpornographic material with serious educational or other value" that might nonetheless be considered offensive in some community.[43] Congress's effort to avoid this problem by creating defenses under which online speakers could make "good faith" efforts to identify and screen out minors were ineffective, as the judges in Philadelphia had found.

But here Justice Stevens waded into an analytical quagmire. First, he said the CDA was unconstitutional unless no "less restrictive alternative" were available that would be "at least as effective in achieving the legitimate purpose that the statute was enacted to serve"—that is, protecting the minds of youth. But then he went on to suggest how the CDA did not in fact serve this "legitimate purpose" because of the substantial amount of valuable speech that it put at risk. This included "any of the seven 'dirty words' used in the Pacifica monologue," as well as "discussions about prison rape or safe sexual practices, artistic images that include nude subjects, and arguably the card catalogue of the Carnegie Library."[44] Stevens then simply hedged his bets: despite all this valuable material that was potentially criminalized by the CDA, he said, "we neither accept nor reject the Government's submission" that the First Amendment permits "a blanket prohibition on all 'indecent' and 'patently offensive' messages communicated to a 17-year-old."

At the very least, though, Stevens said, "the strength of the Government's interest in protecting minors is not equally strong throughout the coverage of this broad statute." Under the CDA, for example, "a parent who sent his 17-year-old college freshman information on birth control via e-mail could be incarcerated even though neither he, his child, nor anyone in their home community, found the material 'indecent' or 'patently offensive,' if the college town's community thought otherwise."[45] But now Stevens switched tracks again and reverted to precisely the assumption of harm to minors that he had just questioned. The government, he said, failed to show why "a less restrictive provision would not be as effective as the CDA" in protecting youth. Possible "alternatives" included "requiring that indecent material be 'tagged' in a way that facilitates parental control of material coming into their homes, making exceptions for messages with artistic or educational value, providing some tolerance for parental choice, and regulating some portions of the Internet—such as commercial Web sites—differently from others, such as chat rooms."[46] None of this "less restrictive alternative" analysis was necessary, of course, if the government's interest in shielding youth from a category of speech as broad as indecency was not "compelling" in the first place.

This strangely shifting aspect of *Reno I*—its repetition of the unanalyzed

"Your Honor, this woman gave birth to a naked child!" Cartoonist Robert Minor's inspired parody of America's chief censor, Anthony Comstock, in the September 1915 *Masses* magazine.

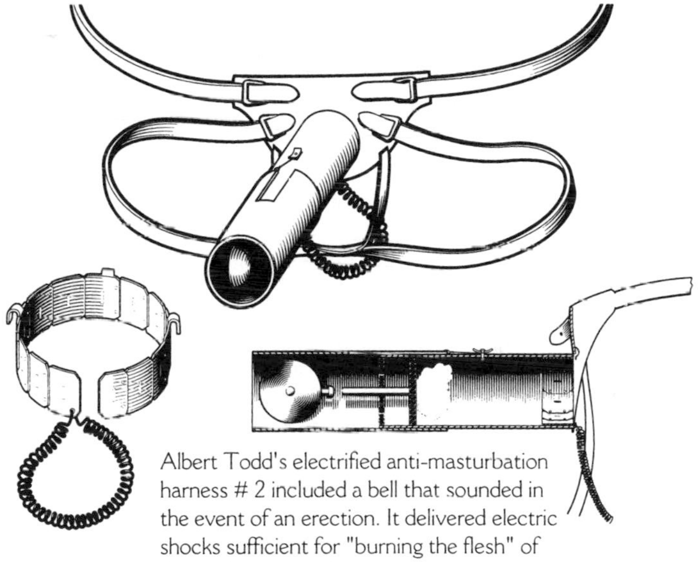

Albert Todd's electrified anti-masturbation harness # 2 included a bell that sounded in the event of an erection. It delivered electric shocks sufficient for "burning the flesh" of determined masturbators.
No. 745,264 (1903)

Myths about the dire effects of youthful masturbation drove 19th-century censorship laws; the myths persisted well into the 20th century. Here, U.S. Patent Office drawings for a device designed to prevent the "secret vice."

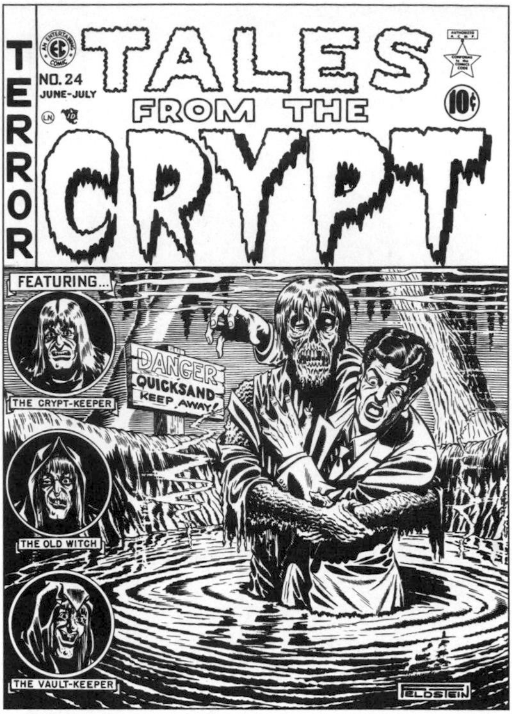

Psychiatrist Fredric Wertham used pseudoscience in his successful crusade against crime, horror, and adventure comics in the 1950s. *Tales from the Crypt*, © 1951, William M. Gaines, Agent, Inc., used with permission. *Crime SuspenStories*, © 1954, William M. Gaines, Agent, Inc., used with permission.

The "School Kids" issue of *Oz*—an occasion for a sensational obscenity trial in Britain. Courtesy of *Oz* magazine.

A frame from *Oz*'s infamous Rupert Bear cartoon, transformed from an original comic strip by Robert Crumb. This parody of a beloved children's book character particularly offended the British government. Courtesy of *Oz* magazine.

OLIPHANT
STUDIO A
YOU SAID CONDOMINIUM— YOU'RE UNDER ARREST!
FCC Radio Police arrested today Surgeon-General Koop for broadcasting AIDS warnings that contained sexual innuendo.

Policing the airwaves. Cartoonist Pat Oliphant comments on the FCC's indecency regime.

FALSO

International sex education materials are considerably less inhibited than those in the United States. Here, Profamilia's *Manual de Educación Sexual* (from the Dominican Republic) deflates masturbation myths but also shows how some pornography can present sexuality in a dehumanizing form.

The Mexican government agency *Conasida* unabashedly counsels safer sex in posters directed to youth. Reprinted with permission.

Como mujer, estoy preparada...

...para prevenir el SIDA
Evita el contagio

TelSIDA 207-40-77

March 14, 1996 http://www.safersex.org/condoms/howtouseacondom.pdf

HOW TO USE A CONDOM

1. USE LATEX CONDOMS. DON'T STORE CONDOMS IN A GLOVE COMPARTMENT OR YOUR WALLET. DON'T USE THEM AFTER THE EXPIRATION DATE. DON'T OPEN THEM WITH YOUR TEETH.

2. PUT THE CONDOM ON AFTER YOU GET HARD. PUT A FEW DROPS OF WATER-BASED LUBRICANT INSIDE THE TIP OF THE CONDOM.

3. SQUEEZE THE TIP OF THE CONDOM TO LEAVE SOME EXTRA SPACE AND ROLL THE REST DOWN THE SHAFT.

4. PUT MORE WATER-BASED LUBRICANT ON THE OUTSIDE OF THE CONDOM

5. AFTER YOU COME, HOLD THE BASE OF THE CONDOM AND PULL OUT. THROW THE CONDOM AWAY; DON'T REUSE CONDOMS.

USE A NEW CONDOM EVERY TIME YOU HAVE SEX

PLAINTIFF'S EXHIBIT
50

THE SAFER SEX PAGE ON THE WORLD WIDE WEB
HTTP://WWW.CMPHARM.UCSF.EDU/~TROYER/SAFESEX.HTML

© 1994 JOHN M. TROYER

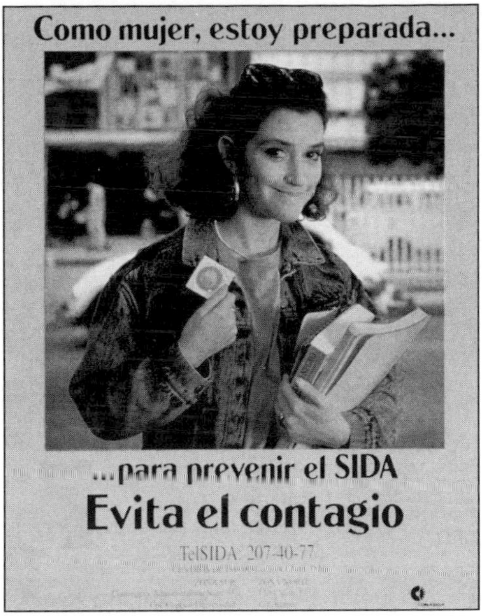

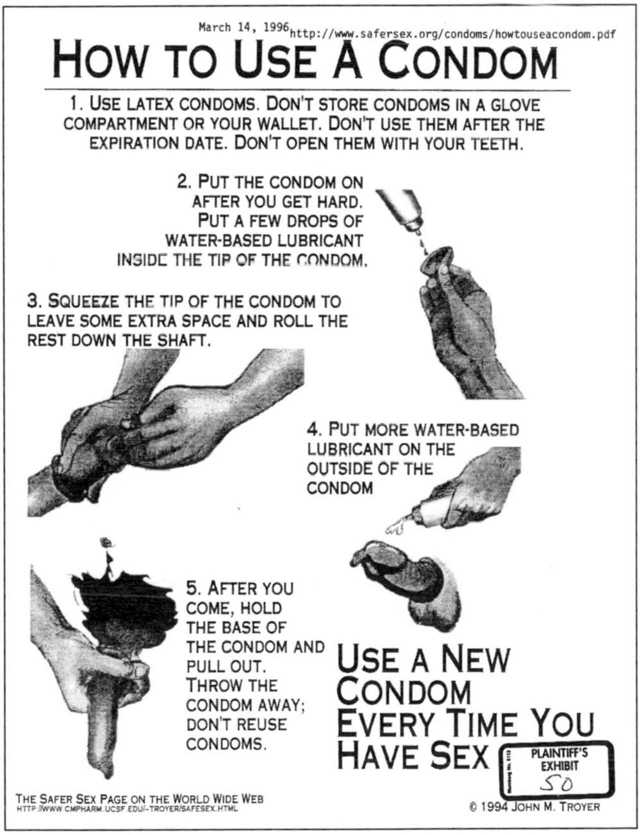

The plaintiffs in *Reno v. ACLU* submitted pages from their Web sites to persuade the courts that not all "indecent" speech is harmful to minors. The Safer Sex Web Page, reprinted with permission.

Trading cards depicting "heinous criminals" and describing their exploits were the subject of a harm-to-minors censorship case in Nassau County, New York. "St. Valentine's Day Massacre," © Salim Yaqub, reprinted with permission. "Jeffrey Dahmer," © Jon Bright, reprinted with permission.

Jeffrey (left) and Jonathan Pyle's challenge to their high school's ban on "vulgar" or "profane" T-shirts led to a students' free-speech victory in Massachusetts. Photo by Christopher Pyle, reprinted with permission.

Jim Borgman, Cincinnati Enquirer

The ironies of the Internet filtering, as depicted by cartoonist Jim Borgman. Reprinted with special permission of King Features Syndicate.

The New York State Liquor Authority banned the Bad Frog beer label because the vulgar gesture might corrupt youthful viewers. Reprinted with permission of Bad Frog, Inc.

FOR THEIR OWN GOOD
It isn't that difficult to shield children from death.
Mommy? Where's Grandpa?
With a little ingenuity, you can keep them in the dark for 15, 16 years—or even more.
Huh?
LIFE IS A MYSTERY
IN YOUR TIME OF SORROW
Our Prayers Are with You
WITH SYMPATHY
SYMPATHY
ACME COLLEGE
We'll start with an easy one: you're watching Bambi, and Bambi's mom gets shot.
FWAKK
Simply look her in the eye and say:
She's fine! I saw her LAST WEEK!! In the woods behind GRAND UNION!!!
Let's say he or she gets curious about cemeteries:
It's a STONE STORE.
Pet death? Watch and learn:
What's wrong with Fifi?
Quick! Look over there.
Do the old switcheroo—
HURL
What? Where? I don't see anything.
—and it's like nothing ever happened.
Fifi had brown stripes.
No, she didn't.
MEOW
Why not keep it on a "need to know" basis? After all—who needs to know?
Grandpa is in the Belgian Congo.
R. Chast

Cartoonist Roz Chast has the last word on protecting youth from the realities of life.

assumption of harm to minors alongside its recognition of the educational, nonharmful nature of much "indecency"[47]—gave the decision an anomalous, unsettled quality despite its importance as a First Amendment landmark. The reason was not difficult to discern. "Harm to minors" from pornography was such a political hot potato that murky equivocation seemed the best approach, especially when that "least dangerous branch" of government, the judiciary, was invalidating an act of the popularly elected legislature.

Justice O'Connor was less ambivalent in her concurrence (joined by Chief Justice Rehnquist). She did not think the indecency standard restricted minors' access to any "substantial" amount of speech that they had the right to read or view, because "the universe of material that is 'patently offensive,' but which nonetheless has some redeeming value for minors or does not appeal to their prurient interest—is a very small one." Thus, while discussions of prison rape or nude art "may have some redeeming educational value for *adults*, they do not necessarily have any such value for *minors*."[48] O'Connor did not indicate whether she was thinking of 7- or 17-year-olds, but her suggestion that nude art (Michelangelo or Botticelli, for example) has no "educational value" for young people was puzzling.

Reno v. ACLU was the first case since Justice Brennan's 1957 peroration in *Roth v. United States* about sex being a "great and mysterious motive force in human life" in which a Supreme Court majority gave serious attention to the educational, artistic, and social value of sexually explicit speech, even for the young. Perhaps for Justice Stevens *Reno* was also an implicit apology for having burdened First Amendment jurisprudence with the intellectually indefensible *Pacifica* decision nineteen years before. If so, however, Stevens's apology was indistinct, for his majority opinion in *Reno* never reconciled its repetition of the harm-to-minors mantra with its disquisition on the evils of the indecency test.

Eight

FILTERING FEVER

The Politics of Filtering—Blocking Sex, Vulgarity, and Dr. Seuss

The Supreme Court's stirring words in *Reno v. ACLU* about the expressive potential of the Internet were exhilarating to First Amendment aficionados but did little to alter the politics of child protection. Just days after the Court struck down the 1996 Communications Decency Act, the White House began to float alternative proposals for controlling cyberspace. The new emphasis was on Internet rating and filtering—software programs of the type the Court had referenced in *Reno* to suggest that "less burdensome alternatives" to the CDA were available to protect minors. Within the month, the White House convened a "summit" meeting to promote filtering; the attendees ranged from online corporations to advocacy groups as disparate as the Enough is Enough antipornography campaign and the Center for Democracy and Technology (CDT), which had helped organize the plaintiff Citizens Internet Empowerment Coalition in *Reno*.

A measure of the new mood was a press release from SurfWatch congratulating itself on the Supreme Court decision, which it attributed "in large part to testimony concerning the effectiveness of Internet filtering," in particular its own software. The release described SurfWatch's "ability to offer daily updates" as giving parents "even more peace of mind" as hundreds of thousands of new pages are "added to the web each day."[1]

Even before the White House summit, the coalition that successfully litigated *Reno* had begun to fragment. While the CDT prepared an "Internet Family Empowerment White Paper" touting rating and filtering,[2] the American Library Association formalized its opposition to Internet filters. Emphasizing that the job of libraries is to provide free access to information, even for minors, the ALA's resolution explained that rating/filtering programs rely either on mindless keyword-based blocking or on subjective, private corporate judgments about offensiveness, and offered examples of librarians' experiences: one program blocked the NASA Web site on exploring Mars because the address (marsexpl.htm) contained the letters SEX; indeed, "any word with SEX as a root would be blocked: sextant, for math, . . . sextet . . . . sextillion, . . . sexton, . . . or sextuplet." Filtering based on "intolerance" restricted research on civil rights and religious cults. Information about drugs, contraceptives, HIV, alcohol, and secondhand smoke "were all off-limits as a result of filtering software."[3]

Despite the ALA's exertions, local libraries were often not able to resist profiltering pressures. The Boston Public Library was one of the first to succumb, announcing in early 1997 that it would install Cyber Patrol on all computers. After public protests, it eventually adopted a compromise: filters in children's rooms only. Of Cyber Patrol's twelve blocking categories (including "violence/profanity," "militant/extremist," and "satanic or cult"), Boston selected three: full nudity, partial nudity, and sex acts.[4] Other products—among them SurfWatch, Net Nanny, CYBERsitter, CyberSnoop, PlanetWeb, Net Shepherd, SafeSurf, Microsoft Plus for Kids, and X-Stop—were now competing as well for lucrative school and library markets. The big ISPs (Internet service providers)—America Online, Prodigy, CompuServe—also offered parental controls, usually relying in turn on SurfWatch or Cyber Patrol software. Microsoft Network simplified the process by making "controls on" the default setting for its browser.[5]

Each of the filtering programs used a combination of keywords and individual site blocking based on human judgment, however fleeting; and each had its own amusing and appalling instances of ideologically based, controversy-averse, or simply mindless overblocking. CYBERsitter, described by *Time* magazine as "the most aggressively conservative filtering program," blocked the National Organization for Women's Web site and virtually all gay and lesbian information. Cyber Patrol blocked the Queer Resources Directory; SurfWatch blocked Associated Press and Reuters articles about AIDS.[6] California's Log-On Data Corporation marketed a "felony load" library version of X-Stop, claiming that it blocked only "illegal" child pornography and obscenity[7]—an impossibility, given that even hard-core pornography is not necessarily obscene until a court or jury decides that it offends "contemporary community standards," appeals to "prurient" interests, and lacks "serious value" under the Supreme Court's three-part *Miller v. California* obscenity test.

More worrisome—because built into computer browsers—was PICS (the Platform for Internet Content Selection). By the fall of 1997, this online technology offered three rating systems: RSACi, Net Shepherd, and SafeSurf. The Canada-based Net Shepherd claimed to have rated by far the greatest number of sites (its estimates ranged from 300,000 to 500,000), but its third-party classification system relied on subjective judgments by volunteers who were paid a few cents per site to judge the "quality" and "maturity level" of various Web pages. RSACi, initially developed by the Recreational Software Advisory Council for video games, relied on self-rating and perhaps for this reason was quickly becoming the industry favorite. For as one executive explained, with "60 million-plus pages on the Web" in 1997, "it takes about one minute per page to rate. To rate every existing Web page," therefore, "would take about 60 million minutes—or one million hours—or over 114 years. Using 114 people working 24 hours a day, the job would take a full year. But the bad news is that as soon as everything was rated, the process would have to start all over again, because within a year the Web would change drastically."[8] Self-rating was the only practical alternative to mindless keyword-based blocking.

RSACi's self-rating system had four categories of disfavored content—nudity, sex, language, and violence—and five settings within each category. Under this scheme, "rape or wanton, gratuitous violence" was rated at level four; sports-related violence at level zero (not blocked). "Frontal nudity (qualifying as provocative display)" ranked at level four; "revealing attire" or "mild expletives" at level one. By the end of 1997 RSACi claimed to have 50,000 self-rated sites (by 1999, it claimed 125,000); the rest of the Internet, including most major newspapers, it automatically blocked. Microsoft Explorer adopted RSACi ratings; and four of the major search engine firms—Lycos, Excite, Infoseek, and Yahoo!—said they would cooperate in "self-regulation" by excluding from their listings any Web sites that did not self-rate. Senator Patty Murray proposed legislation punishing those who "misrated," while her colleague John McCain introduced a bill requiring any public school or library receiving federal aid for Internet connections to install software that labels and blocks "inappropriate" sites. McCain's bill did not pass (he would re-introduce it in subsequent years), but a major step had been taken toward making voluntary filters not so voluntary after all.[9]

A larger "Online Summit" was now planned for December 1997. Christine Varney, a former FCC commissioner, was to chair this conference; a public relations representative for Cyber Patrol handled media registration. Although "parental empowerment" was the dominant theme of the promotional publicity, a careful reading made clear that voluntary filtering on home computers was not the only goal. Netparents.org, a Web site devoted to the Online Summit, explained the virtues of a "Family-Friendly Internet," complete with filtering for schools and libraries.[10] New profiltering groups such as Family Friendly Libraries weighed in with material pressuring libraries to install Cyber Patrol, X-Stop, or Bess (a stand-alone program featuring an adorable golden retriever as its icon) or risk poisoning "young people's minds" with pornography. Enough is Enough was equally unsubtle about countering ALA policy and pushing libraries to adopt filtering.[11] Another Web site promoting the conference, kidsonline.org, advertised what journalist and former *Reno I* plaintiff Declan McCullagh described as "a three-day love-fest for censorware applications like PICS and RSACi." McCullagh reported to his "fight censorship" e-mail list in November that Cyber Patrol had blocked the entire Yahoo! Web site, in addition to about 200 gigabytes of files at mit.edu.[12]

The ACLU and EPIC (the Electronic Privacy Information Center) now became more vocal about the problems with rating and filtering. EPIC's director, Marc Rotenberg, wrote in an open letter to "the Internet community" that "the fundamental purpose of a rating system" is "to allow one person to decide what information another person may receive." Although recognizing that "there is indeed some material on the Internet that is genuinely abhorrent," Rotenberg said, "we do not believe you can hide the world from your children. . . . Good parenting is not something found in a software filter."[13] A few weeks later, the ACLU released *Fahrenheit 451.2: Is Cyberspace Burning?* The "ashes of the CDA were barely smoldering," this pamphlet began, "when the White House called a summit meeting to encourage Internet users to self-rate their speech." Cyber-libertarians at this point became "genuinely alarmed" by the "unabashed enthusiasm for technological fixes" that would "make it easier to block or render invisible controversial speech."

> People who disseminate quirky and idiosyncratic speech, create individual home pages, or post to controversial news groups, will be among the first Internet users blocked by filters and made invisible by the search engines. Controversial speech will still exist, but will only be visible to those with the tools and know-how to penetrate the dense smokescreen of industry "self-regulation."[14]

Explaining that keyword-based technology blocked such sites as www.middlesex.gov or www.SuperBowlXXX.com, while human judgment–based blocking tended to eliminate safer-sex or gay rights information, *Fahrenheit 451.2* tried to justify the ACLU's argument in *Reno I* that the software was nevertheless a " 'less restrictive' means of addressing the government's asserted interest" in protecting youth. While user-based blocking does "present troubling free speech concerns," the pamphlet said, it is "far preferable to any statute that imposes criminal penalties on online speech."[15]

Law professor Lawrence Lessig was not so sure. Taking issue with the ACLU, he argued that *Reno I* "set us in a direction that we will later regret," pushing the " 'problem' of kids and porn towards a 'solution' that will (from the perspective of the interest in free speech) be much worse. The 'less restrictive means' touted by free speech activists in *Reno* are, in my view, far more restrictive of free speech interests than a properly crafted CDA would be."[16] That is, Lessig said, blocking software is "opaque" (the lists of banned sites are secret), and it censors too much material. PICS is even worse: " 'The MIT geniuses who thought it up realized it had broader potential than just blocking indecent speech.' . . . Taken together, filtering software and PICS lead to a hard-wired architecture of blocking that is antagonistic to the original free-wheeling and speech-enhancing values of the Internet."[17]

The December 1–3, 1997, Internet Online Summit was indeed the censorware love-fest that Declan McCullagh had predicted. Its meeting rooms, in a large Washington hotel, were littered with promotional materials and displays of blocking software. A press release from Cyber Patrol announced a new "white list of safe Internet chat and message boards." ("Whitelisting" was a polite term for mechanisms that eliminated the Internet from computers by blocking all of it, except for preselected "safe" sites.) The American Digital Network distributed booklets touting its ISP-based (rather than freestanding) Parent's Choice technology that allowed both control and monitoring of children's online activity. Click & Browse Jr., manufactured by NetWave, offered a whitelist of preselected sites that it was offering free to "America's 86,000 public schools." A press release and glossy brochure from Landmark Community Interests announced that "GuardiaNet, the first server-based Internet filtering package," would include Web sites rated by RSACi, and promised to "make your PC like Fort Knox." Web Chaperone claimed to "scan . . . every Web page as it is loaded, instantly rejecting inappropriate pages"; Two Dog Net traded on endearing puppy pictures to promise a whitelist that "excludes literally all objectionable material"; CyberSnoop's colorful handout, also using a canine motif, promised to deliver

Internet access with "a new leash on life"; while SurfWatch announced a new PICS-compatible version of its product. Like the other promotions, SurfWatch's materials used various terms interchangeably to describe the speech it blocked: "objectionable," "controversial," "inappropriate," "dangerous."[18]

Among the mass of literature were several items from Net Shepherd, which now had a new Family Search site that it said would bring "network television content standards to the Internet." Net Shepherd (whose graphics also featured a happy dog) candidly announced that it "chose to focus its filtering technology on a family-friendly search site simply because, as an advertising supported profit center, it offers the greatest potential for immediate sales revenue." Family Search filtered out sites "judged by an independent panel of demographically appropriate internet users to be superfluous and/or objectionable to the average family."[19]

Family Search, as it turned out, filtered most of the Internet. At a press conference on the opening day of the Online Summit, EPIC released a study showing that Family Search blocked 90 to 99 percent of responsive Web sites when "American Red Cross," "Museum of Modern Art," "National Zoo," or "Dr. Seuss" were typed in as the search terms. Family Search eliminated hundreds of thousands of sites relating to charities, cultural institutions, and basic research information.[20] Net Shepherd responded by acknowledging that its "community of people" rating the Internet were being "very conservative," but that the system was designed "as both a screen for inappropriate content and a lens to find more relevant material."[21]

Vice President Al Gore was the administration's star attraction at the Online Summit the following day. His speech mixed formulaic genuflections to the First Amendment with calls for blocking minors' access to "offensive speech" that he analogized to various physical dangers—live electrical outlets in one metaphor; poisons in the medicine chest a moment later.[22] Such analogies were not, of course, original with Gore: the reductionist equation of disfavored ideas with physical risks, and the consequent failure to appreciate the indirect, multifaceted way in which expression is processed by different individuals had long been a mainstay of harm-to-minors rhetoric.

Just as those who had opposed the CDA broke ranks when it came to rating and filtering, those on the political right were not of one mind on the virtues of the Online Summit. While Enough is Enough had a major role (Donna Rice Hughes, speaking at one panel, complained that without filters "a 14-year-old boy with his raging hormones" could access adult entertainment), the Christian Coalition, the Family Research Council, and the

American Family Association "derided the meeting as a 'love-in' " whose primary goal was damage control for the online industry.[23] *The New York Times*, reporting the controversy, noted that most journalistic Web sites had refused to self-rate under RSACi and that in any event the White House's enthusiasm for filtering had not deterred legislators such as Dan Coats from proposing new online censorship laws.[24] Coats's Child Online Protection Act (COPA), a trimmer version of the CDA, was in fact on its way to passage despite announcements at the industry love-in that "self-regulation" was the answer to online porn.

State Laws, Loudoun County, and Reno II

Despite the Supreme Court's ruling in *Reno*, state legislatures were now passing their own Internet censorship laws. New York's, the first, criminalized communications to minors "which, in whole or part, depict actual or simulated nudity, sexual conduct or sadomasochistic abuse," if they are "harmful to minors" within the meaning of the three-part variable-obscenity test. The ACLU brought a constitutional challenge (with the American Library Association as lead plaintiff), and federal judge Loretta Preska invalidated the law on the ground that it violated the Commerce Clause (Article I, section 8 of the Constitution). That is, the law burdened interstate commerce by imposing New York's censorship standards on "conduct that occurs wholly outside New York," and it intruded into a field that was so intrinsically national rather than local that only Congress could regulate it.[25] While New York did not appeal, New Mexico did—unsuccessfully—when its similar law was struck down in 1998. Georgia, Michigan, and Virginia also passed CDA variants; in all three states, the laws were invalidated, but legislators showed no signs of losing interest in Internet censorship laws.[26]

Just a few weeks after the Online Summit, a citizens group called Mainstream Loudoun filed the first legal challenge to Internet filtering in public libraries. The Loudoun County, Virginia, library board had voted to require that all library computers, "to the extent technically feasible," block both "obscene material" and "material deemed Harmful to Juveniles under applicable Virginia statutes and legal precedents."[27] Presumably because of its claims to block only illegal obscenity, the Log-On Data Corporation's X-Stop program was the chosen filtering product. Web sites blocked using X-Stop's "felony search," however, included the American Association of University Women, Glide Memorial Methodist Church, the Heritage Foundation, Zero Population Growth, and the Yale Graduate Biology Program.[28]

Mainstream Loudoun charged that the mandatory filters burdened its members' First Amendment right "to receive otherwise available speech and information via the Internet," and reduced adults "to even less than material suitable for children." Its federal court complaint described X-Stop's "foul word" function, which blocked any reference to "pussy" (as in "The Owl and the Pussycat") or "bastard" (as in a recent National Book Award finalist, Dorothy Allison's *Bastard Out of Carolina*).[29] Two months later, a group of online publishers, including the Renaissance Transgender Association and the Safer Sex Web Page, intervened in the case, with representation from the ACLU.[30]

This was the first lawsuit challenging online library censorship, and it was carefully watched. Loudoun County's lawyers argued that nobody had any right to see or read anything in particular at a public library—the choices had always been made by library staff—so no First Amendment rights were infringed. The plaintiffs' and intervenors' lawyers responded that X-Stop involved not selection but removal of material already included in the Internet's worldwide library—and removal, moreover, by a private company with undisclosed cultural and moral criteria, which kept its protocols and lists confidential. Even in school libraries, as the Supreme Court had ruled sixteen years before, removal decisions are not immune from constitutional scrutiny and, under the First Amendment, cannot be ideologically motivated. As the ACLU pointed out, Loudoun County's argument meant that "no constitutional violation would be stated if, as a matter of policy, a public library decided that only Democrats had valid ideas and therefore only bought books by Democrats; or if the library purged all books by non-Christians because no religion other than Christianity is valid." Attorney Robert Corn-Revere's brief for Mainstream Loudoun noted that X-Stop added 300 new blocked sites to its list every day, and "could be pursuing an avowedly political or discriminatory agenda for deciding which sites to block, and Loudoun County librarians would never know the difference."[31]

Judge Leonie Brinkema eventually agreed. She ruled that the Supreme Court's 1982 school library decision surely applied to public libraries as well, and limited their ability to restrict access to literature and information within their collections. Nor were Loudoun's asserted interests in "minimizing access to illegal pornography and avoidance of a sexually hostile environment" furthered by reducing all Internet users to the "harm to minors" level or delegating censorship decisions to X-Stop. Among the "less burdensome alternatives" were filters installed on some computers just for minors.[32]

Brinkema did not explain how blocking such items as "The Owl and the Pussycat" would advance the interest in protecting youth; but her minors-only approach soon became the preferred option for many libraries.

As libraries continued to be beset by demands for Internet filtering,[33] frustrations and anomalies multiplied. At one library using filters, patrons received sex-toy Web sites in response to a search request for "toys," but were confronted with screens flashing yellow Cyber Patrol police badges when attempting to research the artists Georgia O'Keeffe and Vincent van Gogh. Federal judges discovered they could no longer access their travel agent online because filtering software blocked the agent's promise of "vacations to *exotic* locales." The American Family Association felt the sting of Internet filters when Cyber Patrol blocked its Web site on grounds of intolerance toward homosexuals. And the Censorware Project reported in 1999 that SmartFilter, used by Utah in all of its public schools and some of its libraries, blocked more than 500,000 sites, among them the Declaration of Independence, the Koran, Shakespeare's plays, and *The Adventures of Sherlock Holmes.*[34]

In Congress, meanwhile, the American Library Association testified against Senator McCain's bill mandating that school and library computers filter out "inappropriate" content as a condition of federal aid. It argued that the overzealousness of filtering deprives both children and adults of information "on subjects ranging from AIDS and breast cancer to religion and politics."[35] Al Gore argued in rebuttal that the McCain bill's vague standard of "inappropriateness" was actually an advantage, in that it would "empower schools to make decisions based on local values."[36] (McCain was to substitute "harmful to minors" for "inappropriate" in his 1999 version of the bill, but he left it up to local school and library districts to decide what the term meant. In late 2000, House and Senate leaders agreed on the filtering mandate, and President Clinton signed the "Children's Internet Protection Act" into law.[37])

Even without a federal mandate, many public schools were signing up for filtering. In November 1998, the entire Tennessee school system adopted Bess, the filter featuring the cute golden retriever, which had thirty-four separate blocking categories, including tobacco, games, medical, alcohol, chat, gambling, "recreation/entertainment," "tasteless/gross," sports, stocks, and swimsuits.[38] A year later, parents and children complained that the New York City schools' computer software blocked "categories like news and sex education, including those of major news outlets, policy groups and scientific and medical organizations"; students were unable to research breast cancer, anorexia, child labor, or AIDS, or to read parts of Steinbeck's *The Grapes of Wrath.* Highlighting the by now recognized "digital divide" that disadvantages lower-income youth in gaining computer skills, *The New York Times* noted that some "prestigious schools" were able to circumvent the filters by accessing university Internet servers.[39]

Filtering euphoria did not, as some of its boosters hoped, forestall more coercive approaches to online speech. In 1998, Congress passed Senator Coats's Child Online Protection Act (COPA), which barred Web sites engaged in commercial activity from expression that violated the *Ginsberg v. New York* variable-obscenity standard. Chris Hansen and Ann Beeson again represented a group of online speakers in challenging the law (the case would be known as *Reno II*); plaintiffs included Androgyny Books, OB/GYN.net, Condomania, Artnet, RiotGrrl, and Powell's Bookstore, a bibliophile's paradise in Portland, Oregon.[40] Although variable obscenity was obviously a tougher standard to challenge than indecency, the ACLU's arguments were basically the same as in *Reno I*: because of the economics and technology of the Internet, COPA had the unconstitutional effect of reducing adults to reading or publishing only what was fit for children; and children, moreover, anywhere from zero to 17 years of age.

Judge Lowell Reed, Jr., invalidated COPA in a February 1999 decision reflecting the same sort of ambivalence that had characterized the Supreme Court's decision in *Reno I.* On the one hand, he suggested, "perhaps we do the minors of this country harm if First Amendment protections, which they will with age inherit fully, are chipped away in the name of their protection." But on the other, he expressed "personal regret" at "delay[ing] once again the careful protection of our children."[41] On appeal, the Clinton Justice Department argued simultaneously that COPA should be narrowly interpreted to bar only material that would lack serious value for older minors, and that the law was necessary to socialize young ones lest pornography "distort their views of sexuality." Voluntary filtering was not an adequate substitute, the government said: whether "because of inertia or distraction" or "because of the technical complexity or cost of blocking software," parents may fail to use it, "thereby leaving their children (and other children that may use their computers) completely unprotected."[42]

There was no recognition here that parents are not all of one view on matters of sexuality and child rearing. Those who eschew Internet filters are not necessarily inert; they may simply disagree with the government's approach to socializing their children.

The Court of Appeals, in any event, agreed that COPA violated the First

Amendment. In a striking decision that put into question the very viability of the legal test for obscenity, the court said that applying "contemporary community standards" in cyberspace would unconstitutionally force Internet speakers to comply with the most conservative communities' notions of what was corrupting or offensive.[43]

Heavy Breathing: The "Harry Met Sally" Case

The same Communications Decency Act whose Internet provisions were struck down in *Reno I* also had a section addressing the presumed harm to minors from "signal bleed"—occasionally images, but mostly sounds, from sex-oriented cable channels that were available only to paying subscribers but that, on some systems, were incompletely scrambled. As a federal court later described it, Congress had received complaints of "partially scrambled images of a nude woman caressing herself" and of "the sounds of what appear to be repeated sexual encounters accompanied by assorted orgiastic moans and groans."[44] Hence the nickname of the law, "Harry Met Sally," in honor of actress Meg Ryan's memorable cries of simulated sexual delight before an astonished delicatessen crowd in the popular film *When Harry Met Sally . . .*

The "Harry Met Sally" law mandated that any "sexually explicit" or "indecent" material on any TV channel "primarily dedicated to sexually oriented programming," if not thoroughly blocked to nonsubscribers (in some systems a prohibitively expensive solution), must be time-channeled to late-night hours.[45] For the Playboy Channel, its imitators, and their subscribers, this was a serious shrinking of available tube-gazing time for adults. Two weeks after President Clinton signed the CDA, Playboy Enterprises and Graff Pay-Per-View (owner of the Adam & Eve and Spice channels) filed a legal challenge. As in the 1994 case of the "heinous crimes" trading cards, "Harry Met Sally" became important because the judges did not rely solely on judicial notions of moral propriety, but actually sought evidence on the harm-to-minors issue.

At the preliminary injunction proceedings, the government introduced psychologist Diana Elliott as an expert witness. She had conducted a study—not peer-reviewed or published—at a Los Angeles child abuse crisis center. The results, she said, indicated that " 'soft' pornography . . . can have a potentially negative effect on children." Those who had seen pornography, according to Elliott, were more likely than others to engage in "sexually reactive" behavior, such as "orally copulating with another child, inserting an object into the anus or vagina of self or same-aged child, simulating sexual intercourse, and excessive masturbation with an object."[46] This seemed like powerful evidence; but these children had all been victims of physical abuse, and the three judges assigned to the case doubted that Elliott's methods shed much light on the question of harm from pornography: "Her results strike us as anecdotal and possibly misleading."[47]

The court nevertheless denied Playboy's preliminary injunction request, citing the 1986 Meese Commission's assertion that pornography causes moral harm to minors, and Supreme Court decisions voicing similar views. But it suggested that if Playboy and Graff planned to pursue the case, they should "provide the court with additional evidence demonstrating the effects of sexually explicit materials on children."[48] Playboy accordingly presented two experts at the trial in March 1998: Richard Green, a psychiatrist specializing in psychosexual development and founding president of the International Academy of Sex Research, and William Simon, a sociologist at the University of Houston. The government presented Elissa Benedek, a child psychiatrist with a practice in Buffalo, New York.

Dr. Green testified that none of the available research—including comparisons of the amount of erotica available in different countries, studies of sex offenders, lab experiments on pornography and violence, and clinical experience worldwide—supported the notion that exposure to sexual explicitness is psychologically harmful to youth. In twenty-five years of clinical practice, much of it with children and adolescents, he had not encountered psychological problems stemming from pornography. "It's reductionist and simplistic," Green said, "to expect that a single variable is going to somehow, in a direct line, lead to some kind of adverse outcome. That's not the way human development evolves."[49]

The three-judge court made little mention of Green's testimony, though, focusing instead on a statement the government had located in a book by Green twenty-four years before that "the visual experiencing of adult sexuality by young children" is "potentially confusing and hazardous."[50] But the court was still faced with what it candidly described as "a paucity" of positive evidence of harm. The Justice Department lawyers had presented "no clinical evidence linking child viewing of pornography to psychological harms," but instead had argued by analogy to television violence studies, a small selection of which they had supplied to Dr. Benedek, who had no previous familiarity with this literature but nevertheless speculated that sexually explicit signal bleed, like violent TV, could lead to "modeling behavior." The judges doubted the analogy was viable. They were equally skeptical of Benedek's opinion that pornography could have a "dysphoric" effect on youngsters. "Dysphoria" simply means "unpleasant feelings," which by Benedek's admission would be "transient," with no long-term effects "in the vast majority of cases."[51] (Some wags commented that it was not dysphoria but euphoria that Congress was trying to prevent with its signal bleed law. As the young winner of a Playboy Foundation First Amendment Award said in 1999, "I haven't read the magazine, but I have watched the Playboy Channel through the squiggly lines."[52])

Although the three judges' opinion in *Playboy v. U.S.* did not mention it, William Simon's testimony had also been a rejoinder to Benedek. Simon wrote in a pretrial statement: "Dr. Benedek's assumptions that exposure to sexually explicit representations is inherently toxic to normal childhood and adolescent development rests on her commitment to traditional Freudian views" regarding necessary repression of sexuality during the "latency" period of childhood, views that "few, including most working within a psychoanalytic tradition, currently hold. Questionable when initially formulated almost a century ago," Simon said, Freudian ideas about sexual trauma

> must command far less credibility in [a] contemporary setting where what might be termed a public erotic landscape appears in abundance, constituting an attended and unattended backdrop to the everyday lives of children, adolescents, and adults.[53]

Beyond the disputes over Freud, of course, there was a deeper trouble with Benedek's testimony. Like experts in earlier eras, she confused psychological harm with departures from social convention. As Stephen Jay Gould has written, efforts to use science to "validate a social preference" can distort both science and public policy, and the risk of distortion is greatest when topics are "invested with enormous social importance but blessed with very little reliable information."[54]

The "Harry Met Sally" court ultimately decided that despite the weakness of the government's case, it had established a compelling need to shield minors from signal bleed. Only a minimal amount of evidence was necessary, the judges said, because Supreme Court decisions from *Ginsberg* to the *Denver Area* cable case had assumed that minors are harmed by sexually explicit speech without requiring empirical evidence to prove the point. Having thus invited psychological testimony, the *Playboy* court ignored it, and ended up back where it had started, with generalizations about moral harm.

Playboy nevertheless won its case in the district court, because the alternative of lockboxes was less of a burden on the First Amendment than the signal bleed law. The relatively small demand for lockboxes (about 0.5 percent) did not demonstrate that the alternative was ineffective, but perhaps only that parents were unaware of lockbox availability, or else did not consider signal bleed a serious problem. In its appeal to the Supreme Court, the Justice Department accordingly argued, as it had in *Reno II*, for governmental power to censor youth in the face of parental "inertia, indifference, or distraction." It reiterated that harm to minors did not require empirical proof; concerns about youthful "exposure to such material are based on commonly held moral views about the upbringing of children."[55]

The usual amicus curiae briefs were filed in *Playboy*—by Morality in Media, the National Law Center for Children and Families, and the Family Research Council on the government's side; and by various media trade and First Amendment groups on Playboy's. An addition to the mix was a brief organized by the National Coalition Against Censorship from sixteen sexuality scholars and therapists urging the Court to affirm the unconstitutionality of the law on the ground that no compelling need to shield minors from signal bleed had ever been established, and that in the absence of psychological harm, sexual conventions and taboos were not sufficient justification for censorship.[56] Another brief, by law professor Laurence Winer on behalf of the Washington, DC–based Media Institute, argued that in this "politically volatile" area of law, simply intoning a governmental interest in "the 'physical and psychological well-being of children' " was meaningless. The state has no general power "to standardize its children," Winer argued; nor has the Supreme Court ever "required a foolproof method of erecting a perfect, hermetic seal" over them.[57]

At the Supreme Court argument in *Playboy*, Assistant Solicitor General James Feldman hammered on the basic theme: "a social interest in the upbringing of children" entitles government to censor when parents don't. Only Justice Ruth Bader Ginsburg questioned this "idea that the government is a sort of superparent." Nobody suggested that watching squiggly lines or listening to the sounds of sex might be a relatively harmless preteen rite of passage or an activity with which youngsters might soon become bored.[58] But in a decision six months later that surprised some Court watchers, a 5–4 majority struck down the "Harry Met Sally" law. Justice Anthony Kennedy's opinion explained that content-based burdens on speech, including indecent speech on cable television, must be strictly scrutinized, and even though the "objective of shielding children" was legitimate, there was scant evidence of an actual problem with signal bleed, and the government's interest in substituting its own judgment for that of "informed and empowered parents" who chose not to block the moans and squiggly lines was not "sufficiently compelling to justify this widespread restriction on speech." The proper course was to publicize the lockbox alternative and let parents decide. Kennedy did not "discount the possibility that a graphic image could have a negative effect on a child," but the government simply hadn't made its case that signal bleed was a pervasive problem.[59] If this was not a rejection of the harm-to-minors rationale, at least it reflected healthy skepticism about how dire the consequences of "indecency" really were.

V-Chips, and Ratings Revisited

In addition to banning Internet indecency and signal bleed, the sprawling 1996 CDA also, for the first time in U.S. history, mandated a rating and blocking system for television. This section of the law required that all TV sets with screens 13 inches or larger, manufactured or distributed in the United States after February 1998, contain "a feature designed to enable viewers to block display of all programs with a common rating"—that is, to have a v-chip. If the TV industry did not, within a year, "voluntarily" develop an "acceptable" rating system to go along with the chip, the FCC would "prescribe" one. Congress specified "sexual, violent, or other indecent material" as the categories to be rated.[60]

The reason for this convoluted procedure was presumably Congress's fear that simply mandating ratings would violate the First Amendment. Indeed, the House Conference Report section on the v-chip provision claimed that "prescribe" did not mean the FCC could "require the adoption of the recommended rating system."[61] But the coercive impact and intent were so plain that, as more than one skeptic observed, the law gave new meaning to the word "voluntary." Quipped attorney Floyd Abrams: "the v-chip is First Amendment–friendly like Henry VIII was wife-friendly."[62]

The v-chip mandate was nevertheless widely touted as a benign species of "parental empowerment" that would simply enable parents to block—in the words of the statute—"programming that they have determined is inappropriate for their children." But parents, of course, would not be "determining" anything about actual programs by activating the chip. The people, or committees, that did the labeling would be the ones to make these subjective judgments about appropriateness, and then only in the categories

Congress had designated: "sexual, violent, or otherwise indecent material." Parents concerned about racism, drugs, drunk driving, religious cults, or homophobia would receive no help from the v-chip law. Nor would parents who sought to make distinctions about what violent or sexual content their children could see: *South Park*, for example, but not Bugs Bunny, or the *Odyssey* but not *Miami Vice*.

The TV industry had lobbied hard against the v-chip law, but once it was in place, the National Association of Broadcasters (NAB), the Motion Picture Association of America (MPAA), and the National Cable Television Association (NCTA) quickly established a committee to design a classification system, with movie ratings czar Jack Valenti in command. In January 1997, Valenti's group submitted its labeling plan to the FCC for approval. The plan had six age-based categories, from TV-Y ("appropriate for all children") to TV-M ("may contain mature themes, profane language, graphic violence and explicit sexual content").[63] The FCC requested comments from the public; the Senate held hearings; and protecting kids from television was once again a front-page story.

John McCain, who chaired the hearings, was "almost literally hoppin' mad," as the session "turned into the proverbial feeding frenzy with senators, and some visiting members of the House, charging forward bravely to go on the record against sex and violence on TV—and to say the new rating system stinks."[64] Advocacy groups objected that the age-based labels did not clearly indicate what content—whether sex, violence, "strong language," or all three—had triggered a particular classification. Representative Tom Coburn denounced NBC's recent broadcast of Steven Spielberg's *Schindler's List*, the first program to receive a TV-M rating: "I cringe," Coburn said, "when I realize that there were children all across the nation watching this program. They were exposed to the violence of multiple gunshot head wounds, vile language, full frontal nudity and irresponsible sexual activity." Displaying either his unawareness of the artistic and historical justifications for violence and nudity in Spielberg's film or his view that children should not learn about the Holocaust, Coburn said the broadcast was proof the new ratings would "only encourage" more sex and violence.[65] Congress generated six new TV bills in the weeks after the Senate hearing—five of them designed to coerce or persuade the industry to suppress disapproved content; and one, authored by then-Representative Charles Schumer, commending NBC for broadcasting *Schindler's List*.

Objections to the absence of content labels in the industry's rating plan poured into the FCC during its February–April 1997 "notice and comment" period. Some were from professional groups like the American Psychological Association (APA), long a believer in the adverse effects of TV violence; others were form letters generated by Morality in Media urging the agency "to take action to rid the TV screen of the violence, sex, anti-Christian innuendoes, profanity and homosexual programs."[66]

The APA argued that content labels were necessary so that parents "can make educated decisions about television programming," because studies showed that viewers become desensitized, or fearful, or learn "specific forms of aggression," from "televised violence." But the APA acknowledged that not all "televised violence" has any of these effects. Violence perpetrated by a hero, for example, or "not portrayed as having long-term consequences for the victim or perpetrator" can lead to imitative behavior, fear, or desensitization; but violence "followed by negative consequences" can teach positive values. That is (so the APA said), TV violence "per se is not the problem; rather, it's the manner in which most violence on television is shown that should concern us."[67]

But if depictions of violence perpetrated by a hero were harmful, presumably material ranging from war movies to cowboy yarns should not be shown. More important, most works of dramatic art—and certainly most news and documentary programs—do not convey such unambiguous messages about the worlds they depict. There seemed little room in the APA's philosophy for inherent ambiguity, irony, complex plot lines, or cathartic entertainment.

In essence, the nation's leading psychological organization was advocating a system in which classifiers would attempt to label each daily TV offering based on whether the sexual or violent content overall seemed to carry a wholesome social message. But as NYU professor Burt Neuborne told the Senate committee, any effort to decide "when speech depicting violence crosses the line from an acceptable exercise in artistic creation, as in *Hamlet*, or *Oedipus Rex*, or *Antigone*, or *The Crucible*, to a forbidden depiction of 'gratuitous' or 'excessive' violence must involve purely subjective notions of taste and aesthetic judgment."[68]

It was clear by this point, however, that the industry would have to add content labels to its proposed rating scheme, and in July 1997, after negotiations with the APA and other groups, Valenti *et al.* announced a revised plan, with a V label for violence, S for sex, L for "coarse language," and D for "suggestive dialogue," on top of the six original age categories. Thus, "crude indecent language" would require a TV-MA, and be labeled TV-MA-L; but "strong, coarse language" only a TV-14-L. TV-PG-S would denote "some sexual situations" and "some suggestive dialogue," while TV-14-V would mean "intense violence" and TV-MA-V would mean "graphic violence." News and sports would be exempt from labeling (but not magazine-style reporting or documentaries).[69]

The FCC now approved the industry's "voluntary" plan. Two networks—NBC and BET (Black Entertainment Television)—rejected the content-based add-ons. Senator McCain, incensed at this rebellion, threatened that he would urge the FCC "to examine in a full evidentiary hearing the renewal application of any television station not implementing the revised TV ratings system"; he also asked each of four new FCC commissioner candidates "to agree to consider a station's use or nonuse of the revised ratings-code as a factor in deciding whether to renew a station's license."[70]

Under the v-chip regime, parents who use the chip will do so on the basis of Congress's determination that it is sex, "indecency," and violence that must be restrained, and the industry's interpretation of "indecent" to mean "coarse" language (L) or "suggestive dialogue" (D). *Schindler's List*, the target of Congressman Coburn, would presumably retain its TV-M classification, with V, S, L, and D added on. And countless other works of film or TV art, from *Bonnie and Clyde* or *Psycho* to documentaries on the civil rights movement, would receive violence ratings.

A 1993 survey of TV violence by Senator Byron Dorgan's office illustrated the point. Prime-time shows found to contain the most violent acts included *The Miracle Worker, Civil War Journal, Star Trek: Deep Space 9, Our Century: Combat at Sea,* and Alfred Hitchcock's *North by Northwest*.[71]

TV ratings, like movie ratings, will push programming in two oddly contrary directions. On the one hand, ratings have a "forbidden fruit" effect. The quest for adventuresome (especially teenage) audiences will cause some producers to *add* sexual or violent content, for what self-respecting adolescent wants to watch a TV-Y-rated show?[72] On the other hand, advertisers will be reluctant to support programs with TV-M, V, S, L, or D labels. Less advertising means less revenue, which in turn means less likelihood that the show will survive—unless, of course, its content is changed. Just as the film director Louis Malle was forced in the mid-1990s to eliminate artistically important scenes from his film *Damage* because of the producers' insistence on obtaining nothing more pejorative than an R classification from the MPAA ratings board,[73] so TV writers will be forced to cut their scripts to achieve desired labels. Those who hope for improved television quality are unlikely to find it in a system that reduces popular art to alphabet symbols.

Meanwhile, it turned out that parents were not so fearful of controversial TV as their legislators had assumed. When the first v-chip circuitry arrived on the market in 1999, the consumer response was underwhelming. "I don't know how the v-chip works," one father of a 6-year-old said, "but I don't really trust that someone else is going to have better judgment than we will." A TV manufacturer remarked: "It's not something that America was clamoring for. It's something that Congress was clamoring for."[74]

But if parents were not clamoring for the v-chip, why did Congress care so much, and why were there so few voices in protest? Indeed, why have sex and violence in the media been such hot political issues at least since the 1954 comic book hearings, if not the Comstockery of a century before? These are complex questions, but in a culture fraught with anxiety over the dangers and temptations that youngsters face, blaming the media had certainly become a habit.

Violence, Curse Words, and Kids at Century's End

In early 1999, two Colorado teenagers styling themselves the "Trench Coat Mafia" gunned down thirteen of their classmates at Columbine High School and then killed themselves. Eric Harris and Dylan Klebold did not model their crime on any particular book or film scenario, but they were reportedly devotees of violent video games, heavy metal music, and hate-oriented Internet sites. They also had assembled an armory of deadly firearms, left a trail of clear warning signs and earlier troubled behavior, and been victims of a high school pecking order where "nerds" and "geeks" are mercilessly hounded by "jocks" and "preps."[75]

Whatever combination of chemical, social, and psychological pressures produced these two sociopathic teenagers, Harris and Klebold became an occasion for intense and unprecedented media bashing. In short order, President Clinton summoned entertainment industry executives to a meeting "to discuss youth violence"; Representative Henry Hyde proposed a "Children's Defense Act of 1999" banning the sale, loan, or exhibition to minors of "sexually explicit or violent material"; and Senator Ernest Hollings introduced a bill banning distribution to the public of "any violent video programming during hours when children are reasonably likely to comprise a substantial portion of the audience."[76]

At Senate hearings a few days after the killings, MIT professor Henry Jenkins tried to explain that neither rock songs nor video games nor "the culture" in general could be blamed for the depredations of Klebold and Harris. Instead, Jenkins said, disaffected young people move "nomadically across the media landscape, cobbling together a personal mythology of symbols and stories taken from many different places," then invest these symbols with their own "personal and subcultural meanings." Jenkins told the senators that the "vocabulary of 'media effects' " in psychology, which for years dominated hearings, studies, and sound bites, had now been "challenged by numerous American and international scholars as an inadequate and simplistic representation of media consumption and popular culture."[77] That is, all of us consume and process art and entertainment, but what use we make of it depends on context, predisposition, and personality.

Jenkins did not get very far in advancing this more-subtle-than-a-sound-bite view of how the media affects human behavior. As he later recounted, he was the only scholar appearing at the hastily convened hearings who questioned the simplistic but popular idea that youngsters directly adopt and imitate the attitudes and behavior they see in media entertainment. When he arrived,

> [t]he Senate chamber was decorated with massive posters of video game ads for some of the most violent games on the market. Many of the ad slogans are hyperbolic—and self-parodying—but that nuance was lost on the Senators who read them all deadly seriously and with absolute literalness. Most of the others testifying were professional witnesses who had done this kind of thing many times before. They had their staff. They had their props. They had professionally edited videos. They had each other for moral support. I had my wife and son in the back of the room. They are passing out press releases, setting up interviews, being tracked down by the major media and no one is talking to me.[78]

The impulse to censor words and images in the interest of youth is centuries old, but as Professor Jenkins discovered, it had attained a circus-like frenzy by the last year of the 20th century. It mattered little that violent juvenile crime in the United States had actually declined 30 percent since 1994 or that, as columnist Frank Rich wrote, "even if Washington could 'clean up' Hollywood without violating the First Amendment, there's scant evidence to suggest that doing so would prevent a single Columbine."[79] Intellectual discourse on the subject had become so impoverished that Jean Bethke Elshtain, a noted scholar, referred in one article to "post–Columbine

High School America" as if that in itself were definitive rebuttal to an argument for minors' First Amendment rights.[80]

Columbine may have suspended reasoned response to the complex relation between culture and behavior, but there were, as always, countervailing signs of iconoclasm. In 1999, film critics protested the MPAA's demand that Stanley Kubrick mask a few fleeting moments of explicit sex during a lugubrious orgy scene in his last film, *Eyes Wide Shut*, in order to obtain an R rating. (Kubrick acquiesced.) "How is it possible," the critics asked, "that a serious movie about human sexuality, made by one of the world's master filmmakers, cannot be seen by American adults in its intended form, when those same adults can watch comparable fare any night on cable television?"[81] In another contretemps the same year—involving Trey Parker's *South Park: Bigger, Longer & Uncut*, a brilliant parody of child-protection politics—the MPAA gave the movie an R rating although an NC-17 was initially in the offing. *South Park* is an allegory in which the animated child characters revel in media-inspired crude language and their affronted parents, to combat the threat, implant a "v-chip" in one child that gives him a shock every time he speaks a naughty word. One critic praised the film's "cheerfully smutty way" of clearing the air of "pompous, hypocritical rhetoric about protecting children from basic if unpleasant realities."

> Beneath the hilarity, the movie is a scathing social parable in which desperate, paranoid grown-ups who long for an impossibly sanitized environment go collectively crazy to the point that they're willing to bring on World War III. And what are they so afraid of? Just some dumb off-color humor about bodily functions.[82]

But if Americans cannot agree whether "dumb off-color humor about bodily functions" is really harmful to kids, the cultural differences in harm-to-minors assumptions outside the United States are even more striking. Comparing U.S. harm-to-minors ideology with that in other countries suggests how widely perceptions differ. The standards are relative, culturally driven, and often employed rhetorically for political ends that may have little to do with any objective showing of harm to youth.

Nine

CULTURAL DIFFERENCES

Minors in the Global Culture

In 1998, the Indian fundamentalist group Shiv Sena organized violent protests against the film *Fire,* the tale of a love affair between two women trapped in oppressive marriages. The film's lesbian theme, ridicule of religious dogma, and portrayal of males as simultaneously tyrannical and ridiculous all contributed to the controversy. By December, Shiv Sena had succeeded in shutting down the film in Bombay, New Delhi, and other major cities, and the government's Censor Board had agreed to reconsider its earlier certificate of approval. "Is it fair to show such things which are not part of Indian culture?" a Shiv Sena leader was quoted as asking. "It can corrupt tender minds."[1]

In India, "corruption of tender minds" was apparently useful rhetoric to advance Shiv Sena's religious and political ends. But if this particular variation on the harm-to-minors theme was based on fundamentalist Hinduism, India also has a British-style obscenity law, a remnant of colonialism, that turns on the sexual anxieties underlying *Regina v. Hicklin.*[2] In 1911, the law was applied to prosecute the publisher of a poetic retelling of a story from the Uriya Haribans, about the erotic dalliances of the gods Radha and Krishna. The prosecutor argued that the work was obscene, that it might "produce impure thoughts," especially among schoolboys, and—foreshadowing England's *Lady Chatterley* trial forty-nine years later—that the offense was aggravated by the cheapness of the publication's price.

In keeping with Indian cultural tradition, however, the obscenity law exempted ancient temple sculptures, paintings, engravings, or other religious images.[3] Although the exemption did not cover the written word, its logic provided justification for an eventual acquittal of the Haribans publisher, on the ground that the poem was "an allegorical representation" of the union of "the supreme with the human soul," and was therefore not likely to deprave and corrupt schoolchildren.[4]

The defendants in a 1952 Indian case were not so fortunate. The court found that their publication of sexually graphic scenes from the walls of ancient Hindu temples, with accompanying text, was deliberately salacious, likely to "arouse sexual passion" among the impressionable and to "contaminate and tend to upset the balance of an ordinary adolescent mind." The judges added: "morbid thoughts about sexual passions are intentionally aroused in the minds of those into whose hands this magazine may and are intended to fall and who are open to such immoral influences."[5]

A 1971 film censorship case brought Indian jurisprudence a step closer to the beliefs that would animate Shiv Sena 27 years later. The Central Board of Film Censors had demanded cuts of nonexplicit prostitution scenes in a documentary film that contrasted luxury and poverty in four Indian cities; the filmmaker sued to challenge the entire regime of prior review and classification. The Indian Supreme Court rejected the challenge, explaining that motion pictures have the capacity to "stir up emotions more deeply than any other product of art," particularly among children and adolescents because "their immaturity makes them more willingly suspend their disbelief." The government's demand for cuts in exchange for a U rating was reasonable given that "censorship is prevalent all the world over in some form or other." Much like the MPAA's (Motion Picture Association of America's) Production Code, abandoned in the United States only a few years before, the Indian board's guidelines banned material that showed sympathy with "crime, wrongdoing, evil or sin," or that would "lower the moral standards of those who see it."[6]

In contrast to the cultural imperatives of postcolonial India or Victorian Britain, Japan has not traditionally associated sex with shame, evil, embarrassment, or sin. Critic Ian Buruma traces sexual themes in Japanese art to a long social tradition: pornographic drawings from at least the 10th century, produced by some of the country's most celebrated artists, were associated with satire and rebellion.[7] Another expert relates the Japanese taste for "fantasy of all kinds" to "the old Confucian puritanism." *Manga*, the ubiquitous contemporary "porno-comics" that mix complex adventure stories with nudity and sex, are "a prevalent addiction because they are an outlet for people whose social codes are rigid and confining."[8]

In 1998, researchers Milton Diamond and Ayako Uchiyama conducted a study of sex crime rates, censorship, and pornography in Japan. They found that although local "Juvenile Protection Ordinances" provided for the identification of items "considered harmful for juveniles," in reality these materials, mostly videos, "remained readily available to persons of any age." A 1993 survey found that about 50 percent of male and 20 percent of female middle and upper high school students regularly read the "porno-comics."[9] Diamond thought this curious contradiction between law and social reality might reflect the culture's "live and let live" attitude, which depends on social pressures "to keep things in line."[10]

Japan's widely available pornography is an often-cited rebuttal to those attempting to blame sexual entertainment for sex crimes. From 1972 to 1995, as Diamond and Uchiyama reported, the incidence of rape and other sexual assault in Japan decreased substantially while pornography's availability notably increased; and rapes committed by juveniles dropped even further, from 33 percent of the total in 1972 to 18 percent in 1995. These statistics were similar to, but "even more striking than, those reported with the rise of sexually explicit materials in Denmark, Sweden, and West Germany."[11] The most common explanation was cultural. As one journalist wrote, Japanese children are heavily socialized in the values of responsibility, obedience, and respect for elders, a process that "is credited, at least in part, with producing the low rates of juvenile crime . . . , teenage pregnancy and drug abuse."[12]

But Diamond and Uchiyama also noted the influence of sex education, standard in Japan's K-12 curriculum since the 1970s. A typical sex ed film, according to one American who taught at a Japanese high school in 1999–2000, was explicit about showing female and male genitalia, the latter in both relaxed and upright positions, and equally straightforward in defining masturbation as "self-pleasure."[13]

Other non-Western societies are even more open about sexual information and youth. West African fairy tales feature "Mr. Penis" and "Mrs. Vulva." In Bali, the child "is made conscious of its sex very early. People pat the little girl's vulva, repeating an adjective for feminine beauty, and applaud the little boy's phallus with the word for 'handsome male.' "[14]

Even within Europe, there are major differences in attitude toward minors and censorship. In 1981, the canton of Fribourg in Switzerland confiscated three sexually explicit paintings by Josef Müller from an art exhibit after a man complained that his young daughter had "reacted violently" to the works. The show would not have raised eyebrows elsewhere in Europe, and indeed, had been mounted without incident in other parts of Switzerland. The artist and several critics, teachers, and other admirers sued, and the case eventually made its way to the European Court of Human Rights, which in 1988 reaffirmed its *Handyside* decision of twelve years before (allowing Britain its "margin of appreciation" to suppress *The Little Red School Book*) and proclaimed that Switzerland had not violated Article 10 of the European Convention on Human Rights (the Convention's free-speech provision) because Fribourg's suppression of the paintings was designed to protect the morals of youth and therefore was "necessary in a democratic society." The international tribunal admitted, however, that "as at the time of the *Handyside* judgment," it is not possible to discern any "uniform European conception of morals."[15]

As in *Handyside*, so in *Müller*, the European Court did not consider the possible right of young people to read or view controversial works. But leaders in the emerging field of international minors' rights were beginning to argue that such a notion should have been considered. By the end of the primary grades, as two legal scholars wrote, "children are well-settled into the political culture in which they are growing up and they have considerable concern with maintenance of those interests that adults associate with human dignity."[16] This minors' rights philosophy found expression the year after *Müller* in the United Nations Convention on the Rights of the Child.

The 1989 UN Convention was a product of political maneuvering. Poland originally proposed it as an Eastern Bloc idea, with emphasis on economic, social, and cultural rights; the United States countered by suggesting additional protections for free expression, access to information, religion, and privacy. Islamic nations objected to the religious freedom clause as inconsistent with the Koran, while East Germany wanted a proviso that expression "could be restricted in the interest of the 'spiritual and moral well-being of the child.' " Eventually, the Convention was adopted with its individual rights provisions intact, although acknowledging the countervailing interests of parents, "public morality," and the state.[17]

Article 17 of the Convention nicely illustrates the tension between minors' rights and ideas about protection. It first recognizes the right to free speech and intellectual inquiry by providing that national governments "shall ensure that the child has access to information and material from a diversity of national and international sources." But it then charges nations with the duty of establishing "appropriate guidelines for the protection of the child from information and material injurious to his or her well-being." Article 17 does not specify what literature might be "injurious," nor does it define "appropriate." The UN Committee on the Rights of the Child, which reviews member nations' reports on children's rights, has paid more attention to this "appropriate guidelines" provision of Article 17 than to youngsters' rights to be free of government censorship.[18]

France's first submission to the Committee, for example, proudly described its law banning material in any publications "intended for young people" that show "in a favourable light banditry, mendacity, theft, laziness, cowardice, hatred, debauchery, or any acts qualified as offences or calculated to demoralize children or young people." As Article 19, the international free-expression group, commented, the provision was "so broad as to potentially preclude almost any piece of fiction or even non-fiction."[19] Indonesia's submission was even more flatly censorial: it boasted that children "receive appropriate information through various reading materials, radio and television" but that "to protect children against hazardous information which is incompatible with the national philosophy and ideology, the Law on Publications restricts certain reading materials, videos and cassettes." Again, Article 19 observed that such restrictions "have no basis in the Convention" and could be used to censor any ideas "which are considered by the government to be controversial or critical." Nigeria, Malawi, Korea, and the United Kingdom were among the other countries whose laws and policies, according to Article 19, "threaten to undermine the child's right of access to information" through broad censorship justified under the rubric of child protection.[20]

The UN Committee did voice some objection to school censorship. It criticized Hong Kong for "certain attitudes" about minors' social roles that "may be delaying the full acceptance" of the Convention's free-expression principles.[21] It made negative comments about Ghana, Denmark, Panama, Togo, and Cyprus, "suggesting that further steps were needed to protect children's freedom of expression within the school system."[22]

A columnist made a similar point shortly after Britain, in 1998, finally incorporated the European Convention on Human Rights into its domestic law. She opined that a 15-year-old girl who had been expelled after criticizing her school in a local newspaper might now have a claim for violation of her free-expression rights.[23]

Indeed, not only the European Convention but other international agreements made it difficult for the separate nations of Europe to remain insular in their censorship regimes. As far back as 1986, for example, the European Court of Justice in Luxembourg ruled that Britain, as a member of the European Community, or EC (later to become the European Union, or EU), was bound by treaty provisions that barred discriminatory treatment of goods imported from other member countries and thus could not ban the import of German rubber "love dolls" when domestic counterparts were available in English shops.[24] As a result of the love doll case, UK Customs had to halt its ongoing Operation Tiger, a campaign against a London bookshop called Gay's the Word. During the eighteen-month campaign, customs officials had impounded works by Oscar Wilde, Gore Vidal, Christopher Isherwood, and Jean Genet.[25] Like the German toys, works by Wilde and his brethren were available domestically, and Britain could not, on grounds of "indecency," discriminate against their imported equivalents.

Hard-core pornography was a different matter, however, and as long as Britain banned it domestically, it could also keep out the imported variety. But even here one could discern the demise of Victorian sexual reticence. The same year that the European Court of Human Rights allowed the government to suppress *The Little Red School Book*, a London jury acquitted a "shoddy little book,"[26] *Inside Linda Lovelace*, of the charge that it depraved and corrupted its likely readers. Pundits opined that the failure of the *Linda Lovelace* prosecution meant that obscenity law "was unlikely to be invoked again against the written word."[27] British prosecutions of pornography continued, however: one court in 1976 rejected the ingenious if circular argument that expert evidence regarding pornography's therapeutic, masturbatory value should have been admitted as relevant to the obscenity law's "public good" defense. As the judges perceived, the characteristics bestowing therapeutic value were "inherent in the self-same quality" that made the works potentially obscene.[28]

Britain provides a fascinating point of comparison with the United States because the two cultures share a tradition of Victorian Comstockery and *Regina v. Hicklin*–style censorship, yet as part of the EU, Britain is distinctly aware that other member nations have radically different ideas about sex, morality, and the upbringing of youth. Particularly in the realms of film, TV, video, and most recently the Internet, struggles in Britain highlight the pervasively political nature of youth censorship, and the difficulty of identifying any objectively based harm from controversial expression.

By 1979, for example, a portion of Britain's legal establishment was ready to recommend the elimination of obscenity laws, as the Lockhart Commission in the United States had done nine years before. A committee appointed by the British Home Secretary and headed by Bernard Williams, provost of King's College, Cambridge, surveyed the sexual entertainment and information then available in Britain; reviewed the relevant psychological and criminological studies; heard from a range of experts; and found no persuasive evidence of harm to minors or adults from pornography.

The Williams Committee reported that research on the possibly harmful effects of sexually explicit literature was necessarily inconclusive because of the different ways in which people define pornography and the difficulty of measuring its effects, given the great range of other influences and stimuli in human life. The Victorian deprave-and-corrupt standard was premised on causal assumptions about deleterious effects, but variations in recent jury verdicts (*Inside Linda Lovelace*, for example) demonstrated that "it is the perception of what is capable of depraving and corrupting that has changed rather than what is actually capable of such an effect." Thus, "harm" was essentially a moral concept; there was little evidence to support the complaints of right-wing groups that pornography wrecks marriages or turns men toward ever more deviant erotic tastes.

As for minors, the Committee canvassed the range of opinion but reached no firm conclusion. It acknowledged that pornographic, like violent, material was "widely seen as particularly dangerous to the young," yet warned that expert opinions differed radically: "this is not a field where much is known." Although children "may be upset or disturbed by watching films," the effects are generally temporary, unless their development "has already been impaired." Even among adolescents, data suggested that "the reaction of the individual appears to relate to his previously established sexual identity rather than influencing the development of that identity."[29]

The Williams Committee ultimately concluded, as the U.S. Meese Commission was to do seven years later, that the basic arguments against minors' as well as adults' exposure to pornography turned on moral ideology. Witnesses feared "cultural pollution, moral deterioration, and the undermining of human compassion, social values and basic institutions." Arguments of this kind "were less concerned with the possibility of specific effects on individual behaviour than with the gradual infecting of society with a disregard for decency" and "a lack of responsibility for others." For the Committee, these fundamentally moral arguments were too broad and unfocused to justify censorship, at least not of written erotica. In any event, it said, Britain's sex censorship law was "a mess," with vague terms like "obscene," "indecent," and "deprave and corrupt" having "outlived their usefulness." Given the lack of demonstrable harm, there should be no restrictions on adults' access to printed material—except for regulations of public display. But the Williams Committee, like the U.S. Lockhart Commission before it, stopped short of urging an end to censorship for youth.[30]

The work of the Williams Committee was noted and praised, but its recommendations were not followed. Political stalemate is neither surprising nor uncommon in this sensitive area, and with the Tories' assumption of power in 1979, the chances for "an end to obscenity" became as remote as in Ronald Reagan's United States. The legal and intellectual morass of Britain's different standards for obscenity and indecency under different laws remained, as did Britain's distinction of having the most repressive approach to sexual expression in Western Europe.

Video Nasties and the Venerable BBFC

The Williams Committee had also been assigned the job of examining Britain's venerable film censorship system, which in 1979 combined "unofficial" ratings and editorial controls by the British Board of Film Censors (BBFC) with local governments' official power to issue, deny, or attach conditions to movie exhibition licenses. The BBFC (later renamed the British Board of Film Classification) had been established by the movie industry in its early days to create a uniform system of vetting that the industry hoped would preempt local authorities' inconsistent and unpredictable licensing decisions. Parliament had blessed the arrangement in 1952 when it directed county councils to ensure that children do not see films designated as "unsuitable" by the "licensing authority or such other body as may be specified in the licence."[31] "Such other body" obviously meant the BBFC, and in time the board's age-based rating categories multiplied—from the original two to seven.

The 1952 film censorship law contained no definition of "unsuitable" for children, and the BBFC over the years prided itself on freewheeling, ad hoc decision making. The board's records from 1939, as documented in scrapbooks at its Soho Square, London, offices, note the rejection of such films as *The Balcony* (1963), *Best of the New York Film Festival* (1975), Pier Paolo Pasolini's *The 120 Days of Sodom* (1963), Andy Warhol's *The Chelsea Girls* (1967), *The Panic in Needle Park* (1971), *Requiem for a Vampire* (1972), *Shock Corridor* (1963), *Snow White and the Seven Perverts* (1973), *Story of O* (1975), *The Wild One* (1954 and 1955), and *The Texas Chainsaw Massacre* (1975).[32]

One safety valve in Britain's film censorship regime is the concept of "exempted exhibitions"—showings by nonprofit ventures, private clubs, or film festivals. These venues do not need BBFC certificates or local authority licenses, thus allowing cinemaphiles, or at least those living in major cultural centers, to see uninhibited films without the indignity of cuts designed to shield youngsters or the "working classes" from corruption.

Until the 1980s, the BBFC could maintain the pretense that it was a voluntary organ of industry self-regulation upon whose judgments licensing authorities simply chose to rely; but anxiety over "video nasties" and Tory dominance in Parliament combined in 1984 to produce a Video Recordings Act, creating for the first time an official national system of prescreening, licensing, and age classification for videos. The Act imposed criminal penalties for any circulation of a videotape without a rating certificate or its distribution to anyone below the age specified in the rating. "Sexual activity," "acts of gross violence," and "human genital organs or urinary or excretory functions" were the areas singled out for restriction. The BBFC was appointed official classifier.[33]

It was under this regime that James Ferman, the BBFC's director for twenty-six years, refused permission for the video of William Friedkin's horror classic *The Exorcist* to be sold in Britain, even though the film was not banned from cinemas. Ferman found *The Exorcist* "deeply unsettling" and felt it endangered teenage girls "who were susceptible to being convinced that evil is a real presence in the world." "We have a responsibility," he said, echoing a theme often heard in Britain. "We can't go the way of America."[34]

Panic over video nasties revived in 1993 when two Liverpool 10-year-olds murdered a toddler, James Bulger, after abducting him from a shopping mall. Publicity surrounding the gruesome crime blamed social phenomena from single mothers to the Pill; and when the horror video *Child's Play 3* was found to have been among those rented by the father of one of the defendants (with whom the boy did not live), the search for an easy explanation, for many pundits, was concluded. There was no evidence that either boy had seen the film, but the trial judge nevertheless opined after the guilty verdicts that "exposure to violent video films may in part be an explanation" for the crime. Members of Parliament immediately called for "tougher action against video and TV violence," while *The Times* editorialized that "screen sadism is immoral whether or not it causes crime."[35] The next year, Parliament amended the Video Recordings Act to require BBFC raters to pay particular attention to depictions of "(1) criminal behaviour; (2) illegal drugs; (3) violent behaviour or incidents; (4) horrific behaviour or incidents; and (5) human sexual activity."[36] Six years later, the European Court of Human Rights ruled that the child defendants in the Bulger case had not received a fair trial or sentence: "massive and highly charged publicity," combined with political pressures, had resulted in intimidating and oppressive proceedings and induced the Home Secretary to increase the punishment.[37]

The BBFC's censorship operation remained idiosyncratic. The Board's brochure explained that there are "no written rules and only general guidelines," partly because standards of taste are "constantly evolving" and partly because every film is unique and must be understood in context.[38] Its six movie ratings ranged from U ("Universal—Suitable for All") (described as nothing "that might be construed as disturbing, harmful or offensive") to 18 (in which "complex sexual relationships" or "controversial religious subjects" could be aired) and R18 (restricted to licensed sex cinemas). In between were PG ("Parental Guidance"—"no serious suggestion of sexual activity" and no "condoning of immoral behaviour unless mitigated by context [e.g., comedy]") and separate categories for ages 12 and 15. Like the MPAA system in the United States, these calibrated categories gave the board leverage in forcing film producers to censor content in exchange for a desired rating.

As one fed-up examiner "confessed" in 1999, "Ferman loved to fiddle, snip and trim." But some trims didn't make sense. The rape scene in *Rob Roy*, for example, "was reduced on film for a 15 cert, and further cut on video following a handful of complaints. Yet many viewers thought the cuts sanitised the rape." Equally important was the plainly political nature of the Board's judgments: "whenever editorials sprang up condemning violent entertainment," there was "a reining in." Controversy "set the board backtracking on policy or retreating into silence. A handful of letters constituted a public outcry."[39]

The BBFC's official rating and certification process provides another point of comparison with the United States, where the private-industry-based MPAA ratings are assigned in secret. Ironically, then, there is more "transparency"—more public awareness and scrutiny of film censorship—in Britain than in the home of the First Amendment. Indeed, analyzing and satirizing the activities of the BBFC is a favorite cultural and journalistic sport. Transparency and the influence of a more sexually liberal European continent also sometimes produce less censorious results. Danish filmmaker Lars von Trier's *The Idiots*, for example, which contains "a rather wobbly orgy scene featuring a split-second glimpse of an erect penis," was passed in 1999 by the BBFC—and by thirty other countries in Europe, South America, and Asia—while in the United States, the MPAA demanded cuts.[40] Adrian Lyne's 1998 cinematic remake of *Lolita*, unavailable in the United States until more than a year after its completion, was exhibited months earlier in central London.

As in the United States, assumptions about imitative or traumatic media effects drove film censorship during James Ferman's reign. Ferman pointed to laboratory experiments by the American Edward Donnerstein and other social scientists that, he said, established a link between sexual violence in films and the actual behavior or attitudes of viewers. He acknowledged that films probably also have cathartic effects, but said that on balance, if a movie is cathartic for 85 percent of its audience but has a triggering or imitative effect for 15 percent, he would still ban it.[41] Predicting harm is "just a balance of probabilities," he said, "there's no proof." Indeed, a 1994 report funded by the BBFC and Britain's three television censorship bodies found no significant difference in film, video, and TV viewing tastes between law-abiding youngsters and juvenile offenders. (*Terminator* 2 was the favorite movie for boys in both groups.) In a preface to the report, Ferman wrote of "the possibility that innocence can be corrupted" by movies or television, but admitted that "few have been able to demonstrate a causal relationship"; "human nature is far too complex to lend itself to simple explanations."[42]

The Home Office commissioned another study; and this time the researcher (Kevin Browne of Birmingham University) concluded that violent offenders were more likely than nonoffenders to prefer violent films. But even here, Browne acknowledged, there was no evidence that viewing violent films *caused* crime. On the contrary, "pre-existing" tendencies probably accounted for the offenders' entertainment tastes; these were due in turn primarily to the influence of parents. "[I]n the absence of parental violence, there was no significant relationship between offending and a preference for violent films." The most that the BBFC could say about this second study was that it showed "that most young people are not strongly influenced by video violence, but some could be."[43]

Ferman was more liberal when it came to nonviolent sexual content, and by the late 1990s this got him into trouble with Tony Blair's New Labour government.[44] Pressure from the Home Office in 1997 caused the BBFC to withdraw an R18 that it had intended for the sex video *Makin' Whoopee* and to deny a certificate altogether; the Video Appeals Committee, a creation of the 1984 law, reversed the decision.[45] Appeals Committee rulings in 1999 again slapped down decisions by the BBFC—now under new leadership—to ban other porn videos. By 2000, this battle had reached the High Court, with the government's attorney arguing on behalf of the BBFC that the videos must be suppressed because of the "risk of 'real and significant harm' to children" if they were sold for home viewing; it was "better not to run the risk," he said, "until more was known." But in May 2000, a judge agreed with the Appeals Committee that the risk of harm to minors was, "on present evidence, insufficient."[46]

As the 1990s ended, the BBFC's aesthetic dilemmas, and its cultural divide from continental Europe, had become ever more precarious. In 1999, Ferman's successor, Robin Duval, and the new BBFC president, Andreas Whittam Smith, passed the "genuinely shocking, slick" French film *Seul Contre Tous* for the 18+ category but only after "optical softening to make two sexual penetration scenes less explicit." "Optical softening" meant blurring a few brief shots of intercourse beyond recognition; only those attending film society showings, exempt from certification requirements, could see the scene unmutilated. Duval and Whittam Smith also struggled over the *The Idiots* before finally approving it without cuts in 1999. (Ferman, shortly before his retirement, had told the film's producer he would pass *The Idiots* with an 18+ rating, but two days later said "he couldn't confirm the 18 certificate because of Home Office involvement."[47] The hot potato was therefore left in the laps of Ferman's successors.[48])

In 1999, the new regime also finally granted certificates to *The Texas Chainsaw Massacre* and the video of *The Exorcist*. Whittam Smith explained that although *The Exorcist* "has a well-reported power to frighten young people and we can't, of course, assume that the 18 certificate for a video means that the under-18s won't see it," nevertheless "lots of people pay good money to be frightened. The question is whether the fright, the terror, could in any way be said to be permanently damaging. . . . And the fact is that there is no solid evidence that *The Exorcist* has been." Whittam Smith noted that *The Exorcist* "has been freely available in the Netherlands and Germany with certificates for 16- and 14-year-olds respectively," a fact demonstrating "the gulf that exists between our own and European standards."[49] It also demonstrated the extent to which censorship of minors turns on cultural attitudes rather than objective determinations of harm.

Cultural change also came to British television. Twenty-six years after an irate citizen had persuaded the courts to halt, albeit temporarily, a planned program about Andy Warhol because of its lesbians, transvestites, and toilet-oriented "flush art,"[50] the country's Broadcasting Standards Commission was only mildly chastising programmers for such improprieties as undue violence on *The Jerry Springer Show*; references to masturbation, imprudently aired on Christmas Day, in the popular sitcom *Men Behaving Badly*; and "inappropriate sexual content" in an ad for an electric shaver because it appeared just after a show "watched by large numbers of children."[51] The Independent Television Commission (ITC), another censorship agency (it has the power to grant or deny licenses to independent commercial networks), admittedly was required by law to monitor programs for "good taste or decency," and restrict violent content when "large numbers" of "children and young persons . . . may be expected to be watching."[52] Its lengthy Programme Code covered "bad language," counseled "special care" with respect to "scenes which may unsettle young children," and banned "demonstrations of exorcisms or psychic or occultic practice" before the 9 p.m. "watershed"[53] (Britain's equivalent of the U.S. safe harbor). But the watershed permitted considerable doses of sex and violence afterward (one wit called it the "waterfall"); and independent channels 4 and 5 continued to push the envelope with shows like *Vice: The Sex Trade* just after 9 p.m.[54]

Colin Shaw, former director of the Broadcasting Standards Commission, argued in a 1999 book that British TV censorship, more sweeping and official than in the United States, actually contributes to freedom and diversity on television because it provides an outlet for complaints and reassures a nervous populace that somebody is "entrusted to look after these things."[55] And it is true that by the 1990s, in contrast to the United States, four-letter words *were* heard on British network TV; condoms were occasionally promoted. Moreover, as Shaw said of the BBC, the venerable publicly funded broadcaster, government support combined with a tradition of editorial freedom protected it from the kind of unofficial censorship pressures by advertisers and ideological groups that are a fact of broadcasting life in the United States.

The French Letter and Internet Watch

Given its tradition of sex censorship, Britain not surprisingly took the European lead in attempts to control the Internet when that revolutionary medium arrived on the scene. An early salvo, in August 1996, was a missive from Chief Inspector Stephen French of London's Metropolitan Police to the country's Internet service providers (ISPs), urging them to remove from their servers some 150 online sites that the police considered "pornographic" and "offensive." (Wags couldn't help dubbing this the "French Letter"—one of England's many euphemisms for a condom.) French warned that obscenity prosecutions could follow if the industry did not "move quickly toward the eradication of this type of Newsgroup from the Internet." His appended list of disapproved online sites began "cleverly," as one reporter observed, with "unpleasantly titled paedophile" groups; it "was only the persistent reader who would realise that the police also wanted to restrict access to newsgroups which clearly dealt with adult consensual sexual activities—many of them lesbian and gay interest groups."[56]

Although civil libertarians protested the French Letter's preemptive demand to purge "offensive" speech without any judicial finding of illegality, the major ISPs were conciliatory. Within a month of the letter, they had negotiated a "Safety-Net Agreement" with the Metropolitan Police, the Home Office, and the Department of Trade and Industry. The Agreement promised that ISPs would work not only to rid computers of Internet content they thought illegal but to develop methods of blocking legal but "offensive" speech by requiring all online speakers to "rate their own web pages" using the RSACi system that had been developed in the United States. ISPs would also "remove web pages hosted on their servers which are persistently and deliberately misrated," though it was not clear who would decide what the correct ratings should be.[57]

The Safety-Net Agreement prefigured the British online industry's formation of the Internet Watch Foundation, or IWF, whose two purposes were to police potentially illegal material (mostly child pornography) and to promote an international rating and blocking system for legal but "offensive" (alternately denoted "potentially harmful") speech. Eager to characterize blocking as benign, informational parental empowerment, fully consistent with free expression, the IWF set about assembling an Advisory Committee, and asked media lawyer Mark Stephens to be the nominee of Liberty, Britain's leading civil liberties group. Stephens called Liberty, whose chief legal staffer agreed to the appointment. The executive director, John Wadham, explained two years later that "no one, including me, on the staff was on top of the issue," but this did not mean "we had given our approval to the IWF, supported its aims, or that we would be seen as being represented on its board."[58]

Mark Stephens chaired the IWF Advisory Committee and became one of the primary authors of its March 1998 report, *Rating and Filtering Internet Content: A United Kingdom Perspective*. The report was circulated months before its official publication date; indeed, its ideas were floated by David Kerr, IWF's director, as early as July 1997, when he told a meeting of European ministers in Bonn that global ratings must be more extensive and wide-ranging than U.S.-based programs. There is a "whole category of dangerous subjects" that demand ratings, Kerr said, including "discussions advocating suicide, information about dangerous sports like bungee-jumping, and more common areas of concern such as drugs, cigarette advertising, sex and violence." Moreover, he said, rating of profanity "needs internationalization: 'The language and references are all American in current rating proposals.' "[59] Kerr did not explain how a global rating system would take account of all the potentially "harmful" or offensive words that might be found in scores of different languages and on millions of Internet sites.

All of these anomalies found their way into the IWF's March 1998 report, which proposed ten subjects that were "unsuitable" or "potentially harmful" for minors. To the four categories already identified by RSACi—"nudity," "sex," "language," and "violence"—the IWF added "personal details," "financial commitments," "tolerance" (actually meant to block intolerance), "potentially harmful subjects," "adult themes," and "context variables." This last category would consist of judgment calls by raters that material fitting into one of the previous nine groups was nevertheless sufficiently valuable from a scientific, journalistic, or literary point of view that users of the filter might want to override it.

To add to the complexity, within each of the IWF's ten categories of "potentially harmful" or "unsuitable" expression it proposed four or five gradations: thus, the IWF adopted RSACi's five levels of "nudity," ranging from "revealing attire" and "partial nudity" to "frontal nudity (qualifying as provocative display)." It likewise adopted RSACi's five levels for "language," from "mild expletive" to "crude, vulgar language" or "extreme hate speech." To these it added five gradations for "tolerance," from "neutral (non-prejudicial) reference to groups or attitudes about them" to advocacy of "action which would cause physical, psychological or economic harm or violence against the group." Its category for "potentially harmful subjects," also with five proposed levels, covered games, hobbies, sports, gambling, and "potential mind-disturbing material, including advocacy of suicide." "Adult themes" was a "catch-all category" that might include "abortion, fetishes, adultery, etc."; no gradations were proposed.

Despite its claims to noncensorial, purely informational intent, the IWF report recommended that browser software be shipped with the default setting to apply ratings. It did not say at which of the many possible levels of blocking the default should be set—if at the maximum, even mildly vulgar language, "kissing related romance," and "neutral (non-prejudicial) reference to groups or attitudes about them" would be blocked. Kerr had no answer when asked where precisely (out of the fifty or so possible permutations) the default should be set under the IWF's plan.[60]

Yaman Akdeniz, a researcher at the University of Leeds and founding director of an anticensorship group, Cyber-Rights and Cyber-Liberties, was one of the first to notice that IWF materials were listing Mark Stephens as Liberty's nominee on the Advisory Committee, thus implying that Britain's major civil liberties organization supported filtering and other government-encouraged efforts at Internet content control. Akdeniz alerted Liberty, which, he said, "did not even know what the heck IWF was at the time when I phoned them." John Wadham agreed: "Liberty did not have its eye on the ball on this issue," and the initial "miscommunication" was "exploited by the IWF to our detriment." A meeting ensued in April 1998, at which a representative of the IWF, Clive Feather, was told that Liberty "is not involved with IWF nor supports private policing schemes."[61]

Yet the IWF continued to assert its civil liberties bona fides, and its Web site continued to identify Stephens as Liberty's nominee through 1998 and much of 1999.[62] David Kerr's explanation, in June 1999, was that Stephens never represented Liberty's views at the IWF, "nomination" not being equivalent to representation, and that "we have never pretended that Liberty supports IWF policies." He added apologies "that we have caused any confusion by not changing the Web site. This was delayed by other pressures and was not meant to deceive anyone. We will remove the reference forthwith."[63] Shortly thereafter, Wadham wrote to Kerr formally requesting the change. But Akdeniz and others protested that the IWF's March 1998 rating and filtering report was still being circulated with Liberty's name. Liberty, meanwhile, approved a statement at its 1999 annual meeting noting the "considerable flaws" in filtering/rating systems, opposing "the imposition of compulsory rating systems and filtering systems on adults" in libraries, and recognizing that children too "have a right to receive information."[64]

If Liberty did not, as Wadham said, have its eye on the ball regarding filtering in 1997, neither did most of the civil liberties world. The question of harm to minors is a difficult one even for people who otherwise oppose censorship; and Mark Stephens's disagreement with Liberty about rating and blocking evidenced a general ambivalence among civil libertarians regarding this politically seductive alternative to the more obviously coercive forms of Internet control. Even the ACLU, litigating *Reno I*, had touted privately marketed labeling and blocking schemes as "less restrictive alternatives" to criminal prohibitions; only later did it publish *Fahrenheit 451.2*, pointing out some of the more conspicuous shortcomings of filtering software. And in Liberty's 1999 book, *Liberating Cyberspace*, Wadham referred to "a legitimate need to ensure that people, including teenagers, are not exposed to offensive or potentially damaging material," and suggested that the need is "more appropriately and effectively" met "through self-regulation and the development of more sophisticated technology"—presumably ratings and filters.[65]

By early 1999, the IWF had helped form an international industry group, INCORE (Internet Content Rating for Europe), and had received a grant of 250,000 euros from the European Union to begin development of an international rating and blocking scheme. Nor was the IWF the only pro-filtering entity to benefit from EU largesse. The London-based Childnet International had received an EU grant to develop Internet complaint hotlines and promotional programs on the virtues of ratings and filters. Childnet was the creation of Nigel Williams, a former officer of the evangelical group CARE (Christian Action, Research and Education). Williams had previously written of pornography that it "trivialises and debases one of God's special gifts. Yet we need not be depressed—seeing through Satan's lies is half the battle."[66] The rhetoric was reminiscent of ideological conflicts over youth, sin, and sexuality going back at least to Victorian times.

The European Union Weighs In

Continental Europe was, in general, less conflicted about youthful sexuality than Britain, but by the mid-1990s its governments were also anxious about sex in cyberspace. Not long after Congress passed the ill-fated 1996 Communications Decency Act, Western Europe was confronted with a Belgian pedophile scandal involving the deaths of four girls and implicating police and high officials in allegations of corruption. In this tense atmosphere, panic about uses of the Internet to entice children into sexual activity spilled over into initiatives that would control minors' simply *reading* pornography or other "objectionable" content.[67]

The EU consisted by the late 1990s of fifteen Member States and was a maze of administrative, judicial, and legislative institutions that governed ever larger portions of Europe's economy.[68] The major administrative body, the European Commission, was headquartered in Brussels and Luxembourg and divided into various DGs (Directorates General) of which two, DG 10 and DG 13, would be most involved in censorship directed at the young. It was DG 10 that administered the 1989 "Television Without Frontiers" Directive, whose main purpose was to remove national barriers to the free flow of TV signals, but which also required Member States to block any shows that "might seriously impair the physical, mental or moral development of minors, in particular programmes that involve pornography or gratuitous violence."[69] The directive offered no guidance on how to distinguish pornography from other sexual expression, or gratuitous from justifiable depictions of violence; and as David Hughes, an official at DG 10, explained, the EU's Member States have extremely diverse ideas about what, if anything, on television "might seriously impair" youthful psyches.[70]

The "Television Without Frontiers" Directive did not stop at proscribing television that "might seriously impair" young minds; it also required the banning or time-channeling of shows "*likely* to impair" them.[71] With respect to the second, presumably less grievous, category of programming, it did not specify what was "likely to impair" minors' development. As the Court of the European Free Trade Association (EFTA) explained in 1997, the directive introduced no "common standard," for "the mental and moral development of minors forms an important part of the protection of public morality, an area where it is not possible to determine a uniform European conception." Thus, neither "serious impairment" nor "likely impairment" has an objective meaning; each country should impose its own version.[72]

The same year as the EFTA decision, the European Parliament directed DG 10 to commission a study of TV rating and blocking, with a focus on the same v-chip device that the U.S. Congress had mandated in 1996 for all TVs 13 inches or larger. The bulky *Final Report: Parental Control of Television Broadcasting*, was produced by the University of Oxford Programme in Comparative Media Law and Policy. Released in February 1999, it surveyed in mind-boggling detail the technical ramifications of TV ratings, the existing classification and censorship schemes in EU Member States, sociological research on the utility of ratings, and data on TV's psychological effects. Although its conclusions were ambiguous—the only clear one being that the v-chip was technologically unfeasible for Europe—the *Final Report* offered insights into European harm-to-minors politics.

The report noted that rating and blocking would suppress valuable information and entertainment for adults as well as youth. It confirmed that the Member States had "highly differentiated approaches" reflecting "their own internal media history" and "social construct," and therefore that "the foundation does not exist, at this point, for extensive harmonisation" in the form of a transnational rating system. France had developed "extremely elaborate" TV rating procedures, for example, while other countries such as Luxembourg had "not implemented any specific systems." The substantive differences, moreover, were striking: the film *Sex, Lies, & Videotape* was 18+ in the UK "while it obtained a 7+ certificate in Sweden and would have even been released within a general audience certificate if it had not contained a violent scene." Only Britain and Italy rated films for bad language; only Germany and the Netherlands rated for fascist ideology or political extremism. France labeled a film for age 12 and up if the national Classification Commission decided that it "might shock the sensitivity of children" through "horrible images" or "representation of traumatic relationship between parent[s] and children." In Britain, by contrast, "sex/nudity related content appears with very sophisticated gradations" in each category of the classification scheme. This concern with sexual content "is not expressed in such a detailed way, nor regulated so carefully in the other countries, and, indeed, in some of them sex is not even perceived as detrimental for minors."[73]

Given this diversity, the *Final Report* said it was "difficult to see how a European-wide classification system could be achieved." But ultimately, the problem with v-chips and other rating and blocking systems was even more basic. Such systems are based on "one dimensional criteria such as age or a basic content descriptor (e.g., sex, violence, incitement to immoral behaviour, crude language), possibly presented in a variety of forms (Sex Level 1, Sex Level 2, Sex Level 3)." Consequently, works are not "appreciated in their complexity and will be rated without an appreciation for context. Risk is also high that certain programmes that would have been of interest for children . . . will fall under these too simplistic criteria and thus never be displayed on the screen." Children too are "individuals with the right to receive information and entertainment."[74]

Having pointed out the difficulties, however, the *Final Report* remained mindful of harm-to-minors politics. It recommended "informational rating systems," which it said would become more common with digital TV set-top boxes and program guides. Indeed, the report looked forward to an electronic world in which a thousand rating systems might bloom, reflecting "religious and cultural preferences, varying philosophies of child-rearing, language training and criteria far removed from the current emphasis on violence and sexually explicit images." Such "niche filtering" admittedly could "be viewed as quasi-censorial," it said, but the "interest in encouraging pluralistic third-party and multiple rating approaches" should "take precedence over this concern."[75]

Finally, the report noted that factors other than the simple presence of media violence determine whether television viewing is harmful. Researchers had found that children "are capable of making varied and complex judgments about violent content," despite "a widespread belief" that they are much less able than adults "to comprehend the context in which violence is shown, and are therefore more susceptible to harm." To the extent bad messages are an issue, the report urged "the enhancement of children's media literacy and critical viewing skills." It noted that Austria, Denmark,

England, Finland, France, Germany, Ireland, the Netherlands, Italy, Scotland, Spain, and Sweden all incorporated critical viewing skills into their public education.[76]

DG 10's David Hughes concurred in the *Final Report*'s conclusions. It had been clear two years earlier, he said, that the v-chip was not feasible for Europe; politics had driven the commissioning of the study. The Bulger murder in Britain, among other factors, "made the debate very passionate and not very rational." TV ratings would be impossible to impose in any standardized way on nations as diverse as those in the EU, said Hughes. Accommodating Muslim cultural values would require rigorous classification of female attire, a standard at odds, to say the least, with most of Western Europe. Yet none of this meant that DG 10 would abandon the ratings game. From the viewpoint of the EU bureaucracy, Hughes said, "it doesn't really matter what the justification" is.[77]

While the massive *Final Report* was in preparation, the European Commission was forging ahead with Internet filtering schemes. At an April 1996 meeting in Bologna, with the Belgian pedophile scandal still in the news, the EU's ministers for telecommunications and culture identified "illegal and harmful content on the Internet as an urgent priority for analysis and action."[78] The European Commission responded the following October with two documents—a *Communication* to the European Parliament and a *Green Paper on the Protection of Minors and Human Dignity in Audiovisual and Information Services*. Both touted filters as a way to protect youth from legal but "potentially harmful" online speech.[79]

The *Communication* started by distinguishing "illegal" from "harmful" but legal expression. Child pornography, for example, is criminal throughout the EU, as is "racist material or incitement to racial hatred," though the authors acknowledged that the "exact definition" of these crimes "varies from country to country." (In fact, there are large differences in the extent to which European nations outlaw racist speech.) As to "harmful" expression, the *Communication* did not essay a definition: it was simply material that "may offend the values and feelings of other persons"—"content expressing political opinions," for example, or "views on racial matters." Indeed, what is considered harmful "depends on cultural differences."[80] It was unclear whether the *Communication* meant to place speech "offensive" to adults in the same category as speech considered "harmful" or "unsuitable" for minors, but this seemed to be the assumption, even while acknowledging that all three concepts vary from one country to another. But if "unsuitable," "offensive," and "harmful" all mean the same thing, then the term "harmful" simply loses its ordinary meaning.

The *Communication* did not clarify these ambiguities but nevertheless recommended the creation of a European-wide Internet labeling and filtering system. It approvingly described the various programs available; and finessing the definitional problem once again, urged the development of European ratings instead of relying on programs devised in the United States, "where there may be a different approach on what is suitable content for minors."[81]

The *Green Paper* was a more discursive "think piece" beneath whose surface hovered a question of political turf: in the brave new world of the Internet, which DG (10 or 13) would administer the Internet censorship rules, and the ensuing funds? Like the *Communication*, the *Green Paper* took pains to distinguish between *illegal* speech in the new media, which the authors said "may be banned for everyone" regardless of age, and *legal* expression that cannot be banned but nevertheless "might affect the physical and mental development of minors" and so should be subject to rating and blocking. The paper used various terms to describe this second category of speech: "questionable," "liable to upset" children, possibly "pos[ing] a problem for minors," possibly "shock[ing] minors," and possibly "harmful to their development." The authors acknowledged not only that attitudes toward socialization of children "vary greatly" among the Member States, but that "a consensus does not necessarily exist, even in medical circles, as to what is likely to affect the moral and physical development of minors." Moreover, "the term 'minors' does not cover a uniform group and it is doubtful whether children of four have the same problems as adolescents of 15." The *Green Paper* nevertheless urged that the EU attempt to "identify shared values" and "areas where there may be a need for common standards," and promote PICS "or equivalent systems with a view to reaching—as quickly as possible—a critical mass of labelled material and navigation systems and parental control devices."[82]

In the next three years, the European Commission, Parliament, Council, and their various committees and working groups were to churn out reports, hold meetings, examine legal ramifications, network with online corporations, and start spending serious money on developing and promoting Internet rating and filtering. Yet all the while, they remained agnostic on the question whether any identifiable category of expression causes identifiable harm to youth. They continued to confuse "harm" with "unsuitability," or offense to moral or cultural values, and to press for standardized labels even while insisting that harm or offense are relative questions to be resolved separately by each Member State.

Thus, a European Commission "working party" reported in March 1997 that industry groups in a number of nations were generating self-regulation schemes not only to remove "illegal" content from their computers (without, however, any judicial determination of illegality) but to provide their customers with classification and filtering systems, develop codes of conduct, encourage online speakers to self-rate, and "deal with cases where the content provider fails to rate properly."[83] A report of the Commission's Legal Advisory Committee the same month applauded both self- and third-party ratings though admitting the difficulty of describing expression in a "value-free" manner.[84] An April 1997 *Resolution* by the European Parliament affirmed the importance of free speech and acknowledged that the notion of "harmful content . . . appertains essentially to the domain of morals," but nevertheless called on the Commission "to encourage the development of a common international rating system compatible with the PICS protocol, and sufficiently flexible to accommodate cultural differences."[85]

Occasional objections were raised within the EU bureaucracy during this labor- and paper-intensive process. The European Parliament's Committee on Women's Rights commented that "parental control" can "be viewed negatively as a means of limiting access to information, thus excluding children and adolescents from a free choice of knowledge."[86] The Economic and Social Committee pointed out that an *Action Plan* proposed by DG 13 for funding rating and blocking schemes was "impracticable" because the information on the Internet was too vast to be classified and labeled, and systems like PICS, although presented as "user-empowering," could become "an instrument of control." Still another committee commented wryly on the amount of paper consumed by the largely duplicative *Green Paper* and *Communication*, suggesting that "as much as Internet content providers compete with each other, Commission DGs also seem to be competing."[87]

"Les Dangers Ubuesques du Filtrage"

By 1998, the EU's plans for international Internet filtering seemed unstoppable, but civil liberties groups did voice their opposition. The Campaign Against Censorship of the Internet in Britain, Feminists Against Censorship, and Cyber-Rights and Cyber-Liberties were joined by Italy's Associazione per la Libertà nella Communicazione Elettronica Interattiva (Association for Freedom in Interactive Electronic Communication), France's Imaginons un Réseau Internet Solidaire (IRIS; loosely translated as Imagining Internet

Network Solidarity), and about thirty others in Europe, the United States, Canada, Australia, and even Singapore in protesting the repressive potential of rating and blocking schemes.

IRIS was particularly imaginative. Its online publications outlined the dangers of rating and filtering, among them the "*liberticide*" that would result from forced self-rating, and the risk that linguistic and cultural minorities would be subject to the tastes and values of "dominant organisms, that is to say, essentially American."[88] IRIS's first *lettre électronique*, in January 1998, contained an "*alerte sur les dangers ubuesques du filtrage*"—that is, a suggestion that the grotesque dictator King Ubu in Alfred Jarry's comic play *Ubu the King* would be quite at home in the world of Internet blocking. IRIS illustrated its point with an "*exemple de blocage*": the Web site of an association for the protection of animals. IRIS commented: "*Disney World s'internationalise, décidément: le père Ubu y a aussi sa place*" (rough translation: Disney World goes decidedly international; King Ubu also belongs there). IRIS particularly objected to the EU's filtering recommendations; to a decision by the French Conseil d'État to make ISPs responsible for online content, and to U.S.-based efforts to suppress racist sites.[89]

In 1997, the civil liberties groups created a Global Internet Liberty Campaign (GILC) to publicize concerns ranging from encryption laws to rating and filtering. GILC protested new PICS rules promulgated by W3C (the World Wide Web Consortium) because they went "far beyond the original objective of PICS to empower Internet users," and instead facilitated "server/proxy-based filtering" that would permit "upstream censorship, beyond the control of the end user."[90] Nine months later, GILC published *"Regardless of Frontiers": Protecting the Human Rights to Freedom of Expression on the Global Internet*, a pamphlet outlining the risks to free expression posed by blocking and labeling systems, particularly when implemented by government institutions like libraries and schools. But the report did not question the necessity of "protecting children from content that is permissible for adults"; it simply argued that the availability of filtering software for parents who want to use it rendered government regulation unnecessary.[91]

The civil liberties opposition did not make much headway against the combined force of the EU bureaucracy and the major online corporations, and by the end of 1998, DG 13's *Action Plan* was in place. The plan encompassed four main projects for 1999–2002—hotlines, "support for self-regulation," "developing technical measures," and "awareness initiatives"—with a total budget of twenty-five million euros. "Technical measures" meant rating and filtering, whose purpose was variously described as dealing with "undesirable content on the Internet," "harmful content," or content "which could be harmful for children." "Awareness initiatives" were activities to persuade governments, Internet speakers, teachers, and parents of the benefits of a classified and filtered online world.[92]

DG 13 now devised "preparatory actions" that different organizations would be paid to undertake in furtherance of the *Action Plan*. INCORE, the industry group largely organized by Britain's Internet Watch Foundation, was the contracting organization for "Preparatory Action 2," a "feasibility study for a European system of content self-rating." Among other things, INCORE would evaluate different filtering programs to determine their respect for "European cultural and linguistic differences" and their ability to "deal with the issue of content which is not appropriately rated."[93] In May 1999, meanwhile, the major online corporations—Microsoft, Netscape, AOL, and Bertelsmann among them—formed yet another international filtering group, the Internet Content Rating Association, or ICRA. Its goal was to "try to create the first world standard" for rating and blocking based on the American RSACi system, whose assets it soon acquired. The new consortium acknowledged that global filtering was not feasible in a cyberworld where "only a tiny proportion—about 1%—of sites have rated themselves," but hoped to drum up enthusiasm "by developing an undisputed standard and boosting awareness of its use through major publicity campaigns." According to the IWF, the companies forming ICRA had "the technical and financial power to complete and implement" global filtering; and they would govern the "new international system" of "voluntary self-rating."[94]

At an "expert meeting" of rating and filtering promoters in Munich that September, Bertelsmann unveiled a new "layer cake" plan for Internet rating and filtering. Incorporated in a *Memorandum on Self-Regulation of the Internet*, the plan had been developed by Yale professor Jack Balkin, with funding from Bertelsmann. The proposed "layers" consisted, first, of PICS-compatible "voluntary" labels or "meta-tags" drawn from a "basic vocabulary" of keywords; then ideologically value-laden "templates" created by different organizations to rate the "meta-tags" based on their varying attitudes toward what is good, bad, or harmful for minors; and finally, third-party ratings of online sites, including whitelists and blacklists that would "provide for more contextualized judgements."[95] In an earlier memorandum, Balkin had proposed that the "common descriptive meta-tags" be "developed by a board of social scientists with reference to relevant and empirical sociological data as to what constitutes 'actual harm' to children." He acknowledged that this would require "difficult tradeoffs" and "adaptability to changing mores,"[96] but failed to note that there is no agreement among social scientists within cultures, no less across them, as to what if anything in the realm of speech or ideas predictably causes psychological harm. Balkin also acknowledged that "his common language will not cover every aspect of content. . . . 'There can be no [common] description for blasphemy in Saudi Arabia.' . . . Neither can hate speech or political speech be satisfactorily rated. 'It's a leaky system,' " he said. " 'But it's the best you can do.' "[97]

GILC made an appearance in Munich to point out the drawbacks of filtering, whether in the form of layer cakes or self-rating. It warned that "the imposition of civil or criminal penalties for 'mis-rating'. . . is likely to follow any widespread deployment of a rating and blocking regime."[98] The online group net.freedom weighed in with an article arguing that if ISPs required self-rating, they would simply be replacing government censors. "Why is this going forward?" the reporters asked. "What happened is the government (the European Commission, in this case) decided to get serious. They buckled down, and at the end of 1998, allocated funds to be spent on the development of a global rating system." With all that money available, "the corporate participants can be reasonably assured of being reimbursed for all their plane fares and hotel costs. (Question: if it's so voluntary, how come the government is paying people to develop it?)"[99]

Even the CDT (the Center for Democracy and Technology), a champion of ratings, critiqued the Bertelsmann plan. It would "jeopardize free expression on the Internet," said the CDT, by "promoting a single, comprehensive, global rating system developed with government involvement or backed by government enforcement"; and "in the name of 'self-regulation,' " would encourage ISPs to collaborate in controlling speech that is legal but "considered offensive by some." ISPs would police the speech of their subscribers, while government regulators would define the standards to be applied.[100]

By early 2000, reports from the first phase of the *Action Plan* were filtering in. INCORE, surveying the European scene, found that too few sites were labeled—especially in languages other than English—to create the "critical mass" necessary for global blocking. It reiterated its view, however, that self-labeling advanced free expression by "reducing pressures on democratic governments to pursue censorship." A report on third-party rating from a French/Italian consortium found serious accuracy problems in the five filtering systems it examined (including Cyber Patrol, SurfWatch, and CyberSnoop). The "precise definition of what is illegal or harmful varies from one country to another," it said; and "the lack of localised versions" made it "difficult to filter slang or swear words." Sixty-four percent of respondents said the software "lacked coherency in terms of filtering results." Improvements—requiring more studies and more funds—were definitely needed.[101]

If INCORE, Bertelsmann, or the European Commission thought that industry-created layer cakes or other rating schemes would forestall direct government censorship, that illusion was soon dispelled by events in Australia. The Australian Broadcasting Authority (ABA) already had an elaborate system for rating TV, films, magazines, posters, and books in order to shield minors "from material likely to harm or disturb them" when, in early 1999, the government persuaded Australia's Internet Industry Association (IIA) to create a Code of Practice that extended the rating system to computers.[102] This "self-regulation" code was not free of official involvement; but even so, it did not satisfy those wanting more forceful controls. A month after the code's appearance, legislation was introduced requiring ISPs to remove "highly offensive or illegal material from their services" upon order of the ABA. The industry protested; the Australian Computer Society said the law would make Australia "the laughing stock of the world";[103] but in June 1999 Australia passed the Broadcasting Services Amendment (Online Services Act).

The law established a complex system for rating and removing "prohibited content" (defined as anything classified RC ["Refused Classification"] or X by the government's Classification Board), or "potential prohibited content" (anything online that has not been classified but if it were, "there is a substantial likelihood" that it would be "prohibited content"). Material would be rated or "potentially" rated as the result of either a private complaint or the ABA's own initiative. Once given the disapproved label, it had to be removed within fourteen hours by the "relevant Internet content host." There was a separate R category for expression that would be prohibited unless subject to a "restricted access system" designed to police Internet content that is "unsuitable for children"[104]—that is, the same age-screening found to be unfeasible two years earlier by the U.S. Supreme Court in *Reno v. ACLU*. By early 2000 the government was ordering ISPs to take down disapproved sites, some of which shifted to overseas servers to avoid the law.[105]

In contrast to the Australian government, the European Union says rating and filtering should be voluntary—for the content provider and the computer user. Yet Richard Swetenham, the DG 13 official in charge of filtering plans, acknowledged that "inducements" to self-rating under an ostensibly voluntary system would inevitably be necessary—and self-rating was the only real option because no third-party rating system could classify even a fraction of the Internet.

Swetenham was well aware of the problems with global ratings. Despite the EU's rhetorical genuflections to cultural diversity, rating systems by definition can only provide a preselected set of adverse labels; and Swetenham wondered how many different categories of potentially undesirable content—not to mention levels within categories—can be created before classifications become unworkable. As for the question of what, if any, online expression might actually harm youngsters, Swetenham was skeptical. "I'm not a psychologist," he said, "and at the end of the day, I don't really care."[106]

Ten

MEDIA EFFECTS

Imitation and Catharsis

While European Union officials exude skepticism about the actual harm to minors from controversial expression, in the United States by the 1990s it was politically almost untenable to question the claim that media violence has been proven to have dire effects on youth. Yet from Dr. Tissot's *L'Onanisme* in the 18th century to campaigns against comic books in the 1950s and TV violence studies a generation later, those favoring censorship have invoked science to bolster their claims. Have the more quantitative studies of recent decades actually added any new knowledge to this endless debate?

Part of the problem has been that the issue of media effects is too often posed in "either/or" terms. Statistical correlations between exposure to films classified as violent by experimenters in a laboratory setting and subsequent behavior deemed aggressive by the experimenters are said to prove that all or a great percentage of children imitate what they see in the media. Catharsis—the therapeutic or "drive reduction" effect of entertainment—has supposedly been disproved by these social science experiments. Rarely do the debaters note that the same work may induce imitation in some viewers and catharsis in others—or that the same person may respond differently to different violent or sexual content. Psychology is "still largely a speculative discipline";[1] it is not the same as physical science.

The unnecessarily divisive conflict between imitation and catharsis as ways of understanding the impact of expression began more than two millennia ago. Plato exemplified the imitation theory when, in the *Republic*, he advocated a thought-control system in which censors allow "any tale of fiction which is good" while rejecting any that is "bad." Mothers and nurses in Plato's ideal world would tell children only "authorized" stories (no Homer or Hesiod, among other banned poets).[2] Aristotle's quite different view in his *Poetics* stressed "the pleasure-giving feature of art." Aristotle "broke with the moralistic attitudes of Plato and asserted the freedom of the arts from moral censorship."[3] He posited that audiences at tragic dramas respond to depictions of even the most appalling events not with anger or frustration, nor by imitating the characters' gruesome deeds, but by identifying with their sufferings and emerging exhilarated and emotionally drained. By exciting spectators' feelings of pity and fear, tragedy effected "the proper purgation of these emotions."[4] Aristotle called this process *katharsis*—a term that still has wide currency in psychology and literature. He opined that catharsis not only permitted feelings that "in real life contain a morbid and disturbing element" to find relief, but produced a "distinctly aesthetic satisfaction" whose effect was to "purify and clarify" the emotions.[5]

Aristotle's theory had tremendous influence. Renaissance writers compared catharsis to medical treatment—as a " physician eradicates, by means of poisonous medicine, the perfervid poison of disease which affects the body, so tragedy purges the mind of its impetuous perturbations by the force of these emotions beautifully expressed in verse."[6] The 19th-century scholar Jakob Bernays averred that theater "provides a harmless and pleasurable outlet for instincts which demand satisfaction, and which can be indulged here more fearlessly than in real life."[7] Others have opined that the ability of bawdy comedy to afford cathartic relief through laughter "may act as a safety-valve without which libidinal pressures become explosive."[8] In his fictional life of Shakespeare, Anthony Burgess suggested that theater's purpose is "the peaceful quelling of the riotous spirits that haunt man's blood," not "their further inflaming"—or "[s]o Aristotle had seemed to say."[9]

One pedagogue who disagreed was Jean-Jacques Rousseau. In his *Lettre à M. D'Alembert* describing the moral perils posed by dramatic works, Rousseau mustered his rhetorical skill to skewer the concept of catharsis: "I know the poetic of theater is supposed to . . . purge the passions in exciting them, but I have trouble understanding this—could it be that, to become temperant and wise, one must begin by being furious and mad?" The pity and terror evoked by tragedy are "fleeting and vain," said Rousseau; the frightful spectacles of Greek drama are more barbarous than the "massacres of gladiators." Comedy is even worse, because of its baleful influence on morals, especially those of women.[10]

Rousseau's didactic approach did not carry the day. Less than a century later, Sigmund Freud identified catharsis as a crucial element of artistic creation, of psychotherapy, and of the fantasies of children at play. Freud thought not only audiences but authors, and indeed all human beings, must at times "throw off the too heavy burden" of life and relieve themselves of painful emotions through creative expression, fantasy, humor, and daydreams.[11] Jean Piaget came to similar conclusions about the function of imaginative play in resolving children's psychological conflicts. Youngsters do in play what they "would dare not" do in reality, Piaget said; cathartic play makes dangerous tendencies acceptable "through canalisation and sublimation."[12]

Bruno Bettelheim pointed out the cathartic function of powerfully charged, often horrific fairy tales. In these violent stories, Bettelheim wrote in *The Uses of Enchantment*, unconscious desires and fantasies are "worked through in imagination" rather than repressed, and their "potential for causing harm—to ourselves or others"—is thereby "much reduced."[13] Bettelheim opposed the "prevalent parental belief" that "a child must be diverted from what troubles him most: his formless, nameless anxieties, and his chaotic, angry, and even violent fantasies." Children's literature that is safe and sunny, and presents "only conscious reality or pleasant and wish-fulfilling images," fails to nourish children's minds. Adults' "widespread refusal to let children know that the source of much that goes wrong in life is due to our very own natures" only makes youngsters feel more anxious about the world and more troubled about their own fears and aggressions.[14] Updating Bettelheim, one commentator on children's theater noted in 1998 that "while object lessons and pithy morals may appeal to parents,"

> children seem to prefer bodily torture. When Snow White's wicked stepmother dances to death wearing red-hot iron clogs in the Young Vic production [in London], we should not be surprised that her frenzied gyrations and chilling screams are punctuated by the sounds of children laughing, delighting in fantasies of revenge.[15]

Two psychologists who generally adhere to imitation theory as applied to TV violence also accept the "importance of fantasy play in cognitive development" and in particular the possibility that "for many poor children whose parents are overworked, inaccessible, or lack cultural orientation to engage in storytelling or reading," television may afford "a remarkable opportunity to come in contact with magic, fantasy, [and] a richer vocabulary."

There is "considerable evidence," they say, "that adults and children who have a well-developed imaginative life are less disposed toward frequent acts of impulsive antisocial behavior or aggression."[16]

Yet despite the eternal appeal of horrific and often erotically charged children's tales, censorship controversies in the 1980s and '90s frequently featured demands that fantasy works incorporating violence, superstition, or gruesome events be kept away from youngsters. In one such incident in 1992, Jacksonville, Florida, moved *Snow White* to a "restricted" list in the school library because of its "graphic violence"; and in 1999 the fantastically popular Harry Potter novels—about the eponymous hero's adventures at the Hogwarts School of Witchcraft and Wizardry—were challenged by parents in a number of communities, and were actually removed from school libraries and reading lists in one Michigan town.[17]

Among literary theorists, James Joyce in his *A Portrait of the Artist as a Young Man* made catharsis a point of dispute between his hero Stephen Dedalus and Stephen's friend Lynch. Stephen the aesthete argues that high art produces catharsis—a "static" emotion—but "improper art" (including pornography) excites only "kinetic" feelings such as "desire or loathing." Lynch is less pontifical: "You say that art must not excite desire," he replies, but even great works sometimes do. "I told you that one day I wrote my name in pencil on the backside of the Venus of Praxiteles in the Museum. Was that not desire?"[18] Lynch seems to have the better of this argument, but Joyce's contemporary D. H. Lawrence agreed with Stephen, defending the sexual explicitness in his own novels while condemning "pornography" as no more than a sickly prod to masturbation.[19] The perilously subjective nature of Lawrence's distinction—he classed *Pamela* and *Jane Eyre* as unwholesomely pornographic—eluded him.

Some of today's pundits follow Lawrence—acknowledging the power of catharsis for serious art but denying it for creations that they consider mere popular entertainment. In her book *Mayhem*, for example, Sissela Bok accepts catharsis but attempts to distinguish between the gruesome depictions of brutality in Picasso's "Guernica" or Steven Spielberg's *Schindler's List* and "the pitilessness that accompanies much entertainment violence." She even praises horror movies or disaster tales in which terror "blends with pity for the victims" or killing is "a dramatic device or a form of closure rather than something savored for its cruelty," and approves the action film *Independence Day* because it reflects the "sense of delight we know from childhood in wreaking havoc, knocking down towers, and seeing fireworks explode and buildings crumble to dust."[20] Bok's distinctions are largely subjective—they seem less about "high" versus "low" art than about movies she enjoys and those she doesn't. The same problem arises in Roger Shattuck's 1996 book *Forbidden Knowledge*, where he agrees with Bettelheim that gruesome fairy tales are cathartic but argues that sadistic works by the Marquis de Sade are appalling and inexcusable.[21]

What authors like Bok and Shattuck overlook is that didactic and cathartic effects may be found in the same work. Indeed, Joyce's masterpiece, *Ulysses*, undermines the dichotomy between static and kinetic art: parts of the novel are arousing, and are probably meant to be (for example, Joyce's mimicking of pornographic romance writing in the "Nausicaa" episode). Blatant eroticism in great works of visual art—the nudes of Titian, for example—also illustrates the point. Renaissance artists often produced such works specifically for patrons to decorate their bedrooms; the intent and likely effect were certainly "kinetic." Nineteenth-century painters produced what Peter Gay describes as "socially acceptable pornography": sensuous nudes, lusty satyrs, "Ottoman merchants exhibiting beautiful naked European captives on the slave market; sculptures that professed to be imparting moral lessons when they only aroused libidinal fantasies."[22] In the century after *Regina v. Hicklin*, its "deprave and corrupt" standard was applied to serious works of literature precisely because they had *both* artistic value and likely libidinous effects.

Sexual entertainment, moreover, has cathartic effects beyond the purely physical. Writing of Japanese pornography, probably the most sadistic in the world, Ian Buruma observes that aesthetic cruelty, "in Japan as elsewhere, is a way of relieving fear, of exorcizing the demons." Rape scenes in Japanese films are fundamentally expressions of a "desperate fear of masculine inadequacy."[23] Though graphic fictions of rape or sexual torture may be distressing to view, their cathartic function for some viewers is suggested by the fact that Japan, for all of its violent pornography, has one of the world's lowest rates of sexual crime.[24]

Even such avatars of direct media effects on human attitudes as the social scientists Edward Donnerstein, Daniel Linz, and Steven Penrod acknowledge that rape is "one of the commonest sexual fantasies"—for women as well as men—"a point that is not lost on the writers of best-selling romance novels." Fantasy is "safe," and does not indicate a desire to experience rape in real life.[25] Likewise, many children and adults enjoy horror movies precisely because they can "experience fear without real danger to themselves" and thereby "tame its effects on the psyche."[26] Henry Jenkins describes four reasons why young people are drawn to violent entertainment: for fantasies of empowerment; fantasies of transgression; acknowledgment that "the world is not all sweetness and light"; and "an intensification of emotional experience."[27] All these can be seen as forms of catharsis.

A modern opponent of catharsis, Bertolt Brecht, scorned the phenomenon precisely because it made people feel better rather than activating them to do something to end the world's miseries. Wanting to teach his audience "a quite different practical attitude," Brecht developed the concept of an Epic Theater in which viewers would be distanced from the characters onstage.[28] But despite Brecht's efforts, his audiences do not generally remain detached from his dramas; nor do they start revolutions upon leaving the theater. Even didactic art of the type Plato favored turns out not to have easily predictable effects.

Disproving Aristotle

Brecht may have disapproved of catharsis, but he did not deny its existence. That task was to be taken up by social scientists in the 1960s and '70s, investigating the mass media's effects on young viewers. These researchers were influenced by the "social learning" or "modeling" school of psychology, whose fundamental tenet is that children learn how to behave through observation and imitation. The founding father of social learning, Albert Bandura, believed we are not born with aggressive impulses; individuals can respond to frustration in various ways, of which aggression is only one.[29] Bandura was surely right that children learn aggression from models they observe in their family and community environments, though it is questionable whether other factors—heredity, brain chemistry, and human passions—can be ignored.[30] But the real problem came when Bandura and his colleagues expanded their generalizations from real-life models to "the symbolic environment"[31] of the mass media.

Bandura supported the conceptual leap on the basis of a famous series of experiments in which nursery school children were shown films of both Herman the Cat and an actual adult hitting a large bouncy "Bobo doll." The children were then frustrated, in order to stimulate aggression, and finally given the opportunity to aggress, in a laboratory setting, against actual Bobo dolls. Those who had viewed the violent films did so in larger numbers than children in a control group; the imitative effect was appreciably greater for boys than for girls.[32] Bandura publicized his findings in a 1963 *Look* magazine article that began with the attention-grabbing proposition that few parents "would deliberately select Western gunslingers, hopped-up psychopaths, deranged sadists, slapstick buffoons, and the like" as role models for their children.[33]

But hitting Bobo dolls is a socially permissible, even encouraged, play activity, and it is not surprising that some young children to whom the activity is suggested on-screen will try it out. As with many laboratory experiments that were to follow, the relevance of the Bobo doll studies to real-world aggressive behavior over the long term was questionable. Seymour Feshbach, one of the few champions of catharsis theory in a field increasingly dominated by social learning enthusiasts, pointed out that most children do understand the difference between fantasy and reality—that the results of "playing war or punching a Bobo doll" are quite different from the results of "kicking one's mother." Violence "in the guise of dramatic fantasy is found throughout history and it seems likely that the vicarious participation in these fantasies does satisfy some human needs."[34] Judith Rich Harris recently reframed the point: children *do* learn by imitation, but selectively. Among other things, they learn that for the most part they cannot simply imitate adults.[35]

The fact that boys' behavior in Bandura's experiments was affected far more than girls' indicated that other factors—cultural, social, biological—were at work in molding the extent to which youngsters, even in the artificial lab setting, imitate actions they see on a TV or movie screen. One might even have interpreted the difference in boys' and girls' emulation of filmed aggression to suggest that the boys were using the toys precisely for their cathartic purpose and would have engaged in *more* aggression outside the laboratory—especially if angered or frustrated—if they had not had the fantasy-play outlet. None of this is meant to suggest that Bandura's experiments, and others that followed, were wholly invalid. They did show short-term imitative effects for some children in a lab setting. But more was claimed for them than could legitimately be extrapolated. And in the political arena, ambiguities and conceptual limitations were easily forgotten.

Bandura's well-publicized experiments came at an opportune political moment. The imitation/catharsis debate is as cyclical as censorship itself, and the social dislocations of the 1960s and early 1970s intensified fears about the impact of television on youth. Academics who developed theories about TV's influence on youngsters were responding to this political climate.[36] When media effects studies began to be done in large numbers in the late '60s and the '70s, their operating hypotheses tended, as one supporter of the school frankly said, "to be grounded on models that *did* predict some type of effect from the media."[37] Or as psychologist Jonathan Freedman, who wrote trenchant critiques of the media effects literature, observed, "it's mostly a political issue, not so much a scientific one"; many psychologists "came to this issue with strong personal dislike of TV violence and a belief that it is harmful." Lab studies supported their view, and they were "predisposed to reject" contradictory evidence.[38]

In the political arena, then, social learning came to overshadow and even obliterate more nuanced understandings of violence and aggression. As a committee of the Association of the Bar of the City of New York noted in a 1997 report, social learning is just one among many psychological perspectives, but its advocates are the ones, primarily, who have researched television and violence. And their results are too equivocal to support the belief that television causes violence in society: "For over thirty years researchers have been attempting to discern the relationship, if any, between aggressive behavior and viewing television violence. The results remain controversial and skeptics abound."[39] Bandura himself acknowledged that social learning is only one among many explanations for how humans develop patterns of aggression, sexuality, or other aspects of behavior. Aggression is "a multifaceted phenomenon that has many determinants and serves diverse purposes," he wrote; even definitions of aggression vary among psychologists, and can include both "direct assaultive behavior" and "remote circuitous acts."[40]

Media effects studies received a windfall in the 1960s and early '70s when the Surgeon General's office, preparing its 1972 report entitled *Television and Growing Up*, devoted $1 million to funding new research. The resulting report was nevertheless guarded about the conclusions to be drawn, noting only a "preliminary and tentative indication" of a causal relation between TV violence and the real-world variety, and then only in children already predisposed to aggression; and cautioning that the "effect is small compared with many other possible causes, such as parental attitudes or knowledge of and experience with the real violence of our society." Despite these reservations, Senator John Pastore orchestrated hearings that distorted the report's guarded conclusions, and in subsequent years the report was often described as validating the imitative effect theory.[41] Social-learning psychologists announced that Aristotle was passé; they had disproved catharsis, or as they phrased it, the theory of "vicarious hostility reduction" through art.[42] Daniel Linz put it even more baldly in an interview: the research is "overwhelmingly clear," he asserted, that media violence has no cathartic effect.[43]

A few studies, primarily by Seymour Feshbach, challenged Bandura.

Measuring aggressive behavior in institutionalized adolescent and preadolescent boys after exposure over a six-week period to violent or nonviolent TV programs, Feshbach found *less* aggression in the group exposed to the violent fare, and posited that the boys used film fantasy as a coping mechanism. Shows in the violent category included (among others) *Batman, Bonanza, Have Gun Will Travel, Superman, Tarzan, Thief of Bagdad, Zorro,* and *Alfred Hitchcock Presents*; in the nonviolent category, *American Bandstand, Bachelor Father, The Donna Reed Show, The Dick Van Dyke Show, Dobie Gillis, Peyton Place, Leave It to Beaver,* and again *Batman*—in acquiescence to the boys' protest at being deprived of this favorite.[44] Feshbach's willingness to compromise the study by allowing the boys in the "nonviolent" group to see *Batman* was one basis for criticizing his work; another was the argument that the boys deprived of their usual violent fare must have acted out in frustration.[45] But in the final analysis, it was the political appeal of the social-learning-inspired experiments rather than any superiority in their methods or results that accounted for the repeated assertion that Feshbach and Aristotle alike had been discredited. For laboratory and field experiments that were said to support the imitation hypothesis also had serious flaws. And occasional studies did still support catharsis. In the late 1980s and early 1990s, for example, a few reported that "adolescents who like heavy metal music listen to it especially when they are angry," that "the music has the effect of calming them down and dissipating their anger," and that "adolescents generally favor music as an aid in coping with their problems."[46]

A measure of the political mood was that although Feshbach contributed an article to the five volumes of papers appended to the 1972 Surgeon General's report, he was not listed ten years later among the experts participating in the next major government survey: the 1982 NIMH (National Institute of Mental Health) report, *Television and Behavior*.[47] Instead, as Jonathan Freedman observed, it was L. Rowell Huesmann, "one of the most avid true believers" in imitative effects, who wrote a review of the social science literature for the 1982 report. And Huesmann "did not really do a review; instead, he referred to a few articles and spent most of the paper on his own research. Thus, no unbiased review was done, and sure enough, the report simply agrees with Huesmann that television violence is harmful."[48] Other reviewers of the 1982 NIMH report, including the National Academy of Sciences' National Research Council, said that its causation conclusions were overstated—based on widely varying definitions of aggressiveness, small statistical differences, dubious lab studies, and inconclusive field experiments.

They noted that the two largest-scale studies had produced similar results, but the authors had interpreted the results in opposite ways.[49]

Definitional Dilemmas

What, then, do studies of media violence or sex actually show? A few preliminary observations about social science research are useful before attempting an answer.

1. First, it's important to identify *what type of effects* social scientists have tried to measure. Researchers differ markedly in describing the effects that they think art, entertainment, and other expression have on youngsters. Some believe that violent content directly inspires imitation. Others say that its primary impact is to desensitize viewers, making them more callous about antisocial or dangerous behavior. Still others advocate an "excitation" theory which posits that physiological arousal—whether from violent entertainment or other sources—can be transferred into aggressive behavior if a person is provoked. Finally, there are champions of the "mean world" effect—a fear of being victimized and a perception that real-world brutality is more pervasive than it actually is.[50]

Many experts acknowledge that not all violent content has any of these possible negative effects. It all depends on context, they say—for example, whether the perpetrator in a violent story is punished. Prominent contributors to a 1998 report identified eleven separate "contextual factors" that they thought influenced a work's impact—among them humor, which they said trivializes violence and "generally contributes to the learning of aggression." (They gave the Three Stooges as an example.)[51]

The variety of different effects posited by social scientists demonstrates the impossibility of pinpointing the overall impact of sexual or violent content in entertainment. Excessive timidity caused by the mean world syndrome is a quite different effect from increased aggression. Different viewers will interpret such "contextual factors" as humor in different ways. One child may think—however fleetingly—that violence is the way to solve problems or gain social status after watching a John Ford Western; another may become fearful; while still a third may interpret the film as pure fantasy without any particular lesson about real-world behavior. As an expert witness in A. S. Byatt's novel *Babel Tower* observes, any mother "knows that some children can take *anything* and some cry and cry over the death of a seal or Bambi and never quite recover."[52]

Sexual material presents the same dilemma. While some children may be frightened or aroused by it, others will be uncomprehending or bored. Even scholars whose work favors media effects have observed that the same content "may create nightmares for one child and be the source of coping skills for another."[53] Dr. Victor Strasburger, a prominent advocate of media effects, agrees that sexual explicitness "could be extremely scary or confusing" for some children and "absolutely harmless" for others.[54]

2. If pinpointing effects is difficult, then *defining what is supposed to cause them* is equally so. Social scientists—not to mention politicians, advocacy groups, and individual parents—may mean many different things when they excoriate "media violence" or (in the words of Congress in its 1996 v-chip law) "casual treatment of sexual material."[55] Definitions in the experimental literature vary from one study to the next, when they are offered at all. And since even media effects enthusiasts tend to agree that expression touching on huge subjects like sexuality or violence is likely to have very different effects depending upon its style, context, and theme, defining what it is that researchers are trying to measure becomes even more treacherous. Thus, the same violent act can be "seen as treason or heroism. Physical discipline of a child may be viewed as appropriate or abusive, depending on viewpoint and culture," and "assault may be viewed as reprehensible conduct or as an appropriate part of a sport or entertainment, like hockey or boxing."[56] The same can be said of hitting Bobo dolls or other violence observed in lab experiments.

Some researchers have attempted to distinguish "good" from "bad" or "gratuitous" media violence. The British Board of Film Classification did so in 1999 when it justified a 15+ rating for *Saving Private Ryan* because "the examiners felt strongly that young people should be able to see this [extremely realistic portrayal] of war."[57] But distinctions based on whether cinematic violence is educational or gratuitous are so subjective, and turn so critically on interpretations that are colored by viewers' psychological, emotional, and cultural background, that quantitative measurement becomes ludicrous. Among other things, trying to shove creative expression into neat categories of "good" and "bad" violence fails to account for such common characteristics as ambiguity, satire, and irony. And there has been no consensus among social scientists on these contextual questions. Some think that depictions of justified violence by heroes who are rewarded, not punished, are in fact far worse than gruesome violence by villains who get their comeuppance in the end.

Other media effects researchers do not even attempt to identify content that they suspect is harmful; they simply examine the effects of TV viewing in general. Their conclusions range from nonempirical predictions that the "idiot box" has fundamentally altered our brains and will lead to the end of literacy to assertions that the very existence of television is responsible for increased rates of violent crime. Whatever their accuracy, studies of this type do not support claims that particular media content is traumatic or causes imitation. Yet even this basic distinction is sometimes lost by those arguing that bad behavior results from bad messages in art or entertainment.

The concept of bad behavior likewise suffers from vagueness and variability. Researchers use widely differing descriptions of the effects they are seeking, ranging from insensitive attitudes or incivility to risky conduct, from violent play with Bobo dolls to violent crime. As the psychologists Kenneth Gadow and Joyce Sprafkin note with considerable understatement, "the term aggression as it is used by researchers in this area is not a unitary concept." In some studies, "a distinction was made between playful and hurtful aggression and in others both peer and adult-directed aggression was studied."[58] The New York City Bar likewise pointed out that "most psychological studies of the effects of television are studies of aggression or aggressive attitudes, not violence. The distinction is significant: many behaviors which few would deem 'violent' may be counted and measured by psychologists as aggressive."[59]

The definitional problems are equally formidable when it comes to sex. If the Supreme Court has had trouble defining obscenity for the legal purpose of distinguishing it from constitutionally protected speech, the problems are truly mind-boggling when terms such as "offensive," "inappropriate for minors," or "casual treatment of sexual material" are deployed. Social scientists Edward Donnerstein, Daniel Linz, and Barbara Wilson offered a good illustration of the point in comments sent to the FCC to correct misstatements in a submission by the American Family Association (AFA) regarding alleged harm to minors from "indecent" radio or television broadcasts. In addition to misrepresenting the results of several studies and confusing youngsters with adults, the scholars said, the AFA confused violent pornography with "indecency." They concluded: "the available social science research does not show that exposure to "indecent' materials has any effect on children."[60]

Thus, Donnerstein and Linz may have believed in adverse effects from viewing violent pornography, but "indecency" was a far broader and vaguer category that included not just "patently offensive" descriptions of sex but four-letter words, innuendos, and bathroom jokes. And even with respect to violent pornography, as Linz and Donnerstein acknowledged, "no one yet has been able to come up with either an acceptable operational definition of aggressive behavior on the part of the subject who is supposedly reacting to the film or other media event, or an acceptable definition of what actually constitutes violence in the media depiction itself."[61]

3. Another big question in social science research is *scientific validity*. At least since the days of *L'Onanisme*, scientific proof has been claimed for what are really just clinical or anecdotal reports of individual cases. Thus, Victor Cline, an early critic of the 1970 Lockhart Commission, has concluded from his clinical experience that adolescent males are "particularly vulnerable" to the "negative and addictive effects" of pornography, which include "having their lives consumed by it: sitting for hours masturbating to adult material and needing progressively stronger, heavier, harder material to give them a bigger kick."[62] Cline offers a number of case histories to support his assertion, but no studies indicating whether it is fair to generalize from his observations. For every case he encountered of a person in need of therapy, there were probably many more who never came to the attention of clinicians and who consumed pornography in moderate doses with no ill effects. A witness in the 1994 "heinous crimes" trading card case made the same point about the evidence adduced by Fredric Wertham in the 1950s against comic books. Wertham interviewed juvenile offenders, she said,

> and asked them if they had read comic books. And they said they had. And he therefore concluded that reading comic books made them into juvenile delinquents. His study is now cited in courses on mass communication as a form of error . . . because you see, had he asked all children of New York City, have you read comics, he would have found that 93 percent of all children had read comics. And they were not all juvenile delinquents.[63]

Judith Harris pithily summarized the problem: "the plural of anecdote is not data."[64] People in therapy (or prison) are not a random cross section of society, and there are not ordinarily control groups when one draws inferences from clinical cases. Although case histories may be both suggestive and compelling (indeed, Freud built a monumental theory around them), they cannot lay claim to proof.

4. Related to the problem of scientific validity is the meaning of *statistics*. In studies that aren't simply anecdotal, researchers rely on statistical correlations to demonstrate imitative effects from violent media. But such

correlations may actually be quite small. Statistical significance in social science generally means a result that would occur no more than once in twenty times by chance. But this doesn't necessarily mean the result occurs very often. In other words, " '[s]ignificant' in the statistical sense does not mean 'important.' It means simply 'not likely to happen just by chance.' "[65]

Thus, a "causation" hypothesis may be borne out, for social science purposes, by an experiment in which the great majority of subjects are unaffected by the particular book, film, or TV show being studied. As Frederick Schauer, the Meese Commission's legal expert, explained, causation in social science is not "deterministic," but "attributive" and "probabilistic."[66] The "identification of a causal relationship under a probabilistic account does not entail the conclusion that the identified cause produces the effect in all, a majority, or even a very large proportion of cases."[67] In the words of one contributor to the 1982 NIMH report, causal inferences in the social sciences "are, at best, approximations."[68]

Obviously, countless violent and sexual acts throughout history have occurred in the absence of any stimulus from television, books, or pornography; likewise, teenage girls became pregnant long before soap operas portrayed illicit sex; and children misbehaved before the introduction of crime comics or Tom and Jerry cartoons. But under the concept of "probabilistic causation," a causal relationship merely means *some* increase, no matter how small, in "the incidence" or "probability" of the effect. Probabilistic causation is not proof and indeed, as Victor Strasburger acknowledged, trying to "tease out the effects of television on human behavior can be a methodologic 'mission impossible' because television is ubiquitous and human behavior is complex."[69]

Researchers differ, moreover, regarding which statistical methods are most reliable: multiple regression analysis, cross-lagged correlations, and many other sophisticated ways of massaging numbers can produce quite different results.[70] Judith Harris describes instances in which social scientists have manipulated data relentlessly to find some sort of positive correlation to support their hypotheses.[71]

Even those who believe that art and entertainment have widespread imitative impact usually acknowledge that social factors such as family environment are far more important influences on children than the media, and have not claimed a "media effect" on attitudes and behavior of more than 5–15 percent.[72] "No reputable scholar," writes Sissela Bok, "accepts the view expressed by 20% of the American public in 1995, blaming television more than any other factor for teenage violence."[73] The National Research Council's 1993 report, *Understanding and Preventing Violence*, does not consider the media a serious factor.[74] Yet politicians, advocates, journalists, and even social scientists have repeatedly used imprecise language in talking about media effects, suggesting that they are large, uniform, and scientifically proven.

With these caveats in mind, what have social "science" media effects studies actually shown? Laboratory, field, and correlational work—the three main types of studies—each has its own large literature and separate strengths and weaknesses. What follows here cannot possibly be a complete description of the vast media effects literature. I have endeavored to put the studies in perspective, describe the highlights, and bring some coherence to what is obviously a daunting and voluminous body of often technical social science work. What must strike any open-minded student of the subject, though, is that despite widely publicized claims that adverse effects have been proven, the studies are ambiguous, disparate, and modest in their results. As Jonathan Freedman described his and his colleagues' eye-opening experience after reviewing what they assumed had been definitely established, "We were initially surprised, then amazed, and finally appalled at the discrepancy between what we found in the research and the way it was generally described."[75] Joyce Sprafkin had a similar experience after her own experiments with emotionally disturbed youths found either no effect of violent television or more aggressive behavior associated with *nonviolent* shows. "I decided to look back carefully at the field and say, well, what have other people really found?" For preschool children, the field studies simply "did not support a special significance for aggressive television."[76]

Despite the ambiguities, contradictions, and deficiencies of media effects studies, however, there ought to be little doubt that art, entertainment, and other forms of expression do have real psychological effects, including, in some cases, imitation. The point is that ultimately these effects are vast and various, and not amenable to quantitative measurement. The basic problem with social scientists' attempts to quantify aesthetic experience is that they "have been looking for simplistic explanations of extremely complex phenomena"; they seek to measure not "chemical bonds or electrical voltage" but "the most subtle human characteristics—the sentiments described so finely by Henry James."[77]

Sex, Violence, and Social Science

The most consistent evidence of media effects comes from *laboratory experiments*—researchers' attempts to manipulate attitudes or behavior in a controlled or "nonnaturalistic" setting. Bandura's Bobo dolls experiments were an early example; similar results were obtained by Leonard Berkowitz when he had an examiner deliberately insult a group of college students to anger them, then exposed them to a boxing movie in which a severe beating takes place. In answering questions afterward, students who were told that the beating was justified expressed "stronger hostility" toward the examiner than those in a control group. From this, Berkowitz concluded that "justified fantasy aggression lowered inhibitions against subsequent hostile responses," and that Feshbach's different results, supporting a catharsis theory, might be explained by his subjects' not considering the movie violence they saw to be justified. "In essence," Berkowitz said, "our findings point to possible dangers in movie and TV adherence to the Mosaic injunction of an 'eye for an eye.' An aggressive villain should perhaps be punished, but apparently not aggressively."[78]

In the field of pornography research, Donnerstein, Linz, and others used similar laboratory techniques. The classic experiment showed male college students explicit films depicting a female victim reacting positively to sexual mistreatment, then asked the students about their attitudes toward rape victims and/or tested their willingness to administer electric shocks or other forms of "punishment" in a lab to a female who was actually a confederate of the researcher and who had previously angered the subjects as part of the experiment. The results generally—but not always—showed greater acceptance of certain rape myths or more "aggressive" behavior toward the female confederate among the young men shown the sexually violent films, though subsequent "debriefing" reversed these effects and sometimes produced more sensitivity to issues of violence against women than the subjects had demonstrated at the outset of the experiment. Donnerstein *et al.* concluded that it was the violent rather than the sexual content that caused aggression, and that R-rated action films were therefore a more serious social problem than pornography.[79]

Other researchers, Dolf Zillmann for example, have disagreed, and focused on "improper" attitudes about sex that they believe are fostered by nonviolent sexual material.[80] Yet family background strongly influenced the subjects' moral responses in Zillmann's studies; and other researchers found that "males who had viewed heterosexual explicitness substantially and repeatedly responded more quickly to the suffering of a female confederate."[81] A cumulative summary, or "meta-analysis," of lab experiments on pornography concluded that angered subjects who had been exposed to images of nudity "diminish in subsequent aggression."[82]

Years of lab studies have left little doubt that experimenters can induce short-term behavioral effects in a statistically significant number of subjects. But it is questionable whether these controlled experimental results have "ecologic validity" in the real world, given "the very artificiality of the circumstances" and "the brevity of both the TV exposure and the effects being measured."[83] Aggression in a laboratory, as the New York City Bar report explained, "is necessarily only an analogue of aggression, such as pushing a 'shock button' or hitting a Bobo doll"; it may be perceived as encouraged and approved by the researchers (the "experimenter demand effect"), "with no possibility of retaliation, sanction, or moral condemnation."[84] Lab studies are also artificial because they are so limited in time and they frequently isolate "selected violent programs or scenes" both from their context in the film and from the larger world in which people are exposed to "a mixture of programming depicting violent and nonviolent activities."[85] The fact that effects for males are almost always more pronounced than for females demonstrates that no simple cause-and-effect relationship exists; ideas are mediated by individuals' varying predispositions and backgrounds before they are absorbed, disregarded, or acted upon.[86]

Donnerstein and other leading researchers have acknowledged the drawbacks of lab studies. In criticizing the Meese Commission on Pornography's misuse of social science data to support its assertion that violent pornography causes sexual crime, they said that lab experiments, including their own, "are susceptible to many criticisms concerning external validity," including the fact that "outside the laboratory violence is not sanctioned, but inside the laboratory aggression is condoned, even encouraged." Moreover, they acknowledged, "usually only studies that obtain positive results are published."[87]

Field studies are an attempt to compensate for the lab experiments' deficiencies by examining media effects in more natural settings—showing movies, for example, to youthful subjects, then observing their subsequent behavior in the real world. But the results of the studies have been "mixed and puzzling": some show that "only initially aggressive children experience heightened aggression after viewing violent films"; others show "heightened aggression only for initially low-aggression children"; still others show "no increase in aggression at all or even a decrease in aggression."[88] Jonathan

Freedman concluded "categorically, with no hesitation," that field experiments provided no "convincing evidence of an effect," and added:

> I am not alone in this. Tom Cook, a highly respected psychologist, wrote a critique of the 1982 NIMH report on television. In it, he and his co-authors said, "[i]n our view, the field experiments on television violence produce little consistent evidence of effects, despite claims to the contrary." Joyce Sprafkin was originally a believer in the effect. In fact, she was a co-author of a book that attacked television. Yet, she has recently changed her opinion. In a review of the evidence written with Kenneth Gadow, they wrote: "[a]t the present time, the findings from the field experiments offer little support for the media aggression hypothesis."[89]

Among the more interesting of the field experiments was one by Sprafkin and others in which previously low-aggression preschoolers showed a threefold increase in aggression after watching not shoot-'em-ups or violent cartoons but *Sesame Street* or *Mister Rogers' Neighborhood*. In another study, emotionally disturbed children, who the researchers thought would be less capable of processing fantasy information and more likely simply to imitate behaviors seen on-screen, responded to nonviolent shows like *Lassie's Rescue Rangers* with more aggressive behavior than they exhibited after viewing violent cartoons featuring Tom and Jerry, Bugs Bunny, and Woody Woodpecker.[90] Sprafkin and her colleagues hypothesized that the nonviolent drama, for all its social uplift, caused anxiety because of its suspenseful plot, and concluded that "commonsense notions about what is harmful or innocent television fare for children are not always on target." Often, "it is the 'control' programs that are the most problematic." "[F]orcing a wholesome television diet on children may be counterproductive."[91]

A field study by Britain's Independent Television Commission attempted to determine the "scare" effect of TV cartoons by interviewing sixty children aged 5 to 9. It concluded that for the most part children are not frightened by cartoons "because they know they are not real." Some older children do feel uncomfortable with stories that relate more obviously to real life, while younger ones "tend not to pick up on scary concepts; they go right over their heads."[92] This study supported the view that unrealistic violence on-screen is unlikely to inspire trauma. Yet Donnerstein and others participating in the 1998 *National Television Violence Study* in the United States asserted that cartoon fantasies are dangerous precisely because they are funny and "trivialize" violence.[93]

Correlational studies are also relied upon to make inferences about media effects. Of course, a correlation between two facts or events does not mean that one caused the other, as any competent researcher will agree. Yet even experts who know better sometimes slide into sloppy language that *suggests*, without quite saying, that an empirical "link" or "association" between two variables (preference for media violence and aggressive behavior, most often) amounts to proof of causation. Perhaps the most shocking such lapse came from the American Psychological Association in the summary section of its 1993 report, *Violence and Youth: Psychology's Response*. There is "absolutely no doubt" of the correlation between viewing TV violence and "increased acceptance of aggressive attitudes and increased aggressive behavior," it said; then leapt to "the irrefutable conclusion that viewing violence increases violence." Nowhere in this summary did the APA acknowledge the difference between correlation and causation—or note that its "irrefutable conclusion" had been questioned many times.[94]

One of the most famous of the correlation studies, by Brandon Centerwall, found a positive relation between homicide rates and the introduction of television in Canada, South Africa, and the United States. (There was no analysis of television content.) On the basis of correlations, Centerwall concluded that television was responsible for a doubling in the number of killings in these countries.[95] The flaws in his logic, and his failure to consider other factors that might account for the rise in homicides, led to widespread criticism. One author noted the lack of violent content on early Canadian TV and the likelihood that political conditions in South Africa accounted for changes in the homicide rate.[96] Ultimately, data showing precisely the opposite correlation (increased TV viewing and reduced homicide rates in many countries) completely undermined Centerwall's claims.[97]

Another oft-cited series of studies found significant correlations between sales of such "men's magazines" as *Playboy* and *Penthouse* and rape rates in different states. The researchers doubted whether the relationship was causal, however, suspecting "some common third variable." And in fact, the correlations "vanish[ed]" when the authors introduced such a third variable, the "Violence Approval Index"—a checklist of "hypermasculine" attitudes—into their statistical analysis. That is, sexist socialization and environment likely accounted for both the magazine sales and the rate of assaults. "Ironically," they wrote, "proposals to regulate pornography have become virtually the only publicly debated approach to reducing rape. This is unfortunate because the scientific evidence does not support the proposition that prohibiting pornography is an effective way to deal with rape."[98]

Although numerous studies have reported correlations between aggressive behavior and preference for violent television, all present essentially the same chicken-and-egg dilemma. That is, it is not clear whether either characteristic causes the other, or whether some third variable or set of variables accounts for both. Thus, for example, an unsurprising correlation between reckless behavior among adolescents and their taste for heavy metal music "did not demonstrate that listening to these types of music causes adolescents to behave recklessly. Rather, both reckless behavior and heavy metal or hard rock music appeal to adolescents who have an especially high propensity for sensation seeking."[99] Similarly, an experiment in 1980 asked 75 adolescent girls, half of them pregnant, about their television viewing habits: it turned out that the pregnant ones watched more TV soap operas and were somewhat less likely to think that their favorite soap opera characters would use contraceptives. The authors acknowledged that it is "difficult to know if television portrayals are encouraging adolescents to be unrealistic about sexual relationships [that is, not use contraceptives], or if unrealistic adolescents identify with the glamorized TV portrayals."[100]

Another study, from a junior high school in North Carolina, found that of 391 students, those who watched sexier TV shows were more likely to have become sexually active in the preceding year. Although "having had intercourse appeared to be related to seeking sexual content on television," the researchers were "unable to determine which came first—sexual intercourse or a proclivity for viewing sexual activity on television."[101] As with the soap opera study, the initial inference might be that television teaches reckless sexual attitudes, but it is at least equally likely that the more sexually adventuresome (or irresponsible) youngsters were drawn to the racier shows, or that parental role models, peer group pressures, or a dearth of straightforward messages and information about sex and contraception were the primary factors influencing both the risk-taking mentality and the preference for sexually oriented TV. The American Academy of Pediatrics (AAP), which for years has expressed concern about the influence of TV, citing such statistics as teenagers' exposure to an "estimated 14,000 sexual references and innuendos per year on television," nevertheless acknowledges that "there is no clear documentation" that the relationship between TV viewing and sexual activity "is causal."[102]

None of this is to say that correlations are meaningless, or that they cannot be bases for further investigation of causative effects—even the "probabilistic" causal effects of social science. Indeed, correlations in Japan and some European countries between availability of pornography and declining sex crime rates[103] suggest that easy access to porn may actually reduce sexual offenses, but they do not prove it. Other studies have found punitive, repressive upbringing, and lack of access to libidinous material, to correlate most strongly with sex crimes. A 1991 study of juvenile offenders reported that although most had seen pornography, the primary causes of sex crimes among these adolescent boys were their own histories of physical and sexual abuse. Some scholars have found "lack of sexual fantasizing" to be correlated with sexual dysfunction.[104]

"Longitudinal" studies, finally, are an effort to examine correlations over time, to see whether quantitative associations can be established between youngsters' television viewing and later, not just contemporaneous, aggressive behavior. One of the more ambitious of these undertakings, the "Rip Van Winkle" study by L. Rowell Huesmann, Leonard Eron, and their colleagues, examined television habits and social conduct among a group of rural New Yorkers at ages 8, 19, and 30. For the males in the study, there was a correlation between violent TV viewing at age 8, one measure of aggression at age 19, and serious crime at age 30. The correlations for females, if found at all, were much lower.[105] Huesmann and Eron said the data supported a finding of "bidirectionality"—that is, aggressive tendencies lead to increased viewing of violent television, and increased viewing in turn increases aggression. In this and other studies, Eron and Huesmann also found strong correlations between aggressive behavior and non-media-related factors such as low parental education and social status, parents' aggressiveness and nonnurturant child-rearing practices, poor school performance, and unpopularity with peers.[106]

Doubters pointed out that other longitudinal studies failed to replicate Huesmann and Eron's findings of a "forward cross-lagged correlation" between males' violent TV preferences at a young age and their later aggression. They also criticized Eron and Huesmann's statistical methods in "Rip Van Winkle" and other experiments, their slim and inconclusive results, their failure to explore other factors associated with violent behavior, their reliance on dubious parental reporting of their children's aggressiveness, and their inability to keep track of many of the subjects over the years of the Rip Van Winkle study.[107] Jonathan Freedman, scrutinizing the first ten years of the Rip Van Winkle study, acknowledged that one correlation for boys was suggestive of causation but doubted whether the study could really support the claims that had been made for it, given that the pattern was not found for girls, and even for boys was found using only one of three measures of aggression: peer reports. Using other measures of aggression chosen by the researchers—self-reports and personality tests—there were no statistically significant correlations. Freedman noted that another large-scale longitudinal study, sponsored by NBC, found "no evidence of a delayed effect of watching television violence," whether based on total samples or subgroups. This NBC study, despite or perhaps because of its corporate sponsorship, was scrupulous in its detail—following about 3,200 youngsters in midwestern cities over a period of three years.[108]

Eron and Huesmann continued to insist that their New York study established causation. As journalist Richard Rhodes recounts, Huesmann used a dramatic bar graph in congressional testimony to illustrate the correlation between early TV viewing and violent crime in adult life. Yet these numbers were not published, and when Rhodes questioned Huesmann years later about the crime data for the 30-year-olds in the study, Huesmann admitted that the correlation was "entirely due to 3 boys who committed violent crimes and had scored high on age 8 TV violence viewing. . . . It is enough to make the results significant according to statistical theory, but if just these 3 boys had behaved differently, all the significant results could have vanished."[109]

Eron and Huesmann conducted further research. In a two-year study of first and third graders in Chicago, they found correlations between violent TV viewing and aggression for both boys and girls, but without the increase in aggression over time that they had argued supported a causal inference in the New York study.[110] Then, in what Freedman described as "a wonderful cross-national study that involved six different countries, with a total of fourteen different groups," all observed over time, Eron and Huesmann found "no significant effect" for Australia, Finland, the Netherlands, Poland, the United States, or kibbutz children in Israel. The only strongly significant effects over time were for two groups of Israeli city dwellers. Yet, as Freedman describes, most of the researchers involved "tried to put the best face on it that they could" in the book that resulted:

> Despite the fact that they had not gotten the effects they wanted, they hedged, did other analyses, and tried to make it sound as if the results supported the initial prediction that television violence would increase aggression. The Dutch group did not hedge. Their write-up came right out and said that there was no evidence of any effect. Well, Huesmann and Eron would not publish their chapter unless

> they revised their conclusions. To this the Dutch replied that they were "competent enough to draw our own conclusions." And they had to publish their report separately. There may be another side to this story, but the fact is that they did publish separately and their view is that their contribution was rejected because they would not change their conclusions. This is an unfortunate incident and indicates, I think, how politicized this issue has become and how difficult it is for some of the researchers to be objective about the research.[111]

The Dutch researchers were unequivocal. They reported positive correlations between aggressive behavior and TV viewing, but these "disappeared almost completely when correlations for the starting level of aggression and intelligence were applied. The hypothesis, formulated on the basis of social learning theory, that television violence viewing leads to aggressive behavior could not be supported."[112]

Huesmann and his colleagues wrote a reply to Freedman's critiques. In it, they minimized the deficiencies of lab experiments, emphasized the "convergence of evidence from different sources" supporting imitation theory, and accused Freedman of "set[ting] an impossible criterion for studies he wants to reject, viz., that they 'demonstrate a causal effect' . . . or 'definitive proof.' " At bottom, they made clear, they simply have a different psychological perspective: their hypothesis about human development is that "aggression as a characteristic way of solving social problems, is learned at a young age and becomes more and more impervious to change as the child grows older."[113] They may well be correct, but their riposte came no closer to demonstrating that "science" had proved it so.

Like Eron and Huesmann, those who believe that adverse media effects have been demonstrated generally adopt a "convergence" approach. That is, they accept the deficiencies of the various methods and the ambiguities of the results, but conclude that cumulatively the studies sufficiently reinforce each other to demonstrate that viewing TV violence causes aggressive behavior.[114] "All studies have drawbacks," as Daniel Linz says; but it is "the cumulation of the evidence" that leaves "absolutely no question" about causation.[115] Similarly, some point to "meta-analyses"—statistical studies that combine the results of many experiments—as proof that the case has been made. But if the underlying studies are flawed, inconsistent, ambiguous in their results, or unable to be replicated, it is not clear that blending them strengthens the case for adverse media effects.

In 1986, Yale professor William McGuire reviewed the previous generation's worth of media effects literature. He concluded that despite the hype, many field and even laboratory studies had found no real-world behavioral impact from TV violence, and those that did reached only a small level of statistical significance. "That myths can persist despite conflicting evidence," McGuire wrote, "is illustrated by the robustness of the belief that television and other media have sizable impacts on the public's thoughts, feelings, and actions even though most empirical studies indicate small to negligible effects."[116] Indeed, the myths about proven adverse effects of media violence were propounded again during the 2000 presidential campaign; a Federal Trade Commission report on entertainment industry marketing targeted at youth became the occasion for threats of government action by candidates Al Gore and Joe Lieberman if industry executives did not "clean up their act." The FTC's report actually contained a balanced survey of the media effects literature acknowledging that "[r]egarding causation," the studies are not conclusive, and that, "whatever the impact of media violence, it likely explains a relatively small amount of the total variation in youthful violent behavior."[117]

Kids, Ambiguity, and the Social Cognition Approach

By the 1980s, a more nuanced "humanistic" or "social cognition" approach to media effects had emerged, centering on "children's appropriation of cultural tools, goals, and activities" as they learn.[118] Even the 1982 NIMH report had noted "a change in psychology since the 1960s when the stimulus-response models of learning began to give way to a broader-gauged cognitive orientation," which understands human beings to respond to new information in varying ways, based on "preestablished schema" that are "built up by many previous interactions with the environment."[119] As psychologist Kevin Durkin put it, broad generalizations about simple, direct effects of art or entertainment on human psyches "do not carry us very far"; television "may be implicated" in child development, but "in different ways at different points in the lifespan." As much depends "upon what the child brings to TV viewing as upon what it extracts."[120]

Durkin describes the social learning school's "waning fortunes" in psychological circles. Youngsters use TV selectively, he says, to "check hypotheses, gather new information, and impose interpretations" on the fictional world that will help them understand the real one. By the age of 7, they do not necessarily accept everything they watch as "realistic or desirable." In short, it is "difficult to disentangle" the media's effects from "the myriad of other social forces conceivably impinging on the developing mind."[121]

By the 1990s, the social-cognitive view of human learning was overshadowing more simplistic media effects theories. Oxford University's 1999 report to the European Commission on the v-chip outlined a range of psychological perspectives, from social learning to catharsis, then focused in some detail on "perceptions research." This approach, the report said, acknowledges that TV violence is commonplace, but asserts that "its significance for the viewer is harder to measure." TV consumers, "young and old, are selectively perceptive and judgmental in their responses to programmes. The ways viewers perceive and evaluate characters and events on television do not always match description incident counts or the meanings inferred from them by researchers."[122] Thus, for example, cartoons like Tom and Jerry contain massive violence, but because of their "fantastical and animated contexts," children tend to perceive them "as containing very little violence at all." One 1996 study sponsored by the British Broadcasting Council reported that "even young children make complex judgments about violence through making a distinction between reality and fantasy," and opined that TV programs that generate such "negative emotions" as sadness or fear may have positive consequences in helping children "learn to cope" with "real-life anxieties and concerns." Children "respond to and make sense of television in the light of what they know about its formal codes and conventions, about genre and narrative, and about the production process. In these respects, they are much more active and sophisticated users of the medium than they are often assumed to be."[123] A 1986 Dutch survey found that by ages 9 to 12, children's perceptions of program content differed little from those of adults.[124]

The social cognition perspective recognizes that different types of expression have different intentions, meanings, and effects. Violence in action movies will be processed by viewers, depending on their ages, temperaments, and other contextual factors, differently from violence in cartoons, Stephen King novels, or interactive Web sites. The same is true of persuasion. Those who cling to a narrowly imitative view of media effects often make an analogy to advertising: corporations, they say, would not invest heavily in TV ads—particularly ads targeting children—unless they were effective. What they overlook is that advertising, like propaganda, is not the same as fantasy, satire, eroticism, pop music, or soap opera. It is a giant leap from acknowledging the power of advertising to accepting the notion that all forms of expression have easily predictable persuasive or imitative effects.

What, then, of catharsis? Obviously, the quantitative methods of social science have not confirmed its existence. But neither have they disproved Aristotle. Highly individualized emotional responses to art are no more amenable to scientific measurement than the imitative effects that social learning psychologists have tried to prove. Just as imitation sometimes occurs, so does catharsis. At least, it is difficult to discount the cathartic responses to art and entertainment that humans have experienced over centuries.

The inability of social science to quantify the impact of art or entertainment obviously does not preclude the existence of a wide range of psychological and behavioral effects, or obviate the need, in a democratic society, for interpretation and critique of media messages. As Victor Strasburger has said, lack of quantitative proof does not mean that objections to TV content cannot exist "on 'purely aesthetic, humanistic, and philosophical grounds.' "[125] Another expert likewise threw up his hands on the causation issue during congressional hearings in 1997 on rock music and teenage angst. Admitting that no studies had established a cause-and-effect relationship, he nevertheless said we should acknowledge "the overall effect music has on people, including adolescents and children."[126]

But as we acknowledge that overall effect, we should also be wary of oversimplifying. The critic Wendy Steiner has bemoaned the literalism, "the collapse of paradox," that in the late 20th century so often reduced art and literature to scripts for indoctrination. There is nothing new about the censorship impulse and the fear of ambiguity in art, Steiner says, noting that it goes back to Plato; but such frightening events as the *fatwa* announced by Iran against Salman Rushdie for insulting Islam in his novel *The Satanic Verses* dramatized the extent to which literalism and reductionism were overwhelming any appreciation for ambiguity. "We will not be led into fascism or rape or child abuse or racial oppression through aesthetic experience," Steiner writes. On the contrary, "the more practiced we are in fantasy the better we will master its difference from the real."[127]

Another critic put the case for catharsis differently. Explaining the popularity of Judy Blume's novels about adolescence and childhood, Mark Oppenheimer said they are cathartic in their appeal to youngsters who have "outgrown the fantastic" and thirst for stories about real life.[128]

CONCLUSION: "THE ETHICAL AND MORAL DEVELOPMENT OF YOUTH"

In September 1999, New York City's mayor, Rudolph Giuliani, tried to close down an art exhibit entitled *Sensation* at the Brooklyn Museum, a venerable institution supported largely with city funds. Among the works on display that the mayor considered "sick" and "disgusting" was the British artist Chris Ofili's "Holy Virgin Mary," a glittering African madonna with an exposed breast of dried elephant dung (a standard ingredient in Ofili paintings) and small photos of unattached female bottoms fluttering cherub-like in the background. As one of his reasons for withholding city funds and filing an eviction action against the museum after it refused to cancel the show, Giuliani noted the institution's own announcement that nobody under 17 would be admitted unless accompanied by an adult. This, he said, violated the museum's lease with the city, which required it to serve the general public, including schoolchildren.

In response, the Brooklyn Museum revoked its "adults only" restriction, but it retained a tongue-in-cheek "Health Warning" that *Sensation* "may cause shock, vomiting, confusion, panic, euphoria, and anxiety." Whatever the purpose of its initial ban on unaccompanied minors—titillation and publicity being among the possibilities—the museum evidently did not feel the specter of psychic harm was so severe that it had to retain the ban once Giuliani had seized upon it as a reason for trying to close the show. When this author visited *Sensation* in early November 1999, several preteenagers were soberly perusing the works without apparent distress.[1]

But the city's lawyers were not inclined to let go of an enticing argument, and on appeal of Judge Nina Gershon's ruling that the mayor's actions had violated the First Amendment, they harped on the harm-to-minors theme. The "vulgar" and "offensive" exhibit, they wrote in their brief, was "antithetical to the public's core values" and clearly "inappropriate" for youngsters; and they singled out two works—one a large graphic photograph of a bullet hole and the other a nude statue entitled "Dead Dad"—that they said "would be extremely disturbing to" children.[2] But if the museum's initial discrimination against youngsters had more to do with art marketing than psychic harm, this revival of the theme in the city's appellate brief had more to do with politics. For the city cited no evidence that "Dead Dad," "Bullet Hole," or any of the other works in *Sensation* would be "extremely disturbing" to young viewers.

Evidence of harm, of course, is often dispensed with in censorship cases where child protection is the proffered justification. In the Brooklyn Museum imbroglio, as in countless others, it was not really fear of any demonstrable psychological harm, but notions of morality and proper socialization that drove New York City's legal rhetoric. As in *Ginsberg v. New York* (the "girlie magazine" case) thirty-one years before, censorship was presumably needed to ensure "the ethical and moral development of youth." The U.S. Justice Department reiterated this theme in the "Harry Met Sally" cable TV signal bleed case in 1999: harm to minors, it said, inheres in material that defies "socially appropriate standards" and "commonly held moral views about the upbringing of children."[3]

FCC v. Pacifica, the famous Supreme Court decision upholding the government's power to censor the "seven dirty words" on television and radio, is perhaps the classic example of the essentially morality-based nature of harm-to-minors censorship. While the five justices in the *Pacifica* majority thought the injury to youngsters from exposure to the vulgarities in George Carlin's comic monologue too obvious even to explain, Justice Brennan, in dissent, protested his colleagues' "depressing inability to appreciate that in our land of cultural pluralism, there are many who think, act, and talk differently from the Members of this Court," including some parents who might "actually find Mr. Carlin's unabashed attitude" toward taboo words to be healthy.[4]

Like concerns about sex or vulgar words, concerns about media violence also have more to do with socializing youth than with objective proof of psychological harm. True, many parents and politicians—bolstered by the claims of one much-publicized school of psychology—do think that television fantasies predictably cause adverse effects in large numbers of children. But their concerns are not borne out by the much-overstated, often frankly ambiguous results of empirical studies. Worries about media violence are thus, like worries about sex and vulgarity, largely symbolic.

This is by no means a reason to belittle them. But we should at least be clear about what is really going on with harm-to-minors rhetoric. As historian Rochelle Gurstein observes, the notion of quantifying aesthetic experience "in a meaningful way is remarkable for both its philistinism and naïveté"; simplistic theories of causation should not be a crutch on which to lean what are essentially moral arguments.[5] The British TV regulator Colin Shaw agrees:

> [I]n the dysfunctional marks of society around us, we think we may be seeing evidence of what television is doing. It is tempting to do so even when we acknowledge, as the majority of people do, the existence of many alternative causes. We want television to ensure that the values which we most esteem are passed on to a new generation and, in order to accomplish that, we want the programmes seen by children to reflect those values in forms which children will comprehend.[6]

What, then, is wrong with censoring minors in the interests of socialization and morality? Most societies, after all, have an impulse to do so, although (as we have seen) the nature of the disapproved subject matter and the extent of censorship vary enormously. The answer, in part, goes back to the beginning of pedagogy—to Plato. Do we really believe that art and entertainment have only those narrow, one-dimensional effects assumed by Plato—or by the judges who quoted him in *Boring*, the school censorship case described at the beginning of this book? The ponderous, humorless overliteralism of so much censorship directed at youth not only takes the fun, ambiguity, cathartic function, and irony out of the world of imagination and creativity; it reduces the difficult, complicated, joyous, and sometimes tortured experience of growing up to a sanitized combination of adult moralizing and intellectual closed doors.

It also deprives youngsters of the ability to confront and work through the messiness of life—the things that are gross, shocking, embarrassing, or scary. From children's fascination with "dirty noses and dirty bottoms"[7] to their pleasure in cartoon violence, adults' efforts to censor may actually get in the way of socialization. Indeed, disadvantaged, at-risk youngsters may be the ones most harmed when discussion about controversial subjects like sex, drugs, or violence is shut down. In the face of the many truly frightening realities of life, one cannot help raising a bemused eyebrow at reports such as one emanating from the Harvard School of Public Health in 2000 that urged the MPAA to modify its rating system to indicate that *Bambi*, *Aladdin*, and *The Lion King* had too much violence for young kids, and opined that even "acts of slapstick comedy, such as Tigger playfully bowling over his friends in 'The Many Adventures of Winnie the Pooh,' " were harmful.[8]

Todd Gitlin has written that the "symbolic crusade against media violence is a confession of despair. Those who embrace it are saying, in effect, that they either do not know how to, or do not dare, do anything serious about American violence. They are tilting at images"; and their "counsel of desperation . . . promises very little practical good."[9] Or, in the words of the much-censored Judy Blume: " 'Children are inexperienced, but they are not innocent.' They need help from adults to figure out how to act in the face of life's realities. . . . We cannot restore a 'lost innocence' that may never have existed, but we can offer perspectives from our experience and help interpreting the world, flaws and all."[10]

Intellectual protectionism frustrates rather than enhances young people's mental agility and capacity to deal with the world. It inhibits straightforward discussion about sex. Indeed, like TV violence, censorship may also have "modeling effects," teaching authoritarianism, intolerance for unpopular opinions, erotophobia, and sexual guilt.[11] Censorship is an avoidance technique that addresses adult anxieties and satisfies symbolic concerns, but ultimately does nothing to resolve social problems or affirmatively help adolescents and children cope with their environments and impulses or navigate the dense and insistent media barrage that surrounds them.

Beyond these large cultural questions about symbolism and socialization, there are some very practical concerns about censorship and classification schemes for youth. As we have seen, fitting art, literature, and entertainment into neat categories for purposes of prohibitions or ratings is not so simple. Censorship—or its milder handmaiden, classification—inevitably falls victim to highly subjective, discretionary decision making that reflects the ideological and personal predilections of the censors and classifiers. The recurring efforts to purge masterworks like *Huckleberry Finn* or *I Know Why the Caged Bird Sings* from American classrooms suggest that bad ideas are not so easy to identify in the arts and entertainment, and that neither pressure groups nor government officials are well qualified to make these literary and pedagogical distinctions. Even the common refrain that children should not be "robbed of their innocence" by exposure to sexual information reflects a far from universal attitude that, when it comes to the subject of sex, ignorance equals innocence and knowledge equals guilt. Gitlin puts it well: "Censorship is a blunderbuss, not a scalpel. Just which violence is supposed to be cleansed, anyway? The number of drops of blood spilled is scarcely the test of an image's vileness or perniciousness. Context is, by definition, unmeasurable."[12]

Finally, there is the not insignificant question of minors' First Amendment rights. This is not some fuzzy, ivory-tower abstraction. Youngsters need access to information and ideas, not indoctrination and ignorance of controversy, precisely because they are in the process of identity formation. They are also in the process of becoming functioning adults in a democratic society and, as the Supreme Court has pointed out, this is not so easy to do if they are shielded from dangerous or disturbing ideas until they are 18. Confrontation with the "bad ideas" they will inevitably encounter is a more likely inoculator than restrictions that only make forbidden fruit more attractive.

Underlying our system of free expression is the principle that government officials cannot ban, burden, or disfavor speech that they find immoral or offensive. Citizens decide these matters for themselves, as federal judge Frank Easterbrook reminded the proponents of an antipornography ordinance back in 1985: "any other answer leaves the government . . . the great censor and director of which thoughts are good for us."[13] The common response here, of course, is that minors are different; they are not sufficiently mature to understand and resist the perils of bad speech. Even John Stuart Mill, the great theorist of intellectual freedom, assumed that youngsters are not capable of handling the liberty of conscience that he championed for adults.[14] The Supreme Court has tended to agree—especially when the subject is sex—but it has also insisted that the First Amendment applies to everyone, and has specifically rejected Plato's procensorship pedagogy (in a case involving music): "From Plato's discourse in the *Republic* to the totalitarian state in our own times, rulers have known its capacity to appeal to the intellect and to the emotions, and have censored musical compositions to serve the needs of the state. . . . The Constitution prohibits any like attempts in our own legal order."[15]

Obviously, very young children have little capacity to enjoy the blessings of First Amendment intellectual freedom. But most of the harm-to-minors debate concerns children beyond the "age of reason" (about 7) and teenagers, at whose socialization "ethical and moral development" arguments are primarily directed. They are the ones, after all, who are using the Internet, playing video games, reading Harry Potter novels, and looking for signal bleed on cable television. They are also the ones whose developing intellectual capacities should be nurtured and respected. Psychologists Lawrence Kohlberg and Carol Gilligan have noted the sophisticated cognitive abilities of many adolescents, and the importance of respecting their "moral relativism," their questioning of social values as they make their way toward adulthood.[16]

Adolescents are sexually charged, skeptical of authority, and hungry for experience. They hardly need television or the Internet to give them sexual ideas; as Victor Strasburger has written, this is a large part of what makes adults so nervous about them.[17] From a purely pedagogical viewpoint, disempowering teenagers through censorship of the information or entertainment they receive is not likely to resolve the emotional and social problems of an age group that in our modern era is already kept in dependency too long. The notion of adolescence as a prolonged period of immaturity, incompetence, and cultural separation is peculiar to the 20th century; as Thomas Hine writes in *The Rise and Fall of the American Teenager*, if they are treated as young adults and allowed to participate in economic, political, intellectual, and even sexual aspects of life, we might find less, rather than more, irresponsible and high-risk behavior.[18]

Harm-to-minors censorship frequently fails to make these age and maturity-based distinctions. Too often, it merges toddlers, grade schoolers, and teenagers into one vast pool of vulnerable youth. If a First Amendment difference is to be maintained between minors and adults, there ought at least to be more thoughtful and finely calibrated judgments about it. As the Supreme Court has said, constitutional rights "do not mature and come into being magically only when one attains the state-defined age of majority."[19]

Europeans sometimes pay closer attention to age differences. The former Norwegian Ombudsman for Children has argued for respecting free-expression rights, and thereby countering feelings of worthlessness, among adolescents who in modern society live for ever longer periods in situations of dependence. She proposes a graduated framework of minors' "rights and responsibilities" in areas from sexual consent to film attendance.[20] Indeed, sexuality education worldwide is also increasingly premised on the need to involve youngsters in designing programs and working as peer counselors.

There are many other affirmative approaches. At MIT, for example, Henry Jenkins's Program in Comparative Media Studies created an online chat room with teens and parents to "encourage conversations about popular culture and media convergence." "Adults dominated discussions" after the mass murders at Columbine High School, Jenkins explained; "[f]ew public fora offered youth a chance to speak or took seriously what they had to say about their cultural environment. The ensuing 'moral panic' reflected a lack of communication between teens and adults about popular culture and media change."[21]

Another promising initiative was YouthARTS, a project created in the late 1990s by arts councils in Atlanta, San Antonio, and Portland, Oregon. (This program was unrelated to the YouthArts Project for gay teenagers described in chapter 7.) The Portland program taught filmmaking, photography, drama, and life skills to youngsters on probation. In Atlanta, young offenders learned painting, sculpture, printmaking, photography, and "business and entrepreneurial aspects of the arts." They were paid five dollars an hour, given assistance in selling their work, and provided with "a sense of accomplishment—and hence, greater self-esteem." In San Antonio, researchers evaluating a program targeted at 11-to-13-year-olds found that they

> gained an increased ability to work on tasks from start to finish. They engaged in less delinquent behavior, and had fewer court referrals than their nonparticipating peers during the program. They showed an improved attitude toward school, improved self-esteem, and greater self-efficacy. And finally, they had a greater resistance to peer pressure.[22]

These results should not have been surprising. As one author has observed, it is better to channel than to deny youngsters' need to create narratives of adventure as part of their process of identity formation and growing up.[23]

Media literacy programs are another antidote to bad ideas generally and electronic bombardments in particular. An established component of public education in Canada, the programs teach critical thinking and viewing skills: understanding how TV and movies create their effects, evaluating ideas and images in both fiction and advertising. Experimental programs in the United States in the 1980s, using role playing and games, covered such topics as "Reality and Fantasy on Television," "Camera Effects and Special Effects," "Commercials and the Television Business," "Stereotypes," and "Violence and Aggression."[24] In the 1990s, a twelve-week media literacy curriculum in Yakima, Washington, explored film technique, media myths, ethics of advertising, journalistic bias, and the question whether media violence causes the real-life variety.[25] Even Rowell Huesmann and Leonard Eron, among the staunchest believers in imitative media effects, reported that teaching critical viewing skills can counteract antisocial messages on television; "we are not helpless," Eron wrote, "in the face of that insidious teacher in our living rooms."[26] Media literacy had become so popular by the end of the 1990s that commercial enterprises like Channel One, which supplies thousands of American schools with prepackaged TV news and advertisements, were trying to co-opt it.[27]

The goal of media literacy, of course, is to foster critical thinking skills. The difference between this educational approach to youth socialization and more censorial techniques was nicely illustrated in a December 1999 exchange at a meeting of the Free Expression Network, a group of anticensorship activists. Stephen Balkam, director of the Internet Content Rating Association (ICRA), asked the group, in essence, Is there no way I can persuade you to support "voluntary" rating and filtering systems? Joan Bertin, the head of the National Coalition Against Censorship, responded that it was not really a matter of tinkering with the system to make it more accurate or fair: "I don't agree with the fundamental philosophy of rating," she said, "that ideas are harmful to children" and should not be discussed but suppressed. David Greene, head of the First Amendment Project in Oakland, California, agreed. We need "a complete paradigm shift" in our approach to the issue, he said—"to a system of critical thinking instead of filtering and rating" for youth.[28]

Sexuality education is another example of an alternative to censorship that advances informed decision making and critical thinking. Good programs address childhood and teenage issues comprehensively rather than relegating the topic of sex to a few obligatory hours of "organ recital." Some programs address peer pressures, media stereotypes, and even the implications of sexual scripts reflected in commercial pornography. Given the ideological minefield that sex ed in the United States had become by the 1990s, church and community programs, books, teen magazines, Web sites, and Dr. Ruth were all alternative, affirmative sources of information to help youngsters cope with the onslaught of sexual signals from popular entertainment, political rhetoric, and peer groups.[29]

By 2000, even the notoriously contraceptive-averse TV networks were beginning to come around. The Media Project, a partnership of Advocates for Youth and the Henry J. Kaiser Family Foundation, had met with several producers to encourage the inclusion of birth control and safer-sex information on popular shows. A panel presentation on European safer-sex commercials "generated amazement among television executives and was cited as the major reason why a major commercial network began to rethink its approach toward sexuality messages."[30]

Even "Monicagate," whose sexually explicit and tawdry details caused much hand-wringing among child-protection advocates, supplied an occasion for useful education. "For some, particularly those dealing with teenagers," *The New York Times* reported, "the President's troubles have provided an opening to discuss basic values, and to engage in genuine dialogue about sexual morality and the dangers of gossip"—not to mention the exploitative potential of relationships consisting largely of female-administered oral sex.[31]

Exploring alternatives to censorship is not meant to suggest that a diet of slasher films and televised sex acts is a great idea for children or adolescents. Unquestionably, much art, literature, and popular entertainment is not very edifying or desirable. But the question is whether taboos and restrictions should be imposed by government or powerful corporations, or whether media literacy, sexuality education, youth arts programs, and training in nonviolent dispute resolution are more likely to be both more effective and less destructive of basic freedoms. Parents in Western culture have long been the primary censors of their children, and are likely to remain so. As children grow older, even parental control inevitably recedes. Government generally has to meet a high threshold of proven harm before it can interfere with parental decisions. When the symbolic and ideological arguments, the distraction from more profitable methods of addressing bad ideas, and the damage caused by censorship itself are considered, a no-censorship policy even for youth should not seem such an alarming prospect.

As usual, Shakespeare had something useful to contribute on this topic. In *Henry IV, Part Two*, the Earl of Warwick tries to assure the king that his delinquent son Hal will not be harmed by his gadding about with lowlifes in London taverns:

> *The Prince but studies his companions*
> *Like a strange tongue, wherein, to gain the language,*
> *'Tis needful that the most immodest word*
> *Be looked upon and learned, which once attained,*
> *Your Highness knows, comes to no further use*
> *But to be known and hated. So, like gross terms,*

The Prince will in the perfectness of time
Cast off his followers, and their memory
Shall as a pattern or a measure live,
By which his Grace must mete the lives of others,
Turning past evils to advantages.[32]

NOTES

These notes generally follow the rules of legal citation. I use *supra* for the first few references to previously cited sources within a chapter; after that, I simply use a shortened citation.

INTRODUCTION

1. *Boring v. Buncombe County Bd. of Educ.*, 136 F.3d 364, 370 (4th Cir. 1998), quoting Plato's *Republic: Book II* (Benjamin Jowett, trans.) (New York: Walter J. Black, 1942), p. 281.
2. *The Republic and Other Works* (Benjamin Jowett, trans.) (New York: Doubleday, 1973), pp. 62–64, 76–78, 86–90. It is, of course, Socrates who dispenses Plato's philosophy in the *Republic* and other dialogues.
3. *Lacks v. Ferguson Reorganized School Dist.*, 147 F.3d 718 (8th Cir. 1998); *Board of Education v. Wilder*, 960 P.2d 695 (Colo. 1998).
4. Personal Responsibility and Work Opportunity Reconciliation Act of 1996, PL 104–93, 104th Congress, 42 U.S.C. §710 (1996).
5. *Bad Frog Brewery v. New York State Liquor Auth.*, 134 F.3d 87, 91 (2d Cir. 1998). The court noted that this hand gesture had been "in use throughout the world for many centuries," tracing it back to Diogenes in ancient Greece.
6. *Id.* at 92, quoting *Bad Frog Brewery v. New York State Liquor Authority*, 973 F. Supp. 280, 285 (N.D.N.Y. 1997).
7. *Id.* at 98, quoting *Sable Communications v. FCC*, 492 U.S. 115, 126 (1989).
8. *Bad Frog*, 134 F.3d at 99, 90.
9. Telecommunications Act of 1996, §502, PL 104–104, 110 Stat. 56.
10. *ACLU v. Reno*, 929 F. Supp. 824, 852–53, 855 (E.D.Pa. 1996).

11. *Reno v. ACLU*, 521 U.S. 844, 878 (1997).
12. On the rise of children's studies, see Edward Rothstein, "How Childhood Has Changed! (Adults, Too)," *New York Times*, Feb. 14, 1998, p. A13; Harbour Fraser Hodder, "The Eroticized Child," *Harvard Magazine*, Mar.–Apr. 1998, p. 22; *The Children's Culture Reader* (Henry Jenkins, ed.) (New York: NYU Press, 1998).
13. See John D'Emilio & Estelle Freedman, *Intimate Matters: A History of Sexuality in America* (New York: Harper & Row, 1988); John Gagnon & William Simon, *Sexual Conduct: The Social Sources of Human Sexuality* (Chicago: Aldine, 1973); Joseph Kett, *Rites of Passage: Adolescence in America, 1790 to the Present* (New York: Basic Books, 1977); Alison Parker, *Purifying America: Women, Cultural Reform, and Pro-Censorship Activism, 1873–1933* (Urbana: U. of Ill. Press, 1997); Peter Gay, *The Bourgeois Experience, Victoria to Freud*, Vol. 2: *The Tender Passion* (New York: Oxford U. Press, 1986).
14. See Michel Foucault, *The History of Sexuality*, Vol. 1: *An Introduction* (New York: Random House, 1978); *The Foucault Reader* (ed. Paul Rabinow) (New York: Pantheon, 1984); Jeffrey Weeks, *Sex, Politics and Society: The Regulation of Sexuality Since 1800* (London & New York: Longman, 1981), p. 11.
15. Sigmund Freud, *On Creativity and the Unconscious* (New York: Harper & Row, 1958), p. 186; see also Freud's *Three Essays on the Theory of Sexuality* (James Strachey, trans.) (New York: Basic Books, 1962), p. 100; Gagnon & Simon, *supra* n. 13, pp. 16–17, 24.
16. Author's telephone interview with Daniel Linz, Nov. 8, 1999.
17. Henry Jenkins, "Professor Jenkins Goes to Washington" (May 8, 1999), posted on various Internet sites including http://www.fiawol.demon.co.uk/FAC, reprinted in "Readings," *Harper's Magazine*, July 1999, p. 19.
18. Paul Veyne, "The Roman Empire," in *A History of Private Life*, Vol. 1: *From Pagan Rome to Byzantium* (P. Ariès & G. Duby, gen. eds.; Arthur Goldhammer, trans.) (Cambridge, MA: Harvard U. Press, 1987), p. 20; see also Elizabeth Childs, "Introduction," in *Suspended License: Censorship and the Visual Arts* (Elizabeth Childs, ed.) (Seattle: U. of Wash. Press, 1997), p. 12.
19. Henry Jenkins, "Introduction," in *The Children's Culture Reader*, *supra* n. 12, pp. 1, 14.
20. *Anheuser-Busch v. Schmoke*, 101 F.3d 325, 330 (4th Cir. 1996) (upholding a city's restrictions on tobacco advertising).
21. See Michael Freeman, "The Limits of Children's Rights," and Gary Melton & Susan Limber, "What Children's Rights Mean to Children," in *The Ideologies of Children's Rights* (Michael Freeman & Philip Veerman, eds.) (Dordrecht: Martinus Nijhoff, 1992), pp. 35, 167, 173; *Children's Competence to Consent* (Gary Melton *et al.*, eds.) (New York: Plenum Press, 1983); Jane Fortin, *Children's Rights and the Developing Law* (London: Butterworths, 1998), pp. 63–70; Michael Grodin & Leonard Glantz, *Children as Research Subjects: Science, Ethics, and Law* (New York: Oxford U. Press, 1994).
22. Rochelle Gurstein, *The Repeal of Reticence* (New York: Hill & Wang, 1996); Neil Postman, *The Disappearance of Childhood* (New York: Delacorte, 1982);

see also Roger Cox, *Shaping Childhood: Themes of Uncertainy in the History of Adult-Child Relationships* (London: Routledge, 1996), p. 180 (summarizing Postman's complaints that children are no longer "immersed in a world of secrets, surrounded by mystery and awe; a world that will be made intelligible to them by adults who will teach them, in stages, how shame is transformed into a set of moral directives").

23. *American Booksellers Ass'n v. Hudnut*, 771 F.2d 323, 330 (7th Cir. 1985), aff'd, 475 U.S. 1001 (1986).

1. "TO DEPRAVE AND CORRUPT"

1. Alexander Nehamas, "Plato and the Mass Media," 71 *The Monist* 222 (1988); for a modern example of moral disapproval in the Platonic vein, see Neil Postman, *The Disappearance of Childhood* (New York: Delacorte, 1982).
2. Mark Golden, *Children and Childhood in Classical Athens* (Baltimore & London: Johns Hopkins U. Press, 1990), pp. 5, 7; see also James Redfield, "From Sex to Politics: The Rites of Artemis Triklaria and Dionysos Aisymnētēs at Patras," in *Before Sexuality: The Construction of Erotic Experience in the Ancient Greek World* (David Halperin *et al.*, eds.) (Princeton, NJ: Princeton U. Press, 1990), pp. 116–28.
3. John Gagnon, *Human Sexualities* (Glenview, IL.: Scott, Foresman, 1977), p. 14; see also Michel Foucault, *The History of Sexuality*, Vol. 2: *The Use of Pleasure* (New York: Random House, 1985); Vol. 3: *The Care of the Self* (New York: Random House, 1986); Nicole Loraux, "Herakles: The Super-Male and the Feminine," in *Before Sexuality, supra* n. 2; François Lissarrague, "The Sexual Life of Satyrs," *id.*, p. 64 ("in Greek practice, there is always a difference of age between male lover and beloved").
4. See Plato, *Symposium*, in *Five Great Dialogues* (Benjamin Jowett, trans.) (New York: Walter J. Black, 1942); Plato, *The Laws* (Trevor Saunders, trans.) (London: Penguin, 1970), pp. 332–41 (condemning sexual acts for purposes other than procreation, and advocating chaste [i.e., "platonic"] relationships); Warner Fite, *The Platonic Legend* (New York: Scribner's, 1934); Roger Cox, *Shaping Childhood: Themes of Uncertainty in the History of Adult-Child Relationships* (London: Routledge, 1996), pp. 3–4.
5. Plato, *The Republic and Other Works* (Benjamin Jowett, trans.) (New York: Doubleday, 1973), p. 79; see also *The Laws, supra* n. 4, pp. 282–92, 300–4.
6. Fite, *supra* n. 4, p. 152; see also *The Laws, supra* n. 4, p. 91 (noting that "virtually all states" except Egypt do not censor music, but allow youngsters to be taught "*anything* by way of rhythm, tune and words," without considering the effect "as regards virtue and vice"). On Plato's puritanism and distrust for any art "outside the full control of the rational mind," see Iris Murdoch, *The Fire and the Sun: Why Plato Banished the Artists* (Oxford: Clarendon, 1977), pp. 12–13; Karl Popper, *The Open Society and Its Enemies*, Vol. 1: *The Spell of Plato* (Princeton, NJ: Princeton U. Press, 1962).
7. John Sommerville, *The Rise and Fall of Childhood* (Beverly Hills: Sage, 1982),

p. 27. Judge Jerome Frank made a similar point when he noted that the correct translation for Plato's "guardians" is "guards," a term that more accurately reflects their totalitarian character. *Roth v. Goldman*, 172 F.2d 788, 796 & n. 33 (2d Cir. 1949) (Frank, J., concurring), citing Fite, *supra* n. 4, p. 14.

8. Aristotle, *The Poetics*, in *Aristotle's Theory of Poetry and Fine Art* (S. M. Butcher, trans.) (New York: Dover, 1951), p. 7.
9. See Elizabeth Belfiore, "Aristotle: Survey of Thought," Richard Janko, "Reception of Aristotle in Antiquity," and Leon Golden, "Reception of Aristotle in Modernity," in *Encyclopedia of Aesthetics*, Vol. 1 (Michael Kelly, ed.) (New York: Oxford U. Press, 1998), pp. 98–99, 104–6, 106–8; John Gassner, "Introduction," in *Aristotle's Theory*, *supra* n. 8.
10. Aristotle, *The Politics* (T. A. Sinclair, trans.; Trevor Saunders, rev.) (London: Penguin, 1962), pp. 446–47. The reference to "scurrilous purposes" is in the reviser's footnotes. Aristotle was apparently thinking of younger children, for he added that censorship is not needed for those who "have reached the age at which they come to recline at banquets with others and share in their drinking; by this time their education will have rendered them completely immune to any harm that might come from such spectacles." *Id.*; see also Gerald Silk, "Censorship and Controversy in the Career of Edward Kienholz," in *Suspended License: Censorship and the Visual Arts* (Elizabeth Childs, ed.) (Seattle: U. of Wash. Press, 1997), p. 283 (noting that age restrictions on viewing "objectionable" works go back to Aristotle's *Politics*).
11. Paul Veyne, "The Roman Empire," in *A History of Private Life*, Vol. 1: *From Pagan Rome to Byzantium* (P. Ariès & G. Duby, gen. eds.; Arthur Goldhammer, trans.) (Cambridge, MA: Harvard U. Press, 1987), p. 79.
12. Peter Brown, *The Body and Society: Men, Women, and Sexual Renunciation in Early Christianity* (New York: Columbia U. Press, 1988), p. 28; Veyne, *supra* n. 11, pp. 20–23; Lloyd de Mause, "The Evolution of Childhood," in *The History of Childhood* (Lloyd de Mause, ed.) (New York: Psychohistory Press, 1974), p. 45.
13. See Walter Kendrick, *The Secret Museum* (New York: Viking, 1987); Alessandra Stanley, "What Scandalous Doin's in the Ruins of Pompeii," *New York Times*, Apr. 6, 2000, p. E1.
14. See Elaine Pagels, *Adam, Eve, and the Serpent* (New York: Vintage, 1988), p. xix; Lawrence Stone, *The Family, Sex and Marriage in England, 1500–1800* (one-volume ed.) (Harmondsworth: Penguin, 1977), p. 125.
15. See Foucault, Vol. 2, *supra* n. 3, pp. 63, 125; Richard Lyman, Jr., "Barbarism and Religion: Late Roman and Early Medieval Childhood," in *The History of Childhood*, *supra* n. 12, pp. 76–87; Stone, *supra* n. 14, pp. 109, 116, 124–25, 145, 254; Sommerville, *supra* n. 7, pp. 52–53; David Archard, *Children: Rights and Childhood* (London: Routledge, 1993), p. 37.
16. Sommerville, *supra* n. 7, pp. 47–49.
17. Peter Brown, "Late Antiquity," in *A History of Private Life*, *supra* n. 12, p. 265; see also Sommerville, *supra* n. 7, p. 60.

18. Mary Martin McLaughlin, "Survivors and Surrogates: Children and Parents from the Ninth to the Thirteenth Centuries," in *The History of Childhood, supra* n. 12, p. 111; Michel Rouche, "The Early Middle Ages in the West," in *A History of Private Life, supra* n. 11, p. 459. Rouche estimates the average life expectancy in 5th-to-8th-century France somewhat higher, at age 45 for males and 30–40 for females.
19. Evelyne Patlagean, "Byzantium in the Tenth and Eleventh Centuries," in *A History of Private Life, supra* n. 11, p. 599.
20. Gagnon, *supra* n. 3, p. 8.
21. See John D'Emilo & Estelle Freedman, *Intimate Matters: A History of Sexuality in America* (New York: Harper & Row, 1988), p. 17; Joseph Illick, "Child-Rearing in Seventeenth-Century England and America," in *The History of Childhood,* p. 330.
22. McLaughlin, *supra* n. 18, p. 120; Rouche, *supra* n. 18, pp. 465–82; see also Stone, *supra* n. 14, pp. 401–2.
23. See, e.g., Stone, pp. 57, 81; Philippe Ariès, *Centuries of Childhood* (Robert Baldick, trans.) (New York: Vintage, 1962), p. 39; Gagnon, *supra* n. 3, p. 14. Linda Pollock, in *Forgotten Children: Parent-Child Relations from 1500 to 1900* (Cambridge: Cambridge U. Press, 1983), contests this thesis, as well as the view of Stone, Lloyd de Mause, and others that children were regularly brutalized until recent centuries.
24. See Stone, pp. 80, 115 (on swaddling); 83, 113 (wet nurses); 84, 113, 120 (apprenticing).
25. McLaughlin, *supra* n. 18, p. 131.
26. See Sommerville, p. 69; Natalie Zemon Davis, *Society and Culture in Early Modern France* (Stanford: Stanford U. Press, 1975).
27. Sommerville, p. 83; see also Leo Steinberg, *The Sexuality of Christ in Renaissance Art and Modern Oblivion* (New York: Pantheon, 1983); James Bruce Ross, "The Middle-Class Child in Urban Italy, Fourteenth to Early Sixteenth Century," and M. J. Tucker, "The Child as Beginning and End: Fifteenth and Sixteenth Century English Childhood," in *The History of Childhood,* pp. 183–228, 229–57; James Fenton, "Leonardo's Nephew," *New York Review of Books,* Nov. 19, 1998, p. 50.
28. George Haven Putnam, *The Censorship of the Church of Rome,* Vol. 1 (New York: Benjamin Blom, 1906, 1967 reissue), p. 185; see also Sue Curry Jansen, *Censorship: The Knot That Binds Power and Knowledge* (New York: Oxford U. Press, 1991), pp. 62–65.
29. Putnam, *supra* n. 28, Vol. 2, pp. 309–10; see also Vol. 1, p. 169 (in the Index of 1758, prohibition of the *Decameron* "was modified so as to cover only the editions printed with heretical commentaries"); Alec Craig, *The Banned Books of England* (2d ed.) (London: George Allen & Unwin, 1962), p. 19. Putnam notes that the first expurgation did not satisfy Pope Gregory XIII, and a second one was undertaken in 1588; this was also unsatisfactory, and "the book remained on the Index, but it continued in general reading, and the authorities

appear finally to have decided to close their eyes to this particular instance of disobedience." Vol. 2, p. 310.

30. Stone, p. 70.
31. William Shakespeare, *Romeo and Juliet*, Act III, sc. ii, ll. 10–28.
32. Ariès, *supra* n. 23, pp. 103, 109, quoting in part Père de Dainville, *La Naissance de l'humanisme moderne* (Paris: Beauchesne et Ses Fils, 1940), p. 261.
33. *Id.*, pp. 116, 119, 411, 413.
34. Davis, *supra* n. 26.
35. Stone, p. 241. Linda Pollock in turn critiques Stone for overstating the pervasiveness of birchings, whippings, and other forms of brutality visited on children, and for simplistically overgeneralizing about changes in social attitudes toward youth. Pollock, *supra* n. 23; see also pp. 1–25 for Pollock's summary of the widely varying views on the history of childhood.
36. Sommerville, p. 94.
37. De Mause, *supra* n. 12, p. 5; see also Elizabeth Marvick, "Nature Versus Nurture: Patterns and Trends in Seventeenth Century French Child-Rearing," in *The History of Childhood, supra* n. 12.
38. Stone, pp. 115–17, 120–22; see also Sommerville, p. 64.
39. Stone, pp. 84, 241–42, 318, 426. As Stone has written, cultural history is less a linear progression than "an unending dialectic of competing interests and ideas." *Id.*, p. 435.
40. Archard, *supra* n. 15, pp. 15–19, 26; see also Henry Jenkins, "Introduction," in *The Children's Culture Reader* (Henry Jenkins, ed.) (New York: NYU Press, 1998), p. 16 (whether or not Ariès "is correct on every particular, his book opened a space for examining the social construction of childhood as an ongoing historical process and for questioning dominant constructions of childhood innocence"); Karin Calvert, "Children in the House: The Material Culture of Early Childhood," *id.*, pp. 72–75; James Kincaid, *Erotic Innocence: The Culture of Child Molesting* (Chapel Hill: Duke U. Press, 1998), p. 53 ("if we think of it as illuminating modern ways of seeing rather than as offering a confident description of the past, the idea of the invented child can be useful"); Anne Higonnet, *Pictures of Innocence: The History and Crisis of Ideal Childhood* (London: Thames & Hudson, 1998), p. 120 (tracing the sentimentalized ideal of sexually innocent, vulnerable childhood in 18th-century Western art and culture; the "Romantic child belongs to the modern affluent west. To anyone outside our culture or not influenced by it, the ideal meanings we have attached to the child's body would be odd if not incomprehensible"); Margaret Talbot, "Against Innocence," *New Republic*, Mar. 15, 1999, p. 27 (discussing "re-Victorianized hypervigilance" about minors' sexuality in the late-20th-century United States); Cox, *supra* n. 4, p. 1, quoting Ariès, *supra* n. 23, p. 125 (Ariès has often been misunderstood: he did not claim that "childhood did not exist" or that children were "neglected, forsaken or despised"; only that in premodern times "awareness of the particular nature of childhood" was lacking). For a simplified view of "the invention of childhood," and complaints about its imminent demise, see Postman, *supra* n. 1.

41. Michel Foucault, *The History of Sexuality*, Vol. 1: *An Introduction* (New York: Random House, 1978), pp. 28, 30.
42. Illick, *supra* n. 21, pp. 303, *passim*, quoting Keith Thomas, *Religion and the Decline of Magic* (New York: Scribner, 1971), p. 111. Stone has expanded on this theme at length, identifying 1500–1800 in England as the period in which "affective bonding" in families developed, and with it a decline in communal life, an increasing sense of personal autonomy, and a lessening association of sex with guilt; see also Jay Fliegelman, *Prodigals and Pilgrims: The American Revolution Against Patriarchal Authority, 1750–1800* (Cambridge: Cambridge U. Press, 1982).
43. John Locke, *Some Thoughts Concerning Education*, in *The Educational Writings of John Locke* (John W. Adamson, ed.) (Cambridge: Cambridge U. Press, 1922); Fliegelman, *supra* n. 42, pp. 1–12 (noting the "enormous political implications" of Locke's *Essay Concerning Human Understanding*, which rejected Descartes's doctrine of innate ideas); Michael Grossberg, *Governing the Hearth: Law and Family in Nineteenth Century America* (Chapel Hill: U. North Carolina Press, 1985), pp. 5–11; see also Stone, pp. 177, 254; Archard, pp. 1–12; Sommerville, pp. 109–24 (Puritans published the "great bulk of child-rearing advice," which generally discouraged parental indulgence, and emphasized "natural love and wise correction"); Pollock, pp. 98–127 (17th- and 18th-century diaries suggest parents believed children were not depraved but pliable and that it was the duty of parents to bend the child's will).
44. Stone, pp. 267–79.
45. Fliegelman, *supra* n. 42, p. 26.
46. Samuel-Auguste Tissot, *A Treatise on the Crime of Onan* (3d ed.) (London: B. Thomas, 1766), p. 22, quoting and paraphrasing *Onania*.
47. See D'Emilio & Freedman, *supra* n. 21, p. 18; Peter Gay, *The Bourgeois Experience: Victoria to Freud*, Vol. 2: *Education of the Senses* (New York: Oxford U. Press, 1984), pp. 295–96; Stone, pp. 311–13, 320–21; Havelock Ellis, *Studies in the Psychology of Sex*, Vol. 1, Pt. 1 (1st ed.) (Philadelphia: F. A. Davis; 1901), pp. 248–49.
48. Tissot, *supra* n. 46, p. 21. On Tissot, *Onania*, and theories relating masturbation to insanity, general paralysis, and other ills, see Robert MacDonald, "The Frightful Consequences of Onanism: Notes on the History of a Delusion," 28 *J. Hist. Ideas* 423 (1967); see also Ellis, *supra* n. 47, p. 249 (*L'Onanisme* was "a production of amusing exaggeration and rhetoric, zealously setting forth the prodigious evils of masturbation").
49. Kendrick, *supra* n. 13, pp. 88–89, citing Peter Gay, *The Bourgeois Experience: Victoria to Freud*, Vol. 1: *The Tender Passion* (New York: Oxford U. Press, 1986), p. 295; see also Stone, p. 311; Steven Marcus, *The Other Victorians* (New York: Bantam, 1967), p. 21; John Gagnon & William Simon, *Sexual Conduct: The Social Sources of Human Sexuality* (Chicago: Aldine, 1973), p. 221 n. 3.
50. Kendrick, *supra* n. 13, p. 89, quoting *L'Onanisme* (6th ed.) (Lausanne, 1775), p. 60.

51. De Mause, p. 43.
52. *Education of the Senses*, *supra* n. 47, pp. 301, 303, 304; see also MacDonald, *supra* n. 48 (describing "contraption patented in the United States in 1908 of 'Sexual Armor,' " that "consisted of a jacket encased in steel armor with perforations, a hinged trapdoor with bolts and a padlock and optional handcuffs"); Kathryn Kelley, "Adolescent Sexuality: The First Lessons," in *Adolescents, Sex, and Contraception* (Donn Byrne & William A. Fisher, eds.) (Hillsdale, NJ: Lawrence Erlbaum, 1983), p. 129. "By the nineteenth century," writes de Mause, the campaign against masturbation "reached an unbelievable frenzy. Doctors and parents sometimes appeared before the child armed with knives and scissors, threatening to cut off the child's genitals; circumcision, clitoridectomy, and infibulation were sometimes used as punishment; and all sorts of restraint devices, including plastic casts and cages with spikes, were prescribed." Graphs assembled by one scholar showed "a peak in surgical intervention in 1850–79, and in restraint devices in 1880–1904. By 1925, these methods had almost completely died out, after two centuries of brutal and totally unnecessary assault on children's genitals." De Mause, pp. 48–49.
53. Ellis, *supra* n. 47, p. 249.
54. Jean-Jacques Rousseau, *Emile, or On Education* (Allan Bloom, trans.) (New York: Basic Books, 1979), pp. 220, 231, *passim*.
55. Priscilla Robertson, "Home as a Nest: Middle-Class Childhood in Nineteenth-Century Europe," in *The History of Childhood*, p. 407.
56. Sommerville, p. 131; see also, on Rousseau, Plato, and totalitarian philosophy, Popper, *supra* n. 6, pp. 246, 257; Michael Ignatieff, *Isaiah Berlin* (New York: Henry Holt, 1998), pp. 202–3.
57. In the Italian, "Oggi donna mi fa palpitar." "Palpitar" is sometimes translated as "tremble" rather than the more clearly sexual "pulsate" or "throb." In the Beaumarchais play on which the opera is based, Chérubin says, "I don't know what's coming over me. For some time I have had such a strange feeling within me. My pulse quickens at the very sight of a woman." Pierre-Augustin Caron de Beaumarchais, *The Barber of Seville & The Marriage of Figaro* (John Wood, ed. & trans.) (London: Penguin, 1964), p. 117. One opera buff calls "Non so più" "a masturbation fantasy, an encyclopedic litany, set to rapid triplets, of what he finds sexually arousing (which is virtually everything he sees)." Sam Abel, *Opera in the Flesh* (Boulder, CO: Westview, 1996), p. 544. The young Octavian in Richard Strauss's *Der Rosenkavalier* is similarly sexually aware: at age 17, he is just winding up a love affair with an "older woman" in her 30s.
58. John Walzer, "A Period of Ambivalence: Eighteenth-Century American Childhood," in *The History of Childhood*, p. 364; see also Joseph Kett, *Rites of Passage: Adolescence in America, 1790 to the Present* (New York: Basic Books, 1977), pp. 41–54 (describing instances of adolescent riot in 19th-century America).
59. Kendrick, pp. 49, 91, 84; D'Emilio & Freedman, *supra* n. 21, p. 71; see also

Kett, *supra* n. 58, p. 200; Foucault, Vol. 1, *supra* n. 41; Thomas Hine, *The Rise and Fall of the American Teenager* (New York: Avon, 1999), pp. 104–5.

60. *The Tender Passion, supra* n. 49, pp. 263–64.
61. Noel Perrin, *Dr. Bowdler's Legacy: A History of Expurgated Books in England and America* (New York: Atheneum, 1969), p. 5; Thomas Bowdler, *The Family Shakespeare, in ten volumes, in which nothing is added to the original text; but those words and expressions are omitted which cannot properly be read aloud in a family* (London: Loman, Hurst, Rees, Orme & Brown, 1818); see also Craig, *supra* n. 29, p. 36; Archard, *supra* n. 15, p. 39; Sommerville, pp. 132, 144.
62. Craig, p. 21; see also See *Regina v. Read* (1708), 11 Mod. 205 (Q.B); *Rex v. Curl* (1727), 2 Str. 789, 93 E.R. 849 (K.B.); Margaret Blanchard, "The American Urge to Censor: Freedom of Expression Versus the Desire to Sanitize Society," 33 *Wm. & Mary L. Rev.* 741, 773 (1992); Frank Fowell & Frank Palmer, *Censorship in England* (New York: Burt Franklin, 1913, 1970); Geoffrey Robertson, *Obscenity* (London: Weidenfeld & Nicolson, 1979), pp. 17–21.
63. Leo M. Alpert, "Judicial Censorship of Obscene Literature," 52 *Harv. L. Rev.* 40, 47 (1938); see also Craig, p. 34; Robertson, *supra* n. 62, p. 23; Stone, p. 335 (describing *Fanny Hill*'s "long and prosperous history").
64. Craig, p. 23 (noting also that Sedley was said to have "excrementiz'd into the street"); see also Alpert, *supra* n. 63, at 41; Robertson, p. 21; *Sir Charles Sydlyes Case* (1663), 1 Keble 620 (K.B.), 83 E.R. 1146; *Le Roy v. Sr. Charles Sidley*, 1 Sid. 168, 82 E.R. 1036 (report in law French as "*indict al common ley pur several misdemeanors encounter le peace del Roy & que fueront al grand scandal de Christianity*").
65. *The Diary of Samuel Pepys*, Vol. 4: 1663 (Robert Latham & William Matthews, eds.) (London: G. Bell & Sons, 1971), p. 209.
66. *Regina v. Read* (1708), 11 Mod. Rep. 142, 88 E.R. 953 (Q.B.) (per curiam).
67. Robertson, p. 22; *Rex v. Curl, supra* n. 62.
68. One judge objected because Curl's behavior really could not be compared to the intemperate antics of Charles Sedley: in the earlier case, "there was a force in throwing out bottles upon the people's heads," *Rex v. Curl, supra*; see the description in *Regina v. Hicklin*, L.R. 3 Q.B. 360, 369 (1868); Craig, p. 34; Theodore Schroeder, *"Obscene" Literature and Constitutional Law* (New York: Privately printed, 1911), pp. 37, 39 (arguing that even in *Curl*, the object was not "to penalize obscenity in literature *as obscenity* rather than as an affront to religion").
69. *The Infamous Essay on Woman or John Wilkes Seated Between Vice and Virtue* (London: André Deutsch, 1972), p. 213. Wilkes was parodying Pope's lines: "Let us (since life can little more supply / Than just to look about us and to die) / Expatiate free o'er all this scene of man; / A mighty maze! But not without a plan." See *Rex v. Wilkes*, 4 Burr. 2527 (D.B. 1770), holding the *Essay on Woman* indictable at common law. Lawrence Stone says that Wilkes's "frank and hedonistic eroticism" would have been "unthinkable in England" before

the 18th century. Stone, pp. 303, 327. Alec Craig, on the other hand, traces free-spokenness in English literature back to Chaucer: it was only in the 19th century that it became " 'the most pudibond, the most respectful of the young person's blush, that the world has ever known.' " Craig, p. 35, quoting Andrew Lang, "The Evolution of Literary Decency," *Blackwood's*, Mar. 1900. Craig probably has the better of this argument. *Aristotle's Master-Piece*, for example, a compendium of sexual advice, was widely available in England, as elsewhere in Europe and in the American colonies, since its publication in the 17th century. It included pictures, discourses on virginity, advice to midwives, and fairly accurate descriptions of the male and female genital organs, confidently identifying the "Clytoris" as "the seat of Venereal Pleasure" in women, as well as "jaunty interpolated verses celebrating the joys of sexual congress." *Education of the Senses, supra* n. 47, p. 367; *Aristotle's Master-Piece* (Anr. ed. 1698), p. 77; see also Marcus, *supra* n. 49, p. 29; D'Emilio & Freedman, p. 46; Lynn Hunt, "Introduction: Obscenity and the Origins of Modernity, 1500–1800," in *The Invention of Pornography* (Lynn Hunt, ed.) (New York: Zone Books, 1996), pp. 9–45; Robertson, p. 25; *United States v. Twelve 200-Foot Reels of Super 8mm Film*, 413 U.S. 123, 133 (1973) (Douglas, J., dissenting); *Commonwealth v. Gordon*, 66 Pa. D & C 101, 120 (1949), aff'd, 166 Pa. Super. 120 (1950); *United States v. Roth*, 237 F.2d 796, 806 (2d Cir. 1956) (Appendix to concurring opinion of Frank, J.).

70. See William Lockhart and Robert McClure, "Literature, the Law of Obscenity, and the Constitution," 38 *Minn. L. Rev.* 295, 325 (1954).
71. Prov. St. 1711–12, c. 6, §19, 1 Prov. Laws, 682; see Sidney Grant & S. E. Angoff, "Massachusetts and Censorship," 10 *BU L. Rev.* 36, 147, 152 (1930); Alpert, at 56; *Roth v. United States*, 354 U.S. 476, 483 (1957).
72. Grant & Angoff, *supra* n. 71, at 147–48; see *Commonwealth v. Isenstadt*, 318 Mass. 543, n. 1 (1945), characterizing the 1711 blasphemy law as "the germ" of Massachusetts's modern obscenity statute, M.G.L. c. 272, §28.
73. The state's high court affirmed the conviction. *Commonwealth v. Holmes*, 17 Mass. 336 (1821). Its view remained unchanged 144 years later when it again found John Cleland's fable obscene; this time, the Supreme Court reversed; see ch. 3.
74. *Commonwealth v. Sharpless*, 2 Serg. & Raw. 91, 101 (Pa. 1815).
75. D'Emilio & Freedman, p. 157.
76. Tariff Act of 1842, c. 270, 5 Stat. 563–66, 27th Cong. (1842); see James Paul & Murray Schwartz, *Federal Censorship: Obscenity in the Mail* (New York: Free Press of Glencoe, 1961), pp. 249–50, tracing the sparse legislative history of the 1842 law and its successors.
77. *Id.*, p. 12.
78. See Hunt, *supra* n. 69, p. 12; James Jones, *Alfred C. Kinsey: A Public/Private Life* (New York: Norton, 1997), p. 67; Alison Parker, *Purifying America: Women, Cultural Reform, and Pro-Censorship Activism, 1873–1933* (Urbana: U. of Ill. Press, 1997); Paul Boyer, *Purity in Print: The Vice-Society Movement*

and Book Censorship in America (New York: Scribner, 1968), pp. 1–52; D'Emilio & Freedman, pp. 130–70; William Leach, *True Love and Perfect Union: The Feminist Reform of Sex and Society* (Middletown, CT: Wesleyan U. Press, 1989), pp. 62–63; Kett, *supra* n. 58, pp. 164–77.

79. See D'Emilio & Freedman, p. 153; Jeffrey Weeks, *Sex, Politics and Society: The Regulation of Sexuality Since 1800* (London: Longman, 1981), pp. 87–88; Constance Nathanson, *Dangerous Passage: The Social Control of Sexuality in Women's Adolescence* (Philadelphia: Temple U. Press, 1991), pp. 75, 199; Viviana Zelizer, *Pricing the Priceless Child* (New York: Basic Books, 1985) (detailing change in the United States from the 1870s "useful child" to the emotionally "priceless" child of the 20th century); Grossberg, *supra* n. 43, pp. 105–44, 278, 301 (describing unsuccessful efforts early in the 19th century to raise the age of consent; and change in attitude after 1850).
80. Parker, *supra* n. 78, p. 19.
81. Weeks, *supra* n. 79, p. 19; see Foucault, Vol. 1.
82. John Chandos, "Unicorns at Play," in *"To Deprave and Corrupt": Original Studies in the Nature and Definition of "Obscenity"* (London: Souvenir Press, 1962), p. 179; see also Craig, pp. 40–43 (noting the popularity, especially among youth, of titillating works by the French novelist Paul de Kock, or the flagellation poetry of Swinburne); Marcus, *supra* n. 49 (describing the pornographic culture of Victorian England).
83. See Sommerville, p. 160 ("[o]ne of the puzzles of our history is the fact that the greatest exploitation of children coincided with the greatest glorification of childhood").
84. Jerome Kagan, *The Nature of the Child* (New York: Basic Books, 1984), p. 267; Postman, *supra* n. 1, p. xii.
85. See Paul & Schwartz, *supra* n. 76, pp. 251, 254–55; Blanchard, *supra* n. 62, at 747.
86. Post Office Act, c. 89, §16, 13 Stat. 504, 507 (1865).
87. *Hansard's Parliamentary Debates*, 3rd Series, Commencing with the Accession of William IV, 1857, Vol. 145 (London: Cornelius Buck, 1857), p. 103; see also J. E. Hall Williams, "Obscenity in Modern English Law," 22 *Law & Contemp. Probs.* 630, 632 (1955); Craig, p. 40. Campbell opined that higher prices were "a sort of check," preventing lascivious publications from getting into the wrong hands. *Hansard's, supra.*
88. Brougham's fears were hardly fantastic: in France, writings by Gustave Flaubert, Charles Baudelaire, and Eugène Sue were prosecuted for offending public morals in the same year that Lord Campbell's Act was passed; see *Education of the Senses*, p. 359.
89. *Hansard's*, Vol. 146, pp. 330–32. Lyndhurst said the paintings "come within the description in this Bill as much as any work you can conceive," yet both are celebrated; the Correggio "hangs in the large square room of the Louvre, right opposite an ottoman, on which are seated daily ladies of the first rank from all countries of Europe, who resort there for the purpose of studying the

works of art in that great gallery"; *id.*; see also pp. 336–37 (Lord Wensleydale opining that "there was not a library in which books could not be found containing passages which a strict dealing magistrate might consider to bring them within the operation of this Bill," including the classics of Lucian, Lucullus, and Juvenal).

90. *Hansard's,* Vol. 146 (June 25, 1857), p. 329.
91. *Id.*, pp. 1152–53, 1355–63.
92. *Regina v. Hicklin,* 3 Q.B. at 362; see Lockhart & McClure, *supra* n. 70, at 325.
93. *Hicklin,* 3 Q.B. at 371.
94. *Id.* at 367, 371–72.
95. *Education of the Senses,* pp. 175–77.
96. Craig, pp. 40–115; see also Edward de Grazia, *Girls Lean Back Everywhere: The Law of Obscenity and the Assault on Genius* (New York: Random House 1992), pp. 40–53; Felice F. Lewis, *Literature, Obscenity, and Law* (Carbondale: So. Ill. U. Press, 1976), p. 24; Robertson, pp. 31–32. Eleanor Marx Aveling (daughter of Karl) was the translator of Vizetelly's edition of *Madame Bovary*; Vizetelly also, at the instance of Havelock Ellis, initiated the celebrated Mermaid Series of English dramatists; see Publisher's Note, *Marlowe* (Havelock Ellis, ed.) (New York: Mermaid Drama Book, Hill & Wang, 1956), p. 345.
97. Weeks, pp. 84–92, 142, 181; see also Craig, pp. 52–65; and Ellis's Foreword to *Studies in the Psychology of Sex, supra* n. 47, pp. ix–xxiii, describing the tortured publication history of the *Studies* following the prosecution of the secretary of the Legitimation League, which had published the original first volume, *Sexual Inversion.*
98. Bill Thompson, *Soft Core: Moral Crusades Against Pornography in Britain and America* (London: Cassell, 1994), p. 17; see also Chandos, "Introduction," in *"To Deprave and Corrupt," supra* n. 82, pp. 27–28 ("for the next ninety-one years" after *Hicklin,* "literature in England and for almost as long in America was subject to a control designed to preserve the innocence or ignorance of a hypothetical adolescent girl, and at times it would seem, a feeble-minded one").
99. See Rebecca Zurier, *Art for the Masses: A Radical Magazine and Its Graphics* (Philadelphia: Temple U. Press, 1988), p. 97. Shaw coined the epithet in 1905 after Comstock called him an "Irish smut dealer" in the wake of the New York Public Library's decision to place an exhibit on Shaw's play *Man and Superman* on restricted view; the library thought Shaw's attacks on social conditions might be misunderstood by children and lead to "juvenile crime." Robert Bremmer, "Editor's Introduction," in *Traps for the Young by Anthony Comstock* (John Harvard Library ed.) (Cambridge, MA: Belknap Press, 1967), p. xxvii, quoting E. L. Bostwick, 39 *Current Literature* 551 (1905); see also Heywood Broun & Margaret Leech, *Anthony Comstock: Roundsman of the Lord* (London: Wishart & Co., 1928), p. 20.
100. Boyer, *supra* n. 78, p. 2; see also Broun & Leech, *supra* n. 99.

101. Bremmer, *supra* n. 99, p. ix; Broun & Leech, p. 26.

102. Anthony Comstock, *Frauds Exposed; or, How the people are deceived and robbed, and youth corrupted* (New York: J. H. Brown, 1880), p. 416.

103. *Traps for the Young*, *supra* n. 99, pp. 240, 132.

104. Weeks, p. 53 n. 14; Jones, *supra* n. 78, p. 54, quoting Ernest Thompson Seton, *Boy Scouts of America: A Handbook of Woodcraft, Scouting, and Life-Craft* (New York: Page & Co., 1910), p. xii.

105. Boyer, pp. 20–21, 281, quoting New York Vice Society, *Annual Report* (1900), p. 12; Boston Watch & Ward Socicty, *Annual Report, 1892–93* (1893); and Watch & Ward Society, "To Every Thoughtful Man Having the Care of Youth" (n.p., 1883; see also David Wilson, "Hysteria Grips U.S. over Violence in Video Games," *Mercury News*, Oct. 9, 1999, http://www.mercurycenter.com/svtech/news/indepth/docs/game101099.htm (describing the 1874 murder trial of a 14-year-old alleged to have been influenced by dime novels until the defendant took the stand and revealed he was illiterate); Todd Gitlin, "Imagebusters: The Hollow Crusade Against TV Violence," *The American Prospect*, Winter 1994, pp. 42–43.

106. D'Emilio & Freedman, p. 16; see also Michael Freeman, *The Rights and Wrongs of Children* (London: Frances Pinter, 1983), p. 17 (the "child-saving" movement that began in the late 19th century "produced a social practice redolent of the rankest repression"); Weeks, pp. 49–50; Nathanson, *supra* n. 79, p. 80; Nicola Beisel, *Imperiled Innocents: Anthony Comstock and Family Reproduction in Victorian America* (Princeton, NJ: Princeton U. Press, 1997) (attributing Comstock's success to the support of social elites concerned that urban immigrants might, through the corruption of sex and other vices, deprive upper-class youth of their privileged position).

107. Parker, *supra* n. 78, pp. 13–19. As late as the 1930s, the ALA recommended against *Little Women* because it "has too much slang and love-making." *Id.*, p. 206 (quoting a prominent children's librarian, writing in the Woman's Christian Temperance Union's 1931 annual report).

108. Mary Gabriel, *Notorious Victoria: The Life of Victoria Woodhull, Uncensored* (Chapel Hill: Algonquin Books, 1998), p. 185.

109. See Broun & Leech, pp. 100–27; Paul & Schwartz, pp. 19–20, 251; Gabriel, *supra* n. 108, pp. 183–229; Lois Underhill, *The Woman Who Ran for President: The Many Lives of Victoria Woodhull* (New York: Penguin, 1995), pp. 228–46; William O'Neill, *Everyone Was Brave: The Rise and Fall of Feminism in America* (Chicago: Quadrangle Books, 1969), pp. 27–29. The 1872 law added to the obscenity ban on books, pamphlets, pictures, prints, or "other publication[s]," the mailing of "any letter upon the envelope of which, or postal card upon which scurrilous epithets may have been written or printed, or disloyal devices printed or engraved." Post Office Act, c. 335, §148, 17 Stat. 283, 302 (1872); see Blanchard, *supra* n. 62, at 746.

110. Paul & Schwartz, p. 21; see also Bremmer, *supra* n. 99, p. xii.

111. Alpert, *supra* n. 63, at 65.

112. An Act for the Suppression of Trade in, and Circulation of, Obscene Literature and Articles of Immoral Use, c. 258, §2, 17 Stat. 598, 599 (1873), 42d Cong., Sess. III. The Act has been amended many times and now appears at 18 U.S.C. §1461.
113. Bremmer, pp. xiii–xiv; Broun & Leech, pp. 141–59.
114. See Martin Blatt, *Free Love and Anarchism: The Biography of Ezra Heywood* (Urbana: U. of Ill. Press, 1989), p. 109; David Rabban, *Free Speech in Its Forgotten Years* (Cambridge: Cambridge U. Press, 1997), pp. 32–37; Leach, *supra* n. 78, p. 42.
115. *Jacobellis v. Ohio*, 378 U.S. 184, 197 (1964) (Stewart, J., concurring).
116. *Commonwealth v. Landis*, 8 Phila. Rep. 453, 454 (Quarter Sess. 1870); see also *Commonwealth v. Havens*, 6 Pa. C.C. 545 (1890) (prosecution of the *National Police Gazette* and *Illustrated Police News*; the test was whether they would "suggest impure and libidinous thoughts to the young and inexperienced"); *United States v. Foote*, 25 F. Cas. 1140, 1141 (Circ. Ct. S.D.N.Y. 1876) (affirming Comstock Act conviction of a physician who had responded by mail to a request for contraceptive information; the court rejected a suggested exemption for physicians on the ground that "any attempt to exclude information given by medical men from the operation of the statute would afford an easy way of nullifying the law").
117. Broun & Leech, p. 192. Bennett was charged under an 1876 recodification of the law; see *United States v. Bennett*, 24 F. Cas. 1093, 1095 (Circ. Ct. S.D.N.Y. 1879).
118. Blatt, *supra* n. 114, p. 105, quoting *Cupid's Yokes, or the Binding Forces of Conjugal Life: An Essay to Consider Some Moral and Physiological Phases of Love and Marriage, Wherein Is Asserted the Natural Right and Necessity of Sexual Self-Government* (Princeton, MA: Cooperative Publishing, 1876), p. 22; see also Rabban, *supra* n. 114, p. 34; Broun & Leech, pp. 185–86.
119. *Bennett*, 24 F. Cas. at 1096; see Rabban, pp. 33–37; Blatt, pp. 59, 115–32.
120. Blatt, p. 118.
121. *Bennett*, 24 F. Cas. at 1101–4.
122. *Ex parte Jackson*, 96 U.S. 727, 732 (1877). This was despite the Court's assertion that "the object of Congress has not been to interfere with the freedom of the press." *Id.*
123. *Education of the Senses*, pp. 301–2.
124. Blatt, p. 106, quoting *The Word*, Feb. 1893, p. 3; on Comstock's persistence and Angela Heywood's role, see also Beisel, *supra* n. 106, p. 101.
125. *United States v. Chesman*, 19 F. 497, 498 (Circ. Ct. E.D. Mo. 1881). A court in Missouri eleven years later condemned *Dr. Clarke's Treatise on Venereal, Sexual, Nervous, and Special Diseases* in addition to two circulars describing venereal ailments; citing *Hicklin* and *Bennett*, the judge told the jury that the Comstock Act was designed to protect "the young and immature, the ignorant, and those who are sensually inclined—who are liable to be influenced to their harm by reading indecent and obscene publications." *United States v. Clarke*,

38 F. 732, 733–34 (E.D. Mo. 1889). The jury returned a verdict of guilty on all counts.

126. *United States v. Harmon*, 45 F. 414, 416 (D. Kan. 1891); *United States v. Smith*, 45 F. 476, 478 (E.D. Wis. 1891).

127. Paul & Schwartz, p. 38.

128. *In re Worthington*, 30 N.Y.Supp. 361, 361–63 (Sup. Ct., N.Y. County, 1894). A New York decision ten years earlier had not focused on youth for the probable reason that the defendant, a bookstore clerk, had sold the works in question (photo reproductions of paintings of female nudes) only to adults. Articulating the early obscenity standard for the state, the New York high court asked whether the images were "naturally calculated to excite . . . impure imaginations" in any spectator. Some of the paintings had been exhibited at the Philadelphia centennial exhibition or the Paris Salon, and the court did admit that banishing all nude art, even if capable of "suggesting impure thoughts," would amount to "false delicacy and mere prudery." It nonetheless deemed these pictures to be unacceptably exciting. *People v. Muller*, 96 N.Y. 408, 411 (1884).

129. *Rosen v. United States*, 161 U.S. 30, 42, 43 (1896). The Supreme Court did reverse a Comstock Act conviction in another 1896 case because the language at issue, although vulgar, was not "calculated to corrupt and debauch the mind and morals of those into whose hands it might fall." *Swearingen v. United States*, 161 U.S. 446, 451 (1896). But the next year, it affirmed the conviction of a Chicago newspaper publisher who had printed advertisements for "Baths" and "Massage." The Court rejected the publisher's argument that the ads were not calculated to deprave or corrupt morals, noting that "persons of ordinary intelligence" would easily "divin[e] the intention of the advertiser." *Dunlop v. United States*, 165 U.S. 486, 501 (1897).

130. *St. Hubert Guild v. Quinn*, 118 N.Y. Supp. 582 (Sup. Ct. App. Term 1909).

131. Schroeder, *supra* n. 68, pp. 307–8. The *Decameron* was held obscene in Massachusetts in 1895, and Rabelais's *Gargantua* and *Pantagruel* in 1903; the former conviction was reversed on appeal, but on the technical ground that the indictment had not identified the material charged as obscene. *Commonwealth v. McCance*, 164 Mass. 162 (1895).

132. See Lewis, *supra* n. 96, pp. 30, 36.

133. *United States v. Kennerley*, 209 Fed. Rep. 119 (1913) (reporter's summary).

134. *Id.* at 120. Hand suggested another test—itself not exactly a model of precision: "should not the word 'obscene' be allowed to indicate the present critical point in the compromise between candor and shame at which the community may have arrived here and now?" *Id.* at 21.

135. *Id.* at 121. Despite Judge Hand's conscientious adherence to the *Bennett/Hicklin* standard, a jury eventually acquitted Kennerley; see Boyer, pp. 46–48.

136. Beisel, *supra* n. 106, pp. 200–2 ("An observer of American politics at the end of the twentieth century can hardly fail to notice the echoes of Comstock's arguments in contemporary political rhetoric").

2. MORE EMETIC THAN APHRODISIAC

1. "The Claims of Psycho-Analysis to Scientific Interest," in *The Standard Edition of the Complete Psychological Works of Sigmund Freud*, Vol. 13 (London: Hogarth Press, 1953), pp. 165, 184; Steven Marcus, "Introduction," in Sigmund Freud, *Three Essays on the Theory of Sexuality* (James Strachey, trans.) (New York: Basic Books, 1962), pp. xx–xxi; "The Sexual Enlightenment of Children," in *Standard Edition*, Vol. 9 (London: Hogarth Press, 1959), p. 152; see generally Peter Gay, "Introduction," in *The Freud Reader* (New York: Norton, 1989), pp. xxii, xi (characterizing Freud as one of a "small handful of supreme makers of the twentieth-century mind"). Another article, in 1908, indicted the sexual ideology of abstinence until marriage: "Civilized Sexual Morality and Modern Nervousness," in *Standard Edition*, Vol. 9, pp. 181, 193; on the impact of "Civilized Sexual Morality," see Rochelle Gurstein, *The Repeal of Reticence* (New York: Hill & Wang, 1996), p. 98; John D'Emilio & Estelle Freedman, *Intimate Matters: A History of Sexuality in America* (New York: Harper & Row, 1988), pp. 171–75.
2. The phrase is Rochelle Gurstein's, *supra* n. 1, p. 99.
3. Michel Foucault, *The History of Sexuality*, Vol. 1: *An Introduction* (New York: Random House, 1978), pp. 104–5, 65; see also Vol. 2, *The Use of Pleasure* (New York: Random House, 1985); Vol. 3, *The Care of the Self* (New York: Random House, 1986); Joseph E. Kett, *Rites of Passage: Adolescence in America, 1790 to the Present* (New York: Basic Books, 1977); Steven Marcus, *The Other Victorians* (New York: Bantam, 1967). Foucault identifies four primary areas in which professional medicine and emerging social science in the 19th century asserted control over sexuality: hysteria among women, youthful masturbation, "socialization of procreative behavior" through prohibitions on contraception, and "psychiatrization of perverse pleasure"—that is, categorizing nonconformist sexuality as pathological. *History of Sexuality*, Vol. 1, *supra*.
4. D'Emilio & Freedman, *supra* n. 1, pp. 277–78.
5. D'Emilio & Freedman, p. 224; see Havelock Ellis, *Studies in the Psychology of Sex*, Vol. 1 (1st ed.) (Philadelphia: F. A. Davis Co., 1901), pp. 248–81; *Of Life and Sex* (New York: New American Library, 1957); Paul Robinson, *The Modernization of Sex* (Ithaca, NY: Cornell U. Press, 1989); Ellen Chesler, *Woman of Valor: Margaret Sanger and the Birth Control Movement in America* (New York: Simon & Schuster, 1992), pp. 110–25, describing Ellis's influence on and affair with Margaret Sanger.
6. See Robinson, *supra* n. 5.
7. Quoted in Gurstein, pp. 92–93. Gurstein's title derives from Agnes Repplier's essay, "The Repeal of Reticence," *Atlantic Monthly*, Mar. 1914, p. 297; Repplier's complaint was "not so much the nature of the information showered upon us," but "the fact that a great deal of it is given in the wrong way by the wrong people"; sex information, for example, was finding its way "into the hands of young women whose enthusiasm for the cause lets down their natural

barriers of defense." *Id.*, p. 298; see also Paul Boyer, *Purity in Print: The Vice-Society Movement and Book Censorship in America* (New York: Scribner, 1968), p. 41 (describing anticensorship sentiment before World War I).

8. Bronislaw Malinowski, *Sex and Repression in Savage Society* (New York: Meridian, 1955) (first published 1927); see also Bronislaw Malinowski, *The Sexual Life of Savages* (Boston: Beacon Press, 1987) (first published 1929); Margaret Mead, *The Coming of Age in Samoa* (New York: Morrow, 1928); Boyer, *supra* n. 7, p.149. Malinowski rejected the "exorbitant claims of psychoanalysis," as well as "its chaotic arguments and tangled terminology"; but nevertheless acknowledged "a deep sense of indebtedness" to Freud "for stimulation as well as for valuable instruction in some aspects of human psychology." *Sex and Repression*, p. 5.
9. See A. A. Brill, "Introduction," in *The Basic Writings of Sigmund Freud* (New York: Random House, 1938); Chesler, *supra* n. 5, pp. 22, 113, 151–60; Leslie Fishbein, "Introduction," in Rebecca Zurier, *Art for the Masses: A Radical Magazine and Its Graphics* (Philadelphia: Temple U. Press, 1988), pp. 3–27; *People v. Sanger*, 222 N.Y. 192 (1918) (affirming Sanger's conviction for dispensing birth control).
10. See Gurstein, *supra* n. 1, pp. 97–98; Gay, "Introduction," *supra* n. 1, pp. xxii–xxiii; Gerald Gunther, *Learned Hand: The Man and the Judge* (Cambridge, MA: Harvard U. Press, 1994). Among other important Freudian acolytes were Emma Goldman, the popular lecturer and anarchist firebrand, and Margaret Sanger, whose campaign for birth control of course violated the Comstock Act's ban on mailing contraceptive devices or information.
11. The phrase is Paul Boyer's, *supra* n. 7, p. 41.
12. Fishbein, *supra* n. 9, pp. 6–7.
13. James Jones, *Alfred C. Kinsey: A Public/Private Life* (New York: Norton, 1997), p. 300.
14. G. Stanley Hall, *Adolescence: Its Psychology and Its Relations to Physiology, Anthropology, Sociology, Sex, Crime and Education*, Vol. 1 (New York: D. Appleton & Co., 1904), p. xiv.
15. *Id.*, pp. xiii, xv, 507–11, 243; Vol. 2, p. 572.
16. *Id.*, Vol. 1, pp. 432–39, 408.
17. Kett, *supra* n. 3, pp. 216, 183, 186; see also Thomas Hine, *The Rise & Fall of the American Teenager* (New York: Avon, 1999), pp. 4–9 (tracing the ideas of adolescent immaturity and angst and the development of an insular, segregated teen culture in the 20th century to Hall's influence).
18. Constance Nathanson, *Dangerous Passage: The Social Control of Sexuality in Women's Adolescence* (Philadelphia: Temple U. Press, 1991), pp. 3–4; see also Henry Jenkins, "The Sensuous Child," in *The Children's Culture Reader* (Henry Jenkins, ed.) (New York: NYU Press, 1998), pp. 212–15 (describing the mid-20th-century influence of behaviorist psychology on child care advice; according to John Watson, the leading behaviorist, the body required "constant discipline," and sensual pleasures from thumb sucking to masturbation were to

be discouraged). Behaviorism, in sharp contrast to Freudianism, "bracketed off questions of interior mental life as ultimately not open to scientific examination, focusing instead on understanding external behaviors." *Id.*, p. 212; see also Erich Fromm, *The Anatomy of Human Destructiveness* (New York: Henry Holt, 1973), p. 24 (behaviorism "does not interest itself in the subjective forces which drive man to behave in a certain way," but only in "the social conditioning that shapes his behavior").

19. See David Rabban, *Free Speech in Its Forgotten Years* (Cambridge: Cambridge U. Press, 1997), for a history of the Free Speech League; *id.*, pp. 311–12, describing ACLU founder Roger Baldwin's refusal to protest the obscenity prosecution of Sholem Asch's play *God of Vengeance* because the issue "is not primarily one of freedom of opinion—it is one of censorship on the ground of morality." See also Theodore Schroeder, *"Obscene" Literature and Constitutional Law* (New York: Privately printed, 1911).
20. Richard Ellmann, *James Joyce* (New York: Oxford U. Press, 1959), p. 370; on *Ulysses*, see *id.*, pp. 391–513.
21. Paul Vanderham, *James Joyce and Censorship: The Trials of Ulysses* (New York: NYU Press, 1998), p. 34. Vanderham's is the most detailed account of the censorship of *Ulysses*; see also Ellmann, *supra* n. 20; Edward de Grazia, *Girls Lean Back Everywhere: The Law of Obscenity and the Assault on Genius* (New York: Random House, 1992), pp. 7–39; Margaret Anderson, *My Thirty Years' War* (New York: Horizon, 1969), pp. 174–75 ("Ezra Pound sent us the first chapter of a manuscript he recommended highly").
22. Vanderham, *supra* n. 21, pp. 32–33.
23. Ellmann, *supra* n. 20, p. 518.
24. *Id.*, pp. 518–19; Vanderham, p. 48; Anderson, pp. 214–22.
25. "Taste, Not Morals, Violated," *New York Times*, Feb. 23, 1921, p. 12.
26. See *Abrams v. United* States, 250 U.S. 616, 624 (1919) (Holmes, J., dissenting); *Whitney v. California*, 274 U.S. 357, 373 (1927) (Brandeis, J., concurring); *Mutual Film Corp. v. Industrial Comm'n of Ohio*, 236 U.S. 230, 241–43 (1915) (noting cinema's potential corrupting influence in the course of rejecting a First Amendment challenge to a film licensing law); Rabban, *supra* n. 19.
27. *Dysart v. United States*, 272 U.S. 655, 656–58 (1926).
28. See Sidney Grant & S. E. Angoff, "Massachusetts and Censorship," 10 *BU L. Rev.* 36, 46–47 (1930); Boyer, pp. 185–87, 192–95.
29. *Commonwealth v. Friede*, 271 Mass. 318, 322–23 (1930). Within the year, Massachusetts amended its obscenity statute to permit works to be judged as a whole, not just on the basis of isolated passages. See William Lockhart & Robert McClure, "Obscenity in the Courts," 20 *Law & Contemp. Probs.* 589, 603 (1955).
30. *United States v. Dennett*, 39 F.2d 564, 565 (2d Cir. 1930); see also Constance Chen, *"The Sex Side of Life": Mary Ware Dennett's Pioneering Battle for Birth Control and Sex Education* (New York: The New Press, 1996), pp. 171–77.

31. Chen, *supra* n. 30, Appendix B (a reproduction of the original pamphlet).
32. *Id.*, Appendix B, p. 11.
33. "The Statues" (1938), in *The Collected Poems of William Butler Yeats* (New York: Macmillan, 1956), p. 322.
34. *United States v. Dennett*, 39 F.2d at 568.
35. *Id.* at 569.
36. *Youngs Rubber Corp. v. C. I. Lee & Co.*, 45 F.2d 103, 108–9 (2d Cir. 1930). The Sixth Circuit followed suit three years later, opining that "the intention to prevent a proper medical use of drugs or other articles merely because they are capable of illegal uses is not lightly to be ascribed to Congress." *Davis v. United States*, 62 F.2d 473, 474 (6th Cir. 1933).
37. Quoted in James Paul & Murray Schwartz, *Federal Censorship: Obscenity in the Mail* (New York: The Free Press, 1961), p. 58; see also Boyer, pp. 218–37.
38. See Paul & Schwartz, *supra* n. 37, pp. 41–42; Boyer, pp. 234–35.
39. See Vanderham, pp. 85–86.
40. Geoffrey Robertson, "Foreword," in *The Trial of Lady Chatterley: Regina v. Penguin Books, Ltd.* (C. H. Rolph, ed.) (London: Penguin, 1961), p. xvi; see also de Grazia, *supra* n. 21, p. 54; Alec Craig, *The Banned Books of England* (London: George Allen & Unwin, 1937), p. 26; Alan Travis, "Secret Files Expose Joyce Fiasco," *The Guardian*, May 15, 1998, Friday Review, p. 1. In 1936, three years after Judge Woolsey exonerated *Ulysses* in the United States, the Bodley Head published a British edition; in response, the government finally acknowledged that *Ulysses* was not obscene. *Id.*
41. Robertson, "Foreword," *supra* n. 40, p. xvi.
42. *United States v. One Obscene Book Entitled "Married Love,"* 48 F.2d 821, 824 (S.D.N.Y. 1931).
43. *United States v. One Book Called "Ulysses,"* 5 F. Supp. 182, 183–85 (S.D.N.Y. 1933).
44. *United States v. One Book Entitled Ulysses by James Joyce*, 72 F.2d 705, 706–7 (2d Cir. 1934). Hand argued that the Supreme Court's 1896 decision in *Rosen v. U.S.*, embracing the *Hicklin* test (see ch. 1), did not require a different result because the actual holding in *Rosen* only involved the specificity of the indictment.
45. *Id.* at 709–11 (Manton, J., dissenting). Manton resigned five years later after evidence surfaced that he had been taking bribes; he was convicted and sentenced to two years in prison. See Joseph Borkin, *The Corrupt Judge* (New York: Clarkson N. Potter, 1962); Gunther, *supra* n. 10, pp. 504–6.
46. *Attorney General v. A Book Named "God's Little Acre,"* 326 Mass. 281, 283 (1950); *Commonwealth v. Isenstadt*, 318 Mass. 543, 549–50 (1945).
47. *New American Library v. Allen*, 114 F.Supp. 823, 834 (N.D. Ohio 1953). The same year, the Ninth Circuit Court of Appeals condemned as obscene Henry Miller's *Tropic of Cancer* and *Tropic of Capricorn*; *Besig v. United States*, 208 F.2d 142 (9th Cir. 1953).
48. *People v. London*, 63 N.Y.S.2d 227, 230 (City Mag. Ct., Mid-Manhattan

1946); see, by contrast, *Parmelee v. United States*, 113 F.2d 729 (D.C. Cir. 1940), finding *Nudism in Modern Life* not obscene; *People v. Gotham Book Mart*, 158 Misc. 240 (City Mag. Ct. 7th Dist. 1936), exonerating the Gotham Book Mart, a New York literary shrine, for selling André Gide's *If It Die*.

49. See de Grazia, pp. 278–79; Paul & Schwartz, pp. 63–137; Boyer, pp. 207–74.
50. *United States v. Levine*, 83 F.2d 156, 156–58 (2d Cir. 1936).
51. Frederic Thrasher, "The Comics and Delinquency: Cause or Scapegoat," 23 *J. Educ. Sociology* 195, 199 (1949), citing Paul Cressey, *The Role of the Motion Picture in an Interstitial Area* (unpublished manuscript on deposit at NYU library); Paul Cressey, "The Motion Picture Experience as Modified by Social Background and Personality," 3 *Am. Sociol. Rev.* 516 (1938); see Willard Rowland, Jr., *The Politics of TV Violence* (Beverly Hills: Sage, 1983), pp. 92–95.
52. Herbert Blumer & Philip Hauser, *Movies, Delinquency, and Crime* (New York: Arno Press & The New York Times, 1970 reprint ed.) (original, New York: Macmillan, 1933), pp. 15, 73.
53. *Hannegan v. Esquire*, 327 U.S. 146, 149 (1946).
54. *Ex parte Jackson*, 96 U.S. 727, 732 (1877).
55. *Hannegan*, 327 U.S. at 156, 157–58.
56. *People v. Doubleday & Co.*, 297 N.Y. 799 (1947), aff'd by an equally divided court, 335 U.S. 848 (1948). The state courts had rejected the publisher's argument that the proper obscenity standard was a work's effect not on "the immature or the depraved" but on "the minds of the mature and those not subject to such influences." William Lockhart & Robert McClure, "Literature, the Law of Obscenity, and the Constitution," 38 *Minn. L. Rev.* 295, 299 (1954), quoting Transcript of Record, p. 48.
57. Lockhart & McClure, *supra* n. 56, at 299, quoting Transcript of Record, p. 48. A later critic said of *Memoirs* that it "possesses a saturnine majesty and passages of ground-breaking sexual realism." John Updike, "The Trashy Years," *The New Yorker*, Nov. 15, 1999, p. 106.
58. Lockhart & McClure, 38 *Minn. L. Rev.* at 298; see also Harry Kalven, Jr., "The Metaphysics of the Law of Obscenity," 1960 *Sup. Ct. Rev.* 1, 4–5.
59. See de Grazia, pp. 273–326, describing Roth's career; William Lockhart & Robert McClure, "Censorship of Obscenity: The Developing Constitutional Standards," 45 *Minn. L. Rev.* 5, 22–23 n. 88 (1960) ("Lockhart & McClure, II"); *Roth v. Goldman*, 172 F.2d 788, 796 (2d Cir.) (Frank, J., concurring), cert. denied, 337 U.S. 938 (1949); Jerome Frank, *Law and the Modern Mind* (New York: Brentano's, 1930) (criticizing "legal fundamentalism" as a remnant of childish wishes for an omnipotent father figure).
60. *Roth v. Goldman*, 172 F.2d at 789.
61. *Id.* at 790 (Frank, J., concurring).
62. *Id.* at 792; see note 72.
63. *Commonwealth v. Gordon*, 66 Pa. D & C 101, 125, 154 (1949), aff'd *sub nom. Commonwealth v. Feigenbaum*, 166 Pa. Super. 120 (1950). Bok added: "I should prefer that my own three daughters meet the facts of life and the litera-

ture of the world in my library than behind a neighbor's barn, for I can face the adversary there directly." *Id.* at 110.

64. *Bantam Books, Inc. v. Melko*, 25 N.J. Super. 292, 318 (1953).
65. See Lockhart & McClure, 38 *Minn. L. Rev.* at 357, noting that "[o]nly in a few reported trial court opinions" before *Hecate County* "was thoughtful consideration given to the constitutional issue," and in only one of these, Judge Bok's opinion in *Commonwealth v. Gordon*, "was the constitutional issue given careful and detailed analysis."
66. There is a large literature on the red-hunting and blacklisting decade after World War II; see, for example, David Caute, *The Great Fear* (New York: Simon & Schuster, 1978); Ellen Schrecker, *Many Are the Crimes: McCarthyism in America* (Princeton, NJ: Princeton U. Press, 1998).
67. U.S. Senate, 81st Cong., 2d Sess., Comm. on Expenditures in the Executive Departments, *Employment of Homosexuals and Other Sexual Perverts in Government* (Washington, DC: Gov't Printing Office, 1950), p. 4; see also John D'Emilio, *Sexual Politics, Sexual Communities: The Making of the Homosexual Minority in the United States, 1940–1970* (Chicago: U. of Chicago Press, 1983), p. 42; Gayle Rubin, "Thinking Sex: Notes for a Radical Theory of the Politics of Sexuality," in *Pleasure and Danger* (Carole Vance, ed.) (London: Routledge & Kegan Paul, 1984), p. 270; Jonathan Katz, *Gay American History: Lesbians and Gay Men in the USA: A Documentary Anthology* (New York: Thomas Crowell, 1976). Replicating the federal government's fixations, the Communist Party-USA also expelled homosexuals in the late 1950s, "on the grounds that their vulnerability to blackmail in the repressive sexual climate of the period would endanger their comrades." Schrecker, *supra* n. 66, 19–20.
68. D'Emilio, *supra* n. 67, p. 41; D'Emilio & Freedman, pp. 292–93.
69. Beauvais Lyons, "Artistic Freedom and the University," 50 *Art Journal* 78 (College Art Ass'n) (1991).
70. See Myron Sharaf, *Fury on Earth: A Biography of Wilhelm Reich* (New York: St. Martin's, 1983), pp. 460–61; de Grazia, pp. 347, 394.
71. U.S. House of Representatives, 86th Cong., 1st Sess., Comm. on Post Office & Civil Service, Subcomm. on Postal Operations, *Obscene Matter Sent Through the Mail* (Washington, DC: Gov't Printing Office, 1959), pp. 1, 14.
72. Alfred Kinsey *et al.*, *Sexual Behavior in the Human Male* (Philadelphia: W. B. Saunders, 1948); Alfred Kinsey *et al.*, *Sexual Behavior in the Human Female* (Philadelphia: W. B. Saunders, 1953); see also Robinson, *supra* n. 5, pp. 42–119; Jones, *supra* n. 13.
73. Jones, p. 563; see also Jonathan Gathorne-Hardy, *Sex, the Measure of All Things: A Life of Alfred C. Kinsey* (Bloomington: Indiana U. Press, 2000); Jeffrey Moran, *Teaching Sex: The Shaping of Adolescence in the 20th Century* (Cambridge, MA: Harvard U. Press, 2000), pp. 135–36 ("So fascinated were Americans with Kinsey's work that word of *Sexual Behavior in the Human Female*'s publication in 1953 pushed off the front pages news of verification of the Soviet hyrogen bomb and Mohammed Mossadegh's surrender in Iran").

74. Jones, pp. 707–11, 712, quoting *New York Post,* Aug. 30, 1953.
75. Robinson, *supra* n. 5, pp. 90–91, 117.
76. Jones, pp. 720–21, 713, 632, quoting Reinhold Niebuhr, "Sex and Religion in the Kinsey Report," *Christianity and Crisis,* Nov. 2, 1953, p. 138; Bishop Schulte's remarks in *Indianapolis News,* Aug. 20, 28, 1953; J. Edgar Hoover, "Must We Change Our Sex Standards?" *Reader's Digest,* June 1948, p. 6; see also Lionel Trilling, "The Kinsey Report," in *The Liberal Imagination* (New York: Anchor, 1953), pp. 223, 225 (originally published in *Partisan Review,* Apr. 1948).
77. See Martin Duberman, "Kinsey's Urethra," *The Nation,* Nov. 3, 1997, p. 40 (faulting Jones for "crude psychologizing [which is really moralizing]" about Kinsey's sexuality); Gathorne-Hardy, *supra* n. 73 (arguing that Kinsey's bisexuality diminished neither his accuracy nor his scientific contribution, and characterizing Jones's as "the Kenneth Starr school of biography," *id.*, p. viii).
78. Jones, pp. 632, 712–23; see also James Jones, "Dr. Yes," *The New Yorker,* Aug. 25 & Sept. 1, 1997, pp. 99, 100.
79. Jones, pp. 715–37; Gathorne-Hardy, p. 408 (the Reece Committee's findings were "demolished" by journalists); Rubin, *supra* n. 67, p. 273; see also Paul Gebhard, "The Institute," in *Sex Research: Studies from the Kinsey Institute* (Martin Weinberg, ed.) (New York: Oxford U. Press, 1976), pp. 10–22.
80. Margaret Blanchard, "The American Urge to Censor: Freedom of Expression Versus the Desire to Sanitize Society," 33 *Wm. & Mary L. Rev.* 741, 789 (1992).
81. See Publisher's Note, in Fredric Wertham, *Seduction of the Innocent* (New York: Rinehart & Co., 1953), p. v (noting Wertham's scientific bona fides); Blanchard, *supra* n. 80, at 788–95; John E. Twomey, "The Citizens' Committee and Comic Book Control: A Study of Extragovernmental Restraint," 20 *Law & Contemp. Probs.* 621, 622, 624 (1955).
82. *Seduction of the Innocent, supra* n. 81, pp. 164, 167, 189–90.
83. *Id.*, pp. 84, 115, 239–41; see also *Ron Goulart's Great History of Comic Books* (Chicago: Contemporary Books, 1986), pp. 263–72 (describing Wertham's influence, and comic book bonfires in several cities); Fred von Bernewitz & Grant Geisman, *Tales of Terror!* (Timonium, MD: Gemstone, 2000), pp. 26–27.
84. Thrasher, *supra* n. 51, at 197, 200; see also Twomey, *supra* n. 81, at 623 n. 11; Blanchard, *supra* n. 80, at 791.
85. Reuel Denney, "The Dark Fantastic" (Book Review), *New Republic,* May 3, 1954, p. 18; see also Dorothy Walter Baruch, "Radio Rackets, Movie Murders and Killer Cartoons," in *New Ways to Discipline: You and Your Child Today* (New York: McGraw-Hill, 1949), excerpted in *The Children's Culture Reader, supra* n. 18, p. 493 (suggesting that more active play outlets for youthful aggression were needed); Reuel Denney, *The Astonished Muse: Popular Culture in America* (New York: Grosset & Dunlap, 1964), p. 164 (Wertham's assertions were "without evidence of any weight").

86. Henry Jenkins, "The Sensuous Child," in *The Children's Culture Reader*, p. 220.
87. *Katzev v. County of Los Angeles*, 52 Cal.2d 360 (1959); see Gail Johnston, "Crime Comics and the Constitution," 7 *Stan. L. Rev.* 237, 238 (1955). The LA ordinance had an exemption for "actual historical events" and "occurrences actually set forth in the sacred scriptures of any religion." Maryland's and Washington's anti-comics laws were invalidated in *Police Comm'r of Baltimore v. Siegel Enterprises*, 223 Md. 110 (1960) and *Adams v. Hinkle*, 51 Wn. 2d 763 (1958).
88. *Juvenile Delinquency (Comic Books)*, 1954: Hearings on S. 190 Before the Subcomm. to Investigate Juvenile Delinquency of the Senate Comm. on the Judiciary, 83d Cong., 2d Sess. (1954), pp. 86, 103; see also *Comic Books and Juvenile Delinquency*, Interim Report of the Senate Comm. on the Judiciary, 84th Cong., 1st Sess.; Blanchard, at 790; Lynn Spigel, "Seducing the Innocent: Childhood and Television in Postwar America," in *The Children's Culture Reader*, p. 117; Rowland, *supra* n. 51, pp. 99–105 (describing Kefauver Committee's examination of violence on television—then in its infancy—as well); *Tales of Terror*, *supra* n. 83, pp. 26–27 (reprinting Senate testimony of EC Comics publisher William Gaines).
89. Blanchard, at 793; Fredric Wertham, *A Sign for Cain: An Exploration of Human Violence* (London: Lowe & Brydone, 1966), p. 197.
90. *Comic Books and Juvenile Delinquency*, *supra* n. 88, p. 14. As for Dr. Wertham, he moved on to other media in the 1960s and '70s, defending "fanzines" as healthy fantasy, but condemning *The Three Stooges* television show as "an ideal primer" for violence. *A Sign for Cain*, *supra* n. 89, p. 194; Fredric Wertham, *The World of Fanzines* (Carbondale: So. Ill. U. Press, 1973), p. 126.
91. Nat'l Council on Freedom from Censorship (organized by the ACLU), *What Shocked the Censors: A Complete Record of Cuts in Motion Picture Films Ordered by the New York State Censors from January, 1932 to March, 1933* (Sept. 1933), p. 2. On the Hays Code, see Leonard Leff & Jerold Simmons, *The Dame in the Kimono: Hollywood, Censorship, and the Production Code from the 1920s to the 1960s* (New York: Doubleday, 1990); Lea Jacobs, *The Wages of Sin: Censorship and the Fallen Woman Film, 1928–1942* (Berkeley: U. of Cal. Press, 1995). The system of film licensing was held in place by a 1915 Supreme Court ruling that movies were just a business, not a form of expression; the Court did not change its mind on this point until 1948. *Mutual Film Corp. v. Industrial Comm'n*, 236 U.S. 230 (1915), contradicted by *United States v. Paramount Pictures*, 334 U.S. 131, 166 (1948). Four years later, it invalidated New York's denial of a license to Roberto Rossellini's *The Miracle*, a film about a simpleminded woman who believes she is the Virgin Mary. (Under pressure from Francis Cardinal Spellman, New York had revoked *The Miracle*'s exhibition license on grounds of sacrilege.) *Burstyn v. Wilson*, 343 U.S. 495 (1952).

92. *Winters v. New York*, 333 U.S. 507, 508, 511 (1948).
93. *Id.* at 523, 530–31 (Frankfurter, J., dissenting).
94. *Id.* at 510.
95. *Chaplinsky v. New Hampshire*, 315 U.S. 568, 572 (1942). *Chaplinsky* held that so-called "fighting words"—words more likely to provoke a fight than invite a conversation—were not protected by the First Amendment. The decision upheld the criminal conviction of a Jehovah's Witness for calling a city marshal a "God damned racketeer" and "a damned Fascist."
96. Zechariah Chafee, Jr., *Free Speech in the United States* (Cambridge, MA: Harvard U. Press, 1941), p. 150.
97. See Rabban, *supra* n. 19; Chafee, *supra* n. 96. Although Chafee believed sexual speech hardly merited the same protection as political speech, he acknowledged that literary censorship had sometimes been excessive. *Id.*, p. 151.
98. Lockhart & McClure, *supra* n. 56.
99. *Id.* at 301.
100. *Id.* at 321, 368. The Communist Party case was *Dennis v. United States*, 341 U.S. 494 (1951), where the Supreme Court majority applied a watered-down "clear and present danger" test to uphold convictions for politically subversive speech even though it presented no imminent threat of violent or illegal conduct.
101. Lockhart & McClure, 38 *Minn. L. Rev.* at 388.
102. *Id.* at 395.
103. Weston La Barre, "Obscenity; An Anthropological Appraisal," 20 *Law & Contemp. Probs.* 533, 533–34 (1955).
104. Melvin Shimm, "Foreword," 20 *Law & Contemp. Probs.* 531, 532 (1955).
105. *United States v. Roth*, 237 F.2d 797, 797 (2d Cir. 1956), aff'd, 354 U.S. 476 (1957).
106. *Id.*
107. *Id.* at 801, 802, 813 (Frank, J., concurring). As a scholar who had written extensively about sociology and law, Frank said he deplored "the use of the word 'scientific' as applied to social studies." *Id.* at 813 n. 33b.
108. *Id.* at 806–7, 809.
109. *Id.* at 815, quoting Jahoda letter. Jahoda's report was *The Impact of Literature: A Psychological Discussion of Some Assumptions in the Censorship Debate* (Research Center for Human Relations, New York University, 1954).
110. *U.S. v. Roth*, 237 F.2d at 816–17.

3. THE GREAT AND MYSTERIOUS MOTIVE FORCE IN HUMAN LIFE

1. *Butler v. Michigan*, 352 U.S. 380, 381 (1957).
2. The quotation is from James Paul & Murray Schwartz, *Federal Censorship: Obscenity in the Mail* (New York: The Free Press, 1961), p. 141; the *Butler* decision does not name or describe the book. William Lockhart & Robert McClure, "Censorship of Obscenity: The Developing Constitutional Standards,"

45 *Minn. L. Rev.* 5, 13 (1960) ("Lockhart & McClure, II"), report that the sale "had been carefully staged" to test the constitutionality of the Michigan law.

3. *Butler*, 352 U.S. at 383–84. Frankfurter did not cite *Hicklin*, or any of the court decisions, from *Kennerley* to *Ulysses*, that had noted its deficiencies. Legal historian Bernard Schwartz reports that after giving some thought to a broader ruling on obscenity, the justices in *Butler* decided to hold off on "full dress treatment" until *Roth*. Bernard Schwartz, *Super Chief—Earl Warren and His Supreme Court: A Judicial Biography* (New York: NYU Press, 1983), p. 219.
4. *Obscenity: The Complete Oral Arguments Before the Supreme Court in the Major Obscenity Cases*, Vol. 2 (Leon Friedman, ed.) (New York: Chelsea House, 1983), pp. 24, 54, 57. At one point, Frankfurter asked Stanley Fleishman, the lawyer for Alberts, whether public opinion on sex represented "established tenets that came from Moses to Sinai via Kinsey." *Id.*, p. 60.
5. American Law Institute, *Model Penal Code, Tentative Draft* No. 6, Comments on §207.10 (1957), p. 10; see also Richard Hixson, *Pornography and the Justices* (Carbondale: So. Ill. U. Press, 1996), p. 21; *Roth v. United States*, 354 U.S. 476, 499 n. 1 (1957) (Harlan, J., concurring in part and dissenting in part) (citing these comments to the *Tentative Draft*). The ALI did not propose any criminal ban on " 'comic' books and other literature emphasizing crime, violence, passion, terror, torture, etc.," noting that "[e]vidence as to any significant relationship between comic book horrors and delinquent juvenile behavior consists largely of undocumented opinion by laymen; the weight of professional opinion based on such studies as have been made is against the hypothesis." Comments, pp. 11–12. The ALI borrowed the phrase "prurient interest" from a 1915 Supreme Court decision denying First Amendment protection to the then-infant art of motion pictures, in part because in presenting cinema "a prurient interest may be excited and appealed to." *Mutual Film Corp. v Industrial Comm'n*, 236 U.S. 230, 242 (1915).
6. *Model Penal Code*, §207.10, Comment, p. 11; §207.10(4)(c), Comment, p. 17. The 1962 *Proposed Official Draft* of the *Model Penal Code* carried over the definitions in the *Tentative Draft* with only minor changes. ALI, *Model Penal Code, Proposed Official Draft*, §251.4 (Philadelphia: ALI, 1962), p. 237.
7. *Sweezy v. New Hampshire*, 354 U.S. 234 (1957) (affirming the right of a Marxist professor not to answer questions put by the state attorney general about the content of his lectures, and recognizing for the first time a First Amendment right to academic freedom); *Watkins v. United States*, 354 U.S. 178 (1957) (imposing relevancy limits on the wide-ranging inquisitions of congressional investigating committees); *Yates v. United States*, 354 U.S. 298 (1957) (interpreting the antisubversive Smith Act of 1940 much more narrowly than the Court had done six years earlier in *United States v. Dennis*, 341 U.S. 494 [1951], when it upheld criminal convictions of Communist Party leaders for their abstract advocacy of socialist revolution); *Service v. Dulles*, 354 U.S. 363 (1957) (ruling that federal agencies cannot ignore their own procedural rules when firing employees for alleged disloyalty).

8. I. F. Stone, *The Haunted Fifties* (New York: Random House, 1963), p. 199.
9. Morton Horwitz, *The Warren Court and the Pursuit of Justice* (New York: Hill & Wang, 1998), p. xii.
10. *Roth v. United States*, 354 U.S. 476, 483–85 (1957), quoting *Chaplinsky v. New Hampshire*, 315 U.S. 568, 572 (1942) (upholding a conviction for so-called fighting words). (The names of the parties in *Roth* were now reversed because Roth was appealing from the Second Circuit decision.) The same day as *Roth*, the court also decided *Kingsley Books, Inc. v. Brown*, 354 U.S. 436 (1957), rejecting a constitutional challenge to a prior restraint scheme in which state authorities could secure a court order banning a publication before it was adjudicated obscene.
11. Harry Kalven, Jr., "The Metaphysics of the Law of Obscenity," 1960 *Sup. Ct. Rev.* 1, 9.
12. *Roth*, 354 U.S. at 486 ("in light of our holding that obscenity is not protected speech, . . . 'it is unnecessary, either for us or for the State courts, to consider the issues behind the phrase "clear and present danger" ' ") (quoting *Beauharnais v. Illinois*, 343 U.S. 250, 266 [1952]).
13. *Roth*, 354 U.S. at 497 (Harlan, J., concurring in part and dissenting in part). A longtime believer in deference to state legislatures, Harlan agreed with the conviction of Alberts but would have reversed Roth's; the "domain of sexual morality is pre-eminently a matter of state," not federal concern, he said, and federalism required deference to the California legislature's judgment that "certain types of literature will induce criminal or immoral sexual conduct," or even if not, will at least "degrade sex, which will have an eroding effect on moral standards." *Id.* at 497–508.
14. *Id.* at 487.
15. *Regina v. Martin Secker & Warburg* (1954), 2 All E.R. 683, 38 Crim.App.Rep. 124, 127–28. The jury got the message and acquitted the publisher of a novel, *The Philanderer*, which recounts the "degeneration of a happily married man whose private insecurity drives him to sexual conquest." Charles Clark, "Obscenity, the Law and Lady Chatterley—Part I" (1961), *Crim. L. Rev.* 157, 158–59. Justice Frankfurter had alerted Brennan to Stable's jury charge, which Brennan liked so much that he intended to include it as an appendix to *Roth*, but Justice Harold Burton dissuaded him. Letter from Frankfurter to Brennan, May 15, 1957; Letter from Burton to Brennan, June 10, 1957, in Brennan Papers, Library of Congress, Part 1, Container 6.
16. *Secker & Warburg*, 38 Crim.App.Rep. at 125, 130. The publisher later wrote a hilarious account of the case, in which he reported that Stable's famous summation "appeared to be unrehearsed." It was later used "by a New York publisher and his wife as their Christmas-card message." Fredric Warburg, "A Slight Case of Obscenity," *The New Yorker*, Apr. 20, 1957, p. 130.
17. *Roth*, 354 U.S. at 489, 487 n. 20.
18. *Id.* at 489 n. 26. See *Commonwealth v. Isenstadt*, 318 Mass. 543, 552 (1945); *Commonwealth v. Gordon*, 66 Pa. D. & C. 101 (Phila. County Ct. 1949);

Lockhart & McClure II, *supra* n. 2, pp. 49–52, demonstrating why the thirteen cases cited by Brennan in support of the "prurient interest" standard were actually all over the lot.

19. *Roth*, 354 U.S. at 491; *Paris Adult Theatre I v. Slaton*, 413 U.S. 49, 84 (1973) (Brennan, J., dissenting). An earlier draft of *Roth* had a discussion of the vagueness issue, but it was deleted from the final opinion. Brennan Papers, *supra* n. 15.
20. *Roth*, 354 U.S. at 495, 496 (Warren, J., concurring).
21. "The Warren Court: Fateful Decade," *Newsweek*, May 4, 1964, p. 28; see also Edward de Grazia, *Girls Lean Back Everywhere: The Law of Obscenity and the Assault on Genius* (New York: Random House, 1992), p. 274. (De Grazia attributed the remark to a conversation that Warren had with his clerks); Jack Harrison Pollack, *Earl Warren: The Judge Who Changed America* (Englewood Cliffs, NJ: Prentice Hall, 1979), p. 355 (" 'I'd punch any man in the face who would show that . . . to one of my daughters,' he shouted at fellow Justices"—no source cited).
22. *Roth*, 354 U.S. at 508–14 (Douglas and Black, JJ., dissenting).
23. Horwitz, *supra* n. 9, pp. 101–3.
24. See de Grazia, *supra* n. 21, pp. 252, 265; Charles Rembar, *The End of Obscenity* (New York: Simon & Schuster, 1968).
25. Rembar, *supra* n. 24, p. 16; see also de Grazia, pp. 88–97; 338–42.
26. *Grove Press v. Christenberry*, 175 F. Supp. 488 (S.D.N.Y. 1959), aff'd, 275 F.2d 433 (2d Cir. 1960).
27. Ed Zern, "Exit, Laughing," *Field & Stream*, Nov. 1959, p. 142.
28. Obscene Publications Act 1959, 11(1) *Halsbury's Laws of England* (4th ed.) (London: Butterworths, 1990 reissue), ¶¶355–61. On the legislative maneuvers and political conflicts that produced the 1959 Act, see Graham Zellick, "Films and the Law of Obscenity" (1971), *Crim. L. Rev.* 126, 128–35.
29. *The Trial of Lady Chatterley* (C. H. Rolph, ed.) (London: Penguin, 1961, 1990); see also *Regina v. Penguin Books* (1961) *Crim. L. Rev.* 176. Other experts who testified at the Old Bailey in defense of the novel included E. M. Forster, C. Day Lewis, and Rebecca West.
30. *The Trial of Lady Chatterley*, *supra*, n. 29, pp. 13, 17, quoting in part *Regina v. Hicklin*, 3 Q.B. 360, 372 (1868).
31. *Id.*, pp. 35, 195.
32. *Shaw v. Director of Public Prosecutions* (1962), A.C. 220, 45 Cr.App.Rep. 113, HL. The publisher was also guilty of conspiracy to corrupt public morals under the common law; see 11(1) *Halsbury's Laws of England* (4th ed., 1990 reissue), ¶62.
33. Barry Cox, *Civil Liberties in Britain* (Harmondsworth, UK: Penguin, 1975), pp. 98–99.
34. *Regina v. Stanley* (1965), 2 Q.B. 327; Post Office Act 1953, 11(1) *Halsbury's Laws of England* (4th ed., 1990 reissue), ¶¶373–75.
35. *Regina v. Clayton & Halsey* (1962), 3 All E.R. 500 (1963), 1 Q.B. 163

(Ct.Crim.App.). Ten years later, the Law Lords (Britain's highest court) rejected an argument that pornographic works were not obscene because their mostly middle-aged male consumers could not be further depraved and corrupted: the Obscene Publications Act, the justices said, was "not merely concerned with the once for all corruption of the wholly innocent, it equally protects the less innocent from further corruption." *Director of Public Prosecutions v. Whyte* (1972), 3 All E.R. 12, 19.

36. *Butler*, 352 U.S. at 383.
37. Lockhart & McClure II, *supra* n. 2.
38. *Id.* at 69–80; see *United States v. 31 Photographs*, 156 F. Supp. 350 (S.D.N.Y. 1957).
39. *Bantam Books, Inc. v. Sullivan*, 374 U.S. 58, 67–71 (1963).
40. *Jacobellis v. Ohio*, 378 U.S. 184, 197 (1964) (Stewart, J., concurring). Two other decisions were handed down the same day as *Jacobellis: A Quantity of Books v. Kansas*, 378 U.S. 205 (1964), established procedural safeguards for the seizure of allegedly obscene literature; and *Grove Press v. Gerstein*, 378 U.S. 577 (1964), reversed without opinion a Florida judgment of obscenity against Henry Miller's *Tropic of Cancer*.
41. A *Book Named "John Cleland's Memoirs of a Woman of Pleasure" v. Massachusetts*, 383 U.S. 413 (1966).
42. *Id.* at 418.
43. *Manual Enterprises v. Day*, 370 U.S. 478, 482 (1962).
44. *Memoirs v. Massachusetts*, 383 U.S. at 460–62 (White, J., dissenting); at 424–33 (Douglas, J., concurring); at 452–53 (Clark, J., dissenting). Hugo Black and Potter Stewart also concurred separately; Harlan wrote a separate dissent.
45. *Id.* at 420 (plurality opinion). In a letter to a judge of the D.C. Circuit, Brennan confirmed that *Memoirs* "leaves the door open for Massachusetts" to prosecute based on pandering "if the evidence is available." March 23, 1966, letter to Judge Charles Fahy, Brennan Papers, Part 2, Container 3.
46. *Ginzberg v. United States*, 383 U.S. 463, 465–68 (1966). The third case decided with *Memoirs* and *Ginzberg, Mishkin v. New York*, applied variable obscenity to find that books appealing to "deviant" rather than average sexual tastes could also be obscene. 383 U.S. 502 (1966).
47. De Grazia, pp. 503, 511; see also Hixson, *supra* n. 5, p. 70.
48. *Ginzberg*, 383 U.S. at 476 (Black, J., dissenting); 497–501 (Stewart, J., dissenting).
49. *New York Times*, Apr. 3, 1966, p. 14E. Brennan had initially voted to hold *Fanny Hill* obscene, but Fortas persuaded him to change his mind. See Lucas Powe, *The Warren Court and American Politics* (Cambridge, MA: Harvard U. Press, 2000), pp. 344–46; see also Bruce Allen Murphy, *Fortas: The Rise and Ruin of a Supreme Court Justice* (New York: William Morrow, 1988), p. 458; *Super Chief, supra* n. 3, pp. 618–23 (recounting the convoluted, shifting alliances in *Memoirs* and *Ginzberg* and reporting that as Brennan announced *Ginzberg* in open court, Warren passed him a note observing "the quizzical expression on the faces of some of the Sol. Gen.'s staff").

50. *Paramount Film Distrib. Corp. v. Chicago*, 172 F. Supp. 69, 72 (N.D. Ill. 1959) (finding the ordinance's provision for an adults-only license "when a film approaches producing a harmful notion in the mind of anyone from one to twenty-one years of age" to be "an insufficient guide to either the censors or those who produce motion pictures," as well as an unjustified imposition on a "twenty year old, married service man [who] would be prevented from seeing a film that might not be suitable for a girl of twelve"); see also Note, "For Adults Only: The Constitutionality of Governmental Film Censorship by Age Classification," 69 *Yale L.J.* 141 (1959).
51. See *Rabeck v. New York*, 391 U.S. 462 (1968), invalidating this earlier law on grounds of vagueness.
52. *Ginsberg v. New York*, 390 U.S. 629, 633 (1968).
53. *People v. Ginsberg*, 56 Misc.2d 882, 883 (1st Dist. Nassau Cty. 1966). The magazines were *Sir, Escapade, Mr. Annual,* and *Man to Man*. On the manufactured nature of the case, see *Ginsberg*, 390 U.S. at 671–72 (Fortas, J., dissenting); Appellant's Jurisdictional Statement in *Ginsberg v. New York*, No. 47 (Oct. term, 1966), p. 5; de Grazia, p. 540.
54. *Ginsberg*, 390 U.S. at 634.
55. *Id.* at 639–41.
56. *People v. Ginsberg*, 56 Misc.2d at 883.
57. *Ginsberg*, 390 U.S. at 639–42.
58. *Id.* at 639–42. "[T]he growing consensus of commentators," Brennan said, is that while studies "all agree that a causal link has not been demonstrated" between obscenity and the ethical development of youth, "they are equally agreed that a causal link has not been disproved either." In a March 4, 1968, letter to Brennan, Byron White praised his "skillful and subtle draft opinion" in *Ginsberg*. White noted the intellectual tension between the argument that variable obscenity is outside the First Amendment and the enumeration of government justifications for banning its distribution to minors. "Perhaps you ride both horses in this case," White wrote. "This is admirable eclecticism if it gets four other guys. In the end, I shall probably be one of them." Brennan Papers, Part 1, Container 169.
59. Willard Gaylin, Book Review, "The Prickly Problems of Pornography," 77 *Yale L. J.* 579, 592–94 (1968), quoted in *Ginsberg*, 380 U.S. at 642 n. 10; revised version reprinted as "Obscenity Is More Than a Four-Letter Word," in *Censorship and Freedom of Expression: Essays on Obscenity and the Law* (Harry Clor, ed.) (Chicago: Rand McNally, 1971), p. 153.
60. *Ginsberg*, 390 U.S. at 650–51, 659 (Douglas, J., dissenting).
61. *Id.* at 674 (Fortas, J., dissenting); see also C. Peter McGrath, "The Obscenity Cases: Grapes of *Roth*," 1966 *Sup. Ct. Rev.* 1, 56 (criticizing variable-obscenity doctrine and calling the Supreme Court's obscenity jurisprudence a "constitutional disaster area").
62. Rita Kramer, "The Dirty Book Bit," *New York Times Magazine*, June 9, 1968, p. 99.
63. *Interstate Circuit v. Dallas*, 390 U.S. 676, 681 (1968). Three years earlier, the

Supreme Court had largely done away with film licensing boards by ruling that they were instruments of "prior restraint" and requiring them to obtain judicial adjudications of obscenity before they could deny exhibition licenses. *Freedman v. Maryland*, 380 U.S. 51 (1965).

64. *Interstate Circuit*, 390 U.S. at 688–89.
65. *Kingsley Int'l Pictures v. Regents of the Univ. of the State of New York*, 360 U.S. 684, 689 (1959). The state had objected to the film's favorable treatment of adultery.
66. *Ginsberg*, 390 U.S. at 637 (majority opinion); 649 (Stewart, J., concurring). At oral argument, Ginsberg's lawyer, Emanuel Redfield, disclaimed any reliance on minors' constitutional rights and based his claims solely on "the right of the vendor or the expresser." *Obscenity*, *supra* n. 4, p. 287.
67. *Tinker v. Des Moines Ind. School Dist.*, 393 U.S. 503, 506–11 (1969) (quoting *West Virginia State Bd. of Ed. v. Barnette*, 319 U.S. 624, 637 [1943]). Only Justice Stewart, concurring in *Tinker*, noted the inconsistency with *Ginsberg*'s ruling the previous year that minors possess limited First Amendment rights. *Id.* at 515 (Stewart, J., concurring). Fortas's opinion in *Tinker* was consistent with his groundbreaking children's rights decision two years earlier in *In re Gault*, 387 U.S. 1 (1967), requiring basic due process protections in juvenile delinquency proceedings. See John Johnson, *The Struggle for Student Rights: Tinker v. Des Moines and the 1960s* (Lawrence: U. Kansas Press, 1997), p. 168.
68. *Shelton v. Tucker*, 364 U.S. 479, 487 (1960).
69. *Epperson v. Arkansas*, 393 U.S. 97 (1968).
70. *Keyishian v. Board of Regents*, 385 U.S. 589, 603 (1967).
71. See *Hill v. Lewis*, 323 F. Supp. 55 (E.D.N.C. 1971); *Eisner v. Stamford Bd. of Ed.*, 440 F.2d 803 (2d Cir. 1971); *Riseman v. School Comm.*, 439 F.2d 148 (1st Cir. 1971); *Fujishima v. Board of Ed.*, 460 F.2d 1355 (7th Cir. 1972); *Shanley v. Northeast Ind. School Dist.*, 462 F.2d 960 (5th Cir. 1972); *Quarterman v. Byrd*, 453 F.2d 54 (4th Cir. 1971); *Nitzberg v. Parks*, 525 F.2d 378 (4th Cir. 1975).
72. *Rosenblatt v. Common Sense Newspapers*, 320 N.Y.S.2d 83, 85, 88 (S.Ct. Dutchess Cty. 1971).
73. *Id.* at 85–90. The injunction was "limited so as only to restrain further distribution to minors under the age of 17 years, and within the school building, or upon the grounds of the Arlington Senior High School or any other public grade or high school"; *id.* at 91.
74. *State v. Vachon*, 306 A.2d 781, 784 (N.H. 1973), rev'd on other grounds, 414 U.S. 478 (1974).
75. *Grosser v. Woollett*, 74 Ohio Op.2d 233, 341 N.E.2d 356, 367–68 (Ct. Common Pleas, Cuyahoga Cty. 1974). The court did allow the school to assign the books where parents had been advised of their "character" and specifically consented.
76. *Cohen v. California*, 403 U.S. 15, 25–26 (1971). Harlan rejected the state's argument that people in the courthouse were a "captive audience" entitled to

protection from offensive messages; this theory, he said, "would effectively empower a majority to silence dissidents simply as a matter of personal predilections." *Id.* at 21–22.

77. *Id.* at 25–26.
78. *Wisconsin v. Yoder*, 406 U.S. 205, 245–46 & n. 3 (1972) (Douglas, J., dissenting.) On minors' rights to receive information over their parents' objections, see Catherine Ross, "An Emerging Right for Mature Minors to Receive Information," 2 *U. Pa. J. Con. L.* 223 (1999).
79. See Rembar, *supra* n. 24.
80. *Report of the Commission on Obscenity and Pornography* (Lockhart Commission) (New York: Bantam, 1970), p. 57.
81. *Id.*, pp. 57–61.
82. *Id.*, pp. 62–63.
83. *Id.*, pp. 578–623; see Powe, *supra* n. 49, p. 357 (Senate voted 60–5 to reject the Lockhart report "before even receiving it").
84. See Zellick, *supra* n. 28; 11(1) *Halsbury's Laws of England* (4th ed., 1990 reissue), ¶372 (common-law offense of "outraging public decency"); ¶376 ("indecent displays"); ¶355 & n. 8 (subjecting films to Obscene Publications Act and exempting them from common-law indecency charges).
85. *Regina v. Stanley*, 2 Q.B. at 333.
86. *Director of Public Prosecutions v. A. & B.C. Chewing Gum, Ltd.* (1967), 1 Q.B. 159, 165, 2 All E.R. 504.
87. *John Calder v. Powell* (1965), 1 Q.B. 509, 515.
88. Philip Meredith, *Sex Education: Political Issues in Britain and Europe* (London: Routledge, 1989), p. 51.
89. Author's interview with Richard Handyside, June 16, 1999; *Handyside Case*, Series A, No. 24 (Eur. Ct. Human Rights, Dec. 7, 1976), at 10. Handyside explained that most of the press run was never seized by police; the books were distributed surreptitiously and made their way into homes and schools.
90. Tony Palmer, *The Trials of Oz* (Manchester: Bond & Briggs, 1971), p. 34. Palmer dedicates the book to his stepdaughter "and all the other seven-year-olds likely to be depraved or corrupted"; see also Geoffrey Robertson's recollection of the trial in *The Justice Game* (London: Random House, 1998), pp. 12–48.
91. *Oz*, School Kids Issue, No. 28, 1971; Palmer, *supra* n. 90, pp. 38–39, 52; Robertson, *supra* n. 90, p. 43; *Regina v. Anderson et al.* (1971), 3 All E.R. 1152, 1157 (Ct.Crim.App.).
92. Robertson, p. 37.
93. Palmer, pp. 27, 193. The judge, Michael Argyle, agreed with Leary's assessment: summarizing the defense testimony of the young law professor Ronald Dworkin with dismissive sarcasm, Argyle said, "he gave us a lecture on public morals which, I am sure, was of great benefit to all who heard it. This prosecution, he said, would be unconstitutional in the United States. That may be. But we are not, as yet, an adjunct of the United States." *Id.*, p. 257.

94. *Id.*, p. 177 (summarizing testimony of psychologist Michael Duane).
95. *Regina v. Anderson* (1971), 3 All E.R. 1152.
96. *Id.* at 1156–57.
97. *Handyside, supra* n. 89, at 14, quoting Inner London Court of Quarter Sessions (Oct. 1971).
98. *Id.* at 15–17.
99. Convention for the Protection of Human Rights and Fundamental Freedoms (1950) (Rome, Nov. 4, 1950); see 8(2) *Halsbury's Laws of England* (4th ed., 1996 reissue) ¶¶102, 122–200.
100. In 1998, Parliament adopted a Human Rights Act that incorporated the European Convention into English law. Human Rights Act 1998, 1998 ch. 42, §§4, 10; see 8(2) *Halsbury's, 1999 Cum. Supp.*, Pt. I, ¶¶101–200 (4th ed. 1999). In one of the more intricate constitutional compromises of the decade, the Act stopped short of empowering courts to invalidate legislation. Instead, British judges could now make "declarations of incompatibility" between domestic laws and Convention rights; such declarations would not affect a law's "validity, continuing operation, or enforcement," but government ministers, if they chose, could propose new legislation to cure the incompatibility.
101. Other exceptions listed in paragraph 2 of Article 10 are "the interests of national security, territorial integrity or public safety, . . . the prevention of disorder or crime, . . . the protection of the reputation or rights of others, . . . preventing the disclosure of information received in confidence," and "maintaining the authority and impartiality of the judiciary."
102. *Handyside*, at 20–22, 27.
103. De Grazia, pp. 560–61; Brennan Papers, Part 1, Container 291; see also Bob Woodward & Scott Armstrong, *The Brethren* (New York: Simon & Schuster, 1979), pp. 196, 244–53.
104. *Miller v. California*, 413 U.S. 15, 24, 30–33 (1973).
105. *Id.* at 32. Burger acknowledged that "[u]nder a national Constitution, fundamental First Amendment limitations on the powers of the States do not vary from community to community," *id.* at 30; but he ignored the point later in his opinion.
106. *Paris Adult Theatre I v. Slaton*, 413 U.S. 49, 63 (1973). Burger had put the point more bluntly at a conference of the justices, describing pornography as "filth in sewers, garbage in dumps." Handwritten notes, Brennan Papers, Part 1, Container 283.
107. *Paris Adult*, 413 U.S. at 84 (Brennan, J., dissenting), quoting Justice Stewart's well-known quip in *Jacobellis v. Ohio*, 378 U.S. at 197. William O. Douglas's dissent in *Miller*, meanwhile, reiterated his long-held view that "highly subjective aesthetic, psychological and moral tests" like "prurient interest," "patent offensiveness," and "community standards" "do not provide meaningful guidance for law enforcement officials, juries or courts," and that "the idea that the First Amendment permits punishment for ideas that are 'offensive' to the particular judge or jury sitting in judgment is astounding." *Miller*, 413 U.S. at 39

n. 5; 44. In a memo to the conference on May 22, 1972, Brennan described Burger's proposed solution to "the obscenity quagmire" as likely to "worsen an already intolerable mess." Brennan Papers, Part 1, Container 279.

108. Nat Hentoff, "The Constitutionalist," *The New Yorker*, Mar. 12, 1990, p. 56.

109. *Paris Adult*, 413 U.S. at 106, 113–14 (Brennan, J., dissenting).

110. *Erznoznik v. City of Jacksonville*, 422 U.S. 205, 212–14 (1975).

111. In a case almost identical to Jacksonville's, a U.S. court of appeals noted the testimony of a psychiatrist that "viewing simple nudity was not harmful to children except to a very small number of them who were reared in what he described as an ultra conservative family environment." Prefiguring *Reno v. ACLU* a quarter-century later, the court noted that children could actually benefit from seeing the nude art objects "found in many museums," and said "even the child's freedom of speech [is] too precious to be subjected to the whim of the censor." *Cinecom Theatres v. Fort Wayne*, 473 F.2d 1297, 1300–2 (7th Cir. 1973), quoting *Interstate Circuit v. Dallas*, 366 F.2d 590, 598–99 (5th Cir. 1966).

112. *President's Council v. Community School Bd.*, 409 U.S. 998, 999–1000 (1972) (Douglas, J., dissenting from denial of certiorari) (quoting *Kleindienst v. Mandel*, 408 U.S. 753, 763 [1972], and *Shelton v. Tucker*, 364 U.S. at 487); *President's Council v. Community School Bd.*, 457 F.2d 289, 291 (2d Cir. 1972). The plaintiffs included three junior high students, their parents, two teachers, a librarian, and a principal. For a more speech-friendly decision in the Second Circuit, see *Thomas v. Board of Ed.*, 607 F.2d 1043, 1045 (2d Cir. 1979) (upholding Granville, New York, high school students' right to publish a satiric magazine containing articles "pasquinading school lunches, cheerleaders, classmates, and teachers," and addressing masturbation and prostitution).

113. *Right to Read Defense Comm. v. School Comm. of Chelsea*, 454 F. Supp. 703, 705 n. 1, 715 (D. Mass. 1978) (quoting *Minarcini v. Strongsville City School Dist.*, 541 F.2d 577, 582 [6th Cir. 1976], which invalidated the removal of Kurt Vonnegut's *Cat's Cradle* and *God Bless You, Mr. Rosewater* and Joseph Heller's *Catch-22* from school libraries, although upholding the school board's refusal to allow the books in the curriculum).

114. *Salvail v. Nashua Bd. of Ed.*, 469 F. Supp. 1269, 1272 (D.N.H. 1979).

115. *Board of Ed., Island Trees School Dist. v. Pico*, 457 U.S. 853, 857 (1982).

4. POLICING THE AIRWAVES

1. *Sonderling Broadcasting Corp.*, 27 Radio Reg. 2d 285, 286 (1973) (Notice of Apparent Liability), reconsid. denied, 41 FCC 2d 777 (1973). The February 21 broadcast was not unique. Two days later, another female caller confided that she had had "a few hang-ups at first" about oral sex, but said, "I have a craving for peanut butter . . . so I used to spread this on my husband's privates and after a while, I mean, I didn't even need the peanut butter anymore." Her advice: "[A]ny of these women that have called and they have, you know,

hang-ups about this, I mean they should try their favorite . . ." "Whipped cream, marshmallow . . ." the host suggested. "You know," the caller said, "it's a little messy, but outside of that it's great." *Id.*

2. William Masters & Virginia Johnson, *Human Sexual Response* (Boston: Little, Brown, 1966); William Masters & Virginia Johnson, *Human Sexual Inadequacy* (Boston: Little, Brown, 1970).
3. *Sonderling*, 27 Radio Reg. 2d at 288–92, aff'd *sub nom. Illinois Citizens Comm. v. FCC*, 515 F.2d 397 (D.C. Cir. 1974) (as amended 1975); Radio Act of 1927, §29; codified at 47 U.S.C. §326 (prohibiting censorship by FCC except for indecency). The indecency ban was deleted from §326 in 1948 and moved to §1464 of the federal criminal code.
4. 27 Radio Reg. 2d at 289–92.
5. *Id.* at 294–98 (Johnson, dissenting).
6. *Illinois Citizens*, 515 F.2d at 404 (panel decision); 409 (Bazelon, J., arguing for rehearing).
7. See *NBC v. United States*, 319 U.S. 190 (1943), relying on the scarcity rationale to justify the FCC's rules against network monopolization and by extension other types of broadcast regulation.
8. Radio Act of 1927, 44 Stat. 1162, superseded by Communications Act of 1934, 48 Stat. 1064, now 47 U.S.C. §§151 *et seq.* The 1934 Act directs the FCC to consider the "public convenience, interest, or necessity" in promulgating regulations, classifying stations, and granting, denying, or renewing licenses. 47 U.S.C. §§303–9.
9. The scarcity justification for public control of broadcasting has always had its critics. They argue that all resources are scarce to some extent, yet we do not permit discretionary licensing schemes for the use of trees, paper, or ink in order to assure that books and newspapers serve a government agency's definition of the public good. Simply because there must be some management of frequencies to prevent broadcast signals from colliding with each other does not necessarily mean that government officials should also control programming. See, e.g., Lucas Powe, Jr., *American Broadcasting and the First Amendment* (Berkeley: U. of Cal. Press, 1987); Matthew Spitzer, *Seven Dirty Words and Six Other Stories* (New Haven: Yale U. Press, 1986); and for a contrary view, Newton Minow & Craig Lamay, *Abandoned in the Wasteland: Children, Television, and the First Amendment* (New York: Hill & Wang, 1995). Minow and Lamay acknowledge that with the proliferation of channels in the 1980s and 1990s, the scarcity rationale for government regulation of broadcast content lost much of its force. *Id.*, p. 67. On the FCC's use of the Fairness Doctrine (which required broadcasters to air competing views) to squelch political opponents, see Powe, pp. 70–161.
10. *Chaplinsky v. New Hampshire*, 315 U.S. 568, 572 (1942); see *Roth v. United States*, 354 U.S. 476, 483–85 (1957).
11. *Duncan v. United States*, 48 F.2d 128, 130–34 (9th Cir.), cert. denied, 283 U.S. 863 (1931), citing *Ex parte Jackson*, 96 U.S. 727 (1877).

12. *Trinity Methodist Church v. FRC*, 62 F.2d 850, 853 (D.C. Cir. 1932), cert. denied, 288 U.S. 599 (1933).
13. Lili Levi, "The Hard Case of Broadcast Indecency," 20 *NYU Rev. of Law & Soc. Change* 49, 108 n. 291 (1992–93); see also Emily Wortis Leider, *Becoming Mae West* (New York: Farrar, Straus & Giroux, 1997), pp. 339–42. Congressmen complained of "the ravishing of the American home" by West's "foul, sensuous, indecent, and blasphemous radio program," which "reduced the Garden of Eden episode to the very lowest level of bawdy-house stuff," and the Commission reprimanded NBC, solemnly emphasizing the need to protect children. See Edythe Wise, "A Historical Perspective on the Protection of Children from Broadcast Indecency," 3 *Vill. Sports & Ent. L. J.* 15, 21 (1996); 83 Cong. Rec. 560–61 (daily ed. Jan. 14, 1938), 75th Cong., 3d Sess.; 83 Cong. Rec. Extension of Remarks (daily ed. Jan. 26, 1938) (quoting letter from Rep. Lawrence Connery to FCC chairman Frank McNinch, and a letter from a constituent). A decade earlier, West had been convicted of obscenity in New York for her stage play *Sex* and sentenced to serve ten days at the women's prison on Welfare Island; Leider, pp. 163–72.
14. *NBC v. United States*, 319 U.S. at 213, 212; see generally Powe, *supra* n. 9.
15. See Spitzer, *supra* n. 9, pp. 53–54, for an economic explanation of why radio, with many more outlets in a given locality, better reflected the diversity of American culture than early, pre-cable television. On the quiescence of broadcasting in the 1950s, see Levi, *supra* n. 13, at 86.
16. The NAB code was ended by court order, after its commercial advertising restrictions were found to violate antitrust laws. See *Primary Jurisdiction Referral of Claims Against Government Defendant Arising from the Inclusion in the NAB Television Code of the "Family Viewing Policy,"* 95 FCC 2d 700, 702 & n. 5, 704 (1983); *United States v. National Ass'n of Broadcasters*, 536 F. Supp. 149, 153 (D.D.C. 1982); Wise, *supra* n. 13, at 23 n. 48; Minow & Lamay, *supra* n. 9, pp. 53–54 (bemoaning the Justice Department's "mindless zeal" in "killing the NAB Code").
17. *Revocation of License of Mile High Stations*, 28 FCC 795, 797–98 (1960) (Appendix to Opinion); see also Powe, p. 166.
18. *Palmetto Broadcasting (WDKD)*, 33 FCC 250, 256–58, 265–80 (1962), aff'd *sub nom. Robinson v. FCC*, 334 F.2d 534, 535 (D.C. Cir.), cert. denied, 379 U.S. 843 (1964); 538 (Wright, J., concurring), citing *NAACP v. Button*, 371 U.S. 415 (1963). The majority had avoided the constitutional issue by ruling that the station owner's false statements justified the license denial.
19. *Pacifica Foundation*, 36 FCC 147, 149–50 (1964); 152–53 (Robert E. Lee, concurring). Two years before the 1964 investigation, the FCC had written to Pacifica about "possible communist affiliations" of some company officers; there followed subpoenas from the Senate Judiciary Committee's Internal Security Subcommittee (SISS), inquiring about a biweekly program on KPFK, Pacifica's Los Angeles affiliate, featuring Dorothy Healey, head of the Southern California branch of the Communist Party. After some internal turmoil,

Pacifica cooperated with the inquisitors, but the FCC refused to act on Pacifica's pending license applications until the investigation was concluded. *KPFA Folio*, Vol. 22, No. 14 (*The Pacifica Papers*) (1972), pp. 6–9; see also *Pacifica Foundation*, 36 FCC at 151.

20. See Powe, p. 170; *Pacifica Foundation*, 2 FCC 2d 1066 (1965).
21. *Jack Straw Memorial Foundation*, 21 FCC 2d 833, 834, hearing ordered on reconsid., 24 FCC 2d 266 (1970), license renewed, 29 FCC 2d 334 (1971). The Commission also approved the station's stated policy of special management review for any "material which raises questions . . . because of some social, moral, aesthetic, or scatological outspokenness." On the historical Jack Straw, see Geoffrey Chaucer, "The Nun's Priest's Tale," in *Canterbury Tales* (A. Kent Hieatt & Constance Hieatt, eds.) (New York: Bantam, 1964), p. 411. Thanks to Dr. Barbara Apstein for the reference.
22. Powe, pp. 173–74.
23. *Jack Straw*, 21 FCC 2d at 841–42 (Johnson, dissenting); 837–38 (Cox, dissenting).
24. *Jack Straw*, 29 FCC 2d at 343.
25. *WUHY-FM, Eastern Education Radio*, 24 FCC 2d 408, 409, 412 (1970).
26. *Id.* at 411–12.
27. *Id.* at 422–23 (Johnson, dissenting); 418, 422 (Cox, dissenting). Johnson added: "Most of the people in this country are under 28 years of age; over 56 million students are in our colleges and schools. Many of them will 'smile' when they learn that . . . an agency of their government, has punished a radio station for broadcasting the words of Jerry Garcia, the leader of what the FCC calls a 'rock and roll musical group.' To call The Grateful Dead a 'rock and roll musical group' is like calling the Los Angeles Philharmonic a 'jug band.' And that about shows where this Commission's 'at.' "
28. Public Notice, *License Responsibility to Review Records Before Their Broadcast*, 28 FCC 2d 409, 414 (1971) (Johnson, dissenting); see also Powe, pp. 176–81. Commissioner Lee's separate statement was even more direct; he hoped that the Public Notice would "discourage, if not eliminate, the playing of records which tend to promote and/or glorify the use of illegal drugs." 28 FCC 2d at 410.
29. See Tom Wheeler, "Drug Lyrics, the FCC, and the First Amendment," 5 *Loyola of L.A. L. Rev.* 329 (1972); Margaret Blanchard, "The American Urge to Censor: Freedom of Expression Versus the Desire to Sanitize Society," 33 *Wm. & Mary L. Rev.* 741, 803–8 (1992); Memorandum Opinion and Order, *License Responsibility to Review Records Before Their Broadcast*, 31 FCC 2d 377, 379 (1971); *Yale Broadcasting Co. v. FCC*, 414 U.S. 914 (1973) (Douglas, J., dissenting from denial of certiorari).
30. Public Notice, 28 FCC 2d at 414–15 (Johnson, dissenting).
31. Wheeler, *supra* n. 29, at 348, 365; *Yale Broadcasting*, 414 U.S. 914 (Douglas, J., dissenting from denial of cert.); see also Powe, p. 179; *Yale Broadcasting Co. v. FCC*, 478 F.2d 594, 603 (D.C. Cir. 1973) (Bazelon, C.J., dissenting from

denial of rehearing *en banc*); Memorandum Opinion and Order, 31 FCC 2d at 379 n. 5.

32. Memorandum Opinion and Order, 31 FCC 2d at 377–79 & n. 5; see *Yale*, 478 F.2d at 596.
33. Powe, p. 181; although the Commission acknowledged that "it is often a most difficult judgment whether a record promotes drug usage," 31 FCC 2d at 378, it ignored the multiple meanings, ironies, and ambiguities that characterize poetic language. As one observer noted, lyrics to the Jefferson Airplane's "White Rabbit" are at points difficult to make out; the Beatles' "I Am the Walrus" is even more obscure. Spiro Agnew mistakenly thought that the Who's "Acid Queen" was "blatant drug-culture propaganda," while an "ironic consequence" of the Notice was the banning of antidrug songs such as "The Pusher" by Steppenwolf; Wheeler, at 351–52, 363.
34. *Yale Broadcasting*, 478 F.2d at 605, 606 n. 24 (Bazelon, C.J.) (quoting *Anti Defamation League of B'nai B'rith*, 6 FCC 2d 385, 398 [1967] [Loevinger, concurring]).
35. *Yale*, 414 U.S. at 916–17 (Douglas, J., dissenting).
36. *FCC v. Pacifica Foundation*, 438 U.S. 726, 729 (1978) (quoting Pacifica's response to the FCC complaint); see also Powe, pp. 185–86. The monologue was recorded on Carlin's album *Occupation: Foole*.
37. *FCC v. Pacifica*, 438 U.S. at 730; see also *Citizen's Complaint Against Pacifica Foundation*, 56 FCC 2d 94, 95 (1975). Lucas Powe points out that Douglas's "young son" was 15, and therefore not likely ignorant of four-letter words. Powe, p. 186.
38. *Pacifica*, 438 U.S. at 751–54 (1978) (Appendix to Opinion of the Court).
39. Albert Bandura, "What TV Violence Can Do to Your Child," *Look*, Oct. 22, 1963, pp. 46–52 (describing experiments in which some children had imitated films of a clown hitting a rubber Bobo doll); see also Thomas Krattenmaker & L. A. Powe, Jr., "Televised Violence: First Amendment Principles and Social Science Theory," 64 *Va. L. Rev.* 1123, 1137–39 (1978). For more on "media effects" psychology, see ch. 10.
40. Surgeon General Jesse Steinfeld wrote in his introduction to the report that media violence is "a very complex issue, for which there are no simple answers"; on the one hand, lurid fantasies can sometimes be cathartic; on the other, some youngsters—depending on a host of other factors in their makeup and background—may imitate aggression seen on-screen. On balance, the "accumulated evidence" did "not warrant the conclusion that televised violence has a uniformly adverse effect nor the conclusion that it has an adverse effect on the majority of children." Moreover, since "a considerable number of experimental studies on the effects of televised violence have now been carried out, it seems improbable that the next generation of studies will bring many great surprises. . . . The lack of uniformity in the extensive data now at hand is much too impressive to warrant the expectation that better measures of aggression or other methodological refinements will suddenly allow us to see a uni-

form effect." Surgeon General's Scientific Advisory Committee on Television and Social Behavior, *Television and Growing Up: The Impact of Televised Violence* (Washington, DC: U.S. Dep't HEW, 1972), pp. iv, 26, 7, 9–10. Steinfeld was criticized for allowing the TV networks to review and veto nominations of experts to the advisory committee that wrote the report and for publishing conclusions that were "too cautious and conservative." *Id.*, p. 118; see also *Television and Behavior: Ten Years of Scientific Progress and Implications for the Eighties*, Vol. 1 (Washington, DC: U.S. Dep't HHS, 1982), pp. 1–2, 36–37 (describing the cautious conclusions of the 1972 report); Robert Liebert & Joyce Sprafkin, *The Early Window: Effects of Television on Children and Youth* (3d ed.) (New York: Pergamon 1988), pp. 59–85; *The UCLA Television Violence Report 1996*, in *The V-Chip Debate: Content Filtering from Television to the Internet* (Monroe Price, ed.) (Mahwah, NJ: Lawrence Erlbaum, 1998), p. 283 (noting concerns in the early '70s over such TV programs as *The Rifleman* and *The Untouchables*); Willard Rowland, Jr., *The Politics of TV Violence* (Beverly Hills: Sage, 1983), pp. 136–96 (recounting the political manipulation of the TV violence issue by legislators, scholars, and industry executives in the early 1970s).

41. Powe, p. 187; see also *Television and Behavior, supra* n. 40, pp. 36–37, describing congressional concern with TV violence since 1952 and pressure on the FCC in the early 1970s; Krattenmaker & Powe, *supra* n. 39, at 1128–34; *UCLA Television Violence Report, supra* n. 40, pp. 282–91; Liebert & Sprafkin, *supra* n. 40, pp. 79–127 (describing politics of TV violence in the early 1970s); Rowland, *supra* n. 40, pp. 199–211; *Writers Guild of America, West v. FCC*, 423 F. Supp. 1064, 1095 (C.D. Cal. 1976), rev'd *sub nom Tandem Productions, Inc. v. CBS*, 609 F.2d 356 (9th Cir. 1979), cert. denied, 449 U.S. 824 (1980).
42. Krattenmaker & Powe, at 1129.
43. *Primary Jurisdiction Referral*, 95 FCC 2d at 702–3. The *Report on the Broadcast of Violent, Indecent, and Obscene Material* is at 51 FCC 2d 418 (1975).
44. *Primary Jurisdiction Referral*, 95 FCC 2d at 700; see Rowland, pp. 239–42.
45. *Tandem Productions*, 609 F.2d 356.
46. *Primary Jurisdiction Referral*, 95 FCC 2d 700. By this time, the NAB Code had been eliminated because of antitrust problems, and the family viewing hour faded into oblivion; see *United States v. NAB*, 536 F. Supp. 149.
47. *Illinois Citizens Committee* 515 F.2d at 404–5.
48. *Report on the Broadcast of Violent, Indecent, and Obscene Material*, 51 FCC 2d 418; on the FCC's use of *Pacifica* to placate Congress, see Krattenmaker & Powe, at 1215.
49. *Pacifica Foundation*, 56 FCC 2d at 97–98. The statute in question was 18 U.S.C. §1464, prohibiting "indecent" as well as "obscene" broadcasting. The Supreme Court precedents that had subsumed "indecent" within "obscene" were *United States v. Twelve 200-Foot Reels of Super 8mm Film*, 413 U.S. 123 (1973); and *Hamling v. United States*, 418 U.S. 87 (1974), interpreting portions of the Comstock law. The same terms were used in 18 U.S.C. §1464.

50. *Pacifica Foundation*, 56 FCC 2d at 100, 95.
51. *Id.* at 98.
52. *Id.* at 102, 103, 108, 111–13 (Robinson, concurring).
53. Glen Robinson, "The Electronic First Amendment: An Essay for the New Age," 47 *Duke L. J.* 899, 948 n. 182 (1998).
54. *"Petition for Clarification or Reconsideration" of a Citizen's Complaint Against Pacifica Foundation*, 59 FCC 2d 892, 892–93 (1976).
55. *Pacifica Foundation*, 56 FCC 2d at 99–100.
56. *Id.* at 99.
57. *Pacifica Foundation v. FCC*, 556 F.2d 9, 10–11 (D.C. Cir. 1977), rev'd, 438 U.S. 726 (1978). Among the myriad deficiencies in the FCC's indecency order, Tamm said, it failed to define children. "Need a nineteen year old and a seven year old be protected from the same offensive language?" *Id.* at 17.
58. *Id.* at 28, 29 (Bazelon, J., concurring) (quoting *Erznoznik v. Jacksonville*, 422 U.S. 205, 212 [1975]).
59. *Id.* at 32–37 (Leventhal, J., dissenting).
60. Petition for a Writ of Certiorari in *FCC v. Pacifica Foundation*, No. 77-528 (October Term, 1977); see *"Petition for Reconsideration,"* 59 FCC 2d at 893.
61. *Landmark Briefs and Arguments of the Supreme Court of the U.S.: Constitutional Law*, Vol. 101 (Washington, DC: University Pubs. of America, 1979), p. 701.
62. Brief of the American Civil Liberties Union *et al.* in *FCC v. Pacifica Foundation*, pp. 24–25. The Appendix to the brief listed forty-five works with taboo words, eleven of them "Children and Young Adults Literature," including Robert Cormier's *I Am the Cheese*, Kurt Vonnegut's *Slaughterhouse Five*, and Alice Childress's *A Hero Ain't Nothin' But a Sandwich.*
63. *Landmark Briefs, supra* n. 61, pp. 690–92.
64. *Young v. American Mini Theatres*, 427 U.S. 50, 70 (1976).
65. *FCC v. Pacifica*, 438 U.S. at 749.
66. *Id.* at 742–50.
67. *Id.* at 733, 750.
68. *Id.* at 743.
69. *Id.* at 745–46.
70. *Id.* at 749; *id.* at 757–58, 761 (Powell, J., concurring) (quoting in part *Ginsberg v. New York*, 390 U.S. 629, 649–50 [1968] [Stewart, J., concurring]).
71. *Id.* at 761.
72. Harry Edwards & Mitchell Berman, "Regulating Violence on Television," 89 *Nw. U. L. Rev.* 1487, 1496 (1995).
73. *Pacifica*, 438 U.S. at 770, 775 (Brennan, J., dissenting). Of the other dissenters, Potter Stewart and Byron White rested on a question of statutory construction: "indecent" under §1464 of the federal criminal code, they said, meant the same as "obscene." Thurgood Marshall joined this dissent but also joined Brennan on the constitutional issue. *Id.* at 777–80 (dissenting opinions of Stewart, Brennan, Marshall, and White, JJ.).

74. John Paul Stevens, "The Freedom of Speech," 102 *Yale L. J.* 1293, 1307–8 (1993).

5. THE REIGN OF DECENCY

1. *WGBH Educational Foundation*, 69 FCC 2d 1250, 1251 (1978) (the case also involved complaints about *Masterpiece Theatre*); *Pacifica Foundation*, 95 FCC 2d 750, 760 (1983); *Infinity Broadcasting Corp. of Pennsylvania*, 2 FCC Rcd 2705, on reconsid., 3 FCC Rcd 930 (1987). See Jason Shrinsky & John Gomperts, "Indecency and the FCC: A Past & Present Perspective," *Radio & Records*, Nov. 6, 1987, p. 14; *Action for Children's Television v. FCC* ("*ACT I*"), 852 F.2d 1332, 1336 (D.C. Cir. 1988); Lili Levi, "The Hard Case of Broadcast Indecency," 20 *NYU Rev. Law & Soc. Change* 49, 90–91 (1992–93) (although *Pacifica* at first "caused much anxiety and uncertainty" in the broadcaster ranks, what in fact emerged from the case was a bright-line test that simply prohibited repeated use of Carlin's immortalized seven dirty words before 10 p.m.; because broadcasters "largely avoided" the seven words "and the Commission held to its narrow interpretation of the indecency standard, the prohibition on indecency nearly fell into desuetude during this period").
2. Quoted in Robert Liebert & Joyce Sprafkin, *The Early Window: Effects of Television on Children and Youth* (3rd ed.) (New York: Pergamon, 1988), p. 50. The FCC also repealed its much-contested Fairness Doctrine in the 1980s, "on the ground that it restricted broadcasters' editorial policies by requiring them to air opposing points of view." Robert Corn, "Tipper's Revenge: The F.C.C. Cleans Up the Airways," *The Nation*, Dec. 5, 1987, p. 681; see *Syracuse Peace Council*, 2 FCC Rcd 5043 (1987), aff'd *sub nom Syracuse Peace Council v. FCC*, 867 F.2d 654 (D.C. Cir. 1989), cert. denied, 493 U.S. 1019 (1990).
3. See, e.g., Andrea Dworkin, *Pornography: Men Possessing Women* (New York: Penguin, 1979); Catharine MacKinnon, *Feminism Unmodified* (Cambridge, MA: Harvard U. Press, 1987).
4. Nan Hunter & Sylvia Law, Brief *Amici Curiae* of Feminist Anti-Censorship Task Force *et al.* in *American Booksellers Ass'n v. Hudnut*, No. 84-3147 (7th Cir. 1985), published in 21 *Mich. J. L. Ref.* 69 (1987–88).
5. *American Booksellers Ass'n v. Hudnut*, 771 F.2d 323, 326, 330 (7th Cir. 1985), aff'd mem., 475 U.S. 1001 (1986).
6. See Robin West, "The Feminist-Conservative Anti-Pornography Alliance and the 1986 Attorney General's Commission on Pornography Report," 4 *Am. Bar Fdtn Rsrch J.* 681–711 (1987).
7. Michael Sniffen, "Panel Is Named to Study Effects of Pornography," *Philadelphia Inquirer*, May 21, 1985, p. 4A. Commission chairman Henry Hudson was a Virginia prosecutor who had eliminated even soft-core materials from his suburban county. Other commissioners included religious-right leader James Dobson; activist priest Bruce Ritter; law professor Frederick Schauer, who

viewed pornography as merely a sex aid, not a form of expression; and psychiatrist Park Dietz, who believed that detective magazines caused crime; see Park Elliot Dietz *et al.*, "Detective Magazines: Pornography for the Sexual Sadist?" 31 *J. Forensic Sciences* 197–211 (1986) (reprinted in Attorney General's Commission on Pornography, *Final Report* [Washington, DC: U.S. Dep't of Justice, July 1986], pp. 58–69). On the commissioners, see Howard Kurtz, "Pornography Panel's Objectivity Disputed," *Washington Post*, Oct. 15, 1985, p. R1; Sniffen, *supra*.

8. Statement of Anne Welbourne-Moglia in *The Meese Commission Exposed: Proceedings of a National Coalition Against Censorship Public Information Briefing on the Attorney General's Commission on Pornography* (New York: NCAC, 1986), pp. 18–19.
9. Quoted in Howard Kurtz, "The Pornography Panel's Controversial Last Days," *Washington Post*, May 30, 1986, p. A13; see also Daniel Linz *et al.*, "The Attorney General's Commission on Pornography: The Gaps Between 'Findings' and Facts," 4 *Am. Bar Fdtn Rsrch J.* 713 (1987); Edward Donnerstein *et al.*, *The Question of Pornography* (New York: The Free Press, 1987), pp. 172–76, critiquing the Meese Commission. The dissenting commissioners, Ellen Levine and Judith Becker, wrote in a separate statement: "Pornography has religious, ethical, social, psychological and legal ramifications. The idea that eleven individuals studying in their spare time could complete a comprehensive report on so complex a matter in so constricted a time frame is simply unrealistic. No self-respecting investigator would accept conclusions based on such a study, and unfortunately the document produced reflects those inadequacies." *Final Report, supra* n. 7, pp. 197–98.
10. *Final Report*, p. 303.
11. *Id.*, p. 344.
12. Quoted in Kurtz, *supra* n. 7; see also *Pornography: Research Advances and Policy Considerations* (Dolf Zillmann & Jennings Bryant, eds.) (Hillsdale, NJ: Lawrence Erlbaum, 1989), pp. xvii, 389.
13. Zillmann & Bryant, *supra* n. 12, pp. xvii, 389. A number of the papers commissioned by the Surgeon General were published in the Zillmann & Bryant anthology.
14. Edward Mulvey & Jeffrey Haugaard, *Report of the Surgeon General's Workshop on Pornography and Public Health* (Washington, DC: U.S. Dep't of HHS, June 22–24, 1986) (manuscript ed.), pp. 57–62.
15. Letter from Brad Curl, National Decency Forum, to Mark Fowler, July 9, 1986. The Forum's letterhead indicated that it was a coalition of groups that included, among others, Citizens for Decency Through Law, National Coalition Against Pornography, C.L.E.A.N. of California, Eagle Forum, Concerned Women for America, and Americans Concerned for Traditional Values.
16. Bob Davis, "FCC Chief Shifts Obscenity View As He Seeks Job Reappointment," *Wall Street Journal*, Dec. 1, 1986, p. 44; Dennis McDougal, "FCC Versus Howard Stern; Agency's 'Indecency' Ruling Hasn't Stopped N.Y. Dee-

jay," *Los Angeles Times*, Aug. 19, 1987, Calendar, p. 1 (recounting taping of show by the mother of a Stern fan); Dennis McDougal, "How 'Jerker' Helped Ignite Obscenity Debate," *Los Angeles Times*, Aug. 18, 1987, Calendar, p. 1 (describing submission of *Jerker* complaint by LA fundamentalist minister Larry Poland). A second complaint against KPFK involved a live performance art show, "Shocktime America." On the two July meetings, see also John Crigler & William Byrnes, "Decency Redux: The Curious History of the New FCC Broadcast Indecency Policy," 38 *Cath. U. L. Rev.* 329, 344–45 (1989); letter from Paul J. McGeady, General Counsel, Morality in Media, to John Smith, Jr., July 23, 1986.

17. Crigler & Byrnes, *supra* n. 16, at 346, quoting letter from John Smith to Donald Wildmon, Executive Director, National Federation for Decency, Sept. 19, 1986.
18. Davis, *supra* n. 16 (noting that Fowler cited as an example of lewdness the broadcast of the film *Looking for Mr. Goodbar* without the editing of a rape scene); see also Crigler & Byrnes, at 344 (picketing to protest Fowler's renomination "seems to be the event" that started the FCC down its new indecency path).
19. Public Notice, *New Indecency Enforcement Standards to Be Applied to All Broadcast and Amateur Radio Licensees*, 2 FCC Rcd 2726 (1987); see also *Infinity*, 2 FCC Rcd at 2706.
20. Quoted in Petition for Clarification of the National Association of Broadcasters, Public Notice Concerning New Indecency Enforcement Standards, FCC 87-365 (June 1, 1987), pp. 3–5.
21. Public Notice, 2 FCC Rcd at 2726; see also *Infinity*, 2 FCC Rcd at 2706; *Pacifica Foundation*, 2 FCC Rcd 2698; *Regents of the U. of California*, 2 FCC Rcd 2703, on reconsid., 3 FCC Rcd 930 (1987).
22. *Infinity*, 2 FCC Rcd at 2705 n. 7.
23. *Pacifica*, 2 FCC Rcd at 2698; *Infinity*, 2 FCC Rcd at 2706; *U. of California*, 2 FCC Rcd at 2703. The punk rock band that performed "Makin' Bacon" was the Pork Dukes.
24. Dennis McDougal, "He's a Crusader Against Indecency," *Los Angeles Times*, Aug. 20, 1987, Calendar, p. 1. The fourth of the April indecency rulings involved bawdy conversations over an amateur radio station whose signals might reach youngsters because, as the Commission noted, "the Boy Scouts of America offers a merit badge for the development of radio skills." *David Hildebrand*, 2 FCC Rcd 2708 (1987). The Commission exonerated "Shocktime America," the other KPFK broadcast under scrutiny, because of its unscripted format and the station's subsequent chastising of its producers.
25. *Infinity*, 2 FCC Rcd at 2706; Press Release, "FCC Takes Actions on Regulation of Indecency and Obscenity," *FCC News*, Apr. 16, 1987, p. 3; see also Crigler & Byrnes, at 347.
26. *Pacifica* 2 FCC Rcd at 2702 (Quello concurring).
27. Letter from H. Robert Showers to Diane Killory, FCC general counsel, July 15, 1987.

28. Crigler & Byrnes, at 335 n. 34.
29. Petition for Reconsideration, FCC 87-365 (June 1, 1987). In addition to ACT, the petitioners included National Public Radio, Motion Picture Association of America, New York Times Company, People for the American Way, Reporters Committee for Freedom of the Press, Association of Independent Television Stations, Capital Cities/ABC, CBS, EZ Communications, NBC, Post-Newsweek Stations, PBS, Radio-Television News Directors Association, and Society of Professional Journalists. The National Association of Broadcasters filed a separate Petition for Clarification, while Morality in Media submitted a brief arguing that the new indecency standard did not go far enough; it should ban from the airwaves any speech that was "more than indelicate and less than immodest." Memorandum Opinion and Order, *Infinity Broadcasting Corp. of Pennsylvania et al.*, 3 FCC Rcd 930, 931 (1987) (quoting petition of Morality in Media).
30. Petition for Declaratory Ruling, *Pacifica Foundation*, FCC C5-574 (May 8, 1987); Supplement to Petition for Declaratory Ruling (June 2, 1987); see Crigler & Byrnes, at 338–41.
31. Bob Davis, "(Bleep) (Bleep) (Bleep) (Bleep) And Yes I Said Yes I Will Yes," *Wall Street Journal*, May 26, 1987, p. 35; Request for Expedition of Declaratory Ruling, *Pacifica Foundation*, FCC C5-574 (May 22, 1987), p. 2.
32. Letter from James McKinney, Chief, FCC Mass Media Bureau, to William Byrnes and John Crigler, June 5, 1987.
33. Application for Review, *Pacifica Foundation*, FCC C5-574 (June 10, 1987), p. 13; see Crigler & Byrnes, at 340. The Commission denied review, 2 FCC Rcd 3957 (1987).
34. E-mail from John Crigler to author, July 20, 1999; Comments of Pacifica Foundation *et al.*, *Enforcement of Prohibitions Against Broadcast Indecency in 18 U.S.C. §1464*, MM Docket No. 89-494 (Feb. 20, 1990), p. 18; Comments of Pacifica Foundation *et al.* in Opposition to Proposed Indecency Ban, *Enforcement of Prohibitions Against Broadcast Indecency in 18 U.S.C. §1464*, GC Docket No. 92-223 (1992), p. 12, citing letter from Alex Felker, Chief, Mass Media Bureau, to Thomas Byrne (April 7, 1988). Joining Pacifica in the 1990 Comments were the National Federation of Community Broadcasters, Alaska Public Radio, Intercollegiate Broadcasting System, PEN American Center, and Allen Ginsberg; in 1992, NFCB, American Public Radio, IBS, National Association of Collegiate Broadcasters, and PEN.
35. Author's interview with John Crigler, Nov. 30, 1999; Dennis McDougal, "Obscenity Issue Still Unresolved," *Los Angeles Times*, Jan. 4, 1988, Calendar, p. 1, noting Pacifica director David Salniker's estimate of "over a quarter of a million dollars" spent on the Carlin case and another $120,000 on *Jerker* and Bloomsday—in addition to free assistance from the ACLU.
36. Comments of Pacifica (Feb. 20, 1990), *supra* n. 34, pp. 3–4, and attached letter from David Salniker to Allen Ginsberg, Oct. 1, 1987; Andrew Yarrow, "Allen Ginsberg's 'Howl' in a New Controversy," *New York Times*, Jan. 6, 1988, p. C22; author's interview with attorney Eric Lieberman, Aug. 3, 1999.

37. Memorandum Opinion and Order, 3 FCC Rcd at 934 n. 47.
38. Quoted in 10 *Pub. Bdcastg Rep.* 3, 4 (Feb. 4, 1988). Participants in the lawsuit were the coalition of broadcasters and public interest groups that had originally sought reconsideration before the FCC, along with a group of intervenors including the ACLU and the National Federation of Community Broadcasters, and friends of the court Allen Ginsberg and PEN.
39. Quoted in Linda Ponce, "Judge Told FCC Ought to Specify What Is Indecent," *Washington Times*, June 2, 1988, p. A3.
40. *ACT I*, 852 F.2d at 1339, 1340–44. The indecency findings against *Jerker* and "Makin' Bacon," aired after the then-existing 10 p.m. safe harbor, accordingly had to be vacated for redetermination, "after a full and fair hearing, of the times at which indecent material may be broadcast."
41. *Id.* at 1342–44, noting FCC counsel's concession at oral argument that the government had no separate interest in censoring minors, apart from assisting parents who wish to do so; see also Crigler & Byrnes, at 351 n. 31.
42. 134 Cong. Rec. S9912 (July 26, 1988).
43. *Id.*, S9913–15.
44. The statute required the FCC, by January 31, 1989, to "promulgate regulations in accordance with Section 1464, Title 18, United States Code, to enforce the provisions of such Section on a 24 hour per day basis." PL 100–459, §608, 102 Stat. 2228 (1988), amending 47 U.S.C. §303, repealed, PL 102–356, §16(b), 106 Stat. 954 (1992); see *Action for Children's Television v. FCC ("ACT II")*, 932 F.2d 1504, 1507 (D.C. Cir. 1991), cert. denied, 503 U.S. 914 (1992).
45. Comments of Pacifica (1990), *supra* n. 34, pp. 7, 9, 12–13.
46. *Enforcement of Prohibitions Against Broadcast Indecency in 18 U.S.C. §1464*, 5 FCC Rcd 5297 (Aug. 6, 1990).
47. *ACT II*, 932 F.2d 1504.
48. Public Telecommunications Act of 1992, §16(a), PL 102–356, 106 Stat. 949 (1992); see *Action for Children's Television v. FCC ("ACT III")*, 58 F.3d 654, 658 (D.C. Cir. 1995) (*en banc*), cert. denied, 516 U.S. 1042 (1996).
49. FCC News Release, "KZKC(TV), Kansas City, MO, Apparently Liable for $2,000 Fine for Indecent Broadcast," June 23, 1988; *Kansas City Television, Ltd. Order*, FCC 88–274 (1988). The agency stayed proceedings due to the pending proceedings in *ACT I*, and eventually vacated the Notice of Apparent Liability; *Kansas City Television, Ltd.*, 4 FCC Rcd 7653 (1988); Levi, *supra* n. 1, at 104 n. 271.
50. Robert Corn-Revere, "New Age Comstockery," 4 *CommLaw Conspectus* 173, 181–82 (1996); author's interview with Robert Corn-Revere, July 20, 1999.
51. *United States v. Evergreen Media Corp.*, 832 F. Supp. 1179, 1185 (N.D.Ill. 1993); letter from James de Castro, President, Evergreen Media Corp., to Edythe Wise, Chief, Complaints & Investigations Branch, FCC Mass Media Bureau, Oct. 10, 1989.
52. Notice of Apparent Liability, *Cox Broadcasting Div., Cox Enterprises*, 6 FCC

Rcd 3704 (1989); Notice of Apparent Liability, *Goodrich Broadcasting*, 6 FCC Rcd 2178 (1991); Memorandum Opinion and Order, *Liability of Goodrich Broadcasting, Inc. (WVIC-FM)*, 6 FCC Rcd 7484 (1991); Notice of Apparent Liability, *Pacific & Southern Co., Inc. (KSD-FM)*, 6 FCC Rcd 3689 (1990). Other cases included an Oregon station, fined for lame jokes about farting and Liberace, and call-in exchanges in which "fuck" and "asshole" were among the epithets heard (Notice of Apparent Liability, *Sound Broadcasting Corp.*, 6 FCC Rcd 2174, reconsid. denied, 6 FCC Rcd 5961 [1991]); a $2,000 fine for repeated use of "fuck" in the Prince song "Erotic City" (*Liability of Nationwide Comm'ns, Inc.*, 6 FCC Rcd 3695 [1990]); and a $25,000 fine for "Candy Wrapper" and "Sit on My Face," a British creation distinguished by the line "Life can be fine if we both sixty-nine" (Notice of Apparent Liability, *KGB, Inc.*, 7 FCC Rcd 3207 [1992]); but see *King Broadcasting*, 5 FCC Rcd 2971 (1990), finding a Seattle sex education broadcast not "pandering, titillating or vulgar" and therefore not indecent.

53. Notice of Apparent Liability, *Sagittarius Broadcasting Corp. et al.*, 8 FCC Rcd 2688 (1992) (imposing $600,000 in fines); Notice of Apparent Liability, *Saggitarius Broadcasting*, 7 FCC Rcd 6873 (1992), reconsid. denied, 8 FCC Rcd 3600 (1993); Notice of Apparent Liability, *Infinity Broadcasting*, 8 FCC Rcd 6740 (1993) (noting repeated problems with Stern mitigated by Infinity's efforts to obey, and imposing total of $400,000 in fines; threatening license revocations if violations continue); see also Levi, at 104–12.
54. Appendix to Notice of Apparent Liability, 8 FCC Rcd 2688.
55. See *KRTH-FM, Assignment of License*, BALH-930618GE (1994) (dissenting statement of Quello); *id.* (statement of Ervin Duggan, indicating he would have denied license assignment to Infinity and supported an inquiry into Infinity's "fitness to remain an FCC licensee"); Steven Nudelman, "A Chilly Wait in Radioland: The FCC Forces 'Indecent' Radio Broadcasters to Censor Themselves or Face the Music," 2 *J. Law & Policy* 115, 117–18, 135–40 (1994).
56. *Sagittarius Broadcasting et al.*, 10 FCC Rcd 12245 (1995); see James Warren, "Radio Indecency Cases Settled," *Chicago Tribune*, Feb. 23, 1994, p. 3; Christine Burke, "Howard's Fine Mess," *New York Post*, Dec. 29, 1997, p. 75. Infinity also promised that it had "implemented various control measures" to guard against future indecency. On the delays and self-censorship pressures in the FCC's enforcement scheme, see Nudelman, *supra* n. 55.
57. Quoted in David Remnick, "The Accidental Anarchist," *The New Yorker*, Mar. 10, 1997, p. 67.
58. Jeffrey Goldberg, "Unfunny Business: Kenneth Starr Makes Howard Stern Look Obsolete," *Slate*, Sept. 26, 1998; www.slate.com/TVReview/98-09-26/TV Review.asp.
59. *Carl v. Los Angeles*, 61 Cal.App.3d 265, 272 (2d Dist. 1976).
60. *Calderon v. Buffalo*, 90 Misc.2d 1033 (NY Sup. Ct. Erie County, 1977); see also *State v. Frink*, 60 Or.App. 209 (1982); *State v. Woodcock*, 75 Or.App. 659 (1985) (striking down Oregon laws that went beyond *Ginsberg*).

61. *Davison v. State*, 288 So.2d 483, 488 (Fla. 1973) (Ervin, J., dissenting).
62. *Virginia v. American Booksellers Ass'n*, 236 Va. 168, 173–75 (1988) (construing the state law in response to "certified questions" from the federal court of appeals, *American Booksellers Ass'n v. Strobel*, 802 F.2d 691 (4th Cir. 1986).
63. *American Booksellers Ass'n v. Virginia*, 882 F.2d 125, 127 (4th Cir. 1989) (decision after remand from the Virginia Supreme Court); see also *American Booksellers Ass'n v. Webb*, 919 F.2d 1493, 1503–4 (11th Cir. 1990); *American Booksellers Ass'n v. McAuliffe*, 533 F. Supp. 50 (N.D. Ga. 1981); *M.S. News Co. v. Casado*, 721 F.2d 1281 (10th Cir. 1983); *Tattered Cover, Inc. v. Tooley*, 696 P.2d 780 (Colo. 1985); *Upper Midwest Booksellers Ass'n v. Minneapolis*, 780 F.2d 1389 (8th Cir. 1985).
64. *Home Box Office v. Wilkinson*, 531 F. Supp. 987, 995–96 n. 16 (D. Utah 1982).
65. *Id.* at 996 & n. 18 (quoting *Erznoznik v. Jacksonville*, 422 U.S. 205, 212–13 [1975]).
66. *Community Television of Utah v. Roy City*, 555 F. Supp. 1165, 1172, 1166 (D. Utah 1982).
67. *Community Television of Utah v. Wilkinson*, 611 F. Supp. 1099 (D. Utah 1985), aff'd *sub nom Jones v. Wilkinson*, 800 F.2d 989 (10th Cir. 1986), aff'd mem., 480 U.S. 926 (1987). Another cable decision, in Florida, invalidated an ordinance banning any distribution "by wire or cable" of "indecent material," defined in the now familiar formula as "a representation or description of a human sexual or excretory organ or function which the average person, applying contemporary community standards, would find to be patently offensive." *Cruz v. Ferre*, 571 F. Supp. 125, 127 (S.D. Fla. 1983), aff'd, 755 F.2d 1415 (11th Cir. 1985).
68. Brief of Action for Children's Television *et al.* as *Amici Curiae* in Support of Appellant/Cross-Appellee, *Sable Communications of California v. FCC*, Nos. 88-515 and 88-525 (Oct. Term, 1988), p. 28.
69. Brief for Appellant/Cross-Appellee, Sable Communications, p. 20, citing *Time*, Mar. 20, 1989, p. 58.
70. *Sable Communications v. FCC*, 492 U.S. 115, 126–28 (1989). On another issue, a challenge to the ban on obscene phone services, Sable was not so successful: the Court rejected its argument that the law unconstitutionally created a national "community standard" rather than the myriad local standards mandated by *Miller v. California*.
71. *Id.* at 126.
72. *Id.* at 131.
73. *Ginsberg v. New York*, 390 U.S. 629 (1968).
74. *New York v. Ferber*, 458 U.S. 747 (1982).
75. *Sable*, 492 U.S. at 130.
76. One decision upbraided the lower court for "brushing aside" the testimony of Park Dietz (recently of the Meese Commission and now an expert witness for the government) "that even minimal exposure to indecent messages can have

damaging psychological effects on children." *Dial Information Services v. Thornburgh*, 938 F.2d 1535, 1541–42 (2d Cir. 1991), cert. denied, 502 U.S. 1072 (1992). The other noted but did not describe "extensive evidence" before the FCC "regarding the effects of pornography on children"; the only source it cited was a group called the Religious Alliance, whose submission had made the remarkable but evidently unquestioned claim that more than 70% of dial-a-porn calls are made by youngsters between 10 and 16. *Information Providers' Coalition for Defense of the First Amendment v. FCC*, 928 F.2d 866, 872 (9th Cir. 1991).

77. 138 Cong. Rec. S646 (daily ed., Jan. 30, 1992); see *Alliance for Community Media v. FCC*, 56 F.3d 105, 117 (D.C. Cir. 1995), aff'd in part and rev'd in part *sub nom. Denver Area Educational Telecommunications Consortium v. FCC*, 518 U.S. 727 (1996).
78. Cable Consumer Protection & Competition Act of 1992, PL 102–385, 106 Stat. 1460, 1486, §§10(a), (b), codified at 47 U.S.C. §§532(h), (j); §10(c), codified at 47 U.S.C. §531(c).
79. *Alliance for Community Media v. FCC*, 10 F.3d 812 (D.C. Cir. 1993), on rehearing *en banc*, 56 F.3d 105 (D.C. Cir. 1995).
80. *Alliance*, 56 F.3d at 124, quoting *Sable*, 492 U.S. at 126.
81. *Id.* at 129–30 (Wald, J., dissenting).
82. Joint Brief of Petitioners, *Action for Children's Television et al. v. FCC*, No. 93-1092 (D.C. Circ. 1993), pp. 33–34, quoting Comments of Action for Children's Television *et al.*, MM Docket No. 89-494, pp. 16–17 & Appendix A (1990). Donnerstein *et al.* added that of eight articles or reports cited by Senator Helms on the Senate floor to support the harm rationale, five concerned violence or suicide, not indecency, and the other three contained only "general speculation about sexually oriented material." These sources, the ACT/Pacifica brief averred, "do not even attempt to document any specific causal relationship between broadcast indecency and harm to children." Joint Brief, pp. 35–36.
83. *Action for Children's Television v. FCC (ACT III)*, 11 F.3d 170, 178 (D.C. Cir. 1993), on rehearing, 58 F.3d 654.
84. *ACT III*, 58 F.3d at 661–62; see *id.* at 670 (Edwards, J., dissenting).
85. *Id.* at 670, 671 (Edwards, J., dissenting), quoting *Alliance*, 56 F.3d at 145 (Edwards, J., dissenting). Edwards opined that the empirical evidence was different with respect to media violence: "[t]here *is*," he said (without the benefit of any argument on the point), "significant evidence suggesting a causal connection" to "antisocial violent behavior." 58 F.3d at 671. He was more circumspect about what social science experiments actually showed in a law review article: Harry Edwards & Mitchell Berman, "Regulating Violence on Television," 89 *Nw. U. L. Rev.* 1487 (1995).
86. 58 F.3d. at 686 (Wald, Tatel, and Rogers, JJ., dissenting).
87. *AIDS Action Comm. v. Mass. Bay Trans. Auth.*, 849 F. Supp. 79 (D. Mass. 1993).

88. *ACT III*, 58 F.3d at 669–70 (majority opinion).
89. *Becker v. FCC*, 95 F.3d 75, 81, 83 (D.C. Cir. 1996). The Washington Supreme Court ten years earlier had forbidden abortion protesters to shout "murder" and related words in order to "avoid subjection of children to the physical and psychological abuse inflicted by the picketers' speech." *Bering v. Share*, 106 Wn.2d 212, 241 (1986).
90. These included failure to "exhaust administrative remedies" (that is, try to persuade the Commission to change its ways); lack of "standing" for all plaintiffs other than Infinity; and as to Infinity, absence of a First Amendment violation despite the "troubling" nature of the Commission's procedures. *Action for Children's Television v. FCC* ("*ACT IV*"), 59 F.3d 1249, 1254-55 (D.C. Cir. 1995), cert. denied, 516 U.S. 1072 (1996).
91. *Id.* at 1263 (Edwards, J., concurring with reservations).
92. *Seyfried v. Walton*, 668 F.2d 214, 217 (3d Cir. 1981).
93. *Bethel School District v. Fraser*, 478 U.S. 675, 683 (1986).
94. *Id.* at 692 (Stevens, J., dissenting).
95. *Hazelwood School District v. Kuhlmeier*, 484 U.S. 160 (1988).
96. *Virgil v. School Bd. of Columbia County*, 862 F.2d 1517, 1525 (11th Cir. 1989); see also Claudia Johnson, *Stifled Laughter* (Golden, CO: Fulcrum, 1994), one plaintiff's story of the *Virgil* case.
97. *McCarthy v. Fletcher*, 207 Cal. App. 3d 130 (5th Dist. 1989); *Wexner v. Anderson Union H.S. Dist. Bd. of Trustees*, 258 Cal. Rptr. 25, 31 (Ct. App. 3d Dist. 1989). *Wexner* was based on California state education law, not the First Amendment, and was later withdrawn because that legal theory had not been briefed by the lawyers. Author's conversation with attorney Ann Brick, Aug. 21, 1999.
98. *Case v. Unified School Dist. No. 233*, 908 F. Supp. 864 (D. Kan. 1995); see *Board of Ed., Island Trees School Dist. v. Pico*, 457 U.S. 853 (1982) (establishing rule against "viewpoint discrimination" in the removal of school library materials). The author was co-counsel for the plaintiffs in *Case*.
99. *Pyle v. South Hadley School Comm.*, 861 F. Supp. 157 (D. Mass. 1994), questions certified to Mass. Supreme Judicial Court, 55. F.3d 20 (1st Cir. 1995). The school dress code also banned messages that "had the effect" of demeaning racial, sexual, ethnic, or religious groups; the trial judge invalidated this anti-hate speech provision.
100. Brief for Plaintiffs-Appellants on a Question Certified from the U.S. Court of Appeals for the First Circuit, *Pyle v. South Hadley School Comm.*, No. 06914 (1995), pp. 32–34. They also argued that the Supreme Court's ruling in the *Fraser* case allowing censorship of "vulgar" speech only applied to school-sponsored activities like assemblies, not to independent messages on buttons or clothing.
101. *Pyle v. South Hadley School Comm.*, 423 Mass. 283 (1996). The federal appeals court had chosen not to address the Pyles' First Amendment arguments about class and culture, but instead "certified" questions to the state supreme court

about the student free-speech law. *Pyle* was a rarity in the annals of T-shirt jurisprudence; most cases went the other way, *e.g., Broussard v. School Bd. of Norfolk*, 801 F. Supp. 1526 (E.D. Va. 1992) (upholding a student's suspension for wearing a New Kids on the Block T-shirt with the message "Drugs Suck"); *Baxter v. Vigo City School Corp.*, 26 F.3d 728 (7th Cir. 1994) (upholding ban on a T-shirt message objecting to grades, racial bias, and certain school policies); *Gano v. School Dist. No. 411*, 674 F. Supp. 796 (D. Idaho 1987) (upholding ban on a T-shirt depicting administrators in an intoxicated state).

102. See *Borger v. Bisciglia*, 888 F. Supp. 97 (E.D. Wis. 1995); "Freedom to Read," *Free Expression* (quarterly of the American Booksellers Foundation for Free Expression) (Winter 1998), p. 1; see also *Desilets v. Clearview Reg'l Bd. of Educ.*, 137 N.J. 585 (1994) (invalidating a principal's censorship of student newspaper reviews of the R-rated films *Mississippi Burning* and *Rain Man* on the ground that the school did not have any policy delineating its legitimate pedagogical concerns). The American Library Association pubished periodic lists of challenged books in public schools and libraries; for the decade of the 1990s, *Huckleberry Finn, Of Mice and Men, I Know Why the Caged Bird Sings, Heather Has Two Mommies*, and *Daddy's Roommate* were among the ten most frequently challenged; see http://www.ala.org/alaorg/oif/top100bannedbooks.html.
103. *Video Software Dealers Ass'n v. Webster*, 968 F.2d 684, 687 (8th Cir. 1992).
104. *Id.* at 688–91.
105. *Davis-Kidd Booksellers v. McWherter*, 866 S.W.2d 520 (Tenn. 1993).
106. Thus, the ordinance banned "heinous crime" trading cards that were "patently offensive to prevailing standards in the adult community as a whole with respect to what is suitable material for minors," lacked serious value for minors, and appealed to the "depraved interest of minors in crime." *Eclipse Enterprises v. Gulotta*, 134 F.3d 63, 64 (2d Cir. 1997). Censorship laws vary in their definition of minority, using 18, 17, or 16 as the threshold of presumed maturity. In New York courts, as the magistrate in *Eclipse* pointed out, 16-year-olds are treated as adults. Transcript, *Eclipse v. Gulotta*, CV-92-3416 (ADS), Mar. 23, 1994, p. 40.
107. *Eclipse*, 134 F.3d at 64–65; Brief for Plaintiffs-Appellees in *Eclipse v. Gulotta*, No. 97-7099 (2d Cir. 1997), pp. 1, 7.
108. Transcript, pp. 65–66, 77–81.
109. *Eclipse*, 134 F.3d at 65–66.
110. *Id.* at 68.
111. *Id.* at 68–69 (Griesa, J., concurring).

6. THE IDEOLOGICAL MINEFIELD: SEXUALITY EDUCATION

1. Wendy Shalit, *A Return to Modesty: Discovering the Lost Virtue* (New York: The Free Press, 1999), pp. 12, 25.

2. Natalie Angier, "A Sex Guide for Girls, Minus Homilies," *New York Times*, Nov. 16, 1999, p. F7.
3. See John D'Emilio & Estelle Freedman, *Intimate Matters: A History of Sexuality in America* (New York: Harper & Row, 1988), pp. 202–21; Bonnie Nelson Trudell, *Doing Sex Education: Gender Politics and Schooling* (New York: Routledge, 1993), pp. 10–13.
4. Trudell, *supra* n. 3, p. 12; see also Diana Trilling, *The Beginning of the Journey* (New York: Harcourt Brace, 1993), p. 15 (describing high school lecture "on what was called sex hygiene. We were told about menstruation and that we must not allow boys to touch us lest it excite them dangerously in ways which girls did not know about—the responsibility was then ours if they went to prostitutes and contracted a venereal disease").
5. Robert Michael *et al.*, *Sex in America: A Definitive Survey* (Boston: Little, Brown, 1994), p. 160 (describing Kellogg's philosophy); see also Peter Gay, *The Bourgeois Experience: Victoria to Freud*, Vol. 2: *The Tender Passion* (New York: Oxford U. Press, 1986), pp. 273–74; Trilling, *supra* n. 4, p. 15 (describing one of Kellogg's books as creating "an unrelieved vista of doom and degradation as a consequence of virtually any sexual activity").
6. See Angier, *supra* n. 2; Ellen Chesler, *Woman of Valor: Margaret Sanger and the Birth Control Movement in America* (New York: Simon & Schuster, 1992), pp. 66, 156.
7. "The Sexual Enlightenment of Children" (1907; first English translation 1924), in *The Standard Edition of the Complete Psychological Works of Sigmund Freud*, Vol. 9 (London: Hogarth Press, 1959), p. 138 ("[w]hat is really important is that children should never get the idea that one wants to make more of a secret of the facts of sexual life than of any other matter which is not yet accessible to their understanding; and to ensure this it is necessary that from the very first what has to do with sexuality should be treated like anything else that is worth knowing about").
8. Jane Brody, "Mary S. Calderone, Advocate of Sexual Education, Dies at 94," *New York Times*, Oct. 25, 1998, p. 52; see also Michael Carrera, *Sex: The Facts, the Acts, and Your Feelings* (New York: Crown, 1981), pp. 308–9; "SIECUS Cofounder Mary S. Calderone Inducted into National Women's Hall of Fame," 26(6) *SIECUS Report* 24 (1998) ("Calderone has helped young people understand and appreciate their own sexuality. Her numerous books have taught thousands of confused and reluctant parents how to explain sex and sexuality to their children").
9. Brody, *supra* n. 8.
10. Janice Irvine, *Disorders of Desire: Sex and Gender in Modern American Sexology* (Philadelphia: Temple U. Press, 1990), pp. 75, 99; "Why the Furor over Sex Education," *U.S. News & World Report*, Aug. 4, 1969, pp. 44–46; Dana Czuczka, "The Twentieth Century: An American Sexual History," 28(2) *SIECUS Report* 15, 17 (Dec. 1999–Jan. 2000).
11. "Why the Furor," *supra* n. 10; People for the American Way, *Teaching Fear:*

The Religious Right's Campaign Against Sexuality Education (Washington, DC: PAW, 1994), pp. 2–3; D'Emilio & Freedman, *supra* n. 3, pp. 346–48; Irvine, *supra* n. 10, p. 99; *Kinsey, Sex, and Fraud: The Indoctrination of a People* (Judith Reisman & Edward Eichel, eds.) (Lafayette, LA: Lochinvar-Huntington House, 1990).

12. *Teaching Fear, supra* n. 11, pp. 2–3; see also Memorandum Opinion and Order, *Mississippi Authority for Educational Television*, 71 FCC 2d 1296 (1979), noting Mississippi law forbidding public broadcasters from airing any programs produced by SIECUS.
13. *Cornwell v. State Bd. of Ed.*, 314 F. Supp. 340 (D. Md. 1969), aff'd *per curiam*, 428 F.2d 471 (4th Cir.), cert. denied, 400 U.S. 942 (1970); *Davis v. Page*, 385 F. Supp. 395 (D.N.H. 1974); *Citizens for Parental Rights v. San Mateo Cty Bd. of Ed.*, 51 Cal. App. 3d 1, 29 n. 18 (1st Dist. 1975), app. dismissed, 425 U.S. 908 (1976); *Unitarian Church West v. McConnell*, 337 F. Supp. 1252, 1253, 1255 (E.D. Wis. 1972); see also *Valent v. New Jersey State Bd. of Ed.*, 114 N.J. Super. 63, 71 (1971), rev'd and dism'd; 118 N.J. Super. 416 (1972) (mandating exemption for three Catholic children from a "Human Sexuality" course that covered sexual intercourse, masturbation, and contraception); *Medeiros v. Kiyosaki*, 52 Haw. 436 (1970) (rejecting parents' challenge to noncompulsory fifth- and sixth-grade sex ed film program); *Ware v. Valley Stream H.S. Dist.*, 75 N.Y.2d 114 (1989) (reversing judgment against parents belonging to the Plymouth Brethren sect who demanded a broader exemption for their children from AIDS education curriculum than was already granted by state law, and ordering trial court to conduct fact-finding on whether the government's interest in mandatory AIDS education was compelling).
14. *Mercer v. Michigan State Bd. of Ed.*, 379 F. Supp. 580 (E.D. Mich.), aff'd, 419 U.S. 1081 (1974); the law was repealed in 1977; see Mich. Compiled Laws, Act 451 (Jan. 13, 1977); A. R. Allgeier, "Informational Barriers to Contraception," in *Adolescence, Sex, and Contraception* (Donn Byrne & William Fisher, eds.) (Hillsdale, NJ: Lawrence Erlbaum, 1983), p. 145.
15. *Tractman v. Anker*, 563 F.2d 512, 517 (2d Cir. 1977); *id.* at 523–26 (Mansfield, J., dissenting). The students' experts also noted that far more graphic sexual information was a daily fact of life for young and old on the streets of New York. *Id.*
16. *Id.* at 519–20; *id.* at 521 (Mansfield, J., dissenting).
17. *Bayer v. Kinzler*, 383 F. Supp. 1164, 1166 (E.D.N.Y. 1974), aff'd, 515 F.2d 504 (2d Cir. 1975); see also *Shanley v. Northeast Ind. School Dist.*, 462 F.2d 960 (5th Cir. 1972) (affirming students' right to publish a school newspaper article on birth control); *Gambino v. Fairfax Cty School Bd.*, 546 F.2d 157 (4th Cir. 1977) (invalidating local school board's ban on article about birth control in student newspaper); but see *id.* at 158 (Russell, J., dissenting) (presaging Supreme Court's 1988 ruling in *Hazelwood School District v. Kuhlmeier* by arguing that school administration has "a legitimate concern in eliminating from its curriculum material which may reasonably be considered conducive to immorality").

18. *Carey v. Population Services Int'l*, 431 U.S. 678, 701 (1977). Justice Brennan wrote this part of the opinion, joined by Stewart, Marshall, Blackmun, White, and Powell.
19. It was, Stevens said, "as though a State decided to dramatize its disapproval of motorcycles by forbidding the use of safety helmets. One need not posit a constitutional right to ride a motorcycle to characterize such a restriction as irrational and perverse." *Id.* at 715 (Stevens, J., concurring).
20. *Id.* at 696, 692–95. This part of Brennan's opinion was joined only by Stewart, Marshall, and Blackmun.
21. *Id.* at 694 n. 17 (Brennan, Stewart, Marshall, and Blackmun, JJ.). The constitutional privacy right had been recognized in 1965 in *Griswold v. Connecticut*, 381 U.S. 479 (1965) (invalidating a law that barred married couples from obtaining contraceptives). Seven years later, the Court extended *Griswold* to unmarried adults, *Eisenstadt v. Baird*, 405 U.S. 438 (1972); and in 1973 came *Roe v. Wade*, 410 U.S. 113 (1973), applying the privacy right to a woman's choice of abortion. Decisions after *Roe* gave minors some abortion rights, but in *Bellotti v. Baird*, 443 U.S. 622 (1979), the Court said states could restrict teenagers' choice of abortion by requiring that they either obtain parental consent or a judicial ruling that they are mature enough to make the decision themselves. *Bellotti* posed "difficult philosophical issues about when childhood should begin and when it should end"; the expert witnesses in the case did not help the justices decide whether minors would be harmed by a grant or denial of reproductive autonomy. Robert Mnookin, *In the Interest of Children: Advocacy, Law Reform, and Public Policy* (New York: W. H. Freeman, 1985), pp. 160, 255.
22. *Carey*, 431 U.S. at 702–3 (White, J., concurring); 713 (Stevens, J., concurring); 719 (Rehnquist, J., dissenting). Justice Powell wrote a separate opinion arguing that New York needed merely to show a "rational" basis for its restriction; but said the state did not meet even this lenient test because its law had no exemption for married teenagers, or for parents who wish to give contraceptives to their children. *Id.* at 705–10 (Powell, J., concurring). Chief Justice Burger dissented but filed no opinion.
23. *Bolger v. Youngs Drug Products Corp.*, 463 U.S. 60, 71-74, & n. 30 (1983). The original Comstock law, of course, banned the mailing of all contraceptive advertisements, but Congress narrowed it in 1970 to cover only unsolicited ads. *Id.* at 70 n. 19.
24. Melvin Zelnik, John Kanter & Kathleen Ford, *Sex and Pregnancy in Adolescence* (Beverly Hills: Sage, 1981), pp. 20–21, 64, 95.
25. Zelnik et al., *supra* n. 24, pp. 20–21, 54, 167, 179; see Donn Byrne, "Sex Without Contraception," John DeLamater, "An Intrapersonal and Interactive Model of Contraceptive Behavior," Paul Abramson, "Implications of the Sexual System," George Cvetkovich & Barbara Grote, "Adolescent Development and Teenage Fertility," A. R. Allgeier, "Informational Barriers," and Elizabeth Rice Allgeier, "Ideological Barriers to Contraception," in *Adolescence*, *supra* n. 14 (considering factors of inadequate sex education, reluctance of teenagers to

acknowledge their sexuality in the face of a "forbidding adult community," guilt, denial, and anxiety).

26. Alan Guttmacher Institute, *Eleven Million Teenagers: What Can Be Done About the Epidemic of Adolescent Pregnancies in the United States* (New York: Planned Parenthood, 1976); *id.*, pp. 34–35 (only 20% of states that require health education mandated sex ed, and only 30% taught about birth control); Alan Guttmacher Institute, *Teenage Pregnancy: The Problem That Hasn't Gone Away* (New York: AGI, 1981).
27. See Tamar Lewin, "Birth Rates for Teen-Agers Declined Sharply in the 90's," *New York Times*, May 1, 1998, p. A21; letter from Alexander Sanger, president of Planned Parenthood of New York City, to *The New York Times*, Week in Review, Oct. 11, 1998, p. 16.
28. See Trudell, *supra* n. 3, p. 15; Preface, and Donn Byrne, "Sex Without Contraception," in *Adolescence, supra* n. 14, pp. ix, 4–5; Constance Nathanson, *Dangerous Passage: The Social Control of Sexuality in Women's Adolescence* (Philadelphia: Temple U. Press, 1991).
29. Phyllis Schlafly, "What's Wrong with Sex Education?" 14 *Phyllis Schlafly Rep.* 1, 2 (Feb. 1981); Phyllis Schlafly, "Classes in Sex, Nuclear War Harm Students," *Conserv. Digest*, May 1984, p. 38; see also Trudell, *supra* n. 3, pp. 17–19; D'Emilio & Freedman, *supra* n. 3, pp. 357–60.
30. Coleen Kelly Mast, *Sex Respect: The Option of True Sexual Freedom* (Bradley, IL: Respect, Inc., 1986, 1990); James Coughlin, *Facing Reality: A Handbook for Healthy Living* (Gulf, IL: Project Respect, 1990); Nancy Roach & Leanna Benn, *Me, My World, My Future* (Spokane, WA: Teen-Aid, Inc., 1987, 1993); Stephen Potter & Nancy Roach, *Sexuality, Commitment and Family* (Spokane, WA: Teen-Aid, Inc., 1990); see discussion in Trudell, *supra* n. 3, pp. 2–4.
31. Mast, *supra* n. 30, p. 6 (1990 ed.); *Coleman v. Caddo Parish School Bd.*, 635 So.2d 1238, 1252 (La. App. 1994).
32. Mast, pp. 35, 41, 45–56; see Annette Fuentes, "No Sex Ed," *In These Times*, Dec. 18, 1997, p. 16; D'Emilio & Freedman, *supra* n. 3, p. 357; *Coleman*, 635 So.2d at 1256–57.
33. *Facing Reality Parent/Teacher Guide* (Gulf, IL: Project Respect, 1990), pp. 6, 24.
34. *Id.*, p. 23; *Teaching Fear, supra* n. 11, p. 8; *Community Action Kit: Information to Support Comprehensive Sexuality Education* (New York: SIECUS, 1997) (review of video *No Second Chance*).
35. Connaught Marshner, "The Growth of Sex Respect," *Conserv. Digest*, Dec. 1988, pp. 41, 46. The graduate student in question was Coleen Mast, author of *Sex Respect*. Marshner reported that the Illinois Public Health Department paid for a mailing of *Sex Respect* brochures to all of the state's middle and high schools; *id.*, p. 41; see also Trudell, pp. 17–18; National Research Council, *Risking the Future: Adolescent Sexuality, Pregnancy, and Childbearing* (Cheryl Haynes, ed.) (Washington, DC: Nat'l Academy Press, 1987), pp. 21–22.
36. Trudell, pp. 3–4.

37. Fuentes, *supra* n. 32. This amounted to about 4,000 of the nation's 16,000 school districts, according to a 1997 report; see Tamar Lewin, "States Slow to Take U.S. Aid to Teach Sexual Abstinence," *New York Times*, May 8, 1997, pp. A1, A22. Most other estimates were lower; see *Teaching Fear*, p. 12 (press reports ranged from 1,500 to 2,400 schools teaching abstinence only); Trudell, p. 18 (about 1,600 districts, according to 1992 report by J. Kerr, "A Is for Abstinence," *City Pages* [Minneapolis], Mar. 4, 1992, pp. 6–8).
38. *Coleman v. Caddo Parish*, 635 So.2d at 1246–47; *Teaching Fear*, pp. 12–15.
39. See National Guidelines Task Force, *Guidelines for Comprehensive Sexuality Education* (2d ed.) (New York: SIECUS, 1996), pp. 58–59; 25(4) *SIECUS Report* 20–21 (1997); SIECUS Fact Sheet, "The National Coalition to Support Sexuality Education," http://www.siecus.org/pubs/fact/fact0005.html. The National Guidelines Task Force had representation from both the American Medical Association and the National Education Association.
40. *Guidelines*, *supra* n. 39, pp. 3, 5; see also Trudell, p. 209 n. 1 (distinguishing the narrow focus of "sex" education on "the anatomical and reproductive aspects," while "sexuality" education "encompasses a wide range of other sexual knowledge, sexual development, reproductive health, gender roles, and interpersonal relationships as well as sexual attitudes, feelings, and behaviors").
41. *Guidelines*, pp. 7–52.
42. *Id.*, p. 1; Trudell, p. 20; Douglas Kirby, *Sexuality Education: An Evaluation of Programs* (Santa Cruz, CA: Network Pubs., 1984); *Risking the Future*, *supra* n. 35, p. 144; Victor Strasburger, "Sex, Drugs, Rock 'n' Roll: Understanding Common Teenage Behavior," 76 *Pediatrics* 704–12 (1985), citing M. Zelnik & Y. J. Kim, "Sex Education and Its Association with Teenage Sexual Activity, Pregnancy, and Contraceptive Use," 14 *Fam. Plng Persp.* 117–26 (1982); Ethan Bronner, "No Sexology, Please. We're Americans," *New York Times*, Week in Review, Feb. 1, 1998, p. 6 (citing SIECUS). Debra Haffner estimated in 1999 that only about four school districts were fully following *Guidelines*; author's interview with Debra Haffner, Nov. 16, 1999.
43. *Risking the Future*, pp. 143–45; Byrne, *supra* n. 28, p. 5 (only one-third of courses in the early 1980s covered birth control); Zelnik, *supra* n. 24, pp. 178–79; Trudell, pp. 6–7, 20, 22 ("activities other than heterosexual intercourse [masturbation, other safer sex activities, and homosexuality]" covered "less frequently"; "pleasures of sexuality. . . . usually omitted from school sex education classes altogether" [citing J. Forrest & J. Silverman, "What Public School Teachers Teach About Preventing Pregnancy, AIDS, and Sexually Transmitted Diseases," 21(2) *Fam. Plng Persp.* 65–72 (1989)]); Michelle Fine, "Sexuality, Schooling, and Adolescent Females: The Missing Discourse of Desire," 58(1) *Harv. Ed. Rev.* 29–53 (1988); Henry J. Kaiser Family Foundation, *Sex Education in America* (Menlo Park, CA, 2000), p. 14 (generally only a few class periods are devoted to sex ed).
44. SIECUS Fact Sheet, "Sexuality Education in the Schools: Issues and Answers" (1997), http://www.siecus.org/pubs/fact/fact0007.html.

45. Trudell, *supra* n. 3, pp. 136–45. Trudell observed this six-hour sexuality segment of a ninth-grade health education class in 1985–86. The topics covered, in order of time spent, were "sexually transmitted diseases (42 minutes), dating (40 minutes), teenage pregnancy consequences (30 minutes), contraception (30 minutes), communicating with parents (29 minutes), adolescent body changes (25 minutes), reproductive anatomy and physiology (21 minutes), marriage and family (18 minutes), saying 'no' to sexual intercourse (15 minutes), pregnancy and prenatal development (13 minutes), love vs. infatuation (10 minutes), childbirth (9 minutes), [and] sexual assault (9 minutes)." Masturbation, sexual response, and homosexuality were not covered, apart from the teacher's occasional comments connecting AIDS almost exclusively with gay men. Condoms were "never mentioned as a possible form for prevention of sexually transmitted diseases." *Id.*, pp. 104–7, 130, 60–61.
46. Author's interview with Debra Haffner, Nov. 16, 1999.
47. Stanley Henshaw & Jennifer Van Vort, "Teenage Abortion, Birth and Pregnancy Statistics: An Update," 21(2) *Fam. Plng Persp.* 85–88 (1989); Elise Jones *et al.*, *Teenage Pregnancy in Industrialized Countries* (New Haven, CT: Yale U. Press, 1986), pp. 21–32, 251–60; Andrew Shapiro, *We're Number One: Where America Stands—and Falls—in the New World Order* (New York: Vintage, 1992), pp. 14–16. See also Centers for Disease Control, "Current Trends: Premarital Sexual Experience Among Adolescent Women," 39(51/52) *Morbidity & Mortality Wkly Rep.* 929–32 (Jan. 4, 1991) (noting that between 1985 and 1988, the percentage of 15-to-19-year-old female nonvirgins in the United States rose to 51%); Freya Sonenstein *et al.*, "Sexual Activity, Condom Use and AIDS Awareness Among Adolescent Males," 21(4) *Fam. Plng Persp.* 152–58 (1989) (nearly half of 17-to-19-year-old males in 1988 reported using no condom at last intercourse); Jones *et al.*, *supra*, pp. 216–17 (noting readier availability of contraceptive services in countries with lower teen pregnancy rates); *The Best Intentions: Unintended Pregnancy and the Well-Being of Children and Families* (Sarah Brown & Leon Eisenberg, eds.) (Washington, DC: Nat'l Academy Press, 1995), pp. 135–37, 193–94 (same; noting also less openness about sexuality in the United States); National Abortion Rights Action League, *Sexuality Education in America: A State by State Review* (Washington, DC: NARAL, 1995); *Risking the Future*, *supra* n. 35, p. 261. In 1997, SIECUS reported encouraging trends: in 1979, fewer than 50% of U.S. adolescents used a contraceptive at first intercourse; by 1988, the number had risen to 65%, and by 1990, more than 70%. Debra Haffner, "What's Wrong with Abstinence-Only Sexuality Education Programs?" 25(4) *SIECUS Report* 9, 11 (1997); see also Sonenstein, *supra*, reporting 15% rise in sexual activity among 17-to-19-year-old males since 1979, with 60% of 15-to-19-year-olds sexually active, half reporting condom use at last intercourse, and double the rate of condom use among 17–19-year-olds since 1979.
48. Shapiro, *supra* n. 47, p. 14, citing Int'l Ass'n for the Evaluation of Educational Achievement, *Science Achievement in Seventeen Countries: A Preliminary Report* (Oxford: Pergamon, 1988).

49. Ira Reiss & Harriet Reiss, *Solving America's Sexual Crises* (Amherst, NY: Prometheus, 1997), pp. 24–25; see also Victor Strasburger, *Adolescents and the Media: Medical and Psychological Impact* (Thousand Oaks, CA: Sage, 1995), pp. 51–52, and, for comparisons with Europe, Colin Shaw, *Deciding What We Watch: Taste, Decency, and Media Ethics in the UK and the USA* (Oxford: Clarendon, 1999), p. 84; Jones *et al.*, *Teenage Pregnancy, supra* n. 47; Elise Jones *et al.*, "Unintended Pregnancy, Contraceptive Practice and Family Planning Services in Developed Countries," 20(2) *Fam. Plng Persp.* 53, 67 (1988); Linda Berne & Barbara Huberman, *Aimer Sans Peur: European Approaches to Adolescent Sexual Behavior and Responsibility* (Washington, DC: Advocates for Youth, 1999).
50. Centers for Disease Control, "State-Specific Pregnancy Rates Among Adolescents—United States, 1992–1995," 47(24) *Morbidity & Mortality Wkly Rep.* 497–504 (June 26, 1998) (pregnancy rates for 15–19-year-olds declined in all 42 reporting states and DC between 1992 and 1995); see also Lewin, *supra* n. 37; "Poll Shows Decline in Sex by High School Students," *New York Times*, Sept. 18, 1998, p. A26; Tamar Lewin, "Youth Pregnancy Rate Falls, Report Says," *New York Times*, Oct. 15, 1998, p. A27; Marc Lacey, "Teen-Age Birth Rate in U.S. Falls Again," *New York Times*, Oct. 27, 1999, p. A16.
51. Alan Guttmacher Institute, *Into a New World: Young Women's Sexual and Reproductive Lives* (New York: AGI, 1998), p. 22.
52. American Library Ass'n, *Newsletter on Intellectual Freedom*, Sept. 1994, p. 150; *Newsletter*, Mar. 1994, p. 54; July 1994, p. 103; Sam Dillon, "Publisher Pulls a Textbook in Furor on Sexual Content," *New York Times*, Mar. 17, 1994, p. C14; see also *Newsletter*, May 1994, p. 87 (*Human Sexuality* pulled in Belleville, Missouri, after parents complained that it "did not concentrate on abstinence" or say whether "sexual relations before marriage, homosexuality, masturbation or abortion are right or wrong"); Jan. 1994, pp. 33–34 (three sex ed books removed from school library in Kenai, Alaska); Sept. 1994, p. 147 (four sex ed textbooks challenged in Sparks, Nevada, public library).
53. *Brown v. Hot, Sexy and Safer Productions*, 68 F.3d 525, 533, 541 (1st Cir. 1995), cert. denied, 516 U.S. 1159 (1996).
54. Personal Responsibility and Work Opportunity Act of 1996, §912, PL 104–193, 110 Stat. 2353, 104th Cong., 2d Sess. (1996), codified at 42 U.S.C. §710. The law did not define the "sexual activity" from which programs must instruct students to refrain, but apparently it included any kind of arousal, not just intercourse. The Medical Institute for Sexual Health (MISH), for example, a Texas-based promoter of abstinence-only materials, defines abstinence as avoiding "any activity involving genital contact or genital stimulation"; and other fear-based curricula, like *Sex Respect*, specifically state that premarital petting leads to problems within marriage. Medical Institute for Sexual Health, *National Guidelines for Sexuality and Character Education* (Austin, TX: MISH, 1996), p. 7; Leslie Kantor, "Scared Chaste? Fear-Based Educational Curricula," 21(2) *SIECUS Report* 1, 4 (1992); *Sex Respect*, p. 31.

55. Mac Edwards, "88 Million Dollars for 'Abstinence-Only,' " 25(4) *SIECUS Report* 2 (1997); Daniel Daley & Vivian Wong, *Between the Lines: States' Implementation of the Federal Government's Section 510(b) Abstinence Education Program in Fiscal Year 1998* (New York: SIECUS, 1999), pp. 7–8. In November 1999, Rep. Ernest Istook secured another $20 million for abstinence-only-until-marriage programs, to be distributed directly by the Department of Health and Human Services rather than through grants to the states.
56. Personal Responsibility and Work Opportunity Act, *supra* n. 54. The other prerequisites for an "abstinence education" program were teaching that "abstinence from sexual activity outside marriage" is "the expected standard for all school age children" ("school age" of course including high school); and that "bearing children out-of-wedlock is likely to have harmful consequences for the child, the child's parents, and society"; as well as teaching "how to reject sexual advances and how alcohol and drug use increase vulnerability to sexual advances"; and "the importance of attaining self-sufficiency before engaging in sexual activity." It was not necessary "to place equal emphasis" on each of the eight elements, but a project could not "be inconsistent with any aspect of the abstinence education definition."
57. According to the most extensive sexuality survey as of 1994, about 15% of men and 20% of women born between 1943 and 1974 said they were virgins when they married. Edward Laumann *et al.*, *The Social Organization of Sexuality: Sexual Practices in the United States* (Chicago: U. of Chicago Press, 1994), pp. 502–3; see also Michael, *supra* n. 5 (the lay version of the Laumann report), pp. 90–96 (few Americans now "wait until they marry to have sex"). A 1999 text reported that only 3% of Americans delayed their first intercourse until the marriage night. Malcolm Potts & Roger Short, *Ever Since Adam and Eve: The Evolution of Human Sexuality* (Cambridge: Cambridge U. Press, 1999), p. 77 (the figure for Britain was 1%). The different numbers probably did not reflect a dramatic change in mores over five years but the fact that Potts and Short were reporting on current practices and Laumann on the experiences of people first married as much as thirty or forty years earlier. Debra Haffner commented that the " 'norm' " of premarital virginity "was probably never true: a third of all Pilgrim brides were pregnant when they were married." Haffner, *supra* n. 47, p. 11.
58. Melody Petersen, "Young New Jersey; Teaching Abstinence: The Price of Federal Money for Sex Education," *New York Times*, July 27, 1997, §13NJ, p. 7, quoting Susan Wilson of the New Jersey Coalition for Comprehensive Family Life/Sexuality Education.
59. Lewin, *supra* n. 37. Maine governor Angus King announced in July 1997 that he was inclined to apply for funds, but agreed that they should not go for school counselors because "they could be hamstrung in what they would be able to tell children." "King May Seek 'Abstinence' Funds," *Portland Press Herald*, July 2, 1997, p. 7B.
60. "Sex Education: Deadline for Abstinence Funds Approaching," *American*

Pol. Network Abortion Rep., July 8, 1997; "States Set to Collect Millions for Abstinence-Only Programs," *Charleston Daily Mail*, July 23, 1997, p. 9A. New Jersey governor Christine Whitman likewise objected to the pedagogical restraints of the program, but finally developed a plan to participate—on condition that "private, non-profit groups teach the abstinence lessons outside of school hours." Petersen, *supra* n. 58, p. 7.

61. Daley & Wong, *supra* n. 55, p. 143.
62. See Petersen, *supra* n. 58; John Dvorak, "Education to Focus on Abstinence," *Kansas City Star*, May 19, 1997, p. Al; Jeff Stryker, "Abstinence or Else! The Just-Say-No Approach in Sex Ed Lacks One Detail: Evidence That It Works," *The Nation*, June 16, 1997, p. 19; Lewin, *supra* n. 37; Jeff Stryker & Maria Ekstrand, "A Campaign Conspicuous by Its Abstinence; Government to Teens: No Sex Education and Please, No Sex," *San Francisco Examiner*, Mar. 17, 1997, p. A17; Anne Grunseit *et al.*, "Sexuality Education and Young People's Sexual Behavior: A Review of Studies," 12(4) *J. Adoles. Rsrch* 421–52 (1997) (of 47 studies evaluating HIV/AIDS and sexuality education, 25 reported neither increased nor decreased sexual activity and "attendant rates of pregnancy and STDs," while 17 reported delays in the onset of sexual activity, reduction in number of sexual partners, or reductions in rates of unplanned pregnancy or STDs, and only three found "increases in sexual behavior associated with sexuality education"); Douglas Kirby, *No Easy Answers: Research Findings on Programs to Reduce Teen Pregnancy* (Washington, DC: National Campaign to Prevent Teen Pregnancy, 1997); Douglas Kirby *et al.*, "School-Based Programs to Reduce Sexual Risk Behaviors: A Review of Effectiveness," 109(3) *Pub. Health Rep.* 339–60 (1994); Jennifer Frost & Jacqueline Forrest, "Understanding the Impact of Effective Teenage Pregnancy Prevention Programs," 27(5) *Fam. Plng Persp.* 188–96 (1995) (finding decreased pregnancy in the two programs, out of five studied, that "were most active in providing access to contraceptive services"); Debra Haffner & Eva Goldfarb, *But Does It Work? Improving Evaluations of Sexuality Education* (New York: SIECUS, 1997); Lynda Richardson, "Condoms in School Said Not to Affect Teen-Age Sex Rate," *New York Times*, Sept. 30, 1997, p. A1.

A 1993 review of existing literature worldwide concluded that, overall, studies showed "no support for the contention that sex education encourages sexual experimentation or increased activity"; if "any effect is observed, almost without exception, it is in the direction of postponed initiation of sexual intercourse and/or effective use of contraceptives." Grunseit *et al.*, *supra*; Anne Grunseit & Susan Kippax, *Effects of Sex Education on Young People's Sexual Behavior* (Geneva: WHO, 1993) (unpublished review commissioned by the Global Programme on AIDS), p. 8; press release, "Sexual Health Education Does Lead to Safer Sexual Behaviour," UNAIDS Joint United Nations Programme on HIV/AIDS, Geneva, Oct. 22, 1997. A 1997 report found that for "interventions to be most effective," teenagers need information about contraception and safer sex "before initiating intercourse." *No Easy Answers*, *supra*,

p. 25; see also *Risking the Future*, p. 147. Abstinence-till-marriage programs, by contrast, did not delay the sexual "debut"; students generally found them "an ineffective deterrent to sexual activity." SIECUS Fact Sheet, "Adolescence and Abstinence" (1997), citing Roper Starch Worldwide, *Teens Talk About Sex: Adolescent Sexuality in the 90s* (New York: SIECUS, 1994), p. 18; *No Easy Answers*, p. 25 (summarizing the six published studies of abstinence-only programs, which found no significant effects in delaying the onset of intercourse). A 1998 study of African-American teenagers by a Princeton psychologist reported that a year after receiving eight hours of abstinence education, 20% had had recent sex, compared with 16.5% in a group that had received eight hours "concentrating on condom use," and 23.1% for a control group. Lindsey Tanner, "Study Urges Lessons on Condoms," *Associated Press Online*, May 20, 1998.

63. Daley & Wong, pp. 86–89, 124, 132, 140; "Keeping an Eye on Abstinence-Only Education," 6(2) *SIECUS Developments* (1998); Martha Kempner, "1997–98 Sexuality Education Controversies in the United States," 26(6) *SIECUS Report* 16–21 (1998); Jodie Levin-Epstein, *Abstinence-Unless-Married Education* (Washington, DC: Center for Law & Social Policy, 1998). In California, the FY 1998 funds were declined after it was learned that previous similar programs "did not increase the number of young people abstaining" but instead, at least in some schools, were associated with increased sexual activity. Daley & Wong, pp. 88–89. A report by the Public Media Center of San Francisco and the Applied Research Center of Oakland, California, concluded that abstinence-only curricula are not only dangerous but illegal because they withhold contraceptive information and fail to mention that condoms do reduce the risk of AIDS. Phyllida Burlingame, *Sex, Lies, and Politics: Abstinence-Only Curricula in California Public Schools* (Oakland: Chardon Press, 1997); see Glen Martin, "Study Blasts Abstinence-Only Sex Education," *San Francisco Chronicle*, April 19, 1997, p. A15.
64. Author's interview with Debra Haffner, Nov. 16, 1999.
65. Jodi Wilgoren, "Abstinence Is Focus of U.S. Sex Education," *New York Times*, Dec. 15, 1999, p. A18; Anne Jarrell, "The Face of Teenage Sex Grows Younger," *New York Times*, Apr. 2, 2000, p. I1 (abstinence is "sole contraception method taught at one-third of all public schools across the country," according to recent Guttmacher Institute poll); *Youth and HIV/AIDS 2000: A New American Agenda* (Washington, DC: White House Office of National AIDS Policy, 2000), p. 15; *Sex Education, supra* n. 43.
66. Michael Carrera *et al.*, "Teens and Sex: How Little They Really Know," 30(3) *Soc. Policy* 41 (2000) (reporting, for example, that only 44% correctly answered "false" to the statement "a female can get pregnant through oral sex," and only 39% to the statement "urinating after sex sometimes prevents pregnancy").
67. *SEX, ETC.: A Newsletter by Teens for Teens*, http://www.sxetc.org; Susan Wilson, "Raising the Voices of Teens to Change Sexuality Education," 28(6) *SIECUS Report* 20 (2000); *id.*, p. 22 (teen editors of *SEX, ETC.* were featured

in *Teen People* magazine); p. 23 (one study showed that "positive attitudes toward postponing sexual activity and negative attitudes about drugs increased significantly among students who read *SEX, ETC.*, especially African-American students"); Angier, *supra* n. 2.

68. David Kaplan, "Teens and Safer Sex," *Washington Post*, Oct. 28, 1998, p. A19 (paraphrasing Berne & Huberman report, *supra* n. 49); National Comm'n on Adolescent Sexual Health, *Facing Facts: Sexual Health for America's Adolescents* (Debra Haffner, ed.) (New York: SIECUS, 1995), pp. 21, 27, 22; Ammie Feijoo & Sue Alford, *Adolescent Sexual Health in Europe and the U.S.—Why the Difference?* 11(3) *Transitions* 1 (2000) (newsletter of Advocates for Youth); see also *Risking the Future*, p. 276, noting successful use of TV and radio contraceptive advertising in Europe.
69. European Charter of the Rights of the Child, Resolution A3-0172/92, §§8.24, 8.32.
70. Author's interview with Vicky Claeys, Mar. 3, 1999.
71. Giustiniana Barbugli & Antonietta Corradini, *Strategie di Educazione alla Contraccezione* (Milan: U.I.C.E.M.P., undated), pp. 3, 14–15.
72. Susan Rose, "Fraught with Fear: The Religious and Sexual Politics of Abstinence-Only" (paper presented at Eastern Sociological Society Meetings, Boston, Mar. 1999), p. 13; see also Philip Meredith, *Sex Education: Political Issues in Britain and Europe* (London: Routledge, 1989), pp. 121–34.
73. Neil Rasmussen, *Sexual and Reproductive Health and Rights for Youth: The Danish Experience* (Danish Family Planning Ass'n, 1996), p. 8.
74. *Case of Kjeldsen, Busk Madsen and Pedersen*, Series A, No. 23 (European Court of Human Rights, Dec. 7, 1976), 1 E.H.R.R. 711, 715 (1976); Andrew Bainham, *Children, Parents, and the State* (London: Sweet & Maxwell, 1988), p. 182.
75. *Kjeldsen*, 1 E.H.R.R. at 716–21; see also Meredith, *supra* n. 72, pp. 126–34; Rasmussen, *supra* n. 73, pp. 17–22.
76. *Kjeldsen*, 1 E.H.R.R. at 730–32, interpreting European Convention on Human Rights, First Protocol, Article 2.
77. Rasmussen, *supra* n. 73, p. 10.
78. Rose, *supra* n. 72, pp. 13–14; Rasmussen, pp. 24–39.
79. Swedish Association for Sex Education (RFSU), *Vision Reality Activities* (Programme of Principles, adopted at RFSU's annual meeting, May 1990) (Stockholm: RFSU, 1990), pp. 7–15; Bainham, *supra* n. 74, p. 182.
80. Meredith, p. 105.
81. Ronald & Juliette Goldman, *Show Me Yours: What Children Think About Sex* (London: Penguin, 1988) p. xxix; *id.*, p. 4 (Swedish children's greater knowledge is partly attributable to their parents' own experience of sex education); p. 35 (Swedish experience demonstrates that children "have the capacity to really understand the process of procreation, from the age of 5 onwards").
82. *Vision Reality Activities*, *supra* n. 79, pp. 48–51.
83. Meredith, p. 118.

84. IPPF European Network, *Health, Choice, Rights: A Decade of Change in Europe* (undated), p. 25; Minou Fuglesang, *"Red Card or Yellow—Are You Still in the Game?": Being Young and Coping with Sexual and Reproductive Health in Tanzania* (Stockholm: RFSU, 1995).
85. Meredith, pp. 29–31.
86. Dep't for Education Circular 11/87, Sept. 25, 1987, ¶¶22, 26. A 1994 circular advised teachers to report a pupil who "has embarked upon, or is contemplating, a course of conduct which is likely to place him or her at *moral* or physical risk." Dep't for Education guidance on sex education, Circular 5/94, reprinted in *Children, Sex Education and the Law* (Neville Harris, ed.) (London: Nat'l Children's Bureau, 1996), pp. 126–37 (emphasis added). The Education Act of 1986 required that any instruction had to "encourage pupils to have due regard to moral considerations and the value of family life." Education (No. 2) Act 1986, §46, 15 *Halsbury's Laws of England* (4th ed., 1997 reissue), ¶403.
87. *Gillick v. West Norfolk & Wisbech Area Health Authority et al.* (1985), 3 All E.R. 402, 409–11, 421, quoting *Regina v. Howard* (1965), 3 All E.R. 684, 685. Lord Fraser added that "there are many girls under sixteen who know full well what it is all about and can properly consent" to sex as well as contraceptives. The Court of Appeal narrowed *Gillick* in a series of later decisions involving youngsters' consent to medical treatment, *Re R* (1991), 4 All E.R. 177; *Re W* (1992), 4 All E.R. 627, but did not contradict the Law Lords' recognition of minors' maturing need for autonomy.
88. Education Act 1993, §241(3), (4), 15 *Halsbury's Laws of England* (4th ed., 1997 reissue), ¶¶404, 405 (carried over from Education Reform Act 1988, §17A).
89. Linda Kirschke, *Kid's Talk: Freedom of Expression and the UN Convention on the Rights of the Child* (London: Article 19, 1999), pp. 32–33.
90. Sarah Boseley, "British Teenagers Have Worst Sexual Health in Europe," *The Guardian*, May 14, 1999, p. 1; see also "UK Top for Single Teenage Mothers," *The Guardian*, May 15, 1998, p. 7; "International Reproductive and Sexual Health Update," 28(4) *SIECUS Report* 4 (2000) (according to European Commission report in March 2000, the UK had the highest teen birthrate in the EU: 22 live births per 1,000, followed by Portugal, with 17); Harris, *supra* n. 86 (documenting British political struggles over sex ed).
91. http://www.lovelife.hea.org.uk.
92. Shaw, *supra* n. 49, pp. 82–83; "Television Grapples to Get Hold on AIDS Messages," *Minneapolis Star Tribune*, Sept. 8, 1987, p. 5C.
93. See Edmund Kellogg & Jan Stepan, "Legal Aspects of Sex Education," 26 *Am. J. Comp. Law* 573, 578–81 (1978); Figen Cook, "Reflections on an Adolescent Sexuality Education Program in Turkey," 28(4) *SIECUS Report* 5 (2000).
94. Rose, *supra*. n. 72, p. 16.
95. Meredith, pp. 150–54.
96. Author's interview with Vicky Claeys, Mar. 3, 1999.

97. Paul Lewis, "A Conference Splits Sharply on Limiting Population," *New York Times*, June 30, 1999, p. A9.
98. See John Gagnon, *Human Sexualities* (Glenview, IL: Scott, Foresman, 1977), p. 92; Carrera, *supra* n. 8, p. 304; Goldman & Goldman, *supra* n. 81, p. 221 ("a true understanding of sexuality is a long and complex process too serious to be left until adolescence").
99. David Archard, *Children: Rights and Childhood* (London: Routledge, 1993), p. 76 (adult euphemisms and equivocations breed bewilderment, anxiety, and mistrust); see also Goldman & Goldman, *supra* n. 81.
100. Gagnon, *supra* n. 98, p. 92.
101. See, e.g., Richard Panzer, *Condom Nation: Blind Faith, Bad Science* (Westwood, NJ: Center for Educational Media, 1997), p. 79; Shalit, *supra* n. 1; Rochelle Gurstein, *The Repeal of Reticence* (New York: Hill & Wang, 1996).
102. Archard, *supra* n. 99, p. 40; see also James Kincaid, *Erotic Innocence: The Culture of Child Molesting* (Chapel Hill: Duke U. Press, 1998); Anne Higgonet, *Pictures of Innocence: The History and Crisis of Ideal Childhood* (London: Thames & Hudson, 1998); *The Children's Culture Reader* (Henry Jenkins, ed.) (New York: NYU Press, 1998).
103. Victor Strasburger, *Getting Your Kids to Say No in the Nineties When You Said Yes in the Sixties* (New York: Simon & Schuster, 1993), p. 94.
104. Kay Smith, "Tough Work at the Chalk-Face," *The Guardian*, May 20, 1998, p. 9.
105. Janice Irvine, *Sexuality Education Across Cultures* (San Francisco: Jossey-Bass, 1995), p. 67; author's telephone interview with Michael Carrera, Jan. 31, 1997.
106. International Planned Parenthood Federation & UN Population Fund, *Generation 97: What Young People SAY About Sexual and Reproductive Health* (London: IPPF/UNFPA, 1997), p. 2.
107. The IPPF is committed "to the empowerment of young people as equal partners in sexual health policy decision making." IPPF European Network, *Make It Happen . . . Make It Now: Young People's Involvement in Family Planning Associations* (London: IPPF, 1996), pp. 4–21. In 1999, FPAs in more than 140 countries were members of IPPF and subscribed to its 1995 *Charter on Sexual and Reproductive Rights*, which recognized a right to sexuality information, regardless of age, and urged governments, "in collaboration with non-governmental organizations," to meet teenagers' needs for education and counseling on "gender relations and equality, violence against adolescents, responsible sexual behavior, responsible family planning practice, family life, reproductive health, sexually transmitted diseases, HIV infection and AIDS prevention." *Charter on Sexual and Reproductive Rights* (London: IPPF, 1996), pp. 14–15, 46–47. Especially in the developing world, where public school sexuality education is less common (and, indeed, the length of schooling may be too short to reach most adolescents), the peer-oriented work of non-governmental organizations like the FPAs has been critical; see *Health, Choice, Rights*, *supra* n. 84; *Into a New World*, *supra* n. 51, p. 42; Population

Action International, *Educating Girls: Gender Gaps and Gains* (Washington, DC: Population Action Int'l, 1998).

108. http://www.advocatesforyouth.org (Aug. 13, 1999); see also "Special Section: Power to Peers," in 30(1) *Social Policy* (1999); http://www.nyclu.org/rrp_thiabout.html (Web site of New York Civil Liberties Union's peer education project on reproductive rights).
109. Carolyn Bower, "Kirkwood Trio Garners National Attention," *St. Louis Post-Dispatch*, Mar. 15, 1999, p. A1; Dick Wehn, "Committee to Review Sex Education Options," *Antrim County* (MI) *News*, Mar. 10, 1999, p. 1A.
110. *Snapshots from the Front Line: Lessons About Teen Pregnancy Prevention from States and Communities* (Washington, DC: Nat'l Campaign to Prevent Teen Pregnancy, 1997), p. 8. Sex educators are also developing curricula sensitive to cultural differences: a 1998 issue of the *SIECUS Report* devoted to "Multicultural Approaches to Sexuality Education" described a "Rites of Passage" program for high-risk African-American teenagers that reflected African traditions of "assisting adolescents in the transition or passage from childhood to adulthood." This meant integrating African history and culture, spirituality, self-esteem, and leadership skills with sexual information. The *Cambios* project in California similarly designed a program for Spanish-speaking teens that did more than simply translate an English-language curriculum. Bilingual facilitators in Los Angeles "helped to uncover concepts, topics, and issues" in standard sex ed "that did not translate in terms of language and cultural appropriateness." Theresa Okwumabua & Jebose Okwumabua, " 'Let the Circle Be Unbroken' Helps African-Americans Prevent Teen Pregnancy," 26(3) *SIECUS Report* 12–17 (1998); Angel Luis Martinez, "*Cambios*: A Spanish-Language Approach to Youth Development," 27(5) *SIECUS Report* 9–10 (1999); see also Irvine, *supra* n. 105.
111. Asociación Dominicana Pro-Bienestar de la Familia, Inc., *Manual de Educación Sexual* (Santo Domingo: Profamilia, 1984), pp. 15–18, 22–24.
112. Elssy Bonilla Castro & Katherine Daraby, *Sex Education in the Dominican Republic: Analysis of a National Program* (Chestnut Hill, MA: Pathfinder Fund, 1986). Profamilia's curriculum was attacked in February 2000 by the archbishop of Santo Domingo; see IPPF Country Profile, *Dominican Republic*, Feb. 24, 2000, http://www.ippf.org/regions/countries/dom/index.htm; Luis Cárdenas, "Profamilia califica de intolerancia los insultos de Cardenal López," *El Siglo*, Feb. 24, 2000, http://www.elsiglord.com/nacionales/2/4.htm.
113. William Fisher & Azy Barak, "Sex Education as a Corrective: Immunizing Against Possible Effects of Pornography," in *Pornography: Research Advances and Policy Considerations* (Dolf Zillmann & Jennings Bryant, eds.) (Hillsdale, NJ: Lawrence Erlbaum, 1989), pp. 289–362.
114. Author's interview with Debra Haffner, Nov. 16, 1999.
115. Ruth Gledhill & Edward Walsh, "Angels Are Out but Onan Is In, Says Vatican," *The Times* (UK), Mar. 19, 1999, p. 5.

7. INDECENCY LAW ON TRIAL: *RENO V. ACLU*

1. Telecommunications Act of 1996, §502, PL 104–104, 110 Stat. 56, codified at 47 U.S.C. §§223(a) and 223(d) (emphasis added).
2. Robert Corn-Revere, "New Age Comstockery," 4 *CommLaw Conspectus* 173, 174 (1996), citing "Comm Daily Notebook," *Comm. Daily*, Mar. 15, 1996, and "Issue of Internet Indecency Tied Up Telco Bills," *Cong. Daily AM*, Dec. 11, 1995; see also the description of the CDA's legislative history in *Reno v. ACLU*, 521 U.S. 844, 858 n. 24 (1997); House Conf. Rep. No. 104-458, 104th Cong., 2d Sess. (1996), pp. 188–89 (defending choice of the *Pacifica* indecency test and insisting that "patent offensiveness" depends on "context" and would not therefore include most material with "serious redeeming value").
3. Codified at 47 U.S.C. §223(e).
4. The other plaintiffs were the Journalism Education Association; National Writers Union; AIDS Education Global Information System; Queer Resources Directory; Electronic Privacy Information Center (EPIC); Electronic Frontier Foundation (EFF); Computer Professionals for Social Responsibility; Clarinet Communications Corp. (an electronic newspaper); Institute for Global Communications (a nonprofit online service provider); Stop Prisoner Rape; Bibliobytes (a producer of electronic books); Declan McCullagh (then a campus activist operating an online free-expression information center); Brock Meeks (editor of the online political newsletter *Cyberwire Dispatch*); and Jonathan Wallace (Internet scholar and publisher of the online magazine *The Ethical Spectacle*).
5. Marty Rimm, "Marketing Pornography on the Information Superhighway: A Survey of 917,410 Images, Descriptions, Short Stories, and Animations Downloaded 8.5 Million Times by Consumers in Over 2000 Cities in Forty Countries, Provinces, and Territories," 83 *Georgetown L. J.* 1849 (1995); Philip Elmer-Dewitt & Hannah Bloch, "On a Screen Near You: Cyberporn," *Time*, July 3, 1995, pp. 38, 45.
6. Henry Jenkins, "Introduction," in *The Children's Culture Reader* (New York: NYU Press, 1998), p. 9, quoting Elmer-Dewitt, *supra* n. 5; Letter to the Editor, *Time*, July 24, 1995.
7. 141 Cong. Rec. S8332-34 (daily ed., June 14, 1995) (remarks of Sen. Coats); 141 Cong. Rec. S8088 (daily ed., June 9, 1995) (remarks of Sen. Exon).
8. This account of the *ACLU v. Reno* litigation is based largely on the author's participation as a member of the legal team. Attorneys David Sobel from EPIC and Michael Godwin of EFF worked with the ACLU on the case.
9. *Fabulous Associates v. Pennsylvania Pub. Utility Comm'n*, 896 F.2d 780, 788 (3d Cir. 1990) (quoting *Sable Communications v. FCC*, 492 U.S. 115, 130–31 [1989]).
10. *Id.*
11. Affidavit of Sister Mary Elizabeth in *ACLU v. Reno*, Civ. No. 96-963 (Feb. 5, 1996).

12. Memorandum Opinion and Order, *ACLU v. Reno*, Civ. No. 96-963 (Feb. 15, 1996).
13. The other plaintiffs were the American Booksellers Association; American Booksellers Foundation for Free Expression; American Society of Newspaper Editors; Apple Computer; Association of American Publishers; Association of Publishers, Editors, and Writers; Commercial Internet Exchange Association; Families Against Internet Censorship; Freedom to Read Foundation (the charitable arm of the American Library Association); Health Sciences Libraries Consortium; Interactive Digital Software Association; Interactive Services Association; Magazine Publishers of America; Microsoft Network; National Press Photographers Association; Netcom Online Communications Service; Newspaper Association of America; Opnet; Prodigy; Society of Professional Journalists; and Wired Ventures, Inc.
14. A third legal challenge to the CDA was filed in New York on behalf of Joe Shea, the editor of an online journal, *The American Reporter*; see *Shea v. Reno*, 930 F. Supp. 916 (S.D.N.Y. 1996) (also invalidating the CDA).
15. See Frank Fisher, "The Ratings Game," *Index on Censorship* (1998), pp. 188, 191–92 (Cyber Patrol "blocks feminist and atheist discussion groups, HIV resource pages, the Animal Rights Resource Site, and criticism of itself and other major players—the popular site 'Why America Online Sucks' is a taboo location for many of these filters"; CYBERsitter blocked Jonathan Wallace's article "Purchase of Blocking Software by Public Libraries Is Unconstitutional"); for more on the shortcomings of filters, see ch. 8.
16. Parties' Stipulation in Preparation for Preliminary Injunction Hearing, *ACLU v. Reno*; *American Library Ass'n v. Reno*, Civ. Nos. 96-963, 96-1458 (Mar. 20, 1996), ¶53. PICS technology was developed by scientists at MIT for the World Wide Web Consortium.
17. Declaration of Kiyoshi Kuromiya (Mar. 8, 1996).
18. Declaration of Patricia Nell Warren (Mar. 16, 1996); Affidavit of Christine Soto (Mar. 7, 1996); Affidavit of Hunter Allen (Mar. 7, 1996).
19. Declaration of Barry Steinhardt (Mar. 27, 1996). Steinhardt, the ACLU's associate director, said that neither screening minors nor creating two separate sites, one for adults and the other sanitized for youth, was financially feasible or consistent with the ACLU's principles. Credit card verification costs were about $1.50 per transaction; bank processing costs even greater. Age verification involved delays ranging from hours to days.
20. Declaration of Robert Croneberger (Mar. 19, 1996). The declaration explained that Carnegie is a public library system encompassing a main building, eighteen branches, one library for the blind and disabled, and several bookmobiles.
21. *ACLU v. Reno*, 929 F. Supp. 824, 857 (E.D.Pa. 1996) (Sloviter, J.), aff'd, 521 U.S. 844 (1997).
22. *Id.* at 883 (Dalzell, J.).
23. Transcript, *ACLU v. Reno*, Apr. 12, 1996, pp. 137–40.

24. Transcript, Apr. 15, 1996, pp. 53–54. Olsen argued that for an online publisher—a large museum, perhaps—the task of tagging each image as it is placed on a Web site would not be onerous. For sites already in existence, he acknowledged that tagging could be time-consuming; to comply with the CDA, however, publishers could either label their entire sites "–L18" until they had time separately to evaluate each page; or, as Chris Hansen put it in his cross-examination of Olsen, to shut the entire site down "for a month or two." Olsen thought labeling the whole site (and thereby rendering it inaccessible to minors) would be "a little less Draconian." Transcript, Apr. 12, 1996, pp. 241–42.
25. Transcript, Apr. 12, 1996, pp. 140–41; author's notes of oral argument, May 10, 1996. Schmidt thought erotic Indian sculptures might be safe as "an educational" or "a cultural thing."
26. Transcript, Mar. 22, 1996, pp. 204–6.
27. *American Booksellers Ass'n v. Hudnut*, 771 F.2d 323, 326, 330 (7th Cir. 1985), aff'd mem., 475 U.S. 1001 (1986).
28. Transcript, Mar. 22, 1996, pp. 221–23.
29. *ACLU v. Reno*, 929 F. Supp. at 844–49. The court's fact-findings acknowledged that "sexually explicit material" exists on the Internet, although there is "no evidence" of its being "the primary type of content on this new medium." It found that almost all sexually explicit online images "are preceded by warnings"; even the government's expert, Agent Howard Schmidt, "testified that the 'odds are slim' that a user would come across a sexually explicit site by accident." *Id.*
30. *Id.* at 852–53, 856 (Sloviter, J.).
31. *Id.* at 859–64 (Buckwalter, J.).
32. *Id.* at 883, 871–72, 882 (Dalzell, J.) (quoting *Simon & Schuster v. New York State Crime Victims Board*, 502 U.S. 105, 116 [1991], and *Turner Broadcasting Sys. v. FCC*, 114 S. Ct. 2445, 2458 [1994]).
33. *Denver Area Educational Telecommunications Consortium v. FCC*, 518 U.S. 727, 732 (1996) (plurality opinion of Breyer, J., joined by O'Connor, Stevens, and Souter); *id.* at 805, 806 (Kennedy & Ginsburg, JJ., dissenting in part) (quoting *Cohen v. California*, 403 U.S. 15, 26 [1971]). Justices Thomas, Rehnquist, and Scalia would have upheld all sections of the law; see ch. 5 for the early stages of the *Denver* case.
34. *Id.* at 759.
35. Linda Greenhouse, "Statute on Internet Indecency Draws High Court's Review," *New York Times*, Dec. 7, 1996, pp. 1, 10.
36. Brief *Amici Curiae* of Enough is Enough *et al.* in *Reno v. ACLU*, No. 96-511 (Jan. 21, 1997), pp. 11–13, quoting Gary Brooks, *The Centerfold Syndrome* (San Francisco: Jossey-Bass, 1995), and Victor Cline, *Pornography's Effects on Adults and Children* (New York: Morality in Media, 1994). The others joining this brief were the National Congress of Black Women; National Council of Catholic Women; Victims' Assistance Legal Organization; Childhelp USA; Legal Pad Enterprises; Focus on the Family; National Coalition for the Pro-

tection of Children and Families; Citizens for Family Friendly Libraries–Georgia; Computer Power Corporation; D/Tex Investigative Consulting; Family Friendly Libraries; Help Us Regain the Children (HURT); Jurinet, Inc.; Kidz Online; Laura Lederer, JD; Log-on Data Corporation; Mothers Against Sexual Abuse; National Association of Evangelicals; One Voice/American Coalition for Abuse Awareness; Oklahomans for Children and Families; Religious Alliance Against Pornography (RAAP); Leonard J. Weitzman, Ph.D.; and Wheelgroup Corp.

37. Author's telephone interview with Dr. Michael Carrera, director of the National Adolescent Sexuality Training Center, Jan. 31, 1997.
38. Enough is Enough brief, p. 10.
39. Brief for the Appellants, *Reno v. ACLU*, No. 96-511 (Jan. 1997), p. 34.
40. The signers of the artists' brief were Robert Altman, Laurie Anderson, Jon Robin Baitz, Eric Bogosian, Robert Beaser, John Corigliano, David Del Tredici, Karen Finley, Timothy Greenfield-Sanders, Emily Hartzell, Jenny Holzer, Tony Kushner, Craig Lucas, Philip Pearlstein, Lou Reed, Cindy Sherman, Kevin Smith, Nina Sobell, Ann Sperry, and Oliver Stone, in addition to Volunteer Lawyers for the Arts and other arts groups.
41. Donna Rice Hughes, "Don't Cry 'Censorship,'" *USA Today*, Mar. 19, 1997, p. 10A.
42. *Reno v. ACLU*, 521 U.S. at 870 (quoting *ACLU v. Reno*, 929 F. Supp. at 842).
43. *Id.* at 877.
44. *Id.* at 878.
45. *Id.*
46. *Id.* at 879.
47. Indeed, Stevens noted without elaboration: "we have repeatedly recognized the governmental interest in protecting children from harmful materials," and (inaccurately) that the plaintiffs "do not dispute that the Government generally has a compelling interest in protecting minors from 'indecent' and 'patently offensive' speech." *Id.* at 875, 863 n. 30.
48. *Id.* at 896 (O'Connor and Rehnquist, JJ., concurring in part and dissenting in part). O'Connor and Rehnquist would have upheld the provisions of the CDA criminalizing the transmission of an "indecent message to a person the sender knows is under 18" and the sending of a "patently offensive" one to a minor. Although some applications of these provisions—particularly messages in newsgroups and chat rooms—would interfere with adults' First Amendment rights, O'Connor and Rehnquist would have narrowed these sections of the law to ban only communications where the speaker "knows that all of the recipients are minors."

8. FILTERING FEVER

1. Press release, "SurfWatch Plays Crucial Role in Overturning Communications Decency Act," June 26, 1997; http://www.surfwatch.com.
2. Center for Democracy & Technology, "Internet Family Empowerment White

Paper: How Filtering Tools Enable Reponsible Parents to Protect Their Children Online" (July 16, 1997). The White Paper was prepared with the help of America Online, AT&T, IBM, Microsoft, and other companies or industry groups with a commercial interest in blocking software.

3. *Resolution on the Use of Filtering Software in Libraries*, ALA Council, July 2, 1997, reprinted in ALA *Newsletter on Intellectual Freedom* (Sept. 1997), p. 119; ALA Intellectual Freedom Comm., *Statement on Library Use of Filtering Software, id.*, pp. 119–20; Remarks of Harriet Silverstone, ALA *Newsletter, id.*, pp. 154–55.
4. "Boston Public Library Censors Kids' Net," *Berkshire Eagle*, Mar. 29, 1997, p. A5; Amy Argetsinger, "Libraries Urged to Nip Internet in the Buff," *Washington Post*, Apr. 21, 1997, p. B1; Maria Seminerio, "Boston Schools Deploy Net Filters," *ZDNN Tech News*, Mar. 22, 1999, http://www.zdnet.com/zdnn/stories/news/0.4586,2229381,00.html. A similar controversy erupted in Austin, Texas, where the compromise solution was to allow four unrestricted, adults-only computers, which minors could not use even with parental permission. See Catherine Ross, "An Emerging Right for Mature Minors to Receive Information," 2 *U.Pa. J. Con. Law* 223, 235 (1999).
5. See Child Advocacy Working Group, *Child Online Safety* (prepared for the Internet Online Summit, Dec. 1–3, 1997), http://www.att.com/projects/tech 4kids, p. 5.
6. Michael Krantz & Declan McCullagh, "Censor's Sensibility," *Time*, Aug. 11, 1997, p. 48; see also Andrew Shapiro, "The Dangers of Private Cybercops," *New York Times*, Dec. 4, 1997, p. A31; Gay & Lesbian Alliance Against Defamation (GLAAD), *Access Denied: The Impact of Internet Filtering Software on the Lesbian & Gay Community* (Dec. 1997); "An Internet Filter Is Eager to Zap the Starr Report," *New York Times*, Sept. 17, 1998, p. G3 (reporting CYBERsitter's announcement that its software would keep youngsters from reading the salacious details of Independent Counsel Ken Starr's report to Congress on the Clinton-Lewinsky affair).
7. See Jonathan Wallace, "The X-Stop Files: Self-Proclaimed Library-Friendly Product Blocks Quaker, Free Speech and Gay Sites," Oct. 1997, http://www.spectacle.org.
8. Gordon Ross, "Censorship and the Internet," Nov. 19, 1997, "fight censorship" e-mail list, Nov. 22, 1997. Ross was the head of Net Nanny. By mid-2000, the number of Web pages was estimated to be more than one billion. Lisa Guernsey, "The Search Engine as Cyborg," *New York Times*, June 29, 2000, p. El.
9. See Shawn Zeller, "A Shaky Deal on Internet Smut," *National Journal*, Nov. 22, 1997, p. 2383; *Fahrenheit 451.2: Is Cyberspace Burning?—How Rating and Blocking Proposals May Torch Free Speech on the Internet* (New York: ACLU, 1997), p. 2, reprinted in *Filters and Freedom: Free Speech Perspectives on Internet Content Controls* (David Sobel, ed.) (Washington, DC: EPIC, 1999).
10. Netparents.org, "Businesses, Public and Private Groups Unite Behind Initia-

tive for Family-Friendly Internet Online World," July 16, 1997, http://www.netparents.org.

11. Jeremy Redmon, "Cyberporn at Libraries Has Smut Foes Furious," *Washington Times*, Oct. 30, 1997, p. C4; 11(4) *Philanthropy* 4 (1997), describing Enough is Enough program in the context of a $160,000 grant from Fieldstead & Co. Family Friendly Libraries was the creation of a Christian-right activist, Karen Jo Gounaud, whose stated goals were to persuade libraries to filter the Internet, to stop promoting "homosexual ideology," and to replace the ALA's *Library Bill of Rights* with a "traditional family"-oriented acquisition policy. This meant, according to Gounaud, more shelf space for material promoting "reparative therapy, ex-gay ministries, or the success stories of the thousands who have made that healing transition." Author's telephone interview with Karen Jo Gounaud, May 17, 2000; FFL Web site at http://fflibraries/org. Another group, Filtering Facts, published *Dangerous Access*, a collection of stories about youngsters (and adults) accessing pornography on library computers. See http://wwww.filteringfacts.org.
12. Declan McCullagh, "Why the Censorware Summit Is a Bad Idea," "fight censorship" e-mail list, Oct. 30, 1997 (commenting: "What's wrong with this idea? Last I checked, the New York Times would never back a 'self-labeling' or 'self-censorship' scheme to stave off a federal censorship law. They'd have the balls to stand up and fight. When faced with presidential pressure to adopt an RSACi-type self-labeling system, the Net should do the same"); Declan McCullagh, "CyberPatrol Blocks Yahoo," "fight censorship" e-mail list, Nov. 16, 1997.
13. Marc Rotenberg, "EPIC Letter to CNET and the Internet Community on Self-Labeling," "fight censorship" e-mail list, July 26, 1997.
14. *Fahrenheit 451.2*, *supra* n. 9, p. 2.
15. *Id.*, pp. 9–12 (noting also that minors have the right to access even "offensive" information—a view that "was considered controversial, even among our allies").
16. Lawrence Lessig, "What Things Regulate Speech: CDA 2.0 vs. Filtering," 38 *Jurimetrics* 629, 632 (1998).
17. Carl Kaplan, "Is a Better CDA Preferable to Opaque Censorship?" *New York Times Online*, Oct. 30, 1997, http://www.nytimes.com (quoting Lessig in part); see also Irene Graham, "Will PICS Torch Free Speech on the Internet?" in *Filters & Freedom*, *supra* n. 9, p. 22.
18. Quotations are from press releases and brochures distributed at the Internet Online Summit, December 1–3, 1997, Renaissance Hotel, Washington, DC. Other companies advertising their wares included EdView, which offered a whitelist of "thousands of sites that have been reviewed and confirmed as being 'secure and smart' "; Microsoft, which touted the PICS-compatible RSACi system; and America Online, which described its "AOL Neighborhood Watch" as allowing separate restricted-access settings for "kids only," "young teens," and "mature teens."

19. Press releases distributed by Net Shepherd at Internet Online Summit, Dec. 1–3, 1997.
20. *Faulty Filters: How Content Filters Block Access to Kid-Friendly Information on the Internet* (Washington, DC: EPIC, 1997), http://www.epic.org, reprinted in *Filters and Freedom*, p. 53.
21. "Net Shepherd Responds to the EPIC Report 'Faulty Filters,' " http://www.netshepherd.com/fsEpicResponse.htm, Dec. 2, 1997; Amy Harmon, "Ideological Foes Meet on Web Decency," *New York Times*, Dec. 1, 1997, p. D1 (quoting Dan Sandford, Net Shepherd's chief executive). The press conference was the first event sponsored by a new coalition called IFEA (Internet Free Expression Alliance), which included, among others, the ACLU, the American Society of Newspaper Editors, PEN, the Society of Professional Journalists, and EPIC. See IFEA *Mission Statement*, http://www.epic.org; Press Release on Internet Ratings and Filters, *Cyber-Liberties*, Nov. 25, 1997, http://www.aclu.org. Filtering companies did attempt to improve their accuracy by using "text strings" in place of single keywords, and sophisticated techniques for identifying nude images on the basis of flesh tones and curves. But the errors did not abate; see, e.g., Dick Kelsey, "Porn-Detection Software Scans Photos," *Computer*, June 1, 2000, http://www.currents.net/news/00/06/01/news2.html (describing Heartsoft, Inc.'s image-scanning software); Declan McCullagh, "Smart Filter Blocks All But Smut," *Wired News*, June 25, 2000, http://www.wired.com/news/technology/0,1282,36923,00.html (describing Exotrope, Inc.'s software, which "incorrectly blocked dozens of photographs including portraits, landscapes, animals, and street scenes"). Filters also sometimes openly discriminated: the same "fulminations against gays and lesbians" that went unfiltered by Cyber Patrol, SurfWatch, and other popular products when found on the conservative Web sites of Focus on the Family and Concerned Women for America were blocked when "duplicated and placed on personal Web pages." Declan McCullagh, "Filters Kowtowing to Hate?" *Wired News*, May 27, 2000, http://www.wired.com/news/print/0,1294,36621,00.html.
22. *Remarks by Vice President Al Gore at the Internet/Online Summit*, Dec. 2, 1997, "fight censorship" e-mail list, Dec. 4, 1997; author's notes.
23. Author's notes (Hughes quote); Aaron Pressman, "Voluntary Internet Measures Endorsed to Protect Kids," Reuters, Dec. 1, 1997, "fight censorship" e-mail list, Dec. 2, 1997.
24. Harmon, *supra* n. 21, p. D6.
25. *American Library Ass'n v. Pataki*, 969 F. Supp. 160 (S.D.N.Y. 1997).
26. *ACLU v. Johnson*, 4 F. Supp.2d 1029 (D.N.M. 1998), aff'd, 194 F.3d 1149 (10th Cir. 1999); *ACLU v. Miller*, 977 F. Supp. 1228 (N.D. Ga. 1997); *Cyberspace Comm'ns v. Engler*, 55 F. Supp. 2d 737 (D. Mich. 1999), aff'd without opinion (6th Cir. 2000); *PSINET, Inc. v. Chapman*, 108 F. Supp. 2d 611 (E.D. Va. 2000) (granting preliminary injunction).
27. Complaint in *Mainstream Loudoun v. Board of Trustees of Loudoun County Library*, No. 97-2049-A (E.D.Va. Dec. 22, 1997). The board called it a "Sexual

Harassment Policy," though it did not address acts of harassment or non-computer-based sexual material.

28. See *Mainstream Loudoun*, 24 F. Supp. 2d 553 (E.D. Va. 1998); Complaint in *Mainstream Loudoun*, ¶¶105, 119; Plaintiff-Intervenors' Complaint (Feb. 5, 1998); Jon Echtenkamp, "Library Picks Software," *Loudoun Times-Mirror*, Nov. 19, 1997, p. A1; Wallace, *supra* n. 7.
29. Complaint in *Mainstream Loudoun*, ¶¶120–24.
30. The other intervenor-plaintiffs were Banned Books On-line; *Ethical Spectacle* online magazine; Books for Gay and Lesbian Teens/Youth Page; artist Sergio Arau; and *San Francisco Examiner* columnist Rob Morse.
31. Brief in Support of Motion to Intervene, *Mainstream Loudoun*, Feb. 5, 1998, p. 13; Plaintiffs' Opposition to Defendants' Motion to Dismiss, p. 16. The Supreme Court's school library case was *Board of Ed. v. Pico*, 457 U.S. 853 (1982); see ch. 3.
32. *Mainstream Loudoun v. Board of Trustees*, 2 F. Supp. 2d 783, 794–95 (E.D.Va. 1998); 24 F. Supp. 2d at 561–57.
33. By the end of 1999, the profiltering group Filtering Facts reported that nearly 1,000 public library systems in the U.S. were using filters on all of their computer terminals. Associated Press, "Libraries Struggle with Pressure to Filter Internet," *Freedom Forum Online* (Dec. 10, 1999), http://www.freedomforum.org/speech/1999/12/10filters.asp. The next year, filtering became a ballot issue in southwestern Michigan, as the American Family Association invested $35,000 in a campaign in the small city of Holland to require library filters. Voters rejected the proposal 55% to 45%, after which the neighboring municipality of Hudsonville rescinded a filtering ordinance its city commissioners had passed the previous December. Keith Bradsher, "Town Rejects Bid to Curb Library's Internet Access," *New York Times*, Feb. 24, 2000, p. A12; Dave Yonkman, "Hudsonville Library Users Have Web Access Restored," *Holland Sentinel*, Feb. 24, 2000, http://www.thehollandsentinel.net/stories/022400/new_hudsonville.html.
34. Katie Hafner, "Library Grapples with Internet Freedom," *New York Times*, Oct. 15, 1998, pp. G1, G8; Wendy Leibowitz, "Shield Judges from Sex?" *National Law Journal*, May 18, 1998, p. A7; American Family Association Action Alert, "Cyber Patrol Filtering Software Blocks AFA Website," May 28, 1998, http://www.afa.net; see also *Censorship in a Box: Why Blocking Software Is Wrong for Public Libraries* (New York: ACLU, June 1998), p. 4, reprinted in *Filters and Freedom, supra* n. 9, p. 121; Courtney Macavinta, "Report Attacks SmartFilter's Blocking Criteria," *CNET News.com*, Mar. 23, 1999, http://www.news.com/News/Item/0,4,34154,00.html; The Censorware Project, *Censored Internet Access in Utah Public Schools and Libraries*, Mar. 1999, reprinted in *Filters and Freedom*, p. 67 (reporting also that SmartFilter censored music lyrics with terms such as "tap" and "surveillance," a scholarly paper about Nazi Germany, a court decision in a drug case, the Iowa State Division of Narcotics Enforcement, and a government brochure, *Marijuana:*

Facts for Teens). The Peacefire Web site eventually published reports on massive overblocking by most filters, e.g., http://www.peacefire.org/censorware/FamilyClick/familyclick-blocked.html (report on AIDS blocked, along with advice for victims of pulmonary disease). The ZapMe Company's computers, provided free to schools, limited students to sites chosen by ZapMe and forced them "to view everything through the ZapMe 'Netspace,' a bordered frame containing a constantly rotating series of ads" for Frito-Lay and Topps bubble gum, among other sponsors. Steven Manning, "Reading, Writing and Candy Ads," *Salon.com*, Aug. 15, 2000, http://www.salon.com/tech/feature/2000/08/15/zapme/index.html.

35. *Statement of American Library Ass'n to U.S. Senate Commerce, Science & Transportation Comm. on Indecency on the Internet*, Feb. 10, 1998, reprinted in *Newsletter on Intellectual Freedom* (May 1998), p. 94; see also "Filtering the Internet," *New York Times*, Mar. 16, 1998, p. A24, noting distinction between parents' choice to install software and government's mandating its use.
36. White House Press Release, Statement of the Vice President on Protecting Our Children from Inappropriate Material on the Internet, Mar. 23, 1998.
37. "Children's Internet Protection Act," Title XVII of the Labor, HHS, and Education Appropriations Act, PL 106–554, 114 Stat. 2763, 106th Cong., 2d Sess. (2000); see "Federal Filtering Mandate Moves Toward Enactment," *EPIC News* Vol. 719 (Oct. 31, 2000); "A Misguided Pornography Bill," *New York Times*, Week in Review, Nov. 12, 2000, p. 14 (editorial on inadvisability of mandated filtering and host of educational sites blocked by filters). In 1999, three states (Arizona, South Dakota, and Michigan) passed laws requiring public libraries to install filters or otherwise develop policies restricting minors' computer access.
38. David Hudson, "Company to Filter Internet Access for All Tennessee Public Schools," *Freedom Forum Online*, Nov. 11; 1998, http://www.freedomforum.org/speech/1998/11/11ena.asp.
39. Anemona Hartocollis, "Board Blocks Student Access to Web Sites," *New York Times*, Nov. 10, 1999, pp. B1, B8. A Commerce Department report earlier in 1999 obliquely made the same point: lower-income youths (who are disproportionately minorities) depend more heavily on public Internet access at community centers, schools, and libraries. National Telecomm'ns & Information Admin., *Falling Through the Net: Defining the Digital Divide* (Washington, DC: U.S. Dep't of Commerce, July 1999).
40. The other plaintiffs were the ACLU; American Booksellers Foundation for Free Expression; Blackstripe (an online forum for gay and lesbian African Americans); Electronic Frontier Foundation; Electronic Privacy Information Center; Free Speech Media (an online host for independent audio and video); Internet Content Coalition (an association of content providers including *The New York Times* and *Time, Inc.*); Philadelphia Gay News; Planetout Corporation (a Web site for "gay, lesbian, bisexual and transgendered persons"); Salon Internet, Inc. (publisher of the popular online magazine); and West Stock,

Inc. (a Web site for the display and sale of stock photographs). All said they engaged in commercial activity, thus subjecting them to COPA.

41. *ACLU v. Reno ("Reno II")*, 31 F. Supp. 2d 473, 498 (E.D.Pa. 1999), aff'd, 217 F.3d 162 (3d Cir. 2000).
42. Brief for the Appellant, *ACLU v. Reno*, No. 99-1324 (3d Cir. July 26, 1999); Reply Brief for the Appellant (Sept. 13, 1999), p. 24.
43. *Reno II*, 217 F.3d. at 173–77. COPA also mandated the creation of a commission to study technological solutions to the problem of online sexual content. Among the witnesses at the commission's hearings in 2000 were antipornography advocates and filtering manufacturers touting their wares, but also EPIC attorney David Sobel, who testified that because the definition of "harmful to minors" is so vague, any discussion of blocking "treads on thin constitutional ice." David McGuire, "Online Porn Panel Wrestles with Age Verification," *Computer*, June 11, 2000, http://www.currents.net/news/00/06/10/news5.html; see also http://www.copacommission.org. As this book went to press, the Supreme Court had not yet ruled on COPA.
44. *Playboy Entertainment Group v. U.S.*, 945 F. Supp. 772, 779 (D. Del. 1996), aff'd mem., 520 U.S. 1141 (1997).
45. See *Playboy Entertainment Group v. U.S.*, 30 F. Supp. 2d 702, 706 (D.Del. 1998), aff'd, 120 S.Ct. 1878 (2000); Telecommunications Act of 1996, §505, PL 104–104, 110 Stat. 56, 136 (1996), codified at 47 U.S.C. §641.
46. Declaration of Diana Elliott in *Playboy*, Civ. No. 96-94/96-107 (D. Del.), May 13, 1996, ¶12.
47. *Playboy*, 945 F. Supp. at 786 n. 25.
48. *Id.*, quoting *Final Report*, Attorney General's Commission on Pornography (Washington, DC: U.S. Dep't of Justice, July 1986), pp. 343–44.
49. Transcript, *Playboy Entertainment Group v. U.S.*, Mar. 5, 1998, pp. 361, 365–67, 397.
50. *Playboy*, 30 F. Supp.2d at 710. Green said his views had evolved since this early, Freudian-influenced work; recent studies of adults who as children had witnessed the "primal scene" indicated no dire effects. Transcript, pp. 418–20.
51. *Playboy*, 30 F. Supp.2d at 716, 711 (criticizing also the government's reliance on the "weakly proven inference" that "the effects of viewing signal bleed of sexually explicit television are the same as viewing sexually explicit television outright").
52. Nicholas Becker, Playboy First Amendment Award Ceremony, New York City, Nov. 15, 1999. Becker won for his conscientious objection to a high school graduation prayer.
53. Exhibit 22, *Playboy Entertainment Group v. U.S.*
54. Stephen Jay Gould, *The Mismeasure of Man* (New York: Norton, 1981), pp. 22–23. Similarly, in the 1940s and 1950s, "medical experts cautioned against thwarting what a group of male doctors told *Life* magazine was a healthy woman's 'primitive biological urge toward reproduction, homemaking and nurturing.' . . . 'To urge upon her a profession in the man's world can ad-

versely affect a girl,' wrote a Yale psychologist, advising against the admission of women to the college." Miriam Horn, *Rebels in White Gloves: Coming of Age with Hillary's Class—Wellesley '69* (New York: Random House, 1999), pp. 7–8; see also Anne Fausto-Sterling, *Myths of Gender: Biological Theories About Women and Men* (2d ed.) (New York: Basic Books, 1988), pp. 207–8 ("there is no such thing as apolitical science. Science is a human activity inseparable from the societal atmosphere of its time and place. Scientists, therefore, are influenced—consciously or unconsciously—by the political needs and urgencies of their society").

55. Brief for Appellants in *U.S. v. Playboy Entertainment Group* (S.Ct. No. 98-1682, Aug. 1999), pp. 35 n. 21, 38–40.
56. Brief *Amici Curiae* of Sexuality Scholars, Researchers, Educators, and Therapists in Support of Appellee, *U.S. v. Playboy Entertainment Group* (Sept. 23, 1999). The author wrote this brief with the help of Joan Bertin and Leonore Tiefer of the National Coalition Against Censorship. The sixteen signers were Elizabeth Rice Allgeier, Vern Bullough, Ulrich Clement, Clive Davis, Milton Diamond, Harold Lief, Konstance A. McCaffree, John Money, Charlene Muehlenhard, Ira Reiss, Stephanie Sanders, Pepper Schwartz, Judith Huffman Seifer, Carol Anne Tavris, Leonore Tiefer, and Carole Vance.
57. Brief of the Media Institute as *Amicus Curiae* in Support of Appellee, *U.S. v. Playboy Entertainment Group* (Sept. 24, 1999), pp. 3–4, 19, 26, 28 (quoting *Reno v. ACLU*, 521 U.S. 844, 869 [1997]; *Wisconsin v. Yoder*, 406 U.S. 205, 232–33 [1972]).
58. Author's notes; Linda Greenhouse, "U.S. Seeks to Restore Limits on Cable Sex Programming," *New York Times*, Dec. 1, 1999, p. A19.
59. *U.S. v. Playboy Entertainment Group*, 120 S.Ct. 1878, 1890–93 (2000). Justice Breyer, in dissent, took the majority to task for implying that the government's interest in protecting children from watching "virulent pornography without parental consent—might not be compelling." Justice Scalia, also dissenting, thought that *Ginzberg v. United States*, the dubious thirty-four-year-old "pandering" decision, justified the law, since the Playboy Channel's purpose was obviously to titillate. Justice Stevens responded in a concurring opinion that *Ginzberg* had been "untenable" even when it was rendered. *Id.* at 1901 (Breyer, J., dissenting); 1896 (Scalia, J., dissenting); 1894 (Stevens, J., concurring).
60. Telecommunications Act of 1996, §551, PL 104–104, 110 Stat. 56, codified in part at 47 U.S.C. §§303(w), (x). Regarding the 13-inch requirement, one wag commented: "Presumably, if the image is small enough, it no longer can be indecent." Michael Noll, "Tele-Perspectives," *Telecommunications*, Apr. 1998, p. 27.
61. House Conf. Rep. No. 104–458, reprinted in 1996 *U.S. Code Cong. & Ad. News*, p. 209.
62. Quoted in Danny Leigh, "Obscured Vision," *The Guardian*, June 16, 1999, §G2, p. 17.

63. Letter from Jack Valenti to William Caton, FCC Secretary, Jan. 17, 1997, reprinted in *The V-Chip Debate* (Monroe Price, ed.) (Mahwah, NJ: Lawrence Erlbaum, 1998), p. 264; Public Notice, *Commission Seeks Comment on Industry Proposal for Rating Video Programming*, FCC No. 97-55 (Feb. 7, 1997). The other categories were TV-Y7 ("may include mild physical or comedic violence"); TV-G ("little or no violence, no strong language and little or no sexual dialogue or situations"); TV-PG ("may contain material that some parents would find unsuitable for younger children," including "infrequent coarse language, limited violence, some suggestive sexual dialogue and situations"); and TV-14 ("may contain some material that many parents would find unsuitable for children under 14," including "sophisticated themes, sexual content, strong language and more intense violence").
64. Tom Shales, "TV's Ratings: G Is for Give Them a Chance," *Washington Post*, Mar. 9, 1997, p. G1.
65. David Bianculli, "Does Schindler's List Critic See the Same Film as the Rest of Us?" *Charlotte Observer*, Mar. 5, 1997, p. 14E; *Television Rating System: Hearings Before the Senate Comm. on Commerce, Science and Transp.*, 105th Cong., 1st Sess. (Feb. 27, 1997), p. 31 (statement of Sen. Patrick Leahy disagreeing with Coburn and reminding his colleagues that laws regulating speech "for the protection of children have no limiting principle"); see also "Censorship and 'Schindler's List,' " *Boston Globe*, Mar. 4, 1997, p. A14 (Rep. Coburn's denunciation of the film "illustrated one of the least acknowledged virtues of free speech . . .—the antiseptic effect of allowing people to air the most obtuse ideas in public").
66. Letter petition to Office of the Secretary, FCC, in No. 97-55, date-stamped Mar. 25, 1997; letter to Chairman Reed Hundt from Patricia Morris, with cc to Morality in Media, date-stamped Mar. 4, 1997. There were many such letters with identical text.
67. Comments of the American Psychological Ass'n, FCC No. 97-55, Apr. 8, 1997.
68. *Hearings, supra* n. 65, p. 326 (written testimony of Prof. Burt Neuborne).
69. Letter Submission of Jack Valenti, President and CEO of the MPAA, Decker Anstrom, President and CEO of the NCTA, and Eddie Fritts, President and CEO of the NAB, to William Caton, FCC Secretary, Aug. 1, 1997, revised Sept. 10, 1997, reprinted in *The V-Chip Debate, supra* n. 63, p. 275. A separate category was added for "fantasy violence" (FV). The other groups participating in the negotiations were the American Medical Association, American Academy of Pediatrics, Center for Media Education, Children's Defense Fund, Children Now, National Association of Elementary School Principals, National Education Association, and National PTA.
70. Letter from Sen. John McCain, Chairman, Sen. Comm. on Commerce, Science, & Transportation, to Robert Wright, President and CEO, NBC, Sept. 29, 1997; Lawrie Mifflin, "Media," *New York Times*, Oct. 6, 1997, p. D11. In July 1999, the FCC reported that all of the top 40 basic cable networks were

encoding or planning to encode, except BET, QVC, and the Home Shopping Network. Thirteen channels, including CNN, ESPN, and Court TV, were "exempt as news or sports programmers." News release, "FCC's V-Chip Survey: Top TV and Cable Networks Encoding TV Ratings Information; Programming Like 'South Park' and 'Jerry Springer' Lagging Behind," July 20, 1999, http://www.fcc.gov/Bureaus/Miscellaneous/News_Releases/1999nrmc9052.html.

71. Press Release from Sen. Byron Dorgan, "Report on Television Violence Shows Fox Network Has the Most Violence Programming," Dec. 16, 1993, and attached report, *Television Violence Demonstration Project Conducted at Concordia College, Moorhead, Minnesota, Sept.–Dec. 1993.*
72. *The UCLA Television Violence Report 1996* found MPAA ratings to be the most potent of eight systems tested in terms of their power to attract children to "restricted" films; in *The V-Chip Debate*, p. 301.
73. See Marjorie Heins, *Sex, Sin and Blasphemy: A Guide to America's Censorship Wars* (New York: The New Press, 1999), pp. 58–59 (describing Malle's cutting, over protest, of *Damage*); Stephen Farber, *The Movie Rating Game* (Washington, DC: Public Affairs Press, 1972), p. 71 (describing cut of line about pubic hair from *The Reivers* to obtain a GP rating); "People," *Int'l Herald Tribune*, Jan. 4, 2000 (reporting cuts in Julie Taymor's *Titus* [based on the Shakespeare tragedy] to achieve R rating); Leonard Leff & Jerold Simmons, *The Dame in the Kimono* (New York: Doubleday, 1990); *Miramax Films Corp. v. Motion Picture Ass'n*, 560 N.Y.S. 730, 734 (Sup.Ct., NY Cty. 1990) (rejecting a legal challenge to MPAA ratings but noting that "films are produced and *negotiated* to fit the ratings. After an initial 'X' rating . . . whole scenes or parts thereof are cut in order to fit within the 'R' category. Contrary to our jurisprudence which protects all forms of expression, the rating system censors serious films by the force of economic pressure.").
74. Catherine Greenman, "The V-Chip Arrives with a Thud," *New York Times*, Nov. 4, 1999, pp. 1, 8. In March 1998, the FCC approved the industry's "voluntary" rating system. News release, "Commission Finds Industry Video Programming Rating System Acceptable," Mar. 12, 1998, http://www.fcc.gov/Bureaus/Cable/News_Releases/1998/nrcb8003.html.
75. Media coverage of the Columbine massacre was intense. This account is drawn from David Von Drehle, "Soul-Searching in School Tragedy Yields Many Warnings but Few Answers," *Int'l Herald Tribune*, Apr. 26, 1999, p. 3; Kevin Merida & Richard Leiby, "Out of the Dark, Into the Mainstream: America's Cult of Violence," *Washington Post*, Apr. 30, 1999, p. 1; "The Guns of Littleton," *The Nation*, May 17, 1999, p. 4; Michael Janofsky, "The Columbine Killers' Tapes of Rage," *New York Times*, Dec. 14, 1999, p. A22. A year after Columbine, families of some of the victims sued school officials, "charging that they knew the two killers' propensity for violence and took no steps to intercede." Michael Janofsky, "Families of Columbine Victims Sue Officials at High School," *New York Times*, July 20, 2000, p. A16.
76. "Children's Protection from Violent Video Programming Act," S. 876, 106th

Cong., 1st Sess. (1999); "Children's Defense Act of 1999," HR. 2036, 106th Cong., 1st Sess. (1999); Lawrie Mifflin, "A Media-Violence Link?" *Int'l Herald Tribune*, May 10, 1999, p. 2; Michael Muller, "Senator Moves Against Violent Games," Apr. 29, 1999, http://www.zdnet.com/zdnn/stories/news/0,4586,2249640,00.html.

77. Henry Jenkins, "Professor Jenkins Goes to Washington" (May 8, 1999), http://www.fiawol.demon.co.uk/FAC; reprinted in *Harper's Magazine*, July 1999, p. 19; reworked as "Lessons from Littleton: What Congress Doesn't Want to Hear About Youth and Media," http://web.mit.edu/cms/news/nais9912/.
78. Jenkins, *supra* n. 77; see also Jonathan Kellerman, *Savage Spawn: Reflections on Violent Children* (New York: Ballantine, 1999), pp. 71, 78 (opining that after every senseless crime, politicians and editorial writers predictably blame the media; "it is the type of facile, glib 'explanation' that is perfectly in sync with today's short-attention-span journalism," and "generates funding for the scores of do-nothing legislative commissions that pass for problem-solving").
79. Jeri Clausing, "Congressional Internet Debate Turns to Issue of Violence," *New York Times on the Web*, May 20, 1999, http://www.nytimes.com/library/te...05/cyber/articles/1congress.html; Frank Rich, "Washington's Post-Littleton Loony Tunes," *New York Times*, June 19, 1999, p. A15; "Violent Juvenile Crime Falls to 10-Year Low," *New York Times*, Nov. 24, 1999, p. A21; Barry Glassner, "School Violence: The Fears, the Facts," *New York Times*, Aug. 13, 1999, p. A21.
80. Jean Bethke Elshtain, "Minors and the First Amendment: A Reply to Marjorie Heins," *Dissent*, Fall 1999, p. 77. Elshtain was responding to the author's article in the previous issue: Marjorie Heins, "Rejuvenating Free Expression: An Argument for Minors' First Amendment Rights," *Dissent*, Summer 1999, p. 43.
81. Bernard Weinraub, "Critics Assault Ratings Board over 'Eyes,'" *New York Times*, July 28, 1999, p. E3. Jack Valenti responded that those critiquing the ratings board were a "'small band of constant whiners' who 'talk to each other, write for each other, opine with each other and view with lacerating contempt the rubes who live Out There, west of Manhattan and east of the San Andreas Fault.'" *Id.*
82. Stephen Holden, "Making a Point with Smut and Laughs," *New York Times*, June 30, 1999, p. E9.

9. CULTURAL DIFFERENCES

1. Barry Bearak, "A Lesbian Idyll, and the Movie Theaters Surrender," *New York Times*, Dec. 24, 1998, p. A4.
2. See Edmund Kellogg & Jan Stepan, "Legal Aspects of Sex Education," 26 *Am. J. Comp. Law* 573, 583–86 (1978).
3. Hari Singh Gour, *The Penal Law of India* (Allahabad: Sardar Patel Marg, 1983), p. 2120, quoting Penal Code, §292.

4. *Kherode Chandra Roy Chowdhury v. Emperor*, Ind. Law Rpts. 39 Calc. 377, 380, 386 (1911).
5. *Sukanta Halder v. State*, 39 A.I.R., Calc. 214, 215–16 (1952).
6. *K. A. Abbas v. Union of India*, 52 A.I.R., C 114, Supr. Ct. 481, 489 (1971).
7. Ian Buruma, *A Japanese Mirror: Heroes and Villains of Japanese Culture* (London: Penguin, 1984), pp. 55, 56.
8. Patrick Smith, *Japan: A Reinterpretation* (New York: Vintage, 1998), pp. 157, 304; see also Kim Hisako Cross, "The Japanese Comic Book: Social Hit or Kiddie Lit?" *Japanophile* (Summer 1999), p. 22; Francine Prose, "Modern Geisha" (review of Gavin Kramer, *Shopping* [New York: Soho Press, 2000]), *New York Times Book Review*, Apr. 23, 2000, p. 26 (describing *manga*, "the telephone-book-size comics," as "the bastard offspring of the classical woodblock print").
9. Milton Diamond & Ayako Uchiyama, "Pornography, Rape and Other Sex Crimes in Japan," 22 *Int'l J. Law & Psychiatry* 1, 5, 7 (1999).
10. E-mail from Milton Diamond to author, Sept. 16, 1998; see also Buruma, *supra* n. 7; Ruth Benedict, *The Chrysanthemum and the Sword* (New York: New American Library, 1946); T. R. Reid, *Confucius Lives Next Door* (New York: Random House, 1999), pp. 88–89.
11. Diamond & Uchiyama, *supra* n. 9, at 11, citing Berl Kutchinsky, "Pornography and Rape: Theory and Practice? Evidence from Crime Data in Four Countries Where Pornography Is Easily Available," 14 *Int'l J. Law & Psychiatry* 47 (1991). Some Japanese scholars believe the correlation is deceptive; they suggest that sexual offenses may be underreported due in part to police insensitivity; e-mail to author from Prof. Satoshi Mishima, Osaka City University Faculty of Law, Jan. 28, 2000. Japan's juvenile crime rates increased in the late 1990s; experts blamed educational pressures and consequent reduction in playtime and family life. Howard French, "Japan's Troubling Trend: Rising Teen-Age Crime," *New York Times*, Oct. 12, 1999, p. A6.
12. Stephanie Strom, "Japanese Family Values: I Choose You, Pikachu!" *New York Times*, Week in Review, Nov. 11, 1999, p. 4.
13. E-mail from Catherine Heins to author, Nov. 1, 1999.
14. Theodore Zeldin, *An Intimate History of Humanity* (London: Reed Int'l Books/Mandarin/Minerva, 1994), p. 101; Margaret Mead, "Children and Ritual in Bali," in *Childhood in Contemporary Cultures* (Margaret Mead & Martha Wolfenstein, eds.) (Chicago: U. of Chicago Press, 1955), p. 42.
15. *Case of Müller and Others*, Series A, No. 133 (Eur. Ct. Human Rights, May 24, 1988), at 9, 22. The European Court was more protective of expression in other cases, *e.g.*, *Open Door Counselling & Dublin Well Woman Centre, Ltd. v. Ireland*, Series A, No. 246, 15 E.H.R.R. 244 (1992) (ruling that Ireland's ban on abortion advice or information violated Article 10); and of bodily integrity for minors, *e.g.*, *A. v. United Kingdom*, 5 Butterworths H.R.C. 137 (1998) (ruling that Britain's allowance of a "reasonable chastisement" defense to a man who severely beat his 9-year-old stepson violated the child's rights under Article

3 of the Convention); *Sutherland v. United Kingdom*, Appeal No. 25186/94 (July 1, 1997) (ruling by the European Commission on Human Rights, an adjunct of the Court, that Britain's higher age of consent for homosexual than heterosexual acts violated the Convention's equality and privacy principles). Compare *Bowers v. Hardwick*, 478 U.S. 186 (1986) (rejection by the U.S. Supreme Court of constitutional challenge to a state's criminalization of homosexual acts).

16. Gary Melton & Susan Limber, "What Children's Rights Mean to Children: Children's Own Views," in *The Ideologies of Children's Rights* (Michael Freeman & Philip Veerman, eds.) (Dordrecht: Martinus Nijhoff, 1992), pp. 173–74; see also Geraldine Van Bueren, *The International Law on the Rights of the Child* (Dordrecht: Martinus Nijhoff, 1995), p. 135. The minors' rights philosophy was a reaction, in part, to a "child saver" approach to children's law that overemphasized protection and paternalism; see, e.g., Michael Freeman, "Introduction: Rights, Ideology, and Children," in *Ideologies, supra*, p. 3; Susan Wolfson, "Children's Rights: The Theoretical Underpinning of the 'Best Interests of the Child,' " in *Ideologies*, p. 8.

17. Cynthia Price Cohen, "The Relevance of Theories of Natural Law and Legal Positivism," in *Ideologies of Children's Rights, supra* n. 16, pp. 62–63; see also Linda Kirschke, *Kid's Talk: Freedom of Expression and the UN Convention on the Rights of the Child* (London: Article 19, 1999), pp. 4–5; Lawrence LeBlanc, *The Convention on the Rights of the Child: United Nations Lawmaking on Human Rights* (Lincoln: U. of Nebr. Press, 1995), p. 161; Göran Therborn, "Child Politics: Dimensions and Perspectives," in *Monitoring Children's Rights* (Eugeen Verhellen, ed.) (The Hague: Martinus Nijhoff, 1996), p. 385. Scores of nations quickly ratified the Convention; by 1999, only Somalia and the United States had not.

18. See UN High Commissioner for Human Rights Web site, http://www.unhchr.ch/hchr_un.htm (urging in a June 1999 report that governments make efforts "to protect children from exposure to harmful information, including violence and pornography"). The UN Convention contains four other speech-related provisions: Article 13 (worded expansively to protect the right not only to "impart information and ideas of all kinds" but to "seek and receive them"; but then [like Article 10 of the European Convention on Human Rights] permitting "certain restrictions," if needed to respect "the rights or reputations of others," public order, or "public health or morals"); Article 12 (giving children a right to be heard in proceedings affecting them); Article 14 (establishing "freedom of thought, conscience and religion," with a caveat recognizing "the rights and duties" of parents or guardians); Article 15 (protecting freedom of association and peaceful assembly).

19. *Kid's Talk, supra* n. 17, pp. 48–49, quoting ¶209, UN Doc. CRC/C/3/Add.15 (1993). The French law also banned material likely to "inspire or promote ethnic prejudices" among the young.

20. *Id.*, p. 49, quoting ¶54, UN Doc. CRC/C/Add.10 (1993); p. 50.

21. *Kid's Talk*, p. 31, quoting ¶137, *Concluding Observations of the Committee on the Rights of the Child: United Kingdom of Great Britain and Northern Ireland: Dependent Territories (Hong Kong)*, UN Comm. on the Rights of the Child, 13th Sess., UN Doc. CRC/C/57 (1996).
22. *Id.*, pp. 32–33.
23. Sarah Wellard, "Society—Children's Rights—Exercise Your Rights," *The Guardian*, Jan. 20, 1999, Society, p. 8.
24. *Conegate v. Commissioner of Customs & Excise* (1986), ECR 1007, 1 CMLR 739, 2 All E.R. 688 (Ct. Justice Eur. Cmties 4th Chamber).
25. See Geoffrey Robertson's rendition of Operation Tiger in *The Justice Game* (London: Random House, 1998), pp. 154–56; Helen Fenwick, *Civil Liberties* (2d ed.) (London: Cavendish, 1998), p. 200. Robertson recounts that Customs also confiscated books by Gay Talese, apparently confused by his name.
26. Robertson, *supra* n. 25, p. 46.
27. Committee on Obscenity and Film Censorship, *Obscenity and Film Censorship: An Abridgment of the Williams Report* (Bernard Williams, ed.) (Cambridge: Cambridge U. Press, 1979), p. 35. The abridgment contains the text of the report but omits the appendices. On *Inside Linda Lovelace*, see also Geoffrey Robertson & Andrew Nicol, *Media Law* (London: Penguin, 1992), p. 107.
28. *Director of Public Prosecutions v. Jordan* (1977), 64 Cr.App.Rep. 33, 38 (HL). The Law Lords (Britain's highest court) affirmed the decision. A few years earlier, Parliament finally ended the nation's regime of theater licensing; drama now became subject to the same censorship standards (obscenity and indecency) as other artistic expression. Theatres Act 1968, 45 *Halsbury's Laws of England* (4th ed. 1985), ¶¶943–55; 11(1) *Halsbury's Laws of England* (4th ed. 1990 reissue), ¶¶362–64. In 1981, Parliament eliminated theaters' liability for common law indecency, see ¶954 & n. 14.
29. *Williams Report*, *supra* n. 27, pp. 2, 4, 56–64, 87–89 (quoting one expert's opinion that exposure to pornography "at a time of stress in the child's process of growing up" could be "very confusing" and, "in constellation with other disturbing factors, could tip the balance toward psychological damage"; another's view that the danger to youngsters was largely in terms of "propaganda for homosexuality"; and still other opinions that prepubescent youngsters would not take much notice of pornography or, if they did, "might be more robust than was commonly assumed"). The Committee noted also that alleged behavioral effects such as increased promiscuity or mistreatment of women were impossible to measure; that sex offenders generally have had less, not more, exposure to sexual materials than others in society; and that there is "no shortage of unpleasant and horrific subjects in traditional children's literature." *Id.*, pp. 11, 89.
30. *Id.*, pp. 87–92, 159–66, 88.
31. *Regina v. Greater London Council, ex parte Blackburn* (1976), 3 All E.R. 184, 187 (Ct. App., Civ. Div.); see also *The British Board of Film Classification: A Brief History*, http://www.bbfc.co.uk; Cinematograph Act 1952, 45 *Halsbury's Laws of England* (4th ed. 1985), ¶¶963–78.
32. Author's notes, Jan. 22, 1999.

33. Video Recordings Act 1984, 45 *Halsbury's Laws of England* (4th ed. 1985), ¶¶1056–1100; 11(1) *Halsbury's* (4th ed., 1990 reissue), ¶¶369–70; Robertson & Nicol, *supra* n. 27, p. 573. The Act provided for classifying and certifying to be done "by a person or persons designated for that purpose by the Secretary of State."
34. "The Power of Religion Is There," BBC News Online, http://news6.thdo.bbc.co.vk/hi/english/entertainment/newsid%5F203000/203768.stm. (Oct. 30, 1998); author's interview with James Ferman, Jan. 22, 1999.
35. See Blake Morrison, *As If* (London: Granta Books, 1997), pp. 26, 155, *passim*; Michael Freeman, *The Moral Status of Children: Essays on the Rights of the Child* (Dordrecht: Martinus Nijhoff, 1997), pp. 238–50, 229; David Buckingham, *Moving Images: Understanding Children's Emotional Responses to Television* (Manchester, UK: Manchester U. Press, 1996), pp. 19–55; Report of the European Commission on Human Rights, *T. v. United Kingdom*, No. 24724/94 (Dec. 4, 1998), ¶¶28, 29; Patrick Wintour, "Bulger Judge Urges Debate on Parenting and Videos," *The Guardian*, Nov. 27, 1993, p. 1; Edward Pilkington, "Boys Guilty of Bulger Murder," *The Guardian*, Nov. 25, 1993, p. 1; "Child's Play," *The Times*, Nov. 26, 1993, p. 21; "Demon Ears," *The Observer*, Mar. 21, 1999, p. 20 (defendants' lawyers, supported by a police inspector, said the boys had not seen *Child's Play* 3).
36. Criminal Justice and Public Order Act 1994, *Halsbury's Laws of England 1999 Cumulative Supplement*, Part II (4th ed. 1999), amending Vol. 45, ¶1058.
37. *T. v. United Kingdom*, No. 24724/94 (Eur. Ct. Human Rights, Dec. 16, 1999); Warren Hoge, "Europe Court Faults Trial of Boy Killers of Toddler," *New York Times*, Dec. 17, 1999, p. A6.
38. BBFC brochure (London: BBFC, undated) (circulated in 1999).
39. Ros Hodgkiss, "BBFC Policy: Confessions of a Censor," http://www.dtaylor.demon.co.uk/bbfcconf.htm.
40. See "Bare-Faced Cheek," *The Guardian*, Feb. 20, 1999, p. 12; Brian Pendreigh, "Everything Was in Place for a Clampdown on Sex and Violence, So Where Is It?" *The Guardian*, Apr. 30, 1999, Screen, p. 6. The BBFC also had to apply Britain's blasphemy law: in 1989, it accordingly refused to issue a certificate to *Visions of Ecstasy*, an experimental cinematic rumination on the psychosexual experiences of St. Teresa of Avila. The imagery in *Visions* was not graphic enough to justify a ban on sexual grounds; the problem, as the board explained, was that "for a major proportion of the work's duration that sexual imagery is focused on the figure of the crucified Christ." After the Video Appeals Committee upheld the ban, describing *Visions* as a "contemptuous, reviling, insulting, scurrilous" work, the director appealed to the European Court of Human Rights; but as in *Handyside* a generation earlier, the Court deferred to Britain's "margin of appreciation," concluding that application of the blasphemy law to *Visions of Ecstasy* was "necessary" in a democratic society. *Wingrove v. United Kingdom*, Case 19/1995/525/611 (1997), 24 E.H.R.R. 1. Britain's blasphemy law prohibits insults only to Christianity; a Queen's Bench decision in 1991 rejected a challenge by Muslims wanting to equalize

matters by banning Salman Rushdie's *Satanic Verses. Regina v. Chief Metropolitan Stipendiary Magistrate ex parte Choudhury* (1991), 1 Q.B. 429.

41. Author's interview with James Ferman, Jan. 22, 1999.
42. Ann Hagell and Tim Newburn, *Young Offenders and the Media: Viewing Habits and Preferences* (London: Policy Studies Inst., 1996), pp. 87, x.
43. *Home Office Research: Effects of Video Violence on Young Offenders*, http://www.bbfc.co.uk; press release, "Home Office Research on Video Violence," Jan. 7, 1998.
44. Ferman applauded sex therapy videos and nonviolent erotica by feminists like the U.S.-based Candida Royalle. His encouragement of the R18 category for pornography aroused the ire of Home Secretary Jack Straw; see "Legalise Hardcore Porn, Says Chief Censor," BBC News Online, http://news.bbc.co.uk/hi/english/ukj/newsid_147000/147753.stm (Aug. 8, 1998). *The Guardian* reported that Ferman, "who had run the BBFC as a personal fiefdom for almost twenty-five years, accused Straw of pandering to the 'puritanical vote.' " Pendreigh, *supra* n. 40, p. 6.
45. BBFC press release, "Video Appeals Committee in Surprise Obscenity Decision," Aug. 13, 1998.
46. BBFC press release, "BBFC Loses Sex Video Standards Appeal," Aug. 16, 1999; "Porn Industry Wins in Landmark Censorship Case," ITN Online, May 16, 2000, http://www.itn.co.uk/Britain/brit20000516/051611.htm; *R v. Video Appeals Committee, The Times*, June 7, 2000, co/4074/99 (Queen's Bench Div.). The seven videos in question were *Horny Catbabe, Nympho Nurse Nancy, T.V. Sex, Office Tart, Carnival International Version (Trailer), Wet Nurses 2 Continental Version*, and *Miss Nude International Continental Version*. The BBFC decided not to pursue further appeals. Members of the Video Appeals Committee included Dr. Philip Graham, chair of the National Children's Bureau; Biddy Baxter, former producer of BBC programs for children; and author Fay Weldon.
47. "Bare-Faced Cheek," *supra* n. 40; Details of BBFC Decision, *Seul Contre Tous*, http://www.bbfc.co.uk (1999); Gaby Wood, "The Censor's Sensibilities," *The Observer*, Mar. 14, 1999, p. 7; Amelia Gentleman, "Explicit Euro-Sex Test for British Censors," *The Guardian*, Feb. 22, 1999, p. 5. The Board justified its eventual passage of *The Idiots* uncut by explaining that even an explicit shot was acceptably "brief and justified by context." News release, *The Idiots*, http://www.bbfc.co.uk (1999). A more graphic French production, *Romance*, about "a nymphomaniac in a sexless marriage," was passed for 12-year-olds in France—an unlikely outcome in Britain. Paul Webster, "French Cinema Seduced by Porn," *The Guardian*, Apr. 13, 1999, p. 12.
48. Attempting to remedy the ad hoc decision making that prevailed under Ferman, Duval announced a code in May 2000 that defined precise "quotas of sex, violence, and bad language" for the 12 and 15 categories—this would allow 15–18-year-olds, for example, to see *The End of the Affair* and *American Beauty*, and 12–15-year-olds to see *Shakespeare in Love*, to which the BBFC

had previously affixed a 15+ rating "even though it had the approval of the Vatican." Nicholas Hellen, "Teenagers to See 'Quota' of Film Sex as Censors Loosen Rules," *Sunday Times*, May 7, 2000, http://www.sunday-times.co.uk/news/pages/sti/2000/05/07/stinwenws01022.html.

49. Ben Fenton, "I'm Not Scared of the Exorcist," *Daily Telegraph*, Feb. 12, 1999, p. 25. As for *The Texas Chain Saw Massacre*, the BBFC said "there is, so far as the Board is aware, no evidence that harm has ever arisen as a consequence of viewing the film"; "by today's standards," the film's visual effects "may seem relatively unconvincing," with the screaming heroine in peril simply "a staple of the cinema since its early days," and "any possible harm that might arise in terms of the effect upon a modern audience . . . more than sufficiently countered by the unrealistic, even absurd nature of the action itself." Details for *The Texas Chainsaw Massacre*, Mar. 16, 1999, http://www.bbfc.co.uk.
50. See *Attorney General (on relation of McWhirter) v. Indep. Broadcasting Auth.* (1973), 1 All E.R. 689, 692 (Ct. App. Civ. Div.), quoting descriptions in the *News of the World* and the *Sunday Mirror*.
51. Broadcasting Standards Comm'n, *The Bulletin*, No. 19 (Mar. 31, 1999), pp. 4–5, 9–11. The Commission lacks coercive power, except to require broadcasters to publish summaries of its decisions and "report on any action they might have taken as a result." *Id.*, inside cover page; see Colin Shaw, *Deciding What We Watch: Taste, Decency, and Media Ethics in the UK and the USA* (Oxford: Oxford U. Press, 1999), pp. 56, 140; Broadcasting Act 1996, *Halsbury's Laws of England, 1999 Cum. Supp.*, Part II (4th ed. 1999), adding to Vol. 45, ¶¶579–86A, 586B.
52. Broadcasting Act 1990, ¶¶6–7; 45 *Halsbury's Laws of England, 1999 Cum. Supp.*, Part II (4th ed. 1999), adding to Vol. 45, ¶¶528–59A; see also University of Oxford, Programme on Comparative Media Law & Policy, *Final Report: Parental Control of Television Broadcasting* (1999), http://europa.eu.int/comm/dg10, pp. 224–26; ITC Programme Code, §1.1, http://www.itc.org.uk.
53. ITC Programme Code, *supra* n. 52, §§1.4–1.6, 1.11.
54. See Will Woodward, "Sex Shows on TV Aired 'Too Early,'" *The Guardian*, Mar. 31, 1999, p. 11; Stuart Miller & Janine Gibson, "Channel 4 Glad to Pioneer the First Gay Drama in British TV," *The Guardian*, Feb. 24, 1999, p. 3; Richard Brooks, "Last Taboo Broken by Sex and the C***," *The Observer*, Feb. 14, 1999, p. 3 (use of word "cunt" in broadcast of *Sex and the City*); Janine Gibson, "Viewers See Sex as Ploy to Boost Television Ratings," *The Guardian*, Jan. 17, 1999, p. 7. Britain still drew the line at hard-core pornography on TV: in 1993, the government squelched an attempt by the pay satellite channel Red Hot Dutch to penetrate the UK market. Red Hot Dutch appealed to the European Court of Justice, but "ran into financial difficulties" and ceased broadcasting before the case was resolved. Stuart Davis, "Still Red Hot: Pornography, Freedoms and Morality," Comment Section (1995), 5 *Ent. L. Rev.* 201; Philip Dann, "The Red Hot Channel: Pornography Without Frontiers," Comment Section (1993), 6 *Ent. L. Rev.* 191.

55. Shaw, *supra* n. 51, pp. 156–57, quoting Michael Grade, former chief of Britain's Channel 4.
56. "Dear Sir/Madam" Letter from Chief Inspector Stephen French, Metropolitan Police Service, London, to "All Internet Service Providers," Aug. 9, 1996, http://www.liberty.org.uk/cacib/theMet.html; Angus Hamilton, "The Net Out of Control: A New Moral Panic—Censorship and Sexuality," in *Liberating Cyberspace: Civil Liberties, Human Rights and the Internet* (ed. Liberty) (London: Pluto, 1999), pp. 174–75. The French Letter arrived in ISP mailboxes about a month after the House of Lords had issued a major report, *Agenda for Action in the UK*, which urged "voluntary" industry self-regulation of Internet content in order to "meet public concerns" about violent, sexual, or extremist online speech and "avoid demands for inappropriate legislation." *Agenda for Action in the UK*, 1995–96, 5th Report (July 23, 1996), http://www.parliament.the-stationery-office.co.uk/pa/ld199596/ldselect/inforsoc/inforsoc.htm. The UK Internet Service Providers Association responded by agreeing to "collaborate in removing 'obscene' material" from online newsgroups. Adam Newey, "Freedom of Expression: Censorship in Private Hands," in *Liberating Cyberspace, supra*, p. 32.
57. See *R-3 Safety-Net: An Industry Proposal*, Sept. 23, 1996, http://dtiinfol.dti.gov.uk/safety-net/r3.htm; KPMG/Denton Hall, *Review of the Internet Watch Foundation* for the Dep't of Trade and Industry and the Home Office, Jan. 22, 1999, http://www.dti.gov.uk/CII/iwfreview/index.html, §§2.1.1–2.1.2; Internet Watch Foundation, *Rating and Filtering Internet Content: A United Kingdom Perspective*, http://www.internetwatch.org.uk/rating/rating_r.html (March 1998); Yaman Akdeniz, "Governance of Pornography and Child Pornography on the Global Internet: A Multi-Layered Approach," in *Law and the Internet: Regulating Cyberspace* (Lilian Edwards & Charlotte Waelde, eds.) (Oxford: Hart, 1997), p. 235.
58. E-mail from John Wadham to author, June 14, 1999; author's interview with John Wadham, Mar. 16, 1999; author's telephone interview with John Wadham, Apr. 7, 1999; author's telephone interview with Alex Hamilton, treasurer and executive committee member of Liberty, Apr. 13, 1999; author's interview with Mark Stephens, Mar. 17, 1999 (recalling that Peter Dawe, a foundation executive who had given the IWF its start-up funding, approached him out of concern that there was "nobody representing civil liberties" on the Advisory Committee, and "asked me if I would do it and would Liberty nominate me").
59. Wendy Grossman, "Europe Readies Net Content Ratings," *Wired News*, July 7, 1997, http://www.wired.com/news/news/politics/story/5002.html.
60. *Rating and Filtering, supra* n. 57; author's interview with David Kerr, Mar. 15, 1999. Kerr indicated during the interview that the "adult themes" category might be dropped.
61. E-mail from Yaman Akdeniz to author, Mar. 19, 1999; author's telephone interview with Alex Hamilton, Apr. 13, 1999; author's interview with John Wadham, Mar. 16, 1999; author's interview with Malcolm Hutty, Mar. 24, 1999. In

1997, Cyber-Rights and Cyber-Liberties published a critique of the IWF's filtering plans: "Who Watches the Watchmen: Internet Content Rating Systems, and Privatised Censorship," http://www.leeds.ac.uk/law/pgs/yaman/watchmen.htm, reprinted in *Filters and Freedom: Free Speech Perspectives on Internet Content Controls* (David Sobel, ed.) (Washington, DC: EPIC, 1999), p. 33.

62. Internet Watch Foundation, *Rating Legal Material*, http://www.iwf.org.uk/rating/rating.html; *Rating and Filtering, supra* n. 57.
63. E-mail from David Kerr to author, June 15, 1999. The author's inquiries in early 1999 precipitated the removal of Liberty's name as a sponsoring organization from the IWF's Web site.
64. E-mail correspondence between Yaman Akdeniz and Clive Feather, Nov. 23, 1999, distributed via http://www.cyberrights.org; Liberty Policy on *Internet Encryption and Rating Systems*, July 1999. In 2000, Malcolm Hutty, director of CACIB (Campaign Against Censorship of the Internet in Britain), agreed to join the IWF board, explaining: "The IWF does constitute a base from which the pro-censorship lobby can work to achieve their goals. I think by having a civil liberties person on the inside many, though probably not all, such poor decisions can be averted." E-mail from Malcolm Hutty to author, May 23, 2000.
65. Liz Parratt & John Wadham, "Introduction," in *Liberating Cyberspace, supra* n. 56, p. 4. One of the contributors to the volume did mention "serious concerns about the effect that centralised rating might have on free expression online": Adam Newey, "Freedom of Expression: Censorship in Private Hands," *Liberating Cyberspace*, p. 44.
66. Nigel Williams, "Pornography," *Nucleus* (Oct. 1997), http://www.cmf.org.uk/pubs/nucleus/nucoct97/pornog.htm; see also Nigel Williams & Claire Wilson-Thomas, *Laid Bare: A Path Through the Pornography Maze* (London: Hodder & Stoughton, 1996), p. 81 (urging prayer and confession as cures for pornography use). Williams should not be confused with the English novelist Nigel Williams.
67. See Penny Campbell & Emmanuelle Machet, "European Policy on Regulation of Content on the Internet," in *Liberating Cyberspace*, p. 140.
68. See Nicholas Rengger, *Treaties and Alliances of the World* (6th ed.) (London: Cartermill Int'l, 1995), p. 252; David Goldberg *et al.*, *EC Media Law and Policy* (London: Addison-Wesley Longman, 1998), p. 8, n. 2; Robert Cottrell, "Europe: So Far, It Flies," *New York Review of Books*, Apr. 8, 1999, pp. 66–73 (describing agreements beginning with the Treaty of Rome that set up the EC or Common Market in 1957—not to be confused with the 1950 Treaty of Rome that produced the European Convention on Human Rights—and continuing through the Treaty of Maastricht that created the EU in 1993).
69. *Television Without Frontiers Directive*, European Parliament & Council, 89/552/EEC (Oct. 3, 1989), as amended by Eur. Parl. & Council Dir. 97/36/EC, reprinted in *Audiovisual Policy of the European Union* (European

Commission, DG 10, 1998); see *Final Report, supra* n. 52, pp. 41–44, http://europa.eu.int/comm/dg10; Goldberg *et al., supra* n. 68, pp. 56–75.

70. Author's interview with David Hughes, Mar. 3, 1999; e-mail from David Hughes to author, Mar. 25, 1999.
71. *Television Without Frontiers, supra* n. 69, Art. 22 (emphasis added).
72. Case E-8/97, *TV 1000 Sverige AB & Norwegian Gov't* (June 12, 1998), ¶¶24, 26.
73. *Final Report, supra* n. 52, Executive Summary; ch. 2.
74. *Id.*, Executive Summary.
75. *Id.*
76. *Id.*, ch. 3.
77. Author's interview with David Hughes, Mar. 3, 1999.
78. European Commission working party on illegal and harmful content on the Internet, *Report* (1997), Introduction, http://www2.echo.lu/legal/en/internet/wpen.html.
79. *Communication* to the European Parliament, the Economic & Social Committee, & the Committee of the Regions, *Illegal and Harmful Content on the Internet* (Oct. 16, 1996), http://www2.echo.lu/legal/en/internet/communic.html; *Green Paper on the Protection of Minors and Human Dignity in Audiovisual and Information Services* (Oct. 16, 1996), http://www2.echo.lu/legal/en/internet/gpen.txt.html, or http://www.europa.int/en/record/green/gp9610/protec.htm.
80. *Communication, supra* n. 79, Introduction, §§3, 5.
81. *Id.*, §5(f).
82. *Green Paper, supra* n. 79, Introduction & Summary; ch. 1, §1, ch. 2, §§2, 2.2, 2.2.2, ch. 3, §3.2.
83. Working party *Report, supra* n. 78.
84. European Commission Legal Advisory Board, *Response to the Green Paper on the Protection of Minors and Human Dignity in Audiovisual and Information Services*, http://www2.echo.lu/legal/en/internet/gplabrep.html, §3.5.2.
85. *Resolution on the Commission Communication on Illegal and Harmful Content on the Internet*, COM(96) 0487-C4-0592/96 (Apr. 24, 1997), http://www.europarl.eu.int.
86. *Opinion of the Committee on Women's Rights, Letter from the Chairperson of the Committee (Nel van Dijk) to Mrs. Hedy d'Ancona, Chairperson of Comm. on Civil Liberties & Internal Affairs*, Jan. 24, 1997 (appended to the *Resolution, supra* n. 85).
87. Economic and Social Comm., *Opinion on the "Proposal for a Council Decision Adopting a Multiannual Community Action Plan on Promoting Safe Use of the Internet,"* Official Journal C 214, July 10, 1998; Comm. on Culture, Youth, Education and the Media, *Opinion for the Comm. on Civil Liberties & Internal Affairs on the Commission Communication on Illegal and Harmful Content on the Internet*; Nov. 19, 1996, and Feb. 27, 1997 (appended to the *Resolution, supra* n. 85).
88. IRIS, *Libertés individuelles et libertés publiques sur Internet*, Oct. 1997, Annexe

VI, François Archimbaud, *Étiquetage et filtrage: possibilités, dangers, et perspectives*, http://www.iris.sgdg/documents/rapport-ce/annex6.html.

89. *La Lettre électronique d'Iris*, No. 1 (Jan. 19, 1998), http://www.iris.sgdg.org/les-iris/li1.html. The Conseil d'État's 1998 report on the Internet surveyed a range of legal issues (privacy, consumer protection, cryptology, domain names); with respect to industry self-regulation, it tended to agree with IRIS that rating and blocking reflected "an Anglo-Saxon behavioural influence that does not correspond to the French ways of thinking and traditions." Council of State, *The Internet and Digital Networks* (1998), http://www.ladocfrancaise.gouv.fr.
90. *GILC Submission on PICS*, Dec. 1997, http://www.gilc.org/speech/ratings/gilc-pics-submission.html, reprinted in *Filters and Freedom, supra* n. 61, p. 103.
91. Global Internet Liberty Campaign, *"Regardless of Frontiers": Protecting the Human Rights to Freedom of Expression on the Global Internet* (Sept. 1998); http://www.gilc.org.
92. *Action Plan on Promoting Safer Use of the Internet: The European Union Adopts Action Plan*, OJ L 98/560/EC Official Journal L 270 (Oct. 7, 1998), p. 48; Decision No. 276/1999 of the European Parliament & Council, Jan. 25, 1999, http://www2.echo.lu/legal/en/internet/actplan.html.
93. *Action Plan Preparatory Actions*, DG 13 Web site, http://www2.echo.lu/iap.
94. IWF press release, "IWFA Founding Member of New Rating Body—ICRA," May 12, 1999; Don Jellinek, "Web Warning on X-Rated Material," *The Guardian*, Online, Apr. 29, 1999, p. 5; ICRA press release, "Committee to Help Revise International Filtering and Labeling System to Protect Children from Harmful Internet Content," Apr. 4, 2000, http://www.icra.org/press/p6.htm (asserting that "to date, more than 130,000 Web sites have rated with the RSACi system, including a great number of the top 100 sites which account for 80% of the web's traffic," and announcing new advisory board members, including Jerry Berman of the Center for Democracy & Technology, Jack Balkin of Yale Law School, and Nigel Williams of Childnet International).
95. Bertelsmann Foundation, *Memorandum on Self-Regulation of the Internet*, and *Comments on the Memorandum*, http://www.stiftung.bertelsmann.de/internetcontent/english/frameset_nojs.htm; Pamela Mendels, "Plan Calls for Self-Policing of the Internet," *New York Times*, Sept. 20, 1999, p. C5; Matthew Yeomans, "The World's Wide Web: The Rating Game," *Industry Standard*, Sept. 30, 1999, http://www.thestandard.com/articles/display/0,1449,6705,00.html.
96. Information Society Project ("an international project, sponsored by the Bertelsmann Foundation"), Yale Law School, *Draft Recommendations for Initiative for Self-Regulation on the Internet: Rating and Filtering*, Apr. 16, 1999, http://www.law.yale.edu/infosociety/filtering_recommendations.html, offering as examples of possible "meta-tag" creators the Catholic Church and the National Abortion Rights Action League.
97. Yeomans, *supra* n. 95.

98. Global Internet Liberty Campaign, *Member Statement Submitted to the Internet Content Summit*, Munich, Germany, Sept. 9–11, 1999, http://www.gilc.org/speech/ratings/gilc-munich.html; see also Mendels, *supra* n. 95; Courtney Macavinta, "AOL, Others Plan Global Net Content Rating System," CNET News.com, Sept. 2, 1999, http://www.news.com/News/Item/Textonly/0.25,41248.00.html.

99. Michael Sims & Jamie McCarthy, "Munich: The Censors' Convention," *Internet Freedom*, Sept. 18, 1999, http://www.netfreedom.org/news.asp?item+87.

100. Center for Democracy & Technology, *First Amendment and Free Expression: An Analysis of the Bertelsmann Foundation Memorandum on Self-Regulation of Internet Content: Concerns from a User Empowerment Perspective*, Oct. 24, 1999, http://www.cdt.org/speech/./991021bertelsmannmemo.shtml.

101. David Kerr, *Final Report: Self-Labelling and Filtering* (INCORE, Apr. 2000), http://www.ispo.cec.be/iap/INCOREexec.html; *Final Report: Review of European Third-Party Filtering and Rating Software Services* (IDATE, Dec. 1999), http://www.ispo.cec.be/iap.IDATEexec.html; Katharine Schmidt, "Babysitter or Big Brother?" *Wall Street Journal*, June 13, 2000, http://interactive.wsj.com/public/current/articles/SB960323393026777 1.htm. ICRA also began to have doubts about the viability of global ratings. A report by its advisory board in August 2000 expressed frustration at "the failure" of RSACi to achieve wide acceptance among either online publishers or parents, and recommended more reliance on third-party blacklists, especially for difficult categories like nudity, language, and sports violence. *Report of the Advisory Board*, Aug. 4, 2000, http://www.icra.org/adreport.htm. In Britain, meanwhile, the IWF announced that, at the behest of the government, it would begin to police online racism. But because it was often difficult to determine the legality of offensive speech about race, the IWF would not "ask anyone to remove material unless government prosecutors 'say they would be able to get a result in court.' " David Kerr said: " 'Quite frankly, to an extent this is a hot potato for the government, and we are not going to allow them to dump it on us.' " Lakshmi Chaudhry, "British ISPs Crack Down on Hate," Jan. 25, 2000, http://www.wired.com/news/politics/0,1283,33906.00.html; Alan Travis, "Watchdog Moves to Curb Racist Websites," *The Guardian*, Jan. 26, 2000, http://www.newsunlimited.co.uk/ uk_news/story/0,3604,128923.00.html.

102. See Office of Film & Literature Classification, *Guidelines for the Classification of Films and Videotapes* (Sydney, July 1996) (mandatory classification system); *Printed Matter Classification Guidelines* (Sydney, July 1992) (voluntary classification system for "printed matter," which nevertheless mandated that unclassified publications had to "observe requirements" regarding display and access by youngsters "that would attach to such publications if classified"); Internet Industry Association, *Internet Industry Code of Practice*, Feb. 12, 1999, http://www.IIA.net.au/Code4.html (agreeing that companies would label and segregate "content, the possession of which while not illegal . . . , is nevertheless determined by the Relevant Authority to be unsuitable for minors in ac-

cordance with the National Classification Code"; "Relevant Authority" meant any group authorized by "statute, ministerial direction or parliamentary intent" to assign classifications, "including the Telecommunications Ombudsman, the Australian Broadcasting Authority, and the Federal or State Police).

103. James Glave, "No Smut Please, We're Australian," *Wired News*, Apr. 22, 1999, http://www.wired.com/news/news/politics/story/19268.html; see also Adam Creed, "Australian Net Regulation Plans Draw Industry Fire," *Newsbytes*, Mar. 21, 1999, http://www.newsbytes.com; "Stop! Police!" *Sydney Morning Herald* online, May 8, 1999, wysiwyg://73/http://www.smh.com.au/icon/990508/cover.html.
104. Broadcasting Services Amendment (Online Services Act); Pt. 3, Div. 1, cl. 10–11; Pt. 4, Div. 1–3; Pt. 1, cl. 4. The law also provided for industry self-censorship codes, to be supplemented or replaced by governmental standards if not considered adequate, *id.*, Pt. 5.
105. Stewart Taggart, "Australian Net Censor Law Passes," *Wired News*, July 7, 1999, http://www.wired.com/news/print_version/politics/story/20499html (reporting Electronic Frontiers Australia's description of the law as "political posturing, designed to create the illusion that the government was 'cleaning up the Internet,' while in fact the amendments have done nothing to stop any end-user accessing anything they please"); Luisa Bustos, "ABA Starts Cleaning Up the Web," *Network Today World*, Jan. 21, 2000, http://www2.idg.com.au/nww; Simon Hayes & James Riley, "Censor to Face High Court Test," *Australian IT*, Jan. 31, 2000, http://www.australianit.com.au/com (reporting Eros Foundation's plan to bring a constitutional challenge to the law); Jamie Murphy, "Australia Using Law to Go After Objectionable Sites," *New York Times on the Web*, Feb. 19, 2000, http://www.nytimes.com/library/tech/00/02/cyber/articles/19australia.html.
106. Author's interview with Richard Swetenham, Mar. 2, 1999.

10. MEDIA EFFECTS

1. Andrew Hacker, "The Unmaking of Men," *New York Review of Books*, Oct. 21, 1999, p. 25.
2. Plato, *The Republic and Other Works* (Benjamin Jowett, trans.) (New York: Doubleday, 1973), pp. 62–63.
3. John Gassner, "Introduction," in *Aristotle's Theory of Poetry and Fine Arts* (4th ed.) (New York: Dover, 1951), p. xi; see also Samuel Butcher, in *id.*, p. 238 (although not wholly rejecting the earlier didactic theory, Aristotle "never allows the moral purpose of the poet or the moral effects of his art to take the place of the artistic end"); Stephen Halliwell, *Aristotle's Poetics* (Chapel Hill: U. of North Carolina Press, 1986), p. 15.
4. *The Poetics*, in *Aristotle's Theory*, *supra* n. 3 (S. H. Butcher, trans.), p. 23.
5. Butcher, *supra* n. 3, pp. 254–55. Merely "being enabled by the artist to stand at some distance from a painful experience, to observe and understand it, can in itself afford some release from our tensions." Gassner, *supra* n. 3, pp. lx–lxi.

Aristotle thought epic poetry, with its "Reversals of the Situation, Recognitions and Scenes of Suffering," produced a similar effect. *The Poetics, supra* n. 4, p. 91.

6. Butcher, p. 247, n. 1, quoting Minturno, *L'Arte Poetica* (Venice, 1564), p. 77.
7. Butcher, p. 245; see also Adnan Abdulla, *Catharsis in Literature* (Bloomington: U. of Indiana Press, 1985), pp. 16, 27–28; Halliwell, *supra* n. 3, p. 197; Frederic Raphael, "After Pity and Terror, Knowledge," *Times Literary Supplement*, May 14, 1999, p. 14.
8. Abraham Kaplan, "Obscenity as an Aesthetic Category," 22 *Law & Contemp. Probs.* 544, 555 (1955); see also Halliwell, p. 200; Gassner, *supra* n. 3; Abdulla, *supra* n. 7, pp. 7, *passim*.
9. Anthony Burgess, *Nothing Like the Sun: A Story of Shakespeare's Love-Life* (New York: Norton, 1975), p. 80.
10. Jean-Jacques Rousseau, *"Lettre à M. D'Alembert sur les spectacles,"* in *Oeuvres Complètes*, Vol. 5 (Paris: Chez Dalibon, 1824), pp. 29, 35, 49, 51, 73–74, 134.
11. Sigmund Freud, "Creative Writers and Daydreaming," in *The Freud Reader* (Peter Gay, ed.) (New York: Norton, 1989), pp. 436–43; Sigmund Freud, *On Creativity and the Unconscious: Papers on the Psychology of Art, Literature, Love, Religion* (New York: Harper, 1958); see also Raphael, *supra* n. 7, p. 15 (arguing that "the cathartic affectations of psychoanalysis" resemble "Aristotelian *katharsis*" because Freud's idea "was to enable a patient, by dramatic re-presentation, to come through his or her fears [and self-pity] and to reach a stage where reason could influence and civilize the mind").
12. Jean Piaget, *Play, Dreams and Imitation in Childhood* (New York: Norton, 1962), pp. 132–33, 158; see also Erik Erikson, *Childhood and Society* (New York: Norton, 1950), p. 215 (noting that according to cathartic theory, "play has a definite function in the growing being in that it permits him to work off pent-up emotions and to find imaginary relief from past frustrations").
13. Bruno Bettelheim, *The Uses of Enchantment: The Meaning and Importance of Fairy Tales* (New York: Penguin, 1975), p. 7; see also John Sommerville, *The Rise and Fall of Childhood* (Beverly Hills: Sage, 1982), pp. 136–38 (describing the psychological value of the romances, fairy tales, and nursery rhymes that 16th- and 17th-century pedagogues tried to suppress).
14. Bettelheim, *supra* n. 13, p. 7; see Joan Acocella, "The Big Bad Wolf Is Back," *The New Yorker*, Nov. 30, 1998, p. 112; Henry Jenkins, "Lessons from Littleton: What Congress Doesn't Want to Hear About Youth and Media," http://web.mit.edu/cms/news/nais9912 ("Bettelheim argues that the violence and darkness of fairy tales is important for children to confront as a means of acknowledging the darker side of their own nature. Without such a depiction, children might take their own transgressive impulses as evidence that they are a 'monster,' rather than learning how to recognize and control those aspects of themselves").
15. Maria Tatar, "It's Time for Fairy Tales with the Bite of Reality," *New York Times*, Arts & Leisure, Nov. 29, 1998, pp. 1, 10.

16. Jerome Singer & Dorothy Singer, *Television, Imagination, and Aggression: A Study of Preschoolers* (Hillsdale, NJ: Lawrence Erlbaum, 1981), pp. 4–5, 7. The Singers note Konrad Lorenz's belief that aggression is a fundamental human drive, and characterize Freud's view that symbolic expressions of aggression have at least a partially drive-reducing function as "a scientific translation of Aristotle's early concept of catharsis." *Id.*, p. 97; see Konrad Lorenz, *On Aggression* (New York: Harcourt, Brace & World, 1963).
17. "Tale of Evil, or Evil Tale?" *New York Times*, Mar. 22, 1992, p. 10; " 'Muggles for Harry Potter' to Fight Censorship," FEN Newswire, Mar. 7, 2000, http://www.freeexpression.org; "Network Opposes Potter Policy," Letters to the Editor, *Holland Sentinel*, Apr. 19, 2000, http://www.thehollandsentinel.net/stories/041900/opi_letters.html. The school superintendent later withdrew some of the restrictions.
18. *A Portrait of the Artist as a Young Man*, in *The Portable James Joyce* (Harry Levin, ed.) (New York: Viking, 1947), p. 470.
19. D. H. Lawrence, *Pornography and Obscenity*, in *The Portable D. H. Lawrence* (Diana Trilling, ed.) (New York: Viking, 1946), pp. 646–71.
20. Sissela Bok, *Mayhem: Violence as Public Entertainment* (Reading, MA: Addison-Wesley, 1998), pp. 28, 43.
21. Roger Shattuck, *Forbidden Knowledge* (New York: Harcourt Brace, 1996), pp. 227, 323. Shattuck, who relies on sources as dubious as Fredric Wertham, the Meese Commission, and the death-row claims of sex murderer Ted Bundy to support his argument for the pernicious effects of sexual violence in art, also acknowledges Aristotle's "theory of catharsis or purgation" along with Plato's "theory of infection or corruption" as explanations of human responses to artistic works. *Id.*, pp. 227, 241–42, 291–92 (art " 'has the power to intensify [not just to purge] emotions' "), quoting Edgar Wind, *Art and Anarchy* (2d ed.) (New York: Vintage, 1969) (in the 3d ed., Chicago: Northwestern U. Press, 1985, p. 94); see also Bok, *supra* n. 20, p. 41 ("As both Plato and Aristotle pointed out, we do delight in representations of objects and emotions that would evoke altogether different responses in real life; but most of us side with Aristotle in refusing to regard this as corrupting or maiming in its own right").

    In a version of Shattuck's argument, former FCC chair Newton Minow and his co-author, Craig Lamay, dismiss catharsis as having no relevance to television despite its acknowledged role in fairy tales filled with "murdering witches" and "cannibalistic giants." The latter, they say, like modern children's literature, were "developed in the service of children's moral education"—a dubious proposition in light of Bettelheim's critique of just this didacticism in modern children's literature; see Newton Minow & Craig Lamay, *Abandoned in the Wasteland: Children, Television, and the First Amendment* (New York: Hill & Wang, 1995), p. 35. Wertham made the same distinction, contrasting "the popular folk wisdom" of fairy tales with "the violence hackwork of the mass media." Fredric Wertham, *A Sign for Cain: An Exploration of Human Violence* (London: Lowe & Brydone, 1966), pp. 219–23.

22. Charles Paul Freund, "Buying Into Culture," *Reason*, June 1998, pp. 24–32; Peter Gay, *The Victorian Experience: Victoria to Freud*, Vol. 5: *Pleasure Wars* (New York: Norton, 1998), p. 195. On the cathartic, orgasmic effect of pornography, see Robin West, "The Feminist-Conservative Anti-Pornography Alliance and the 1986 Attorney General's Commission on Pornography Report," 4 *Am. Bar Fdtn Rsrch J.* 681, 685 n. 12 (1987) (noting that the Meese Commission discussed "harms" but not "benefits" of pornography for some men as well as women); Eberhard & Phyllis Kronhausen, *Pornography and the Law* (New York: Ballantine, 1959), pp. 273–74 (reporting that comic books, lewd magazines, and even hard-core pornography are "more often than not a *safety valve* for the sexual deviate and potential sex offender"); D. W. Abse, "Psychodynamic Aspects of the Problem of Definition of Obscenity," 22 *Law & Contemp. Probs.* 572 (1955); Robin West, "Pornography as a Legal Text: Comments from a Legal Perspective," in *For Adult Users Only: The Dilemma of Violent Pornography* (Susan Gubar & Joan Hoff, eds.) (Bloomington: U of Indiana Press, 1989), pp. 151–52 (discussing "purgative" and "exemplary" models of pornography's impact); and, generally, *Pleasure and Danger: Exploring Female Sexuality* (Carole Vance, ed.) (London: Routledge & Kegan Paul, 1984); *Bad Girls and Dirty Pictures: The Challenge to Reclaim Feminism* (Alison Assiter & Avedon Carol, eds.) (London: Pluto, 1993).
23. Ian Buruma, *A Japanese Mirror: Heroes and Villains of Japanese Culture* (London: Penguin, 1984), pp. 55, 61.
24. Milton Diamond & Ayako Uchiyama, "Pornography, Rape, and Sex Crimes in Japan," 22 *Int'l J. Law & Psychiatry* 1, 14 (1999); see also Berl Kutchinsky, "Pornography and Rape: Theory and Practice? Evidence from crime data in four countries where pornography is easily available," 14 *J. Law & Psychiatry* 47 (1991) (noting similar correlations in European countries).
25. Edward Donnerstein *et al.*, *The Question of Pornography* (New York: The Free Press, 1987), p. 184; see also Kronhausen, *supra* n. 22, p. 267 (contending that it is not pornography but "guilt-based sexual inhibitions, restrictions, and repressions" that cause mental illnesses and antisocial behavior).
26. David Blum, "Embracing Fear as Fun to Practice for Reality: Why People Like to Terrify Themselves," *New York Times*, Oct. 30, 1999, p. B11. Margo Jefferson similary argued in defending popular entertainment: "the need for escape is surely as pure as the need for truth or beauty. How often are we allowed to leave our lives completely behind and suffer no ill effects when we return?" Margo Jefferson, "A Bout of Bad Taste Can Make a Day Worthwhile," *New York Times*, Feb. 25, 1998, p. E2. A defender of violent movies opined that the "adrenaline rush has supplanted the tearfest" as a source of "emotional catharsis." David Gilbreth, in "The Mail," *The New Yorker*, May 18, 1998, p. 9; see also Daniel Mendelsohn, "Working Their Way to the Top" (review of W. S. Merwin's translation of Dante's *Purgatorio*), *New York Times Book Rev.*, July 23, 2000, p. 8 ("who among us doesn't go skimming for shocks every now and then?"). An opera lover, equating musical and sexual climaxes, cited the gorgeous three-soprano trio at the end of Richard Strauss's *Der Rosenkavalier*

as an example of "that sense of engagement, fulfillment and exhaustion that Aristotle calls catharsis." Sam Abel, *Opera in the Flesh: Sexuality in Operatic Performance* (Boulder, CO: Westview, 1996), p. 92.

27. Jenkins, *supra* n. 14.
28. Bertolt Brecht, *Brecht on Theatre* (John Willett, ed. & trans.) (New York: Hill & Wang, 1964), pp. 57, *passim*; see also Halliwell, *supra* n. 3, p. 316.
29. See Albert Bandura, *Aggression: A Social Learning Analysis* (Englewood Cliffs, NJ: Prentice-Hall, 1973); Albert Bandura, *Principles of Behavior Modification* (New York: Holt, Rinehart & Winston, 1969); Albert Bandura, "Social Learning Theory of Aggression," *J. Comm'n* 12–29 (Summer 1978); Ted Rosenthal & Barry Zimmerman, *Social Learning and Cognition* (New York: Academic Press, 1978); Richard Evans, *Albert Bandura: The Man and His Ideas—A Dialogue* (New York: Praeger, 1989); Kevin Durkin, *Television, Sex Roles and Children: A Developmental Social Psychological Account* (Milton Keynes, UK: Open U. Press, 1985), pp. 42–46; Robert Liebert & Joyce Sprafkin, *The Early Window: Effects of Television on Children and Youth* (New York: Pergamon, 1988), pp. 65–79; Thomas Krattenmaker & L. A. Powe, Jr., "Televised Violence: First Amendment Principles and Social Science Theory," 64 *Va. L. Rev.* 1123, 1134–42 (1978).

    Bandura emerged from an era in which American psychology was dominated by behaviorism, which rejected Freud and subjective psychological forces generally, and focused on the social conditioning that shapes human behavior. See Erich Fromm, *The Anatomy of Human Destructiveness* (New York: Henry Holt, 1973), pp. 24–98; Judith Rich Harris, *The Nurture Assumption: Why Children Turn Out the Way They Do* (New York: The Free Press, 1998), pp. 4–5; *id.*, p. 107 (in rejecting the theory that aggressiveness is at least partly inherited, behaviorists ignored evidence going back to prehistoric times that "waging war and slaughtering our enemies are things we knew how to do long before we learned how to leave written records").
30. See, *e.g.*, Harris, *supra* n. 29, pp. 107, 185; Lorenz, *supra* n. 16; Fromm, *supra* n. 29 (describing destruction and cruelty not as "instinctual drives, but passions rooted in the total existence of man"); Debra Niehoff, *The Biology of Violence* (New York: The Free Press, 1999) (describing sources of aggression in brain chemistry, which in turn is shaped by the environment); Jonathan Kellerman, *Savage Spawn: Reflections on Violent Children* (New York: Ballantine, 1999) (positing that aggression, like other behaviors, results from the interaction of inborn traits with environmental influences, with media having little direct impact); Rollo May, *Power and Innocence: A Search for the Sources of Violence* (New York: Norton, 1972) (describing, *inter alia*, positive and negative types of aggression; Alfred Adler's theory that aggression is a primary human urge, fundamental to life; and the cathartic "ecstasy of violence" in drama and literature); Eric Negourney, "The Chemistry of Unchecked Aggression," *New York Times*, Feb. 1, 2000, p. F8 (describing relation between hormone levels and aggressiveness in children).
31. Evans, *supra* n. 29, p. 6.

32. See Albert Bandura, Dorothea Ross, & Sheila Ross, "Imitation of Film-Mediated Aggressive Models," 66 *J. Abnormal & Social Psych.* 3–11 (1963).
33. Albert Bandura, "What TV Violence Can Do to Your Child," *Look*, Oct. 22, 1963, pp. 46–52.
34. Seymour Feshbach & Robert Singer, *Television and Aggression: An Experimental Study* (San Francisco: Jossey-Bass, 1971), pp. 1–2, xiv.
35. Harris, pp. 10–11, 50–70. Similarly, sociologist Paul Hirsch commented: "You could argue that the kids were invited to hit the doll. They saw a grown-up do it and then they were left alone in the room with the doll to do whatever they felt like. I don't know that I'd base any sweeping social changes about TV on research like that." Quoted in Patrick Cooke, "TV or Not TV," *In Health*, Dec.–Jan. 1992, p. 39.
36. See Liebert & Sprafkin, *supra* n. 29, pp. 59, 60–64, 113–58 (describing successive government investigations that spurred the research work: Sen. Estes Kefauver's Committee on Juvenile Delinquency in 1954; Sen. Thomas Dodd's hearings in 1961; the Senate Subcommittee on Juvenile Delinquency in 1964; the National Commission on the Causes and Prevention of Violence in 1968; and the Surgeon General's study in 1972, which was followed by more hearings); Willard Rowland Jr., *The Politics of TV Violence* (Beverly Hills: Sage, 1983) (tracing the political ascent of behaviorist communications scholars, to the detriment of more nuanced or humanistic explorations of mass media, and their use of, and by, both politicians and the TV industry).
37. Edna Einseidel, "Social Science and Public Policy: Looking at the 1986 Commission on Pornography," in *For Adult Users Only*, *supra* n. 22, p. 91.
38. Author's telephone interview with Jonathan Freedman, Nov. 3, 1999; Jonathan Freedman, "Television Violence and Aggression: What Psychologists Should Tell the Public," in *Psychology and Social Policy* (Peter Suedfeld & Philip Tetlock, eds.) (New York: Hemisphere, 1991), p. 185.
39. Committee on Communications & Media Law, "Violence in the Media: A Position Paper," 52(3) *Record of the Ass'n of the Bar, City of New York* 273, 283–86 (1997); see also Alexis Tan, "Social Learning of Aggression from Television," in *Perspectives on Media Effects* (Jennings Bryant & Dolf Zillmann, eds.) (Hillsdale, NJ: Lawrence Erlbaum, 1986), p. 41 ("after two decades of intensive research, there is still considerable disagreement within the research community on whether television violence causes aggression in the real world").
40. Bandura, "Social Learning Theory," *supra* n. 29, pp. 12–13.
41. Surgeon General's Advisory Committee on Television and Social Behavior, *Television and Growing Up: The Impact of Televised Violence* (Washington, DC: Gov't Printing Office, 1972), pp. 4, 7, 67 (noting that evidence did not "warrant the conclusion that televised violence has a uniformly adverse effect" or "an adverse effect on the majority of children," and that many studies "fail to show any statistically significant effects in either direction"—that is, imitation or catharsis). On Senator Pastore's falsely manufactured consensus, see

Rowland, *supra* n. 36, pp; 171–96; see also National Research Council, *Understanding and Preventing Violence* (Albert Reiss, Jr., & Jeffrey Roth, eds.) (Washington, DC: Nat'l Academy Press, 1993), p. xi (noting Surgeon General's "conflicting evidence and findings of small, if any, impact"). Meanwhile, government money spent on social science research "was diverted from the National Institute of Mental Health budget by reducing support for the construction of community mental health centers." Richard Rhodes, "Hollow Claims About Fantasy Violence," *New York Times*, Week in Review, Sept. 17, 2000, p. 19.

42. See Bandura *et al.*, *supra* n. 32, p. 3; Leonard Berkowitz & Edna Rawlings, "Effects of Film Violence on Inhibitions Against Subsequent Aggression," 66 *J. Abnormal & Soc. Psych.* 405–12 (1963); Russell Geen & Michael Quanty, "The Catharsis of Aggression: An Evaluation of a Hypothesis," in *Advances in Experimental Social Psychology*, Vol. 10 (Leonard Berkowitz, ed.) (New York: Academic Press, 1977), pp. 2–37; Einseidel, *supra* n. 37, p. 91; Evans, *supra* n. 29.
43. Author's telephone interview with Daniel Linz, Nov. 8, 1999.
44. Feshbach & Singer, *supra* n. 34; see also Seymour Feshbach, "The Catharsis Hypothesis, Aggressive Drive, and the Reduction of Aggression," 10 *Aggressive Behav.* 91–101 (1984); Feshbach, "Reality and Fantasy in Filmed Violence," in *Television and Social Behavior*, Vol. 2 of the Surgeon General's report, *supra* n. 41, pp. 318–45.
45. See Krattenmaker & Powe, *supra* n. 29, pp. 1142–44 (collecting sources and describing experiments with results contrary to Feshbach & Singer's); Liebert & Sprafkin, pp. 76–78; Singer & Singer, *supra* n. 16, pp. 99–101; *Television and Growing Up*, pp. 65–67 (describing a study that failed to replicate Feshbach's findings).
46. Jeffrey Arnett, "The Soundtrack of Restlessness: Musical Preferences and Reckless Behavior Among Adolescents," 7(3) *J. Adol. Rsrch* 313 (July 1992) (summarizing Jeffrey Arnett, "Adolescents and Heavy Metal Music: From the Mouths of Metalheads," 23 *Youth & Society* 76–98 [Sept. 1991]); see also Lawrence Kurdek, "Gender Differences in the Psychological Symptomatology and Coping Strategies of Young Adolescents," 7 *J. Early Adol.* 395–410 (1987) ("heavy metal music, with its angry and aggressive sound, is especially useful to adolescents in purging anger"); Donna Gaines, *Teenage Wasteland—Suburbia's Dead End Kids* (Chicago: U. of Chicago Press, 1990), pp. 177–216 (documenting troubled youngsters' use of rock music and noting that Tipper Gore had "not a clue about how music works in kids' lives," *id.*, p. 207).
47. *Television and Behavior: Ten Years of Scientific Progress and Implications for the Eighties* (Washington, DC: U.S. Dep't of HHS, 1982).
48. Jonathan Freedman, "Viewing Television Violence Does Not Make People More Aggressive," 22 *Hofstra L. Rev.* 833, 836 (1994).
49. Thomas Cook *et al.*, "The Implicit Assumptions of Television Research: An Analysis of the 1982 NIMH Report on *Television and Behavior*," 47(2) *Pub.*

Opin. Q. 161, 179–92 (1983); Nat'l Academy of Sciences News Report, *Minutes: Workshop on Television and Violent Behavior* (Washington, DC: Nat'l Institute of Justice, Dec. 10, 1982).

50. See University of Oxford Programme in Comparative Media Law & Policy, *Final Report: Parental Control of Television Broadcasting* (1999), ch. 3, "Media Theories Background," http://europa.eu.int/comm/dg10; Stacy Smith *et al.*, *National Television Violence Study* 3 (Thousand Oaks, CA: Sage, 1998), p. 10; Mike Allen & Dave D'Alessio, "A Meta-Analysis Summarizing the Effects of Pornography II Aggression After Exposure," 33 *Human Comm'ns Rsrch* 258 (1995); George Gerbner & Nancy Signorielli, *Violence and Terror in the Mass Media* (Paris: UNESCO, 1988); George Gerbner *et al.*, "Living with Television: The Dynamics of the Cultivation Process," in *Perspectives, supra* n. 39; George Gerbner *et al.*, "The 'Mainstreaming' of America: Violence Profile No. 11," *J. Comm'n* 10–29 (Summer 1980); *Pornography and Sexual Aggression* (Neil Malamuth & Edward Donnerstein, eds.) (New York: Academic Press, 1984); Daniel Linz *et al.*, "The Attorney General's Commission on Pornography: The Gaps Between 'Findings' and Facts," 4 *Am. Bar Fdtn Rsrch J.* 713, 720–26 (1987); Daniel Linz & Edward Donnerstein, "The Effects of Violent Messages in the Mass Media," in *Message Effects in Communication Science* (J. J. Bradac, ed.) (Newberry Park, CA: Sage, 1989); Daniel Linz *et al.*, "Effects of Long-Term Exposure to Violent and Sexually Degrading Depictions of Women," 55 *J. Personality & Soc. Psych.* 758–68 (1988); Denise Caruso, "Linking Entertainment to Violence," *New York Times on the Web*, Apr. 26, 1999, http://www.nytimes.com.library/tech/99/04/biztech/articles/26digi.html.

51. *Nat'l Television Violence Study, supra* n. 50, pp. 11–20.

52. A. S. Byatt, *Babel Tower* (New York: Vintage, 1996), p. 581.

53. Aletha Huston & Dolf Zillman, "Media Influence, Public Policy, and the Family," in *Media, Children, and the Family* (Dolf Zillmann *et al.*, eds.) (Hillsdale, NJ: Lawrence Erlbaum, 1994), p. 6.

54. Author's telephone interview with Victor Strasburger, Jan. 13, 1997.

55. Telecommunications Act of 1996, PL 104–104, §551(a), 110 Stat. 56 (1996), published in the Historical and Statutory Notes to 47 U.S.C. §303(w) (announcing Congress's "findings" that "children exposed to violent video programming at a young age have a higher tendency for violent and aggressive behavior later in life than children not so exposed," and "are prone to assume that acts of violence are acceptable behavior"; and that "children are affected by the pervasiveness and casual treatment of sexual material on television, eroding the ability of parents to develop responsible attitudes and behavior in their children").

56. "Violence in the Media," *supra* n. 39, p. 284; see also *Final Report, supra* n. 50, ch. 3, "Media Theories Background" (without attending to style, genre, quality, nuance, and context, "a children's cartoon or a Shakespearean drama are rated as depicting the same level of violence as an action or horror film").

57. M. L. Poulter, "Report from BBFC's Consultation Evening, The Watershed, Bristol, 15 Nov. 1999," e-mail distributed from plmpl@eis.bris.ac.uk, Nov. 19, 1999.
58. Kenneth Gadow & Joyce Sprafkin, "Field Experiments of Television Violence with Children: Evidence for an Environmental Hazard?" 83(3) *Pediatrics* 399, 401 (1989).
59. "Violence in the Media," p. 296; see also Rowland, *supra* n. 36, p. 125 (noting experimenters' confusion between laboratory-induced or play aggression and real-world violence); Federal Trade Comm'n, *Marketing Entertainment Violence to Children: A Review of Self-Regulation and Industry Practices in the Motion Picture, Music Recording, and Electronic Game Industries*, appendix A, "A Review of the Research on the Impact of Violence in Entertainment Media" (Washington, DC: FTC, Sept. 2000), http://www.ftc.gov/reports/violence/vioreport.pdf (noting the wide variety of different effects posited by social scientists, and the weakness of the empirical evidence).
60. Edward Donnerstein, Daniel Linz, & Barbara Wilson, *Comments on the Submission to the FCC by the American Family Association et al.*, MM Docket No. 89-494 (FCC, undated).
61. Linz *et al., supra* n. 50, 4 *Am. Bar Fdtn Rsrch J.* at 722.
62. Victor Cline, *Pornography's Effects on Adults and Children* (New York: Morality in Media, 1994), pp. 15, 3.
63. Testimony of Catherine Yronwode in *Eclipse Enterprises v. Gulotta*, CV-92-3416 (ADS), Transcript, May 23, 1994, pp. 92–93.
64. Harris, *supra* n. 29, p. 214.
65. David Moore, *Statistics: Concepts and Controversies* (4th ed.) (New York: W. H. Freeman, 1997), pp. 486–90. Sometimes, more rigorous measures of once in 100 times are used.
66. Frederick Schauer, "Causation Theory and the Causes of Sexual Violence," 4 *Am. Bar Fdtn Rsrch J.* 737 (1987).
67. Schauer, "Causation Theory," *supra* n. 66, at 752–54, citing Hubert Blalock, Jr., "Multiple Causation, Indirect Measurement and Generalizability in the Social Sciences," 68 *Synthese: An International Journal for Epistemology, Methodology, and Philosophy of Science* 13 (1986); Paul Humphreys, "Causation in the Social Sciences: An Overview," 68 *Synthese* 1 (1986).
68. Eli Rubenstein, "Introductory Comments," in *Television and Behavior, supra* n. 47, Vol. 2, p. 104.
69. Victor Strasburger, *Adolescents and the Media: Medical and Psychological Impact* (Thousand Oaks, CA: Sage, 1995), p. 13; Victor Strasburger, "Children, Adolescents, and Television—1989: II. The Role of Pediatricians," 83 *Pediatrics* 446–48 (Mar. 1989). Dolf Zillmann, a prominent champion of media effects, also acknowledged that the "research on many potentially significant aspects of the influence of pornography on beliefs, attitudes, and behaviors cannot be definitive"; it "leaves us with considerable uncertainty about exposure consequences at the societal level." Dolf Zillmann, "Pornography Re-

search, Social Advocacy, and Public Policy," in Suedfeld & Tetlock, *supra* n. 38, p. 174; see also Kellerman, *supra* n. 30, pp. 72–73 (establishing a causal link is methodologically almost impossible because virtually every child in Western society "watches oodles of TV, so it is difficult to come up with control groups and to otherwise tease out specific effects of media violence"). A senior researcher at the University of Pennsylvania put it more boldly: "You can never prove anything in social science." Statement of Dr. Amy Jordan, senior researcher at Penn's Annenberg Public Policy Center, at a meeting of the Free Expression Network, Washington, DC, Mar. 22, 2000 (author's notes). Dr. Jordan may have spoken too broadly: many social science measurements are not empirically problematic. It is the subjective nature of judgments about media content and human attitudes that make them impossible to quantify.

70. See Schauer, *supra* n. 66; Rubenstein, *supra* n. 68, p. 2; Jonathan Freedman, "Effect of Television Violence on Aggressiveness," 96 *Psych. Bull.* 227 (1984).
71. Harris, pp. 18–23, 215; see also Hubert Blalock, Jr., *Casual Inferences in Nonexperimental Research* (Chapel Hill: U. of North Carolina Press, 1964), p. 5 ("causal inferences [in social science] are made with significant risk of error").
72. See, *e.g.*, Victor Strasburger, "Television and Adolescents: Sex, Drugs, Rock 'n' Roll," 1 *Adol. Medicine—State of the Art Reviews* 161, 172–73 (1990); Bok, p. 85 (repeating the 5–15% figure but noting that such estimates "are rarely specific enough to indicate whether what is at issue is all violent crime, or such crimes along with bullying and aggression more generally").
73. Bok, pp. 85, 5, 57 (identifying "more direct" causes of violent conduct to include family breakdown, child abuse, firearms availability, and overindulgence in drugs and alcohol; and acknowledging that "it will always be difficult to disentangle the precise effects of exposure to media violence from the many other factors contributing to societal violence"); see also Nat'l Research Council, *supra* n. 41 (emphasizing genetic, social, and family influences on violent behavior—including alcohol abuse and availability of guns).
74. Nat'l Research Council, *supra* n. 41; see also Franklin Zimring & Gordon Hawkins, *Crime Is Not the Problem: Lethal Violence in America* (New York: Oxford U. Press, 1997) (availability of firearms—not media imagery or even the general crime rate—accounts for the high rate of lethal violence in America); Kellerman, *supra* n. 30 (focusing on psychopathology, produced by a combination of hereditary and environmental factors, and excoriating pundits who predictably blame the media after every senseless crime).
75. Freedman, 22 *Hofstra L. Rev.*, *supra* n. 48, at 837. See also Jib Fowles, *The Case for Television Violence* (Thousand Oaks, CA: Sage, 1999), pp. 20–50 (summarizing the dubious results of media-violence research).
76. Testimony of Joyce Sprafkin in *Eclipse v. Gulotta*, Mar. 28, 1994, pp. 112–13.
77. David Buckingham, *Moving Images: Understanding Children's Emotional Responses to Television* (Manchester, UK: Manchester U. Press, 1996), p. 8; Howard Gardner, "Do Parents Count?" *New York Review of Books*, Nov. 5, 1998, p. 20.

78. Berkowitz & Rawlings, *supra* n. 42, p. 411; see also Krattenmaker & Powe, at 1140; "Violence in the Media," at 286–87, citing Heath *et al.*, "Effects of Media Violence on Children: A Review of the Literature," 46 *Arch. Gen. Psychiatry* 376 (1980).
79. Edward Donnerstein & Daniel Linz, "Mass Media Sexual Violence and Male Viewers: Current Theory and Research," 28 *Am. Behav. Sci.* 601 (1986); Donnerstein *et al.*, *The Question of Pornography, supra* n. 25; Linz *et al., supra* n. 50, at 719, 723–26; Linz & Donnerstein, "The Effects of Counter-Information on the Acceptance of Rape Myths," in *Pornography: Research Advances and Policy Considerations* (Dolf Zillmann & Jennings Bryant, eds.) (Hillsdale, NJ: Lawrence Erlbaum, 1989), pp. 259–83.
80. Althea Huston & Dolf Zillmann, "Media Influence, Public Policy, and the Family," in *Media, Children, and the Family, supra* n. 53; Dolf Zillman, "Effects of Prolonged Consumption of Pornography," in *Pornography: Research Advances, supra* n. 79, pp. 127–54; *The Question of Pornography, supra* n. 25, at 79–83, describing studies finding no increase in callousness after viewing full-length porn films.
81. Kathryn Kelley *et al.*, "Three Faces of Sexual Explicitness: The Good, the Bad, and the Useful," in *Pornography: Research Advances, supra* n. 79, p. 60; see also Alison King, "Mystery and Imagination: The Case of Pornography Effects Studies," in *Bad Girls, supra* n. 22, pp. 57–83, analyzing the conservative ideological suppositions in Zillmann's work from a feminist anticensorship perspective.
82. Allen & D'Alessio, *supra* n. 50, p. 12.
83. Strasburger, *Adolescents and the Media*, p. 166.
84. "Violence in the Media," at 287–88; see also Freedman, "Television Violence," *supra* n. 38, pp. 179–89; Krattenmaker & Powe, at 1150–57; Mike Allen & Dave D'Alessio, "The Role of Educational Briefings in Mitigating Effects of Experimental Exposure to Violent Sexually Explicit Material: A Meta-Analysis," 22 *J. Sex Rsrch* 135 (1996).
85. "Violence in the Media," at 228–29; Liebert & Sprafkin, p. 141; see also Krattenmaker & Powe, at 1150–57; Strasburger, "Television and Adolescents," *supra* n. 72, pp. 161–94; Jonathan Freedman, "Television Violence and Aggression: A Rejoinder," 100(3) *Psych. Bulletin* 372–78 (1986); Freedman, 22 *Hofstra L. Rev.* 833; Robert Kaplan, "Television Violence and Viewer Aggression: A Reexamination of the Evidence," 32(4) *J. Soc. Issues* 35–70 (1976); and "TV Violence and Aggression Revisited Again," 37(5) *Am. Psychologist* 589 (1982).
86. University of Exeter professor Brian Young made this point in *Emulation, Fears and Understanding: A Review of Recent Research on Children and Television Advertising* (London: ITC, 1998), pp. 8–9; see also Cook *et al., supra* n. 49.
87. Linz *et al., supra* n. 50, at 722.
88. "Violence in the Media," p. 289.

89. Freedman, 22 *Hofstra L. Rev.* at 842 (quoting Cook *et al.*, pp. 181–82; Gadow & Sprafkin, *supra* n. 58, pp. 399–405).
90. Joyce Sprafkin, Kenneth Gadow & Patricia Grayson, "Effects of Viewing Aggressive Cartoons on the Behavior of Learning Disabled Children," 28(3) *J. Child Psych. & Psychiatry* 387–98 (1987); Gadow & Sprafkin, *supra* n. 58.
91. Sprafkin, Gadow, & Grayson, *supra* n. 90, at 394; Gadow & Sprafkin, p. 403. Alternatively, they proposed that it is not any particular content but simply the "hot" medium of television that increases arousal levels and thereby induces antisocial behavior. See also Singer & Singer, p. 40 (noting that "frenetic activity" in TV game shows may contribute to aggression by children).
92. Sue Chambers *et al., Cartoon Crazy?: Children's Perceptions of "Action" Cartoons* (London: ITC, 1998), p. 5.
93. *National Television Violence Study*, p. 183.
94. American Psychological Association, *Violence and Youth: Psychology's Response*, Vol. 1: *Summary Report of the American Psychological Association Committee on Violence and Youth* (Washington, DC: APA, 1993), p. 133. The chairman of the APA committee was Leonard Eron, one of the most prominent believers in imitative media effects.
95. See Brandon Centerwall, "Exposure to Television as a Risk Factor for Violence," 129 *Am. J. Epidemiology* 643–52 (1989); Brandon Centerwall, "Television and Violence: The Scale of the Problem and Where to Go from Here," 267 *JAMA* 3059–63 (1992).
96. "Violence in the Media," pp. 292–93; Marcia Pally, *Sex & Sensibility: Reflections on Forbidden Mirrors and the Will to Censor* (Hopewell, NJ: Ecco, 1994), pp. 108–12; see also Strasburger, "Television and Adolescents," critiquing Centerwall for overstating his statistics.
97. See "Violence in the Media," at 292–93; Bok, p. 86; Zimring & Hawkins, *supra* n. 74, pp. 133–34, 239–43; Judith Levine, *Shooting the Messenger: Why Censorship Won't Stop Violence* (New York: Media Coalition, 2000), p. 7.
98. Larry Baron & Murray Straus, *Four Theories of Rape in American Society: A State-Level Analysis* (New Haven: Yale U. Press, 1989), p. 189; see also Larry Baron & Murray Straus, "Sexual Stratification, Pornography, and Rape in the United States," in *Pornography and Sexual Aggression, supra* n. 50, pp. 186–208; Larry Baron & Murray Straus, "Four Theories of Rape: A Macrosociological Analysis," 34 *Soc. Probs.* 467–89 (1987); *The Question of Pornography, supra* n. 25, pp. 66–67; King, *supra* n. 81, pp. 74–75.
99. "The Soundtrack of Restlessness," *supra* n. 46, at 325.
100. Charles Corder-Bolz, "Television and Adolescents' Sexual Behavior," 3 *Sex Ed. Coalition News* 3, 5 (1981); see also Strasburger, *Adolescents and the Media*, p. 49.
101. Jane Brown & Susan Newcomer, "Television Viewing and Adolescents' Sexual Behavior," 21 *J. Homosexuality* 77, 84, 88 (1991); see discussion in Strasburger, *Adolescents and the Media*, p. 49; *Risking the Future: Adolescent Sexuality, Pregnancy, and Child-bearing* (Cheryl Haynes, ed.) (Washington,

DC: Nat'l Academy Press, 1987), p. 249 (noting that no study "has convincingly linked program content and exposure to adolescent sexual attitudes and behavior").

102. American Academy of Pediatrics, "Children, Adolescents, and Television," 96(4) *Pediatrics* 786 (1995).

103. See Diamond & Uchiyama, *supra* n. 24, at 11; discussion in ch. 9; Berl Kutchinsky, "The Effect of Easy Availability of Pornography on the Incidence of Sex Crime: The Danish Experience," 29 *J. Soc. Issues* 163–81 (1973); Berl Kutchinsky, "Pornography in Denmark: A General Survey," in *Censorship and Obscenity* (Rajeev Dhavan & Christie Davies, eds.) (Totowa, NJ: Rowman & Littlefield, 1978), pp. 111–26; Berl Kutchinsky, "Pornography and Its Effects in Denmark and the United States: A Rejoinder and Beyond," 8 *Comp. Soc. Rsrch* 301–30 (1985); *Obscenity and Film Censorship: An Abridgment of the Williams Report* (Bernard Williams, ed.) (Cambridge: Cambridge U. Press, 1979), pp. 61–95.

104. See, *e.g.*, Diamond & Uchiyama, at 15–19 (citing additional sources); Paul Gebhard *et al.*, *Sex Offenders: An Analysis of Types* (New York: Harper & Row, 1965), pp. 670–78; Bill Thompson, *Soft Core: Moral Crusades Against Pornography in Britain and America* (London: Cassell, 1994), p. 133 (collecting sources); *The Question of Pornography*, pp. 32–37, 70–71; Michael Carrera, *Sex: The Facts, the Acts, and Your Feelings* (New York: Crown, 1981), p. 41; Judith Becker & Robert Stein, "Is Sexual Erotica Associated with Sexual Deviance in Adolescent Males?" 14 *Int'l J. Law & Psychiatry* 85–91 (1991); Kelley *et al.*, *supra* n. 81, p. 67; Kronhausen, *supra* n. 22, pp. 273–74 (quoting the chief psychotherapist at St. Elizabeth's Hospital in Washington, DC, to the effect that "people who read salacious literature are less likely to become sexual offenders . . . , for the reason that such reading often neutralizes what aberrant sexual interests they may have").

105. See L. Rowell Huesmann *et al.*, "The Stability of Aggression over Time and Generations," 20 *Devel. Psych.* 1120 (1984); Leonard Eron *et al.*, "Does Television Violence Cause Aggression?" 27(4) *Am. Psychologist* 253–63 (1972); Leonard Eron, "Parent-Child Interaction, Television Violence, and Aggression of Children," 37(2) *Am. Psychologist* 197–211 (1982); discussion in Freedman, *supra* n. 70, at 239–41; "Violence in the Media," at 293–94.

106. "Violence in the Media," at 294; see L. Rowell Huesmann *et al.*, "Intervening Variables in the TV Violence-Aggression Relation: Evidence from Two Countries," 20 *Devel. Psych.* 746, 773 (1984); Freedman, "Rejoinder," *supra* n. 85, p. 376.

107. See David Sohn, "Television Violence and Aggression Revisited," 36(2) *Am. Psychologist* 229–31 (1981); David Sohn, "On Eron on Television Violence and Aggression," 37(11) *Am. Psychologist* 1292–93 (1982); Herbert Kay, "Weaknesses in the Television-Causes-Aggression Analysis by Eron et al.," 27(10) *Am. Psychologist* 970–73 (1972); Gilbert Becker, "Causal Analysis in R-R Studies: Television Violence and Aggression," 27(10) *Am. Psychologist*

967–68 (1972); Krattenmaker & Powe, at 1148–49; Freedman, *supra* n. 70, at 235–43 (acknowledging that numerous studies have found correlations between aggressive behavior and preference for violent television, but pointing out that none establishes causation).

108. Freedman, *supra* n. 70, at 241–43, citing J. Ronald Milavsky *et al.*, *Television and Aggression: A Panel Study* (New York: Academic Press, 1982). Milavsky *et al.* described their work as "the most extensive study of television effects on child and adolescent aggression that has appeared in the scientific literature." *Id.*, p. xviii.
109. Richard Rhodes, "The Media Violence Myth," *Rolling Stone*, Nov. 23, 2000, p. 55; e-mail from L. Rowell Huesmann to Richard Rhodes, Mar. 13, 2000.
110. See Freedman, *supra* n. 70, at 241; Leonard Eron, "Parent-Child Interaction," *supra* n. 105.
111. Freedman, 22 *Hofstra L. Rev.* at 849–51, citing Oene Wiegman *et al.*, *Television Viewing Related to Aggressive and Prosocial Behavior* (The Hague: Stichting Voor Onderzoek van het Onderwijs, 1986); see also Wiegman *et al.*, "A Longitudinal Study of the Effects of Television Viewing on Aggressive and Prosocial Behaviors," 31 *Brit. J. Social Psych.* 147–64 (1992); Freedman, in Suedfeld & Tetlock, *supra* n. 38, pp. 182–84. The book resulting from the cross-national study was *Television and the Aggressive Child: A Cross-national Comparison* (L. Rowell Huesmann & Leonard Eron, eds.) (Hillsdale, NJ: Lawrence Erlbaum, 1986).
112. Wiegman *et al.*, "A Longitudinal Study," *supra* n. 111, at 147.
113. L. Rowell Huesmann *et al.*, "The Effects of Television Violence on Aggression: A Reply to a Skeptic," in Suedfeld & Tetlock, pp. 192, 197, 198.
114. See, *e.g.*, *Television and Behavior*, p. 37.
115. Author's telephone interview with Daniel Linz, Nov. 8, 1999.
116. William McGuire, "The Myth of Massive Media Impact: Savagings and Salvagings," in *Public Communication and Behavior*, Vol. 1 (George Comstock, ed.) (New York: Academic Press, 1986), p. 174; see also Robert Kaplan & Robert Singer, "Television Violence and Viewer Aggression: A Reexamination of the Evidence," 32 *J. Soc. Issues* 35–70 (1976); Robert Kaplan, "TV Violence and Aggression Revisited Again," 37(5) *Am. Psychologist* 589 (1982); Fowles, *supra* n. 75, pp. 20–50; Donn Byrne & Kathryn Kelley, "Basing Legislative Action on Research Data: Prejudice, Prudence, and Empirical Limitations," in *Pornography*, *supra* n. 79, pp. 363–86. In the related field of TV's effect on children's cognitive development, a Department of Education–sponsored study concluded that most of the research was either shoddy or inconclusive or both, and was plagued by preconceptions. David Anderson & Patricia Collins, "The Impact on Children's Education: Television's Influence on Cognitive Development," Working Paper No. 2 (Washington, DC: U.S. Dept. of Ed., Office of Educational Research and Improvement, Apr. 1988).
117. *Marketing Entertainment Violence*, appendix A, *supra* n. 59; David Rosenbaum, "Panel Documents How Violent Fare Is Aimed at Youth," *New York*

Times, Sept. 12, 2000, p. Al; Katharine Seelye, "Before a Hollywood Crowd, Democrats Lower the Volume," *New York Times*, Sept. 20, 2000, p. Al. A month before the release of the FTC report, the American Academy of Pediatrics and three other professional groups issued a joint statement claiming "a strong consensus" within the "public health community" on the ill effects of entertainment violence, and referring to "well over 1000 studies" that "point overwhelmingly to a causal connection between TV violence and aggressive behavior." American Acad. of Pediatrics, American Psychological Ass'n, American Medical Ass'n, American Acad. of Child & Adolescent Psychiatry, *Joint Statement on the Impact of Television Violence on Children*, July 26, 2000, http://www.aap.org/advocacy/releases/jstmtevc.htm. The "1000 studies" were not for the most part reports of experiments but summaries, interpretations, and commentaries. Jonathan Freedman commented: "The scientific evidence does not support what they are saying." Assertions based on "intuitions and experiences" would not be objectionable, but "putting it in terms of what scientific evidence shows is irresponsible and absolutely wrong." Cheryl Arvidson, "Statement Linking Media Violence to Violence in Kids Draws Criticism," *Freedom Forum Online*, http://www.freedomforum.org/news/2000/07/2000-07-31-08.htm.

118. Sara Meadows, *The Child as Thinker: The Development and Acquisition of Cognition in Childhood* (London: Routledge, 1993), p. 344.
119. *Television and Behavior*, Vol. 1, pp. 87–91, 20.
120. Durkin, *supra* n. 29, p. 3; see also Jenkins, *supra* n. 14 (because consumers respond to the same media in different ways, "universalizing claims are fundamentally inadequate in accounting for media's social and cultural impact"); Nat'l Research Council, pp. 101–2 (media effects theories are oversimplistic because they fail to consider either how different individuals respond to identical stimuli or how various factors—psychosocial, neurological, and hormonal—*interact* to produce particular behavior).
121. Durkin, pp. 43, 87, 118, 17; see also Jane Brown, "Theoretical Overview," in *Media, Sex and the Adolescent* (Bradley Greenberg *et al.*, eds.) (Cresskill, NJ: Hampton Press, 1993), p. 21 (viewers and listeners "do pick and choose among the variety of available images and messages"; the problem with the social learning perspective is that not all people, young or old, interpret the same expressive content in the same way); Strasburger, *Adolescents and the Media*, pp. 13, 89 ("different viewers may process the same content differently"); Barrie Gunter, *Dimensions of Television Violence* (New York: St. Martin's, 1985), p. viii (discussing "the complexity and variety of violence forms on television, and more importantly, of viewers' appraisals of them").
122. *Final Report*, *supra* n. 50, Annex 3, "Media Theories Background," quoting Barrie Gunter, "The Importance of Studying Viewers' Perceptions of Television Violence," 7 *Curr. Psych.* 26–43 (1988).
123. Barrie Gunter & Adrian Furnham, "Perceptions of Television Violence: Effects of Programme Genre and Type of Violence on Viewers' Judgments of Vi-

olent Portrayals," 23 *Brit. J. Social Psych.* 155–64 (1984); see also Buckingham, *supra* n. 77, pp. 5, 310 (the "theoretical and methodological weaknesses of media effects research are well-documented"; the notion of media effects "has, it would seem, been irredeemably contaminated with the behaviourialism and empiricism of mainstream psychology; it is seen to be fundamentally incompatible with a truly complex social theory").

124. T. H. A. Van der Voort, *Television Violence: A Child's Eye View* (Amsterdam: Elsevier Science Pubs., 1986).
125. Strasburger, "Children, Adolescents, and Television," 83 *Pediatrics* 446–48 (quoting Gadow & Sprafkin, p. 404).
126. David Stout, "A Hearing Focuses on Lyrics Laced with Violence and Death," *New York Times*, Nov. 7, 1997, p. A21, quoting Frank Palumbo's testimony for the American Academy of Pediatrics.
127. Wendy Steiner, *The Scandal of Pleasure: Art in an Age of Fundamentalism* (Chicago: U. of Chicago Press, 1995), pp. 117–18, 211.
128. Mark Oppenheimer, "Why Judy Blume Endures," *New York Times Book Review*, Nov. 16, 1997, p. 44.

CONCLUSION

1. The museum later said that its original ban on unaccompanied minors "was a responsible position for us to take," citing the example of restrictions on R-rated movies. The "Health Warning," it added, was "a tongue-in-cheek advertising strategy" unrelated to the exclusion of minors. Letter from Judith Frankfurt, Deputy Director for Administration, to author, Sept. 15, 2000. On the Brooklyn Museum brouhaha, see David Barstow, "Seeking Buzz, Museum Chief Hears a Roar Instead," *New York Times*, Sept. 25, 1999, p. B1; David Barstow, "Giuliani Ordered to Restore Funds for Art Museum," *New York Times*, Nov. 2, 1999, p. A1. Judge Nina Gershon's decision summarizes the sequence of events, *Brooklyn Institute of Arts & Sciences v. New York*, 64 F. Supp. 2d 184 (E.D.N.Y. 1999). On the "aura of illicitness" created by "adults only" classifications, see Christoph Zuschlag, " 'Chambers of Horrors of Art' and 'Degenerate Art': On Censorship in the Visual Arts in Nazi Germany," in *Suspended License: Censorship and the Visual Arts* (Elizabeth Childs, ed.) (Seattle: U. of Wash. Press, 1997), p. 214.
2. Appellants' Brief, *Brooklyn Institute v. New York*, No. 99-9326 (Nov. 24, 1999), p. 13. The appeal was dismissed after the city agreed to settle the case by restoring the museum's funds and abandoning its state court eviction suit.
3. Brief for Appellants in *U.S. v. Playboy Entertainment Group* (S.Ct. No. 98-1682, Aug. 1999), pp. 35 n. 21, 38–40.
4. *FCC v. Pacifica Foundation*, 438 U.S. 726, 775, 770 (1978) (Brennan, J., dissenting); see also Catherine Ross, "Anything Goes: Examining the State's Interest in Protecting Children from Controversial Speech," 53 *Vand. L. Rev.* 427, 521–22 (2000) ("the government's professed interest in reinforcing

parental authority often clashes with principles of family autonomy and cultural pluralism that are central to the Constitution. The state's evaluation of speech undercuts the authority of parents who do not share normative cultural values.").

5. Rochelle Gurstein, *The Repeal of Reticence* (New York: Hill & Wang, 1996), p. 249.
6. Colin Shaw, *Deciding What We Watch: Taste, Decency, and Media Ethics in the UK and the USA* (Oxford: Clarendon, 1999), p. 59.
7. The phrase comes from A. S. Byatt's fictional expert witness in *Babel Tower* (New York: Vintage, 1996), p. 581. On children's perennial fascination with bathroom matters, see Martha Wolfenstein, *Children's Humor: A Psychological Analysis* (Glencoe, IL: Free Press, 1954) (scatology and sexual body parts are normal subjects of childish curiosity and humor); Barbara Meltz, "Why Good Children Use Bad Words," *Boston Globe*, At Home, Sept. 24, 1992, p. A1; "Keeping the World Safe for Comfy Underwear," *New York Times*, Apr. 10, 2000, p. C19 (describing popular series of "epic novels," *The Adventures of Captain Underpants*, whose fourth volume—*Captain Underpants and the Perilous Plot of Professor Poopypants*—had "climbed to No. 2 behind Harry Potter" on one children's best-seller list in April 2000).
8. Paul Farhi, *Washington Post Online*, May 24, 2000, http://www.washingtonpost.com/wp-dyn/articles/A59337-2000May23.html. Studies in Britain, by contrast, have indicated that most children understand cartoon fantasies not to be prescriptions for real-world behavior; see ch. 10.
9. Todd Gitlin, "Imagebusters: The Hollow Crusade Against TV Violence," *The American Prospect*, Winter 1994, pp. 46–47.
10. Joan Bertin, "Views on the News from the Executive Director," National Coalition Against Censorship, *Censorship News*, Winter 1998, p. 3, quoting Judy Blume in part.
11. William Fisher & Azy Barak, "Sex Education as a Corrective: Immunizing Against Possible Effects of Pornography," in *Pornography: Research Advances and Policy Considerations* (Dolf Zillmann & Jennings Bryant, eds.) (Hillsdale, NJ: Lawrence Erlbaum, 1989), p. 303.
12. Gitlin, *supra* n. 9, p. 47.
13. *American Booksellers Ass'n v. Hudnut*, 771 F.2d 323, 330 (7th Cir. 1985), aff'd, 475 U.S. 1001 (1986).
14. John Stuart Mill, *On Liberty*, in *Essential Works of John Stuart Mill* (Max Lerner, ed.) (New York: Bantam, 1961), pp. 263, 323, 327.
15. *Ward v. Rock Against Racism*, 491 U.S. 781, 790 (1989). This decision upheld New York City's regulation of the sound level at open-air concerts, but recognized music's expressive value and First Amendment protection.
16. Lawrence Kohlberg & Carol Gilligan, "The Adolescent as Philosopher," 100 *Daedalus* 1051 (1971); see also Michael Freeman, "The Limits of Children's Rights," and Gary Melton & Susan Limber, "What Children's Rights Mean to Children," in *The Ideologies of Children's Rights* (Michael Freeman & Philip

Veerman, eds.) (Dordrecht: Martinus Nijhoff, 1992), pp. 35, 167, 173; Jane Fortin, *Children's Rights and the Developing Law* (London: Butterworths, 1998), pp. 63–70; Michael Grodin & Leonard Glantz, *Children as Research Subjects: Science, Ethics, and Law* (New York: Oxford U. Press, 1994), pp. 63–70; Ross, *supra* n. 4, at 466 & n. 181.

17. Victor Strasburger, *Getting Your Kids to Say No in the Nineties When You Said Yes in the Sixties* (New York: Simon & Schuster, 1993), p. 62; see also Kohlberg & Gilligan, *supra* n. 16, p. 1060 (if "there is anything which can be safely said about what is new in the minds of adolescents, it is that they, like their elders, have sex on their minds"); Erik Erikson, *Identity: Youth and Crisis* (New York: Norton, 1994), p. 118; Erikson, *Childhood and Society* (New York: Norton, 1950), pp. 263–66; Paul Abramson, "Implications of the Sexual System," in *Adolescents, Sex, and Contraception* (Donn Byrne & William A. Fisher, eds.) (Hillsdale, NJ: Lawrence Erlbaum, 1983), pp. 56–60.
18. Thomas Hine, *The Rise and Fall of the American Teenager* (New York: Avon, 1999); see also Leon Botstein, "Oh, Grow Up," *New York Times Book Review*, Oct. 10, 1999, p. 28 (reviewing Hine); Joseph Kett, *Rites of Passage: Adolescence in America, 1790 to the Present* (New York: Basic Books, 1977); Henry Giroux, *Channel Surfing: Race Talk and the Destruction of Today's Youth* (New York: St. Martin's, 1997), p. 31 (noting the importance of providing "opportunities for kids to voice their concerns" and allowing them "to reconceptualize themselves as citizens and develop a sense of what it means to fight for important social and political issues that affect their lives").
19. *Planned Parenthood of Missouri v. Danforth*, 428 U.S. 52, 74 (1976) (invalidating restrictions on minors' access to abortion); see also the English House of Lords decision in *Gillick v. West Norfolk & Wisbech Area Health Authority et al.* (1985), 3 All E.R. 402 (discussed in ch. 6).
20. Mălfrid Grude Flekkøy, *A Voice for Children* (London: Jessica Kingsley Pubs., 1991); see also *The Ideologies of Children's Rights*, *supra* n. 16.
21. "MIT to Host On-line Conversations with Teens About Popular Culture and Media Convergence," Mar. 13, 2000, http://www.teen.com/mit.html.
22. Americans for the Arts brochure, *YouthARTS—Arts Programs for Youth at Risk: The Tool Kit* (undated); see also President's Comm'n on the Arts & Humanities, *Coming Up Taller: Arts and Humanities Programs for Children and Youth at Risk* (1996), http://www.cominguptaller.org.
23. Cynthia Lightfoot, *The Culture of Adolescent Risk-Taking* (New York: Guilford Press, 1997).
24. Robert Liebert & Joyce Sprafkin, *The Early Window: Effects of Television on Children and Youth* (New York: Pergamon, 1988), pp. 117, 226–29; Victor Strasburger, *Adolescents and the Media: Medical and Psychological Impact* (Thousand Oaks, CA: Sage, 1995), p. 5. For links to detailed information, curricula, and media literacy organizations, see Ontario Media Literacy Homepage, http://www.angelfire.com/ms/MediaLiteracy/index.html;http://www.ritsumei.ac.jp/kic/so/semminor/ML/linkor-e.html (from Ritsumeikan University in Japan).

25. Molly Berger, *Media Class 7th-8th Grade Twelve Week Elective*, http://interact.uoregon.edu/MediaLit/FA/MLCurriculum/Mediaclass.html.
26. Leonard Eron, "Parent-Child Interaction, Television Violence, and Aggression of Children," 37(2) *Am. Psychologist* 197, 209 (1982); see also Liebert & Sprafkin, *supra* n. 24, p. 228.
27. See Steven Manning, "Channel One Enters the Media Literacy Movement," 14(2) *Rethinking Schools* (1999), http://www.rethinkingschools.org.
28. Author's notes, Dec. 2, 1999.
29. Popular parenting guides are generally more open and sex-positive than public school curricula; see, *e.g.*, Laura Nathanson, *The Portable Pediatrician's Guide to Kids: Your Child's Physical and Behavioral Development from Ages 5 to 12* (New York: Harper Perennial, 1996), p. 17 (noting that masturbation is normal); Laurence Steinberg & Ann Levine, *You and Your Adolescent: A Parent's Guide for Ages 10–20* (New York: HarperCollins, 1997), pp. 102, 108 ("sexual desires and fantasies are normal and common"; the only "real-harm in sexual fantasies is guilt"; soft-core pornography, "used as a means of satisfying curiosity, or as an accessory to masturbation, . . . will not speed up, slow down, or otherwise disrupt a young person's sexual development"); but see *id.*, pp. 108–9 (arguing that hard-core pornography [defined as "magazines and books with graphic pictures or descriptions of people violating sexual taboos"] is "not appropriate for young teenagers").
30. Kate Langrall Folb, " 'Don't Touch That Dial!': TV as a—What!?—Positive Influence," 28(5) *SIECUS Report* 16, 17 (2000).
31. Tamar Lewin, "Mommy, What's an Intern? And Other Hard Topics," *New York Times*, Feb. 1, 1998, p. 20.
32. William Shakespeare, *Henry IV, Part Two*, Act IV, sc. iv, 11. 67–78.

INDEX